BLAKE AND SPENSER

BLAKE

AND

SPENSER

ROBERT F. GLECKNER

THE JOHNS HOPKINS UNIVERSITY PRESS
Baltimore and London

The publication of this book has been aided by grants
from The Carl and Lily Pforzheimer Foundation, Inc.,
and the National Endowment for the Humanities.

The Johns Hopkins University Press
701 West 40th Street
Baltimore, Maryland 21211
The Johns Hopkins Press Ltd., London

*The paper in this book is acid-free and meets the guidelines for
permanence and durability of the Committee on Production
Guidelines for Book Longevity of the Council on Library
Resources.*

Library of Congress Cataloging in Publication Data

Gleckner, Robert F.
Blake and Spenser.

Bibliography: p.
Includes index.
1. Blake, William, 1757–1827—Criticism and
interpretation.   2. Spenser, Edmund, 1552?–1599—
Influence—Blake.   3. Spenser, Edmund, 1552?–1599.
Fairie queene.   I. Title.
PR4147.G546   1985   821'.7   85–45
ISBN 0-8018-2521-0 (alk. paper)

FOR GLENDA

Contents

Acknowledgments   ix

ONE. *Spenser and Blake*   1

TWO. *The Torments of Love and Jealousy*   27

THREE. *Roads of Excess*   71

FOUR. *Calling and Naming*   117

FIVE. *The Characters in Spenser's Faerie Queene, I*   158

SIX. *The Characters in Spenser's Faerie Queene, II*   196

SEVEN. *The Characters in Spenser's Faerie Queene, III*   222

EIGHT. *Spenser's Spenser and Blake's Spenser*   263

APPENDIX A. *Spenser and Blake's Thel*   287

APPENDIX B. *Blake, Bunyan, Pilgrimages, and Allegory*   303

APPENDIX C. *Allegory and Typology*   308

APPENDIX D. *Spenser's Ireland and Blake's Erin*   311

Notes   319

Index   391

Acknowledgments

Much of the research for, as well as the writing of, this book has been generously supported by a series of research grants from the Duke University Research Council. I am also indebted to the Carl and Lily Pforzheimer Foundation and the National Endowment for the Humanities for their handsome contributions to the book's publication costs. For permission to reproduce Blake's plates and pictures I am grateful to the Cultural Committee of the City of Manchester Art Galleries, the Paul Mellon Collection, the Trustees of the British Museum, the Pierpont Morgan Library, and the National Trust; also, for their several courtesies in helping me secure the photographs and permissions, Christopher Beharrell, Historic Buildings Representative, the National Trust, Southern Region; Timothy Clifford, City of Manchester Art Galleries; Mary Ann Thompson, Secretary, Paul Mellon Collection; C. A. Ryskamp, Director, the Pierpont Morgan Library; Thomas Yoseloff, Associated University Presses; Patrick Noon, Curator of Prints and Drawings, Yale Center for British Art; the Photographic Services Section of the Wilson Library, University of North Carolina, Chapel Hill; and the Audiovisual Education Department of the Duke University Medical Center.

My personal debts are many. Those to other scholars, Spenserians and Blakeans alike, should be obvious from my frequent quotations from and citations of their work. But if this book might well have emerged without his influence and guidance in all manner of Spenserian matter, it would have been singularly the poorer for my colleague A. Leigh DeNeef's absence, not only from its pages but from my mind in its writing. If there are gaffs herein, they are not his but my inadequacies in dealing with what he knows of Spenser so commandingly. At the other end of my literary spectrum, Joseph Anthony Wittreich, Jr.'s, and David V. Erdman's scrupulously detailed reading of my manuscript reminded me of what I should have known, rescued me from assorted slips and errors, and engaged me (as I engage them in these pages) in the "mental fight" in which friendships are nurtured and sustained—the kind of engagement that should be the business of all of us who profess. If it would be egregiously arrogant to claim thereby that out of all my mental engagements the truth now shines clear, what glimmerings are herein owe much to Leigh, Joe, and David.

Finally, to Deborah Gilliland my warm appreciation for unfailing efficiency and promptness as typist and catcher of stupidities.

BLAKE AND SPENSER

CHAPTER ONE

Spenser and Blake

I N H I S 1 9 6 5 *Blake Dictionary* S. Foster Damon summed up
the status of investigations into the relationship between Blake
and Spenser this way: "Blake's criticism of Spenser is to be found
in his painting 'Spenser's *Faerie Queene.*'"[1] While Damon is correct in
the sense that this painting constitutes the only documentary evidence
we have of Blake's "reception" of Spenser's poetry,[2] I want to suggest that Blake's "criticism" of Spenser is, in a variety of ways, part
of the fabric of most of his other works as well. Yet Spenser is rarely
apparent (in the root sense of that word) in Blake's poetry in the same
way that, say, the Bible and Milton are, the "ways" in which he does
appear being inherent in and absorbed by Blake's own poetic
"ways." The most obvious of these are his habitual techniques of
contextualized allusion and buried quotation (or near-quotation),
about which I have already had something to say in several articles
and in my study of Blake's *Poetical Sketches*.[3] I shall not repeat that
evidence here *in extenso* but shall try to build upon it with respect to
some of Blake's works that are largely untreated, or dealt with only
minimally, in those previous discussions. Such building will not take
the form of conventional source hunting or mere listings of allusions
but rather will be in the spirit of my development in *Blake's Prelude* of
what I called there Blake's technique of significant allusion and its
implications for, and consequences in, Blake's own mode of contextualized literary criticism.

Briefly, significant allusion has more to do with borrowed contexts
than with borrowed lines or phrases or even words—although the
former, of course, are energized by the latter. John Hollander makes
a similar point in his fascinating little book, *The Figure of Echo*. Usefully distinguishing among quotation, allusion ("overt" or intentional), and echo (unintentional, appealing "not to the audience for
an allusion, but to the surrounding poem itself"), he also identifies a

1

kind of allusive echo: ''The fragmentations and breakings-off of intertextual echo can result in pieces of voice as small as single words, and as elusive as particular cadences''—although most commentators, ''employing the genially open philological 'Cf.,''' shun ''the caves of ambience and the chambers of meaning.''[4] In his essay ''Influence and Independence in Blake,'' John Beer proposes a distinction between the ''mere coincidence'' of seemingly echoed phrasings and the ''intensive'' and ''extensive'' effects in a work which are caused by its alluding to a ''distinctive element'' in the source, ''which raises probability above the level'' of ''mere coincidence.''[5] Beer's focus, however, is more on distinguishing between apparent and real allusion than on defining the nature and functioning of the allusion itself. While Blake's wide and often eccentric reading makes it difficult to decide whether an apparent allusion is really meaningful, his significant allusions tend to vitiate that problem by drawing with them into his context an appropriate borrowed context, one that more often than not inverts, subverts, or otherwise comments upon the significance or direction of the Blakean context into which it has been inserted. The point may be made the other way around as well—Blake's context inverting, subverting, or otherwise manipulating the borrowed context to its own ends or purposes, a kind of catachresis or *abusio*.[6] Such a technique, related to satire, is essentially a poetic-technical version of Los's ''Striving with Systems to deliver Individuals from those Systems'' in *Jerusalem*,[7] the erring systems (or images, locutions, verbal enactments of belief) thus being subjected to the ''correction'' or revivification of Blake's imaginative perception of the truth of the matter. His contextualized literary criticism thus also becomes contextualized philosophical, religious, political, social, and psychological criticism, a poetical *modus operandi* that draws into itself what oft was thought about the eternal verities, not to express them more felicitously or powerfully but to redeem them from the error of their previous or conventionally accepted expression.

Beyond such an elaborate and complex allusionary technique is the far more difficult area of the ''general influence'' of Spenser on Blake, the sort of indebtedness that is not only undocumentable by anything in Blake's prose comparable to his essay on *The Canterbury Tales* or even to his book annotations but is also not apparent even in his most deeply buried allusions. This sort of relationship is succinctly summarized by Damon in citing Spenser as ''Milton's 'original,' and Milton in turn [as] Blake's original, thus establishing the symbolic line in English literature.''[8] ''Symbolic line'' is a rather fuzzy label to apply here; Joseph Anthony Wittreich's more extensive and detailed analysis of the ''line of vision'' is far more to the point, especially as his conception of the "line" establishes the Bible, and particularly the prophets and the Book of Revelation, as the line's origin.[9] Despite my obvious debts to Wittreich's work even beyond my specific acknowledgments, I prefer a somewhat different approach to the line than what he has offered—one that concentrates less on the nature of epic-prophecy and its evolving literary forms and apocalyptic implications than on what I regard to be, in its broadest sense, Blake's preoccupation with the nature of allegory. To put the question in somewhat oversimplified fashion, Revelation and Milton are, in Blake's terms, clearly "sublime allegories," but is that an accurate definition of *The Faerie Queene*—or for that matter, of the minor poems (some of which Spenser refers to as "visions") or of *The Shepheardes Calender, Amoretti, Epithalamion, Prothalamion*, and the *Fowre Hymnes*? That is, however much some (or even all) of these poems may be seen by Spenserian critics and scholars as something other than mere allegory (or whatever they *seem* to be), how did Blake perceive them? To say, with Damon, that "*The Faerie Queene* is an allegory, of which Blake disapproved" is to say the obvious, to point only to the tip of the iceberg; Damon's subsequent commentary on the painting of *The Faerie Queene* characters shows, unfortunately, little sense of the applicability of his critical truism to the painting itself, much less to Spenser as a whole.[10] John E. Grant and Robert E. Brown are far more ambitious in this respect in their "Report and . . . Anatomy" of the painting,[11] but I hope to be able to go beyond their essentially taxonomic study to provide a kind of critical or investigatory pattern upon which future study of Spenser's influence on Blake may build. For just as no one has yet had the last word on the Blake-Milton relationship, the following pages on the Blake-Spenser relationship are but a step—I trust a forward step.

I have been somewhat severe with Damon, a scholar to whom all Blakeans owe much, precisely because of the influential nature of his achievement and the titular authoritativeness of his last book, *A Blake Dictionary*. His entry under Spenser in the *Dictionary* provides some clues and directions for the sort of analysis of the Blake-Spenser relationship I essay here. "Blake evidently found the epic [*The Faerie Queene*] to be 'full of vision,' like *Pilgrim's Progress*," he writes, citing the *Vision of the Last Judgment* assertion, "Fable or Allgory [*sic*] is Seldom without some Vision Pilgrims Progress is full of it the Greek Poets the same." Just prior to this, Blake had pronounced "The Hebrew Bible & the Gospel of Jesus" as "not Allegory but Eternal Vision or Imagination of All that Exists" (E554). It is a nice point to try to understand what "some Vision" means to Blake. If "Eternal Vision" is an "Imagination of All that Exists" "Really & Unchangeably'' (E554), is ''some Vision'' a sort of diluted eternal vision or a vision of some of what exists, really and unchangeably? In his annotations to Bishop Watson's *Apology for the Bible*, which was written in response to Paine's *Age of Reason*, Blake maintains (in connection with Watson's discussion of Moses' authorship of the Pentateuch) that ''historical facts can be written by inspiration,'' a distinction between history writing or history painting and poetry or true art that Blake will often return to. In these terms ''Miltons Paradise Lost is as true as Genesis. or Exodus'' even though ''the Evidence is nothing'' (E617). Milton's poem is thus regarded by Blake as all vision (Milton was solidly of the devil's party in the famous *Marriage of Heaven and Hell* phrase) despite the obscuring of that vision by Milton's spectrous self and his adherence to the conventionalities of the politics, religion, and ethics of his day. With apparently no vision at all, Dryden ''degraded Milton'' with his ''Niggling & Poco Piud'' ''completion'' of *Paradise Lost*.[12] Somewhere in between, presumably, lie Bunyan and the Greek poets—and, I believe, Spenser.

In the penultimate textual plate of *Jerusalem*, the most stirring apocalypse and ''paradise regained'' in English poetry, ''The innumerable Chariots of the Almighty appeard in Heaven,'' among them ''Bacon & Newton & Locke, & Milton & Shakspear & Chaucer'' (97:8–9, E257). Elsewhere, and in other but similar terms, Michelangelo, Raphael, Dürer, and Giulio Romano join this visionary company.[13] It is startling, to say the least, to find Blake's infernal triumvirate—Bacon, Newton, and Locke—in this company, for their inclusion strongly suggests Blake's final judgment of them as redeemable, as being possessed of vision after all, no matter how devastatingly and debilitatingly deformed that vision might be in their works. In recent years Donald D. Ault, F. B. Curtis, and Stuart Peterfreund have shown how this can be, at least with respect to Newton, but the redeemability of Bacon and Locke still lacks champions.[14] What is even more disturbing, however, is the consistent absence of Spenser's name from Blake's visionary company. Does this mean that he is somehow in the company of those lost causes, Dryden and Pope, or Correggio, Titian, Rubens, and Rembrandt?[15] I think not—although I cannot explain thereby the steady absence of his name from Blake's habitual groupings of the beautiful and the damned in both his prose and his poetry.[16]

Blake's few references to Spenser by name are ambiguous, that very ambiguity suggesting at least that Spenser cannot be all bad. The earliest is in *Poetical Sketches*, in the title of the poem *An Imitation of Spencer*. Since I have dealt with this poem at some length elsewhere, suffice it to say here that the poem does not, as Damon claims, "prove that Blake admired him early."[17] It does suggest that Blake read him early, however, albeit much in the spirit of other eighteenth-century imitators who found Spenser a poet to emulate for his diction, his mellifluousness, and his "Gothic" stanza.[18] The *Imitation* aside, elsewhere in the *Sketches*, particularly in *To the Evening Star*, *To Morning*, and *To the Muses*, there is abundant evidence of Blake's having read Spenser both extensively and with considerable care—moreover, with a sharply critical eye and intelligence. Damon's "admiration" may be the better word here, but if it is, clearly that admiration is carefully qualified. "Some vision" in the *Epithalamion* and *The Teares of the Muses* (as well as, to a lesser extent, other of the "minor poems" and, of course, *The Faerie Queene*) may be the operative occasion for that admiration.[19] Moreover, it is difficult to imagine Blake's being oblivious to, or uninterested in, the conjunction of text and design in *The Shepheardes Calender* and perhaps as well in the *Theatre for Worldings*.

It is a truism that, in some sense, all of Blake's works tend toward a "marriage"—at least from the *Songs of Innocence and of Experience* and *The Marriage of Heaven and Hell* on. Without going into the complexities of Blake's idea of a marriage, there still can be little doubt that this is one of the reasons he was attracted to Spenser's *Amoretti*, *Prothalamion*, *Epithalamion*, and even *The Faerie Queene*. At the same time, there is even less doubt that Blake would have been unimpressed with a marriage of the Thames and Medway,[20] if indeed that had any meaning for him at all. Similarly, though less harshly, the marriages celebrated by the epithalamic hymns and the one indicated by the sonnet sequence were conceptually flawed in various ways. If "some Vision" inhered in the idea of marriage itself in Spenser's poems, their bondage to time (as Blake saw it) dimmed that vision considerably. Blake's critique of the issue is launched in careful detail in "To the Evening Star" and "To Morning" in the *Poetical Sketches*, both constituting, as I have shown in *Blake's Prelude*, a kind of anti-epithalamium in their exploitation of Spenser's emphasis on the "timeliness" of his marriages. This "attack" is similar in kind and technique to that in Blake's four seasons poems upon the conceptual and philosophic substructure of Thomson's *Seasons* (and the satellite poems of others that it spawned)—not to mention the conventions of Spenser's *Shepheardes Calender*, his pageant of the seasons, months, and days in the Mutabilitie Cantos, Pope's *Pastorals*, and the rest of what Rosemond Tuve called "the commonplaces of seasons poetry."[21] And, as I shall show in the next chapter, with a studied and deliberate obtuseness Blake interprets the *Amoretti*—as if not flawed enough in its conception of marriage—as a kind of epitome of Petrarchan error, a model indeed for his own preoccupation with the literal "war of the sexes" in the fallen worlds of *The Four Zoas, Milton,* and *Jerusalem,* the seeds of which may be found in *The Book of Thel, Visions of the Daughters of Albion,* and the early, shorter "prophecies."[22]

The next reference to Spenser by name cannot be so easily dated. (As a matter of fact neither can the "Imitation," despite a "publication" date of 1783 for *Poetical Sketches*; my guess is that the poem is very early, perhaps 1771.) It is in his *Notebook* accompanying a four-line quotation from Book II of *The Faerie Queene,* assigned by Blake to one of the series of emblems he entitled "Ideas of Good & Evil," the preliminary version of *For Children: The Gates of Paradise.* The earliest of these emblems to which a date can be assigned with reasonable confidence is, as Erdman has shown, 1787–88.[23] If this is so, and if (as Erdman argues) the rest of the emblems, or indeed the idea of an emblem series, had not yet eventuated, the "Spenser emblem" would thus fall somewhere between 1787–88 and 1793, at the very least twenty years after the Spenser imitation and perhaps ten years after Blake's critical wrestling in *Poetical Sketches* with *Epithalamion, The Teares of the Muses, The Shepheardes Calender,* and possibly other shorter poems—of those *Amoretti* being the best guess.

The quotation from the second canto of Book II of *The Faerie Queene* is, if not an obscure one to Spenser scholars, at least a part of a relatively unmemorable (to eighteenth-century readers) and even "minor" episode in Guyon's adventures, but it is of particular interest here.[24] Redcrosse and the Dragon, Una, Archimago, Duessa, and a number of other "major" characters and episodes would seem to characterize *The Faerie Queene,* or at least to invoke its fullness and narrative-allegorical panoply, better than Amavia and the bloody-handed child Ruddymane. The obscureness of the quotation, to which Blake dutifully attaches Spenser's name, may indicate that by 1787–93 he knew *The Faerie Queene* so intimately that he could, with confidence, "evoke" it this way, even for an audience that was likely less knowledgeable about such "minor" specifics (albeit acquainted with the poem in general or "on the whole," as the spate of Spenserianism in the latter quarter of the eighteenth century amply testifies). Yet, one hesitates to apply to Spenser Thomas Minnick's claim that Blake knew *L'Allegro* and *Il Penseroso* by heart and may indeed have held much, if not all, of *Paradise Lost*—not to mention the Bible—in his memory as well.[25] But there is, I think, considerable evidence, well before his painting of *The Faerie Queene,* that Blake knew the entire poem far more than casually or "in general."

An additional conclusion is also possible on the basis of the *Notebook* entry and Erdman's analysis of its dating: somewhere between 1777–80 and, say, 1787, Blake was spurred to read *The Faerie Queene* as extensively and intensively as he apparently had read other Spenserian poems prior to his writing *Poetical Sketches*. Alas, there are no surviving letters from this period, but his reading of Lavater's *Aphorisms on Man* sometime early in 1789 may have had something to do with his wanting to investigate further what Spenser had done with the conventions of virtues and vices. Moreover he had read by this time Swedenborg's *The Wisdom of Angels, concerning Divine Love and Divine Wisdom*, not to mention the earlier *Treatise concerning Heaven and Hell, and of the Wonderful Things therein, as Heard and Seen*. His annotations to the former include his first efforts at the distinction between ''Essence'' and ''Identity'' as well as some discussion of ''Substances'' (E604, 606–7)—matters taken up by Spenser in a number of places in *The Faerie Queene* but most particularly in the Garden of Adonis episode and in the Mutabilitie Cantos. Indeed, it is tempting to refer one of Blake's marginal comments in *The Wisdom of Angels* directly to the Garden of Adonis section. Swedenborg had written that there is a progression of forms ''from first Principles to Ultimates, and from Ultimates to first Principles.'' Blake's ''gloss'' is ''A going forth & returning'' (E607). Spenser's ''version'' of this phenomenon is: he (the porter Genius)

> sendeth forth to live in mortall state,
> Till they againe returne backe by the hinder gate.

The relationship between the two passages seems less than compelling unless one recalls Blake's much later verbatim repetition of his annotational phrase in a context that clearly suggests his intent to rectify Spenser's error in the Garden of Adonis:

> All Human Forms identified even Tree Metal Earth & Stone. all
> Human Forms identified, living going forth & returning wearied
> Into the Planetary lives of Years Months Days & Hours reposing
> And then Awaking into his Bosom in the Life of Immortality.

This is the finale of Blake's apocalyptic conclusion to *Jerusalem* (plate 99, E258) and also his most glorious ''redemption'' of the natural cycle into the eternal moment of living, human identity. It is, in fact, an enactment of Blake's oft-repeated dictum that generation is an *image* of regeneration, that is to say, *merely* an image of regeneration. Such an image is what Spenser provides, cyclical in shape and process: ''So like a wheele around they runne from old to new'' (*Faerie Queene*, III,vi,33). For him all things that are created ''grow'' from eternal substance to form, each taking its proper form (''Meet for her temper and complexion''), whether that ''for reasonable soules'' or for beasts, birds, fish, ''natures fruitfull progenyes'' (vi,38,35). These forms are bodies within which substance then ''invades''

> The state of life, out of the griesly shade.
> That substance is eterne, and bideth so,
> Ne when the life decayes, and forme does fade,
> Doth it consume, and into nothing go,
> But chaunged is, and often altred to and fro.
>
> (vi,37)

Moreover these forms ''are variable and decay / By course of kind, and by occasion,'' for ''all that liues, is subiect to [the] law'' of ''wicked *Time*'': ''All things decay in time, and to their end do draw'' (vi,38-40). For Blake, this familiar generational and reincarnational cycle is a benighted ''image'' of natural regeneration, the image itself a product of man's reasoning process, which is itself a reflection of natural cycles. The ''bottom line'' of this total conception is, of course, Spenser's famous phrase, imaged by Adonis himself, ''eterne in mutabilitie'' (vi,47).

Blake's contrary, and hence redemptive, vision is that of the eternality of the identity of human forms, even those human forms of ''Tree Metal Earth & Stone.'' These are not merely the identities or forms into which eternal substance materializes for a span, but the living identity and indivisibleness of Spenser's substance and form, essence and manifestation, divinity and humanity, imagination and the Spenserian concept of ''reasonable soules.'' Generation and re-generation are, in these terms, un-concepts, for there is only an eternal, present-participial ''living,'' a ''going forth & returning'' that is an eternal ''Awaking into his Bosom in the Life of Immortality'' (E258). In more conventional terminology, the vision of plate 99 of *Jerusalem* is an enactment of the fact that ''Man has no Body distinct from his Soul for that calld Body is a portion of Soul discernd by the Five Senses. the chief inlets of Soul in this age'' (*Marriage of Heaven and Hell*, E34)—and in Spenser's age as well, with its militantly dualistic (that is to say, generational, sensory, and rational) perception of the nature of things.[26] ''In Eternity one Thing never Changes into another Thing Each Identity is Eternal,'' not merely its essence or only its soul, Blake says elsewhere. ''All Things are comprehended in their Eternal Forms in the Divine body of the Saviour the True Vine of Eternity The Human Imagination''—*are* (my emphasis), not will be.[27] Finally, to Spenser's view that

> in the wide wombe of the world there lyes,
> In hatefull darkenesse and in deepe horrore,

> An huge eternal *Chaos*, which supplyes
> The substances of natures fruitfull progenyes,
>
> (III,vi,36)

Blake retorts pointedly in his *A Vision of the Last Judgment*,

> Many suppose that before the Creation All was Solitude &
> Chaos This is the most pernicious Idea that can enter the
> Mind as it takes away all sublimity from the Bible & Limits
> All Existence to Creation & to Chaos To the Time & Space
> fixed by the Corporeal Vegetative Eye & leaves the Man
> who entertains such an Idea the habitation of Unbelieving
> Demons Eternity Exists and All things in Eternity
> Independent of Creation. (E563)

Unlike Spenser, and despite the judgment of some critics that plate 99 of *Jerusalem* is cyclical in nature, Blake, as E. J. Rose points out, "is no prophet of eternal recurrence." I cannot agree, however, with Rose that he is "fundamentally" a "Christian poet" who "conceives of time as a pilgrimage toward eternity."[28] As Blake's ambiguous syntax in plate 99 demonstrates, "going forth & returning" are the same act, which he defines as "Human Forms identified, living." The "direction" of the going forth and returning is governed by "Into" in line 3 of the plate, as are "reposing / And then Awaking." Spatially and temporally, this is the eternal moment in which "Planetary lives of Years Months Days & Hours" is (the singular verb required here) "the Life of Immortality" *in* Christ's "Bosom." In such a moment "the Outline the Circumference & Form" are identical "for ever," the "Circumscribing . . . excrementitious / Husk & Covering" that the senses perceive to be there are "circumcised" "into Vacuum," where they "belong" imaginatively, so that "the [eternal] lineaments of Man" are revealed (*Jerusalem* 98:18–22, E257), "All Human Forms identified."

I have pursued this rather long excursus not only to identify early a key aspect of Blake's quarrel with Spenser but also to demonstrate the extraordinary persistence in his imagination of the conception, images, and language of the Garden of Adonis section of *The Faerie Queene*, from his *Poetical Sketches*, Lavater, and Swedenborg days to the final apocalypse of *Jerusalem* some forty years later. If we return now to those early days of Blake's acquaintanceship with Spenser's poetry in the context of his reading of Lavater and Swedenborg, it is more than coincidental that the preoccupation of all three of these figures with the conventional wisdom of virtues and vices not only led to Blake's own proverbial wisdom in *There Is No Natural Religion* and *All*

Religions Are One (1788) but may well have prompted him to a more intensive study of Spenser's epic than he had hitherto accorded it.

In light of this, the "Spenser emblem" in the *Notebook* takes on even greater significance as part of a germinating presentation of "Ideas of Good & Evil." It will bear, then, a second look here, one that will enable us to see that the quotation seems displaced from its pictorial accompaniment. The emblem itself (No. 3, p. N18 in Erdman's edition of the *Notebook*) is of a mounted knight apparently deserting (or indifferently passing by) a kneeling, imploring woman, who may or may not have a babe in her arms (Keynes says yes, Erdman no).[29] Behind them is "a machicolated tower," suggesting a castle. By itself there is nothing remarkable about the drawing, certainly nothing that is unequivocally Spenserian about it aside from the suggestiveness of castle, damsel in distress, and knight errant. Taken along with *The Faerie Queene* quotation glossing Emblem 4, however, suggestion seems to become identity. Emblem 4 has a clothed boy trying to capture a flying babe in his hat, with another (dead?) figure at his feet—Blake's sketch for plate 7 of *The Gates of Paradise*. The quotation is:

> Ah luckless babe born under cruel star
> And in dead parents baleful ashes bred
> Full little weenest thou what sorrows are
> Left thee for portion of thy livelihed.

Erdman says that the legend "can apply" to the boy, the figure lying dead, the one still flying, and even to the reader.[30] But can it not also be applicable to Emblem 3, the "cause" of Ruddymane's plight in Spenser's story? The Spenserian cause is Sir Mordant's desertion of Amavia for the bliss of Acrasia's bower. Is this the subject, then, of Emblem 3, as Emblem 4 pictures Ruddymane's likely life thereafter? There is no way to know, of course, but what is clear is that by this time Blake seems to be deliberately putting Spenser's *Faerie Queene* to work for his own purposes, as he was already doing extensively with the Bible and Milton.

With such suggestiveness as inheres in these two emblems, it is tempting to search elsewhere in the *Notebook* series for corroboration of Spenser's impact on Blake in the context of "Ideas of Good & Evil."[31] I shall resist that temptation here (although I hope others will yield to it) in favor of considering the more solid evidence inherent in Blake's final two references to Spenser by name. They occurred somewhere between 1794 and 1804, one in Blake's illustrations to Gray's poems and the other a labeled portrait of Spenser in his series of tempera "Heads of the Poets" done for William Hayley (see figure

1). Although the two are related in certain ways, as Irene Tayler has observed in her fine study of the Gray illustrations,[32] let me take up the latter first since it is essentially simpler than the Gray.

The portrait of Spenser was part of a commission from Hayley (who had been instrumental in attracting Blake and his wife and sister to Felpham in 1800) for a series of "heads" of great authors to be used as a frieze in Hayley's library at Turret House. Of the list of those authors to be included, which was revised several times, eighteen of Blake's portraits still exist, a number of them in an unfinished state.[33] Although Hayley himself no doubt chose the poets to be included, he obviously talked with Blake about the project and may even have accepted advice from him. Those finally selected are an odd galaxy and hardly a Blakean pantheon: Homer, Cicero, Dante, Demosthenes, Chaucer, Tasso, Spenser, Shakespeare, Camoëns, Milton, Dryden, Otway, Pope, Cowper, Voltaire, Ercilla (a Spanish epic poet), Klopstock, and Thomas Alphonso Hayley, William's illegitimate son who died in May 1800. In 1925, when the series was first published, the condition of the Spenser had deteriorated so badly— "paint peeling off and varnish bad"—that little is discernible in that reproduction other than the head itself in its laurel frame. An editorial note under the portrait reads, in part, "it is receiving the attention of the Committee."[34] The committee apparently did authorize the portrait's restoration, for in the Manchester City Art Gallery exhibit of 1969 (if not earlier) it was in sufficiently good shape to be photographed, along with the other "heads" displayed at the gallery, and published in William Wells's catalogue of the exhibit. As Wells indicates, Blake's model for the Spenser was an engraving by George Vertue; to a generally faithful rendition, Blake added a large medallion around Spenser's neck with a portrait of Queen Elizabeth on it. Outside the laurel wreath and paralleling its contours is a ring of fairies dancing-flying, to the left Elizabeth herself in royal dress sitting in a crescent moon, to the right an old shepherd with staff.

Tayler describes Spenser's look as one of "supercilious elegance" (104). However different the look from that in Vertue's original, I should be hard-pressed to define it so absolutely. Of greater importance is Elizabeth's powerful presence in the painting. She hangs heavily from Spenser's neck, as it were, as well as "ruling" on the left as the chaste Cynthia. Tayler's conclusion seems to me correct: "the design synopsizes Blake's view of Spenser" (104), a view that is sharply divided between the efficacy of the fairy dreams that circle his head, on the one hand, and the aged pastoral (with staff, not pipe or harp) and queen-dominated poet, on the other. Spenser's look, then, supercilious or no, is hardly a happy one, matching Blake's own atti-

FIGURE 1.   Blake, *Edmund Spenser*, from *Heads of the Poets*
(courtesy of the City Art Gallery, Manchester)

tude; in Tayler's words, "he felt that the greatest danger to [Spenser's fairy] vision might be epitomized in the figure of a coyly demanding virgin queen" (105). And, one might add, pastoral innocence, as the aged shepherd indicates, is long gone. My analysis of the Britomart and Calidore figures in Blake's painting of *The Faerie Queene* (see chapter 7) comes to much the same conclusion.

The idea of Spenser's "fairy way" of writing, of course, is quite consonant with the later eighteenth century's new championing of Spenser—in the work of Warton and Hurd, for example, among a host of lesser advocates of what Hurd called "the charms of *fairy*."[35] More important to Blake, however, was the linkage between the world of Fairy and the structure of Spenser's poem, the latter more often than not described as Gothic, which Blake, from his earliest apprenticeship days, defined as "Living Form"—as distinct from the "Mathematic Form" of the "Classics."[36] Although Blake's appropriation of the Gothic for his own purposes is quite different from Warton's and Hurd's defense of the structure of *The Faerie Queene* on the basis of their understanding of Gothic architecture (neither Warton nor Hurd, for example, prefers Gothic to classical epic; for them the two styles are simply different), at the base of both is the creative power inherent in the land of Fairy. Thus, where Gray has his Bard say,

> The verse adorn again
> Fierce War, and faithful Love,
> And Truth severe, by fairy Fiction drest,

he is quite within the critical currents of his day. Similarly attuned, Blake entitled his illustration to these lines (he checked the third one above as the focus of his illustration) ''Spenser creating his fairies''[37] (see figure 2).

There is no evidence in Gray's poem, aside from the phrase ''by fairy Fiction drest,'' that he was anywhere near as ecstatic about Spenser's *idea* of Fairy as were Hurd, the Wartons, and others. Indeed, in *The Progress of Poesy* Spenser is omitted entirely, the divine line leaping from Shakespeare to Milton.[38] This is not to say that Gray did not borrow heavily from Spenser and most particularly from *The Faerie Queene*. But he borrowed from everyone—almost indiscriminately. As Roger Lonsdale notes, ''Gray's poetry is often a remarkable tissue of the phrases of other poets,'' to the point where Gray himself even feared being called ''Plagiary.'' But Gray once told his friend Norton Nicholls that ''he never sat down to compose poetry without reading Spencer for a considerable time previously.''[39] From the pattern of his allusions to Spenser as well as to other poets, contemporary and early, it is clear that Gray's purpose in such allusions (*intention* may be a better word) was to incorporate in his own poetry *le mot juste*, what was ne'er so well expressed: Spenser, then, as the poet's poet.[40] While Blake obviously found Gray's ''Gothicism'' in the Norse bardic poems to his liking, he quite clearly found no ''fairy world'' or fairy way of writing in Gray (again quite in tune with the eighteenth century's general reception of Gray's poetry).[41]

What Gray *did* find in Spenser, aside from the brilliance of his diction and phrasing, was ''Fierce war, and faithful Love, / And Truth severe'' as well as ''Pale Grief and pleasing Pain, / With Horror, tyrant of the throbbing breast'' moving ''In buskined measures.''[42] The ''fairy Fiction'' was but the ''dress'' of all of this, a separation of content and form that Blake would have regarded as the poetical equivalent of the separation of soul and body. Blake's illustration to Gray's lines reflects this duality in Gray and criticizes the similar duality in Spenser. The dominant figure in the illustration is a very youthful, robed Spenser, as unlike *The Heads of the Poets* portrait as it can possibly be. In fact, at least in the context of the Gray illustrations, Spenser's face is reminiscent of that of the ''Pindaric Genius'' of Blake's title-page illustration—surely less Gray himself (as the immediately subsequent Gray ''portraits'' in the illustrations to the ''Ode on the Spring'' make clear) than Blake's pictorialization of *his* idea of the ''Poetic Genius,'' the ''true Man.''[43] Although Tayler does not remark upon it, Blake portrays Gray himself, ''writing his poems,'' as so heavily robed that his human lineaments are all but totally obscured—always a bad sign in Blake's designs. In sharp contrast are the naked ''purple year'' of plate 3 and, most especially, the

FIGURE 2. Blake, *Spenser Creating His Fairies*, plate 12 of his illustrations to Thomas Gray's *Poems*

(from the collection of Mr. and Mrs. Paul Mellon)

proliferation of human-formed insects, zephyrs, flowers, and so on that crowd this same design. "It is not Gray who personifies the flowers," Tayler observes, "but Blake" (p. 48). Gray's own poetic creativity in the title-page design to the Spring Ode ironically eventuates in nothing more than the mechanical listing of Blake's own six designs by title. The sixth design seems to confute my point about Gray's human-form-obscuring robes, for it presents him in a familiar Blakean form-fitting body suit. But he has his back to us; neither his hands nor a pen is visible to create anything on the writing scroll before him. And, as Tayler notes (p. 52), he is firmly planted by Blake on the huge roots of the equally huge tree that dominates the left side of the picture, one branch of which hangs ominously over the entire scene, its pitifully few leaves reaching toward the ground. The scene is clearly not auspicious, and Blake accentuates its inauspiciousness by having, as his own title indicates, two "Summer Flies reproaching the Poet" with severely accusing fingers.

Despite Blake's own identification of the root-bound figure as "the Poet," it looks less like the Gray "portraits" in designs 2 and 4 than it does like the "purple year" of design 3. The "confusion" seems to me to be deliberate. The year and the poet, here conflated, join with the "sportive kind" of design 5 in succumbing to time; as Gray's penultimate line reads, "Thy sun is set, thy spring is gone," the Blakean reference being to the huge sun that pours light (as it turns out, vainly) onto the figure of Gray writing his poems in design 2. Gray is, as the "sportive kind" say, but a "Poor Moralist" after all, his "doom" foretold in the fourth design with its idle pen, severely staring eyes, monumental barren tree and rocks in the background, and the waters of materialism in the foreground. The human lineaments of the sixth design, then, are a kind of fraud or pretence, at worst a human form *human* on its way to the "grave" of Nature, emblemized by the massive tree roots as well as the barren, rocky landscape.

If we return now to *The Bard* illustration of Spenser, I believe we can "read" it more intelligently. Blake prepares for it in the two preceding designs, King Edward III in full armor, stunned and grieving over his dead queen, and Elizabeth I herself, protected and supported by Edward's reincarnation in "a Baron bold," both (with the text box) hovering above three bards. The reincarnation idea is not, I think, fanciful, for what Tayler describes as merely "a huge plume adorning" the Baron's helmet (p. 103) includes a plumed helmet, forehead, eye, and bridge of nose facing left, back to the previous design of Edward. Furthermore, Gray's own language must have seemed ominous to Blake, to say the least, for the bards are "Girt

with many a Baron bold'' as well as "gorgeous Dames, and States-
men old / In bearded majesty," all of whom "appear" in Gray but
are nowhere in evidence in Blake's illustration. Like a rayed sun,
however, the "form divine" of Elizabeth hovers in the clouds over
the text and the bards. She is, says Gray, "of the Briton-line" with

> Her lion-port, her awe-commanding face,
> Attempered sweet to virgin-grace.

All this seems unpropitious for the bards, but turning from this image
of Elizabeth to Blake's later portrait of Britomart in *The Faerie Queene*
painting, one is struck by its likeness to Blake's version of Gray's
Elizabeth. I shall deal in detail with the painting later, but here I want
to note that Spenser's association of Britomart with Amoret, Belphoebe, and Florimell and his summing-up of all three in Elizabeth
herself bode ill for the future of visionary poetry in her age.[44]

This identification (after the fact, of course, since *The Faerie Queene*
painting is still some years off) is nevertheless corroboratable by the
reference in the text of Blake's tenth Gray design (Edward and the
dead Eleanor) to the legendary idea of Arthur's return, the fundamental mythological basis for Spenser's entire poem. It includes the
blurring of all the knights into Arthur to parallel the blurring of all
virginal females into the Faerie Queene herself. The "issue" Gray
speaks of in the penultimate line of design 10, then, may be Arthur,
but Blake, like everyone else, knew Gloriana-Elizabeth's issue to be
nonexistent.

In the twelfth design, Blake accordingly inserts Spenser as Elizabeth's "minion," puissant in his youthfulness but unpromisingly
draped in heavy folds. The "fairy Fiction" he produces to "dress"
his "Truth severe" (to use Gray's terminology) is spectacularly out
of his element, as that "element" has been presented in the two previous designs. To accent this jar, Blake paints "fairy Fiction" as most
timorously "advancing" upon Elizabeth's, Edward's, and Arthur's
world, looking back apprehensively as if contemplating hasty retreat,
his hands held cautioningly or even in trepidation, if not outright
fear. Spenser holds back the text with the palm of his right hand as if
to clear the way, but the "way" pictured is the "Truth severe" of
Mammon's cave, into which Guyon is about to be shoved by Mammon's constant guardian, the "vgly feend . . . / The which with
monstrous stalke behind him stept" (II,vii,26). The other "truth" is
the Cave of Despair, complete with Despair's offering of a suicidal
knife to the naked human (clearly not a knight, or at best a totally
disarmed knight) before him; a second nude male is lying in the foreground, knife in his chest, oozing blood.[45] Blake thus takes Gray's

reference to Grief, Horror, Despair, and Care and transfers it directly to Spenser's two caves, whether Gray intended such specific reference or not. Among Mammon's cohorts in *The Faerie Queene* are Revenge, Despight, Treason, Hate, Jealousy, Fear, Sorrow, Shame, Disdain, Horror, and Care, the last not only not "sceptred" as in Gray but "selfe-consuming" (II,vii,22–23, 25). No "pleasing pain" here, as Gray (or his Bard) would wish. Given the nature of this world, Spenser's poor fairy may remind us of Blake's "Infant Sorrow":

> Into the dangerous world I leapt:
> Helpless, naked, piping loud;
> Like a fiend hid in a cloud.

(E28)

The fairy's "dangerous world" is Spenser's "Truth severe," the same world upon which Gray's poem concentrates. It is one fit for neither fairies nor bards, and we would not be surprised to find the tiny figure in Spenser's hand joining Gray's bard in his leap from the cliff into "endless night." In neither Gray nor Blake does that occur, but the fantasy, it seems to me, is not illegitimate.

The two figures to the right of the text box are more troublesome. Tayler identifies them as "Truth severe" on the left, and "fairy Fiction" on the right, the latter, she says, looking remarkably like the Spenser of the *Heads of the Poets* (p. 104). Although there are some difficulties with her identification of the two figures (which Tayler herself admits), it is impossible not to acquiesce in what seems to be Blake's literal illustration of the line he checked—the Spenser figure, the fairy himself, and *The Faerie Queene* allusions being his imaginative version of the line. As we have seen, though, that imaginative version is auspicious neither for Gray nor for Spenser (perhaps not even for the Bard who speaks the line). Accordingly, it is probable that Blake had other things in mind for the two figures aside from merely personifying Gray's abstractions. The clue to these "other things" seems to me to lie in Tayler's shrewd observation that "fairy Fiction" is "dressed in what appears to be a theatrical outfit" (p. 104). Exactly. Both figures are, in fact, on a stage—the one on which, in Gray's lines,

> In buskin'd measures move
> Pale Grief, and pleasing pain.[46]

While Horror too, "tyrant of the throbbing breast," is on Gray's stage, Blake has relegated him, in a nice visual pun, to Despair's cave with a knife in his chest. "Pale Grief" slowly moves forward in his/

17

her (it is impossible to be certain which) buskined measure, reading the book of consolation, totally withdrawn into his/her self, eyes downcast to the book, carefully composed. Next to this figure, with a look that must be "pleasing pain," is his/her companion actor in this allegorical minipageant, in a costume topped by a curious scalloped collar that almost harlequinizes his demeanor. Grief's book, Tayler suggests (pursuant to her identification of this figure as Truth), implies the "rigidity of doctrine" while pleasant pain's (Fairy fiction's) open scroll signifies "a creative product" (p. 104). Perhaps. But perhaps they are merely learning their scripts for the play, which itself will be a moralistic, perhaps even sentimental, parody of the stark realities of *The Faerie Queene* vignettes. If the two children on the cloud above their heads are in any sense versions of the Piper's inspiration in the frontispiece to *Songs of Innocence*, their tune will have to be a good deal more strenuous here to breathe life and "reality" into these pasteboard masks. Even so, they may represent the "voice" that Gray's Bard hears—"as of the cherub-choir"—that is, Milton's poetry will supersede Spenser's ineffectual, even misguided, efforts with a prophetic voice like the Bard's own. However congenial Spenser's creation of fairies was to the eighteenth-century critical establishment, Blake's focus on that Lilliputian creation immediately preceding the fatal plunge of the Brobdingnagian Bard suggests a poetical figure as impotent as Gray himself in the Spring Ode—"Poor Moralist" after all, perhaps, but with a modicum of vision at least sufficient to portray some of the eternal realities of intellect in *The Faerie Queene*. The precise nature and manifestations of that ambiguous attitude are the subject of this book.

II

Before turning to that subject in its fullness and complexity, however, something must be said about Blake's use of Spenser's texts. More specifically, which edition did he use (perhaps even own)? The question involves more than idle curiosity, for there is good reason to believe that Blake learned some things, particularly about *The Faerie Queene*, from Spenser's editors—in addition to what he learned from the Wartons, Hurd, and others, not to mention his own shrewdly critical reading.

Although it is possible that Blake saw or read a pre-eighteenth-century edition of *The Faerie Queene*, there were a number of eighteenth-century editions of the poem that were far more readily available. Furthermore, of the books that we know he had in his own library, only two were published before 1744 (the date of Blake's copy of Berkeley's *Siris*): a 1616 Chapman's *Homer* and a pre-1600 edition of Allessandro Vellutello's *Dante*, which the *Literary Gazette* says he used for his Dante drawings near the end of his life.[47] Given his habitually precarious financial circumstances, it is difficult to conceive of Blake's library as large or containing many expensive editions, Frederick Tatham's contrary testimony about Blake's "large collections" notwithstanding.[48] He could have borrowed an earlier Spenser, of course, but the range of his intimacy with Spenser's works, and particularly with *The Faerie Queene*, argues against mere short-term possession.

John Hughes's *The Works of Mr. Edmund Spenser* in six volumes (London: Jacob Tonson, 1715) must be considered a likely possibility. It is the first "modern," scholarly edition by a practicing literary critic of some repute, and it is also the first fully illustrated edition of Spenser, containing nineteen engravings by Louis DuGuernier— some eight of *The Faerie Queene*, ten of other poems, and one of Spenser's tomb. Based largely on the 1679 folio (said to have been overseen by Dryden), although making some effort to restore earlier quarto readings, the Hughes edition is now regarded as at best "a compromise . . . only fitfully and capriciously" carrying out the editor's original intention to correct earlier editions "and to preserve the Text entire," even "to follow . . . for the most part, the old spelling."[49] As Ernest de Selincourt puts it, in accepting the third folio as his basis Hughes also accepted "many of its errors and modernizations," and "many of his emendations" showed "an inadequate knowledge of the earlier stages of the language." Nevertheless, Hughes was "a capable editor" and "there can be no doubt that [his] edition did much for the reputation of Spenser in the eighteenth century." It is not true, however, that "all later editions before Todd [in 1805] were content with reprinting their text from Hughes," as will be seen below.[50]

The 1715 edition was reprinted in 1750 with minor changes (but without the DuGuerniers), thus perhaps increasing its availability to Blake. But is is precisely the third folio's and Hughes's modernizations that suggest Blake's use, and perhaps ownership, of this edition, for the only example of Blake's quotation of more than a phrase from Spenser is the *Notebook* legend to Emblem 4:

> Ah luckless babe born under cruel star
> And in dead parents baleful ashes bred
> Full little weenest thou what sorrows are
> Left thee for portion of thy livelihed.

All eighteenth-century editions other than Hughes's that Blake might have had access to before quoting this passage employ various versions of Spenser's Renaissance spelling. Hughes's is as follows:

> Ah! luckless Babe, born under cruel Star,
> And in dead Parents baleful Ashes bred,
> Full little weenest thou, what Sorrows are
> Left thee for Portion of thy Livelihed.

Except for the pointing and the familiar eighteenth-century conventions of capitalization, the quatrain is identical with Blake's. This does not mean, of course, that the Hughes text is the one Blake used consistently or even solely. Hughes provides a glossary of Spenserian words but, as every editor since Upton in 1758 has pointed out, it is filled with errors. There are some "scholarly" and textual notes, but for the most part they are relatively inconsequential. Moreover, Hughes's preliminary "Essay on Allegorical Poetry" in Volume 1 is distressingly conventional and filled with confused terminology. If it did anything for Blake, it merely confirmed his worst fears about Spenser's allegory. Allegory is, Hughes says, "a kind of Poetical Picture, or Hieroglyphick, which by its apt Resemblance conveys Instruction to the Mind by an Analogy to the Senses; and so amuses the Fancy, whilst it informs the Understanding" (1,xxix). It is also "a kind of continu'd Simile, or an Assemblage of Similitudes drawn out at full length" (ibid.), and finally, "the whole literal Sense of [allegories] is a kind of Vision, or a Scene of Imagination, and is every where transparent, to shew the moral Sense which is under it" (xxxix). In Blake's several definitions of sublime allegory, as distinct from allegory addressed to the corporeal powers, such terms as "Poetical Picture," "Hieroglyphick," "Resemblance," "Analogy," and "Fancy" play no part. To make matters worse, Hughes later confounds or blurs allegory, fable, and "literal Sense" (xlvii). If, then, Blake may have agreed with Hughes's general definition of allegory, he would have been appalled at the undiscriminating terminology, and although he may have been pleased to find Hughes acknowledging the prophetic books of the Bible as being the highest kind of such poetry (liv), the "such poetry" Hughes defined obviously would not have accorded with Blake's championing of the Bible as "prophecy" in his visionary sense.

Hughes's "Remarks on the Fairy Queene," also in his first volume, is equally conventional and notably unhelpful, except in the most rudimentary of ways. Essentially a tissue of oohs and ahs, the brief essay presents Spenser in his old-hat role of exceller in description (as distinct from Chaucer's excellence in character depiction) and "an admirable Imager of Vertues and Vices, which was his particular Talent" (xxvii). Indeed, this simple sort of allegory *is* Spenser, according to Hughes: "the *Fairy Land* of Poetry, peopled by Imagination; its Inhabitants are so many Apparitions; its Woods, Caves, wild Beasts, Rivers, Mountains and Palaces, are produc'd by a kind of magical Power, and are all visionary and typical" (xxxiv). He does defend *The Faerie Queene*, however, against the charges of disunity and even incoherence leveled against it by the staunch maintainers of "the Rules of Epick Poetry, as they have been drawn from the Practice of *Homer* and *Vergil*" (lx), thus establishing the fundamental principle of Spenser criticism that was pursued later more eloquently by Warton, Hurd, and others. The distinction is made vigorously, of course, in Blake's curious etched plate containing both "On Homer's Poetry" and "On Virgil" (E269–70).

But if Blake learned little or nothing from Hughes's essays (assuming he even read them with any care), Hughes's listing of the woods, caves, beasts, rivers, mountains, and palaces as productions of "a kind of magical Power" and as "all visionary and typical" has a familiar ring. In plate 11 of *The Marriage of Heaven and Hell*, on the origin of priesthood, Blake's list of "sensible objects" that "the ancient Poets" animated includes "woods, rivers, mountains, lakes, cities, nations" (E38). The similarity of the lists, however, is only apparent, for Hughes is not interested in the imaginative animation of these objects but simply in their presence in *The Faerie Queene* as allegorical constructs. John Upton's introduction to his 1758 edition of *Spenser's Faerie Queene*, though, does say something strikingly similar to Blake's point: "Every part therefore of the universe was thought to be under the particular care of a tutelar deity; when not only the sun, moon, and planets, but mountains, rivers, and groves; nay even virtues, vices, accidents, qualities, &c. were the objects of veneration and of religious dread."[51] Just prior to this, Upton had cited "Hesiod's Generation of the Gods" as "properly the generation of the world . . .: he gives life, energy, and form to all the visible and invisible parts of the universe"(1,xxvi). As I indicated in an earlier note, it is possible that Blake had read Hesiod's *Theogony* for himself even before executing his 1817 set of engravings after Flaxman's designs— and hence before the creation of *The Marriage*—Thomas Cooke's translation of 1728 being the likely edition readily available to him.[52] But nowhere in Hesiod is this idea of animating sensible objects expressed as Upton presented it. Frye has suggested that Blake's Leutha in *Visions of the Daughters of Albion* may derive from Hesiod's Eleuther (the "fertile earth") and Enion from Hesiod's Eione; Thaumas (perhaps an antecedent of Blake's Tharmas) is also in the

Theogony, "born of Earth."[53] But surely more interesting to Blake than the names was Hesiod's account of Jove's plotting of man's destruction by creating a "fair virgin":

> From her, the fatal guile, a sex derives
> To men pernicious, and contracts their lives,
> The softer kind, a false alluring train,
> Tempting to joys which ever end in pain.
>
> (Ll. 874–77)

Be that as it may, Cooke's quoting of a passage from Bacon's *Wisdom of the Ancients* in his appended "A Discourse on the Theology and Mythology of the Ancients" is even more tantalizing, for it begins with Bacon's acknowledgment that such poetic "fictions" as Hesiod and others write are "liable to be wrested to this or that sense" or even to have such meanings applied to them "as were not thought of originally." This "license of the few" (Blake's priests in plate 11 of *The Marriage?*), Bacon says, should not blind us to the essential allegorical intent and value of these "fables of the ancient poets," for there is in them "such coherence in the similitudes with the things signified . . . and in the propriety of the names which are given to the persons or actors in the fable" that they appear to him to be intended allegories.[54] Blake may well have read the Bacon essay himself, prefatory to Bacon's own elucidations of the meanings of familiar classical myths and personages,[55] but whether or not he did, it is striking to find this collocation of "Blakean" ideas in Hesiod, Bacon, Cooke, and Upton.

Far beyond what Hughes achieved, Upton's edition of *The Faerie Queene* is a full, careful, discriminating (and learned) scholarly work, with almost half of its second volume devoted to textual and glossarial notes. It was, I am convinced, "Blake's Spenser" (excepting, of course, the "minor poems," for which he may well have continued to consult Hughes), and its notes provided him with a wealth of material and suggestions for his painting of *The Faerie Queene* characters if not with his first thorough understanding of Spenser's epic as a whole. Let me here cite but two instances. In *The Faerie Queene*, II,vii,8, Spenser writes, in the accepted reading,

> God of the world and worldings I me call
> Great *Mammon*, greatest god below the skye.

That Blake would have noted the passage especially is attested to by the Gray illustration alone. Upton says, however, that the reading should probably be "God of THIS world" on the authority of John 12:31 ("the prince of this world"), 1 Cor. 2:6 ("the princes of this world''), and Milton's *Paradise Regained* IV,203 (''God of this world''). To be sure, Milton's precedent would have been sufficient sanction for Blake's famous phrase, but the scholarly to-do about it that Upton creates also would have attracted his attention.[56]

My other citation of Upton's notes is a composite, having to do with names and identities in *The Faerie Queene*. ''Britomartis,'' he writes, ''is the same as Diana, Cynthia, or Belphoebe'' (2,515); Artegall's ''name corresponds to his Christian name *Arthur*, and means *Arthur's peer*'' (2,527); and in creating Archimago, Spenser ''very plainly'' had in mind Chaucer's ''Monk and Frears'' (2,346). As we shall see, Blake makes use of (or otherwise reflects) each of these rather striking pronouncements, which either led him to read *The Faerie Queene* far more sensitively than Hughes's introduction would have prompted or (to allow Blake his due as a splendid critic in his own right) firmly corroborated his own perception of what is *really* ''going on'' in Spenser's poem.

Finally, two other eighteenth-century editions of Spenser and one dating from the early nineteenth century should at least be noticed— those edited by Thomas Birch in 1751, Ralph Church in 1758, and John Aikin in 1802. The first two, in their own ways, represent an advance over Hughes's edition, but neither provides the sort of interpretive, textual, or glossarial help that Upton's does; the third is of interest less for Aikin's editing (which was based on an amalgam of earlier editions) or for his life of Spenser than for its illustrations (first added in an 1806 edition) by Stothard, whose ''version'' of Chaucer's Canterbury pilgrims so enraged Blake.

Church's four-volume *The Faerie Queene by Edmund Spenser* (London: William Faden) includes ''Some Account of the Life and Writings of Edmund Spenser,'' written, according to Church's Preface, ''at my request, and communicated, in an obliging manner, by a Friend'' (1,xi). Insofar as I know, the friend has never been identified, but no matter—his ''account'' is limited to Spenser's life and details of his publishing career. Although Church provides footnotes that are somewhat more extensive than those of Hughes, they are mostly textual, minimally glossarial, and considerably thinner than Upton's— as is Church's glossary proper, which is appended to volume 1. Birch's edition (which Church ignores) does claim special interest for its sumptuousness—a three-volume quarto ornamented with thirty-two designs engraved by an unknown hand from drawings by William Kent.[57] Since Kent died in 1748 at the age of 64, the drawings were among his last artistic achievements, perhaps even the last— although at his death he was ''still busy with his finest domestic work, Holkham,'' Thomas Coke's remarkable house in Norfolk, which one twentieth-century architectural historian has adjudged "perhaps the finest of all the English houses of the eighteenth century."[58] No comparable judgment can be made of Kent's *Faerie Queene* illustrations, however. Much inferior to his famous designs for Thomson's *The Seasons* (1730), which, in their conceptual synopticalness, are similar to his earlier designs for Gay's *Fables* (1727), the *Faerie Queene* pictures represent a return to what Jeffrey Eichholz calls the "insipid style" of Kent's illustrations to Gay's *Poems on Several Occasions* (1720). Although Eichholz is not quite correct in describing each of the plates as revealing "a single narrative event" (on several occasions Kent conflates more than one event in a single design), his explanation of "some of the odd effects in these designs" probably approaches the truth, generously interpreted: "The result of the artist's conscious abandonment of certain rules of perspective and proportion, . . . Kent's only method, perhaps, of producing an impression of the fanciful in visual terms."[59] Nearer to the untarnished truth, however, is Walpole's judgment, albeit perhaps overly severe, as a reflection of the orthodox critical dicta of his day. To him, as to Eichholz and others, Kent's Spenser illustrations, although "exceedingly cried up by his admirers," displayed "wretched drawing . . ., total ignorance of perspective, . . . want of variety, . . . disproportion of . . . buildings and . . . awkwardness of attitudes" of the various figures. Although the book engravings were, as Walpole also acknowledges, "ill-executed" (something Blake would have noticed immediately, had he seen the edition), of greater significance is the distressingly conventional (and simple) nature of the illustrations; neither character nor landscape is reminiscent of anything in Blake's works. The whole set, ambitious as it may seem, is uncompelling.[60] If, as Margaret Jourdain claims, they "bear traces of Italian influence,"[61] the Italian progenitors were not among Blake's pantheon of artistic models. I doubt that Blake looked at or was even aware of either Birch or Church.

It is equally dubious that Blake knew of Stothard's illustrations in Aikin's edition (which was published first in 1802, without the Stothards), for there is no mention of it—as one might otherwise have expected—in Blake's *Descriptive Catalogue* (1809), where he pillories Stothard's Chaucer painting. I should not go so far as to claim of the Spenser, as Blake does of his rival's Chaucer, that "All is misconceived, and its mis-execution is equal to its misconception" (E540), but Stothard's plates (engraved by Heath) are hardly remarkable. Moreover, obvious liberties have been taken with Spenser's text, the sort of deviations Blake pounces upon in his *Descriptive Catalogue* excoriation of Stothard's Chaucer, leading to his conclusion, "When men cannot read they should not pretend to paint" (E539). To cite only the errors in the first plate (depicting Redcrosse and Una, captioned by the first two and a half lines of I,iv), Stothard gives Redcrosse neither a red cross nor a shield but does supply him with a lance, a glittering suit of black armor (showing no "old dints of deep wounds" nor "cruell markes of many a bloudy fielde"), a helmet with a gigantic brush-plume, and a flying cape fluttering behind his shoulders as if upheld by a gale. The dwarf is partly visible over the rump of Una's "Asse more white than snow," dressed (as nearly as one can tell) like a court page with immaculately bobbed hair. Una's look *may* be of "one that inly mournd," but her blank stare (she wears no veil) looks more trancelike than reflective of "some hidden care." Blake clearly would have had a field day with this, as well as with the other nine— had he seen the volume. Nevertheless, like the Kents, these illustrations deserve more attention than they have been accorded to date, even though they clearly are not the products of the sort of painterly genius Hazlitt called for in order to do Spenser justice.[62]

Not until H. J. Todd's great 1805 edition of the *Works* (in eight volumes) would Upton be superseded in the scholarly world of Spenser studies, although, as the *Spenser Variorum* eloquently testifies, Upton's notes are still (or were in 1932) a power to be reckoned with, as they were for Todd and all subsequent editors.[63] Since Blake's painting of *The Faerie Queene* characters dates from no earlier than 1815 (Keynes's conjecture) and more probably should be assigned to about 1825, it is certainly possible that Blake used Todd's edition. But, since the first substantial evidence of Blake's more-than-casual interest in Spenser's poetry was in the *Poetical Sketches* volume of 1783, it seems justifiable to conclude that the Spenser edition he may have owned would have predated Todd's. And given his extremely limited means, it is most unlikely that, when Todd's edition appeared, Blake ran right out to buy it. Operating on this premise, I give this edition (as well as the minimally glossed Hughes) short shrift in the following pages and, where useful and appropriate, rely on Upton.

One final word by way of introduction. In looking at the English epic tradition to see whether it is "Hellenic or Hebraic in shape," Northrop Frye speculates that a "peculiarity of English literature," namely, "that its national and religious mythologies do not have the same origin," may account for the fact that in its "early 'Gothic' period it did not produce a poet corresponding to Homer or Virgil":

It is not until after the religious capital of England had
been moved from Rome to London that Spenser gives us a
full epic synthesis of English Christianity in a "darke conceit" which is partly a vision of the purified English Chris-

tian Church and partly a vision of English history in terms
of Arthurian symbolism. . . . Spenser has a clear grasp of
the unity of British and Christian mythology, but perhaps
Blake would have said that an orthodox censor in his mind
causes him to make more use of disguise and camouflage in
working out his theme than a prophet should do. For example, he proposes to present in Prince Arthur a Renaissance
"complete man," and as to a Christian the only complete
man is also complete God, the association of Arthur with
Jesus would take him straight into the symbolism of Blake's
great hymn, "And did those feet in ancient time," which
opens *Milton*. But it is not clear that he has the nerve for
this.[64]

Whether it is not clear to Frye, or to me, or to Spenser's critics at
large, is not to my point—though it is, of course, a nice point of contention in all Spenser studies. What *is* clear to me, although apparently not to Frye, is that *Blake* charged Spenser with this failure of
nerve, a failure inherent in what Frye describes as "disguise and
camouflage," that is, the trappings of Spenserian allegory. If that is
so, and if Blake perceived the "true poet" in Spenser to be redeemable from the suffocating trammels of conventional morality (and indeed from conventional institutionalized religion and its self-perpetu-
ating sectarian wars), we must find evidence of Blake's turning the
"angelic" Spenser against himself to reveal the devilish Spenser that
was hid (to use Blake's labels from *The Marriage of Heaven and Hell*). In
other words, we should be able to see him emulating his own Los,
laying

his words in order above the mortal brain

As cogs are formed in a wheel to turn the cogs of the adverse wheel.

(*Milton*, 27:9–10, E124)

As Frye says, "our task would be much easier if Blake had left us an
extended comment on Spenser paralleling his essay on Chaucer."[65] I
have already suggested that Blake's pictorializing of the characters of
The Faerie Queene is that "extended comment," and I shall turn to it in
due course. But if indeed it was completed only in 1825, two years
before Blake's death, and if, as I have shown, Blake was reading
Spenser as early as 1780 or so, there must have been some indirect or
implicit mini-"commentary" punctuating his works in those forty-
five intervening years which served as a genuine prelude to his culminating rescue of Spenser from his demons, whoever or whatever they
were. It is to some of those minicommentaries, then, that I shall turn
first.

CHAPTER TWO

The Torments of Love and Jealousy

THE RANGE, subtlety, and sophistication of Blake's allusions to and use of Spenser's poetry in his own first volume of poetry, *Poetical Sketches*, are astonishing. The *Amoretti, Colin Clouts Come Home Againe, Epithalamion, Fowre Hymns, Muiopotmos, Prothalamion, The Shepheardes Calender, The Tears of the Muses, Virgils Gnat*, and a wide variety of episodes in *The Faerie Queene*, including prominently the Mutabilitie Cantos, all figure in the book to a greater or lesser extent. These poems therefore constitute a substantial beginning to a steady interest in, and commentary on, Blake's great Renaissance predecessor. I have explored the nature of this early commentary in detail elsewhere,[1] and although much of what I have argued with respect to Blake's "reception" of Spenser is pertinent to the present discussion, it would be impossible, not to say untoward, to re-present it in summary fashion here. I trust that it is not untoward, then, to refer my readers to that "prelude" as the originating force for my advance into—to change the Wordsworthian metaphor—the gothic church of which *Poetical Sketches* is the antechapel. Wordsworth is of course speaking of *The Recluse*, for which the passage he quotes in his preface to *The Excursion* is "a kind of *Prospectus*," *The Prelude* a "preparatory poem," and the "minor Pieces . . . when they shall be properly arranged will be found by the attentive Reader to have such connection with the main Work as may give them claim to be likened to the little cells, oratories, and sepulchral recesses, ordinarily included in . . . edifices" such as Gothic cathedrals.[2]

On the face of it, it seems absurd to consider all of Blake's works between *Poetical Sketches* and *The Characters in Spenser's Faerie Queene* merely as little cells, oratories, and sepulchral recesses, but one need not align Blake's career precisely with the particulars of Wordsworth's metaphor to recognize that, in one very important sense at least, all of Blake's works prior to the Spenser painting constitute "a kind of *Prospectus* of the design and scope of the whole Poem" that is the painting. Whether cells, oratories, recesses, antechapels, or the cathedral itself, then, in the next several chapters I enter into a substantial part of the body of Blake's poetical works in search of the ways in which Spenser's achievement impinges on it, is absorbed in it, is transmuted by it, and is otherwise "used"[3] to build on but go considerably beyond the allusionary experiments (and triumphs) of *Poetical Sketches.* Because I intend to focus on the "ways" of allusive usage rather than on isolated and individual ends susceptible to explication merely for its own sake, I begin with what appears to be a "theme" in Blake's poetry but will emerge, I trust, as a typical *modus operandi* for his sustained and developing apprehension and critique of his sense of what Spenser was all about.

Two of Blake's earliest poems, *To Morning* and *To the Evening Star*, deal intensively with ideas of love and marriage. They are, indeed, the beginning of his life-long exploration of these themes, which constitutes so concerted an effort that Jean Hagstrum was led to remark that "Blake may be justly considered the greatest love poet in our language."[4] *The Book of Thel*, some of the *Songs of Innocence and of Experience*, *Visions of the Daughters of Albion*, and several of the early, short prophecies come immediately to mind. But *The Four Zoas* is subtitled, in part, "The torments of Love & Jealousy" (E300); *Milton* is described in its opening lines as a "journey . . . thro' [the] Realms / Of terror & mild moony lustre, in soft sexual delusions" (E96); and *Jerusalem*, broadly speaking, is "about" the divorce of Albion and his "emanation" and their reunion.

Over thirty years ago, in identifying "female-worship" in Blake as "disguised nature-worship," Northrop Frye suggested that "all Petrarchan and chivalric codes directed to the adoration of a mistress are imaginatively pernicious for that reason."[5] There is no evidence that Blake read Petrarch or Tasso, although he probably did read some Ovid; nor, for that matter, are there any clear signs that he traveled widely in the realms of gold of the Elizabethan sonneteers. But he did read Shakespeare early, as the quasi-Shakespearean *King Edward the Third* of the *Poetical Sketches* testifies, and he read Spenser. Here I propose to look carefully at a work usually ignored even by those Blake scholars who mention Spenser at all, the *Amoretti*, which I believe had a considerable impact on Blake's conception of the fallen female (especially what he called the "Female Will") and on his familiar analogizing of love and war.[6]

Frye's insight is the more revealing if we recognize in a passage from *The Marriage of Heaven and Hell* a kind of extrapolation of his point:

> All Bibles or sacred codes. have been the
> causes of the following Errors.
> 1. That Man has two real existing principles
> Viz: a Body & a Soul.
> 2. That Energy. calld Evil. is alone from the
> Body. & that Reason. calld Good. is alone from
> the Soul.
> 3. That God will torment Man in Eternity for
> following his Energies. (plate 4, E34)

Compounding these errors, the Petrarchan or Platonic code not only
promulgated with equal insistence the first two of these propositions;
in effect, it prescribed Woman's torment of Man on earth as, paradoxically, "punishment" for his adherence to that code—a torment
that reinforces the separateness of body and soul, desire and love, the
"real woman" and the ideal form (*Idea*). Energy, in the code, is not
only *not* "the only life" (as *The Marriage* passage says it is); it is a force
that must be circumferenced virtually to the point of extinction. To
Blake, Petrarchan restraint of energetic gratification of desire is a sec-
ularized version of priest-ridden religion, the Female Will acting as a
surrogate God whom the lover worships precisely as man worships
the gods of poetic fictions, once those "mental deities" have been
"certified" as real by priests (*Marriage*, plate 11, E38). Appropriately, the passage of *The Marriage* immediately following the attack on
sacred codes deals with this Petrarch-sanctioned self-restraint:

> Those who restrain desire, do so because
> theirs is weak enough to be restrained; and the
> restrainer or reason usurps its place & governs
> the unwilling.
> And being restraind it by degrees becomes
> passive till it is only the shadow of desire. (E34)

That is to say, the unwillingness of love's energies to brook delay collapses into the willingness to deify virginity (theologically, socially,
and sexually to be "good").

In his *Hymne of Heauenlie Love* Spenser concludes with the image of Christ as heavenly love. "Thou must him loue," he admon-
ishes:

> All other loues, with which the world doth blind
> Weake fancies, and stirre vp affections base,
> Thou must renounce, and vtterly displace.

(Ll. 261–64)

Desire must also be displaced (or sublimated):

> Then shalt thou feele thy spirit so possest,
> And rauisht with deuouring great desire
> Of his dear selfe, that shall thy feeble brest
> Inflame with loue, and set thee all on fire
> With burning zeale, through euery part entire,
> That in no earthly thing thou shalt delight,
> But in his sweet and amiable sight.
>
> (Ll. 267-73)

The Blake-like locution (which is also, of course, a staple of the poetry of mysticism), "rauisht with deuouring great desire," leads Spenser to his logical conclusion: "all worlds desire will in thee dye," and, blinded by "that celestiall beauties blaze," man "shall plainely see / Th'Idee of his pure glorie."[7] Translated, if crudely, into Blakean language, to be blind is to see, and to see in such fashion is to "realize" (that is, make real) an abstraction—precisely as the enslaving priests of plate 11 of *The Marriage* do. Sadly, Milton made essentially the same error, and his history of this willing restraint of desire, Blake charges, "is written in Paradise Lost. & the Governor or Reason is call'd Messiah" (E34).

No doubt any discussion of the theme of love in Spenser (as Blake might have perceived it) should begin with *The Shepheardes Calender*. Mine does not. Of all Spenser's poems, Blake seems to have been attracted to it least as a specific resource for his imaginative reconstruction (or deconstruction) of Spenserian values or poetic practice.[8] There are, insofar as I have been able to determine, no allusions to individual poems or passages of the *Calender* in Blake's poetry, and even the "pastoralism" of the designs to the *Songs of Innocence and of Experience* owes nothing to what one might expect to be of real interest to the composite artist, the *Calender*'s graphic emblems. Such "commentary" on the *Calender* as there is in Blake, then, seems to me implicit in the sophisticated attack on all cycles and sequences, seasonal and diurnal, in his *Poetical Sketches* volume—and, more muted, in his later poems. He would have perceived quickly that, as Isabel MacCaffrey puts it, *The Shepheardes Calender*'s "circumscribing frame" is "at once linear and cyclical" and that "time dominates" it "as a geometric pattern which may be described schematically as a circle intersected by linear tracks."[9] If, as Kathleen Williams observes, "for us the natural cycle is in itself the way to death, and we will gain life only by looking to the cycle's source,"[10] Blake clearly would have agreed, but only in part. His "translation" of Williams's point might be phrased as follows: "For us the natural cycle is in itself the way to

30

death, and we will gain life only by recognizing the error of its source.'' That source is Urizen, not, as Williams suggests, the Christian tradition, or, more properly, the source is Blake's Old Testamental god, Nobodaddy:

> To God
> If you have found a Circle to go into
> Go into it yourself & see how you would do.
>
> (*Notebook*, E516)

In Blake's myth, the circle-cycle is Vala, Nature; even old Nobodaddy-Urizen-God does not do too well in it, for MacCaffrey's idea of formal circumscription is, to Blake, ''excrementitious'' and must be, rather marvelously, ''circumcised'' ''into Vacuum evaporating'' (*Jerusalem* 98:18–19, E257). It is no accident, then, that Blake's own ''shepherd's calendar,'' the *Songs*, radically avoids anything like the temporal structure of Spenser's, and that they are more remarkable for what they do with the idea of pastoral than for what they do specifically to, or with, Spenser.

I begin, then, with neither the *Songs* nor the *Calender* but with *The Book of Thel*, written about the same time as the *Songs*. Variously interpreted, depending upon whether Thel is identified as unborn spirit or innocent or already lapsed soul, the poem has also provoked considerable argument over the significance of Thel's entering her own grave plot and of her climactic, precipitous flight back to the ''vales of Har.''[11] The symbolic values of the grave itself, however, are uniformly accepted as those of Blake's state of Experience, the world of the body and the senses. But he substantially enriches and intensifies those values by defining this underworld in terms of a parodic Petrarchism, his likely source of which is Spenser's *Amoretti*, though he might well have read some Sidney, Daniel, and Drayton in addition to Shakespeare.[12] Even had he not read much Renaissance poetry aside from Spenser, he could scarcely have been unaware of the largely moribund residuum of Petrarchism in the eighteenth century, a lack of status in large measure precipitated by the seventeenth-century French critics' repudiation of it even as a poetic device. But in those versified embarrassments, he would have missed the full panoply of the tradition as it emerged out of the fundamental seriousness behind the ''play'' of courtly love—and, prior to that, out of the passionate genuineness of Petrarch's love for Laura.[13]

Well before the eighteenth century the familiar conceits had been domesticated, emptied of emotional power, and energetically debased into limp verbal constructs—or, occasionally and more vitally, resurrected into wonderful absurdity in such works as *The Rape of the*

Lock and, far less grandly, in this 1730 gem from Dodsley's *Miscellany*:

> But when her charms are in the dance display'd,
> Then every heart adores the lovely maid:
> This sets her beauty in the fairest light,
> And shews each grace in full perfection bright;
> Then, as she turns around, from every part,
> Like porcupines, she sends a piercing dart:
> In vain, alas! the fond spectator tries
> To shun the pleasing dangers of her eyes,
> For Parthian-like, she wounds as sure behind,
> With flowing curls, and ivory neck reclin'd.[14]

Such a dying, or ossifying, of belief into convention merely exacerbated what for Blake was the passive derivativeness of eighteenth-century art—inspired by the Daughters of Memory and valorized by the doctrine of Imitation. However amused he may have been at Belinda's fate, he never admitted Pope to his "devil's party," as his wonderful *Notebook* epigram entitled "Imitation of Pope: A Compliment to the Ladies" indicates:

> Wondrous the Gods more wondrous are the Men
> More Wondrous Wondrous still the Cock & Hen
> More Wondrous still the Table Stool & Chair
> But Ah More Wondrous still the Charming Fair.

> (E506)

Such non-art was not worth Blake's care, only his summary dismissal. Milton and Spenser were another matter.

To return, then, to *The Book of Thel* and to Spenser and Petrarchan sublimations of the senses and desire, what galled Blake most was the lover's willingness to restrain desire to the point of its becoming but "the shadow of desire" (*Marriage*, E34)—an extraordinary mind-forged self-manacling counterpointed by the hyperbolic physicality of the mistress's cruelty, disdain, torment, and warlike assault upon him. The poet-lover, as Sidney writes in *Astrophel and Stella* 61, may "invade her ears" with his "slow words" and "dumb eloquence," but it is *her* sweet voice that summarily undoes *him* to the point of his rejoicing in his pain. "Why cannot the Ear be closed to its own destruction?"—the first line of the voice of sorrow's speech in *The Book of Thel*—in this sense parodies a typical lover's complaint, brutally unplaintive to poor Thel's ears as it rises from the "hollow pit."[15] Undone already, but anticipating even more delicious undoing, all Petrarchan lovers (and, often, their mistresses) are similarly all ears, but the vehemence of Blake's line on the ear is strikingly reminiscent of Spenser's Sonnet 86 on the "false forged lyes" of jealous tongues:[16]

> Venemous toung, tipt with vile adders sting,
>> of that selfe kynd with which the Furies fell
>> theyr snaky heads doe combe, from which a spring
>> of poysoned words and spitefull speeches well.

The comparably devastating power of jealousy in Blake's fallen world needs no comment here.

The power of Blake's parodic construct is intensified by his apparent reversal of Petrarchan sex roles, the usual interpretation of the voice of sorrow's speech being that of the cruel male who terrifies Thel with a forecast of the sexual cruelty and warfare awaiting her in the "real" (that is, unpastoral) world. There is little doubt that, in one sense, such an interpretation is correct, as I demonstrate below with reference to Spenser's House of Temperance episode. At the same time, it must be recognized that Blake is at some pains to make the sex of this voice ambiguous, that is, to allow the voice to be, in effect, Thel's own as well, very much as Amoret's perception of and participation in the Mask of Cupid in Busirane's Castle are a hallucination precipitated by her sexual fears. Thus, the voice of sorrow's speech amalgamates both the victimizer and the victim of sexual torment, the eye, for example, receiving "the poison of a smile" while also "stord with arrows ready drawn" and with "fighting men in ambush." Similarly, the tongue is "impress'd with honey from every wind" yet also obviously feeds the ear with oral destructiveness; the mouth forms smiles that are poisonous, and the nostril inhales terror. The final two lines of the voice's speech not only refer significantly to "the youthful burning boy" and his "curb" in the third person but include both sexes in the plural of "our desire."[17] Sexual warfare in Blake's fallen world is no respecter of conventional sex roles—nor, as we shall see, is it a simple reversal of Petrarchan fictions. With this in mind, let us return to the language of the voice of sorrow's speech and its extraordinary ambiguity of allusion.

The Petrarchan mistress's most fearful weapon is, of course, her eyes, to which Blake accordingly devotes almost half of the grave-speech:

> Why cannot the Ear be closed to its own destruction?
> Or the glistning Eye to the poison of a smile!
> Why are Eyelids stord with arrows ready drawn,
> Where a thousand fighting men in ambush lie?
>> Or an Eye of gifts & graces, show'ring fruits & coined gold!

Daniel speaks of "murdring eies" (*Delia*, 37), Drayton of eyes as "turrets" and as sending "poyson" "to his hart" (Sonnets 130, 134), but Spenser devotes an entire sonnet (47) to the visceral cruelty of "smyling lookes":

> Trust not the treason of those smyling lookes,
>> vntill ye haue theyr guylefull traynes well tryde:
>> for they are lyke but vnto golden hookes,
>> that from the foolish fish theyr bayts doe hyde:
> So she with flattring smyles weake harts doth guyde
>> vnto her loue, and tempte to theyr decay,
>> whome being caught she kills with cruell pryde,
>> and feeds at pleasure on the wretched pray:
> Yet even whylst her bloody hands them slay,
>> her eyes look louely and vpon them smyle:

—the lover all the while luxuriating "in her cruell play." "Eyelids stord with arrows ready drawn / Where a thousand fighting men in ambush lie" is perhaps the most conventional conceit in Blake's grave passage. Sidney, for example, figures Stella's brows as bows, "And in her eyes . . . arrowes infinite" (Sonnet 17); for Drayton, eyes are "christall quivers" (126). But the trope of the mistress-warrior is of course ubiquitous from Ovid to Petrarch, Desportes, Ronsard, Barnes, Linch, Lodge, and other better-known English Petrarchists. It is one of Spenser's favorites as well, and Blake's language argues his recollection of *Amoretti* 12, 16, and 57. Sonnet 12 recounts the speaker's efforts "to make a truce." Under his white flag,

> all fearlesse then of so false enimies,
> which sought me to entrap in treasons traine,

he disarms himself only to be betrayed:

> a wicked ambush which lay hidden long
> in the close couert of her guilefull eyen,
> thence breaking forth did thick about me throng.

In Sonnet 16 the ambushers are "legions of loues" flying "in her glauncing sight,"

> darting their deadly arrowes fyry bright,
> at euery rash beholder passing by.

In Sonnet 57 the poet-lover again tries to sue for peace with his "Sweet warriour," no longer able to endure the grievous wounds of the "thousand arrowes, which your eies have shot." But of course he does endure, often ad nauseam, "weeping upon the threshold" (as Blake artfully describes the recalcitrant lover Theotormon in *Visions of the Daughters of Albion*) or, again like Theotormon, sitting "Upon the margind ocean conversing with shadows dire" (E47, 51).

Poetic convention is thus transformed by Blake into the all too real *quidditas* of sexual warfare in the world of the senses, a warfare whose destructiveness is inherent in (not merely the result of) an imaginative blindness to the fact that the very conventions thus made real are but the same fictions that, in *The Marriage*, poets create, priests "realize," and the vulgar accept—"choosing forms of worship from poetic tales" (E38). Apocalypse (or more simply, salvation) comes about, Blake tells us, by an *improvement* of sensual enjoyment (*Marriage*, E39). But more often than not (as in *Visions of the Daughters of Albion*), innocence that is "honest, open, seeking / The vigorous joys of morning light; open to virgin bliss" is perverted to "the modest virgin" dissembling "With nets . . . to catch virgin joy," turning "the wheel of false desire" and being an "artful, secret, fearful, cautious, trembling hypocrite." Worst of all, this calculated program is then sanctioned *and* sanctified by what Blake calls "Religious dreams and holy vespers" (E49). In the *Visions*, Theotormon is, says the frustrated Oothoon, a "sick man's dream," and if she subscribes to his code, she will become "the crafty slave of selfish holiness" (E50). The language and theological overtones here not only viciously parody Petrarchism but also lead to the even more devastatingly self-destructive "self-enjoyings of self-denial":

> the youth shut up from
> The lustful joy. shall forget to generate. & create an amorous image
> In the shadows of his curtains and in the folds of his silent pillow
>
> (E50)

—an image to which, no doubt, he will write Petrarchan love poems.

In the grave passage of *Thel*, Blake next refers to "an Eye of gifts & graces" that showers "fruits & coined gold." Though hardly conventional, the line is a cunning piece of Petrarchan deceit, one that strikingly, if surprisingly, includes an echo of *Samson Agonistes*, that splendid Blakean essay on the Female Will and self-enslavement.[18] The Chorus at one point describes Samson as

> solemnly elected,
> With gifts and graces eminently adorned,
> To some great work.[19]

In *The Book of Thel* that "great work" becomes a shower of gold that Blake surely associated with Zeus's rape of the imprisoned Danaë. It seems unlikely that Blake did not know Titian's famous painting (in which the gold is clearly "coined gold"),[20] but he also recalled, I think, the House of Busirane in Book III of *The Faerie Queene* (not coincidentally a book on Chastity), where, in the gold and silken arras, Zeus's "golden showre" that "Did raine into [Danaë's] lap an hony dew" is portrayed (xi,31). This stunning conflation of Petrarchism, classical myth, and Milton's God equates Zeus's lust (his gift to Danaë) both with God's gift, which is spurned by the lovesick self-restrainer Samson, and with the prostitution of love to battlings for dominion and also to money. Even Samson himself decries Dalila's "Spousal embraces, vitiated with gold" (l. 389). As Blake wrote more sweepingly later on, "Money . . . is The Great Satan or Reason the Root of Good & Evil In The Accusation of Sin" (*Laocoön*, E275).

The *Laocoön* equation is especially apropos at this point in *Thel*'s grave passage, since Blake next maneuvers his depiction of the senses and sexual warfare toward an explicit attack on the imputation of sinfulness to the gratification of desire (male *and* female) and to what he must have regarded as the paradoxical Petrarchan notion of "pure and chaste desyre" (*Amoretti*, 22):

> Why a Tongue impress'd with honey from every wind?
> Why an Ear, a whirlpool fierce to draw creations in?
> Why a Nostril wide inhaling terror trembling & affright.
> Why a tender curb upon the youthful burning boy!
> Why a little curtain of flesh on the bed of our desire?

This focus on the tongue, the ear, and the nostril in addition to the eyes incorporates into Blake's construct another Miltonic scene. Satan's intricate temptation design is initiated by appeals to Eve's senses: "fruit of fairest colors mixed, / Ruddy and gold"; the "savory odor" of the apple sweeter than the "smell of sweetest fennel"; the "sharp desire . . . / Of tasting"—all cast in what Milton describes as "honied words" (perhaps the seed of Blake's line on the tongue).[21] Milton's scene, of course, is prefigured by Eve's dream, in which her ear quite literally "draws in" the "creations" of Satan that raise in her "distempered, discontented thoughts, / Vain hopes, vain aims, inordinate desires / Blown up with high conceits" (IV,800–809).

Nostrils seem only bizarrely Petrarchan, and there is nothing similar in either Spenser or Milton; but Blake would not have forgotten that, as Adam and Eve indulge their lust after the "curb" has been lifted by their disobedience,[22] Milton again focuses on the scent of the apple:

> Soon as the force of that fallacious fruit,
> That with exhilarating vapor bland
> About their spirits had played, and inmost powers
> Made err, was now exhaled, and grosser sleep
> Bred of unkindly fumes, with conscious dreams
> Encumbered, now had left them,

they arise from their "unrest" with "darkened" minds, naked "To guilty Shame," "in face / Confounded . . . as strucken mute" (IX,1046-64). Adam is no "youthful burning boy," of course, but there is little doubt that Blake saw in him the lineaments of the human form divine grotesquely disguised in theocratic suppressed desire—the "curb" more appropriate to horse than to man—now erupting in bestial lust.

Finally, the curtain of flesh of the voice of sorrow's speech to Thel obviously echoes, perversely, the Hymen of Spenser's *Epithalamion* as well as all Petrarchan hymens, an echo that ramifies into what Blake calls later the

> Sexual Garments, the Abomination of Desolation
> Hiding the Human Lineaments as with an Ark & Curtains.
> (*Milton* 41[48]:25-26, E142)

Blake's redaction of Milton's phrase, the "fleshly tabernacle," in *Paradise Regained* (IV,599), is little short of remarkable. Only Jesus, the Imagination, can rend those garments finally in the infinite improvement and expansion of sensual enjoyment—in contradistinction to sublimated Petrarchan consummations, where curtains of flesh are indeed rude and drossy barriers. In the *dolce stil nuovo* tradition, as O. B. Hardison observes, the divinely virtuous lady after death "becomes a disembodied spirit—literally *angelicata*, 'made into an angel'"—an evolvement that "carries with it a suggestion of contempt for the world, since by contrast to the spiritual excellence of the lady, human glory becomes 'worthlesse.'"[23] The earth is "lothsome and forlorne," as Spenser says in Sonnet 13, the flesh "drossy slime." In this light, Thel *is* the disembodied spirit some have claimed her to be, the *angelicata* whose sense of her own uselessness leads her momentarily to reenter the world of sexuality and generation. But if, as Hardison argues, Spenser's Easter sonnet (68) reconciles *angelicata* and "cruel fair," flesh and spirit, desire and worship, in the context of Christian love and marriage, there is no such reconciliation in *The Book of Thel*.[24]

The reasons for Thel's failure are not hard to find. In a sense she is, in Arnold's terms, "wandering between two worlds" "With nowhere yet to rest" her head. She wishes to be of "use" but to be unused, to be prolific without being devoured, to be "found" without being "lost," to be reborn without dying (precisely as in the Renaissance double entendre).[25] In short, she longs for transcendence, the perverse innocence of ignorance Blake figured so devastatingly in the mock-pastoralism of the Vales of Har in *Tiriel*, a realm presided over by a personification of Memory (even his punning here on the word "Vales" is to my point). There, like Har and Heva, she would be able to "[play] with flowers. & [run] after birds . . . / And in the night like [an infant sleep] delighted with infant dreams" (E277).

But *angelicata* or not, Thel is a Spenserian Alma, that "virgin bright" in Book II of *The Faerie Queene* "That had not yet felt *Cupides* wanton rage" (ix,18). Yet Blake, shrewdly following Spenser, merges Thel-Alma's virginal image with that of the House of Temperance itself, fiercely besieged by the senses' excesses. "Against the bulwarke of the *Sight*" a "monstrous rablement" battered, Spenser turning Petrarchan convention to his own uses:

> And euery one of them had Lynces eyes,
> And euery one did bow and arrowes bear:
> All those were lawlesse lustes, corrupt enuies,
> And couetous aspects, all cruell enimies.
>
> (II,xi,8)

Hearing is attacked by

> Slaunderous reproaches, and fowle infamies,
> Leasings, backbytings, and vaine-glorious crakes,
> Bad counsels, prayses, and false flatteries.
>
> (xi,10)

Smell is "cruelly assayd" by "hideous shapes . . . like to feends of hell" that besiege the sense "with light illusions" (xi,11, clearly one of the origins of Milton's temptation scene). Taste suffers the onslaught of

> luxury,
> Surfeat, misdiet, and vnthriftie wast;
> Vaine feasts, and idle superfluity.
>
> (xi,12)

And Touch suffers from the "most horrible of hew, / And fierce of force" of all, significantly replete with Petrarchan weapons:

> Armed with darts of sensuall delight,
> With stings of carnall lust, and strong effort
> Of feeling pleasures . . .
>
> (xi,13)

Citing Britomart's rescue of Amoret from Busirane's castle, William C. Johnson argues that for Spenser, reason is "the one effective weapon against the hyperbole of the courtly love language and the allegorized dangers involved in sustained belief in passion for its own sake."[26] Blake characteristically stands this idea on its head. For him, reason produces the hyperbolic conventions and allegorizations as much as it infuses the idea of temperance or the Palmer's prudential steering of Guyon toward and through the Bower of Bliss. I have said that Thel aspires to transcendence. She does. But in typically perverse fashion, Blake couples this idea with her wish to reason her way to the wisdom of Eden or Eternity rather than to risk her "place," her virginity, and her sense of self in the threatening excesses of the wars of experience. To her, the very idea of improving sensual enjoyment is an absurd tautology, inimical to her vision of herself as an Alma-like Queen of the Vales of Har, perched (however precariously) on her "pearly throne." To Blake, however, she is what he calls in his poem *Europe* a "nameless shadowy Female" (E60), "the shadow of desire," an incipient Vala whose cruelties swarm through all the prophetic books.

It has been said of Sidney's *Astrophel and Stella* that its dramatic power inheres in the "confrontation between desire and convention," the sexually frustrated speaker emblemizing "the impact of desire on a convention manifestly inadequate to cope with it." Whether or not we can agree further with this same critic that Sidney's "ulterior motive" is to "bed" Stella,[27] the point about reason and convention is pertinent here; for Blake could not have been insensitive to the fact that Spenser's *Amoretti* is "remarkably free of expressions of strong physical desire."[28] Restrained desire thus produces not only the ugliness of secret lust but also the very literary form and convention in which it is sublimated to a desideratum, and Blake's attack is as much on the autocracy of the literary form as it is upon the perniciousness of that form's content. Thel's flight from the grave, then, appropriately is to what Blake describes elsewhere as "an allegorical abode where existence hath never come" (*Europe* 6:7, E62)—in other words, to a pastoral fiction where, as a proleptic Heva (in *Tiriel*), she may, *like* a child (Blake's language is careful), sit "beneath the Oak" and be

as the shadow of Har. & as the years forgotten
Playing with flowers. & running after birds . . .
And in the night [an infant sleep] delighted with infant dreams.

(E277)

Despite this (slightly) anachronistic reference, the fundamental identity of Thel and Heva seems to me confirmed in the twelve lines deleted in the *Tiriel* manuscript (E815). The first seven are a radical, and far more violent redoing of the voice of the grave speech (or perhaps its origin, since we do not know precisely the dates of composition of either poem):

> Dost thou not see that men cannot be formed all alike
> Some nostrild wide breathing out blood. Some close shut up
> In silent deceit. poisons inhaling from the morning rose
> With daggers hid beneath their lips & poison in their tongue
> Or eyed with little sparks of Hell or with infernal brands
> Flinging flames of discontent & plagues of dark despair
> Or those whose mouths are graves whose teeth the gates of
>   eternal death.
>
> (E815)

As insidious as Petrarchism was to Blake, pastoralism was, in a sense, worse. Tiriel's rejection of its comforts, games, and song is an instructive comment on Thel's defection—no matter how misguided his motivation and direction (he "seeks the woods" in somewhat the same maniacally determined fashion the speaker of Blake's *Mad Song* makes *his* world consistently dark—and, one might add, error-ridden).

Nevertheless, it seems to me possible to argue that, for Blake, Spenser—for all his benightedness—was redeemable in a way that, say, Pope was not. If, for the latter, "Whatever is, is right," Blake's response was the wry but unequivocal maxim:

> What seems to Be: Is: To those to whom
> It seems to Be, & is productive of the most dreadful
> Consequences to those to whom it seems to Be . . .
> (*Jerusalem* 32[36]:51–53, E179)

On the other hand, Blake may have regarded Spenserian allegory, whether Petrarchan or pastoral,[29] as but a fashionable mask hiding the lineaments of the true poet, a "system" as it were, not an ontology. Infected by the Daughters of Memory, Spenser's "fable" was not "without some Vision," whereas in Pope "Reality was Forgot & the Vanities of Time & Space only Rememberd & calld Reality Such is the Mighty difference between Allegoric Fable & Spiritual Mystery" (*Vision of the Last Judgment*, E554–55). Milton's problem was the same as Spenser's: only the names have been changed, the Puritan dispensation usurping the pernicious fictions of courtly love and its religious underpinnings. Such, it seems to me, are the systems from which it is Los's task in Blake's prophecies to "deliver Individuals"

(*Jerusalem* 11:5, E154). And so it is Blake's task. But if there are hints in *The Book of Thel* that Spenser is one of those individuals, we have a long way to go to solidify suggestion into fact.

Returning now to that poem, we can appreciate the full pertinence of Spenser's Busirane (to whom I alluded briefly above) to Blake's conception. Amoret, we recall, is the twin of Belphoebe, a coupling of Love and Virginity which compellingly poses the central questions of Blake's poem. For if Belphoebe is Virginity, not merely virginal, she is also the abstract embodiment of repressed desire, of abstinence.[30] Accordingly, Spenser's initial description of her is in the very terms that fill the *Amoretti*. If, as Harry Berger argues, she is a fine example of his notion of "conspicuous irrelevance" and as such imitates "the poet's [Petrarchan] presentation of her," she is also, in Rosalie Colie's terms, an "un-metaphored character, a character quite literally created out of the stock literary metaphors"; she is an "artifice," "an abstraction, a perfection whose origin is not human existence but the artistic imagination." She is, in other words, a deliberate fiction, just as her informing metaphors derive from an ultimate and even more fundamentally pernicious fiction, Petrarchism.[31] She is in *Thel* the Vales of Har, so to speak, as Amoret is the grave.[32]

It has often been observed that *Thel*'s Vales of Har markedly resemble Spenser's Garden of Adonis, to which Venus conveys the infant Amoret "To be vpbrought in goodly womanhed" (II,vi,28).[33] The garden has two gates, guarded by the porter Genius, "the which a double nature has": "He letteth in, he letteth out to wend, / All that to come into the world desire." On the way out, the "naked babes" are clothed with "fleshly weedes"—Spenser's coordinate phrase is "sinfull mire"—but on their return they "grow afresh, as they had never seene / Fleshly corruption, nor mortall paine" (III,vi,32–33). Contravening Spenser's paradigm of "eterne in mutabilitie," Blake's porter opens the gate to the grave with all its fleshly weeds and sinfull mire, the Clod of Clay's invitation to Thel to return as well as to enter satirically mimicking the naked babes' rebirth, free of "Fleshly corruption" and "mortall paine." The Spenserian cycle is thus short-circuited by Thel's retreat, Blake condemning both the "wisdom" of the natural-cyclical paradigm as well as Thel's reasoned preference for the pleasanter of two fictions. In this light, the apparent wisdom of the Clod of Clay's invitation to Thel to enter world of mutability—of the eternal cycle of birth, decay, death, and rebirth—is severely undercut, for that world constitutes the same dull round of Nature that Blake so consistently inveighed against. Spenser's Nature metaphor, "the wide wombe of the world" (III,vi,36), is thus most apt, and it is one that Blake adapts for his "Natures wide womb'' in the *Book of Urizen* (4:17, E72) and elsewhere in the prophetic books. In fact, the impact of the Garden of Adonis paradigm calls into question *all* of the advice given to Thel by her interlocutors, for each of them rests his or her case on the desirability, the ''eternity,'' of natural cycles. As Spenser puts it, ''So like a wheele around they runne from old to new'' (III,vi,33). The ''lesson'' Thel learns from the Lily, Cloud, and Clod, then, is precisely the ''lesson'' of the Garden of Adonis, that ''All things decay in time, and to their end do draw'' (vi,40). What she does not seem to see is ''that *Time* their troubler is,'' so that only if it were not for Time, everything that grows in the garden ''*Should* happie be, and haue immortall blis'' (ibid., my italics). When she flees the ''wide wombe of the world'' that is, as the Clod of Clay says, the earth's ''house'' and thus the violent obverse of the garden's (Vales of Har's) pleasantness and ''pleasures manifold,'' she flees from time into time, self and virginity intact, neither a Spenserian Venus nor a Psyche.[34]

Turning now to Busirane's castle and Spenser's Amoret-Belphoebe narrative, we recall that Belphoebe is taken to a Nymph ''to be upbrought in perfect Maydenhed'' (III,vi,28), unlike Amoret's ''goodly womanhed.'' When Amoret is captured by Busirane, then, she is Belphoebe-Thel plunged into the terrifying world of her own sexual desires and fantasies.[35] In that world, figured as Busirane's castle, Jove's lustful exploits, including (as I noted earlier) the shower of ''fruits & coined gold,'' adorn the tapestries, and in that world Amoret marches in the hallucinatory Mask of Cupid, her virgin ''brest all naked,''

> Of her dew honour . . . despoyled quight,
> And a wide wound therein (O rueful sight)
> Entrenched deepe with knife accursed keene,
> Yet freshly bleeding forth her fainting spright.
>
> (III,xii,20)

Her heart ''drawne forth, and in silver basin layd,'' Amoret is followed by Cupid himself and his terrible train—all, Spenser tells us outright, ''phantasies / In wauering wemens wit'' (xii,21,26). Amoret's metaphorical ''return'' from this mental ''grave'' is effected by her reassertion of her chastity—an escape-pattern Milton borrowed for his Lady in *Comus*. That is to say, Britomart appears, dispells Amoret's psychosomatic ''dying,'' and in Spenser's original version, returns her to Scudamore's embrace and a kind of Blakean hermaphroditic union. But if C. S. Lewis is correct about the Busirane episode's recording of the final literary defeat of the ideal of courtly love by the ideal of marriage, Blake would have seen Spenser's hermaphrodite as a bizarre and pernicious "solution" to a pernicious problem—indeed, as the ultimate confession by Spenser of the fundamental error inherent in the thrust of the *Amoretti* toward betrothal and holy matrimony. For Blake, hermaphroditism is "a sterile state of unreconciled and warring opposites," a "Twofold form" that is "The Female-male & the Male-female."[36]

As I have already noted, Thel, like Amoret, was terrified by the harsh reality of her fantasy—that is, the reality lurking beneath the Petrarchan fictions—and fled back to her more comfortable original fiction, pastoral innocence (becoming once again "like" Belphoebe). But no Scudamore awaits her with his "long embracement" and the mutual "despoiling" of "loues bitter fruit" (xii, original stanzas 45, 47). It was given to Thel to enter and return; Amoret "More easie issew now, then entrance late" finds, the vanished flame at the gate giving "her leaue at pleasure forth to passe" (xii,43). But true to Spenser's revised conception, I think we must regard the aftermath of Thel's flight back to the Vales of Har as Amoret's "gentle sprite" feeding "on hope" alone (xii,44). Whether Thel, like Amoret, is "thereof beguyled" and "fild with new affright" (ibid.), we cannot know, of course, but it is, in Blake's conception, far from likely. If, as Janet Gezari notes, "the players in the Masque of Cupid are activated Petrarchan metaphors" belonging not to the reality of nature but to the "reality" of poetic conventions that have captured Amoret's mind,[37] the knight in shining armor with whom Amoret hopes to be reunited is a comparable fiction, the same one Spenser dramatized in his rejected five stanzas. Similarly Thel, as incipient Heva, will be reunited in sterile memory to an aged Har, both pitiful emblems of "the years forgotten," huddling "for refuge in Mnethas [Memory's] arms" from the tyranny of age and mortality, as those are embodied in Tiriel himself (*Tiriel*, E277).

Many commentators on *The Book of Thel* remark upon its pastoralism: the Vales of Har (so this scenario goes) constitute a state of innocence and pastoral unity where human beings can converse directly with natural creatures that see no conflict between life and death. In Blake's later parlance, this is the state of Beulah. In fact, however, pastoral worlds, as Blake perceived from the beginning, were illusory retreats from the very world of cyclicity that Thel herself perceives the Vales of Har to be and that her interlocutors—the Lily, the Cloud, and the Clod of Clay—paradoxically confirm them to be in their efforts to assuage her sense of fading and decay. The poem's terse conclusion, then, is Blake's exploding of a double fiction, Thel's shrieking flight a classic out-of-the-frying-pan maneuver. The "fire," of course, crackles menacingly beneath the apparent comfort and invulnerability of the Vales of Har precisely as the searing quiddities of Brigants lurk beneath Meliboe's fancied Elysium in Book VI of *The Faerie Queene*. Thus, the Vales of Har must be seen as Blake's fallen world of Generation disguised as Beulah; in other words, it is an allegory. As another of Blake's fallen females (Enitharmon) cries at one point,

> Go! tell the human race that Womans love is Sin!
> That an Eternal life awaits the worm of sixty winters
> In an allegorical abode where existence hath never come.[38]

Clearly a Thel redivivus, Enitharmon's progeny are what Blake calls "nameless shadowy females," fictional products of a fiction. Named, they become "real" allegorical personages, as unsubstantial as the abstracted and realized God that the priests maneuver into being in *The Marriage of Heaven and Hell*.

Thel is Blake's first portrait of this "shadowy female," and both she and Blake are so insistent about her "shadowiness" that virtually all early interpreters (and some even today) regard Thel as an "unborn spirit." If, as is claimed, her name derives from the Greek for "will" or "desire" or "wish," all three significations are equally damning—the "will" becoming Blake's destructive Female Will and the "wish" underscoring the folly of her desire to remain in the never-never land of her illusion.[39]

A final note with respect to the most persuasive interpretation of *The Book of Thel* that we have to date, Mitchell's, in *Blake's Composite Art*. Although his reading wobbles somewhat uncertainly between the very contrasting interpretations (or judgments) that his own presentation is at some pains to establish as, in a sense, equally true (almost in Blakean fashion), he comes solidly to the conclusion that Thel's flight from the grave is a positive rejection (if I may employ that oxymoron) of "the hell of pain and terror she encounters in the underworld and the pastoral evanescence of the Vales of Har" (p. 83). Somehow, then, Thel does not "fail" (as the most common reading, including mine in *The Piper and the Bard*, would have it). Yet, in using "her reasoning powers," she retreats from and evades experience (p. 90); "instead of finding herself she creates what Blake was later to call the 'Selfhood' or 'spectre,' an 'abstract objecting power' which reduces the contraries of life to negations, and objectifies the human self to itself (*Jerusalem* 10:14–15, E151 [i.e., E153])." Although I did not allude to this later Blakean idea above, Blake's idea of negation is perfectly consonant with my point about Thel's preference for the illusory pastoralism of the Vales of Har, for the "abstract objecting power" is also the power that creates and sustains allegories and systems like Petrarchism—and, by extension, Spenser's poetry.

Mitchell himself tends to lean in this direction, but without embracing the Petrarchan implications as fully as I have. So he can describe the "love" implicitly defined by the voice of sorrow as "romantic love, that curious combination of pleasure and pain, guilt and idealism. . . . it will produce 'prisoners of sex.'" Thus,

> Blake fills the "voice of sorrow" with the love-language of
> Donne, Shakespeare, and the Petrarchan sonneteers to
> stress the larger cultural and historical implications of
> Thel's private sorrow. But Renaissance protests against the
> pathological character of love never take on the exaggerated
> anxiety one feels in Thel's voice of sorrow. They do not
> ask, "Why a tender curb upon the youthful burning boy?"
> because they think they know the answer. . . . Carefully
> sublimated sexual love may even lead us up a Platonic lad-
> der to that ideal realm. (pp. 93–94)

Just so. As I have indicated, Spenser's Alma is very much there as the Platonic soul, and, as Mitchell acknowledges (without reference to Spenser), "the senses are seen as breaches in the defenses of the self through which beguiling, destructive forces may enter, or as offensive weapons designed for the entrapment and destruction of others" (p. 91). If, then, Mitchell reads the totality of *Thel* as ambiguous, with Blake raising problems there which he "could solve only by writing more poems" and which we can "solve only by reading on through the illuminated books" (p. 87n), and if Mitchell perceives Thel herself caught between, and rejecting, "irrelevant idealism" on the one hand (the advice of her three interlocutors) and "intolerable realism" on the other (the voice of sorrow from the grave), his interpretation is not so different from mine after all. For, to my mind, it is not possible to regard Thel's flight as positive (certainly not "a revelation") if she becomes therewith an abstract reasoning power rather than an imitation of Christ—in my terms, a Petrarchan "heroine" rather than the anti-Petrarchan lover Blake portrays in the figure of Oothoon in *Visions of the Daughters of Albion*.

Indeed, in the *Visions* (E45–51) Blake provides a number of variations on Petrarchan themes as well as on the Spenserian error of Christian marriage as a solution to the "problem." Theotormon, the Petrarchan lover-poet, so to speak, not only writes no love-poems but is stunned into almost absolute silence (aside from tears and sighs) at the destruction of what he clearly had thought of as his Petrarchan mistress, Oothoon, who is brutally ravished by Bromion as she unliterarily flies to "where [her] whole soul seeks" (1:13). Bromion, in turn, will solve the problem of her soiled virginity by allowing

Theotormon to "marry Bromions harlot, and protect the child / Of Bromions rage, that Oothoon shall put forth in nine moons time" (2:1–2). Theologically self-manacled within the terms of love conventions, Theotormon cannot even contemplate such a course. Oothoon, recognizing this, tempers her "impetuous" desire for him (1:15) to the language of Petrarchism, calling upon Theotormon's Old Testamental (and, of course, Promethean) "Eagles" to

> Rend away this defiled bosom that I may reflect
> The image of Theotormon on my pure transparent breast
>
> (2:15–16)

—clearly a version of the love-sonnet tradition of the lover's "image pure" reflected in the mirrors of his mistress's eyes. She will even use the "weapons" of Theotormon's deluded image of her to defeat his courtly inaction:

> But silken nets and traps of adamant will Oothoon spread,
> And catch for thee girls of mild silver, or of furious gold;
> I'll lie beside thee on a bank & view their wanton play
> In lovely copulation bliss on bliss. . . .
>
> (7:23–26)

For in the very "jaws of the hungry grave" that so terrifies Thel, Oothoon can see "a palace of eternity" (6:1) if one will only "take [his] bliss" (6:2) "in the heaven of generous love" (7:29); in religious abstinence "the worm erect[s] a pillar in the mouldering church yard" (5:41), and marriage is a binding of one "who burns with youth . . . / In spells of law to one she loaths" (5:21–22)—another way of saying that the object of one's desire, once possessed in "selfish holiness," becomes the object of loathing. In a very real sense, then, in the terms of my analysis of *The Book of Thel*, Oothoon rejects her Petrarchan role as the image or fiction Theotormon insists on in favor of the anti-Petrarchan role of active lover. The former demands only "The self enjoyings of self denial" in which "the horrible darkness is impressed with reflections of desire," both the result of "seek[ing] religion" and its "rewards" for "continence" (7:8–11); the latter is the perception that "acts are . . . lovely" (7:10) or, as Blake put it in his earlier radical revaluing of conventional moral terminology, "all Act is Virtue" and "the omission of act in self & the hindering of act in another . . . Vice" (Annotations to Lavater, E601; cf. *The Marriage* 3, E34).

Finally, if for Spenser, Castle Joyous is an "*in malo* version of the Garden of Adonis,"[40] one might well argue that Blake perceived it to be the place within which Oothoon would procure for Theotormon girls of silver and gold. For "Such loue is hate" to Spenser, "such desire is shame" (III,i,50), and Theotormon, Britomart-like, will surely "dissemble it with ignorance" (ibid.), preferring the indulgence of egregious self-pity at the loss of his "image" of "chaste desires," which, for Spenser (sadly, to Blake's mind), "nourish" the "mind" (III,i,49). The risks in identifying Oothoon with Malecasta are substantial, of course, for Oothoon's notion of "happy happy Love! free as the mountain wind!" (7:16) is not exactly Spenser's lust. But neither is her magnanimous offer to Theotormon the road to the palace of wisdom. She may behold the "eternal joy" (8:8), but the gates of its palace remain forever closed to her in the poem (she can merely "wail" every morning, uncomforted by her clear perceptions that "every thing that lives is holy" and that the "soul of sweet delight" can never be defiled—8:10, 1:9), even as the grave is eternally open to Thel. Both will become contrary aspects of Blake's Female Will, Thel the autocratic Petrarchan mistress and Oothoon one of the very Daughters of Albion who, "Enslav'd" (1:1), weep endlessly at her plight and "eccho back her sighs" in a kind of demonic parody of the echoing in Spenser's *Epithalamion*.[41]

The later "torments of Love & Jealousy," not only in *The Four Zoas* but also in *Milton* and *Jerusalem*, are thus, in part at least, outgrowths of Blake's antipathies to the *dolce stil nuovo* tradition as well as to the errors of assorted other allegories. Before turning to those expansive forms, however, two other poems, significantly later (i.e., circa 1800–1804) than *Thel* and the *Visions*, may serve both as a useful transition from a more explicit to an increasingly subsumed (or assimilated) Petrarchism and as an indication of the steady persistence of that tradition and its tropes in Blake's creative imagination.

There has been little disagreement about *The Golden Net*,[42] the consensus arguing that the three females are a composite representation of external nature; the net (in some sense identifiable with them) symbolizes the restraint of desire, which in turn modulates into the net of natural religion and the tree of mystery. Each of the virgins is an image of self-repression, and in his misguided sympathy for them, the speaker himself falls under the net, paradoxically entreating its other victims for aid. Nets, of course, are ubiquitous in Blake, associated variously with religion, fallen nature, Vala, Urizen, the restraint of energy and desire, the Mundane Shell, and so on. Sexually they are female and implicitly, if not explicitly, threefold—that is, for Blake, representative of jealousy and warring sexuality, which achieve their most terrifying avatar in *Jerusalem*:

Such is the nature of Ulro: that whatever enters:
Becomes Sexual, & is Created, and Vegetated, and Born.

. . . their vegetating roots [spread] beneath Albion
In dreadful pain the Spectrous Uncircumcised Vegetation.
Forming a Sexual Machine: an Aged Virgin Form.
In Erins Land toward the north, joint after joint & burning
In love & jealousy immingled & calling it Religion.

(39[44]:21–27, E186–87)

When he was drafting *The Golden Net*, however, Blake's mind was too full of Milton (he was laboring at his poem *Milton*) to achieve such a brutal intensity. Since among other things, the poem *Milton* prominently includes Milton's struggles with his sixfold emanation (wives and daughters) and hence with the Female Will, Blake's imagination teemed with the nets, traps, and gins, the woven hypocrisies of the fallen female. And he had already borrowed from Michael's prefiguration to Adam of the world's future in *Paradise Lost* for his own vision of Thel's grave plot:

a place
Before his eyes appeared, sad, noisome, dark,
A lazar-house it seemed. . . .
. . . .
Dire was the tossing, deep the groans; Despair
Tended the sick, busiest from couch to couch.

(Ll. 477–90)

With all this in mind, it is not surprising to find Blake turning again to *Paradise Lost* to anchor his *Golden Net* poem. In summoning up for Adam a vision of "the tents / Of wickedness," Michael presents the "just men" who "Long had not walked" on the plain

when from the tents behold
A bevy of fair women, richly gay
In gems and wanton dress; to the harp they sung
Soft amorous ditties, and in dance came on:
The men, though grave, eyed them, and let their eyes
Rove without rein, till in the amorous net
Fast caught, they liked, and each his liking chose.

(XI,607–8, 577–87)

In *Paradise Regained*, Belial's advice to Satan in his quest for means to corrupt Christ echoes this scene:

Set women in his eye and in his walk,
Among daughters of men the fairest found;
Many are in each region passing fair
As the noon sky, more like to goddesses

> Than mortal creatures, graceful and discreet,
> Expert in amorous arts, enchanting tongues
> Persuasive, virgin majesty with mild
> And sweet allayed, yet terrible to approach,
> Skilled to retire, and in retiring draw
> Hearts after them tangled in amorous nets.
>
> (II,153–62)

Satan, of course, rejects the lascivious Belial's suggestion in favor of "manlier objects" (1. 225) to try Christ's constancy, but the net imagery is precisely Blake's—as well as that of Spenser and the other Petrarchan sonneteers.

Sidney Lee states flatly that Spenser, in the *Amoretti*, follows "Petrarch in describing his imprisonment in the net of his mistress's golden tresses," though he admits that "it is not always possible to determine whether he is the immediate debtor of Petrarch or of Petrarch's followers in Italy and France."[43] The editors of the *Spenser Variorum* point out even more cautiously that hair as gold wire, and hence as a potential net, has served poets well since medieval times.[44] Nevertheless, I have found no evidence to suggest Blake's awareness of the trope earlier than Elizabethan poetry or, for that matter, in such obvious places as Castiglione, Ficino, or DuBellay. But there is plenty of golden hair flowing throughout English poetry and, more to the point, many hair-nets. Sidney's phrase is Cupid's "day-nets" (Sonnet 12), and in another sonnet (103) he imagines the "wanton winds, with beauties so divine" (as those of Stella), "Ravisht" in such a way that

> in her golden haire
> They did themselves, O sweetest prison, twine.

Daniel's version is the more sinister "snary locks" and "nets" (Sonnet 14), and Drayton, reversing the sex roles, has his speaker contemplate "binding" his mistress with his own "torne-tressed haire" (115). But of the Elizabethan sonneteers, it is Spenser who makes the most sustained use of the convention. *Amoretti* 37, based in part on Petrarch's *Rime* 59, is as follows:

> What guyle is this, that those her golden tresses,
>   she doth attyre vnder a net of gold:
>   and with sly skill so cunningly them dresses,
>   that which is gold or heare, may scarse be told?
> Is it that mens frayle eyes, which gaze too bold,
>   she may entangle in that golden snare:

>　　and being caught may craftily enfold,
>　theyr weaker harts, which are not wel aware?
>Take heed therefore, myne eyes, how ye doe stare
>　henceforth too rashly on that guilefull net,
>　　in which if euer ye entrapped are,
>　　out of her bands ye by no means shall get.
>Fondnesse it were for any being free,
>　　to couet fetters, though they golden bee.

Aside from its rather startling pertinence to Blake's poem, the sonnet is of particular interest for Spenser's dramatic explication, as it were, of the trope. The mistress's hair and the golden net are at first distinct, only to blur into each other through mutual goldenness and finally to be identified. Further, as the mistress "enfolds" her hair in the net, so the lover is entrapped by her "sly skill," cunning, and craft. Quite literally, he becomes clothed with her guile as her hair is clothed with the net.

The Golden Net seems to begin where Spenser leaves off, with the attempted escape of the young man. Yet, in its erratically punctuated manuscript form (the only form we have), Blake's opening couplet, on second look, constitutes an odd fragment. Although the fourth line provides a finite verb for the apparent subject of the sentence—"Three virgins"—lines 2 and 3 seem interruptively exclamatory:

>　　　Whither young Man whither away
>　　　Alas for woe! alas for woe!

If we take the lines to be spoken by the three virgins, as line 4 seems to indicate, we encounter an immediate paradox. Since it is the virgins who are "Clothd" in "flames of fire," "iron wire," and "tears & sighs," in what sense are we to understand their apparent question to the young man (whoever he is) who seems to be leaving them? Perhaps they wish company in their misery. Perhaps it is an expression of their suppressed desire and longing. Perhaps. More trenchantly, the "question" of line 2 may also be taken as a punning imperative: "Wither, young man, wither away." That is to say, the young man's very perception of the three virgins and their "situation" is evidence of, or even constitutes, *his* bondage well before the golden net descends upon him. Nevertheless, just as in *Jerusalem* Erin bitterly laments that "By Laws of Chastity & Abhorrence I am witherd up" (49:26, E198), so Blake's three virgins consume themselves witheringly in the "ungratified desires" that are emblemized in the flames of fire, iron wire, and tears and sighs that are their "clothing." (Indeed, for "iron wire" Blake originally wrote "sweet desire.")[45] These accouterments of the Petrarchan lover's misery become, then, a mutual withering away, so destructive to the human form divine that the form becomes the physical embodiment of those accouterments. Even merely clothed with flames, iron wire (surely a torture-chamber version of the "golden wire" of Petrarchan hair), and tears and sighs, the three virgins' essential humanness has become the very engine of torture they inflict mercilessly upon the lover *and* themselves, in the service of the Petrarchan code. The "Net of Golden twine" itself, which they hang "upon the Branches fine" of the tree (under which, presumably, the young-man-speaker of the poem languishes) is a product of their flames, wire, tears, and sighs; but it is also a modulation of all of these, by way of the Petrarchan golden hair that ensnares the poet-lover, into an archetypal Blakean net.

It is unnecessary to invoke the manifold significances of nets in Blake's poetry to understand his point here, but we should remember that all his nets are "knotted" and "twisted like to the human brain," as he tells us in the *Book of Urizen* (E82). They are, in other words, mental constructs, allegories, self-conceived and self-imposed by the "weak" who allow their desires to be restrained because their desires are weak enough to be restrained. As Blake writes in *The Four Zoas*,

> the weak
> Begin their work; & many a net is netted; many a net
> Spread & many a Spirit caught, innumerable the nets
> Innumerable the gins & traps. . . .
>
> (II, E319)

These nets are not only made attractive and valorized by Petrarchan love poetry; they are also quite extraordinarily the very instruments of Petrarchan song:

> & many a soothing flute
> Is form'd & many a corded lyre, outspread over the immense
> In cruel delight they trap the listeners, & in cruel delight
> Bind them, condensing the strong energies into little compass.
>
> (*Four Zoas* II, E319)

"Every energy [is] renderd cruel," as Los says in *Jerusalem* (38[43]:26, E185), the "pale artifice" of the lover *and* mistress "spread[ing their] nets upon the morning" (*Four Zoas* II, E325) "to catch the joys of Eternity" (*Song of Los* 4:2, E67).

In literary terms, this entire process is precisely that by which vision becomes allegory. In plate 11 of *The Marriage*, to which I have already had occasion to allude, the imaginative realities of "sensible objects" that the "ancient Poets animated" are separated from their titular and tutelary deities by priests who "realize" (that is, make real) or "abstract" (that is, paradoxically make real by separating *verba* from *res*) "the mental deities from their objects" (E38). The erstwhile signifier is sanctioned (indeed pronounced) as the signified, the abstraction is personified, and rational-mechanical allegory triumphs over its imaginative bases, over "what Eternally Exists. Really & Unchangeably." "Allegories," Blake wrote simply, "are things that Relate to Moral Virtues Moral Virtues do not Exist" (*Vision of the Last Judgment*, E554, 563). Accordingly, he locates the scorn and jealousy raging between his epic males and females "In the little lovely Allegoric Night of Albions Daughters,"[46] that is, in the world of the unimaginative allegorical poet. One might say, without stretching the point too far, that Blake's divine artificer, Los, when fallen, becomes an allegorist, creating not only a system by which individuals may be delivered from systems but also an allegory by which readers may be delivered from allegories.

If we return to *The Golden Net* with all this in mind, we may see that the speaker's fundamental error is his belief in the realness of the allegory. As a result of this imaginative myopia, *he* weeps pityingly "to see the woe / That Love & Beauty undergo," reversing the roles of mistress and poet-lover. And in pitying, as so often in Blake, he becomes what he beholds—revealing himself to be the victim of the very burning fires and ungratified desires his tears seem calculated to ameliorate. Appropriately, the virgins—now no longer victims but victimizers—smile a "beguiling" smile (clearly not the "Smile of Smiles" that is "an end to all Misery" in the preceding Pickering Manuscript poem) and bear "the Golden Net aloft" in an apparent gesture of release for the speaker, only to cover the entire "Morning of [his] day" with it. And he becomes the now totally lost and fallen Petrarchan poet-lover, a full-fledged Blakean spectre:

> Underneath the Net I stray
> Now intreating Burning Fire
> Now intreating Iron Wire
> Now intreating Tears & Sighs[47]

—praying, that is, not to the Mercy, Pity, Peace, and Love that are, corporately, "The Divine Image" but to the allegorical abstractions now "realized" by his minimal twofold perception. In his *Notebook* Blake wrote:

> The look of love alarms
> Because tis filld with fire
> But the look of soft deceit
> Shall Win the lovers hire.

(E474)

Spenser's "flatt'ring smyles" that "weake harts doth guyde" and "the treason of those smyling looks" are not submerged very deeply in the deceitful smile of *The Golden Net*.

The poem ends with the speaker's pitiful cry, "O when will the morning rise,"[48] his erstwhile sympathy for the three virgins now come full circle to self-pity, and the poem come full circle to its first line. As Blake concluded in the dizzy spiralings of *The Mental Traveller*, "And all is done as I have told" (E486).

That spiraling or circularity is true as well of another "transitional" Petrarch-based poem, *The Crystal Cabinet*, also from the Pickering Manuscript. If the fact that the speaker-lover of the poem finds himself captured by a maiden, locked up with a golden key, and burning like a flame signals at least a residual Petrarchism functioning in the poem, the titular image is hardly as patent as that of *The Golden Net*. Nevertheless, it seems to me incontrovertible that the crystal cabinet is a remarkable conflation of Petrarchan eyes and mirrors. The poem is generally recognized to be one of Blake's presentations of his threefold state of Beulah, but it is too often forgotten that Beulah is also the realm of sexuality. "The Sexual is Threefold," Blake writes in *Milton*; the "Human is Fourfold" (4:5, E97). Threefoldness, while protectively "moony,"[49] and from its biblical origins associated with marriage, is also delusory—or, as Blake has it in the above *Milton* passage, "Woven," just as golden nets are woven. Cabinets, though, are rare in Blake. Indeed, his only use of the word outside of this poem is in *Milton* (28[30]:8, E125), in a context at least related to his conception of Beulah. In Daniel's *Delia* 60, however, the mistress's eyes are "cabinets of love," the paradise to which the lover's soul aspires. While it is true that this is not a consistent, or even a frequent, Petrarchan conceit, the assignment of crystal to eyes is common, from Daniel's Sonnet 14 to Shakespeare's 46 to Drayton's "Christall quivers of her eyes" (126, strikingly amalgamating eyes as mirrors, as the fountain source of tears, and as an armory of arrows) to Spenser, whose *Amoretti* 45 is the likely source for Blake's conception in *The Crystal Cabinet*:

> Leaue lady in your glasse of christall clene,
>   your goodly self for euermore to vew:
>   and in my selfe, my inward selfe I meane,
>   most liuely lyke behold your semblant trew.
> Within my hart, though hardly it can shew
>   thing so diuine to vew of earthly eye,
>   the fayre Idea of your celestiall hew,
>   and euery part remains immortally:

And were it not that through your cruelty,
  with sorrow dimmed and deformd it were:
the goodly ymage of your visnomy,
  clearer than christall would therein appere.
But if your selfe in me ye playne will see,
  remoue the cause by which your fayre beames darkned be.

As usual, what Blake has done to his source is crucial. Whereas Spenser presents his poet-lover as conceiving of his mistress viewing herself in his eyes, as in her own mirror, and even more truly in his "inward selfe" (which reflects her "semblant trew"),[50] Blake transforms this rather commonplace trope into an action: the maiden catching the speaker and putting him into the world of her eyes, where he sees another England, London, Thames, and Surrey as well as "Another Maiden like herself." It is an intricate Chinese-box effect: (1) the maiden sees the speaker, which is to say he enters her mental world; (2) the speaker's image is reflected in her eye, which physically, as well as from his perceptual vantage, places him in the "world" of her perception; (3) the speaker sees his own image in her eyes and thus becomes both perceiver and perceived in the mental drama that follows; (4) the maiden's mental-perceptual world, of which the speaker's image has become a part, includes the sum of her other perceptions, her mental-"real" world, as it were, replete with cities, towers, hills, bowers, and, most importantly, her self—or, more accurately, similitudes (to use a Blakean word) of all these things. The illusoriness of it all—that is, the mental constructs such a world consists of—is sundered by the speaker's attempt to physically "sieze the inmost Form." In literary terms, it is as if the personified abstractions of an allegory were to try to embrace a "real" woman inhabitant of the world of external realities from which the allegory was abstracted, or as if two abstractions suddenly decided to act as if they were really real, as the allegorist-priests of *The Marriage* pronounced them.[51] In any case, with that action, the crystal cabinet bursts and the speaker finds himself, like Keats's knight, alone and palely loitering—in Blake's terminology, "in the outward air again." This is, I suggest, a precise reversal of what happens in Spenser's sonnet, where the mistress's image, "the fayre Idea of your celestiall hew," "resides" in *his* mental world (heart) "immortally." But his tears, caused by her cruelty, distort that inner reflection (seen by her through *his* eyes now) which ought to be "clearer than christall"; if she would only recognize that her disdain distorts her own image in him, she would then "remoue the cause by which your fayre beams darkned be."

No such remediation, or possibility of remediation, occurs in

Blake's poem. Both the speaker and the maiden see themselves in (and perhaps through) the other's perceptions (eyes), producing thus a double illusion: the lovely maiden "shining clear" is "really" the "Weeping Woman pale reclind," and the speaker, not "really" "dancing merrily" in the "Wild," is instead "A weeping Babe upon the wilds" filling "with woes the passing Wind."[52] The entire action of the poem, then, is a kind of frustrated wish-fulfillment, a psychological, vicarious sexual adventure complete with beautiful girl and a soap-opera-ish "another world." The fantasy (which Blake may be presenting as adolescent if we can attach that implication to the speaker's "dancing merrily" in a kind of *Songs of Innocence* setting) is intensified by the inherent artificiality of the Petrarchan tropes and code out of which Blake constructs this paradigm of perverse (or perverted) imagination; but his own work also provides an intensifying richness to the poem as well as corroboration of the ultimate Petrarchan sources. For example, in Night the Fifth of *The Four Zoas*, the fallen Vala is described as "that once fair crystal form divinely clear" from whom now—in a striking echo of Drayton—"rage on rage shall fierce redound out of her crystal quiver" (E340). A series of actions analogous to the whole of *The Crystal Cabinet* occurs in Night the Seventh. There Los feels

> a World within
> Opening its gates & in it all the real substances
> Of which these in the outward World are shadows which pass away
> Come then into my Bosom & in thy shadowy arms bring with thee
> My lovely Enitharmon. I will quell my fury & Teach
> Peace to the Soul of dark revenge & repentance to Cruelty.
>
> (E368)

Similarly, in Night the Ninth, as the sun arises "in the crystal sky" of impending apocalypse, Vala calls upon Enion to

> awake & let thine innocent Eyes
> Enlighten all the Crystal house of Vala awake awake
> Awake Tharmas awake awake thou child of dewy tears
> Open the orbs of thy blue eyes & smile upon my gardens.
>
> (E399)

But, as the speaker of *The Crystal Cabinet* finds out, the crystal house of Vala is no paradise. It is but "a little lovely Moony Night," at best a sort of holding pattern in sleep prior to the real awakening to Eden and fourfold life and Imagination, at worst a sexual battleground or the very woven net of hypocrisies and ungratified desires that Blake surely saw embedded in his carefully chosen word "cabinet."[53]

Blake's speaker has merely exchanged one unimaginative reality for another, and thence falls into a third, where, as a belated "Infant Sorrow," he must now think of what's best for himself just as the maiden, now a "Weeping Woman pale reclind," must also. As Blake's Petrarchan eye and mirror images make clear, he who sees himself only, sees the ratio only (to reverse an early Blake dictum).

Blake's most devastating visions of this perverse Beulah—this illusory threefoldness—are in *Jerusalem* where, although the germinal Petrarchism has been all but totally subsumed, *The Crystal Cabinet* allusions sustain its impact. For example, Vala, now become "the Covering Cherub . . . majestic image / Of Selfhood," is equated with

> .a Tabernacle
> Of threefold workmanship in allegoric delusion & woe.
> (89:9-10, 44-45, E248-49)

Within this tabernacle of delusion sits a

> Double Female . . . .
> Religion hid in War, a Dragon red & hidden Harlot
> Each within other, but without a Warlike Mighty-one
> Of dreadful power, sitting upon Horeb. . . .
> (89:52-55, E249)

And, even more terrifying, from plate 70 (an ambitious reworking of *The Crystal Cabinet*):

> Imputing Sin & Righteousness to Individuals; Rahab
> Sat deep within him [Albion]hid: his Feminine Power
>   unreveal'd
> Brooding Abstract Philosophy. to destroy Imagination, the
>   Divine-
> Humanity A Three-fold Wonder: feminine: most beautiful:
>   Three-fold
> Each within other. On her white marble & even Neck, her
>   Heart
> Inorb'd and bonified: with locks of shadowing modesty,
>   shining
> Over her beautiful Female features, soft flourishing in beauty
> Beams mild, all love and all perfection, that when the lips
> Recieve a kiss from Gods or Men, a threefold kiss returns
> From the pressd loveliness: so her whole immortal form three-
>   fold
> Three-fold embrace returns: consuming lives of Gods & Men
> In fires of beauty melting them as gold & silver in the furnace

Her Brain enlabyrinths the whole heaven of her bosom &
    loins
To put in act what her Heart wills; O who can withstand her
    power
Her name is Vala in Eternity: in Time her name is Rahab.

(E224)

In an unpublished essay, Thomas Vogler has advanced the idea that *The Crystal Cabinet* is a manipulation of Blake's detestation of Lockean epistemology and metaphysics into poetic argument. In his view, the cabinet is the human mind, not merely the eye, "an epistemological prison governed by Locke's two-stage theory of human understanding," that is, the passive reception of sensory stimuli followed by reflection operating on the sensory data. But, shrewdly citing Blake's transformation of Locke's name in *An Island in the Moon* into "John Lookye," as well as "Lock" (E456), he associates the idea of a *crystal* cabinet with the familiar Renaissance crystalline humor of the eye as well as Newton's famous *camera obscura* experiments with a prism. I need not go into all of the details of Vogler's argument for one to see the remarkable appropriateness of his conception to my own analysis of the perceptual errors dramatized in Blake's poem. Locked in the crystal cabinet of his eye (and hers), all reality becomes mere reflection, a little lovely moony night of illusion which, to the speaker, appears so real (as did Newton's "image" of the sun on the wall) that he seeks to grasp it physically—thereby shattering the illusion and leaving him once again imprisoned within his "Vegetative Eye." "In chains of the mind locked up," Vogler suggests, alluding to the bounding and bound Urizen (E75), and, as a consequence, "in the outward air again," as Blake has put it in *The Crystal Cabinet.*

This penultimate line of the poem deserves some final comment. In its simplest sense it is, as I noted earlier, the return to "reality" from the perceptual errors that led into the world of the cabinet. But that "reality," as we have seen, is equally delusory, for it too is a product of the speaker's fallen perception. A brief passage from *The Four Zoas* will illuminate the point. On his "Couch of death Albion" turns "his Eyes outward to Self. losing the Divine Vision."[54]

We are, of course, a long way from Petrarch here, and from Spenser; but the consistency with which Blake manipulates the basic ingredients and conceits of the courtly love code and the persistence of those in his poetry, at least through the first decade of the nineteenth century, bespeak a steady fascination for what he shrewdly recognized as the psychological realities underlying the literary conventions—the very sorts of realities explored by Wilkie and Johnson in their recent study of *The Four Zoas.*[55] Or perhaps turning that around a bit, it is wise and more accurate to say that Blake invests with salvational significance and evangelical fervor a literary mannerism that essentially and politely (to Blake cruelly) masked the imaginative realities inherent in all human relationships, despite the games people play.

Those games, as I noted in the beginning of this chapter, are, in a sense, the *modus operandi* (or one of several modes) of each of Blake's epic prophecies, though they are, of course, not their "subject" and the game-players are hardly courtly lovers. My previous glances forward to passages in *The Four Zoas*, *Milton*, and *Jerusalem* to help illuminate the precise nature of Blake's earlier anti-Petrarchism (and, thereby, a portion of his critique of Spenser) indicate in some measure the pervasiveness of the traditional tropes in his imagination. What happens to those tropes in the major prophecies, however, reflects a considerable advance over, and often a radical transmutation and intensification of, the tropes themselves into the visceral realities of which they were, to Blake, temporarily useful but finally unsatisfactory emblems. It is as if, once having pillaged the tradition to mercilessly expose the perniciousness of its fictions (in the *Songs*, early short prophecies, and the "new" lyric form of the Pickering Manuscript poems), Blake, in turning to epic forms, saw that he must, like Spenser in *The Faerie Queene*, demote Petrarchism to a role at best subsidiary to a focus on (in C. S. Lewis's words, quoted earlier) "the deep human suffering which underlies" courtly love. There is a paradox in such a move, of course, for the earlier poems— *Thel*, *The Golden Net*, and *The Crystal Cabinet*—function in the human realm of love, lust, and jealousy, the characters recognizably like ourselves. What happens in the epics is that Blake subtracts the "like ourselves" part of the equation, leaving thereby the naked passions themselves as his central characters. Thus, when he subtitles *The Four Zoas* "The torments of Love & Jealousy," he means that Love and Jealousy themselves, in all their complexities and nuances, will battle it out in the arena of the human mind. The rest of the subtitle clearly points the way: the torments will take place "*in* The Death and Judgement of Albion the Ancient Man." Cementing this radical change of tactics is Blake's appended quotation (in the original Greek) from Ephesians: "For our contention is not with the blood and the flesh, but with dominion, with authority, with the blind world—rulers of this life, with the spirit of evil in things heavenly" with "principalities" and "powers."[56] Blake's poetic mode (he says) will therefore be "heroic," as is appropriate "for the day of Intellectual Battle" (E300).

To put this all rather too crudely, but I think not outrageously, Blake will now write his *Faerie Queene* and leave his *Shepheardes Calender* and *Amoretti* behind. Another passage in chapter 6 of Ephesians is to the point: Paul urges his audience to pray "always with all prayer and supplication in the Spirit"; "to take unto you the whole armour of God"; to have "your loins girt about with truth" and "have on the breastplate of righteousness"; to take "the shield of faith, wherewith ye shall be able to quench all the fiery darts of the wicked"; to "take the helmet of salvation, and the sword of the Spirit, which is the word of God" (vv. 13–17). I find it difficult not to believe that Blake associated this familiar imagery with Spenser's knights (as Spenser himself did in the Letter to Raleigh, with respect to his creation of Redcrosse—and perhaps Arthur). Blake's own hint of this may be in the passage at the top of page 4 of the *Zoas* manuscript, in which Blake's *unfallen* poet, Urthona, propagates "in the Auricular Nerves of Human Life / Which is the Earth of Eden . . . / Fairies of Albion afterwards the Gods of the Heathen" (E301). In any case, Blake was acutely aware that *all* mythologies have a habit of deteriorating into "realized" heathen gods and into systems that enslave their very makers as well as the "vulgar" upon whom all systems are so rudely and tyrannically imposed. Thus, for Blake, even the Bible's mythology had to be read in its infernal sense, as did the Greek Poets and Milton—and Spenser.

By the time he was in the midst of his monumental struggle with the abortive *Four Zoas* manuscript, he came to realize that Petrarchism was not so much a mythology as an enabling means of sustaining the regnant mythology in the context of human intercourse. It would have been no revelation to him to discover that courtly love was a "love religion," the lady significantly virginal as well as cruel (and "holy"), the lover an abased eremite at her shrine. And if he was aware that Ovid and some of his French followers produced what Lewis calls "impudent" parodies "of the practices of the Church, in which the *Ars Amatoria* becomes the gospel,"[57] that would only have confirmed the perniciousness of the "system" and its allegorical embalmings. *The Four Zoas*, then, as well as *Milton* and *Jerusalem* later on, are, among other things, Blake's efforts to annihilate the power of all mythologies, not merely their operative agents, or what I have called their enabling means.[58] To do that obviously required what he called "the march of long resounding, strong, heroic Verse" of epic prophecy (or prophetic epic), the origins of which he found in Daniel, Isaiah, and Revelation. The pastoralism of *The Book of Thel* (for all the terror of its mythological descent into the entrails of the grave), Blake's militant antibiblical stance in the earlier short prophecies, his concerted attempts to rewrite history, and his narrow focusing on vehicular metaphor in the later lyrics, were all, in a sense, false starts—

something like anatomies of symptoms rather than a concerted attack on and "cure" for root causes.[59] Those causes, of course, are in the human brain, "Living Creatures" nonetheless, the natures of which (Blake wrote) only "the Heavenly Father" knew. What *The Four Zoas* essays, then, is no less than an effort to *know* them, even while Blake admits at the outset that "no Individual" knoweth them, nor "Can know in all Eternity" (E301). Is it any wonder that he never wrestled the poem into final form? In its apocalyptic conclusion, even as Blake envisions Urthona (his delusive phantom, the fallen Los, now departed) rising

> from the ruinous walls
> In all his ancient strength to form the golden armour of science
> For intellectual War The war of swords departed now
> The dark Religions are departed & sweet Science reigns,
>
> (E407)

he knows that he has now but come to *know* those zoas better and that the "real" "Intellectual War," not the "war of swords," is still ahead of him. The "Greek and Roman Models" he rejects in the Preface to *Milton* (E95), the Miltonic model he implicitly rejects on the title page of that poem by claiming that his purpose is "To Justify the Ways of God to Men" (E95), the absorption of Spenser's "Fairies of Albion" into his own idea of spectres and emanations, *and* his concomitant embrace of the prophetic books of the Bible—all signal the demise of "mere" Petrarchism, or anti-Petrarchism, in his own version of epic.

Verbal remnants do remain, however, and it is not without significance that the stirring prefatory hymn in *Milton* adapts Petrarchan metaphors to "Mental Fight":

> Bring me my Bow of burning gold:
> Bring me my Arrows of desire:
> Bring me my Spear: O clouds unfold!
> Bring me my Chariot of Fire.[60]

Milton's bows, arrows, spears, and chariots are here also, of course, as are those of Homer's warriors, gods, and goddesses and those of Spenser's knights and assorted allegorical figures. But the "Sword" that Blake says shall not "sleep in his hand" is the sword, *minus* its initial "s," of Revelation, the prophetic and apocalyptic sword-word out of the mouth; the bow has been taken out of Cupid's silly hands as well as out of the savage hands of man, god, angel, and devil alike, to be Miltonized into the rainbowed end of Book XI of *Paradise Lost*, God's final convenant with man:

> when he brings
> Over the earth a cloud, he will therein sit
> His triple-colored bow, whereon to look
> And call to mind his cov'nant.

(Ll. 895–98)

And when "fire purges all things new, / Both heav'n and earth, wherein the just shall dwell," so too will Blake and *his* disciples build Jerusalem "In Englands green & pleasant Land."

But Spenser is here too, I think. However much Blake may have cringed at Redcrosse's humbling instruction in the House of Holinesse, the vision of Hierusalem to which he is led would have impressed him. It is "a goodly Citie" whose "wals and towres were builded high and strong / Of perle and precious stone." For Spenser, it is God that "has built" it

> For those to dwell in, that are chosen his,
> His chosen people purg'd from sinfull guilt.

(I,x,57)

Again Blake would have demurred, but I think he also would have remembered with pleasure that Cleopolis, "for earthly frame, / The fairest peece, that eye beholden can," is the image of Jerusalem on earth, and Redcrosse, "sprong out from English race," will in effect build at least a metaphorical Jerusalem in England as its patron saint (ll. 60–61). But to do this, Redcrosse must—as Spenser must (the latter suggests it by conflating Sinai, the Mount of Olives, and Parnassus in stanzas 53–54) and Blake must—not remain "in peace" in Celia's house contemplating his future "long voyage" to the cabin in the sky but must "turne againe / Back to the world" and with his knightly weapons (now translated into the nice Blakean metaphor of the plough) build that new Jerusalem *in* England's green and pleasant land (63, 66). The ultimate source of all this building, of course, is the Bible, in the Psalms, Isaiah, Daniel, and elsewhere, but perhaps most particularly in Revelation. There the "new Jerusalem," John says in a usefully ambiguous grammatical construction, comes "down out of heaven from my God" (21:1). Jerusalem is not, as in Spenser, built "out there" somewhere but rather is *re*built continuously, that is, redeemed, descended anew "out of heaven from God" (Rev. 21:10). In Blake it descends to, is redeemed in, is built in England, which is Albion, who is Jerusalem, which is Imagination, the site of Blake's poem—as it is, without their knowing it to a greater or lesser degree, the site of Milton's great epics and Spenser's fairy cosmos.

We are by now a long way from Petrarch and the courtly code, this excursus intended, in part at least, to measure that enormous distance. Nevertheless, as I indicated earlier, the trappings of Petrarchism remain, and a brief look at one or two of these remnants will, I think, be sufficient to show how the increasingly receding *Amoretti* and its metaphorical world get absorbed into the very sinew of prophecy.

Certainly one of the most stunning of these absorptions is what Wilkie and Johnson call, perceptively, Enitharmon's "canticle" in Night II of *The Four Zoas*: "Delivered with sensuous languor, the canticle is the definitive prescription of how to tame men by alluring and emasculating them at the same time (and is thus, among other things, both an exposition and an exposé of the tradition of courtly love)." Equally important, "Enitharmon's ability to unman Los is made possible by her allegiance to her 'God' Urizen."[61] The canticle begins with Enitharmon's extraordinary evocation of pastoral landscape brought into being by the sound of her Orphic "sphery harp": "the Golden sun arises from the Deep," and Blake dazzlingly figures the echo of that "first Sound" as waking "the moon to unbind her silver locks" (E323). But the very triteness of the language signals the inefficacy of its metaphysical assumptions, and the song itself quickly emerges as diabolical:

> The joy of woman is the Death of her most best beloved
> Who dies for Love of her
> In torments of fierce jealousy & pangs of adoration.
>
> (E324)

In the world of Nature, however, the same one Spenser figures in his Garden of Adonis, this "time" is one of rejoicing in the fullness of "living harmony":

> The birds & beasts rejoice & play
> And every one seeks for his mate to prove his inmost joy.
>
> (E324)

Spenser's version of this is:

> All that in this delightfull Gardin growes,
> Should happie be, and haue immortall blis:
> For here all plentie, and all pleasure flowes,
> And sweet loue gentle fits emongst them throwes,
> Without fell rancor, or fond gealosie;

> Franckly each paramour his leman knowes,
> Each bird his mate, ne any does enuie
> Their goodly meriment, and gay felicitie.

(III,vi,41)

Moreover Venus, "when euer that she will, / Possesseth" Adonis "and of his sweetnesse takes her fill" (46). In turn, Blake's version of that is Enitharmon's ecstatic "Arise you little glancing wings & sing your infant joy / Arise & drink your bliss / For every thing that lives is holy" (the echoing of Oothoon's cries in *Visions of the Daughters of Albion* is an insistent undertone).

But just as Time, in Spenser's conception, is the "troubler" of the garden, preventing ultimate happiness and "immortall blis," so in Enitharmon's fallen world, no matter how hard she tries to "plant a smile / In forests of affliction," her "sweet bliss" is but to "tremble & wither across the heavens / In strong vibrations of fierce jealousy" (E323). The "cause" of this is her paramour Los's fancied (or real— they are the same to Enitharmon) dalliance with "Ahania's image" or "the virgins / Of summer" (E322–23). "Thou art mine," she firmly pronounces just before her canticle, "Created for my will my slave tho strong tho I am weak" (E323). Having sung her song "in Rapturous delusive trance," she leads Los "into Shadows," and he, now equally deluded by her song and its vision of what they once were (summarized in ll. 9–15 on E322), "siezd her in his arms delusive hopes." From his grasp (precisely that of the speaker in *The Crystal Cabinet*, equally futile) she "thence fled outstretchd / Upon the immense like a bright rainbow weeping & smiling & fading" (E324). Blake shrewdly makes this fading an echo of Los's own earlier on the same page:

> Therefore fade I thus dissolvd in rapturd trance
> Thou canst repose on clouds of secrecy while oer my limbs
> Cold dews & Hoary frost creeps tho I lie on banks of summer
> Among the beauties of the World.

"Cold & repining" like a true Petrarchan lover, "Los / Still dies for Enitharmon" till she revives him again "with [her] sweet song" (E323), and, as in *The Mental Traveller* paradigm, "all is done as I have told," over and over and over again.

The entire passage is well-nigh inexhaustible in its echoing and counterechoing brilliance, and it is tempting to pursue it further. But, as C. S. Lewis says at one point in *The Allegory of Love*, "the chief duty of the interpreter" is "to begin analyses and to leave them unfinished." In that way he will awaken "the reader's conscious knowledge of life and books in so far as it is relevant, and then . . . stir the less conscious elements in him which alone can fully respond to the poem'' (p. 345). For all the wisdom and tact of that dictum, I cannot resist a final word—perhaps an allusion:

> he onely ioyed
> In combats of sweet loue, and with his mistresse toyed.
>
> (V,v,24)

These lines from *The Faerie Queene* evoke Hercules' taking up the distaff for Iola's sake, the mythological allusion characterizing Artegall's self-submission to Radigund's ''crueltie.'' ''Seruing proud *Radigund* with true subiection'' (26), Artegall in turn becomes the object of her lust, and she proceeds to suffer all the woes of a Petrarchan lover with ''loue-sicke hart'':

> And still the more she stroue it to subdew,
> The more she still augmented her owne smart,
> And wyder made the wound of th' hidden dart.
>
> (V,v,28)

Clarinda, her go-between, then insinuates herself into the picture, *her* heart by now in thrall. Thus, unto Artegall

> all her subtill nets she did vnfold,
> And all the engins of her wit display;
> In which she meant him warelesse to enfold,
> And of his innocence to make her pray.
> So cunningly she wrought her crafts assay,
> That both her Ladie, and her selfe withall,
> And eke the knight attonce she did betray:
> But most the knight, whom she with guilefull call
> Did cast for to allure, into her trap to fall.
>
> (V,v,52)

Whether or not this is a ''source'' for Blake's *Four Zoas* wars of the sexes is less important than Blake's discovery in *The Faerie Queene* of Spenser's own employment of the Petrarchan tradition in ways he himself had done and would continue to do. Nothing in the *Amoretti* would have prepared him for that sort of subversion (including the ''Blakean'' reversal of the courtly love sex roles). Thus it seems to me quite proper to argue that Blake's careful reading of *The Faerie Queene*, in some measure at least, helped to pave the way for such poems as *The Golden Net* and *The Crystal Cabinet*, not to say *The Four Zoas*. Blake would have abhorred, of course, Artegall's rescue by the embodiment of virginity, Britomart—though he may secretly have found a certain satisfaction that, in Radigund's fatal fight with her, the "dainty parts" of both were "hackt and hewd, as if such vse" as they were created for "they hated" (V,vii,29). It is difficult to find anywhere in Spenser a more graphic and grisly image of Blake's conception of love debased to war.

Wilkie and Johnson (p. 60) remark of *The Four Zoas* episode I have been concentrating upon that it seems "to reflect the so-called anti-feminine side in Blake," but they go on to point out that "an indictment of either sex exclusively" was not Blake's intent (as the echoed delusion and fading of Los and Enitharmon that I noted earlier indicate). Moreover, the Los-Enitharmon struggle is juxtaposed sharply to Urizen's brutal treatment of *his* emanation, Ahania, in Night II and especially in Night III of the poem. Nevertheless, it is difficult not to agree with those commentators who argue that Blake's idea of the divinely ordained subservience of the female stems in large measure from Milton. What is less often remarked is that Milton more than likely borrowed the idea from Spenser (all the while mindful, of course, of Eve's "birth" out of Adam). Spenser attributes Radigund's cruelty to her shaking off of

> the shamefast band,
> With which wise Nature did them strongly bynd,
> T'obay the heasts of mans well ruling hand,
> That then all rule and reason they withstand,
> To purchase a licentious libertie.
> But vertuous women wisely vnderstand,
> That they were borne to base humilitie,
> Vnless the heauens them lift to lawfull soueraintee.
>
> (V,v,25)

The exception is Queen Elizabeth, the Faerie Queene herself, and the passage is impossible to reconcile with, say, the marriages of the *Epithalamion* and *Prothalamion*. Rule and reason in the above passage become the province of Urizen in Blake's poetry, and the treatment of Ahania he pursues throughout the prophetic books is ample evidence that Blake thought Spenser quite wrong about that. However, "licentious libertie" was not a pillar of his credo nor, of course, was "base humilitie." It was not, then, merely the notion that an "indictment of either sex exclusively would be a falsification of reality" (Wilkie and Johnson, p. 60) that leads Blake to accord equal time to male and female cruelties, but rather the idea, fundamental almost from the very beginning, of the relationship between prolific and devourer. Religion, we recall from *The Marriage of Heaven and Hell*, whether the *Amoretti*'s, the *Epithalamion*'s, *The Faerie Queene*'s, or *Milton*'s, "is an endeavour to reconcile the two'' in the peace that is, according to ''The Human Abstract'' of *Songs of Experience*, ''mutual fear'' (E40, 27). Instead, Blake says, somewhat cryptically and anti-epithalamically, ''These two classes of men are always upon earth, & they should be enemies; whoever tries to reconcile them seeks to destroy existence'' itself (E40). The key, then, is in the nature of this ''enmity.'' ''Opposition is true friendship'' (E42); ''Altho' our Human Power can sustain the severe contentions / Of friendship, our Sexual cannot.'' It is from the latter that ''arose all our terrors in Eternity,'' those that ''led to War the Wars of Death'' (*Milton* 41[48]:32–36, E143).

He who would see the Divinity must see him in his Children
One first, in friendship & love; then a Divine Family, & in the midst
Jesus will appear. . . .

(Jerusalem 91:18–20, E251)

And more majestically, five plates later on:

Wouldest thou love one who never died
For thee or ever die for one who had not died for thee
And if God dieth not for Man & giveth not himself
Eternally for Man Man could not exist. for Man is Love:
As God is Love: every kindness to another is a little Death
In the Divine Image nor can Man exist but by Brotherhood.

(96:23–28, E256)

This is about as close as Blake ever comes to defining the indefinable—love.[62] And he found that definition not in Spenser or Milton, not even in the Bible, but in his own imagination and his struggles with those other ''systems.''

Its definitional opposite is just as eloquent:

Every ornament of perfection, and every labour of love,
In all the Garden of Eden, & in all the golden mountains
Was become an envied horror, and a remembrance of jealousy:
And every Act a Crime, and the fallen Albion the punisher & judge.

(Jerusalem 28:1–4, E174)

For love has become, in a remarkable phrase, ''unnatural consanguinities and friendships / Horrid to think of where inquired deeply into'' (ibid.). Blake inquires into them in this *Jerusalem* passage only to assert that ''willing sacrifice of Self'' has become ''sacrifice of (miscall'd) Enemies'' on the altars of ''Justice, and Truth'' (28:20–23, E174).

I am sensible at this point that we have moved considerably beyond the torments of *The Four Zoas* into the very heart of *Milton* and *Jerusalem*. But in so doing, I trust that the increasing subsumption of Petrarchism into Blake's own myth has become clearer. What may still be unclear is the reason for this subsumption. Petrarchism, at least after *The Four Zoas*, has served its purpose for Blake's evolving conception of the complexities (and dualities) of his states of Beulah-Ulro and Generation-Regeneration, that purpose largely the establishment of a context within which *Milton* and *Jerusalem* could function meaningfully and to which they may allude without further exposition. As Helen McNeil observes in a fine, unduly neglected essay, "more than any other of Blake's poems about universal disaster and ultimate recovery, *The Four Zoas* operates without a context, even a Blakean one."[63] That is, its contexts are created in the very "action" of the poem's "characters," which are thrown at us, so to speak, with little or no preamble or definition. At the same time, *The Four Zoas* is no mere psychomachia, the very admission inherent in my negative constitutive of the "context" in which the poem functions. And a contributory part of *that* context is Petrarchism—though, more often than not, a Petrarchism crudely cartoonized, as in the scatological and pornographic drawings that fill the poem's manuscript pages.[64]

In "the hands of Urizen" (here most simply ratiocinative reason), "in the shadows of Valas Garden" (that is, in the love conventions of all amatory fictions), Blake says there are only "the *impressions* of Despair & Hope" (my italics: the word is deliberately Lockean); it is a "land of doubts & shadows sweet delusions unformd hopes." Existing within "their orbed senses within closd up," Blake's archetypal lovers, Luvah and Vala, wander "in the dreams of Beulah" where "They heard not saw not felt not all the terrible confusion" of "the wracking universe" (E395). This is the world of allegory, of poetic convention—a delicately poised refuge from the wars of the world, wars of all kinds—but in its delicacy and beauty (for it is beautiful and safe), its poise is infinitely precarious, always in danger of collapsing into that sinister world of division and fallen vision. What *The Four Zoas* seems to me to demonstrate is that the poise is always collapsing, even as it is "achieved"—which is to say, the achievement itself is a self-delusion, manufactured out of Urizenic myopia. In the "reality" of the mental-visceral world of *The Four Zoas, thought is act*. The word, literary convention, or allegory merely incarnates what has already been "done" and will continue *being* done. "Words are as irrevocable as incidents: however mistaken or inadequate a phrase is, once it has entered the world of the Zoas it must be coped with as fully as any more recognizable act."[65] That is precisely what "happens" to Petrarchism and its cerebrated tropical language. Put simply, the words become real and thus gradually abandon their reliance on, or even connection with, a metaphorical tradition that militantly declared their unreality.

Jean Hagstrum once remarked that "metaphors have a way of taking over in Blake."[66] Indeed. But, as Blake demetaphorizes poetic convention to expose its underbelly of (usually) terrifying and ugly reality, he also remetaphorizes it, often even more terrifyingly. For example, in this extraordinary reworking in *Milton* of a passage from *The Four Zoas* (E404–5), we see not only "war . . . associated with sado-masochistic perversion, and with the naturalizing of imaginative energy"[67] but also a radical transformation of the central images and motifs of, say, Spenser's *Amoretti* (see sonnets 10, 11, 22, 24, 30, 31, 42, and 47):

> in the Wine-presses the Human grapes sing not, nor dance
> They howl & writhe in shoals of torment; in fierce flames
>   consuming,
> In chains of iron & in dungeons circled with ceaseless fires.
> In pits & dens & shades of death: in shapes of torment & woe.
> The plates & screws & wracks & saws & cords & fires & cisterns
> The cruel joys of Luvahs Daughters lacerating with knives
> And whips their Victims & the deadly sport of Luvahs Sons.
> They dance around the dying, & they drink the howl & groan
> They catch the shrieks in cups of gold, they hand them to one
>   another:
> These are the sports of love, & these the sweet delights of amorous
>   play
> Tears of the grape, the death sweat of the cluster the last sigh
> Of the mild youth who listens to the lureing songs of Luvah.
>   (27[29]:30–41, E124–25)

Poetically, what underlies this passage is both the sexual explicitness of *The Four Zoas* text and illustrations and their antecedent Petrarchisms as well as Blake's confident assumption that characters, powers, images, metaphors, and even individual words can be introduced in the full knowledge that his reader will recognize the "antecedent cultural images" that constitute their present context.[68] To oversimplify, we need to know the *Amoretti* here, but we also need to know what Blake did with its Petrarchism in *The Four Zoas* to "realize" the full horror and significance of a passage like this and its "place" in a poem like *Milton*. Blake once wrote of his archetypal prophet Los,

> he lays his words in order above the mortal brain
> As cogs are formd in a wheel to turn the cogs of the adverse wheel.
>   (*Milton* 27[29]:9–10, E124)

There is, I think, no more succinct explanation of Los's role in all of Blake's work. He is an allegorical antiallegorist, just as he is a Petrarchan anti-Petrarchist, a poetic antipoet.[69] In his career, he too listened "to the lureing songs of Luvah" (who is also called, significantly, "Prince of Love"), but he has now turned that song back on itself to produce the ultimate antisong that is the Song of Songs—delivering us, thereby, from *all* systems, including his own, into the realms of Imagination. In those realms, in Eternity, the wars between the sexes

> are wars of life, & wounds of love,
> With intellectual spears, & long winged arrows of thought:
> Mutual in one anothers love and wrath all renewing.
> (*Jerusalem* 34[38]:14–16, E180)

Once Eternity is sundered, the problem is to prevent its falling endlessly into nonentity or eternal death. Thus, Los hammers out on his anvil

> a World of Generation from the World of Death:
> Dividing the Masculine & Feminine. . . .
> (58:16, 18–19, E207)

Generation is thus not merely the "*Image* of Regeneration"; it is also its enabling means. What happens next, however, is unfortunate, if inevitable, and as neat an epitome of the nature and fate of Los's "allegory" as we might find:

> The Feminine separates from the Masculine & both from Man,
> Ceasing to be His Emanations, Life to Themselves assuming!
> (90:2, E249)

Blake's language is characteristically precise: what remains after this separation is not Man and Woman (least of all the minute particularity of Adam and Eve), but rather the personified abstractions, Masculine and Feminine. They, in turn, begin "to form Heavens & Hells in immense / Circles: the Hells for food to the Heavens: food of torment, / Food of despair"; and their heavens are named "Chastity & Uncircumcision" (49:61–64, E199). As Blake says elsewhere, "Man must & will have Some Religion; if he has not the Religion of Jesus, he will have the Religion of Satan" (*Jerusalem* 52, E201)—or make one of his own. In other words, what the Masculine and Feminine abstractions have is an allegorical world in which, by the very rules that govern their creation of that world, they become real. Such allegories rend what Blake calls "the fibres of Brotherhood," give rise to wars for dominion, and are dedicated to the destruction of "all who do not worship Satan under the Name of God''—Satan in this sense being a compendium of all created, realized, or abstracted gods (ibid.). Finally, and most crucially, all such allegories are ''Feminine,'' that is, their god is female, virginal, cruel, unforgiving, utterly destructive, and her subjects are Petrarchan lovers.

But if allegories *are* feminine, must one annihilate the feminine to redeem the masculine? This would indeed be the rational way, for, as Blake's archetypally feminine Vala herself says,

> I alone am Beauty
> The Imaginative Human Form is but a breathing of Vala
> I breathe him forth into the Heaven from my secret Cave
> Born of the Woman to obey the Woman. . . .
>
> (*Jerusalem* 29[33]:48–51, E176)

But of course Vala is quite wrong:

> In Great Eternity, every particular Form gives forth or Emanates
> Its own peculiar Light, & the form is the Divine Vision
> And the Light is his Garment This is Jerusalem in every Man
> A Tent & Tabernacle of Mutual Forgivness Male & Female
> Clothings.
>
> (54:1–4, E203)

It is this light that must be rekindled to effect the destruction of allegories; or, to reverse the proposition, the destruction of allegories is that rekindling, whereby the Divine Vision's ''Garment'' is the ''Clothings'' of ''Male & Female'' and their garments are Jerusalem, the bride of Christ. In Genesis, ''God created man in his own image,'' *but* ''male and female created He them''; no wonder Blake persists— with conscious blasphemy but true Christian imagination—in reading the Bible in its infernal sense. God was, simply, wrong. Eternal or Redeemed humanity (Albion, not Adam) ''is far above / Sexual organization; & the Visions of the Night of Beulah,'' where ''the Masculine & Feminine are nurs'd into Youth & Maiden'' (79:73–74, 76, E236). Blake's final use of Petrarchan metaphor, now magnificently transmuted, announces the proper ''organization'' (or reorganization). Albion's

> . . . Bow is a Male & Female & the Quiver of the Arrows of Love,
> Are the Children of this Bow: a Bow of Mercy & Loving-kindness; laying
> Open the hidden Heart in Wars of mutual Benevolence Wars of Love.
>
> (*Jerusalem* 97:12–14, E256)

CHAPTER THREE

Roads of Excess

FRYE'S FINE ESSAY entitled "The Road of Excess" was succeeded a year later by Martin Price's book, *To the Palace of Wisdom*.[1] Although the latter does not refer to the former, both titles come from one of Blake's famous Proverbs of Hell in *The Marriage of Heaven and Hell*: "The road of excess leads to the palace of wisdom." Frye's allusion, in his half of the proverb, is to the extremity of "Blake's statements about art," which demands "some kind of mental adjustment to take them in." Price, on the other hand, says that the proverb reminds us "that all literature thrives on risk and overstatement, thrusts beyond the measured and judicious, and strains against order, if only to make us know what measure and order mean." With both of these applications in mind I too take up Blake's proverb, in an attempt to provide a critical entrée into an odd *ménage à deux* indeed—Blake and Spenser in the "house" of *The Marriage of Heaven and Hell*.

Although all sensible Blakeans acknowledge that *The Marriage* is some sort of satire, the butt of which (Swedenborg) is merely a target of convenience or avenue to much larger concerns, I for one am dissatisfied with all interpretations of the work—which are, perhaps for reasons that I shall adduce here, not particularly numerous, given its apparent centrality and seminal nature in the canon[2]—not because they *mis*read exactly but because no guiding principle of interpretation has yet been advanced that will account for the apparent shifts in the authoritativeness of the several speakers. More simply, when is Blake speaking "in his own voice," and how do we know? In posing to himself the same question ("Where does Blake speak straight?"), Bloom is quite right to say that "the usual misinterpretation of Blake's contraries" in *The Marriage* "is that they represent a simple inversion of orthodox moral categories. . . . Blake of course is doing nothing of the kind; he is denying the orthodox categories altogether, and opposing himself both to moral 'good' and moral 'evil.' "[3] Frye suggests that this sort of misinterpretation is due to our ignoring the fact that Blake attaches two meanings to the word *hell*, one real and the other ironic.[4] I'm not sure that's quite satisfactory as a "guiding principle," although it will certainly help. As Bloom remarks, after quoting Frye's idea, the "voice of the Devil" is "Blake's own, but diabolical only because it will seem so to Swedenborg or any other priestly Angel." So far, so good. But when Bloom goes further to say, in plate 4 ("The voice of the Devil"), that "Blake speaks straight for once" for he "really does believe that Energy is the only life, and is from the body," are we meant to understand *these* words of the devil (for they are the devil's words) as Blakean gospel, *despite* our being "priestly angels"? Apparently—for energy, Bloom later and rather surreptitiously translates into "energetic world of imaginings" and "creative exuberance." The transition as such is merely stated rather than examined: "sexual exuberance, breaking the bounds of restraint and entering a fullness that Angelic Reason considers excess, will lead to a perception of a redeemed nature, though this perception itself must seem unlawful to fallen reason."[5]

The problem here is not that Bloom is wrong (indeed, his essay in *Blake's Apocalypse* and its predecessor in article form are, to my mind, still the best commentaries on *The Marriage*) but that there is no clear way for one immersed in Blake to know why he is wrong. And for the non-Blakean, his rightness almost becomes a matter a faith. This problem is at its most intense in the Proverbs of Hell. Though "of Hell," they are not spoken by a devil but rather by a Lucianic traveler in Hell who, like a good tourist, has collected some proverbs, "thinking that as the sayings used in a nation, mark its character," so these will reveal the Nation of Hell's wisdom "better than any description of buildings or garments."[6] In assuming that Blake here speaks *in propria persona*, Bloom establishes a quadripartite structure for the proverbs as a whole, based on his assumption that they "exist to break down orthodox categories of thought and morality." Nevertheless, they "form overlapping groups" that are "largely defined by their imagery." The fact that the imagery "is presented in a variety of ironic disguises" does not inhibit Bloom's conveniently translating it into the four-square paradigm. Finally, we are left with this: "the Proverbs should mean a variety of things, quite correctly, to different readers." If they do, as indeed they have proved to have done, precisely how we are to identify "the laws of artistic creation" that Bloom sees Blake creating in this series of aphorisms is left unspoken.[7] The Devil's initiatory "sentence" ("now percieved by the minds of men, & read by them on earth'') with which the proverbs are launched is, we forget to note, not a statement but a question:

> How do you know but ev'ry Bird that cuts the airy way,
> Is an immense world of delight, clos'd by your senses five?

How indeed?

It is well known that Blake adapted these lines from Chatterton's *Bristowe Tragedie*. But, if Blake meant it "to serve as an introductory motto" to the Proverbs of Hell, with Chatterton thus serving as "a prophet of later poets' sensibilities,"[8] the choice is an odd one. The lines are spoken by Syr Charles Bawdin, who is about to be executed; the particular context of the lines is his memory of escapes from death in battle and the consequent irony of his present predicament. The absurd irrelevance to Blake's context and apparent purposes makes one wonder what point he had in mind in making the allusion at all— if indeed the lines are more than an unconscious (or perhaps conscious) echo of a felicitous phrase. Yet such unwilled echoes or borrowings for essentially extrinsic purposes are rarely Blake's way. The trope of "cutting the air" (or water) has a venerable history in literature as far back as Homer, Virgil, and Ovid. Nevertheless, there is a distinct and recognizable allusion in Chatterton's lines—to Spenser. In Book II of *The Faerie Queene*, overcome by his three-day ordeal in Mammon's cave, Guyon's "enfeebled spright" is "laid in swowne" and hence made vulnerable to capture and certain "execution" by Pyrochles and Cymochles. But at this critical moment, Spenser materializes for Guyon a guardian angel, among whose accouterments are

> two sharpe winged sheares
> Decked with diuerse plumes, like painted Iayes,
> [That] were fixed at his backe, to cut his ayerie ways.
>
> (viii,5)

This miraculous intercession is preceded by Spenser's account of "care in heauen" for "creatures bace, / That may compassion of their euils moue." This care consists of "heauenly spirits" who

> with golden pineons, cleaue
> The flitting skyes, like flying Pursuiuant,
> Against foule feends to aide vs millitant.
>
> (viii,1–2)

Guyon's particular heavenly spirit is, says Spenser,

> Like as *Cupido* on *Idæan* hill,
> When hauing laid his cruell bow away,

> And mortall arrowes, wherewith he doth fill
> The world with murdrous spoiles and bloudie pray.
>
> (viii,6)

Chatterton, an inveterate and incorrigible literary thief, has here stolen quite marvelously, translating Spenser's Cupid simile, with its Petrarchan murder, darts of love, and bloody prey, into the visceral cruelty of Syr Charles's imprisonment and impending death—all the while alluding to the Spenserian ministrations of a heavenly spirit. We should not be surprised, then, to find Syr Charles, in the rest of the poem, reasserting the righteousness of his life and career and his readiness to die in the knowledge that a future life awaits him in "the land of bliss" with "God in Heaven."

The Devil's question in *The Marriage*, then, is at least in some measure answered by the Chatterton-Spenser allusion (there is no doubt, I think, that Blake knew both passages): we know that every bird that cuts the airy way is an immense world of delight because of "th' exceeding grace / Of highest God" who sends such "blessed Angels . . . to and fro" (viii,1). But something is still awry; grace of this kind is hardly a Blakean tenet, and even if it were, the love of God that inspires such grace hardly seems appropriate to the Proverbs of Hell.[9] In *An Hymne of Heauenlie Love,* however, the nine orders of angels are equipped "with nimble wings to cut the skies, / When he [God] them on his messages doth send" (ll. 66–67), a passage that may very well have suggested to Blake an appropriate conversion of angel-messengers into a Devil who delivers his message to "the minds of men" "with corroding fires."

Despite the attractiveness of the Spenser-Chatterton connection to Blake's "introduction," it does not exhaust Blake's remarkable pattern of allusion. Milton's Satan and his hosts are habitually cloud-enwrapped, but in *Paradise Regained* "the Adversary" summons "all his mighty Peers, / Within thick clouds and dark tenfold involv'd" (I,38–41), and the Deluge is presaged by clouds "with black wings / Wide hovering" (XI,738–39). In *Paradise Lost* Beelzebub's advice to the fallen angels is not "to sit in darkness here / Hatching vain empires" but rather, in Milton's own words, "earth with hell / To mingle and involve" (II,377–78, 383–84); he then calls for a champion to

> tempt with wand'ring feet
> The dark unbottomed infinite abyss
> And through the palpable obscure find out
> His uncouth way, or spread his airy flight
> Upborne with indefatigable wings

> Over the vast abrupt, ere he arrive
> The happy isle. . . .
>
> (II,404-10)

Later in his confrontation with Sin and Death, Satan announces his mission of treading

> Th' unfounded deep, and through the void immense
> To search with wand'ring quest a place foretold.
> . . . .
> Created vast and round, a place of bliss.
>
> (II,829-33)

"Into this wild abyss, / The Womb of Nature and perhaps her grave," "the wary Fiend" stands "on the brink of hell and looked a while" (II,910-11, 917-18), just as earlier "those bad angels" were "Hovering on wing under the cope of hell / 'Twixt upper, nether, and surrounding fires" (I,345-46).

Here then are both Blake's "abyss of the five senses" (Milton's Hell and Chaos) and his "present world," his Devil-Satan about to discover the "immense world of delight" (see V,88) that is the unfallen Eden, where "Nature's whole wealth" is "To all delight of human sense exposed" (IV,206), a world that he will corrupt by means of the abyss's very senses that are "delighted." Furthermore, the "immense world of delight" also seems to be Beelzebub's vision of the fallen angels' possible reentry into heaven, their escape from "corroding fires":

> or else in some mild zone
> Dwell not unvisited of heav'n's fair light
> Secure, and at the bright'ning orient beam
> Purge off this gloom; the soft delicious air
> To heal the scar of these corrosive fires
> Shall breathe her balm.
>
> (II,397-402)

The permutations are dazzling, for Blake at once celebrates and condemns Milton's fallen host and leader, as if to warn us not to take his diabolical gospel (and its book of proverbs) uncritically or unilaterally. Satan's energy may be impressive, but he is also a destructive manipulator of the senses; however prolific (in Blake's sense of that term in *The Marriage*), he is as much a devourer as the maw of his progeny, Sin and Death.[10] Furthermore, the immense world of delight which he suggests is somehow "in" every bird that cuts the airy way (as distinct from Blake's more famous "World in a Grain of

Sand," E490) is equally ambiguous; it is Milton's Eden, but it may also be Blake's (they are obviously not the same). And finally, while Blake's Devil employs his corrosives creatively to etch the plates that will be perceived by the minds of men, Milton's devils seek an immense world of delight that is both free of "corrosive fires" and mild and balmy to the senses.[11]

If we return now to the Proverb of Hell with which we started, several corrosive "sentences" may now be perceived by our minds. For Milton, the road of sensory excess clearly does not lead to the palace of wisdom, though that is precisely the bottom line of Satan's temptation of Eve. To her, the fruit of the forbidden tree is itself "excess" (IX,648), and, once fallen, she and Adam are perceived by God as "Bewailing their excess" (XI,111). And, of course, Eve's expression of gratitude to the most "precious of all trees / In Paradise" includes its opening for her of "wisdom's way" (IX,798, 809). But to assume from this that Blake, pursuing his already announced dissatisfaction with *Paradise Lost* earlier in *The Marriage*, therefore does believe that the road of excess leads to the palace of wisdom is to attribute to him the same error of either/or that so infuriates him in Milton's conception. One should be reminded here that, as Milton says earlier, in another context of excess,

> neither man nor angel can discern
> Hypocrisy, the only evil that walks
> Invisible, except to God alone,
> By his permissive will, through heav'n and earth;
> And oft though wisdom wake, suspicion sleeps
> At wisdom's gate, and to simplicity
> Resigns her charge, while goodness thinks no ill
> Where no ill seems.
>
> (III,682–91)

Thus, even Uriel, the "sharpest-sighted Spirit of all in heav'n," is beguiled by Satan's desire to know God's full creation so that he may praise "The Universal Maker." Uriel's response to Satan is directly apropos Blake's proverb:

> "Fair Angel, thy desire which tends to know
> The works of God, thereby to glorify
> The great Work-master, leads to no excess
> That reaches blame, but rather merits praise
> The more it seems excess. . . ."[12]

The critical points to be adduced from all of this with respect to the authoritativeness of any "sentence" in *The Marriage of Heaven and Hell* are at least two: (1) Milton's Satan, and hence Blake's Devil, is not always "right" nor are angels always wrong; and (2), most important, the authority of rightness resides more often than not in our perception and understanding of the nature of Blake's allusions.[13] Another way to state the first of these is to say that all "conventional wisdom" in *The Marriage* is not to be merely turned upside down or inside out to arrive at Blakean "truth" (the point that Bloom makes); and another way to state the second is to say that whatever Blake ricochets off of the conventionalities of Spenserian or Miltonic (and, we should add, biblical) texts is to be taken as the "real" truth. Thus, as plate 5 of *The Marriage* imperiously declaims, in *Paradise Lost* Messiah is "Reason" and "the original Archangel or possessor of the command of the heavenly host, is calld the Devil or Satan." Hence, according to "The Devils account," it is "Messiah" who "fell. & formed a heaven of what he stole from the Abyss" (E34–35)—that is to say, put bluntly, Milton's cosmic geography is upside down. Now in one sense, this may indeed be "surpassingly excellent [literary] analysis," as Bloom says,[14] but in another it is arrant nonsense. And, more to the point, Blake knows it is nonsense, as the ridiculously pedantic "Note" at the end of the passage, with its wry political metaphor, suggests. "Parties" have nothing to do with the matter. If Milton were of the Angels' party, he would be Swedenborg and *Paradise Lost* would be just another spiritual travelogue. That the poem as we have it is, in Blake's view, redeemable argues Milton's confusion, not a fundamental error.[15] The negations of nonpoetry (unpoetry) are not redeemable, as Swedenborg is not; the eternal contraries are. "Error can never be redeemd in all Eternity." Man, and poets, can only be redeemed from "Errors Power,"[16] *from* Satan who, *in propria persona*, "fall'n from his station . . . never can be redeem'd" (*Milton* 11:22, E105).

In some sense, then, we are called upon in *The Marriage* to redeem the diabolical Blake from the excesses of his own apparent "correctives" to Swedenborgian, angelic, Spenserian, Miltonic "error"—which we can do not by simply reading in an infernal sense but by perceiving with our whole minds. Hell may be, as Frye says, "this world as it appears to the repressed imagination" (angels), but it is equally true that this world is "heaven" only in the eyes of devils, the unrepressed imagination. In fact, *this* world is neither—nor, more importantly, is it merely a "balance" between the two. "Balance," as Eaves correctly argues, "avoids both extremes of imbalance," a kind of *via media* or *discordia concors* that is, to Blake, but a benighted accommodation to an erroneous perception. "Wholeness," Eaves goes on, "is itself an extreme, its opposite being 'fragmentation.'"

Bloom seems to me as wrong as the advocates of such a Blakean accommodation when he argues that the reader must "move constantly from a defiant celebration of heretofore repressed energies to a realization that the freed energies must accept a bounding outline, a lessened but still existent world of confining mental forms."[17] If Reason, as *The Marriage* tells us, "is the bound or outward circumference of Energy" (E34), then Energy must be the center that is mentally confined. However, if Energy is the bound or outward circumference of Reason, the geometric metaphor remains just as geometric—no matter who or what does the confining. One metaphysic is no less tyrannical than another. For Blake, Dryden is a perfect instance of this in his attempt to "finish" *Paradise Lost* and thus to put it right, only to "degrade" Milton.[18] If the Devil's sentence in *The Marriage*, then, is now "read by [men] on earth," Blake clearly hopes that such readers will read with their whole "intellect," which, as Shelley also knew, is both center and circumference. Only in that way may we emulate the prophetic Los, who "reads the Stars of Albion" while his rational spectre "reads the Voids / Between the Stars" (*Jerusalem* 91:36–37, E251). The latter is "the Newtonian who reads Not & cannot Read" because he "is opressed by his own Reasonings & Experiments" (letter to Richard Phillips, E769).

In the same letter from which this last phrase is taken, Blake concludes with uncharacteristic humility, "We are all subject to Error" (E769). Yes—but the road of excess is not, thereby, the way to infallibility, for Blake or for Adam and Eve. It is rather (as I now revive Spenser from the limbo of this prolegomenon) the way to, among other places, the Bower of Bliss. Blake, of course, did not need to open his Spenser to discover the age-old ideas of temperance, moderation, and the golden mean.[19] In *Milton*, for example, he cites the familiar classical quaternion of "Temperance, Prudence, Justice, Fortitude" as "the four pillars of Tyranny" (29[31]:49, E128). And there is no specific "Bower of Bliss" in his works. Nevertheless, it is difficult to imagine his being indifferent to the central principles (and principals) of Book II of *The Faerie Queene*, which I believe stuck in his memory (and in his craw) as vividly as the equally widespread and commonplace Petrarchisms of the *Amoretti*.

What seems striking at first glance to the student of Blake, as Guyon and the Palmer enter upon the road to the bower, are the apparently minor roles Spenser assigns to both Excesse and Genius, both of whose allegorical names might well be straight out of Blake. Blake's idea of Genius, of course, underlies virtually all his thought, most centrally that "the Poetic Genius" is "the true Man," and "that the body or outward form of Man is derived from the Poetic

Genius. Likewise that the forms of all things are derived from their Genius. which by the Ancients was call'd an Angel & Spirit & Demon" (*All Religions Are One*, E1). Thus, it is not that "energies" ("the Poetic Genius") "accept" a confining form but rather that energies exfoliate into the "forms of all things," including man. But the "form" of man is his soul-body, the Human form divine rather than the human abstract. Only to the fallen does it appear that Reason is the bound or outward circumference of energy.

Spenser's version of this is defined in Book II as a "contrary" to the false Genius at Acrasia's gate, who is "quite contrary" to

> that celestiall powre, to whom the care
> Of life, and generation of all
> That liues, pertaines in charge particulare,
> Who wondrous things concerning our welfare,
> And straunge phantomes doth let vs oft foresee,
> And oft of secret ill bids vs beware:
> That is our Selfe, whom though we do not see,
> Yet each doth in him selfe it well perceiue to bee.
>
> (xii,47)

This "true" Genius, Agdistes, Spenser assigns to the Garden of Adonis, and he is "a God" as "sage Antiquity / Did wisely make" him (xii,48). What is missing from Spenser's conception of the essential self "we do not see" but know is there is Blake's qualifying adjective, the idea of the Imagination in every man as his true self (as Milton's true self is Milton as "true Poet"). It is possible, however, that Blake built this idea at least in part upon Spenser's notion of "that celestiall powre" which "straunge phantomes doth let vs oft foresee," although he certainly would not have been pleased by Spenser's choice of words. At the same time, the Genius of the Garden of Adonis could not have satisfied him at all as the ushering agent into an endless cycle of birth, life, decay, and death.

Even more ominously, though, Acrasia's Genius is an agent of illusion, a "foe of life, that good enuyes to all," and, most importantly, who "secretly doth vs procure to fall, / Through guilefull semblaunts, which he makes vs see." Blake would not have missed the echoes of this guilefulness in Milton's Satan (not to mention Archimago and Duessa), and the nature of this connection ought to give us pause when our minds rush to embrace as "Blakean" the excesses of Satan as desiderata. Spenser's Excesse is a similarly ambiguous figure. Although minor in the sense of her brief role in canto xii, she is in many ways the presiding allegorical power of the entire book, manifest in Mordant, Perissa and Elissa, Furor and Occasion, Pyrochles

and Cymochles, Phaedria, Mammon, and Maleger, as well as a
number of lesser figures and allegorical landscapes and loci. Her ambiguity (for Blake) inheres in the fact that, although she stands in firm
opposition to the prudence and temperance of Guyon and the Palmer
(both these virtues, we recall from *Milton*, among the pillars of tyranny), subscribing to her creed leads not only to the animalistic excesses of Maleger's troops assailing Alma's castle but also to the
"lewd loues, and wastfull luxuree" in which Acrasia's "lovers"
spend their days, goods, and bodies in sterile and "horrible enchant-
ment" (II,xii,80). The fundamental horror is the transformation of
man into beast—for Blake, the defacing of the human form divine
into the "donghill kind" represented by Grille (the same transformation, of course, that Blake knew in the Circe myth but also, closer to
his heart and mind, in *Comus*—and, retransformed, in his own
poems, *The Human Abstract* and *A Divine Image*).

For Spenser and Milton this situation involves no dilemma: temperance and/or chastity and/or prudence and/or moderation—as well
as, even more fundamentally, the reasonable mind that gives birth to
and sustains those virtues—solve all such apparent problems. Spenser's Medina is one of the classic instances of the establishment and
maintenance of the golden mean; her two sisters, Perissa and Elissa,
are the too-much and too-little extremes. Of these, the "excessive"
Perissa had

> No measure in her mood, no rule of right,
> But poured out in pleasure and delight;
> In wine and meats she flowd aboue the bancke,
> And in excesse exceeded her owne might.
>
> (II,ii,36)

Her suitor is properly Sans-loy. Milton's version of this is inherent in
Comus, but he articulates the principle more precisely in Spenser's
terms (as well as Aristotle's and Seneca's before him) in Book XI of
Paradise Lost. There Michael tells the fallen Adam:

> "There is . . . if thou well observe
> The rule of *Not too much*, by temperance taught
> In what thou eat'st and drink'st, seeking from thence
> Due Nourishment, not gluttonous delight."
>
> (Ll. 530-33)

Michael's maxim is immediately followed by "another sight" that he
conjures up to Adam (one to which I alluded in the previous chapter),
the "bevy of fair women, richly gay," who sashay into the sight of the
apparently "just men." "In gems and wanton dress" they were and

> to the harp they sung
> Soft amorous ditties, and in dance came on:
> The men, though grave, eyed them, and let their eyes
> Rove without rein, till in the amorous net
> Fast caught, they liked, and each his liking chose.
>
> (Ll. 577, 582–87)

Adam mistakes this vision for a portent of "peaceful days" wherein "Nature seems fulfilled in all her ends" (Ll. 600–602), and Michael abruptly corrects his judgment:

> Those tents thou saw'st so pleasant, were the tents
> Of wickedness . . . ,

and

> that fair female troop thou saw'st, that seemed
> Of goddesses, so blithe, so smooth, so gay,

are "empty of all good,"

> Bred only and completed to the taste
> Of lustful appetence, to sing, to dance,
> To dress, and troll the tongue, and roll the eye,

the result of all of this being the just men's yielding up of "all their virtue" and swimming in excess of "joy." And, Michael adds in language Blake clearly borrowed for one of his Proverbs of Hell, for this excessive joy "The world erelong a world of tears must weep" (ll. 607–8, 614–16, 618–20, 623, 627). Blake's version is "Excess of sorrow laughs. Excess of joy weeps," just as his version of Michael's initial maxim is the coda of the Proverbs of Hell: "Enough! or Too much" (or, the earlier proverb: "You never know what is enough unless you know what is more than enough").

In this last proverb, the mental battle between Blake and his two predecessors seems to me joined, and our final understanding of the "wisdom" of Blake's apparently sanctioned "road of excess" inheres in our previous understanding of what he means by "enough." "Reason," in the sense employed by Spenser and Milton (and in both classical and Christian traditions), is clearly anathema. For Blake *that* reason is fallen Urizen, whose iron decalogue consists of

> One command, one joy, one desire,
> One curse, one weight, one measure
> One King, one God, one Law.
>
> (*Book of Urizen*, E72)

The vertical symmetry here is striking: command-curse-King, joy-weight-God, desire-measure-Law—each quite literally undermining the triplets just above:

> . . . peace, . . . love, . . . unity:
> . . . pity, compassion, forgiveness.

The equable oneness of "the human form divine," announced so stirringly in *The Divine Image*, here becomes the one law of the one self-appointed god and king, reigning (and warring) under the banner of reason. At the other end of the scale, "too much," or (in Milton's words) "more than enough," is established, as it were, for both Milton and Spenser by God through Nature only so "that temperance may be tried" (*Paradise Lost*, XI,805).

The "doctrine of enough" is far from explicit or even clear in Blake, his discussion of it limited entirely to the passages in *The Marriage* I have cited; except for a handful of conventional poetic usages, he seems to reserve the word for equally conventional use in his prose. We must, then, look elsewhere to get to the center of the question of "Enough! or Too much" and the analogous problem of the true relationship between "excess" and "wisdom." Bloom (and others) explains away the problem by relegating the terms to an "antinomian rhetoric" whose "shock value" is geared "to clarify the role of the contraries."[20] While that is difficult to disagree with, I do not believe that it is the whole story. Closer to the whole story is Bloom's *en passant* remark with which I have already taken issue: "Blake asks . . . his reader . . . to move constantly from a defiant celebration of heretofore repressed energies to a realization that the freed energies must accept a bounding outline, a lessened but still existent world of confining mental forms." To make the sentence mean what I think Bloom intends it to mean (or what I would like to think it means) necessitates a clearer understanding of Urizen. "Reason *and* Energy," *The Marriage* announces clearly, "are necessary to *Human* existence" (my italics). Furthermore, "Energy . . . is alone from the Body" and "Reason . . . is alone from the Soul." So far, so good. But then we are told that "Man has no Body distinct from his Soul," hence no Energy "distinct" from Reason. What is "calld" Body-Energy "is a portion of" Soul-Reason "discernd by the five Senses, the chief inlets of Soul in this age." The labeling or naming of body as "Body" (and energy as "Energy"), then, is a product of sensory perception plus reason, an "idea" in Locke's sense of that word. But "inlets" is a curious word here. In *Europe* the senses are *outlets*:

> . . . . thro' one he breathes the air;
> Thro' one, hears music of the spheres; thro' one, the eternal vine

Flourishes, that he may recieve the grapes; thro' one can look.
And see small portions of the eternal world that ever groweth;
Thro' one, himself pass out what time he please, but he will not.

(E60)

That seems clear, but if we change the senses to inlets and especially "inlets of Soul," we are (or Blake is) in the peculiar position of saying that, through the senses, "portions" of soul (and therefore portions of reason) infiltrate the body; or, given the ambiguousness of the prepositional construction, the Soul's-Reason's capacity to perceive (receive) "reality" is severely limited by the age's reduced perceptual capacities—in the language of the *Europe* passage just alluded to, by having "infinite Window" reduced to "five windows."[21]

The Devil's conclusion to this crucial section of *The Marriage* thus emerges in its ambiguous confutation as Blake's "correction" of the Devil's one-sided diabolism: Energy may be the only life and is from the body, and Reason is the bound or outward circumference of Energy, but we already know from the preceding "principle" that "Man has no Body distinct from his Soul." Thus, if Reason is the bound or outward circumference of energy, the traditional conception of the soul within the prison of the body is turned inside out; the soul (Reason) is now the sheath or envelope within which Body-Energy resides, and its perceptual and experiential *outlets* are the five senses of *Europe*. Blake's quarrel with Spenser and Milton, then, is not merely over their separation of body and soul but over their myopic inversion of the nature of that separation—which is to say their erroneous and pernicious "calling" of the "real" body "Soul," and the "real" soul "Body." The *Blakean* truth of "the road of excess" proverb is, then, the seemingly curious but meticulously prepared-for proverb that his speaker could not find in Hell: the road of sensory excess leads to the soul's "enough," which is the "All" that "satisfies" Man (*There Is No Natural Religion*, E2). Or, to return to Blake's own terminology, "Energy is *Eternal* Delight" (my italics) because Energy is not distinct from Reason but only that portion *of* Reason "discernd by the five Senses." In this world, *mere* energy (the excesses of the body) leads only to bowers of bliss, Comus's orgies, Eve's fall, and, in Blake's prophetic terms, the sensual agonies and perversion of Vala's world. And *mere* reason leads but to the endless destruction of bowers of bliss. Analogously, Urizen's world (*fallen* Reason, the fallen soul) is "the outward circumference" (in the language of *The Marriage*) of that of Vala (the body of Nature); yet, at the same time, his world *is* hers and he is "Stung with the odours of Nature" as he explores "his dens around" and uncreates the world in good Genesis (and Miltonic and Spenserian) fashion:

> He form'd a line & a plummet
> To divide the Abyss beneath.
> He form'd a dividing rule:
>
> He formed scales to weigh;
> He formed massy weights;
> He formed a brazen quadrant;
> He formed golden compasses
> And began to explore the Abyss
> And he planted a garden of fruits
>
> (*Book of Urizen*, 20:31–41, E80–81)

—right in the middle of *Paradise Lost* and the Garden of Adonis. And, like Milton's and Spenser's God,

> he saw
> That no flesh *nor spirit* could keep
> His iron laws one moment.
>
> (23:25–26, E81; my italics)

"For he saw that life liv'd on death," necessitating the spinning, weaving, and knotting of "The Net of Religion" *in* "the human brain." In turn, the human brain (that is to say, the fallen soul)

> form'd laws of prudence, and call'd them
> The eternal laws of God
>
> (23:27, 24:21–22, 28:6–7, E81–83)

—yet another naming rationally to circumference an "idea."

It is a stunning history. But for my purposes here, we must not lose sight of its origins in *The Marriage* and its contraries. Spenser's and Milton's problem was not that they did not recognize the eternal contraries as "necessary to Human existence," but rather that they had them backward. The antinomian rhetoric of *The Marriage*, then, is in part calculated to reverse that fundamental error. At the same time, however, that same rhetoric, "read" by imaginative minds (not that of Devils *or* Angels), is calculated to reveal the eternal oneness of the contraries that, in the fallen world ("Human existence"), are torn asunder—thus making them merely "necessary." "Hell is the outward or external of heaven," Blake wrote as early as his annotations to Swedenborg's *Heaven and Hell*, but even more crucially, hell "is of the body of the lord. for nothing is destroyd" (E602). And, succinctly, "Heaven & Hell are born together" (annotations to Swedenborg's *Divine Love and Divine Wisdom*, E609).

To put the matter in terms of perception, an infinite sense perception is imaginative perception.[22] Thus on plate 12 of *The Marriage*,

Isaiah can say in apparent contradiction, "I saw no God. nor heard any, in a finite organical perception; but my senses [that is, my infinite "organical perception"] discover'd the infinite in every thing" (E38). Similarly, "The ancient Poets" (Blake's "Poetic Genius" who "is the true Man") perceived *their* world with "enlarged & numerous senses" (ibid). In one sense, this means that such men contain their worlds precisely as the four redeemed zoas (senses) *are* the Eternity (at the apocalyptic close of *Jerusalem*) in which they walk "To & fro . . . as One Man reflecting each in each & clearly seen / And seeing" (E258). They are both the center, from which they drive "outward the Body of Death in an Eternal Death & Resurrection," and "the Outline the Circumference & Form, for ever" (E257). More simply, the eternal senses redeemed are the Imagination; Urizen redeemed is Imagination (Reason, not reason); the body redeemed is Imagination (soul); hell redeemed is Imagination (heaven); and so on. If "Heaven & Hell are born together," their subsequent "marriage" is possible only if they are perceived to be born apart. Thus in plate 3 of *The Marriage* "a *new* heaven is begun," but it is only thirty-three years later that (presumably) the old "Eternal Hell revives" (E34; my italics). Under all its antinomian rhetoric, then, as well as its diabolical "wisdom," lies the Blakean wisdom that the "world" of hell is just as illusory as the "world" of heaven. Each represents a "metaphysics" that each imposes on the other. The imaginative truth of the matter is the *eternal* state of "marriage" in which all things eternally are. Blake's anti-Swedenborgian, anti-Miltonic, anti-Spenserian, and antibiblical propaganda document is, imaginatively, not a program (or "progression") which, if followed, will lead to a marriage, but rather a continuous and repetitive reassertion and celebration of the eternality of Marriage. That is to say, it is not, nor did Blake intend it to be, anything like "The Bible of Hell" or any other kind of bible or "sacred code."[23] It is, instead, the ultimate epithalamium for the marriage that is the composite art of *The Marriage*. It is also a glorious celebration of the resurrection, for in the eternal body of Christ, The Marriage takes place, and "none shall want her mate" for "his spirit it hath gathered them"; and "they shall possess it for ever, from generation to generation shall they dwell therein" (Isaiah 34:16–17). Or, as Blake put it, citing Isaiah 34 and 35, this is "the return of Adam to Paradise"—the *eternal* paradise that "revives" (lives again, anew, still), not "the Eternal Hell."[24]

At this point the reader may be pardoned for wondering what all this has to do with Spenser directly, and with *The Faerie Queene* and Guyon particularly, for there is no question that Blake hardly needed to turn to Spenser, or to Milton, to find benighted ideas against which to levy the arsenal of his mental warfare. And in any case, Milton, whom we know as an early mentor of and persistently powerful influence on Blake, was much nearer to hand than Spenser if he decided he needed a specific target. The general point to be made in this regard is a simple one: both Spenser and Milton were *poets*, not philosophers or theoreticians, so that in a fundamental sense (to Blake) they should have known better. Milton "*was* a true poet," Blake says unequivocally, but then, consistent with the studied perversity apparent elsewhere in *The Marriage*, the gratuitous and ultimately misleading "equivalent" of the first phrase: "of the Devils party without knowing it." Nowhere does he say either of Spenser. I said at the outset that Blake's "road of excess" proverb provides us with an entrée into the Blake-Spenser relationship in *The Marriage*. It does. But by dealing largely with the figure of Excesse herself—along with Genius, Guyon, the Palmer, and the Bower of Bliss—I did not bring the story to its appropriately Blakean close. Aghast at what he sees of Acrasia's "paradise of pleasure and ennui" (as Byron puts it tellingly),[25] Guyon, belying his allegorical signification even while still closely attended by the prudent, cautious, reasonable Palmer, wreaks havoc on the Bower of Bliss: "All those pleasant bowres and Pallace braue," Spenser begins his five-stanza conclusion to the book (his language openly regretting his own character's surrender to excess despite his "training" in the earlier cantos),

> *Guyon* broke downe, with rigour pittilesse;
> Ne ought their goodly workmanship might saue
> Them from the tempest of his wrathfulnesse,
> But that their blisse he turn'd to balefulnesse:
> Their groues he feld, their gardins did deface,
> Their arbers spoyle, their Cabinets suppresse,
> Their banket houses burne, their buildings race,
> And of the fairest late, now made the fowlest place.

(II,xii,83)

The wanton excess of destruction here Blake surely would have regarded as a most unholy "wisdom," least of all a "redemption." Excess is thus destroyed by excess, and Excesse maintains her mastery over the "The Legend of . . . Temperance." At least that is the way I think Blake read these closing stanzas.[26] But while he might well have regarded the conclusion as a kind of poetic justice levied on Spenser's moral structure, he would also have remembered, with equal satisfaction, that it is not in Guyon's power to undo Acrasia's Circean transformations of man into brute. Only the Palmer's "vertuous staffe" seems to have that power, and even he, for all the magic of his rational prudence, can reverse only part of the damage. The beasts become men again, "Yet being men they did vnmanly looke." And the one that "had an hog beene late, hight *Grille* by name,"

> Repined greatly, and did him miscall,
> That had from hoggish forme him brought to naturall.
>
> (II,xii,86)

Guyon then pontificates in the self-inflation of his "victory" (which Grille's very existence argues is Pyrrhic at best):

> See the mind of beastly man,
> That hath so soone forgot the excellence
> Of this creation, when he life began,
> That now he chooseth, with vile difference,
> To be a beast, and lacke intelligence
>
> (II,xii,87)

—the "intelligence" and "excellence," of course, that Guyon sees in himself. To Blake, the Palmer's coda would have sounded precisely right to eternize the "failures" of both exemplars of the book's virtues:

> The donghill kind
> Delights in filth and foule incontinence:
> Let *Grill* be *Grill*, and haue his hoggish mind.
>
> (II,xii,87)

As if they had a choice.[27]

Blake was so taken with this marvelous demonstration of Guyon's and the Palmer's self-confutation and allegorical ineptitude that he borrowed from it directly for another of his poems, "I Saw a Chapel All of Gold" (*Notebook*, E467–68), which includes several other Spenserian allusions—all focused now on the codified forms of moral virtue called religions. We need to recall here that it is "the religious" who call the eternal contraries "Good & Evil," heaven and hell, and that Religion itself is the "reconciler" of—that is, reciprocal canceller of the power of—the very contraries its agents name and hence "realize" (*Marriage*, E34, 38). And, as I have indicated with respect to reading *The Marriage* in Blakean terms, in "I Saw a Chapel" Blake's allusions are not only integral to the poem's total meaning but, in effect, determine for us where Blake (as opposed to his speaker in the poem) stands on the whole matter.[28] While there is insufficient evidence to argue that Blake's poem owes its inception to Spenser, a key passage from *The Ruines of Time* informs "I Saw a Chapel" in an important way. After listening to the long lament of the spirit of Verulam,[29] the speaker of Spenser's poem has a series of visions "Like tragicke Pageants seeming to appeare" (l. 490), the first of which is as follows:

> I saw an Image, all of massie gold,
> Placed on high vpon an Altare faire,
> That all, which did the same from farre beholde,
> Might worship it, and fall on lowest staire.
>
> (Ll. 491–94)

If, as Renwick suggests, Spenser's "point of departure" was the statue of Zeus at Olympia (as mentioned, for example, in his *Ruines of Rome*, l. 20) and the "great image" in Daniel 2:31–35,[30] Blake's poem radically alters both the biblical theme of the ultimate fall of the four empires at the coming of Christ and the Spenserian theme of the frailty and vanity of all sublunary things. Taking his cue from Spenser's comparison of this "Image" with that "great Idoll"

> To which th'*Assyrian* tyrant would haue made
> The holie brethren, falslie to haue praid,
>
> (Ll. 495–97)

Blake constructs an image of false, idolatrous religion that, in its forbidding power and above all its secrecy (*vide* the closed door that prevents all entrance except apparently by force), deters even mistaken worship except from afar and without. Spenser's worshipers too, we note, "did . . . from farre beholde" the idol placed on high and could reach only the "lowest staire," certainly sufficient hint—whether or not it was Spenser's intention—for the inaccessibility of Blake's chapel.[31] Moreover, that "worship" is associated not with eternal or spiritual life but with death:

> And many weeping stood without
> Weeping mourning worshipping.

One is reminded of the end of *The Book of Urizen* after the formation of the self-strangling "Net of Religion":

> And their children wept, & built
> Tombs in the desolate places,
> And form'd laws of prudence, and call'd them
> The eternal laws of God.
>
> (28:4–7, E83)

As Hazard Adams suggests,[32] Blake here has taken a step beyond his song of experience, *The Garden of Love* (written at about the same time), where

> A Chapel was built in the midst,
> Where I used to play on the green.
>
> And the gates of this Chapel were shut,
> And Thou shalt not. writ over the door;
> So I turn'd to the Garden of Love,
> . . . .
> And I saw it was filled with graves,
> And tomb-stones where flowers should be:
> And Priests in black gowns, were walking their rounds,
> And binding with briars, my joys & desires.
>
> (E26)

This garden of love may distantly owe its origins to *The Romance of the Rose*, the *Song of Solomon*, and the entire *hortus conclusus* tradition, but more proximately it echoes Geryoneo's usurpation of Belge's kingdom in *The Faerie Queene*:

> . . . he had brought it now in seruile bond,
> And made it beare the yoke of inquisition,
> . . . .
> So now he hath new lawes and orders new
> Imposed on it, with many a hard condition,
> And forced it, the honour that is dew
> To God, to doe vnto his Idole most vntrew.
>
> To him he hath, before this Castle greene,
> Built a faire Chappell, and an Altar framed
> Of costly Iuory, full rich beseene,
> On which that cursed Idole farre proclaimed,
> He hath set vp, and him his God hath named.
>
> (V,x,27–28)

The pertinence of this sequence to both *The Garden of Love* and "I Saw a Chapel" is obvious, but we need to recall as well another passage in *The Ruines of Time*:

> Then did I see a pleasant Paradize,
> Full of sweete flowres and daintiest delights,
> Such as on earth man could not more deuize,
> With pleasures choyce to feed his cheerefull sprights.
>
> (Ll. 519–22)

But characteristically Blake transforms Spenser's emphasis on the delights of the flesh—"earthlie blis, and ioy in pleasures vaine" that inevitably lead to the garden's being "wasted quite" (ll. 528–29; the anticipation of Guyon's destruction of the bower is obvious)—into an emblem of innocence and the joyous unrestraint of desire, whose "destruction" is not due to time but rather to the fallen state of the speaker of the poem, who now sees the garden of love as a graveyard in whose midst is the "idol" of religious law, the chapel with gates shut and "Thou shall not. writ over the door."[33] These Thou-shalt-nots, the self-imposed impossibility of entering into (that is, perceiving) the oneness that is both sexual and imaginative (generation as an *image* of regeneration), Spenser's idolatrous image to which the "holie brethren" are made falsely to pray, and the self-repression of desire (as well as perception) Blake conflates rather spectacularly in his vision of the serpent's violent rape (the imagery of stanza 2 is unmistakable) of the chapel all of gold.

In this sense Adams is right in seeing the serpent as Orc-like (p. 240), the spirit of wrathful revolution against all forms of repression, but like Guyon's human rage and vengeance that belies his fairy status and allegorical signification, Orc is also the perversion of love into sexual warfare (Blake's intuitive sense of the "meaning" of rape that we have "discovered" in the twentieth century is remarkable). While the tigers of wrath may be wiser than the horses of instruction, according to Hell's wisdom (E37), such wrath, erupting out of repression and unilluminated by imaginative vision, finally leads to the promulgation of new tyranny to replace the old.[34] In the language of another of Blake's manuscript studies for *Songs of Experience*, significantly entered into his *Notebook* just prior to "I Saw a Chapel," the fury of the speaker's "wind" "blight[s] all blossoms fair & true" even as it nourishes others:

> all blossoms grew & grew
> Fruitless false tho fair to see
>
> (E467)

—a grotesquely parodic version of the Garden of Love. Rage, then, no matter how seemingly worthy its enterprise (again Guyon comes to mind), is seen by Blake to be as negating as abstinence, which

> sows sand all over
> The ruddy limbs & flaming hair
> But Desire Gratified
> Plants fruits of life & beauty there.
>
> (*Notebook*, E474)

While Blake's serpents are confusingly various, the one in "I Saw a Chapel" is with deliberate ambiguity both phallic and Orc-like as well as repressively priestlike, an embodiment of natural religion. Thus, Blake first establishes—at least in part by reshaping two of

Spenser's "visions"—the indissoluble relationship among false religion, repressed desire (hence, frustrated sexuality), death, and the mind-forged manacles of reason which prevent the union of human with human as well as with divinity (the worshipers do not "enter in" not because they cannot but because "none did dare"). Then he turns in his second stanza from Spenser to Milton's Samson. Not only is his destruction of the "theater / Half round on two main pillars vaulted high" (ll. 1605–6) the triumph of God's power over the idolatrous Philistines' worship of Dagon (who is at least reminiscent of Spenser's "Idoll"), but his resistance of Dalila's blandishments constitutes (among other things) his triumph over sexuality that is prostituted to political and religious purposes. But taking his cue perhaps from the Semichorus's later description of Samson—"His fiery virtue roused" as "an ev'ning dragon" (serpent) come to assail the "tame villatic fowl" (ll. 1690, 1692, 1695)—Blake daringly transforms the Miltonic positiveness of Samson's destruction of the Philistines[35] into a graphically melodramatic rape of the established church and its sacraments. The transformation is made all the more extraordinary by the allusion to *Paradise Lost* in the last line of the second stanza. In Book V of Milton's epic, Raphael begins his descent from Heaven to earth at God's behest by flying "through the midst of heav'n"

> till at the gate
> Of heav'n arrived, the gate self-opened wide
> On golden hinges turning, as by work
> Divine the sov'ran Architect had framed.
>
> (Ll. 251, 253–56)

Similarly, in Book VII,

> Heav'n opened wide
> Her ever-during gates, harmonious sound
> On golden hinges moving, to let forth
> The King of Glory in his powerful Word
> And Spirit coming to create new worlds.
>
> (Ll. 205–9)

While this last allusion provides an obvious commentary on the unopened (locked?) doors of Blake's chapel, regardless of the fact that, in both passages, Milton is speaking of egress from Heaven, Blake clearly sets his rape against the Miltonic background of both an open, unsecret religion (Milton was indeed "of the Devils party" after all) and the idea of the freely opening gates of heaven. At about the same time as the composition of "I Saw a Chapel," Blake used this motif of the open/closed door in *America*, where the door represents not only closed secret religion but also the gates of the five senses (here consumed in the "fierce flames" of Orcian revolution) and Milton's gates of Heaven: on plate 16 of *America* the "ancient Guardians" of the law

> slow advance to shut the five gates of their law-built heaven
> Filled with blasting fancies and with mildews of despair
> With fierce disease and lust, unable to stem the fire of Orc;
> But the five gates were consum'd, & their bolts and hinges melted
> And the fierce flames burnt round the heavens, & round the
>   abodes of men.
>   (16:17–23, E57–58)

Another gate image strikingly similar to its use in "I Saw a Chapel" is found in *The Four Zoas*, where the "Gates of Enitharmons heart" are

> burst . . . with direful Crash
> Nor could they ever be closd again the golden hinges were broken
> And the gates broke in sunder & their ornaments defacd
> Beneath the tree of Mystery. . . .
>   (VII, E360)

Finally, and even more startling, is Blake's pencil sketch executed at about this same time of a spikily crowned female figure (Enitharmon?) whose genitals are represented as a small Gothic chapel containing a figure that is possibly an idol.[36]

Thus, Blake characteristically adopts at face value Samson's heroic annihilation of idolatrous religion only to escalate and radicalize it into an un-Miltonic forceful opening of the gates of a closed and secret heaven, a revolt against restrained desire and enforced virginity, the destruction of the gates of the five senses (and hence the reawakening of imaginative vision), and the revival of life against a religion of death. At the same time, for Blake the heroic, selfless act of Milton's Samson is ultimately an act of corporeal war, destructive of archenemies, to be sure, but nonetheless breeding new tyranny.[37] Just so, in *The Four Zoas* the successful revolutionist, Orc, "began to Organize a Serpent body" and, turning light into "flaming fire," "affection into fury & thought into abstraction," he becomes "A Self consuming dark devourer rising into the heavens" (Night VII, E356). Accordingly, in *The Four Zoas* Blake establishes the "pavement sweet / Set with pearls & rubies bright" along which the serpent draws his "slimy length" (on his way to "Vomiting his poison" on the bread and wine) as the rich garb of the transformed Orc—who thus takes on the accouterments of the very religion he has ostensibly destroyed:

Beneath down to his eyelids scales of pearl then gold & silver
Immingled with the ruby overspread his Visage. . . .

"Emerald Onyx Sapphire jasper beryl amethyst"—all strive "in ter-
rific emulation" to gain "a place / Upon the mighty Fiend" (VIII,
E373), each gem a perversion of the pavement of love in the Song of
Solomon (3:10).

The unregenerate Orc first follows the advice Blake later has Los
deliver in *Jerusalem*:

> . . . overthrow their cup,
> Their bread, their altar-table, their incense & their oath:
> Their marriage & their baptism, their burial & consecration.
> (91:12–14, E251)

And then, by his ambiguously regenerative yet destructive act, the
chalice of wine becomes the "Cup / Of fornication," the bread the
"food of Orc & Satan, pressd from the fruit of Mystery." As a result,

> The Ashes of Mystery began to animate they calld it Deism
> And Natural Religion as of old so now anew began
> Babylon again in Infancy Calld Natural Religion.
> (*The Four Zoas* VIII, E386)

It is at least possible that Blake found some sanction for this ambiguity (although he rarely needed sanction for anything) in Spenser's
Faerie Queene. In Book VI, for example, the Blatant Beast breaks

> into the sacred Church . . .,
> And robd the Chancell, and the deskes downe threw,
> And Altars fouled, and blasphemy spoke,
> And th'Images for all their goodly hew,
> Did cast to ground. . . .
> (xii,25)

And though Calidore "supprest and tamed" the beast (xii,37), Blake
well might have read this attack on the iconoclasm of the Puritan ex-
tremists as a desirable smashing of idolatry and secret religion. At the
same time, he would have recognized that the Blatant Beast's violence is but the obverse of Guyon's, the excess of reforming zeal that
re-forms new codes even as it destroys old ones. Thus, the "new religion" of the Blatant Beast is never quelled in *The Faerie Queene* as
Spenser left it, and "he raungeth through the world againe," his
power unrestrained, "Barking and biting all that him doe bate"
(VI,xii,40). In Book I of *The Faerie Queene*, the passage Hazard Adams
alludes to (but does not quote) in his analysis of "I Saw a Chapel"

(p. 240) is in some respects the other side of the coin, although it has its own ambiguity, from Blake's point of view:

> Therewith she spewd out of her filthy maw
> > A floud of poyson horrible and blacke,
> > Full of great lumpes of flesh and gobbets raw,
> > Which stunck so vildly, that it forst him [Redcrosse] slacke
> > His grasping hold, and from her turne him backe:
> > Her vomit full of bookes and papers was,
> > With loathly frogs and toades, which eyes did lacke,
> > And creeping sought way in the weedy gras:
> Her filthly parbreake all the place defiled has.[38]

What Spenser's full allegorical intent was here probably mattered little to Blake, but the fact that this serpentlike creature was the embodiment of error (especially religious error) was surely a happy discovery. In his own poem, then, he has Spenser's Errour defile the sacraments as if she were the radically iconoclastic Puritan Blatant Beast; but he severely undercuts the desirability and even the validity of that iconoclasm by having the Beast vomit out Errour's poison. In all cases (and we can add here Guyon in the Bower of Bliss as well as Milton's Samson), "positive" act becomes visionless destruction.

Blake concludes "I Saw a Chapel" with the speaker laying himself down in a sty among the swine. Interestingly containing the only use of *sty* in all of Blake and one of only two uses of *swine*, this passage is often viewed as merely a revulsion from the violence of the rape. Damon, for example, says the whole poem "is based on the thesis that a forced and unwanted act of sex . . . is a pollution of the sacrament of real love."[39] While in one sense that is true, such an interpretation is far too narrow (as well as orthodoxly religious) to account for the poem's intricate ambiguities. After all, *The Marriage* seems to sanction such excesses in its campaign to liberate desire from self-repression. Part of Damon's difficulty lies in his not recognizing the final literary allusions in the poem—to Milton's *Comus* and to Spenser's antecedent conception in Book II of *The Faerie Queene*. Comus, we recall, is the son of Circe and, emulating her employment of a "charmed Cup" (l. 51), he too offers

> > > to every weary traveler
> > His orient liquor in a crystal glass,
>
> . . . .
>
> > Soon as the potion works, their human count'nance,
> > Th' express resemblance of the gods, is changed
> > Into some brutish form of wolf, or bear,
> > Or ounce, or tiger, hog, or bearded goat,

> All other parts remaining as they were;
> And they, so perfect is their misery,
> Not once perceive their foul disfigurement,
> But boast themselves more comely than before,
> And all their friends, and native home forget,
> To roll with pleasure in a sensual sty.
>
> (Ll. 64–65, 68–77)

The allusion is many-faceted and, as usual, is an example of Blake's wrenching of his borrowings out of context (yet retaining some residue of that context) for his own purposes. Obviously no advocate of chastity, he sides here with Comus's antipathy to restraint:

> welcome joy and feast,
> Midnight shout and revelry,
> Tipsy dance and jollity.
>
> . . . .
>
> Rigor now is gone to bed,
> And Advice with scrupulous head,
> Strict Age, and sour Severity,
> With their grave saws in slumber lie.
>
> . . . .
>
> Venus now wakes, and wakens Love.
>
> (Ll. 102–4, 107–10, 124)

In the same vein the Attendant Spirit, in describing Comus and his sport to the two brothers, says he

> to every thirsty wanderer,
> By sly enticement gives his baneful cup,
> With many murmurs mixed, whose pleasing poison
> The visage quite transforms of him that drinks,
> And the inglorious likeness of a beast
> Fixes instead, unmolding reason's mintage
> Charactered in the face. . . .
>
> (Ll. 524–30)

In Spenser, as Guyon approaches the Bower of Bliss, he first meets Genius (as noted earlier in this chapter), who "secretly doth vs procure to fall, / Through guilefull semblaunts," and who, like Circe and Comus, is equipped with "A mighty Mazer bowle of wine" to "gratify" all guests (II,xii,48–49). No "orient liquor" or "pleasing poison," this mere alcoholic enticement Guyon easily (and "disdainfully") destroys (st.49). But next he meets Excesse, the presiding *genius loci*:

> In her left hand a Cup of gold she held,
>> And with her right the riper fruit did reach,
>> Whose sappy liquor, that with fulnesse sweld,
>> Into her cup she scruzd. . . .

(xii,56)

This too Guyon dashes down, and he moves on unscathed into Acrasia's bower with all its luxurious delights—as well as its transformed men:

>> Whylome her louers, which her lusts did feed,
>> Now turned into figures hideous,
>> According to their mindes like monstruous.

(xii,85)

Retransformed to men by the Palmer's "vertuous staff," "they comely men became" again, Spenser's adjective borrowed by Milton for the *Comus* passage cited above. But even more important, with respect to Milton's inclusion of a hog and a sty in the same passage, is Spenser's concluding vignette of Grille, the epitome of the "donghill kind" that "Delights in filth and foule incontinence" because his "*mind*" is "hoggish" (my italics).

The attractiveness of this collocation of ideas and images to Blake for the purposes of "I Saw a Chapel" is obvious. While seeming to undercut the Homeric, Spenserian, and Miltonic emphasis on Circean charms and magic, Blake has his speaker "[turn] into a sty" in what appears to be a nice bit of studied ambiguity.[40] But one need not insist on such cleverness. The speaker, as Hazard Adams suggests, is repelled "not at sexuality itself, but at the hypocrisy of the moral law toward it" (pp. 240–41). Hence, he opts "To roll with pleasure in a sensual sty"—or, translating Spenser and Milton into Blake, to "improve" sensual enjoyment to the point where "the whole creation will be consumed, and appear infinite. and holy whereas it now appears finite & corrupt" (*Marriage*, E39). Such sensual enjoyment is pointedly opposed to "Rigor," the "Advice" of "scrupulous heads," "Strict Age," "sour Severity," and "Grave Saws," all of which the Proverbs of Hell rail against. Still, Comus's "unmolding" of "reason's mintage / Charactered in the face" as well as Acrasia's turning men "into figures hideous, / According to their mindes like monstruous" seem hardly Blakean desiderata either—though they might very well be, in *The Marriage*, a Devil's. As much as he was repelled no doubt by the deification of reason by both his predecessors, his own human form divine looks no more like Grille than like Milton's human face divine.

Despite his helpful reference to the Orc cycle, then, Adams's conclusion about "I Saw a Chapel" is no less narrow and misleading in its own way than is Damon's comment on the poem as a whole. As in Blake's perception of Book II of *The Faerie Queene*, no one wins. Guyon "conquers" Excesse only to fall victim to excess; the Palmer transforms the beasts back into men but "Yet being men they did vnmanly looke" and Grille insists on and succeeds in remaining Grille. Temperance conquers Excesse in the allegory, but in *this* world excess destroys temperance. In Blake's poem the serpent destroys the tyranny of false religion but, in the excess of his Guyon-like reformation, forces the "freed" speaker-worshiper to embrace the dehumanizing and dehumanized "religion" of Comus and Grille. If, as Damon says, the speaker "rejects" the serpent because his "cure" is even more diseased than the disease itself, he also rejects the forbidding tyranny and bleakness of the religion of death with which the poem opens. Both rejections are "negations" in Blake's precise sense of that word, and, as a result, the speaker's embrace of the sty and the swine is an anti-act, a negating of his fundamental and divine humanness in the service of excessive revulsion. It is Guyon's final destructive act all over again, which, as I have said, vaporizes his allegorical signification and aligns him with the very Excesse who rules the world of Book II. As Blake wrote tellingly in *A Vision of the Last Judgment*, "he who is out of the Church & opposes it is no less an Agent of Religion than he who is in it" (E562).

To Blake, then, Spenser's vision at the end of Book II of *The Faerie Queene* was righter than he knew—or intended. Despite reason's power and the sun-clad power of chastity (the bound and outward circumference of energy personified), Grille is still out there along with the Blatant Beast, and Comus holds his Cotyttoan rites nightly—all impervious to the onslaughts of a misconceived and misdirected poetics. In this sense both Spenser and Milton are allegorists (the false poet that is an incrustation over their true-poet imaginative selves), for "Allegories are things that Relate to Moral Virtues Moral Virtues do not Exist they are Allegories & dissimulations. . . . by their Works ye shall know them" (*A Vision of the Last Judgment*, E563–64).

Thus far in this chapter I have been arguing implicitly that, although there are abundant Spenserian echoes or analogues in the works I have focused on, Book II of *The Faerie Queene* was, for Blake, an especially enduring, vivid, and detailed memory. It is now time to escalate implicitness to explicitness with respect to *The Marriage of Heaven and Hell*, especially in light of its usual interpretation as a "litany of excess."[41] As I noted in chapter 1, it is no accident that the only passage Blake ever quotes directly from Spenser is a quatrain from Book II; but even more compelling, when added to the passages I have already examined in connection with *The Marriage*, is the quite extraordinary uses to which Blake puts the Guyon-Mammon episode in his "Memorable Fancy" of the "Printing house in Hell" (plate 15, E40).

The standard (indeed, so far as I know, the only) interpretation of this passage is as a kind of allegory of Blake's unique process of "illuminated printing." Briefly, and oversimplified, that process was essentially relief-engraving whereby the text and design were drawn on a copper-plate with an impervious liquid and the surrounding areas eaten away with acid (and/or gouged out with a burin or graver) to leave the text and design raised for printing—after which the printed design was touched up with a quilled pen or brush and hand-colored. As Erdman puts the matter succinctly, with respect to Blake's "Memorable Fancy,"

> Each metal plate, cut and burnt into by tool and acid fire,
> is a "cave," each process the cave goes through is a
> "chamber" in his printing house. But the result of the
> process, the surface of the paper printed and coloured,
> which we also call a "plate," is a "cave" too; the student
> enters it to find the immense palaces the poet-artist has
> built for his delight.[42]

The graphic details that accompany the text of the printing house in Hell both contribute to and confirm this allegorical reading, with a miniature burin or graver leading to the words describing the first chamber, assorted cliff edges (the edges of the cavities cut or acid-burned into the plate), various leafy hieroglyphics for the leaves of a book, and so on. At the foot of the plate is a large eagle with a long, looped serpent in its talons, which Erdman interprets as "the serpent of temporal delineation" collaborating with "the eagle of spatial illustration"—in other words, text plus graphic design.[43]

The unequivocally positive thrust of this interpretation seems unexceptionable. It does, however, assume the identity of the speaker as Blake himself and, to maintain the autobiographical Blakeanism of the plate's "message" (or iconicization), it also glosses over some rather crucial issues and words and ignores the polemical antinomianism that constitutes the entire work's efficient form.

Blake himself provides unmistakable clues to a less "Blakean" reading of the plate than Erdman and others have offered. In the first place, it is labeled "A Memorable Fancy." If the several "Fancies" in *The Marriage* are part of Blake's satire on Swedenborg's stodgy and unfailingly dull "Memorable Relations" in his *Treatise concerning Heaven and Hell, and of the Wonderful Things therein, as Heard and Seen*, the deflation, or trivializing, of "Relations" (narratives of "fact") to mere "Fancies" is an effective, if simple, satiric ploy. As we learn on plate 21, what Swedenborg fancied new "is only the Contents or Index of already publish'd books." The "Fact" is, as Blake's speaker goes on to say, that Swedenborg's facts are "all the old falshoods" (E42). It is abundantly clear, however, and universally acknowledged that *The Marriage* is considerably more than an anti-Swedenborgian diatribe, the latter merely the vehicle for the point of the former.[44] Swedenborg aside, then, suitably put in his place as both a servile copier (a blind one at that, for he copies only errors) and an idle fantasist, what exactly does Blake imply by the titular phrase "A Memorable Fancy"?

The first thing that should strike us is Blake's yoking of memory and fancy in a way roughly anticipative of Coleridge's more famous definition some thirty years later (which is itself a redaction of Lockean epistemology). Fancy, Coleridge says, as distinct from the creative (and perceptive) imagination, is "the aggregating power"; it is "always the ape . . . of our memory" and thus "has no other counters to play with, but fixities and definites."[45] Blake's most mature "definitions" of fancy seem to argue that he is quite in tune with the prevailing aesthetics of his day, which regarded *fancy* and *imagination* as interchangeable terms. In 1799, for example, he tried to correct the obtusely conventional Rev. John Trusler's "Mistakes" in saying "that the Visions of Fancy are not be [*sic*] found in This World. To Me This World is all One continued Vision of Fancy or Imagination" (E702). Complaining in another letter a few days later to artist friend George Cumberland about his frustration with Trusler, Blake charges the latter with attempting to make him "Reject all Fancy from his Work" (E703). Similarly, in the later *Vision of the Last Judgment*, he uses "Imagination" synonymously with "Visionary Fancy" as the faculty by which "the Prophets" perceive and employ "their various sublime & Divine Images as seen in the Worlds of Vision" (E554–55).

But all of these instances of Blake's use of the word *fancy* occur well after the completion of *The Marriage of Heaven and Hell*. What about earlier? His first use of the word is in *Poetical Sketches* (1783), in the Gothic "potboiler" entitled *Fair Elenor*, where it is simply contrasted to conventional reality. Similar occurrences of the word in this ordinary sense, still current today, punctuate the volume; but in one poem there is a striking adumbration of Blake's linking of memory and fancy in *The Marriage*. In *Memory, Hither Come*, memory is plaintively besought by the speaker and, while its "music floats" upon the winds of his mind, he'll

> pore upon the stream,
> Where sighing lovers dream,
> And fish for fancies as they pass
> Within the watery glass.

(E415)

The idle fatuity of this surrender to memory and illusion is, I think, rather finely done, Blake's speaker wallowing in the sentimental conventionalities of the ubiquitous memory-inspired love lyrics of the eighteenth century, "inspired" by the Renaissance preoccupation with such lovesickness and its fanciful conceits. It is perhaps not unwarranted to suggest that Blake's later judgment of Swedenborg's "Memorable Relations" is that they are but fancies fished from the stream of sensory impressions "Within the watery glass" of his mirrorlike memory. As Eaves says, Blake's "strongest criticism of Swedenborg in *The Marriage* . . . is that he is not original."[46] His "Memorable Relations," then, are not merely "Memorable Fancies" but are the relatings of "facts" remembered. This ought to tell us something of Blake's narrator in *The Marriage*. Bloom argues that "the *Marriage* is written out of the state of Generation, our world in its everyday aspect."[47] But this is to confuse Blake with his speaker, for it is the latter, not the former, whose point of view is of this world. As a result, the speaker's antinomianism should be just as suspect as Swedenborg's nomianism. Both are the products of seeing-is-believing-is-remembering, both (to Blake) utter fancy.

To return to linguistic history, the word *fancy* does not appear in *Songs of Innocence*, nor does *memory* (though the former may well be implied in the little lost boy's momentary mesmerization by the *ignis fatuus*, and the latter in "Old John's" memory of his carefree childhood), but in *Tiriel* we are presented with a parodic Adam and Eve living out their lives, under the tutelage and protection of Memory (Mnetha), in a "fancy" of their unfallen state. Moreover, as Essick has demonstrated in impressive detail, their entire existence is an allegory of eighteenth-century artistic principles and practice as Blake, in deliberately oversimplified fashion, conceived it: sensory imitation, memory, fancy-imagination.[48] It is meet and right, then, that Tiriel himself is blind and, even with surrogate eyes (his "daughter" Hela), commands his daughter to lead him to Har and Heva, where he may "with pleasure . . . dwell" in their fancied Eden. One need not meticulously trace this evolution in all its stages to recognize that, by the time of *The Marriage*, Blake has refined eighteenth-century epistemology and aesthetics into myopic vision, a perception of the fractionalized "ratio only," and then equated that with fancy and its "images" derived from memory. From this point it is but a short leap to the explicitness of *Jerusalem*: "when separated / From imagination," the aggregate of sense impressions closes

> itself as in steel, in a Ratio
> Of the Things of Memory. It thence frames Laws & Moralities
> To destroy Imagination. . . .
>
> (74:10–12, E229)

To recapitulate, for Blake, fancy produces "images" that are presented as "real" by clothing them in garments derived from the memory's storehouse of sense impressions. Such images, we should now see, are allegories in the same sense that the names the ancient poets gave to "things," thus animating them, were abstracted by priests from those things, pronounced real, and given form as "gods." This extraordinary mental maneuvering or prestidigitation leads, rather startlingly, to the conclusion that *The Marriage* is narrated by an allegorist. Lest that leap seem totally foolhardy at this point—that is, before my entering the patent allegory of the Printing house in Hell—let me cite some revealing, although usually overlooked, language in *The Marriage*.

The *just man*, the *villain*, the *perilous path*, the *paths of ease* and other comparable terms in "The Argument" might well serve in the most simplistic of allegories, polarizing our readerly perceptions in precisely the way such allegories, not to say "arguments," do. In fact, the poet who writes "The Argument" should appear to us as a sort of unimaginative Isaiah (from whose "book" virtually the entire "poem" is stolen), who, lest we miss his point, must translate his own allegory: the serpent, for example, must be a "sneaking serpent." On plate 3, "Hell revives" and a series of capitalized abstractions are said to be "necessary to Human existence." If "the religious" derive their abstractions from these, they are but further removed than the speaker himself from whatever "sensible objects" lie "behind" his abstractions, an instance then of the pot calling the kettle black. On plate 5, "the restrainer" is "reason," who both "usurps" and "governs," and the rest of the plate argues that *Paradise Lost* is an allegory in which Milton simply attaches the wrong significations to his allegorical figures. That is, he "called" them by the wrong names.[49] The correct names, says the speaker, are "the Father" as "Destiny," "the Son" as "a Ratio of the five senses," and "the Holy-ghost, Vacuum"—punctuating his arrogant rectification with an exclamation point and a scholarly footnote to this "argument."

The proverbial wisdom of the Proverbs of Hell is almost entirely couched in language that either allegorizes "truths" openly or encourages us to read them allegorically. Even the human form divine, which, in the *Songs of Innocence*, is the virtues it "contains" (not merely emblemizes), becomes in the Proverbs a structure of abstractions (Sublime, Pathos, Beauty, Proportion—this last the "kicker" that should undermine the entire conception if our imagination has not been entirely blunted by the earnestness of Blake's narrator). Plate 11, then, properly comes last in this opening series, for although it represents the speaker still maintaining his antinomian stance and rhetoric, it is also Blake's revealing to us the error of our sympathetic, nodding agreement with the "obvious" rightness of the speaker's diabolic wisdom thus far. The spoof that follows in the "Memorable Fancy" of dining with Isaiah and Ezekiel (E38–39) ought to convince us further that something is amiss, but the soberness and colloquial "realness" of the question and answer conversation instead continue to impose power upon us—to the point where all readers to date, so far as I know, simply do not recognize that both prophets confess to having done precisely what plate 11 has described. Their discussion centers on "the first principle of human perception," just as the opening paragraph of plate 11 presents what the ancient poets' "enlarged and numerous senses could perceive." But instead of creating poetry out of those perceptions, Isaiah and Ezekiel assume that their version of the perceptual principle is the "right one," and hence they "despised" all the "Priests & Philosophers of other countries . . . prophecying that all Gods would at last be proved. to originate in ours. . . . and we so loved our God. that we cursed in his name all the deities of surrounding nations, and asserted that they had rebelled." "This," says Ezekiel, "like all firm persuasions, is come to pass" (that is, "the vulgar came to think that all nations would at last be subject to the jews"), and now "all nations believe the jews code and worship the jews god, and what greater subjection can be." What indeed![50]

Plate 14 (E39) is again a retailing of what the speaker has "heard from Hell," but even more striking is the insolent self-righteousness of his "command" that the "cherub with his flaming sword . . . leave his guard at tree of life," an audacity that severely calls into question his pontifical conclusion, "This [the apocalypse] will come to pass by an improvement of sensual enjoyment." "But first," he says, I've got to "expunge" your (the reader's) erroneous notions about bodies and souls. By this time, if we are paying attention to Blake's language, we should be sick of the fellow, who clearly has "the vanity to speak of [himself] as the only wise" (E42)—but we go on listening, and believing, and become trapped thereby in the peculiar metaphysics of the Printing house in Hell (plate 15). More of that "Memorable Fancy" in a moment. Meantime, plate 16 (E40) "corrects" other errors that we clearly have: "in truth" these "Giants" are not giants at all but the "causes of" sensual existence "& the sources of all activity." The cause-and-effect reasoning here seems to have disturbed no reader of *The Marriage*, even though Blake carefully provides clues to its error: "Thus" such and so, the speaker goes on; "But . . ."; "Some will say," but "I answer . . ."; the "two classes of men . . . should be enemies," and whoever says they are not "seeks to destroy existence"—or, even worse, whoever tries to reconcile these two classes is "religious." And, as in the critical essay on *Paradise Lost* in plate 5, the treatise of plate 16 ends with a pompous, pedantic footnote that refers us to the biblical parable of the sheep and goats, which, translated into the speaker's terms, necessitates consigning the goats (the devourers) to perdition and the sheep (the prolific) to "inherit the kingdom prepared . . . from the foundation of the world" (Matt. 25:32ff.), precisely an "Angelic" program for reform.

Then follows Blake's own parable (E41–42) which fundamentally explicates his own technique in *The Marriage*—an Angel and the speaker imposing on each other their respective metaphysics, both of which are "phantasies." *The Marriage* proper closes with the self-righteous condemnation of Swedenborg's lack of originality, the Swiftian irony of the speaker's revelation of his own vanity totally lost on him—as well as, apparently, on the readers of *The Marriage*, despite the tone of "Now hear a plain fact," "Now hear another," "And now hear the reason," "Thus . . .," "Have now another plain fact" (E43). By this time we are persuaded that we really have no choice. When the confuted Angel becomes a Devil in the final "Memorable Fancy" (E43), we ought not to care one way or the other; and the fact that he becomes the speaker's "particular friend" does not speak especially well for him at this point. "One Law for the Lion & Ox *is* Oppression" (my italics), as the closing line of plate 24 says (E44), but what it does not say (though Blake rather grandly does in the structure of the whole *Marriage*) is that *any* "One Law . . . is Oppression"—and, alas, we the readers are left with the one law that is a result of the speaker's only conversing with Devils, who are all irreligious, and not with Angels, who all love religion, "for he was incapable thro' his conceited notions" (plate 21, E43). There is no marriage in *The Marriage* for the simple reason that heaven and hell and angels and devils simply do not exist except in the minds of the fallen, who allegorize "Good" into "Heaven" and "Evil" into

"Hell." Only the "Chorus" at the end of "A Song of Liberty" (E45) proclaims that "everything that lives is Holy"—wholly. Two makes an allegory.

If we return at long last to the Printing house in Hell (E40), we ought to note fundamental problems in what seems so hellishly "right" about "Blake's" allegory. For example, the printing house is dedicated to transmitting "*knowledge* . . . from generation to generation" (my italics). Although Blake often uses the word *knowledge* interchangeably with *wisdom*, he is also fairly consistent in condemning the tree of knowledge for its association with good and evil. Moreover, before the writing of *The Marriage*, he inevitably regarded knowledge as that of Lockean epistemology. Thus, in *All Religions Are One*, "the true method of knowledge is experiment," and "from already acquired knowledge Man could not acquire more"; the "faculty of knowing" is merely "the faculty which experiences" (E2). In a manuscript fragment, Reason is described as "once fairer than the light" but is said to be now "fould in Knowledges dark Prison house" (E438), a soul-body metaphor so clearly anticipative of *The Marriage* that one is emboldened to regard this last phrase as the progenitor of *The Marriage*'s libraries as well. Even more to the point is the idea of a library itself, which is a kind of institutionalized memory in "the forms of books . . . arranged"—quite in the sense, as we shall see, of Spenser's Eumnestes. It is no accident that, in *An Island in the Moon*, it is "the Lawgiver" who frequents libraries, "taking extracts from Herveys Meditations among the tombs & Young's Night thoughts" like a good country squire or societal young lady improving her mind in her copybook (E446)—or like Swedenborg's "recapitulation of all superficial opinions."[51] Countering such "libraries" Blake, with the divinely inspired Bible in mind, persists in calling much of his own work (after *Songs of Innocence and of Experience*) the book of this, the book of that, book the first, and so on. As I have argued in *Blake's Prelude*, these are actually anti-books in much the same way that the "Bible of Hell" we are promised at the end of *The Marriage* (E43) is an anti-Bible and Blake's invention of "composite art" is an anti–illustrated book.[52]

Blake's "Memorable Fancies," then, are anti–Memorable Relations, but as such, their contrariness deliberately seduces us into the very error they are calculated to dispel, one that only our alertness to their allusive power enables us to resist. To effect the power of the "angelic" contrary to the Devil's (or Hell's) persistent embodiment of his metaphysics and to thus sustain the mental warfare of the contraries that ever threatens to dissolve into a mere debate, in the printing house "Fancy," Blake has rather astonishingly appropriated

Spenser, allegorist extraordinaire and therefore, to Blake, a devotee of memory, reason, and the moral virtues.

The allusions are basically to two different but related episodes in Book II of *The Faerie Queene*, conflated by Blake in such a manner that his use of them constitutes a criticism of Spenser as well as of angelic, Swedenborgian wisdom and library (or Lockean) storehouses of memory. The two episodes are Guyon's visit to the Cave of Mammon[53] and his later restorative sojourn in Alma's House of Temperance. The first of these is a version of the mythical descent into Hell, of which *The Marriage* itself is another version. Mammon first appears at the entrance to his "hole." He is appropriately coated with soot, his "cole-blacke hands" seeming "to haue beene seard / In smithes fire-spitting forge." His "nayles like clawes appeard" (vii,3), a detail that may well lie at the base of Blake's transformation of Mammon into the dragon-forms (Blake's are always clawed) that hollow out the cave of Hell's printing house. It may also be the first clue to the "real" relationship between the eagle pictured on the plate and the serpent it not only holds firmly in its claws but also seems, at least, to be pulling upward away from its eating into the rocky cliff at the lower left of the plate. More of this in a moment. While there is no "rubbish" to be cleared away from Mammon's cave-mouth, upon Guyon's approach, Mammon does

> remoue aside
> Those pretious hils [of gold] from straungers enuious sight,
> And downe them poured through an hole full wide,
> Into the hollow earth, there them to hide.
>
> (vii,6)

With that, Mammon conducts Guyon on his tour through a hellish landscape from which Blake borrowed in remarkable detail:

> That houses forme within was rude and strong,
> Like an huge caue, hewne out of rocky clift,
> From whose rough vaut the ragged breaches hong,
> Embost with massy gold of glorious gift,
> And with rich metall loaded euery rift.
>
> (vii,28)

No "vipers" fold "round the rock" or adorn the cave "with gold silver and precious stones" as in Blake, but the interior of Mammon's abode is no less gorgeous in its several chambers. Roof, floor, and walls in one "were all of gold" (vii,29), in another

> Many great golden pillours did vpbeare
> The Massy roofe, and riches huge sustayne,

And euery pillour decked as full deare
With crownes and Diademes.

(vii,43)

If no eagle causes "the inside of the cave to be infinite," Mammon's
accumulation "of richesse" is such that

Ne euer could within one place be found,
Though all the wealth, which is, or was of yore,
Could gathered be through all the world around,
And that aboue were added to that vnder ground.

It is, of course, no less than a bower of bliss, a place of excess, as
Spenser himself reminds us: "Loe here the worldes blis," Mammon
says, "To which all men do ayme" (vii,32). Moreover, the infiniteness of man's desire, greed, and lust in Spenser's conception has,
with equal effectiveness, made Mammon's Cave its symbol.

Another stop on Mammon's tour (perhaps not coincidentally the
fourth chamber of the infernal "house") is particularly pertinent to
the Printing house in Hell, for it is there that

an hundred raunges weren pight,
And hundred fornaces all burning bright.

(vii,35)

Blake's "Lions of flaming fire, raging around & melting the metals
into living fluids" do not labor here, but amid "fiers *Vulcans* rage"

By euery fornace many feends did bide,
Deformed creatures, horrible in sight,
And euery feend his busie paines applide,
To melt the golden metall, ready to be tride.

(vii,35)

"Here is," says Mammon in Spenser's savagely ironic phrase that
Blake would not have missed, "the fountaine of the worldes good"
(vii,38), received by men (no less than books are in Blake's "Fancy")
in "the forms" of the world's currency and the icons of power
("crownes and Diademes").[54]

It is difficult not to believe that Blake made precisely this connection between books and worldly power (indeed it may well be one of
the seeds of Urizen and his massy books), for the currency of received
knowledge and the coined currency of power, dominion, war, treason, jealousy, lust, and all the host of allegorical abstractions that
populate Mammon's Cave are equally dehumanizing and self-enslaving. To try to put us, the reader-viewers of the plate, straight on
this score, Blake rather shrewdly (and all too subtly as it has turned

out) shifts his allusionary context to Alma and Spenser's elaborate allegory of the human body and mind in the ninth canto of Book II of *The Faerie Queene*, where Guyon is strictly lessoned in the virtues of temperance, restraint, and the well-ordered body—the excesses of his experience in Mammon's cave having exhausted his "vitall powres" and "laid [him] in swowne" (vii,66; viii,proem). Again, as in the case of Acrasia's Bower, no palace of wisdom lies at the end of this road of excess but rather the "palace" of Philotime, so large

> As it some Gyeld or solemne Temple weare:
> Many great golden pillours did vpbeare
> The massy roof, and riches huge sustayne.

> (vii,43)

In it are the crowns of power and "titles vaine / Which mortall Princes wore, whiles they on earth did rayne." In Spenser's conception of Alma, however, there is a "palace of wisdom," but Arthur, not Mammon, guides Guyon on the road to it.

This "palace" is besieged by excess, now in the form of Maleger and his ruffian band of senses. Blake, one might imagine, gloated some to discover that Guyon deserts Alma's besieged castle after having been carefully instructed as to how to combat excess, leaving the fight against the sensual besiegers to Arthur. Be that as it may, with respect to the now severely undercut "Blakeanism" of the printing-house Memorable Fancy, Blake allusively imports an ersatz corrective to Mammon's influence.

Alma's "house" is not a "cave," but it does have many chambers—six to be exact, as in Blake's plate: the Hall of Diet and Appetite, the Kitchen "vaut" manned by Concoction and Digestion, the "Parlor" of the Affections, and the tripartite "Turret" of the head, this last in the charge of three monitors: Phantastes, an unnamed "man of ripe and perfect age," and Eumnestes.[55] This threesome is glossed by Spenser scholars, pursuant to conventional Renaissance psychology, as, respectively, Imagination or Fancy, Reason or Understanding, and Memory. I do not believe it necessary, or even desirable, to try to match Alma's six "chambers" with the six of Hell's printing house to recognize the uses to which Blake puts Spenser's allegory. In the kitchen, which Spenser aligns firmly and purposefully with Mammon's furnace chamber,

> There placed was a caudron wide and tall,
> Vpon a mighty furnace, burning whot.

> (ix,29)

With its "vaut," "raunges," smoke, furnace, and cauldron, Blake would not have missed the Mammon allusion, which Spenser signals by quoting himself: "Some scumd the drosse, that from the metall came" in the earlier episode, "And euery one did swincke, and euery one did sweat" (vii,36). In Alma's kitchen "some" were assigned "to remoue the scum, as it did rise" and all "did about their businesse sweat" (ix,30–31), the scum in both instances the origin perhaps of the "rubbish" being cleared away by the dragon-man in Blake's first chamber. To Spenser, Alma's kitchen (and her entire "house") is the "good" contrary to Mammon's excess, lust, and sensual-monetary self-imprisonment. Everything in her castle is orderly, proportional, proper, and temperate, even to the excreting of "all the liquor, which was fowle and wast" (ix,32). To paraphrase Mammon to Guyon, here is the fountain of the body's good.[56]

But Blake characteristically (and predictably) will have none of that sort of "good" either, however orderly. He therefore turns Spenser's contrast between the two episodes into a synonym. The "living fluids" that Blake's flaming lions cast "into the expanse" are thus, from one point of view, Spenser's liquid waste, now not excreted circumspectly as in Alma's castle (ix,32) but broadcast upon the world. Lest this seem not only gratuitously gross but interpretatively excessive, one needs to recall here a passage from Blake's *Descriptive Catalogue* (E546) which describes one of Blake's paintings (now lost). Given the anti-Swedenborgianism of *The Marriage*, that the subject "is taken from the Visions of Emanuel Swedenborg" is rather spectacularly coincidental. That subject is "The Learned, who strive to ascend into Heaven by means of learning" and who appear to the imaginative "like dead horses" (akin no doubt to the *The Marriage*'s "horses of instruction"). Moreover, these horses are emblematic of that species of "Learning" that has been placed above "Inspiration" by "corporeal demons" who have entered "into disease and excrement, drunkenness and concupiscence" in their "possession" of the "bodies of mortal men." As a result, Blake concludes, "the doors of the mind and of thought" (that is, imagination) are "shut," and "knowledge" derived from experience, sense perception, and reason are substituted for imaginative wisdom. In *Jerusalem*, it is the "Spectre," the reasoning power in man, who remakes man in his own fallen image, as Spenser's Mammon tries to do with Guyon:

> The Man who respects Woman shall be despised by Woman
> And deadly cunning & mean abjectness only, shall enjoy them
> For I will make their places of joy & love, excrementitious.
>
> (E247)

Toward the end of *Jerusalem*, in its ringing apocalypse, "the excrementitious" is associated with the fallen senses (and, one might add, therefore with the fancy), a "Husk & Covering" that must be annihilated to reveal the eternal lineaments of Imaginative Man (98:18–19, E257).

The agency by which that husk and covering are created is the memory, hence Blake's allusive move in his Memorable Fancy from Alma's kitchen to the "turret," where Memory and his two compatriots, Understanding and Fancy, reside. The first of the turret's three chambers is Phantastes', filled with all manner of the "creations" that populate the Printing house in Hell: dragon-men, vipers, eagles, and lions (ix,50). All are, Spenser says,

> idle thoughts and fantasies,
> Deuices, dreames, opinions vnsound,
> Shewes, visions, sooth-sayes, and prophesies;
> And all that fained is, as leasings, tales, and lies.
>
> (51)

To Spenser these fantasies are at once visionary poems (lies) and the allegorical monsters and "shewes" of an uncontrolled imagination or fancy.[57] Blake's imagination, however, is Spenser's Phantastes elevated to deific status. Implicit here, as well as in the received reading of Blake's allegory with which we began, is a severe condemnation of the elder poet's implicit condemnation of Phantastes, uncontrolled by the denizens of the turret's two other chambers, Reason or Understanding (its personification unnamed by Spenser) and Memory (Eumnestes). The latter's chamber (to Blake, in light of his and Spenser's excursus on excrement, appropriately "th' hindmost roome") is not merely full of the past, *all* the past, but is called a "Librarie" of "rolles," "old records," "long parchment scrolles"—and books (ix,57–59). These books are history books, of course, the repository of the world's memory, arranged according to the ordering principles evident in Spenser's second turret chamber (Reason and Understanding) and accessible by consulting (that is what "auise" in stanza 59 means) "antique Registers." On the walls of this second chamber are painted

> memorable gestes,
> Of famous Wisards, and with picturals
> Of Magistrates, of courts, of tribunals,
> Of commen wealthes, of states, or pollicy,
> Of lawes, of iudgements, and of decretals;
> All artes, all science, all Philosophy,
> And all that in the world was aye thought wittily.
>
> (ix,53)

All these books and paintings, which Spenser himself calls "memorable," are the very excrementitious husks that must be corrosively etched away in Blake's printing process to reveal the "real" infinite wisdom or "history" that was hidden. For Spenser, however, all three chambers must function together, as they do in the tight regimen of Alma's castle, each a check or tempering influence on the other two, their collaborative product (to Spenser) wisdom—which consists of counseling "fair *Alma*, how to gouerne well."[58] To Blake, such counsel is antiart, the "ratio" implicit in all self-limiting allegories.[59]

The printing-house plate, then, is a "Fancy" indeed, a memorable product of Alma's turret—and hence, knowledge and worldly power, not wisdom; excrement, not "the fountaine of the worldes good"; memory embalmed in books, not inspiration or imagination engaged in mental fight; allegory, not vision. Or perhaps it is a parable of imagination gone wrong, the "metals" that are cast "into the expanse" by the ominous "Unnam'd forms" and there "reciev'd by Men" who turned them into "mere" books "arranged." At the same time, it would be a mistake not to see Blake's printing house as what Erdman and others say it is. But what they say it is must also be seen as an allegorical antiallegory. As Blake's surrogate poet-prophet-artist in his epic poems, Los says at one point in his struggle against the trammels of fancy, reason, the senses, and memory,

> I must Create a System, or be enslav'd by another Mans
> I will not Reason & Compare: my business is to Create.
> (*Jerusalem* 10:20–21, E153)

What we tend to forget in reading these all-too-familiar lines is that Los is a *fallen* Zoa; moreover, he is reacting to the disastrous action of the fallen "Sons of Albion," who make of the eternal contraries first "Qualities" (which they "name . . . Good & Evil"), then "From them they make an Abstract"—precisely as the Priests of plate 11 of *The Marriage* do with the "sensible objects" named and animated by "The ancient poets." This "Abstract . . . is a Negation"

> Not only of the Substance from which it is derived
> A murderer of its own Body: but also a murderer
> Of every Divine Member: it is the Reasoning Power
> An Abstract objecting power, that Negatives every thing.
> (*Jerusalem* 10:7–14, E152–53)

In order to rescue these negations from eternal nonentity (irretrievableness), to fix them in the world of events where they are susceptible to imaginative retransformation into the external "substance" from which the sons of Los derive them, Los is forced, in his fallen state, to employ the metaphysical tactics of his enemy. That is to say, he objectifies the abstractions that Albion's sons, in their purblindness, have pronounced real by way of their "objecting power"— "Till a system was formed," as *The Marriage* puts it.

That "system," Los's system, is what I have called an allegorical antiallegory, a "Fixing" of

> Systems, permanent: by mathematic power
> Giving a body to Falshood that it may be cast off for ever.
> With Demonstrative Science piercing Apollyon [the angel of
>   the bottomless pit in Revelation] with his own bow!
> (*Jerusalem* 12:12–14, E155)

As grand and triumphant as this sounds, it is but half the job. What remains is the "system" Los himself creates so that he will not "be enslav'd by another Mans." It is in the language of that system, in its systematic antisystemizing, that Blake, not Los, strives with *all* "Systems to deliver Individuals from those Systems" (*Jerusalem* 11:5, E154). Including Los's. The ultimate deliverers, of course, are Blake's readers, for it is we who must recognize Blake's imaginative deallegorizing in Los's antiallegorical allegory. Otherwise, we either accept Los as our "priest"—or Swedenborg, or Milton, or the God of the Old Testament. Or Spenser. Los's "system," I submit, is the allegorical antiallegory. The only alternative is the system of belief (or allegory) of another man, whether a Swedenborg or a Spenser. "Striving with Systems to deliver Individuals from those Systems," as Los says, is the true artist's task, his only task (*Jerusalem*, E153). And we, the reader-spectators, are those individuals.

If I am correct about this dizzying mental warfare, we must, I think, look with as much suspicion at the graphic "emblem" Blake attaches prominently to the printing-house Fancy as we have at the text itself. Erdman describes it as eagle and serpent "married," soul and body, artist and poet, genius and craftsman, "collaborating to produce linear text and infinite illumination."[60] The visual impact of the illustration, to be sure, is a rising of eagle and snake out of the pictured clouds (of allegory) that they both push asunder, into the expansive imagination of the Memorable Fancy itself. The fact that the "Fancy" is a fantasy of memory should give us pause at this point, but that aside for the moment, let us push on to extend this interpretation. Without violation, we might say, then, that the books at the end of the Memorable Fancy are neither placed nor arranged in libraries at all. With but a little vision of our own, we can discover in Blake's final sentence a nagging grammatical ambiguity: the metals cast into the expanse "were reciev'd by Men who occupied the sixth chamber, *and took* the forms of books & were arranged in libraries" (my italics). If the phrase "metals [melted] into living fluids" constitutes the subject of "took," all well and good; Blake's illuminated books are indeed inscribed with living fluids. At the same time, "took" is also governed by "Men" as well as by the second use of the word *metals*. In this sense, it is men who become the "books" whose form the metals take. That is to say, they become Spenser's Eumnestes, whose library is but an externalization of himself. As Greenberg suggests, they become what they behold, repositories of "things foregone" (*FQ* II,ix,56). The ambiguity is a nice one, but since its subtlety may dissuade complete acquiescence, let us now return to the eagle and the snake.

If the vipers of Blake's text fold "round the rock & the cave . . . adorning it with gold silver and precious stones" (which Erdman interprets as the coloring of the "printed" paper), then the eagle's function in the next chamber seems to undo what has just been done—for "he [causes] the inside of the cave to be infinite" even as his cohorts, "Eagle like men," counterproductively build "palaces in the immense cliffs" (Erdman's "getting the text on to the plate" and thence onto the paper). This in turn is followed by the etching process in the fourth chamber. *After* the printing? Aware of the dilemma, which is exacerbated by other problems in the sequence of Blake's procedure, Erdman more or less side-steps it by describing Blake's allegorical version of the process as "elliptical" or "a conflation of processes."[61] Why it should be that way he does not say. One possibility is that Blake here intends to desequentialize the mathematical neatness of Spenser's allegory—allegorically to antiallegorize in a mechanical sense. But that hardly seems likely, and Los is as yet unborn. The other possibility (aside from simple confusion on Blake's part) is inherent in the Spenserian origins of the printing house. We recall that, when Guyon enters Mammon's cave, an "vgly feend" immediately stalks him:

> Well hoped he, ere long that hardy guest,
>   If euer couetous hand, or lustfull eye,
>   Or lips he layd on thing, that likt him best,
>   Or euer sleepe his eye-strings did vntye,
>   Should be his pray. And therefore still on hye
>   He ouer him did hold his cruell clawes,
>   Threatning with greedy gripe to do him dye
>   And rend in peeces with his rauenous pawes,
> If euer he transgrest the fatall *Stygian* lawes.
>
> (*Faerie Queene* II,vii,27)

Since Guyon here is as much the Lucianic traveler in Hell as is Blake's speaker in *The Marriage*, Blake may be telling us via his illustration that his speaker has succumbed to the "wisdom" of Mammon's Cave and its temptations and thus has fallen victim to the foul fiend's vengeance. Such an interpretation gains some credence from Blake's Spenser illustration to Gray's *The Bard*, in which the foul fiend is bat winged, as well as from the fact that the eagle's head and beak, indeed his entire rising vector, lead directly to the word *libraries*, as curious a place for the "marriage" of body and soul as it is for Blake's corrosive "books." And yet that is where Guyon ends up in Alma's castle, eagerly consuming the golden apple of "knowledge" that has been transmitted by books "from generation to generation"—a knowledge that extends from the creation of man by Prometheus to the ascendancy of Gloriana, the Faerie Queene. In sum, the conflation of cantos vii and ix which Blake exploits in his text he also employs in his illumination of that text.

Blake was no doubt delighted to find that Spenser uses the word "Beguild" to describe the effect of this reading on both Guyon and Arthur, the latter of whom reads, we recall, the "true" history that is the "matter of just memory" (II,proem,1). In their blithe assumption of the truth of what they both have read, it is meet and right that Mammon's ugly fiend take them as his prey—"snatcht away," as Spenser says in a passage Blake may have had in mind, "More light than Culver in the Faulcons fist" (II,vii,34). The problem here is that Guyon is no viper and Mammon's fiend is hardly an eagle. At this point, it is well to remember that the entire thrust of the "Fancy" has been to deallegorize, not to reallegorize, in whatever sense of correctness our own minds assume and impose. Thus, if for Spenser Guyon is (or emblemizes, or enacts in some fashion) the virtue of Temperance, it is insufficient to understand Blake's "version" of the fairy knight as merely Excess. But, if we take our cue to Blake's "meaning" in the illustration from the eagle's flight toward the word *libraries* as well as from the Spenserian origins of the entire plate, we will find a most interesting passage in the tenth canto of Guyon's errantry. Reading in his book, Guyon finds first

> how . . . *Prometheus* did create
> A man, of many partes from beasts deriued,
> And then stole fire from heauen, to animate
> His worke, for which he was by *Ioue* depriued
> Of life him selfe, and hart-strings of an Aegle riued.
>
> (x,71)

If Erdman is correct (as I think he is) in interpreting the viper's activities in the text as "*illuminating* the plate,"[62] which is both a cave and rock, then Guyon's descent into Mammon's cave is a rather remarkable and devastating parody of both this viperish illumination and Prometheus's (as Guyon's ancestral creator) "animation" of the human form by fire. For insofar as Guyon illuminates the darkness of Mammon's cave at all, he does so with his armor: his "glitter and armes . . . / . . . with their brightnesse made that darknesse light" (vii,42). Such presumption very nearly earns Guyon his quietus from Disdayne, but more important, it earns him, in Blake's reinterpretation, the wrath of the "God of the world," "Great *Mammon*, greatest god below the skye" (vii,8). He calls down upon Guyon the famous Jovian eagles to deprive him "Of life him selfe" as well as to rive his "hart-strings" (x,70)—as Spenser "erroneously" has it—to the consternation of his commentators.[63]

If indeed Blake's eagle is "genius" married to craftsmanship (Erdman's view), then the marriage must be one of eternal torment and punishment. In Spenserian terms, the erstwhile illuminating viper, who is firmly in the clutches—and hence in the service—of the god of this world, is, as we know from Urizen's metallic books, a bookmaker-librarian-lawgiver, as distinct from the "eagle of genius" as he can possibly be.[64] And Blake would have remembered that Spenser endows Mammon himself with his fiend's "nayles like clawes" (vii,3). Lest this all seem impossibly fanciful, not to say pedantically overingenious, we need to remind ourselves of Blake's preoccupation in the early 1790s with the Prometheus myth.

I have already argued that there is something fundamentally Orcian about Guyon's final destructive excessiveness in the Bower of Bliss. We should not be surprised, then, to find in *America*, dated on its title page 1793—the year Blake was completing *The Marriage*—that Orc is presented as the "Eternal Viper":

> Ah rebel form that rent the ancient
> Heavens; Eternal Viper self-renew'd, rolling in clouds
> I see thee in thick clouds and darkness on America's shore.
> Writhing in pangs of abhorred birth . . .
>
> (9:14–17, E54)

Just prior to this passage Blake reinvokes, in a self-identifying speech by Orc, the "rebellion" of Oothoon against the active physical tyranny of Bromion and the passive mental tyranny of Theotormon, both of which are incorporated into Theotormon's eagles, dutifully called down to "rend" the "defiled" Oothoon.[65] Orc will "renew the fiery joy" that is emblemized in Oothoon's

> coarse-clad honesty
> The undefil'd tho' ravish'd in her cradle night and morn:
> For every thing that lives is holy, life delights in life;
> Because the soul of sweet delight can never be defil'd.
>
> (8:11–14, E54)

Orc will also "stamp to dust" the "stony law" and "scatter religion abroad / To the four winds as a torn book" (8:5–6), the same book(s) "formed" in the sixth chamber of the Printing house in Hell, or in Alma's chamber of memory.

But though a viper, Orc's Prometheanism is established as well by Blake in the Preludium to *America*, where the "father stern abhorr'd" of the "shadowy daughter of" the earth (and hence the god of this world) "Rivets [Orc's] tenfold chains while still on high [his] spirit soars; / Sometimes an eagle screaming in the sky" and sometimes a "serpent folding" (1:11–15, E51). Thus, as both eagle and serpent, Orc is the revolutionary version of the eagle and serpent of the printing-house plate; but as Guyon-Mammon-fiend the plate's eagle and serpent must be seen as Orc gone wrong, an unmarriage as it were, rising toward the very books of this world he dedicates himself corrosively to destroy—just as Guyon perversely surrenders to the excess that his allegorical signification is dedicated to eradicate.[66] It is in this sense, then, that Guyon as viper may be seen to capitulate to the Mammon-fiend. Not only will he read and believe the books in Eumnestes' library but he will also become rich and powerful in his possession of both versions of the "*worldes* blis" (II,vii,32; my italics). As for the impact of all this upon *The Marriage* and in particular plate 15, it is, to say the least, to de-Blakeanize it devastatingly: the printing house itself is Mammon's cave and Alma's House of Temperance, the vipers are Orc gone wrong, the eagles who make the cave infinite end up as the tools of the god of this world, Prometheus's fire and Blake's corrosives give birth only to brazen books, and the marriage of eagle and serpent is an abomination. The limitations of a conventional Hell as a Blakean desideratum could not be dramatized more thoroughly.[67] We should remember more often than we do that "In Hell all is Self Righteousness" (*Vision of the Last Judgment*, E565), a self-righteousness "conglomerating against the Divine Vision" (*Jerusalem* 13:52, E157), both of these points later articulations of the central point of plate 21 of *The Marriage*.

If, as many argue, Blake was slow to recognize the ultimate perniciousness of his Orc, phasing him gradually into the more enlightened Los, *The Marriage*'s printing-house Fancy seems to me to argue precisely the opposite. Allowing for his outdated terminology, Plowman was right.[68] Genius must take Orc in tow firmly—perhaps like good predators, must eat (absorb) Orc's viperishness, and thereby translate it into mental rather than corporeal ends. For such ends constitute "the palace of wisdom," which, in the language of 1 Chronicles, is "the palace . . . not for man [i.e. fallen man], but for the LORD God" (29:1).

CHAPTER FOUR

Calling and Naming

O F   L A T E , Blake has been linked steadily with a "line of vision" extending from the Bible through Spenser to Milton, a line drawn largely by way of these three poets' reliance on Revelation as a model, as providing "the divine analogy to their art."[1] The essential characteristics of Revelation that make drawing this line possible—aside from the poets' allusions to the biblical book—are, in Joseph Wittreich's analysis, for example, a mixture of genres, obscurity, and an elaborate allusiveness (most particularly to the prophetic books of the Old Testament).[2] It is a "gathering of all forms into one central form" whose structure is neither dramatic nor narrational but nonlinear, even labyrinthine, "wherein events instead of succeeding one another are, through a system of synchronisms, made to mirror one another." If it is dramatic in any sense, it is interiorized drama, a "drama of perspectives," which leads to an epiphanic recognition of error. "John's prophecy," Wittreich reminds us, "is about *seeing*" rather than doing,[3] a distinction Blake "marries" in his pithy saying, "Thought is Act."[4] Thus, the battles of good and evil in apocalyptic prophecy are "mental fight" rather than corporeal war, psychomachias rather than physiomachias.

This brief summary of what has been elaborated on by a variety of biblical, Spenserian, and Miltonic scholars is intended here as an acknowledgment of the general rightness of this view; it is certainly incontrovertible with respect to Blake and readily demonstrable in Milton's "sequence" of *Paradise Lost*, *Paradise Regained*, and *Samson Agonistes* (this last, of course, a poem about seeing). Spenser, however, more often than not has been described as a nonapocalyptic poet even while being aligned with the biblical prophets in a variety of other ways and even while being credited with patterning much of *The Faerie Queene* on Revelation.[5] I do not wish here to enter the quarrel over whether Spenser is prophetic, apocalyptic or neither, or whether, if he is prophetic and/or apocalyptic, he is a conservative or a radical revolutionary, as Northrop Frye makes that distinction.[6] There is no doubt in my mind, though, that Blake regarded Spenser as at least a prophet *manqué*—though perhaps also (or instead) a failed prophet. I address this issue directly in the next three chapters. Here I wish to focus on several other aspects of Blake's efforts to redeem his Renaissance predecessor, particularly with respect to *The Faerie Queene*.

We have seen so far that there is an important and revealing relationship between Blake's exploitation of the Spenserian contraries of excess/temperance, imagination/memory (the senses), sexual war/mental fight, and the relationship between these contraries and Blake's distinction between allegory addressed to the corporeal powers and that addressed to the imagination. At the heart of this latter contrariety, which at once absorbs and underlies the others, is Los's (Blake's) fundamental struggle to redeem the former by means of the latter, or more broadly, to annihilate all systems (including linguistic systems) by constructing a countersystem, as it were, that self-destructs.[7] The problem is that both the error and the means to right it are "stubborn structures." Hazard Adams has argued that "Los's eternal act of building the 'stubborn structure of the language' [*Jerusalem* 36[40]:59, E183] can be seen as a struggle with a spectral or 'allegorical' system grown like a 'polypus' from his original system (original not in the historical sense but in the sense that his system represents the fundamental nature of language—its metaphorical nature)."[8] While in essence correct, Adams's statement of Los's problem and task is, in my judgment, rather seriously flawed in its own language, for it is not *Los's* "original system" that becomes debased but rather the Word *Him*self (or, as Blake dramatizes that in *Jerusalem*'s apocalypse, the "conversation" of Eternity that is a "[walking] / To & fro . . . as One Man reflecting each in each & clearly seen / And seeing" [98:28, 38–40, E257–58]). Blake says that Los creates his "stubborn structure" lest Albion become "a Dumb despair" (36[40]:60, E183), that is to say, lest Albion be both wordless and Wordless.

Maureen Quilligan argues that "redeeming language" is "fundamental to the genre of allegory," a redemption effected through wordplay (for her the pun) whereby "the polysemousness of language becomes the correction for its own ambiguity and abuse."[9] But, as she does not point out, polysemousness in turn lends itself to simply "doubling" or personification allegory and hence, as Murray Krieger notes, to a subservience to the normal incapacities of language.[10] Those normal incapacities have been interpreted by Samuel

Levin as a "latent predisposition . . . that makes personifications" eminently viable, indeed natural and inevitable; for "the language contains more nouns than predicates," and the nouns convey the "other" meaning of the allegory. More pointedly, "the entire range of volitional, affective, emotional, moral, and ethical states, dispositions, and activities, the predicates that the language makes available, are specific to humans." [11] This is the "rough basement" upon which Los perforce must build his linguistic "structure" (or system) and which he must then wrestle into its unfallen status of (to put it somewhat bluntly) the humanized noun-verb/verb-noun of *Jerusalem*'s apocalyptic being-conversation-action. "Like Langland" before him, Quilligan says, Spenser also "set himself the task of redeeming language." [12] The question, then, is whether Blake perceived (or to what extent he perceived) that that was what *The Faerie Queene* was "about."

We need to approach this issue, however, in the context of some larger "facts" about Spenser. As Wittreich usefully reminds us, "even if Spenser, like Milton, exercises the mind of his reader, his objective is not to overthrow the reigning orthodoxies, political and religious, but to effect a deeper understanding of them and consequently to confirm them." [13] Spenser scholars make the same point by analyzing Spenser's focus "on the Christian call to honourable action in this world," an interpretation encouraged by Spenser himself in the Letter to Raleigh. [14] In one sense, at least, Blake's antipathy for the idea of a "gentleman" and "honourable action in this world" is launched in *The Marriage of Heaven and Hell* and most especially in the Proverbs of Hell, with their sometimes virulent attacks on the conventional wisdom of Solomon and Ecclesiastes and on the "Spenserian" virtues of holiness, temperance, prudence, chastity, and justice. Nevertheless, as he could with Milton, Blake was able to distinguish Spenser the poet from Spenser the theologian, moralist, philosopher, or social scientist; and as might be expected, Blake found one crucial basis for the distinction in Spenser's handling of individual characters, in the particulars rather than in the abstract or generalized meanings attached by Spenser to those particulars. I say meanings "attached by Spenser" *to* the particulars, rather than meanings abstracted *from* the particulars not to beg the important question of whether Blake regarded Spenser as the allegorizer or the reader as allegorizer of Spenser, but rather to give Spenser his due. Although there is continuing debate over the matter, I think it fair to say that more critics than not these days subscribe to Rosalie Colie's perception that "things and personages in *The Faerie Queene become* metamorphosed into their essences. . . . They become their being.''[15] More simply, Kathleen Williams argues that Spenser's personages "are not in themselves virtues but specialized versions of ourselves. . . . The virtues do not define the books which they name or the knights by whom they are defended; the books and actions of the knights define the virtues, by working them out through the narrative in human terms."[16]

The major evidence of Blake's focusing on individual characters in Spenser is, of course, his painting of *The Faerie Queene*, not coincidentally called *The Characters in Spenser's Faerie Queene*. The "in" is crucial. This is no illustration *of* the poem *The Faerie Queene*; Blake's painting is a "vision," on the pattern of *A Vision of the Last Judgment* or, more obviously, his painting of *Chaucer's Canterbury Pilgrims* (not of *The Canterbury Tales*). In the latter, as his *Descriptive Catalogue* essay on Chaucer elaborates, "Every Class [of men] is Individual" (Annotations to Reynolds's *Discourses*, E648); "The Combats of Truth & Error" are "not only Universal" (that is, general) "but Particular." In his painting of the Last Judgment, "Each are Personified There Is not an Error but it has a Man for its [Actor, *deleted*] Agent that is it is a Man. There is not a Truth but it has also a Man" (*Vision of the Last Judgment*, E563). Not only is "All Knowledge . . . Particular" but "Singular & Particular Detail is the Foundation of the Sublime"— that is, of Vision (Annotations to Reynolds, E648, 647). "He who wishes to see a Vision; a perfect Whole / Must see it in its Minute Particulars; Organized" (*Jerusalem* 91:20–21, E251).

From this point of view, *The Faerie Queene* may be a "continued allegory" in its outward form, but, Blake acknowledges, "Allegory is Seldom without some Vision"—even those of Bunyan and the Greek poets. Only "The Hebrew Bible & the Gospel of Jesus"—and, of course, Blake's own prophecies that he was never loath to regard as *the* "everlasting gospel"—are "Eternal Vision or Imagination" (*Vision of the Last Judgment*, E554). The "some Vision" that Blake discerned in Spenser lies in part in Spenser's minute particularity of character, but at the same time—and paradoxically—it also lies in the sort of shifting identities of those characters which I explore as functioning in Blake's painting.[17] Blake learned the resolution of this apparent paradox, I believe, from Spenser. The *locus classicus* of the latter's resolution is in the Garden of Adonis:

> That substance is eterne, and bideth so,
> Ne when the life decayes, and forme does fade,
> Doth it consume, and into nothing go,
> But chaunged is, and often altred to and fro.

> The substance is not chaunged, nor altered,
> But th' only forme and outward fashion.
>
> (II,vi,37–38)

Spenser's "substance," much to Blake's displeasure, is "The substance of natures fruitful progenyes" stored in the "wide wombe of the world," "An huge eternall Chaos."[18] Blake's "translation" of Spenser's language is crucial. As early as his annotations to Lavater's *Aphorisms on Man*, he distinguishes "substance" from "Essence," aligning the former with "accident" (E596). For him that which "is eterne" is "the word of God & everything on earth is the word of God & in its essence is God" (E599). Thus, the eternal "I" and "Thou" in *The Four Zoas* VII (E359) "walkd about" in "mild fields of happy Eternity / . . . in undivided Essence." Substance is Nature; Aristotle's "matter . . . in itself is not this or that" until it is endowed with "shape or form." Spenser's "forme and outward fashion," then, become Blake's "substance," the accidence of time and space. "Substance," Blake allows, "gives tincture to the accident," but it does not alter essence. Instead it makes the accidence of essence "physiognomic" (E596), a point to which he returns in his Chaucer essay. Thus, "thought," for Blake, has no substance, as Oothoon's attack on Bromion's epistemology in *Visions of the Daughters of Albion* indicates. If it did, to pursue her recalcitrant lover Theotormon's absurd abstraction of this attack, thought would be "made" of substance, joys would grow in gardens, sorrows would swim in rivers, and shadows of discontent would wave on mountains (3:2–25, 4:1, E47–48). One does not need to argue that such gardens allude to the Garden of Adonis—which they may very well—to make the point, or to see Blake's point. Spenser was simply wrong about the matter, his innate genius tainted by his age's epistemology and natural science, not to say by its religion.

For Blake, Spenser's "huge eternall *Chaos*" is terrifyingly temporal—as Spenser says, "created"—hence both "petrific" and "abominable," and "the unreal forms of Ulro's night," "a formless unmeasurable Death / Whirling up broken rocks on high into the dismal air / And fluctuating all beneath in Eddies of molten fluid." It is these "Ruind Furnaces / Of Urizen" that Los, "affrighted / At the formless unmeasurable death," hammers into form on his "Anvils of Iron petrific," lest all of eternity (and hence man) fall into eternal death and nonentity.[19] What he creates is the form of Urizen in Blake's parodic Genesis, *The Book of Urizen* (which is largely incorporated into *The Four Zoas*).[20] More specifically, "the death-image of Urizen" (*Book of Urizen* 15:2, E78) is created. That is to say, "Natures wide womb" (*Urizen* 4:17, E72; the echo of Spenser has not been noted here) contains not the eternal Spenserian-Aristotelian substance of "natures fruitful progenyes" but is, rather, "A void immense, wild dark & deep, / Where nothing was" (4:16–17, E72), a material absence of all substance. Out of this illusion (even as he is identified with it), Urizen is "born," "Unknown, unprolific! / Self-closed, all-repelling," "A self-contemplating shadow" (3:2–3, E70; 3:21, E71). Once formed of this nothingness, Urizen creates his own garden of Adonis: "he planted a garden of fruits" (20:41, E81); but, just as in Spenser's garden "Infinite shapes of creatures . . . are bred, / And vncouth formes, which none yet euer knew" (III,vi,35), so Urizen's "garden"

> teemd vast enormities
> Frightning; faithless; fawning
> Portions of life; *similitudes*
> Of a foot, or a hand, or a head
> Or a heart, or an eye, they swam mischevous.
>
> (23:2–6, E81; my italics)

In human terms Los's "creation" is the delimiting of the Fall in man:

> There is a limit of Opakeness, and a limit of Contraction;
> In every Individual Man, and the limit of Opakeness,
> Is named Satan: and the limit of Contraction is named Adam.

From this latter limit, "the Saviour in mercy . . . / . . . forms Woman: That / Himself may in process of time be born Man to redeem." The marvelous grammatical squinting here makes it clear that man redeems man, for "there is no Limit of Expansion! there is no Limit of Translucence. / In the bosom of Man for ever from eternity to eternity" (*Jerusalem* 42:29–36, E189).

That infiniteness of expansion and translucence refers to the Imagination, which, in Blake's system, replaces Spenser's eternal substance,[21] and Spenser's substance in turn becomes what "Accident" forms by the "cruelties of Demonstration":

> It became Opake & Indefinite; but the Divine Saviour,
> Formed it into a Solid by Los's Mathematic Power
>
> (*Milton* 29[31]:35–38, E128)

—that is, into Satan and Adam, antitranslucence (hence anti-Christ) and antiexpansiveness (hence sensebound, timebound, spacebound man, the human form of anti-Christ). When

> the Bodies in which all Animals & Vegetations, the Earth & Heaven

Were containd in the All Glorious Imagination are witherd &
darkend,

when "The Lungs, the Heart, the Liver, shrunk away far distant
from Man," what is left is "a little slimy substance floating upon the
tides" (*Jerusalem* 41:13–18, E198).

It is in light of such passages that we must understand Blake's
seemingly inconsistent use of the word *substance* elsewhere, a use that
seems to echo that of Spenser. For example, in his *Descriptive Catalogue*
discussion of Chaucer's characters, Blake writes: "nothing new occurs in identical existence; Accident ever varies, Substance can never
suffer change nor decay" (E532). But substance here means the eternal lineaments of human, created character, identities, not what
Blake earlier called *essence*. This confusion was one of Swedenborg's
errors that Blake quickly corrected: "Essence is not Identity but from
Essence proceeds Identity & from one Essence may proceed many
Identities" (*Annotations*, E604). It is *accident* that varies (or to the corporeal eye seems to vary) *identity*. Thus, "characters" are "repeated
again and again, in animals, vegetables, minerals, and in men";
"consequently they are the physiognomies or lineaments of universal
human life, beyond which Nature never steps" (*Descriptive Catalogue*,
E532–33). Nor does the Garden of Adonis. The point is the same one
that Blake makes in the Lavater annotation, where substance "tinc-
tures" accident "& makes it physiognomic." [22] It is these physiognomies that constitute the species of the abstract genus, "the classes of
men" that "Chaucer numbered" just as "Newton numbered the
stars, and as Linneus numbered the plants." [23] The dire implications
of the analogy and Blake's own verb choice ("numbered") could not
be clearer and may very well constitute as severe an attack on
Chaucer's procedure in *The Canterbury Tales* as the painting of Spenser's characters is on Spenser's allegorical procedure. When Blake, in
a letter to Hayley informing him of progress on the "Heads of the
Poets" series for Hayley's library, remarks that these poets' "physiognomies have been [his] delightful study," we can understand even
more the nature of Blake's vehement criticism inherent in his "head"
of Spenser (see figure 1 and my commentary in chapter 1 above).

The ultimate perversion of essence or Imagination in Blake is inherent in the uses to which it is put—a process parallel to that of the
priests in *The Marriage of Heaven and Hell* forming a religion from "poetic tales." In *Jerusalem* "the Sons of Albion" are the offenders:

They take the Two contraries which are calld Qualities, with which
Every Substance is clothed, they name them Good & Evil
From them they make an Abstract, which is a Negation

Not only of the Substance from which it is derived
A murderer of its own Body: but also a murderer
Of every Divine Member.

$$(10:8-13, E152-53)$$

This passage is worth examining carefully, for it is an extraordinary epitome of the evolution of error, the sequence of mental gymnastics performed by "the Holy Reasoning Power" in man. Eternally (or, in temporal terms, in the beginning), there is the Divine Body of Imagination (the Word), the Divine Marriage of the eternal contraries ("conversation"). The fallen mind, however (actually Mind self-abstracted from the Divine Body), interprets the contraries to which it "belonged" and in which it has its eternal being as mere qualities, Lockean ideas, which by their very nature are abstractions from sense (in Blake, from the "substance" of essence). These in turn become the "clothing" of mortal substance, thence to be named and "realized" as independently existent—precisely as the priests of *The Marriage* reify the ancient poets' names. Such abstract existences are then further abstracted into "a Negation" not only of the created substance but of the Divine Body from which the abstract qualities and their substantiations are originally derived. The "murderer" in Spenser is "wicked *Time*" (III,vi,39); in Blake it is man's "Holy Reasoning Power," his capacity for abstraction and the ontological arrogance of his making "real" what he abstracts—not to say of his pronouncing in self-appointed "Holiness" that this abstraction from an abstraction is (w)hole.

We may now return to Spenser's characters, those particulars that are physiognomic "substance" but in whose substance the eternal forms may be perceived if our own imaginations are energetic enough to do so. Among the characteristics of prophecy is obscurity, the most detailed explication of which is Michael Murrin's in *The Veil of Allegory*. I need not go into his elaborate argument and documentation nor (at least for the moment) the connection he makes between allegory and prophecy to point out here that for Murrin the archetypal veil and revelation is the Exodus account of Moses' several trips to the mount to receive the Word of God and deliver it to the people. Although that particular exemplum hardly would have pleased Blake, Murrin is certainly correct in concluding that "a late classical critic would have agreed perfectly" with Blake's distinction between allegory addressed to the corporeal powers and that addressed to the intellectual or imaginative powers. Indeed Murrin goes on to suggest that Blake's idea of Vision (as distinct from allegory) is "what Spenser would call allegory." [24]

A substantial element in the obscurity or "dark conceit" of allegory-prophecy is disguise. "In *Paradise Lost* and *Paradise Regained*, no less than in *The Faerie Queene*," Wittreich maintains, "disguises engage protagonists and readers alike in an unmasking process: both experience, or should experience, an epiphany; and that epiphany is marked by an unveiling, a sudden recognition of error—an apocalypse."[25] "For I discern thee other than thou seem'st," Christ in *Paradise Regained* says to Satan, who has appeared to him as "an aged man in rural weeds" (I,348,314)—Archimago redivivus, of course (as well as his Satanic descendant in Giles Fletcher's *Christ's Victory on Earth*). All the more devastating (and horrifying), then, is Blake's Nurse's prophecy of her innocent charges' future in *Songs of Experience*:

> Then come home my children, the sun is gone down
> And the dews of night arise
> Your spring & your day, are wasted in play
> And your winter and night in disguise.
>
> (E23)

In Book IV of *Paradise Regained*, Milton adds another dimension to disguise: "plaine thou now appear'st," says Christ, "That Evil One, Satan for ever damned" (ll. 193–94). He is not now merely "other than thou seem'st"; he is identified, which is to say he is named.

In *Paradise Lost*, echoing Revelation 3:5, Milton reports that the fallen angels' names are

> blotted out and razed
> By their rebellion from the Books of Life.
> Nor had they yet among the sons of Eve
> Got them new names.
>
> (I,361–65)

Once busy in the world,

> By falsities and lies the greatest part
> Of mankind they corrupted to forsake
> God their Creator, and th'invisible
> Glory of him that made them to transform
> Oft to the image of a brute, adorned
> With gay religions full of pomp and gold,
> And devils to adore for deities.
>
> (I,367–73)

Then they became "known to men by various names" (l. 374), Milton's cue for one of his majestic catalogues—the sum of the names of which is "Satan." "His former name" was Lucifer, Raphael reminds Adam and us (V,658),

> (So call him, brighter once amidst the host
> Of angels than that star the stars among).
> (VII,132–33)

In Blakean terms, Lucifer (whose name, we should remember, is itself a simile) falls into the state "called Satan" (appropriately Blake's "Limit of Translucence"), where he says, "I glory in the name" (X,386). In *The Marriage of Heaven and Hell*, Blake's "ancient Poets" not only "animated" all things "with Gods or Geniuses" but "[called] them by the names"—thus repeating in the finite mind the act of creation in the infinite I AM, as Coleridge explains the processes of the primary imagination. More precisely, these gods are imaginative "visions of . . . eternal attributes, or divine names" (*Descriptive Catalogue*, E536), "mental deities," "sensible objects" imaginatively perceived. Priests then "realize" (make "real") or "abstract the mental deities [that is, the poetic names] from their objects" to form a system (Grecian polytheism or any other theism) to enslave the vulgar, arrogantly sanctifying their procedure by "pronouncing" that the very gods they have iconicized out of names "orderd such things." As Blake says later in his *Descriptive Catalogue*, these divine names, "when erected into gods, become destructive of humanity. They ought to be the servants, and not the masters of man, or of society. They ought to be made to sacrifice to Man, and not man compelled to sacrifice to them" (E536).

This fundamental error is at the heart of Blake's attack on Milton in *The Marriage*. *Paradise Lost*, he says, is "the history of this . . . & the Governor or Reason is *call'd* [by Milton] Messiah." Even worse, "the original Archangel or possessor of the command of the heavenly host, is *calld* the Devil or Satan and his children are *call'd* Sin & Death" (my italics). In the Book of Job, however, "Miltons Messiah is call'd Satan."[26] In his role of diabolical priest, Blake's speaker simply takes the process of Milton's error to its logical conclusion, creating an abstract out of what Milton has already abstracted from the "imaginative facts": "the Father is Destiny, the Son, a Ratio of the five senses. & the Holy-ghost, Vacuum"—and, we might add, *Paradise Lost* is an even more debased allegorical theodicy than Blake thought it was. The folly of identifying Blake willy-nilly with his speaker in *The Marriage* could not be more patent, for, sensitive to the personal, political, and religious pressures hovering over the exercise of Milton's poetic genius, Blake *in propria persona* recognizes elsewhere that Milton's imaginative self entirely contradicts the error-ridden Milton of *The Marriage*. As Michael foretells, corrupt priests

> all the sacred mysteries of heav'n
> To their own vile advantages shall turn

Of lucre and ambition, and the truth
With superstitions and traditions taint,
Left only in those written records pure,
Though not but by the Spirit understood.
Then shall they seek to avail themselves of names,
Places and titles, and with these to join
Secular power, though feigning still to act
By spiritual, and to themselves appropriating
The Spirit of God.

(Paradise Lost XII,509–19)

Such naming as I have been describing derives from the first chapter of Genesis and the parallel between God's creating-naming and Adam's naming of the creatures. "Naming is properly apotropaic," Patricia Parker reminds us; "it allows something to be placed at a distance, outside the self." In another sense, it is "making approachable and indeed domestic a Titanic and rude disorder."[27] Both senses of the act pertain, of course, to God, who functions in time even before he "creates" light and darkness: "*In the beginning* God created the heaven and earth" (my italics). In addition, the "waters" are "there" before he "creates" (thus Blake's allegorization, the "waters of materialism"), God's main action with regard to them being, significantly, a Urizenic division or separation. And it is his separations that he names. Once the earth "brings forth" or generates, God forms man out of the dust of this ur-generative power, Adam thus becoming a form generated out of a created form ("let the dry land appear"), which is the substance of no known essence. That is to say, Adam is made an identity and acts as Adam in chapters 2 to 4, even though he is not named until chapter 5: "In the day that God created man, in the likeness of God made he him; Male and female created he them; and blessed them, and called their name Adam, in the day when they were created."[28] Tannenbaum's point, mentioned earlier, is thus well taken: "Genesis is a justification of the Angels' party,"[29] for Adam is immediately put to work in the service of God and the creation, "to dress it and keep it"; and at the same time he becomes the first victim of a "Thou shall not": "But of the tree of the knowledge of good and evil, thou shalt not eat of it: for in the day that thou eatest thereof thou shalt surely die" (2:15, 17).

If, as Tannenbaum argues according to conventional exegesis, biblical naming is "using language to reproduce the creative power of God" ("to give something a name is to call it into existence by incorporating it into a language and thus into consciousness"), the "creative power of God" that we witness in Genesis is that of Urizen in Blake's *Book of Urizen*. Each naming there, Tannenbaum acknowledges, "proclaims a further separation between the human and the divine; each calls into existence another error, a new bane rather than a new blessing."[30] Neither Adam nor Eve, nor the tree of knowledge of good and evil in Genesis, read literally, constitutes a "blessing" for very long.

As to Adam, initially separated both from the divine and the earth, he is further apotropaically distanced by being named; and being named, he becomes thereby endowed with the power of naming that which has already been created out of the same Adamic dust. No poet like the ancient poets of *The Marriage*, Adam animates nothing. He merely "adorns" with names, which is essentially the same power granted him by God to "have dominion over the fish of the sea, and over the fowl of the air, and over every living thing that moveth upon the earth" (Gen. 1:28). What God leaves unspoken is the phrase, "as I have dominion over you." Milton makes the implication clearer. His Adam's naming is not merely a "poetic" mental conferral but an exercise in power, for as God says in *Paradise Lost*, " 'I bring them [the creatures] to receive / From thee their names, and pay thee fealty / With low subjection' " (VIII,343–45). What he has no power over, he cannot name. Thus, "to the heav'nly Vision" he says,

> O by what name, for thou above all these,
> Above mankind, or aught than mankind higher,
> Surpassest far my naming.
>
> (VIII,356–59)

The hierarchical order of authority, including the authority of naming, is thus established. Adam acknowledges it explicitly:

> Hast thou not made me here thy substitute
> And these inferior far beneath me set?
>
> (381–82)

It is this "fit and meet" arrangement (VIII,448) that is at the heart of Blake's use of names and most particularly at the heart of his distinction between "The Divine Names" and those that "in Selfhood" are appropriated, "seeking to Vegetate the Divine Vision / In a corporeal & ever dying Vegetation & Corruption." When these names "mingle" into "One. they become One Great Satan" (*Jerusalem* 90:40–43). And in this particular passage, Satan is named "Hand & Hyle & Bowen & Skofeld," just as elsewhere in Blake his names are legion. The remainder of this *Jerusalem* passage is apropos as well since it is, in a sense, yet another Blakean redaction of Genesis. Here God becomes "the Individual" who "appropriates Universality" (again we are reminded of the opening line of the Preludium of *The*

Book of Urizen), and when he does, "He divides into Male & Female," who in turn "Appropriate Individuality" only to "become an Eternal Death. / Hermaphroditic worshippers of a God of cruelty & law!" (90:52–56, E250).

In Blake's eyes, then, Genesis is a perverse analogy to the Word becoming flesh. "In the beginning," according to the Gospel of John, "was the Word, and the Word was with God, and the Word was God" (1:1). Adam's name and being are its earthly parallel: he is *a* word made flesh as Christ is "*the* Word . . . made flesh" (John 1:14). In Revelation, then, as in Blake's *Jerusalem*, the names of the fallen *is* Satan, the names of those who stand with the Lamb *is* "his Father's . . . written on their foreheads" (14:1). In an important essay, V. A. DeLuca summarizes Blake's "philosophy of names" as follows:

> The autonomy of mythic names and their formulaic arrangements imply that they function collectively as a principle of structure in Blake's works and not a principle of conceptual reference. They serve to separate the world of Divine Vision from that of space and time and yet to enforce their necessary confrontation. If they compose *in toto* a "stubborn structure," a multi-latticed gate repelling or inviting our entrance into the Divine Vision, according to the variation of our perceptions, each separate name may be considered as a fragmented individuation of that structure, pointing to the hypothetical existence of some name-less *Ur*-name, the name of the Divine Vision itself.[31]

But "the hypothetical existence" is not hypothetical at all to Blake, nor is it an *Ur*-name. It is the Word, *the* Name, one and the same. It may be "Unutterable" to Satan's minions (*Milton* 11[12]:14, E104), but that is only because, unable to perceive its "embodiment," they know it/Him not. Blake's poem *The Lamb* is the simplest and most exquisite contrary of this:

> He is called by thy name,
> For he calls himself a Lamb:
> He is meek & he is mild,
> He became a little child:
> I a child & thou a lamb,
> We are called by his name.

> (E9)

Put somewhat crudely, but no less accurately, we are Him (or, I and thou are He). The same logic of name and eternal identity is at the heart of *Infant Joy* (E16), which is a vision, as it were, of the Divine Vision—albeit punctuated by the imminence of its fall ("Sweet joy befall thee") into Generation, that is (in the terms I have been developing here), into its *proper name*.[32] When Joy's tongue, to borrow the language of *To Tirzah*, is closed "in senseless clay" and he is "to Mortal Life" betrayed (E30), the imaginative logic (the "sense") of

> I happy am
> Joy is my name,

is no longer possible—or is only possible once again through the Herculean imaginative effort that effects the apocalyptic retransformation of names into beings: "& every Word & Every Character / Was Human," and "they walked / To & fro in Eternity as One Man reflecting each in each & clearly seen / And seeing" (*Jerusalem* 98:35–36, 38–40, E258). By this time in *Jerusalem*, as DeLuca notes, names drop out of existence, most notably "Los" (absorbed in "Jesus"), "Jesus" itself in plate 96, and "Albion" in plate 97, "until all the diverse attributes of Humanity converge to be identified in one name." "Jerusalem," at the end of the poem, thus becomes "a name to destroy the power of the mystery of names."[33]

The pertinence of Blake's "philosophy of names," as well as of the idea of naming, to Spenser may be obvious by now, but what I wish to suggest is that it is Spenser's practice from which Blake learned what DeLuca properly calls this "structural principle." While it would be absurd to exclude the biblical origins of the process and implications of naming—and Milton's careful elaboration of those origins—as important antecedents to Blake's own practice, it is in Spenser that Blake would have found that practice most widely used and elaborated.[34] More importantly, he saw it at the core of Spenser's own distinction—unformulated in discursive prose but implicit in the Letter to Raleigh—between allegory and vision. Without retreading the all-too-well-trodden, now even muddied, ground of Blake's own attempts to make this distinction clear, one should be able to see, at the heart of that distinction, his "philosophy of names." In his Chaucer essay, "visions of the eternal attributes" are "divine names," "eternal principles" incarnated in the "characters of human life." When the visions are "erected into gods," they "become destructive to humanity," which "is" (not is named) "Jesus the Saviour, the vine of eternity" (*Descriptive Catalogue*, E526). Blake's echoing of plate 11 of *The Marriage* is instructive, for the religion the priests create there from "poetic tales" is an allegory, an antiimaginative perversion of the visionary "what-is" (achieved by "The ancient Poets'' through ''their enlarged & numerous senses'') into an earthly pilgrimage, or progress, toward what might be—if the pilgrims are ''good.'' *Religion*, then, is not quite the right word here, at least by itself; Blake does not use it in the passage. Instead, priestcraft creates ''*forms* of worship'' (my italics) based on the abstraction of names (deities) from their objects and the pronouncing of those names as ''real.'' The mimicry of John's gospel is staggering in its arrogant self-righteousness, precisely the self-righteousness of the God of Genesis.

From this, one might well argue that Blake's effort in his prophetic books, artistically speaking, is to redeem Vision from Allegory. Although Karl Kroeber's wish to deliver *Jerusalem* from its commentators seems to me misguided as an overall critical position, he is certainly correct in wanting to deliver it from its allegorizers—as Newman Ivey White did many years ago for Shelley.[35] Although Kroeber does not make the distinction in the same way I do, his point about Blake's verse being ''anti-paradigmatic'' is apropos: ''Albion does not represent, say, mankind'' any more than any other character ''stands for'' or ''represents'' (or merely re-presents) anything.[36] Blake's point, however, which Kroeber ignores, is that most of the characters in Blake's prophetic books, early and late, are deliberately presented to us as ''meaning'' something. *The Book of Urizen* is perhaps the clearest (and the earliest) sustained example of this—though Blake flirted with the idea before (in *The French Revolution*, most notably, where the Bastille prisoners are blatantly allegorically named). Much of *The Book of Urizen* has to do with how ''meaning'' emerges as more real, so to speak, than the object to which it is ostensibly attached. When ''a shadow of horror'' is first seen and mysteriously ''described'' by Blake with a series of conflicting adjectives and nouns, ''Some said / 'It is Urizen''' (3:5–6, E70). Later the Eternals say he *is* ''Death'' (6:9, E74), but what Urizen really ''means'' in this world is King, God, Law, Sin, Religion, Man, the creatures of Genesis, Science, Jealousy, and on and on. He is the disposition to, or act of, reason, that is, a self-generation of his own signification parallel to his self-generation of his very being.[37] At no point does Blake name him Reason—or even associate him with reason. *We* do, accommodatingly falling into Blake's allegorical trap, as I have just demonstrated by my lengthy ''equation.''

If, as Kroeber claims, ''the progressive movement of *Jerusalem* as a whole is meant to bring us to a point of transformation at which we awake to the existent reality which we have been concealing by self-created illusion'' (and I believe that is true), that ''existent reality'' is not words ''*both* as verbal symbols *and* as visual artifacts''[38] but names purged of their attached meanings, which is to say, words that are not "artifacts" but the eternal attributes of the human form divine.

For all its problems, Kroeber's essay is, in its fundamental perceptions if not its articulations, more right than E. J. Rose's unequivocal assertion that "Neither in theory nor in practice does Blake adopt the techniques of the fable or of simple allegory." Hence, he must conclude logically that Blake "seeks to *replace*" allegory with myth (my italics).[39] Replacing is not the point. Just as Blake reminds us that all allegories contain some vision, so his visions of necessity have some allegory in them. Without the latter, the former is impossible or, more accurately, unnecessary. Although, as W. J. T. Mitchell observes, "we must avoid the abuse of systematic allegory involved in assigning rigid moral identities to Blake's characters," many of those characters are presented to us as allegories. Part of the reason is inherent in Mitchell's subsequent remarks, though he does not apply them to precisely my point: "Los can make mistakes; Satan and Urizen are capable of prophetic perception and action."[40] Exactly so—except that when any character makes a "mistake," the mistake is deified in a name, whereby its "meaning" is made "real"—for all spectres in Blake "take refuge in Human lineaments" and are clothed by the Daughters of Los in "integument soft" (*Milton* 28[30]:28, 20). That is, they are "veiled" with a name and an identity so that, if Los's labors are not in vain, they may be recognized as the error they are and annihilated.[41] Thus, when Milton comes "in Self-annihilation" (41[48]:2, E142), what he annihilates is his "Selfhood," which is named "Satan" (14[15]:30, E108); he also casts off "the rotten rags of Memory" (allegorical names, among other things) so that his "Human Lineaments" will shine clear (41[48]:4, 26). What is shed is "the Not Human" as well as the Not-Poetry, the "imitation of Natures Images drawn from Remembrance" (41[48]:1, 24). This redemption is a resumption of the "time" when "eternal life sprung," when "Earth was not" and "Death was not" (*Book of Urizen* 3:36, 39, E71). These last two locutions are crucial. While they "mean" that this state of existence is prior to God's creation in Genesis as well as prior to Urizen's creation (and self-creation) in *The Book of Urizen*, they are also a denial of the imaginative validity of God's naming. "Earth was not" is not equivalent to "There was no earth" just as it does not equal "nothing was" (*Urizen* 4:16, E72). What "was" (and eternally is) is "eternal life," the "Immortal" expanding and contracting "his all flexible senses" in the eternal wars of intellect, that is to say, "the Wars of Eternal life" of the closing lines of Night I of *The Four Zoas* (E313) and the "conversations" of *Jerusalem* 98 (E257–58).

I I

What Blake perceived as "going on" in *The Faerie Queene* is precisely this battle between allegory and vision—with, alas (as his painting eloquently demonstrates), allegory all too often winning out. At the center of this victory—which, for Blake, was capped in the fragmentary seventh book by what must have seemed to him the nonargument between Nature and Mutabilitie (either's "defeat" would be a victory for the power of this world)—is the fact that, as Morton Bloomfield says, in any age "committed to a set of organized beliefs," what are merely personified abstractions to us were "real to begin with, simply *because* they were 'names.' And names could be representations in much the same solid-feeling way as things were."[42] Angus Fletcher interprets the same basic principle in terms of religious allegory: "A monotheism," he writes, "requires . . . agents [dæmons] to exist because it needs to have objects of heretical worship; it needs the petty, schismatic little gods which are created by popular superstition and fancy. These fractionations of the One become proper objects of attack, since they are the cause of schisms within the orthodox belief." But, as a result of this simple dichotomizing of good and evil, right and wrong, The Way and other ways, "the reader is forced into an attitude either of acceptance or rebellion."[43] No other response is possible.

Blake's allegorical antiallegory, *The Marriage of Heaven and Hell*, is such a rebellion, producing in turn the "new orthodoxy" in the form of diabolical allegory. *The Faerie Queene* is such an acceptance—at least in its primary and formally announced function to "fashion a gentleman or noble person in vertuous and gentle discipline," who will be a model of, as we say, coping with and in this world. Thus, *"in the person of* Prince Arthure" Spenser says he will "sette forth magnificence," as "in" Redcrosse he will "expresse Holynes," "in" Guyon he will "sette forth Temperance," and "in" Britomart he will "picture Chastity"—my italicization underscoring the personification allegory. "The stress in most personification allegory is on the action," Bloomfield says, the personifier throwing "his creativeness into what he has his figures do."[44] While the otherness of the meaning of the allegory is conveyed by the nouns, it is the humanizing predicates that finally "realize" the named abstractions,[45] that is to say, they animate the "pictures," to use Spenser's term for Britomart. The sharp distinction between this cerebral process and John's gospel is crucial, for there God's uttered Word *is* his Son, Blake's Imagination, John's "Light"—all the verbs attached to It/Him being forms of the verb *to be* until he is *"made* flesh" in this world "and dwelt among us" (1:1–2, 14). Spenser's "incarnations," however, are devised for "exploits" and "adventures" that they perform. They are, in other words, what Owen Barfield calls "representations" that are just as "real" (to readers and to Spenser) as things[46]—and just as "real" as Blake makes Reason, Imagination, Time, Space, Religion, Prudence, and so on.

Were that all there was to Spenser, Blake would not have given him a second thought or would have placed him in that special hell (or Non Ens) to which he consigned Pope, Dryden, Titian, Rembrandt, et al. Blake knew that what he said of Chaucer's Knight was as imaginatively wrong as it was logically correct: "The Knight is a true Hero, a good, great, and wise man . . . and is that species of character which in every age stands as the guardian of man against the oppressor" (*Descriptive Catalogue*, E538). As early as *King Edward the Third* in *Poetical Sketches* he put that grievous error to rest, as he did again, with specific reference to Spenser, in Emblem 3 in his *Notebook*, which depicts an armed knight regally indifferent to the kneeling, imploring woman.[47] In her provocative article, "The Artistic and Interpretive Context of Blake's *Canterbury Pilgrims*," Betsy Bowden notes what Karl Kiralis, in his pioneering study of the painting, ignores— that there is more often than not a fundamental "ambiguity inherent in all but a few of these 'eternal principles or characters of human life.'" This discrepancy is sometimes discernible in Blake's "portrait" itself, but it more frequently lies between the visual icon and what Bowden calls Blake's "abstract verbal praise" in his *Descriptive Catalogue* essay on the painting. Thus, Chaucer's Knight "seems not merely unparticularized" in the sense of his appearance's not matching Chaucer's description "but also sinister." In corroboration of her perception (which itself seems to me accurate), she cites Blake's description of the Knight's costume as "without ostentation" and as "unaffected simplicity," whereas the pictured Knight "wears many layers of clothing" and is otherwise elaborately, not to say ostentatiously, outfitted (see figure 3 below). If he is an "eternal type," she concludes, he defines "man's oppressor. And with the rules and trappings of chivalry, he guards against forces that man—if left to his own inspiration—might embrace rather than fear."[48] While it would be absurd to claim that Blake therefore "embraced" the diabolism of that old Dragon, Duessa, Acrasia, et al., it is equally absurd to claim that he saw Spenser's knights as embodiments of the Imagination. Such a readerly resolution of the problem would simply be a repetition of the usual interpretation of the Angels and Devils of *The Marriage of Heaven and Hell*.

Kathleen Williams makes an important distinction that is to the point here. "The virtues," she writes, "do not define the books which they name or the knights by whom they are defended; the books and the actions of the knights define the virtues, by working them out through the narrative in human terms." Rather than being Holiness, then, or "expressing" it or being a picture or image of it, Redcrosse battles (as it were) both "in, and for, his own soul or for the release of Adam who is himself." [49] Coleridge was right about Fairieland being the realm of mental space. But, if Blake recognized this even before Coleridge did, the question before us is whether, as for Coleridge, Williams, and other Spenserians, that creation of mental space was in itself sufficient to redeem the intransigence of the allegory which both constructs and sustains that space. Or, to put the matter another way, was Spenser's conception of mind, to Blake, enlightened or benighted? To speak to that question it will be useful to recur to the Busirane episode of *The Faerie Queene*, which I discussed in a different but related context in chapter 2.

Amoret's imprisonment by Busirane, as most Spenserians now agree, is a "state" of Amoret's mind, "an imprisonment in her own mind," [50] the use of the noun *state* in such a locution being very close to Blake's understanding of the word:

Distinguish therefore States from Individuals in those States.
States Change: but Individual Identities never change nor cease:
· ·
Satan & Adam are States Created into Twenty-seven Churches
And thou O Milton art a State about to be Created
Called Eternal Annihilation that none but the Living shall
Dare to enter: & they shall enter triumphant over Death
And Hell & the Grave! States that are not, but ah! Seem to be.
(*Milton* 32[35]:22-29, E132)

As the subsequent passage makes even clearer, for Blake, states are allegorical. Only "The Imagination is not a State: it is the Human Existence itself," whereas "Falshood," properly nurtured, becomes "a Space & an Allegory around the Winding Worm." [51] Busirane's castle is thus a state, as are the myriad caves, castles, woods, and so forth that crowd Spenser's landscape of the mind. It is especially appropriate, then, that Busirane's castle be populated by Ease, Fancy, Desyre, Doubt, Daunger, Feare, Hope, Dissemblance, Suspect, Griefe, Fury, Displeasure, Pleasance, Despight, and Cruelty, not to mention the sixteen other allegorical "realities" in Cupid's entourage.

Such a conception is but one of many in *The Faerie Queene*, and there is little point in enumerating them here; but the Busirane episode is archetypal (pace Kroeber) in a special way for my purposes. All the allegorical personages, Spenser tells us, are "phantasies / In wauering wemens wit"; "disguized . . . in masking wise" (that is, abstractions made "real" and named, as in a masque or morality play), the personages march about in Amoret's mind, locked up there in that "enchaunted Chamber" as fast as the chamber that Britomart, for all her power and might, is unable to open (III,xii,26, proem). The next day, however, Britomart enters the chamber before the masque begins anew, only to find that "all those persons, which she saw without" were "vanisht all and some" (stanza 30). In their place, seated before the physically shackled Amoret, is "the vile Enchaunter" himself (stanza 31). But he is not alone. Spenser has merely moved us into the mind (Amoret's) that created "all those persons" in the first place, via her diseased imagination (that is, Busirane himself). His/her "persons" are now the "straunge characters of his art" that "With liuing blood" he continues to write on Amoret's brain, and it is Amoret's blood, of course, that "animated" these abstractions for the masque.[52] Seeing Britomart, Busirane throws his "wicked bookes" aside and tries to stab Amoret—which is to say, in shame and despair, she is at the point of suicide. As an allegory herself, Britomart still does not comprehend and is about to slay Amoret's "fancy" (Busirane), to perform a lobotomy as it were; but Amoret, not so far gone as to be unaware of this curious new threat, now from without, stays Britomart's hand and has her force Busirane, in effect, to march Cupid's procession right out of her mind and back safely into his allegorical compendium or book. She is miraculously healed of her wounds and freed of her chains "as she were never hurt" (stanza 38), a "perfect hole"—which is to say, Spenser's version of a human form divine, its contraries of mind and heart married once more, her virginity restored, ready to be reunited with Scudamour.

Spenser's cancellation of his original concluding stanzas of Book III celebrating the Hermaphroditic union of Amoret and Scudamour no doubt suggested to Blake some glimmering of hope for Spenser after all, for hermaphroditism to Blake was the falsest of marriages, even an antimarriage; but Spenser's replacement of his first ending with Amoret, Thel-like, feeding on hope alone and "fild with new affright" at Scudamour's absence from their rendezvous might well have confirmed Blake's sense of Spenser's fundamental error in the entire episode. With her reason once more in control of her fancy or imagination, hermaphroditism was her appropriate Blakean destiny—and, if that were not to be so, her remaining alone and palely loitering were even more appropriate. "Thought alone can make monsters," Blake once said very early in his career, "but the affections cannot" (*Annotations to Swedenborg*, E603). That saying is a measure of his unhappiness with Spenser, for Amoret's "affections" are clearly her "phantasies," products not merely of her sexual fears but also of her imagination (of Phantastes in Alma's tripartite turret of the head). It is "Thought" (Britomart) that comes to her rescue as the monster-slayer rather than the monster-maker, a true knight "errant" for Blake, since she is not merely Reason but Chastity, the latter a "monster" created by the former. No wonder Britomart fares so badly under Blake's furious brush in *The Faerie Queene* painting, and no wonder, therefore, that Blake's central figure in that painting is, in Angus Fletcher's words, "Gloriana . . . the unapproachable yet infinitely desirable object of courtly desire . . . the avenging Britomart, the melting Amoret, the chaste, athletic Belphoebe, the transparently beautiful Florimell, the just Mercilla, the truthful Una."[53] It is only with the last that I quarrel.

In any case, at this point in Spenser's poem, Busirane disappears as a "character," although his mental signification endures throughout *The Faerie Queene*, both before and after Book III, in a variety of guises. He is like a Chaucerian pilgrim to Blake, one of the "physiognomies . . . of universal human life' (E533), the eternal framer of frauds (III,xii,43), the ilk of Archimago and Duessa, a habit or faculty of mind whose "worke" this time was "wasted" (and that "deepe engrieved him") but whose power always makes another time. He is eternally reincarnated in readers and poets alike. It is possible that Spenser's fear at the end of Book VI of the newly loosed power of the Blatant Beast over his own poem extenuated his "guilt" somewhat in Blake's eyes—for surely the Beast is, at least in one sense, Busirane redivivus in even more vicious form. His "venemous despite" leveled at Spenser's "homely verse, of many meanest," very well might be constitutive of a simple allegorical reading, creating thereby a treatise, however amusing and exciting its "plot," on the moral virtues, dull in the extreme. If this is so, the Mutabilitie Cantos, alas, allow Busirane full reign—with their personified Mutabilitie and Nature, their Greek and Roman gods and goddesses, their masquelike procession of the seasons, months, days, and hours. Even "*Life*" was only "*like* a faire young lusty boy" (VII,vii,46), but a faint similitude, as Blake might say, of eternal identity in the Divine Vision. For the latter, for "that Sabaoths sight," which will yield "that same time when no more *Change* shall be" (my italics), Spenser can only pray (VII,viii,2).

I I I

We may now return to the matter of "disguise" in *The Faerie Queene* and the concomitant process of naming. Just as much of the poem is patterned on the archetypalism of Book I, so disguise has its "eternal" avatar in that book. A. Bartlett Giamatti has provided a valuable analysis of Proteus in myth, literature, and art as both *vates* and *magus*, a dual significance well established before Spenser wrote and used by Spenser in both negative and positive capacities.[54] For the moment, let us concentrate on the former, his capacity for deception. Like Jove and Cupid, he can take many "formes and shapes" (I,ii,10) and can also create false images out of the "Sprights" that inhabit the realms of Pluto, Gorgon, and Cocytus (i,37–38). His major effort in this latter capacity is the false Una ("that misformed spright"—i,55), who comes lasciviously to Redcrosse's bed and subsequently appears staining her honor in the bed of another. To Redcrosse, the first is a bad dream that becomes "real," only to fade into "That troublous dreame" once more; but the second scene, in its total otherness, stuns his senses and causes him to desert Una (II,3–6). It is at this point (stanza 11) that Archimago transforms himself into not merely Redcrosse but "*Saint George* himself" (at least so "ye would haue deemed him to be"). His St. George, however, is, to use Spenser's word, a "semblaunt"; what Archimago "puts on" is not merely the outward accouterments of knightliness but "the *person* . . . / Of that good knight." That is, to whomsoever shall perceive him as such, he *is* Redcrosse. So perfect is the semblance that Una, seeing Archimago as Redcrosse for the first time since she was deserted, "By his like seeming shield, her knight *by name* / She weened it was" (I,iii,26), "the truest knight aliue" (37; my italics).

The sequence is most instructive, and the Blake of *The Marriage* as well as of the prophecies would have appreciated it: "True *Saint George*" (ii,12) becomes a St. George semblant whom Truth perceives to be the name of the true St. George; and to compound the ironies, Spenser has Lawlessness expose the error while Truth looks on haplessly. Except for Sansloy's unmasking, Blake employs the identical process several times in *The Four Zoas*, that most Spenserian of his major prophecies. For example, in Night III when Enion wanders "like a cloud into the deep / Where never yet Existence came" (thus paralleling Una's wandering in the dream-world of Archimago's magic), Tharmas complains of her "fading lineaments" that make his "eyelids fail":

What have I done! both rage & mercy are alike to me
Looking upon thee Image of faint waters. I recoil

From my fierce rage into thy semblance. Enion return
Why does thy piteous face Evanish like a rainy cloud
Melting. a shower of falling tears. nothing but tears! Enion:
Substanceless. voiceless, weeping, vanishd. nothing but tears! Enion
Art thou for ever vanishd from the watry eyes of Tharmas.

(E330-31)

Blake concludes, ''For now no more remaind of Enion in the dismal air / Only a voice eternal wailing in the Elements.'' I do not mean that this relationship holds any of the ''meaning'' of the Una-Redcrosse-Archimago relationship, but the perceptual position of Tharmas vis-à-vis Enion is clearly that of Una vis-à-vis Redcrosse, even to the ''realizing'' (to use Blake's verb from *The Marriage of Heaven and Hell*) of a ''semblance.''

It should be noted, however, that Blake has expertly revaluated Spenser's semblants. Enion's problem is that, as an ''aspect'' of Tharmas (his tears or pity, in contrast to his present wrath in the passage cited), she is fading into nonentity, that irretrievability against which Los's creative, formative efforts are directed endlessly. Similarly, in Night VII Enitharmon's bosom (pity in one of her significations, as well as space) is the ''soft repose for the weeping souls / Of those piteous victims of battle,'' where ''embodied semblances'' are ''fabricated.'' These are the Los-shaped ''forms *sublime* / Such as the piteous spectres may assimilate themselves into / They shall be ransoms for our Souls that we may live'' (E370). The *vates* aspect of Proteus-Archimago is thus translated by Blake into Los's emulation of the Divine Hand's placing the two limits to the Fall, Satan and Adam. Both of these, true to Proteus's dual nature as ''good'' and ''bad'' *magus*, are as much semblances as the false Una or the false Redcrosse. To perceive either as ''real'' in and for itself is to pronounce the Divine Vision, the Divine Body of Imagination, Jesus, to be no more.

Archimago's name—Arch-Magus, the agent of deceit and falseness; Arch-Imager, the giver of form to deceit and falseness; and Arch-image, the form itself of deceit and falseness—must have attracted Blake. In the proem to the second canto of Book I, Spenser himself pays tribute, as it were, to the effectiveness of his reality-creating image making. When Archimago parts ''The Redcrosse Knight from Truth,'' into Truth's ''stead faire falshood steps,'' ''image of truth new-born'' to misappropriate Milton's phrase from the Nativity Ode. As early as the manuscript poem, ''Then she bore pale desire,'' Blake establishes his conception of images: ''Pride made a Goddess. fair or Image rather till knowledge animated it. 'twas Calld Selflove'' (E448). Archimago's magic could hardly be defined more

139

succinctly. Quality becomes image becomes animate, is named. In the Enion-Tharmas passage cited earlier, Enion has become merely an "image of grief," and there are countless other passages throughout the works in which Blake employs the idea of images in the same way. Such images are created by the mind of man, that is to say, abstracted from The Divine Image, which is the Human Imagination, "the All in Man" (*Annotations to Berkeley*, E663). The latter is the stuff of Vision, the former, of Allegory. Archimago, the Arch-Imager, then, is an allegorist even as he is himself an allegory; rather than Giamatti's *vates* (an aspect of the Protean tradition about which Blake gives little evidence of knowing), he is for Blake the false prophet, the archetypal Priest who appropriates names (the "eternal principles" of Blake's Chaucer essay) and gives them "substance" and form. Despite the seeming similarity here to Los's function, neither Archimago nor Blake's Priest "realizes" error so that it will be annihilable but rather so that it will be deified, named, and thus made The Divine Name.[55] In one sense, then, Blake's "problem" with *The Faerie Queene* is the relative distinguishability of Spenser from Archimago—or Spenser from Blake's own Priest.

Duessa is Archimago's female counterpart in the sense that she, as her name tells us, is already two. Not only can she misshape (let us say, a Fradubio, Fidessa, or Fraelissa), but she herself is "misshapen" (I,ii,41). Even her "house" is "misinformed" (stanza 43). To use Blake's term, she is a "similitude," an image, a seeming. In Spenser's own terminology, she is not merely a woman who is false, she is "this false woman" (xii,32) or, as Una describes her, "the face of falshood" (x,49); and he insists (through Redcrosse's confession in canto xii) on the "realizing" power of her name: she is

> *Fidessa* hight,
> *Fidessa* hight the falsest Dame on ground,
> Most false *Duessa*, royall richly dight,
> That easie was t'inuegle weaker sight.
>
> (St. 32)

At her stripping by Arthur, she becomes the falsehood for which she is an image (or the face), an abstraction now (in the literal sense) deformed. One is reminded here of Urizen's exploration of his self-created world in *The Book of Urizen*:

> And his world teemd vast enormities
> Frightning; faithless; fawning
> Portions of life; similitudes

140

>   Of a foot, or a hand, or a head
>   Or a heart, or an eye.
>
>   (23:2-6, E81)

Thus, Duessa, "Such as she was," is portioned into the similitudes of a filthy hag, a fox, dung, an eagle, a bear, and contrahuman parts that add up to no shape or form except the forms of de-formity, falsehood itself. She is, then, as Acrasia is in Book II, not merely "a demonic allegorist," as Berger characterizes the latter,[56] but allegory itself, a congeries of semblances. When she is finally brought to the bar of justice in Mercilla's palace in Book V, it is meet and right that "good" allegorical figures testify for her, and Murder, Sedition, Incontinence of Life, Adultery, and Impiety are called as witnesses against her.

Although the *Spenser Variorum* is remarkably silent on the matter of Duessa's trial and Mercilla's ultimate judgment (except for its endless pursuit of the historical allegory), more recently, some scholars have addressed the surreptitiousness with which Spenser alludes to Duessa's death. I doubt that Blake noticed or cared, but I cannot conceive his being less than outraged at the idea of extending mercy to a pernicious allegory, even as he might have laughed at the notion that allegory can be sentenced to death. The issue for Blake was not whether, as the beginning of the tenth canto argues, "it is better mercifully to reform than judicially to kill"[57] but rather whether a "system" founded on Justice (Artegall) and Mercy (Mercilla) is any "better" than one governed by Duessa's equally abstract semblances—which is to say that for Blake the "issue" was a nonissue. Spenser does not know, Blake surely felt, that allegories are allegories: "bad" ones are hardly redeemable by "good" ones, since the very bases of both are founded in errors of perception, abstractions made "real." To Blake, then, Mercilla's mercy is appropriately unexercised, and had Blake known of the historical-allegorical constraints under which Spenser was laboring, the latter's awkward attempt to accommodate them would only have exacerbated his basic error in handling the entire matter of Duessa's fate. In addition, although justice is never pronounced openly, it is executed according to "the reformative expedience of the 'common wele,'"[58] an equally abhorrent alternative to Blake. Blake would have perceived Duessa's "dying" offstage as Spenser's confession that he did not know how to rid his poem of her. Abstractions are not annihilable but, rather, when embodied, they become susceptible to being unperceived: Error "is Burnt up the Moment Men cease to behold it" (*Vision of the Last Judgment*, E565). That is to say, what is annihilable is the habit of mind that makes abstractions real. Having no power over such matters, Mercy merely weeps, arises, and presumably exits (V,ix,50)—as do Arthur, Artegall, and all the personified abstractions—leaving the habit of mind to be imaged again and again in *The Faerie Queene*, most notably perhaps in that other allegorist, the Blatant Beast.

As if all this were not self-damning enough, Spenser's most grievous error occurs before Duessa's trial. Mercilla is presented as a paragon, yet another of Elizabeth's alter egos in the poem:

> She Angel-like, the heyre of ancient kings
> And mightie Conquerors, in royall state,
> Whylst kings and kesars at her feet did them prostrate.
> Thus she did sit in souerayne Maiestie,
> Holding a Scepter in her royall hand.
>
> (V,ix,29–30)

At her feet "Virgins clad in white" sit adoring (and adorning) "her royall state," along with Elizabeth's Lion (stanzas 31–33). But in the very temple of this perfection of "high soaring thought" (stanza 34), Bon Font, whom Blake would have regarded as an embodiment of the poetic genius, has his tongue "Nayled to a post, adiudged so by law." His crime was blaspheming "that Queene," but more fundamentally he had had the audacity to take on "the bold title of a Poet" (stanzas 25–26). It is difficult not to imagine Blake seeing himself in the same position in his world. Perhaps the binding of the "Human Form" "upon the Stems of Vegetation," including fastening "with a screw of iron / . . . this ear into the rock" and "circumscribing" the tongue, is a distant echo of Spenser's conception.[59]

With such unequivocal evidence of an "Angelic" imagination at work, the key question I have been investigating presents itself again in the extraordinary iconography of the nailed tongue. Put simply, if Spenser could "allow" Mercilla to execute such judgment (hardly merciful, yet somewhat "right" in the context of Elizabeth-Gloriana's paradise on earth), in what sense can he be regarded as redeemable, as of the devil's party without knowing it? A. Leigh DeNeef, without respect to Blake, poses the issue rather neatly in Spenser's own terms:

> Did Bon Font actually write "lewd poems," or were his
> verses, like Spenser's own . . . , simply misread? Did he
> actively seek evil or was he merely "likened . . . to a
> welhed / Of evill words"? Anyone who is so "bold" as to
> take upon himself the title and obligations of a Poet runs
> the risk of having his good name similarly effaced. . . .
> Spenser confronts that risk directly. He realizes that by his

very aims the poet places himself at the mercy of his readers, who can either applaud him as Bon Font or accuse him as Malfont.[60]

I have already argued how *The Marriage of Heaven and Hell* seduces us, indeed almost coerces us, into misreading, how even the apparent diabolical processes of Blake's art in the Printing house in Hell lend themselves to ready misconstruction, how Thel's "misreading" of the voice from the grave merely confirms her continued existence in an allegorical abode where existence has never come, and how the speaker of *The Marriage* misreads *Paradise Lost* and thereby rescues it from its "bad" allegory only to transform it into a "new," diabolical allegory.

If we consider Blake's Spenser painting, it may well be that some sense of mutual predicament led Blake to group Duessa, Archimago, and the Blatant Beast, rather ineffectually "under control," at the end of his procession of the *The Faerie Queene* characters (see figure 4 below). If, as most Spenserians argue, the poem functions cumulatively, the sum of all morally pernicious allegories in the work resides in this infernal trinity. Or, to extrapolate a bit, each of these figures in his/her/its (a significantly inclusive gendering) own way is the author of all allegories, not to mention their being the "wicked tongues" that unstintingly attack the truth of vision, which destroys all allegories. There is little need to document extensively Blake's own fears about the way his works were being received by the "clods" of this world, but we might note a few. His friend and fellow artist Fuseli, "Indignant" at the reception of his art by an art world ruled jointly by Reynolds and Gainsborough, "almost hid himself." Blake adds: "I am hid." And again: "To defend the Bible in this year 1798 would cost a man his life" for "The Beast & the Whore rule without controls."[61] But the most fundamentally human of these complaints is Blake's 23 August 1799 letter to the Rev. John Trusler, who had obviously attacked Blake's idea of "Moral Painting" as well as his "method of Study" (E702). What Trusler wanted, what he thought any artist should be doing, was "realistic" allegorical painting. His being a minister would have been signal enough to Blake of his obtuseness, but anyone who could write *Hogarth Moralized* or *The Way to be Rich and Respectable* was surely possessed of a Duessa-Archimago-Blatant Beast mind. To such a mind, a mind like Blake's was surely "dim'd with Superstition," one that, alas, cannot deal with "living with This World" and hence with following *"the Nature of it."*[62] Similarly dimmed with superstition, Spenser, perhaps only in those revealing moments of great personal and artistic uncertainty, transcended the prison of his own allegory, although Blake saw those moments all too clearly as heavily overshadowed by the power of the allegory, gauged to speak to "living in This World" and to following "the Nature of it."

On the Archimago-Duessa paradigm are built all the manifold disguises of *The Faerie Queene*, some accurately imaging their wearers' significance (the simple or naïve allegories), some belying the characters' true essences or divine images. The former need not detain us; in their simplicity and patency—their inevitable attachment to moral virtues and vices—they constitute much of Spenser's "angelicism" to Blake. The others were of far greater interest to him, for they evidenced the pattern of disguise he himself chose for his own "allegory." Of these, Britomart is by far the most complex and multivalent. In Book II Spenser writes of Duessa:

> Her purpose was not such, as she did faine,
> Ne yet her person such, as it was seene,
> But vnder simple shew and semblant plaine
> Lurckt false *Duessa* secretly vnseene.
>
> (i,21)

The description and terminology are equally applicable to Britomart. Without pressing the analogy unduly, it should also be noted that Glauce is the inspiration for Britomart's disguise throughout *The Faerie Queene*, thus placing herself in precisely the same position to Britomart—disguised as her squire—as Archimago is to Duessa in Book II. Spenser accuses Glauce of having a "foolhardy wit" (III,iii,52), but foolhardy or no, Glauce "Conceiu'd a bold deuise":

> Let vs in feigned armes our selues disguize,
> And our weake hands (whom need new strength shall teach)
> The dreadfull speare and shield to exercize.
>
> (St. 53)

Verbal deceit accompanies this plotted disguise, as it usually does, for Glauce, using a wonderful Spenserian double-pejorative verb, goes on to argue that, since Britomart is "tall, / And large of limbe," the disguise will not "misseeme" her; and besides, there were other great women warriors, especially Angela, the Saxon Virgin queen (stanzas 53–56). Spenser's extraordinary multilayered conception would not have been lost on Blake: Petrarchan woman, lovesick and languishing, becomes knight-warrior becomes angel, each charactered layer belying the essential nature of its predecessor. For Blake, if not for Spenser, that line of belying goes back even further than the Petrarchan mistress, for she is but a fictional image of woman in the first place, as much an abstraction of womanness as Britomart's Chastity is. It is right, then, that the new knight and her squire enter the allegory proper "Couered with secret cloud of silent night" (stanza 61), for Duessa's power and very being emanate from that realm (see I,v,27).

Blake's portrayal of Britomart in his *Faerie Queene* painting is based on his perception of this fundamental deception, one that (for Blake at least) colors whatever Britomart does in the rest of the poem. Her own myopia, evidenced in her falling in love with "'th' only shade and semblant of a knight, / Whose shape or person yet [she] neuer saw" (ii,38), would have been icing on the cake for Blake. Her manifold "disguises" throughout the poem are thus predictable, the most obvious being Belphoebe, Amoret, and Florimell. She is also Venus and Diana (as Upton notes, in Cicero, Glauce is the mother of Diana) and a host of other classical avatars, not to mention, most crucially, Radigund, who literally enslaves Artegall, turning him into a woman just as Artegall's image in the mirror enslaves Britomart.[63] Were her Petrarchan origins and such alter egos not enough to convince Blake of Britomart's essential Duessanism, the fact that Spenser aligns her with Gloriana as well would have been her ultimate damnation (she is thus figured in Blake's painting as Rahab, the Whore of Babylon, and others of that Blakean-biblical ilk). But since, except for a few well-known moments, Britomart maintains her disguise as a knight throughout the poem (the only major knight, be it remembered, who pursues no knightly quest), she is also Redcrosse, Guyon, Artegall, Calidore, and even Arthur—with all the questions inherent in their make-up that Blake felt compelled to address in the painting. Lest this characteral mélange seem somehow excessive, one must recall Spenser's language during Britomart's initial transformation at Glauce's instigation: she will become "a mayd Martiall" (III,iii,53)—that is, as the careful capital and punning verb tell us, she is artifically remanufactured as Mars (more accurately, Venus armata)—an image (as Williams puts it) of "completeness as woman and warriour . . . in whom feminine and masculine qualities are balanced," which would have viscerally repelled Blake.[64] Its Blakean perverseness is accented by the fact that the Isis priest's vision is a version of Merlin's forecast of Britomart's future, a prophecy that is unfulfilled in the poem, as we have it. Moreover, Britomart's other "revelation," her dream, is equally un-Blakean: Isis-woman-Britomart standing with one foot on Osiris-man-Artegall, the perfect image of the Female Will (V,vii,12–16, 22); and the priests of Isis Church who interpret her dream "tied were to stedfast chastity, / And continence of life," mortifying their flesh (stanza 9). The entire scene, then, had to

epitomize for Blake Spenserian misvision and its devastating consequences.

Britomart's own disguise breeds a number of others, including
some extraordinary variations on the theme. After she has revealed
her face in Castle Ioyeous, for example, Guyon asks her why she is
disguised (Spenser's language in the passage is at least interesting if
not curious): "what inquest / Made her dissemble her disguised
kind."[65] It may be that Spenser himself is telling us here that her
essential (real, true) "kind" is disguised as the "Faire Lady she . . .
seemd, like Lady drest," which in turn is dissembled in her guise as
the "fairest knight aliue" (III,ii,4). But that essentially Spenserian—
rather than Blakean—question aside, in Book IV Spenser himself addresses Britomart as that

> Vnluckie Mayd to seeke her enemie,
> Vnluckie Mayd to seek him farre and wide,
> Whom, when he was vnto her selfe most nie,
> She through his late disguizement could him not descrie.
>
> (v,29)

Aligned with all the other quests against great enemies, Britomart's is
for an "enemy" that is a friend, as well as for a friend who is in turn
disguised as her enemy: in III,ii,8, Artegall is "one, that hath vnto
me donne / Late foule dishonour and reprochfull spight, / The
which I seeke to wreake"; and in IV,iv,44, Artegall, "In quyent disguise," as Britomart was in the Temple of Isis, is unceremoniously
dumped by Britomart from his horse as the enemy knight in Satyrane's tournament—only to ride "Against her" again "full of des-
piteous ire, / That nought but spoyle and vengeance did require"
(IV,vi,11), both bathing "their hands in bloud of dearest freend"
(vi,17).

Britomart is not merely "unlucky," then, as Spenser knows full
well. In her own way, though it is unlikely that Spenser would go as
far in the matter as I believe Blake did, she is an antiknight, whose
misperceptions of her Love (and of herself) precipitate a mock quest
that will end, if it ever ends, with her foot on her lover's neck. On the
opposite side of the looking-glass, so to speak, is the witch's son's reaction to Florimell's presence in their hut. Stunned by her "image"
he demands of his mother, "What mister wight that was, and whence
deriued, / That in so straunge disguizement there did maske"
(III,vii,14). Thus, Beauty itself is charged by an Arch-Image-
maker's son with being merely a semblance. His mother, the necro-
mancer herself, similarly has the gall to charge that Florimell has
been thither brought by some "deuill" (vii,8)—some other, even

more diabolical, allegorist. In effect, the son becomes the allegorical Beastly Lust that his mother summons "out of [the] hidden cave" of her mind, seeking to devour Florimell whole. She escapes, of course, to continue her endless flight in the poem, while Satyrane tames the beast with Florimell's magic girdle that she has dropped.

My point here is not that the Florimell story parallels any of Britomart's, but rather that the entire *Faerie Queene* is, in a sense, imaged in the two episodes. Disguise breeds disguise, error breeds error, names breed names.[66] Perhaps the epitome of this last is III,i,45, again in connection with Britomart: Gardante, Parlante, Iocante, Basciante, Bacchante, and Noctante are all born of one parent (it is difficult to believe that the parent is not the Argante of III,vii,47, although Spenser does not say so). It is little wonder that, when the truth appears in its own guize, it is thought to be an allegory of error, like all the rest. Only Una, as A. C. Hamilton observes, needfully reminding us of the obvious, "cannot be divided *in* herself, being one."[67] Perhaps she is the Virgin Mary, Elizabeth, Chaste Love, True Church, et al., as Edwin Honig claims,[68] but she herself is oneness. As such, she, in effect, needs no rescuing; it is her parents who require that. More important, she needs no other quality or virtue or faculty to complete herself, as she demonstrates so vividly, standing alone at the end of Book I as Truth deserted by Holiness—yet again. Angus Fletcher has suggested that all of Spenser's knights are "subcharacters" whom Arthur generates.[69] This is precisely DeLuca's point about Blake's names, the clearest example of which (on the pattern of Gardante, Parlante, et al.) is Enitharmon's nine children in *Europe* (E65–66), all of whose names (except for Orc) reflect "phonetic elements of Enitharmon's name, as if a primary name matched its referent in propagating descendants." Blake's proliferation of names, then, is "suggestive of a shattered unity, and in their aggregate of its potential restoration."[70]

But clearly the same can be said, and indeed has been said, of Spenser's characters. The crucial difference, it seems to me, is in the nature of the unity out of which the characters emerge. If Arthur is, in one sense, the sum of all the other knights and Elizabeth of all the "good" female characters, their anticipated union would seem to parallel that of Blake's Albion and Jerusalem. In fact, the difference between the two "marriages" is enormous, not least because Spenser's never comes about in the poem, and in history it can never come about. And so he offers us a variety of earthly or fairy surrogates patterned, as Nohrnberg argues, on Venus, who "hath both kinds in one, / Both male and female, both vnder one name" (IV,x,41)— thus the "impending mutualization" of Scudamoret, Britomartegall,

Osirisis, Paridellenore, Thamedway, Claribellamour, and so on.[71] But the surrogates are either fitful or abortive. Redcrosse deserts Una before the marriage is consummated, Guyon has no mate or coupling namesake, Britomart is a female-male or male-female unto herself, the announced titular knight of Book IV (Telamond) never appears, Artegall disappears at the end of Book V (alone except for Talus), and Calidore leaves Pastorella with her parents to continue his chase after the Blatant Beast. Meantime, Arthur's composite "gentleman or noble person" of "vertuous and gentle discipline" yields the poem to Nature and Mutabilitie—or to Blatant Beasts.

Spenser's names then are a taxonomic calendar of what has already been created, an Adamic naming; and insofar as the names are joinable, they are so only mechanically, as Nohrnberg has demonstrated: one added onto the other to form not The Divine Name or the Divine Body of the Imagination but an hermaphroditic parody or sexual perversion of the androgyne. As Diana Hume George reminds us, "for Blake, the hermaphrodite . . . represents the sterile fusion of masculine and feminine in collusion against the human."[72] Thus, though somewhat overly severe, Russell Fraser is correct (at least from Blake's point of view) in regarding the "arbitrary correspondences of the *Faerie Queene*" as "a kind of architecture whose function is not philosophical [Blake would have said 'imaginative'] but placatory"; its "compulsive design . . . replaces real turbulence with an appearance of order, which is often apprehensible in diagrammatic ways and is thereby the more airless and evidently controlled."[73] If, then, Spenser "creates" Genesis-like, he offers his creation to "the rational consciousness" as "a way of regulating imaginative materials that otherwise appear confounded by contradictions and bristling with destructive implications."[74] Blake's way, however, is to "deregulate" those same "materials" in such a way that, so liberated, they may confront their own contradictions and grapple with their own destructiveness, in short, work out their own salvations. For such an endeavor, similitudinous continued allegory is seriously deficient, embalming (as it were) its own errors in its very structure. As William Nelson observes, "the whole Tenor of the Knights' adventures insists upon the point that man is incapable of achieving his own salvation."[75]

If Angus Fletcher is right about Arthur's generating his subcharacters, insofar as any of Spenser's knights generate subcharacters, what is produced, as Fletcher himself acknowledges, is plot symmetry; and this in turn "enforces an allegorical interpretation, since, in effect, we always want to know which is the genuine and which the false representation."[76] Blake, I think, saw both representations as false. That is why, in his eyes at least, Duessa may be tried but neither convicted nor executed. And that is why, in his own version of *The Faerie Queene* characters, we cannot know "which is the genuine and which the false representation"—except as that is revealed to us by our own imaginative penetration of Spenser's allegorical disguises. Precisely the same imaginative act is requisite to "understanding" Blake's own works—verbal, pictorial, and composite. Allegory is the artistic guise of Blake's Generation. *The Faerie Queene* functions in that realm; its aim is not to justify the ways of God to man but the ways of man to man. If Colie, like a number of other Spenserians, prefers to see the things and personages in *The Faerie Queene* becoming, gradually and cumulatively, metamorphosed into their essences, becoming "their being," I am perfectly prepared to believe that that is true; but Blake did not see the poem that way. Calidore's blundering, in full armor, into the dance of the Graces is a fitting image of Blake's final perception of Spenser's poem: the vision vanishes when disguise or allegory appears.[77] The futility of the one to even assist, much less maintain, the other is emblemized negatively at the far right of Blake's Spenser painting: Calidore, in his armored dress or skin, gestures vainly to Duessa, Archimago, and the Blatant Beast to stay out of the poem (see figure 8 below).

In his extensive discussion of Blake's idea of "sublime allegory," Wittreich leans heavily on Colie's claim to fix Blake firmly in a line of vision and of epic-prophecy that includes Spenser as well as Revelation and Milton. *The Faerie Queene*, he says, collapses all its "typological struggles" and its performing figures "into a single figure and a single momentous action." That figure and action are the "One Man" and the internalized-in-the-mind fall from paradise and its recovery.[78] This, I fear, is not only to misread Spenser but to misread Blake. Nothing of the sort "happens" in *The Faerie Queene*. Indeed, in one sense at least, Book VI and the Mutabilitie Cantos militate against even the possibility of such an eventuation. As for Blake, pace Wittreich and Tannenbaum, he is no typologist. Typology functions only *in* time, even as its "terminus," a *forma perfectior*, denies temporality. The typological values of an event or character are not even discernible or identifiable except in retrospect—at which "point in time" the typologies should collapse into the eternal reality of which they are mere shadows. To read retrospectively is to valorize time, and in thus identifying typologies, such reading is itself allegoresis. Neither events nor characters can be foreshadowed in Blake, nothing can be construed as pointing *to* (though that is what Tannenbaum argues), because there is no "to" or "from." "Progression" is "necessary" only to human existence, as *The Marriage* reminds us; just so,

allegory is "a *continued* . . . darke conceit," a "historye." As Blake
says of Bunyan and the Greek poets, it may contain "some vision"
(or strive toward vision), but it is not vision.[79] Wittreich's own case is
fatally compromised, it seems to me, by his admission later in the
same essay, that "Spenser usually counts on a 'stock response,' " that
he asserts (implicitly as well as explicitly) a "moral superiority" over
his readers, and that, "like his epic predecessors [he] allegorized a
received tradition of beliefs."[80] While none of these admissions damage the validity of Wittreich's claim for Spenser's rightful place
among the visionary company of prophets, they do describe succinctly the basis of Blake's somewhat less-than-urgent need to correct
or redeem him (although, the more—and the more intensively—
Blake read Spenser, the clearer his "hidden" poetic genius or true
poetness tended to become). Milton's and Blake's superiority to
Spenser, in Blake's eyes, quite rightly resides in the fact that they are
"generators" of values rather than conformers to those that already
exist—in Aristotle, the Bible, wherever, it does not matter.

This latter point, as well as Wittreich's prior three "admissions,"
are surely composite reason enough why there is no poem entitled
Spenser. It is the reason, as well, why Spenser's name never appears in
Blake's works, poetry or prose, except as an acknowledgment of his
authorship of the single sustained quotation from him that Blake
gives us, the *Notebook* quatrain I have commented upon in chapter 1.
And, finally, it is the reason Blake's painting of the characters in *The
Faerie Queene*, like virtually all of his illustrations to other poets, is
more critical, even judgmental, than it is redemptive. There are no
poems entitled *Young* or *Gray* or *Bunyan* or *Dante* or *Virgil* or *Homer* or
Ovid, either. None of them, in Blake's judgment, had sufficient visionary power to leaven their "allegories," though one could argue, I
think, that, once the aging Blake read Dante in the original, his earlier attitudes, expressed in his annotations to Boyd's translation,
changed sufficiently for him to accord that poet the magnificence of
what we have of his planned "visual poem."[81] I realize that such an
argument risks having to say something comparable about Blake's
even more ambitious, indeed herculean, task of "illuminating"
Young's *Night Thoughts*, so I shall not pursue it further. Suffice it to
say that, before the mideighteenth century in England, Dante was
not a power to be reckoned with (indeed had not yet been translated
into English), certainly not as he would be shortly for Coleridge,
Shelley, Keats, and Byron. The *Commedia* was not on coffee tables;
Young's poem, like Gray's *Elegy*, was. To Blake's mind they needed
a Blake, as it were, to disabuse the public of Error that had become
not only common practice but the "law."[82] As early as *An Island in the*

Moon, Blake fretted over such "blindness" becoming law, for there he has "Steelyard the Lawgiver, sitting at his table taking extracts from Hervey's Meditations among the tombs & Youngs Night thoughts" (E456). Blake's graphic *Epitome of James Hervey's "Meditations Among the Tombs"* is the "answer" to the former, as the *Night Thoughts* illuminations are to the latter—and, as *Chaucer's Canterbury Pilgrims* is to *The Canterbury Tales* and *The Characters in Spenser's Faerie Queene* to *The Faerie Queene*.

One final note. Hamilton concludes his fine essay in *A Theatre for Spenserians* as follows:

> Through his art of language Spenser seeks to purify words
> by restoring them to their true, original meanings. When
> Adam fell, he lost that natural language in which words
> contain and reveal the realities they name. Though
> corrupt, languages remain divinely given and the poet's
> burden is to purify the language of his own tribe. Words
> have been "wrested from their true calling": the poet
> attempts to wrest them back. Spenser "writ no language,"
> as Jonson noted: that is, he avoids a fallen language which
> would only confirm man in his state of bondage.[83]

The pertinence of this idea to the study of Blake may be obvious, but its relationship to the twin ideas of naming and allegorizing in both Blake and Spenser requires a brief discussion.

In Blake, concomitant with the emergence from Eternity of the self-separated Urizen is the utterance of "Words articulate, bursting in thunders / That roll'd on the tops of his mountains" (*Book of Urizen* 4:3–5, E71). Although, as usual in this work, the syntax is extraordinarily crabbed, ambiguous, and puzzling (for reasons that I have suggested elsewhere),[84] "myriads of Eternity" in the final line of plate 3 seems to be the subject of the sentence. The phrase is of especial interest since it stands midway between Eternity itself (or *the* Eternals)— that is, when "Earth was not"—and the myriads who will fall in Urizen's wake (more properly, the myriads of which Urizen is composed). It is possible for us to "see," therefore, that these articulated "thunders" will become in the Fall (that is, in Creation) some of the many "solid[s] without fluctuation" that fallen consciousness seeks. Appropriately, then, later in plate 4 we learn that the "origin" (as well as the end) of these articulations is Urizen's "books formd of metals" in which he has "written the secrets of wisdom" (ll. 24–25). Moreover, that "wisdom" (comparable clearly to the Word's perversions in the proverbs of Solomon and Ecclesiastes) is derived from

Urizen's "dark contemplation" upon the "the wars of Eden," the "Mental . . . Wars of Eternity," the "Wars of Eternal life,"[85] which now to his dimmed perception seem an eternal dying or living "in unquenchable burnings" (4:12-13, E71)—or in "battles dire / In unseen conflictions with shapes" (3:13-14, E70); or, once more,

> fightings and conflicts dire,
> With terrible monsters Sin-bred:
> Which the bosoms of all inhabit;
> Seven deadly Sins of the soul.
>
> (4:27-30, E72)

It is difficult not to associate these mental maneuverings by Urizen with Spenser's *Faerie Queene* and its monsters, its fightings and conflicts, and its sins, all of which (from Spenser's—and Blake's anti-Urizenic—perspectives) do inhabit all fallen bosoms. In the terms I have been developing, however, we are witnessing here yet another version in Blake of the origins of allegory, the only "form" appropriate to fallen language. "Rent from Eternity" (6:8, E74), Urizen becomes an allegory of himself—which is to say, in Blake's cosmology, creation (what he will later call Generation) is an allegory, or an allegorized "version" of Vision or Eternity.

Among Los's many counterefforts, then, is his rebuilding (reforming) of language: he "calls" some of the emanations of Albion (whose fall is the same as Urizen's but differently perceived) Chichester, calls Winchester a "son of Los," "his Emanations / Submitting to be call'd Enitharmons daughters, and be born / In vegetable mould" (*Jerusalem* 36[40]:49-55, E182-83). At this point in *Jerusalem*, there follows a Spenserian-Miltonic catalogue of English place names, which Los tells us are given because "English" is "the rough basement" from which his task of building "the stubborn structure of the language" must begin,

> acting against
> Albions melancholy, who must else have been a Dumb despair.
>
> (Ll. 59-60, E183)

This "stubborn structure" is the linguistic counterpart of Satan, "the limit of opakeness," and Adam, "the limit of Contraction." Blake might well have called it the limit of Abstraction. Such a limit is double-edged. Put to Urizen's use (as it always will be), it becomes the law in one sense, in another the "similitudes / Of a foot, or a hand, or a head" which become the fractionated materials of allegory. Los's linguistic efforts are understandable in terms of the famous paradigm of creating a system, not only that he may not be enslaved by another man's, but that he may thereby deliver individuals from all systems (*Jerusalem* 10:20, E153; 11:5, E154). In other terms one plate further on, Los's countersystematizing is inherent in his being "the finger of God," writing prophecies as in the famous wall-writing episode in the Book of Daniel:

> Fixing their [Albion's Sons'] Systems permanent: by mathematic power
> Giving a body to Falshood that it may be cast off for ever
> With Demonstrative Science piercing Apollyon with his own bow!
> (*Jerusalem* 12:10–14, E155)

This he will do—this Los, Finger of God, Poet-Artist, Blake—"by printing in the infernal method, by corrosives, . . . melting apparent surfaces away, and displaying the infinite which was hid" (E39). While this locution is from *The Marriage*, in the very passage of *Jerusalem* where he strives with systems to deliver individuals from systems, Los

> in his ladles the Ore
> He lifted, pouring it into the clay ground prepar'd with art.
> (11:3–4, E154)

The "apparent surfaces" are words, allegorical abstractions enshrined in the fallen language of Urizen (or in the language of the fallen mind), whose "apparent" surfaces speak to our senses and corporeal understanding—like proverbs or allegories, prose or poetry in the fetters of rhyme, the "rhetoric of substantiality."[86] It might well be said that reason-created language speaks only to reason, Urizen thus talking to himself. In any case, the "infinite" "hid" therein has been chained in names, separating identity from identity (or identities from Identity) as the Genesis God creates Adam in his own image, names him, and then separates Eve from him—"till a system was formed," which is Urizen's net of names (the biblical begettings), the Religion of Moral Virtues and labeled contraries whose labels have been made "real" and hence are no longer marriagable, but hermaphroditically attachable (and detachable).

What the poet writes, then, if he is doing his job, is an allegory to deliver individuals from allegories. In the preface to *Jerusalem*, Blake addresses his reader ("the Public") directly, asserting (among other things), "nor vain my types shall be" (E145). These "types" are at once his mode of illuminated printing (the phrase I have quoted is preceded by "Therefore I print") and his allegories—not, as has been claimed, his typologies. "Mark well my words!" cries the Bard of *Milton* repeatedly, "they are of your eternal salvation" (2:25,

E96). Blake's point is not that we should listen to the Bard's words and thereby be saved. Neither he nor the Bard (nor Los) is a preacher. Their words are *of* our salvation, which is to say, they are allegories to deliver us from the abyss of allegories. Elsewhere in *Milton*, Los's "Printing-Press," which is the wine press of the apocalypse that (among other things) presses the vinous eternal realities of intellect out of the husks of words, is the "place" where

he lays his words in order above the mortal brain
As cogs are formd in a wheel to turn the cogs of the adverse wheel.
(27[29]:9–10, E124)

That is, the printing press is a mill created to deliver individuals from mills with "complicated wheels" (*There Is No Natural Religion*, E2). Los's words are thus calculated to reverse the cycling of the same dull round over again, unwind the complications, and thereby re-turn language to the humanized "conversation" of the final plate of *Jerusalem*.

The Spenserian "parallel" to this is instructive. Busirane is forced by Britomart to unsay his spell, to dearticulate it, so that Amoret may be rescued from her own literary fantasy (much as Shelley's Prometheus unsays his curse upon Jupiter). Britomart, however, is as unlikely a Los as is Busirane himself, and Amoret is hardly the human form divine. What is important in Blake's conception is not merely release from fiction's power (though that is part of it) but rather a release of language from rational, solipsistic articulation (Urizen talking to himself) into the conversation of "Visionary forms dramatic" that redound from tongues to walk "To & fro in Eternity as One Man," as one Word. Los, we might note finally, does not do it for us; as the fallen form of Urthona, he provides but the means our "mortal brains" must grasp to effect our own salvation, to do our own re-turning.

If we now return to the quotation from Hamilton with which I began, certain important "translations" or interpolations need to be made if it is to be an acceptable gloss on the way Blake (not Hamilton nor even Spenser) regarded Spenser's language. Adam, for Blake, is already "fallen," in that his humanness is divorced from the Divine Body of Imagination. As a result, Blake's Adam loses no "natural language" at all but rather loses the "language" of eternal names. My point is more than a quibble over Hamilton's language, for it defines at least one fundamental aspect of Blake's "quarrel" with Spenser. If, as Hamilton says, Spenser's "burden is to purify the language of his own tribe" (as I think it is), Blake's is not—as Los's building *on* the rough basement of the English language suggests. He does not wish to "purify" that basement but rather to employ it in such fashion that individuals are entirely delivered from it as well as from the stubborn structure that arises on its base. In this sense, having already been delivered from it (at least upon his completion of *Milton*), Blake in "writing" *Jerusalem* may be described, as Jonson described Spenser with very different intent, as having "writ no language." Hamilton characterizes this "no language" as Spenser's avoidance of that which would only "confirm man in his state of bondage." But such an avoidance is a manifest impossibility: that "no language" has to be silence, literally no language. Hamilton escapes his dilemma by invoking the principle of the "purity" of Adamic language, that "natural language" Adam uses when "he gives names to his creatures which express their natures." Precisely. Pace Hamilton's good intentions, that is the way Blake perceived Spenser's language—much to his distress—identifying it as one of the critical aspects of Spenser's work that demanded redemption, or at least correction.

The key question with respect to Blake's overall attitude toward Spenser, then, arises in Hamilton's final words, as well as in Quilligan's thesis in *The Language of Allegory*. Spenser's "word-play" (which has been the subject of his entire essay), Hamilton argues—but not quite so intensively as Quilligan—"is not an idle game but a sustained and serious effort to plant words as seeds in the reader's imagination. In Jonson's phrase he 'makes their minds like the thing he writes.'" So far so good, for so does Blake. But when Hamilton says that Spenser thus "restored at least those words which are capable of fashioning his reader in virtuous and gentle discipline," he has moved his entire analysis of Spenser's language precisely in the direction to which Blake most objected, so much so that in all likelihood Blake was unable to appreciate (fully, if at all) the kind of "word-play" in Spenser that Hamilton analyzes, the same kind Blake himself employs to "reveal the infinite which was hid."

It is tempting in all this (and by way of conclusion, I shall not resist the temptation) to turn to Spenser's own comments on language in his epistle to Gabriel Harvey, prefatory to *The Shepheardes Calender*, the main source for Hamilton's claims. There Spenser makes his familiar claim for Chaucer as "the Loadestarre of our Language"—not exactly Los's "rough basement" but close enough to encourage us to read on. The language of Spenser's compliments to Chaucer aside (they would not have pleased Blake), that first of the English poets had "the sound of those ancient Poetes still ringing in his eares." Although Spenser attributes the achievement to Livy, he might very well have been understood by Blake as saying that Chaucer too labored "to set forth in hys worke an eternall image of antiquitie" (hence the nature of his painting of Chaucer's Canterbury Pilgrims), a "portraict" molded by "good and naturall English words" restored "to theyr rightfull heritage." From Blake's point of view, this is indeed Los's basement—where any poet must begin. It is as well the language Spenser used, however refined and purified in his graduation from pastoral to prophetic epic (a "journey" that Blake himself pursued from *Songs of Innocence* to *Jerusalem*).

For Blake, it remained to Milton to raise the language above its basement. Though infected by Spenser's disease, not only in the blatant allegorical passages on Sin and Death but much more fundamentally in the abstractions that are Milton's Father, Son, and Holy Ghost (see Blake's *Marriage*, E35), to Blake, Milton's language soared to the sublime of Revelation, *Paradise Regained* especially redeeming such allegory in its portrayal of the Eternal Imagination. As Wittreich tellingly observes, "If we are to continue to talk about 'the Devil's or Blake's version' of the poems Blake illustrates, then we should acknowledge, when we come to the *Paradise Regained* series, that here Milton's voice is the voice of a true poet who read the Bible in its infernal sense." Moreover, he goes on to argue, conventional typology is all but ignored by Blake in these designs, for his "point, like Milton's, is that Christ's resurrection occurs now, paradise is regained now, not in some typologically (allegorically) assumed future time."[87] In collapsing time to an infinite moment, both Blake and Milton annihilate the basis of twoness, on which both Duessan typology and Duessan allegory are built; and in collapsing conventional space, both "place" the drama in the theater of the mind, precisely that "mental space" Coleridge claimed for *The Faerie Queene*. It is not merely coincidental that Blake's illustrations for *Paradise Regained* were executed during his composition to *Jerusalem*. Not only was *Paradise Regained*, to Blake, "free from the impedimenta of the classical epic tradition,"[88] it was free from allegorical impedimenta as well. If, as E. J. Rose contends, "Milton's error" in Blake's eyes was that he did not distinguish "clearly between 'Allegory & Vision' and was drawn into categories of metaphor and a conception of metaphor which caused him to write 'in fetters,'"[89] that may be true of *Paradise Lost* but clearly not of *Paradise Regained* (Rose neglects to remind us that Blake's attack on Milton in *The Marriage* is limited to *Paradise Lost*). *Paradise Regained* presents, nay it is, the very vision accomplished *in perpetuo* that Spenser despairs of attaining at the end of Book VI of *The Faerie Queene*: "A fairer Paradise is founded now" (*Paradise Regained*, IV,613).

Now. It is the now of "that same time when no more *Change* shall be" (*Faerie Queene* VII,viii,2) purged of its future tense; and it is the now of plate 99 of *Jerusalem*, when "All Human Forms" are "identified," not as Adam (or even the Genesis God) identifies and hence separates them but as the God of John's gospel identifies them in The Word, those "Visionary forms dramatic" that have been "delivered" from all allegorical systems. Words have "become their being."[90]

CHAPTER FIVE

The Characters in Spenser's
Faerie Queene, I

I N LIGHT OF the general ignoring of Spenser in Blake studies in favor of Milton and the Bible, it is not surprising that his
tempera, *The Characters in Spenser's Faerie Queene*, has received little
attention, as John E. Grant and Robert E. Brown note in one of the
two major efforts to give it some regard, ''Blake's Vision of Spenser's
Faerie Queene: A Report and an Anatomy.'' The other is S. Foster Damon's discussion in *A Blake Dictionary*, which Grant and Brown acknowledge as ''the only attempt at a systematic exposition'' of the
painting.[1] Although I do not intend here merely a third ''exposition,'' one that purports to identify all of the minute particulars of the
painting, I would hope some advance over these two previous discussions will emerge in this and the following two chapters. I wish to
address the way in which Blake perceived (read) *The Faerie Queene* as
well as the method(s) he chose to correct its ''errors'' of vision. Once
we have a surer grasp of this graphic ''poem'' against the background
of the sort of verbal and conceptual imitation-criticism I have already
examined, we should be prepared to say something reasonably definitive on the question of Spenser's redeemability in Blake's eyes. I begin, then, with some important critical issues raised by both previous
discussions of the painting, issues that neither of them speaks to, at
least directly. In doing so I must also refer to Karl Kiralis's ground-
breaking analysis of Blake's earlier (1810) painting of *Chaucers Canterbury Pilgrims*, which set the pattern for the two subsequent analyses of
the Spenser.[2]

Kiralis's analysis assumes (properly, I think) that Blake's ''illustration'' to Chaucer is similar in kind and intent to his verbal and pictorial ''commentaries'' on Homer, Virgil, Dante, Spenser, Shakespeare, Bacon, Bunyan, Newton, Locke, Milton, Reynolds,
Berkeley, Wordsworth, Byron, and others—that it is, in other words,
''an acutely perceptive, imaginative'' piece of criticism (KK139).

Citing Blake's own urging that "the Spectator [must] attend to the Hands & Feet to the Lineaments of the Countenances they are all descriptive of Character & not a line is drawn without intention & that most discriminate & particular," Kiralis also points out, like a good Coleridgean, that we must at the same time "consider the larger elements," the whole picture. He addresses this latter principle first, for he believes that "to appreciate the comparative placement of the Pilgrims is vital to understanding what Blake is doing with this picture" (KK140).

What he finds in this "comparative placement" is that Blake—unlike Thomas Stothard, who stole the idea from Blake and did his own, more popular *The Procession of Chaucer's Pilgrims to Canterbury* (1808)— honored Chaucer's "hierarchical views" that dictated the Knight and the Squire (rather than the Miller, as in Stothard) to be appropriately at the head of the procession. Kiralis makes the point only to drop it, however, in favor of attention to various groupings of characters. As a result, the hierarchical order to which Chaucer and his age subscribed is given little or no attention in the rest of Kiralis's essay, except as that seems to dovetail with his interpretations of individual characters and groups of characters. To be sure, he frequently cites the penetrating appreciation by Blake of Chaucer's precise language with respect to a number of the characters (unlike Stothard's carelessness in this matter), but to all intents and purposes, Chaucer's views are all but totally submerged by Kiralis's attempts to elucidate Blake's perception of Chaucer. One must acknowledge, however, that Kiralis is a good enough critic to recognize, though he does not consistently demonstrate, that Blake's perception of the pilgrims is "surprisingly like Chaucer's and that [therefore] the archetypal nature of their thought allows Blake's somewhat unorthodox criticism to throw a fresh and illuminating light on Chaucer's genius" (KK167). Nevertheless, his overriding conclusion is that "Blake forces his readers to understand Chaucer in his own [that is, Blake's] image" (KK167).

That image is revealed most tellingly in "the careful placements of the entire group of Pilgrims and specific arrangements of smaller groups" (KK167) (see figure 3). Thus, the Miller, for example, is located "just behind the Wife of Bath that he may leer at his sexual soul-mate," and the Merchant "also peers intently upon her" (because of his tale of cuckoldry). There is, thereby, a "triangular arrangement with the Wife of Bath at its apex" (KK141). Other triangular arrangements include those at the head and rear of the procession (Knight-Squire-Squire's Yoeman, Poet-Chaucer-Clerk) and, as a "counterpart" to the Wife of Bath triangle, one centering

FIGURE 3. Blake, *Chaucers Canterbury Pilgrims*
(*courtesy of the British Museum*)

about the Prioress, whom Kiralis interprets as Blake's Tirzah to com-
plement the Wife of Bath's Rahab. Together, he argues, they constitute "the essential counterparts of woman hood [*sic*] as Blake conceives it" (KK142).

I confess to seeing the Prioress's triangle as considerably less defined than Kiralis does. Moreover, that she is said to be "framed by
the Pardoner (the corrupt Church) and the Knight (the highest member of the aristocracy present)" argues at least a certain confusion
with respect to triangular arrangements (KK158). The Monk, for example, looks at the Prioress with fully as much lechery as that of the
Miller and the Merchant, and the other apex of the base of this "triangle" is the tightly trifold image of the Nun's three priests, who do
not look at the Prioress at all. If the latter is a Tirzah, we must also
recognize in her certain ambiguities, for, to Blake, "the essential
counterparts" of *all* womanhood are hardly limited to Rahabs and
Tirzahs. I shall attend to these ambiguities shortly. On the matter of
triangles, we should also note the clearer (and far more striking) triangle formed by the Pardoner, the Friar, and the Manciple which
Kiralis says nothing about. The most extraordinary aspect of this triangle is Blake's sexually ambiguous portrayal of the Pardoner—with

muscular torso, haunches, and legs but feminized face and head and rather daintily gloved right hand. As such, the Pardoner may very well be part of Blake's composite female character in the painting.[3] And one may well wonder where Jerusalem is.

But for the moment, let me resist further second-guessing of Kiralis's interpretations, which he offers as "samplings" (KK167), and turn to his implicit critical principles and assumptions. In addition to the triangles, he finds a variety of pairings (most often contrasting), many of which intersect with the triangles or suggest contrasting triangles: Knight-Poet, Squire-Clerk, Pardoner-Parson, Wife of Bath-Prioress, Plowman-Miller, and so on. And then there are the more "difficult . . . to explain . . . asymmetrical configurations" (KK145) that we would not even see or pay attention to if we were not equally well versed in the whole of Chaucer's *Tales* and Blake's works. Kiralis's prime example includes Physician-Franklin-two Citizens. These various groupings, symmetrical and asymmetrical, are fitted by Blake into the larger "pairing" suggested by Harry Bailey's central position in the procession and his broad arm-gesturing. This "splits the group in two: the foremost unit constituting essentially the upper social level . . . and the other unit basically a lower social

group'' (KK142). But, unlike his earlier appeal to Chaucerian orthodox hierarchy, which he leaves at that, Kiralis demonstrates here how
Blake deliberately makes use of the two groups and hence of the hierarchy. Not only are the two groups dominated (at least in some sense)
by the Prioress and the Wife of Bath (Tirzah-Rahab perhaps, but perhaps also Jerusalem-Vala), but the nature of the latter part of the pilgrimage tends to suggest that, for Blake, it should be leading the procession—not of course to Canterbury but to Jerusalem. Let me leave
that most important interpretive point in abeyance for the moment,
however, in order to identify Kiralis's second basic critical principle—in addition to figural conformations.

The second principle has to do with the relationship between the
foreground and background, on the one hand, and between this spatialization and the characters themselves, on the other. Damon's suggestion that the morning star and the rising sun in the background
represent Chaucer and (perhaps) Shakespeare, respectively, seems to
me a poor guess (it ignores the clouds, the possibility that it is evening, the two colors—and perhaps kinds—of birds flying ''above,''
and the at least ambiguous backlighting of the landscape); but, it is
incontrovertible that ''the placing of the two forms of churches over
specific characters,'' as Kiralis argues, ''is not by accident'':

> The hollow shell of the tower of a late Gothic church is
> mainly above the Wife's head, though also above the Mer-
> chant's, obviously to show the emptiness of their faith in
> spiritual concerns, more pointedly illustrated by the Wife;
> whereas a solid church tower is over the head of the Parson
> to confirm that his enthusiastic superstition is for him a
> true religion, a spiritual reality and not a dead orthodoxy.
> The horizontal line of march headed by the Parson, includ-
> ing the Plowman [who, Kiralis suggests, is Blake himself]
> and the Franklin, is enclosed by a second solid church
> structure over the heads of the two Citizens. (KK149-50)

Similarly, church towers ''are conspicuously absent in the background of the entire front group''—''though the Squire and his Yeo-
man may have a spark of religion left since each is directly under what
may be construed as a tower'' (KK149). One may quarrel with this
interpretation, particularly as it tends to confuse ''Chaucer's religion'' with Blake's idea of religion, but the critical principle is surely
sound. More firmly ''Blakean,'' says Kiralis, is the cottage above the
Host's horse, which suggests marriage as ''based on mutual love that
encompasses mutual forbearance, forgiveness, and understanding''
(KK151). Perhaps this is true for Chaucer, but hardly for Blake;

thus, we are once again shuttled between Chaucerian ideas and those of Blake without clear indication as to how we are to know one from the other or the relationship between them—in the picture as well as in the mind and imagination of its creator. It is indeed something like the interpretive problem I identified previously in my discussion of "authority" in *The Marriage of Heaven and Hell* (see chapter 3).

Finally, Kiralis refers abundantly to the writings of both poets to try to clarify matters, including (where it seems appropriate or useful) some analysis of the content of various of the pilgrims' tales, both with respect to the character of the teller and that of other pilgrims as well. Chaucer's own point of view is derived, as it should be, not only from the General Prologue but also from his manner in the tales themselves; and Harry Bailey's point of view ("the Host's wisdom as exhibited in his perception and consequent treatment of the characters as well as in the ordering of the tales," KK167) is attended to even more carefully with revealing results. That the problem of point of view (and hence "final meaning," if there is such a thing) is forbiddingly complex is amply demonstrated by Kiralis's maneuvering from one view to another as seems most useful or pertinent. It is difficult to know how to do otherwise. But a major consequence of this maneuvering is often to confuse Blake's view (in his picture) with Chaucer's, with the Host's, and with those of the several characters. The basic critical principles necessary are there, then, in Kiralis's essay, but his own blurring of them or expedient extrapolation from them often leads to confusion—or at least to questionable conclusions that are frequently what we know Blake would or might have thought, given his total career up to 1810, not to say what he thought, wrote, and painted-engraved between that time and his death.

I I

The main principle by which to date we have been taught to "read" Blake's painting of Spenser's characters in *The Faerie Queene* is that "it was obviously planned as a companion piece to 'Chaucer's Canterbury Pilgrims'" (Damon, p. 383). Once we assume that, Kiralis's principles of analysis follow inevitably. Thus, Damon says, putting the cart before the horse,

> In order to make the pictures balance, there is some correspondence between the two sets of characters. Redcrosse, like Chaucer's Knight, leads the cavalcade; Una, next to him, balances the Prioresse; Sir Guyon looks backward,

FIGURE 4.   Blake, *The Characters in Spenser's Faerie Queene*
(courtesy of the National Trust, Petworth; Photograph: Courtauld Institute of Art)

just as does the Pardoner; then with extended arms Amoret
holds the center of the picture, like Harry Bailey. (see figure 4)

Almost as if he were aware in midsentence that these "balancings"
are wildly confusing (even if we ignore the questionable identification
of Amoret), Damon quickly adds, "But these parallels are aesthetic
only [whatever that "only" means]; for the deeper significance, we
must study the symbols in the skies above them"—that is, Kiralis's
second critical principle, which Kiralis clearly relegates to a subsidiary, sort of generally governing, place in his own critical procedure.
One gets the sense in reading Damon's analysis of what Grant and
Brown call the supernal regions that he sees the progression of Spenser's characters "from Babylon to the New Jerusalem" as determin-
ing the identification of characters and icons in the supernal regions
(his own reference to the characters' "deeper significance" residing
"in the skies above them" to the contrary notwithstanding). Although it seems unrelated to his basic principle (right or wrong),
Damon firmly establishes Blake's characters as being "aligned in
Spenser's own order"—that is, book by book, if not canto by canto—
which in turn leads him to interpret part of the supernal region (above
the figure he calls Amoret) in terms of her character, or more pre-

cisely, in terms of his identification of Blake's central figure as Amoret. And despite Blake's clear blocking off of his foreground characters into six segments (one of which is occupied by Arthur, who thus presents a major interpretive problem), Damon sets Arthur aside, as it were (somewhat as Spenser does in his book-by-book structure), gives Amoret two books (III and IV) and therefore must claim that Britomart does not appear in the painting at all, and "assigns" to Redcrosse-Una, Guyon-Palmer, Artegall, and Calidore-Blatant Beast their respective single books.

Grant and Brown both elaborate and refine on, as well as "correct," Damon's perceptions. But they accept without question Damon's underlying critical principle: "that Blake intended [the *Chaucer* and the *Spenser*] to be companion pictures" (GB57). Thus, there are "striking" similarities between Blake's Prioress and Una and between the Wife of Bath and Britomart (Damon's Amoret); "and the further similarity between the gestures and positions of Harry Bailey and Britomart must be meaningful" (GB58). Grant and Brown do go beyond Damon's summary observations, however, in contrasting the apparent "progress" of Chaucer's pilgrims (whether in the "right" direction or not) with the generally stalled configuration of the *Spenser*. If the latter's characters are really going to get to what is assumed to be (according to Damon) the New Jerusalem in the upper left, we can tell only on the basis of what we are "able to gather about the proportions of Good and Evil revealed in the heavens of Spenser" (GB59)—again, a Damonian principle. Finally, Grant and Brown also accept (with some refinement and elaboration) the validity of Kiralis's critical procedure: (1) attention to Blake's minute particulars of posture, gesture, sight-lines, clothing, and mounts (or lack thereof); (2) pairings and groupings of characters, including Kiralis's idea of the composite feminine principle; (3) the relationship (by spear, gesture, proximity, vertical line, and the like) between individual characters, or pairs or groups of characters, to characters and icons in the supernal regions; (4) "cross-references to some other Blake works which contain figures that seem to have resemblances to those in the Spenser procession" (GB59)—this point analogous to Kiralis's reliance on Blake's "critical essay" on Chaucer as well as on some of Blake's graphic works; and (5) due and careful attention to the poet's own text (character descriptions, relationships, and so on). One final principle is commandingly operative, and that is the order of the characters, who are assumed to conform to Spenser's book-by-book arrangement—though Arthur, as I have noted, causes difficulties by "usurping" Book V in Blake's sequencing, not to mention Blake's sentencing of Duessa and Archimago, along with the properly placed but improperly still-under-control Blatant Beast, to the tail end of the procession. Kiralis, as we have seen, handles this "principle" rather loosely, whereas Damon asserts it flatly and unequivocally, interpreting the supernal-region "sequence" (Babylon to the New Jerusalem, Justice to Mercy—ignoring sun to moon) as therefore proper.

As in my dealings with Kiralis and Damon, I do not intend here a critique of Grant and Brown's specific interpretations, which they advance, disarmingly, as secondary to their descriptive and identifying intent as well as tentative. Rather, I wish to focus on the critical principles that inhere even in their descriptions and identifications, as well as in whatever interpretive comment they consequently offer. The most crucial of these principles is one borrowed from Damon: the order of the characters reflects the order of Spenser's books. Blake seems to sanction this by placing Redcrosse, Una, the lion and ass, the Dwarf, and the Dragon at the head of the "procession." If Chaucer's Knight is there at least in part because of late medieval hierarchical concerns (not to mention his telling the first tale), Spenser's Redcrosse has little to do with such hierarchy—either in Spenser or in Blake. If hierarchy were a matter Blake perceived in either poet, his placing of a child at the head of the human procession must be interpreted as a critical comment on such a conception. But in fact, it is the Dragon's head that "leads" the Spenserian characters, albeit about to be crushed by the hooves of Redcrosse's horse, not pierced by his spear or trusty (but in Blake absent) sword. This conforms as little to Spenser's arrangement as Archimago's bringing up the rear (he disappears vaguely in the middle of *The Faerie Queene*, though his falseness, to be sure, lives on in a variety of other guises).

What then are we to make of the still-alive Dragon leading the way, albeit "accompanied" by the apparently fearless (oblivious?), haloed Dwarf-child? Or of the muzzled Blatant Beast stared at (sympathetically?) by an exposed, and hence defeated, Duessa and a bound Archimago bringing up the rear—even if we "know" that one of these three remains captured or defeated in *The Faerie Queene*? Is this the reason Blake has so carefully "stalled" his "procession," wherever it may be "headed"? And what are the reasons that, out of twenty-four human figures (including "Ruddymane" but excluding the mysterious torsoless head below Calidore's horse), only three are looking directly forward: the Dwarf-child, the figure Grant and Brown identify as Scudamore, and Talus. (Unless otherwise noted, in this portion of my discussion, I shall employ the identifications that Grant and Brown supply.) But even Talus stands stolidly sideways and Scudamore's face is slightly turned to his left (just as Timias is clearly facing Belphoebe). Of these same twenty-four (an interesting multiple of six),[4] a full thirteen are looking back in one fashion or another, including five of the six "major" mounted characters (all, that is, except Arthur, who looks up in rather silly fashion—perhaps Blake's comment on Spenser's notion of spiritual vision). In addition, those who "lead" horses (Palmer, Satyrane, Talus) stand stock-still and sideways—contrasting sharply with the Dwarf-child, who really does lead in full stride. And all the arm waving has more the earmarks of a curtain call (with perhaps the exception of Calidore, who "holds" Duessa and Archimago in their place) than meaningful gesture or the purposive pointing to supernal regions that Grant and Brown make much of. No lance is at battle-ready, no sword unsheathed, even though several of the horses seem eager for action; and again only Calidore seems to be "spurring" his horse (though, like all the riders, he wears no actual spurs). He is also the most completely armored of all the knights, fitting Arthur's description in Spenser much more than Blake's Arthur does: "From top to toe no place appeared bare" (I,vii,29). I shall return to this point presently.

We can thus conclude, I think, that, like Spenser himself and unlike Chaucer (and Blake's *Chaucer*), Blake did not envision the characters of *The Faerie Queen* as a procession. Tableau is closer to the mark, but I hesitate to employ that word because of its rather narrow aesthetic implications, even though it could be argued that, for Blake, a tableau would be an appropriately graphic structural epitome of allegory (one thinks of his painting entitled *Epitome of James Hervey's "Meditations Among the Tombs"*).[5] For a better description, let us turn to Spenser himself in his Letter to Raleigh: "The generall end . . . of all the booke is to fashion a gentleman or noble person in vertuous and gentle discipline. . . . I labour to pourtraict in Arthure, before he was king, the image of a braue knight, perfected in the twelue priuate morall vertues, as Aristotle hath deuised, the which is the purpose of these first twelue bookes." Further, "in the person of Prince Arthur I sette forth magnificence in particular, which vertue for that . . . it is the perfection of all the rest, and conteineth in it them all, therefore in the whole course I mention the deedes of Arthure applyable to that vertue, which I write of in that booke." I do not wish to belabor a matter well known to Spenserians, but the crucial word here for us, and (I think) for Blake, is "conteineth": Arthur contains in himself and his magnificence all the other virtues expressed in their perfection *as they occur in each book* of *The Faerie Queene*. Ergo, each book (and its main character) is an aspect of Arthur portrayed. Spenser then goes on to explain his full plan, the Faerie Queene's "Annuall feaste" of twelve days, the twelve virtues, the twelve adventures, and so on—concluding with: "Thus much Sir, I haue briefly ouerronne to direct your vnderstanding to the wel-head of the History, that from thence gathering the whole intention of the conceit, ye may as in a handfull gripe al the discourse, which otherwise may happily seeme tedious and confused."

What Blake has given us in the painting, I think, is this "al" in a "handfull," the entire discourse at once, as it were, not in sequence—or at least not merely in sequence. Just as Spenser planned twelve to equal one, so too Blake portrays six in such fashion as to equal one—on the pattern of his zoas, as four that equal one. Such a perception of oneness, of course, in Spenser or Blake's "version" of Spenser, depends upon our imaginative power. Seen as a procession, like the *The Canterbury Tales* as well as Blake's graphic presentation of the pilgrims, Spenser's characters become what neither he nor Blake perceived them to be—pilgrims, whether to a shrine or to the New Jerusalem. Arthur does not need to make such a journey, though we may; and if we do, we will make it in our imaginative pilgrimage through Spenser's book, not on any earthly road.

Blake was well aware, however, that Spenser subscribed to sequences, cycles, and other such structures (of art and of belief), *The Shepheardes Calender*, the *Amoretti*, the *Epithalamion*, and the Mutabilitie

Cantos being only among the most prominent of these. All of them are "timely"—focusing on time, functioning in time, relying on time. Yet, at the same time, Blake may have perceived what Spenser himself intended (though to Blake, imperfectly executed)—that all these are visions of eternity even as they are productions of time (as *The Marriage* puts it)—not precisely "eterne in Mutabilitie" but immutably eterne (a critical difference with Spenser, as we have seen in previous chapters). If, in each case, our reading relies on the final efficacy of time, we shall be left with *The Ruines of Time*.[6] Eternity may be "in love with the productions of time" from the confusing diabolical-angelic shifting perspective of *The Marriage of Heaven and Hell*, but it is the ruins of those productions, not Time itself, that "builds mansions in eternity." What is unbuilt builds; "productions" obscure. Thus, those mansions that our imaginations are led to see by the artist are unbuildings, precisely in the sense of Orwell's marvelous coinage, "unpersons," disengendered from time. Cycles and sequences—of days, months, seasons—are the structures of the sublunary, vegetable world, where ends are consolable only in terms of the sequence proceeding or the cycle recycling.[7]

With this fundamental principle in mind, let us look at the supernal regions of Blake's Spenser painting. The span of time that "governs" the progression is one day, from the archer-sun to the Cynthia-moon; the latter may be rising out of her sphere only to arch back to where light rises. This collapsing of time into a kind of symbolic or visionary moment forces us to perceive the entire "procession" coinstantaneously—as we do the *Vision of the Last Judgment* or the "epitome" of Hervey's *Meditations*. While such an "instavision" is *physically* impossible (an impossibility Blake accentuates by the horizontal elongation of his painting), it is to Blake imaginatively possible if we do not *visually* proceed from left to right, as Spenser's narrative compels us, or from right to left as the painting urges us to do. Instead, this double horizontal axis forces us to abandon seeing merely "with the eyes" (a procedure that ultimately leaves us either walleyed or cross-eyed) in favor of attempting at least to see "through our eyes." "We are led to Believe a Lie," Blake wrote in *Auguries of Innocence*, "When we see not Thro the Eye" (E492); or again, even more appropriately, in *The Everlasting Gospel*:

> This Lifes dim Windows of the Soul
> Distorts the Heavens from Pole to Pole
> And leads you to Believe a Lie
> When you see with not thro the Eye.

> (E520)

The resultant imaginative-palimpsest effect (its verbal equivalent being a palindrome) is described by Blake in *A Vision of the Last Judgment*:

> All Things are comprehended in their Eternal Forms in the
> Divine body of the Saviour the True Vine of Eternity The
> Human Imagination who appeard to Me as Coming to
> Judgment. among his Saints & throwing off the Temporal
> that the Eternal might be Establishd. around him were seen
> the Images of Existences according to [their aggregate
> Imaginations (deleted by Blake)] a certain order suited to
> my Imaginative Eye.[8]

The central regnant figure to either corporeal or imagination eye is God—that is Blake's Christ-Jehovah, in whose gestural embrace the entire procession functions. My hyphenation of Blake's divinity betokens not uncertainty but rather a holding action, pending a fuller "explication" of that figure in the painting. Suffice it to say here, as Henry Summerfield points out in an important essay,[9] that by the time of the Spenser painting Blake had developed "a daring theology rooted in Boehme to enable him to sustain with equal fervor a passionate devotion to the trinitarian God of Christianity and an unremitting protest against the life-denying cruelty of the moral law and the created universe." Separated from Christ, Jehovah becomes cruel, tyrannical, destructive, and "leprous," the god of this world, ensconced on his throne "out there" and therefore distinct from the Divine Humanity in every man. But the "Names Divine" are "Jesus & Jehovah" (E269), Their-Its-His spectrous shadow the Angel of the Divine Presence.[10] In Blake's painting, at the still point of the heavenly bodies' diurnal movement, "God" appears quite obviously as what he "seems" to be, the Urizenic God of this (and Spenser's) World, whose agents on earth are the very corporeal, warlike (or otherwise fallen) creatures below. The figure with the scales to his left is with equal clarity Justice or Astraea, one who brings "out number weight & measure in a year of dearth" (*Marriage*, E36), whose abode is the stars, who holds her balance beneath what may be (if we can credit Grant and Brown's shrewd guess) the Covering Cherub or Nature or the Angel of the Divine Presence (or all three), and who looks (if at anyone) at the fiercest and most ominous human figure in the painting, Talus. In *Milton*, Blake puts the case for justice in his universe succinctly: "Temperance, Prudence, Justice, Fortitude the four pillars of tyranny."[11] But, lest I get too far ahead of myself, let us return to the geography and population of the painting's supernal realm.

Though hardly a dominant figure, the poet-artist seated in the clouds above the left hand of the God of This World, and to the immediate right of Justice's scales, claims immediate attention if only because he is so obviously not a "character" in *The Faerie Queene* (for a blow-up of this section of the painting, see figure 9). The figure is a fascinating conflation of at least two of Blake's previous graphic-poets, one in *All Religions Are One*, the other in the twelfth illustration to Gray's *The Bard*. The former Erdman identifies persuasively as "a youthful John the Baptist" seated with legs crossed, as in the Spenser painting, "the prophetic mantle on his knee."[12] The inscription on the plate is "The Voice of one crying in the Wilderness," rather splendidly appropriate to the poet-prophet-artist in a Spenserian universe dominated by the God of this World. The Gray illustration is of Spenser himself "creating his fairies" (Blake's own title to the picture), one of whom stands, somewhat timorously, on Spenser's left palm (see figure 2).[13] While there is little physical likeness between these two—the Gray figure clad in a full-length robe with legs uncrossed and John the Baptist naked except for the mantle on his thigh—the latter does look at least a little like the Spenser-painting figure. Grant and Brown suggest Blake's *Il Penseroso* design entitled "Milton and His Dream" and the small figure at the lower left of *Jerusalem* 36[41] as possible clarifiers "of this enigmatic area of the Spenser picture" (GB83). I find no clues in the Milton illustration but the *Jerusalem* "poet-figure" is tantalizingly pertinent. Erdman identifies him unequivocally as Blake,[14] pen at rest on his left thigh after having inscribed in mirror-writing on a gigantic scroll,

> Each Man is in his Spectre's power
> Untill the arrival of that hour,
> When his Humanity awake
> And cast his Spectre into the Lake.
>
> (E184)

The poet-figure is (possibly) naked and is looking up solicitously to the gargantuan despairing Albion, for whom, at the conclusion of the previous plate, Los has already begun to build "the stubborn structure of the Language, acting against / Albions melancholy, who must else have been a Dumb despair" (ll. 59–60, E183).

This concatenation of echoes or analogues suggests that the figure in the Spenser painting is either Blake (Los) or Spenser, depending upon how we look at it. The former's book (or drawing board), in which he writes (or on which he draws or engraves) without looking at it, generates a winged figure flying upward, its left wing cutting the "rainbow-roofed enclave made up of a cloud streamer from the cloud halo of Jove . . . and the right wing of Nature, the Spread-winged

Presence";[15] the latter creates the "History" that unfolds itself below. But what disturbs this rather neat, not to say convenient, ambiguity is the presence of "a slightly smaller 'double' figure" that "appears to be seated" on the poet-artist's left thigh and from whom "two or more figures" seem to issue "and then go up the cloud-steps, which are on a wall above the scales of Justice, to the bent right leg of the Spread-winged Presence" (GB83). If Grant and Brown are correct here (this area of the painting is frustratingly faint and indistinct), it would seem that the "double" is Spenser, whose creations (fairies or not) find their "home" only in the world of the ominous Angel of the Divine Presence and its less ominous appearing but no less pernicious goddess of earthly justice and punishment. The book on which the "Blake-Los figure" leans his left arm may thus be *The Faerie Queene* itself, firmly closed and unenterable except via the imaginative inventions of the "true artist," who writes-engraves-paints without consulting it. This last detail, I should add, differs from plate 10 of *The Marriage of Heaven and Hell*, in which "Blake," as Erdman calls him, sits cross-legged to the devil's left and copies down in the book on his lap the Proverbs of Hell on the devil's scroll.[16]

That the figure in the Spenser painting is Blake, The Prophet, his vision unclouded and undeterred by the Spenserian demon who would dictate to him the truths contained in the book, is attested to not merely by the John the Baptist allusion but also by the striking similarity of his pose to Blake's wash-drawing after one of Adam Ghisi's engravings of Michelangelo's Sistine frescoes—the one representing Daniel, the only prophet-figure included in that series of drawings (see figure 5). "In the original fresco," as Jenijoy LaBelle points out, "a shadowy spirit hovers behind Daniel's left shoulder," one that Ghisi changes into "a fat-cheeked baby who seems to be speaking," a detail that Blake repeats but lightens considerably into a wraithlike presence.[17] One wonders whether the "double" in the Spenser painting is a child (it is impossible to distinguish it sharply enough to be sure), or Michelangelo's original "shadowy spirit," or both. If both, the child would be analogous perhaps to the child on the cloud of the *Introduction* to *Songs of Innocence*, "inspiring" the piper—the hovering, intimidating presence in the Spenser painting therefore Spenser himself with his book. In any case, Blake's Daniel figure has a heavy tablet or volume or drawing board on his lap and, while looking at it, copies out onto a drawing board to his right what he reads/sees—or perhaps, as LaBelle suggests, writes "a commentary on it,"[18] just as the Blake figure in the Spenser painting "writes" his commentary on *The Faerie Queene*.

Blake, of course, is a commentator par excellence on his own po-

FIGURE 5.   Blake, drawing after Adam Ghisi's engraving of
Michelangelo's *Daniel*

(courtesy of the British Museum)

etry, most obviously by way of his illuminations but also, as I have argued earlier in this book and elsewhere, via his manipulations of contextualized allusions that provide various angles of perception by which to construe his own poetry as well as to probe its "greater truth." In this context, and that of the poet figure in the Spenser painting, one must at least wonder whether he was critically sophisticated enough to recognize Spenser's proems in *The Faerie Queene* as commentaries on the poet's own text rather than, or in addition to, their being "introductions" to their respective books. While I do not think I can answer that question definitively, let me hazard some guesses (based largely on Leigh DeNeef's provocative analyses of the proems)[19] that may well have some bearing on the mysterious poet and his hovering presence in Blake's Spenser painting.

In the proem to Book I, for example, Spenser asserts his guidance by Clio (the muse of history), Cupid, Venus, Mars, and Elizabeth, aligning himself as well with Virgil. Obviously none of these hovering ghosts would have pleased Blake at all. Spenser's effort was therewith fatally compromised from the start—a self-damning cemented by the proem's concluding abasement of Spenser before Elizabeth, his "thoughts too humble and too vile," his style too "afflicted." Analogously, we may regard the painting's poet-figure as Blake hovered over by Spenser, but wraithlike enough to call into question any suggestion of inspiration, much less Blake's self-abasement. Or, more interestingly (and characteristically), we may be invited to regard the poet figure as Spenser, in "lowly . . . weeds" but otherwise unidentifiable as shepherdlike, hovered over intimidatingly by Blake. If, as DeNeef argues, "the proems seek 'rightly to define' the metaphor that expresses the poet's presence in the poems" (p. 91), Blake's visual "metaphor" may be explicated, depending upon how we "read" the painting, as a Virgil-haunted Spenser, a Spenserian Blake, or a Blakean Spenser. Or, to put the cart and horse in proper order, the way we "read" *The Characters in Spenser's Faerie Queene* is determined by the nature of our perception of its "author." That is to say, if the ultimate authority for our interpretation is Spenser (emulating Virgil and inspired by Elizabeth), we will see him in Blake's poet-figure and interpret the characters, scenes, and icons in that light. This is essentially Grant and Brown's procedure, qualified by their knowledge of Blake (as it would not be if the painter were unknown or known to be someone other than Blake). If the authority is a Spenserian Blake, we will read Blake's painting as an illustration of *The Faerie Queene*, faithful to its text and differing only in degree or emphasis from an unknown painter's pictorialization. But, if the poet-figure is a Blakean (or Blakeanized) Spenser, the "rules" of interpretation change radically.

Something of the same relationship as this last obtains in Spenser's consciousness of his relationship as poet to his created poet-figure, Archimago. As Nohrnberg points out, echoed by DeNeef, the potential analogy between the two figures "offers to equate Archimago's activity with the imagination concurrently shaping Spenser's poem," Nohrnberg adjudging this equation positively.[20] But, as DeNeef goes on to argue, the relationship cannot be so unequivocally estimated, for Archimago is "the duplicity that inhabits all metaphors" (p. 97). He is thus the progenitor of all subsequent "false-speakers" in *The Faerie Queene*, and Spenser "defines the success of his own heroes as a process of 'defacing' the false fictions created by his poetic antagonists" (pp. 97–98). Here, it seems to me, is an invaluable clue to

Blake's poet figure—if not to his "absolute" identity, at least to his function in the painting. As what I have awkwardly called "Blakean Spenser," he is Archimago-like in deliberately misreading as well as misspeaking (mispainting) *The Faerie Queene*, much as the Devil in *The Marriage of Heaven and Hell* misspeaks all the eternal verities. But, as such, Blake is shrewdly aware, as he was in *The Marriage*, that Archimagos, like Spenserian poets, "create 'feigned images' by metaphors and parodic doubling" (p. 99). Thus, if Spenser invites us "to question a poetic method [the dark conceit] that so willingly adopts the strategies of its announced antagonists" (p. 104), we know already that, by the time of his Spenser painting, Blake had developed a long history of doing precisely that—verbally, graphically, and compositely. Los creates systems not merely to be free of another man's, but to free individuals (readers) from all systems. Turning the world upside down results but in the same old world, upside down. A thoroughly Blakeanized Spenser, instead of a Virgilian or Ariostoan or Spenserian Spenser, is neither illuminating nor, more importantly, redemptive.

If, as DeNeef claims, Spenser appropriates Archimagoan strategies "to defend [himself, and his text] against those antagonists" (p. 104), Blake goes him one better. Self-defense is not the issue. The imaginative freedom of the reader is. Therefore, Blake will risk Archimagoan "deceit" to purge Spenser of Archimagoism; he will create "feigned images" by "metaphoric and parodic doubling," which, by means of their very duplicity, will rescue Spenser's true poetness from its "aboundance of an idle braine / . . . and painted forgery" to reveal not its "matter of just memory" (*Faerie Queene* II,proem,1) but its "matter" of just imagination. And he will "deface" the "false fictions created by" the Spenser who, in these terms, is his *poetic antagonist.* "Opposition is true Friendship" (E42), we recall. That Blake found in Spenser's proems, or in *The Faerie Queene* as a whole, precedent for his own Los-like procedure seems to me most unlikely, but even if glimmers of Spenser's sensitivity to the perils of his own *modus operandi* shone through now and again, Blake not only would have been pleased, but clearly would have regarded such critical diabolism as a sign of Spenser's redemptiveness. Those glimmers, then, may be inherent in the complexity of Blake's poet-artist character in this alien poetic land of another poet-artist. Perhaps he is Archimago redeemed, not merely shackled, as Blake portrays him, like a Michelangeloesque slave and, like the Blatant Beast, still powerfully present in Spenser's world. One suspects that Blake knew full well, and meant us to see, that handcuffing Archimago is like imprisoning Proteus in a sieve.

Grant and Brown, then, seem to offer false alternative readings of the scene:

> It would appear that the Artist does not need a book open before him to do his work; Blake's license with Spenser's text is consistent with this principle. But the appearance of a double (Spectre of Los) in the lap of the Artist, together with the evident stream of figures to [the Spread-winged Presence], would imply that the Artist is less liberal than he would like to think. Whether this is Blake's assessment of Spenser's limitation or whether it is Blake's confession of his own shortcomings is hard to decide. (GB83)

The artist is not copying *The Faerie Queene*, nor is he imitating Spenser. He is instead copying his imagination of *The Faerie Queene* even as he reproduces its external, visible form. "Men think they can Copy Nature as Correctly as I copy Imagination this they will find Impossible" (*Public Address*, E574). "License" or "liberality" has nothing to do with the matter. As Daniel reads the words of the writing on the wall, he interprets its truth—that Belshazzar's kingdom has been "numbered" by God, and He has finished it; that Belshazzar "art weighed in the balances, and art found wanting"; and that his "kingdom is divided" (Dan. 5:25–28). Moreover, Daniel's final vision is of apocalypse, given him and interpreted first by Gabriel, then by Michael; and Michael concludes by saying, "But thou, O Daniel, shut up the words, and seal the book, even to the time of the end" (Dan. 12:4). Perhaps this is the same closed book the artist in the Spenser painting leans on, now transformed from *The Faerie Queene* to the Book of Revelation.

That Blake's artist-prophet does not reign in the world of the painting is clear (despite his head's being fractionally higher than the God of This World's); but he does seem to be unaffected by the God's sceptre or rod and is oblivious to (or studiously ignores) Justice and her scales. Nevertheless, he is functioning under the grotesque parody of the Holy Ghost, the Spread-winged Presence, which may constitute, therefore, the necessary conditions of art in this world. Yet, as physically unprepossessing and unphysically dominant as he is, he remains eternally youthful, despite the passage of time before his face. Sitting behind the entire panorama, he is the behind-the-scenes god of this picture's universe. He is not the Los who forges abstractions into existence; he is the Los of the eternal printing press. More grandly, he is the Imagination itself, whose titanic power is displayed in the Christ-Jehovah figure with the universe in his lap. "Know that after Christs death, he became Jehovah" (*Marriage of Heaven and Hell*,

E35), the Jehovah who, as Summerfield points out, "is Jehovah the Divine Humanity whose Covenant is the forgiveness of sins, whose Spirit is the Divine Mercy, whose visions inspire the poet."[21]

III

What I have been suggesting with respect to the painting's supernal realms (and by extension to the mortals below) may be summed up as a kind of phantasmagoria in which each character and thing is, and is not, merely itself. What it is imaginatively can only be determined by our imaginative "gripe" of the whole in our hand, precisely along the lines of Blake's famous quatrain:

> To see a World in a Grain of Sand
> And a Heaven in a Wild Flower
> Hold Infinity in the palm of your hand
> And Eternity in an hour.

(E490)

(It is not often enough remarked that Blake says here, in order to "see" the infinite world, we must "hold" in our hand the physically unholdable "objects" that are in our minds and very being.) Another way to express this principle is to say that the painting depicts Spenser's characters frozen into an eternal moment that negates (or supersedes) their fundamental temporality, as that is governed by the "movement" of sun (upper right) to moon (upper left) as well as by the suggestion of cyclical time in Cynthia's graceful curving upward to "become" once again the archer-child of the sun. Spatially speaking, the characters ought to be moving, as Damon suggests, from the Babylonian Tower of Babel in the upper right to the New Jerusalem in the upper left but, as we have seen, virtually nothing below moves at all. At the same time, the archer-sun and Cynthia-moon are totally dominated (perhaps even stalled) by the eternal, fantastically haloed sun of Jove-Urizen-Christ-Jehovah. This domination is accentuated by the moon's being but a thin crescent, lit only on the right by the eternal sun's rays (surely not by the infant archer far to the right); by the "world," despite its angelic cradlers, being totally Jove's oyster; and, finally, by the unmoving symmetry of the entire supernal realm. We need to look further at the particulars of that realm.

If the presence of the poet in "eternity" seems proper and right, we must wonder about Astraea with her anti-Blakean scales and the stars that halo (and thus compromise) her halo—for it is between her and the God of This World that the poet is both squeezed in, as it were, and dwarfed. All of her signa are unpropitious. Except in the apocalypse of Blake's great paintings of the Last Judgment, ever since *The French Revolution* (see ll. 211–19, for example: E295–96), stars are inevitably associated with, and allegorically constitutive of, Urizenic tyranny, the oppressive solar system with its concentric, imprisoning circular orbits ("starry wheels") ever turning, ever grinding like a mill with complicated wheels. But Blake's astronomy is far more precise than this generalization suggests. The *locus classicus* of this precision is Book 2 of *Milton*, with its geography and genealogy of the "Covering Cherub" and the "Mundane Shell" (37[41]–38[43], E137–38). No matter at the moment that these are "in" Milton himself; most germane to my purposes here is that we first see the "Twelve monstrous dishumanizd terrors Synagogues of Satan" that are, in Damon's words, "all the old, false mythologies," based in large part on Milton's catalog in *Paradise Lost* (I,392–521) of the fallen angels as the future gods of the heathen religions.[22] But they are also the zodiacal characters, of which Blake's four zoas ("Four Starry Universes," E393) are the "redeemed" (that is to say, humanized) version. The "dishumanizd terrors" are also part of the Mundane Shell's galaxy of the Ptolemaic forty-eight constellations that include the zodiac, fifteen constellations in the southern hemisphere, and twenty-one in the northern hemisphere. Blake lumps the hemispheric divisions under, respectively, Orion (the giant slain by Diana, the goddess of chastity) and Ophiucus (the giant who, as in Blake's *Laocoön*, was caught in the embrace of the twin serpents of good and evil, the "cloven fiction" of "fallen morality").[23]

Other numerical permutations suggest themselves here and are employed by Blake (for example, the forty-eight Levite cities), but they need not detain us beyond recognizing the astral universe Blake has created in his Spenser painting. With some imagination, we may find the entire zodiac herein pictured, although for the moment I wish to concentrate on Blake's Astraea (see figure 9 for a blow-up of this section of the painting). She is the constellation Virgo holding the constellation Libra in her right hand; thus, she is not merely Justice and the daughter of Zeus and Themis (herself a goddess of law and justice) but Blake's archetypal Virgin, Whore of Babylon, Female Will. Moreover, Blake surely knew that Astraea deserted the earth when men grew corrupt, thus becoming the sort of virginal sky-god that, for him, epitomizes all such sterile, allegorical separations and abstractions—indeed, all religions.[24] As Spenser put it succinctly, she

> Return'd to heauen, whence she deriu'd her race;
> Where she hath now an euerlasting place,
> Mongst those twelue signes, which nightly we doe see
> The heauens bright-shining baudricke to enchase;

And is the *Virgin*, sixt in her degree,
And next her selfe her righteous ballance hanging bee.[25]

I do not suppose Blake "needed" this passage to create his supernal Astraea figure, but that he did have it in mind is suggested by her textual proximity in *The Faerie Queene*, and her spatial relationship in Blake's painting, to Talus, Spenser's juistically retributive man "of yron mould, / Immoueable, resistlesse, without end," who executes "her stedfast doome" (VI,i,12). As Upton remarks in his edition of *The Faerie Queene*, "who is ignorant of Talus, mentioned by Plato, Apollonius Rhodius, etc. and by almost all the mythologists?" In that tradition, Talus (or Talos) is denominated "brazen" for his carrying around with him the laws carved on brazen tablets.[26] The relevance of this to Blake's Urizen and his brazen and iron books and laws needs no further comment here, but I shall have more to say of Talus later.

A word more needs to be said of Astraea's scales. They are as pernicious as stars and, without exception in Blake's works, as Urizenic as brazen quadrants and golden compasses. In a unique passage in *The Four Zoas*, we learn how those scales got "out there" in Astraea's hand: they were "rent from the faint Heart of the Fallen Man" (*Four Zoas* II, E319), which, as we know from *The Divine Image* of *Songs of Innocence*, is not merely the seat of mercy but *is* Mercy (E12). For Blake that is the only justice; he will have no "truck" with the idea of Truth and Justice returning to men, Mercy sitting between, as in Milton's *Nativity Ode*. Perhaps even closer to Blake's conception is Spenser's Mercilla, about whom I have already spoken (from Blake's point of view) pejoratively, but who, despite her virginal, queenly status and accouterments of majesty, at least initially (or is it, merely, ostensibly?) does resist the demands of the bloodthirsty witnesses against Duessa for "justice." She,

> whose Princely breast was touched nere
> With piteous ruth of her so wretched plight,
> Though plaine she saw by all, that she did heare,
> That she of death was guiltie found by right,
> Yet would not let iust vengeance on her light;
> But rather let in stead there of to fall
> Few perling drops from her faire lampes of light;
> The which she couering with her purple pall
> Would haue the passion hid, and vp arose withall.
>
> (V,ix,50)

But, as Seneca noted, clemency is one thing, pity another. Indeed, the latter is as much a "vice" as is its opposite, the barbarity of Talus.[27] The bloodiness of Book V as a whole submerges the Mercilla episode so effectively that Spenser scholars to this day must, rather acrobatically, refine the book's purpose to what they regard as Spenser's overall intent. Perhaps one of Spenser's turn-of-the-century editors is right about Mercilla: "it is a meagre conception, and is not born of sympathetic imagination."[28] Whether that is at least one way Blake read the passage we have no way of knowing, but had he known (as he probably did from Upton) that the entire episode is a kind of whitewash of Queen Elizabeth's deciding upon the fate of Mary, Queen of Scots, he would have peremptorily abandoned his momentary affection for Mercilla and put her in orbit with Astraea-Virgo.

If Blake's Astraea, then, is "really" Mercy, she is more Mercilla than she ought to be for the good of Spenser's characters beneath. It may be a hopeful sign that no Urizenic "massy weights" freight the pans, as they do in *The Book of Urizen* (20:36–37, E80), and that what may be a human figure issues from the left pan; but I tend to think that the latter (he, she, or it) is probably only a Scorpio escaping from Libra as Blake's zodiac moves toward the Sagittarian poet-figure in one of his guises, Blake (he was born 28 November). As an archer, his sign is far more appropriate than the little archer of the sun Blake pictures, for Blake's arrows are "the Arrows of Love" and "of Intellect," his bow "Mercy & Loving-kindness" (*Jerusalem* 97:12–13, 98:7, E256–57)—or, in another verbal incarnation, "the bows of my Mind & the Arrows of Thought" (letter to Butts, E722). Moreover, in its nonrainbow signification, the hovering presence (clearly ominous) is directly above the scales, and hence above the Urizenic, Satanic Talus. Directly pertinent to this aspect of Presence-Scales-Talus is a passage from *Jerusalem* that is so relevant to *The Faerie Queene* as a whole that one wonders if it is a Blakean summary of the "dark" side of Spenser's conception, that is, that side emergent when Spenser was most clearly not of the devil's party:

Envying stood the enormous Form at variance with Itself
In all its Members: in eternal torment of love & jealousy:
Drivn forth by Los time after time from Albions cliffy shore,
Drawing the free loves of Jerusalem into infernal bondage;
That they might be born in contentions of Chastity & in
Deadly Hate between Leah & Rachel, Daughters of Deceit & Fraud
Bearing the Images of various Species of Contention
And Jealousy & Abhorrence & Revenge & deadly Murder.
Till they refuse liberty to the male.

(69:6–14, E223)

When this happens, all

The Jealousies become Murderous: uniting together in Rahab
A Religion of Chastity, forming a Commerce to sell Loves
With Moral Law, an Equal Balance, not going down with decision.
Therefore the Male severe & cruel filld with stern Revenge:
Mutual Hate returns & mutual Deceit & mutual Fear.
(69:33–37, E223)

Thus, hate balances hate, deceit deceit, fear fear, the moral law in equilibrium without decision. Such a conception applies at least to much, if not all, of *The Faerie Queene* when read in simplistic allegorical terms; but its more specific and direct pertinence is to Spenserian Justice as that is incorporated into Artegall, Talus, and Arthur, who are the three main figures, as identified by Grant and Brown, below Astraea and her scales.

Although there are other scales in Blake, in the graphic as well as the poetic work, the most striking analogue to the Astraea figure is the gigantic crowned female in the *Night Thoughts* series, illustrating, according to Blake's mark in Young's text, the line "When faith is virtue, reason makes it so." If that were not pernicious enough, Blake found Young writing earlier on the same illustrated page:

reason rebaptized me when adult;
Weigh'd true and false in her impartial scale;
My heart became the convert of my head;
And made that choice, which once was but my fate.
On argument alone my faith is built:
Reason pursued is faith.[29]

Obviously nothing has been learned from Spenser's day to Young's.

Although I am reasonably convinced of the justness of the foregoing analysis, it is difficult not to be disturbed by the fact that a good deal of what I have ascribed to "Astraea" is applicable as well to the seemingly compensatory soaring figure in the upper left (see figure 7). For, as the virginal moon-goddess Cynthia, she is also Spenser's Elizabeth and therefore the Faerie Queene herself. She emanates out of the dark side of the moon whose (presumably) benign rays (Blake's state of Beulah) shine away from her—unless we are to take her to be a humanized version of this radiation; and, with a facial expression that appears to me less benign than Astraea's more-or-less neutral look, she flies above the Palmer (Prudence, rationality), her moon hovering over the figure Grant and Brown identify as Belphoebe, that is, Virginity. Furthermore, spatially she "balances" the sun in the upper right far more symmetrically than she would if acting (as we might expect her to do were she Blake's moony realm, Beulah) as a contrary to Astraea, who in fact has no figure to "balance" her in the supernal realm. Thus, Damon's pronouncing her "Mercy" (the expected and conventional contrary of Astraea-Justice) is clearly in error—as Grant and Brown note.

Then there is Cynthia's moon itself. In his study of "Blake's Moon-Ark Symbolism," Nicholas Warner identifies all crescent moons as moon-arks and therefore of good omen—associated with Beulah, Noah, Ololon, and, more broadly, with Blake's "themes of spiritual degeneration and ultimate redemption through the saving power of the imagination and of Christ's mercy." The moon-ark image itself is "an image of both spiritual illumination and spiritual transportation from one state of moral consciousness to another."[30] All of the moon-arks he discusses, however, are those astronomically impossible figures that "float" either on air or water, horns upward as prow and stern. Clearly Cynthia's is not one of these—or if it is, we must see it as in the process of spilling out its precious cargo of "saved" souls who somehow, happily, fly safely away. The closest analogue to Cynthia's crescent in Blake's graphic works is one Warner does not comment on, though he does comment at some length on the plate. It is plate 33 of *Jerusalem*, the bottom third of which is occupied by what Warner describes as an "Ulroic scene . . . presided over by a bat-winged creature."[31] It is indeed a scene of dread and chaos, brooded over (mimicking the Holy Ghost as dove) by the archetypal spectre, who even causes the lighted crescent of the moon to be turned away from the sun's source of its light. No such spectre controls Cynthia in the Spenser painting, and her lighted crescent is toward the sun, suggesting at least some form of redemption taking place, despite the nagging negatives of virginity and queenly sovereignity.

A possible clue to this redemptiveness is in Blake's *Vision of the Last Judgment*, in which "the Church Universal" is "represented by a Woman Surrounded by Infants." This "State," which is "of the Innocent Heathen & the Uncivilized Savage who having not the Law do by Nature the things contained in the Law . . ., appears like a Female crownd with Stars driven into the Wilderness She has the Moon under her feet" (E559). In the painting of the Last Judgment itself, her posture and bordering children parallel the Spenser painting figure, which "is honored with a plate halo which is surrounded by clouds and perhaps by multitudes. . . . In the train of her outspread arms many indistinct figures are indicated" (GB81). She may, then, as Grant and Brown suggest, be Blake's Ololon, these two identifiable by way of their mutual ''mooniness'' with Beulah. In *Milton*, for example, ''the Sons & Daughters of Ololon descended'' into Beulah,

> Crying with one voice. Give us a habitation & a place
> In which we may be hidden under the shadow of wings.
>
> (30:4, 24–25, E129)

But if, in *Milton*, Milton reunites with his emanation, Ololon, no such reunion (or any other kind of union) occurs for Cynthia in the Spenser painting. She is, nevertheless, the ''highest'' figure in the panorama, indeed about to soar out of sight into some supersupernal realm—or, more germanely, out of *The Faerie Queene*. She is also, despite Blake's characteristic skewing or violation of perspective and therefore of respective sizes, the closest ''human'' figure to the New Jerusalem in the upper left, which is, in this sense, the ''real'' sun as opposed to that in the upper right. In this light, it can be argued that her soaring from the moon's dark side is ''right,'' the Copernican-Newtonian solar system that dictates the configuration of her brilliant crescent being deserted for that greater light that is Jerusalem. Pressing Blake's imaginative logic to its extreme, one can argue that ''Cynthia'' is thus Beulah becoming Jerusalem (the woman as well as the city), which is, for both Milton and Blake, that brighter Sun-Son.

Lest such an interpretation of the upper left of the painting be thought entirely idiosyncratic, we should recall Damon's brilliant suggestion that the ''Church Universal'' of the Last Judgment painting and the Cynthia-Mercy-Moon goddess of the Spenser painting are not only one and the same but that both are identifiable with ''the woman of *Revelation* with the moon under her feet.'' Damon has the chapter wrong, but he is nonetheless right.

> And there appeared a great wonder in heaven; a woman clothed with the sun, and the moon under her feet, and upon her head a crown of twelve stars:
> And she being with child cried, travailing in birth, and pained to be delivered.
> And there appeared another wonder in heaven; and behold a great red dragon, having seven heads and ten horns, and seven crowns upon his heads.
> And his tail drew the third part of the stars of heaven, and did cast them to the earth: and the dragon stood before the woman which was ready to be delivered, for to devour her child as soon as it was born.
> And she brought forth a man child, who was to rule all nations with a rod of iron: and her child was caught up unto God, and to his throne.

> And the woman fled into the wilderness, where she hath
> a place prepared of God. (Rev. 12:1–6)

We recall that, in his description of the Last Judgment painting,
Blake presents his "Church Universal" as "a Female crownd with
Stars driven into the Wilderness She has the moon under her feet."
The allusion to Revelation is unmistakable. Moreover, in having
Cynthia-woman of Revelation swoop up over Una and her compan-
ions (including what Revelation calls "that old serpent" and Spenser
"that old dragon"), Blake reminds us of Spenser's reliance on Revelation, especially in Book I of *The Faerie Queene*. But there, of course,
there is no "man child." Just a dwarf, whom Blake converts into the
haloed leader of Spenser's "procession," armed not with Talus's flail
(the "rod of iron" of Revelation) but with "the blood of the Lamb,
and by the word of their testimony" (Rev. 12:11). Hence, almost certainly, Blake carefully absents Una's lamb, for she has given birth to
The Lamb, "The Word of God," out of whose "mouth goeth a sharp
sword, that with it he should smite nations: and he shall rule them
with a rod of iron" (Rev. 19:13, 15).

Finally, one of the seven angels calls John to "Come hither, I will
shew thee the bride, the Lamb's wife."

> And he carried me away in the spirit to a great and high
> mountain, and shewed me that great city, the holy Jerusa-
> lem, descending out of heaven from God. (Rev. 21:9–10)

But he "saw no temple therein: for the Lord God Almighty and the
Lamb are the temple of it" (Rev. 21:22), that is, we enter into the
Divine Body of Imagination just as it is in us, eternally, if we would
only find the way.

Spenser simply had it wrong, or, at the very least, Redcrosse perceives it wrong. For him the New Jerusalem *is* a city, the road to
which is an arduous and "painefull pilgrimage," and the entry into
which God has jealously reserved

> For those to dwell in, that are chosen his,
> His chosen people purg'd from sinfull guilt.
>
> *(Faerie Queene* I,x,61,57)

Even worse, once Redcrosse has won his "famous victorie" over
"that old Dragon" (x,60; xi,proem), he deserts the Truth, abandons
the long, hard road to the New Jerusalem, and "Vnto his Faerie
Queene" does "back . . . returne" "and *Vna* left to mourne"
(xii,41). It is she, not Blake's "Cynthia" in the painting, who is the
real "Sunne of the world, great glory of the sky," "Diuine re-
semblaunce, beauty soueraine rare, / Firme Chastity" (VI,x,28,

27). Had he recalled this particular passage (or any number of others like it) Blake would have been appalled, not merely because "Sunne of the world" echoes his own "God of this world," but because Elizabeth here is a "sky-god" and, compounding her perniciousness, merely a "resemblance," an allegory, of chastity. In a classic double take, we see Blake's Cynthia to be Cynthia after all, her telltale eyeline, as Grant and Brown note, being toward Britomart—who is, as we shall see, Cynthia. "He who sees the Ratio only sees himself only" (E3). Beulah is safe in Jerusalem's bosom and/or the Divine Body of Imagination, who (as the Dwarf-Child) calmly, amid all the bustle and confusion, walks "forward thro' Eternity" (*Milton* 21[23]:14, E115), taking Jerusalem with him. That is the "pilgrimage" to end all pilgrimages, or better yet, the pilgrimage that annihilates the validity of all earthly pilgrimages, however "bright"; for the little child that shall lead them leads them but in the mental-imaginative travel of which Blake's *Mental Traveller* is the Urizenic-Orcian parody, the dance macabre of cycles:

> the Babe the Babe is Born
> . . . .
> And none can touch that frowning form
> Except it be a Woman Old
> She nails him down upon the Rock
> And all is done as I have told.
>
> (E486)

Now that we have toured the heavens of Blake's painting, it is time to recapitulate a little and to regroup toward one final assault on its seemingly endless shifting values. It is not only possible but indeed we may be invited by Blake to see the entire supernal realm as symmetrical, not only in time but also in space: the God of This World at center, Babylon and the New Jerusalem on his far left and right respectively, archer-sun and Cynthia-moon similarly arranged. The poet-figure aside for the moment, Astraea, especially given her imposing size, seems the only oddly placed figure—at least until we recognize that she is "balanced" by the myriad human figures to Jove's right (see figure 10). They include what may be the horsemen of the apocalypse or merely Grant and Brown's unidentifiable "two or more elongated horses with riders blowing horns" (GB81), a few moving upward from St. Paul's and the "Gothic portal" (GB82), most of them sweeping, in one fashion or another, toward the moon and Cynthia.[32] No comparable human movement clusters around or near Astraea, who may be seen to be functioning, then, in a nonhumanized (not inhuman but unhuman, Urizenic) world, a kind of translation by

Blake of her mythical flight from the decadent earth to become a sky-god.

If this symmetrical spatialization is indeed as I have described it, Blake has presented us in the supernal realms with both "procession" and an evocation of contraries. The former "moves" in the same direction as *The Faerie Queene* characters below, while its fluidity increases markedly as the eye moves from right to left. The most obvious signs of progression are from the Tower of Babel on the far right to Jerusalem on the far left, from the sun to the moon, from the unpeopled city below the sun to the swarming humans leading to, and surrounding, Cynthia. Concomitantly, we are moved from the inhuman, virgin-inspired and virgin-dominated justice of Astraea to the modern institutionalizing of religion in the vaginal "church" and St. Paul's Cathedral (both "ministering" to humans who, like the children in *Holy Thursday* of *Songs of Innocence*, soar in song and "radiance" past these structures to "the seats of heaven among"— E13)—thence to, and through, Beulah to Jerusalem, the city and "church" that is itself human.

In one sense, this "progression" is Blake's "correction" of Arthur's quest for the Faerie Queene, as that is imaged in small by Redcrosse's tutelage in the House of Holinesse, where Faith, Hope, Charity, and Mercy (which Blake might well have been attracted to) are, to Blake's mind, overwhelmed by the likes of Humility, Zeal, Reverence, Obedience, and, worst of all, Penance (with his "yron whip"), Remorse, and Repentance (I,x,4–34)—all based on a conception of "religion" that was anathema to Blake. Even if he were able to "stomach" the flagellations of the House of Penance, Blake would have been repelled by the fact that Spenser's Hierusalem is merely the heavenly Cleopolis presided over by the virgin Fairy Queen Elizabeth. As Blake put it, making the same point in his own mythopoeic context, "the Shadows of Beulah terminate in rocky Albion" (*Milton* 31[34]:11, E130), that is to say, the realm of "The Rocky Law of Condemnation & double Generation, & Death" (*Jerusalem* 44[30]:37, E193). This rocky law is that "Judgment" (like Astraea's, the God of This World's, Nature's, Spenser's)

> that is arisen among the
> Zoa's of Albion where a Man dare hardly to embrace
> His own Wife, for the terrors of Chastity that they call
> By the name of Morality.
>
> (*Jerusalem* 32[36]:44–47, E179)

If Satan's "Watch Fiends" ever found this "place" (Beulah), "they would call it Sin / And lay its Heavens & their inhabitants in blood of punishment" (*Jerusalem* 37[41]:19–20, E183), precisely what happens to Redcrosse in the House of Penance. There, in Blake's "version," the "Shadowy Female," "outstretching her Twenty seven Heavens over Albion,"

> will put on the Human Form & take the Image of God
> Even Pity & Humanity but my Clothing shall be Cruelty
> And I will put on Holiness as a breastplate & as a helmet
> And all my ornaments shall be of the gold of broken hearts
> And the precious stones of anxiety & care & desperation & death
> And repentance for sin & sorrow & punishment & fear.
>
> *(Milton* 18[20]:2-3, 19-24, E111)

Both Spenser and Blake are drawing on Ephesians, but Blake's diabolizing of both the Bible and Spenser by making his Christian warrior the nameless shadowy female not only ruthlessly subverts the conventional trope but also provides us invaluable clues to his pictorial interpretation of both Redcrosse and Arthur.

Passages like the one I have just quoted are legion in Blake's writings, all of them emblemizing the visceral cruelty of the religion of holiness—centered on the notion of "sin" (and the therefore necessary "whips of stern repentance"); the reader may consult them at his leisure. I will cite one last passage, however, this a prose summary of Blake's key point about such religions and therefore a keystone in the tomb he sees Spenser building for his own poetic genius. It is from *A Vision of the Last Judgment*:

> Men are admitted into Heaven not because they have
> curbed & governd their Passions or have No Passions [cf.
> Guyon's and the Palmer's roles in *The Faerie Queene*] but
> because they have Cultivated their Understandings [i.e.,
> Imaginations]. The Treasures of Heaven are not Negations
> of Passion but Realities of Intellect from which All the
> Passions Emanate Uncurbed in their Eternal Glory The
> Fool shall not enter into Heaven let him be ever so Holy.
> Holiness is not The Price of Enterance into Heaven Those
> who are cast out Are All Those who having no Passions of
> their own because No Intellect. Have spent their lives in
> Curbing & Governing other Peoples by the Various arts of
> Poverty & Cruelty of all kinds Wo Wo Wo to you
> Hypocrites Even Murder the Courts of Justice more
> merciful than the Church are compelld to allow is not done
> in Passion but in Cool Blooded Design & Intention
> The Modern Church Crucifies Christ with the Head
> Downwards. (E564)

So does Spenser's.

If Spenser's Cynthia is transformed by Blake into Beulah and the Church Universal, and therefore partakes equally of the "influence" of the New Jerusalem and of the identically haloed Una-Truth immediately below her (I shall have more to say of her anon), then Astraea is Generation, the world of the cities in the upper right (London and Babylon) and the Religion of Holiness—the world of the material sun (rent from Mars's "red sphere," as Blake says in *America* 5:5, E53). Early on, Orc is associated with the "fiery red" sun and "the strife of blood" (*Europe* 15:3, 11, E66), but more importantly, Urizen's sons, in Blake's maturer conception in *The Four Zoas* VII,

> took the Sun that glowd oer Los
> And with immense machines down rolling. the terrific orb
> Compell'd. The Sun reddning like a fierce lion in his chains
> Descended to the sound of instruments that drownd the noise
> Of the hoarse wheels & the terrific howlings of wild beasts
> That dragd the wheels of the Suns chariot & they put the Sun
> Into the temple of Urizen to give light to the Abyss
> To light the War by day to hide his secret beams by night
> For he divided day & night in different orderd portions
> The day for war the night for secret religion in his temple.
>
> (E361)

The pertinence of this passage to what I have had to say in chapter 4 about Blake's interpretation of Genesis is, I trust, obvious. But that relationship aside, the sun of *The Four Zoas* seems to me to be that of Blake's Spenser painting, whose archer presides over what Damon describes as "the sacrifice of the baby of the two parents standing at the flaming altar" below and to the left of the archer (see figure 8). Grant and Brown reject this interpretation in favor of the archer's being simply "a counterpart of Cynthia . . . and thus an avatar of Apollo" (GB85). This seems to me to be only half-right, and only if this "avatar of Apollo" is associatable with Apollo's fall in Milton's *Nativity Ode*. Moreover, Grant and Brown's interpretation ignores the proximity to the archer of Nimrod's tower and Babylon. Although they discover no child being sacrificed, their further rejection of Damon's identification of the archer as "Molech" is short-sighted. As the "god for whom children (especially first sons) were burned alive," Molech surely was associated by Blake with the God who orders Abraham's sacrifice of Isaac and later Jephthah's daughter. In *Paradise Lost* he is a spirit of war; in *Jerusalem* Molech "rejoices thro the Land from Havilah to Shur: he rejoices / In moral law & its severe penalities," and is associated with the Moabite god Chemosh, Bacchus, Venus (the mistress of Mars), Thor, and Friga (the Scandi-

navian Venus). The last two, along with Woden, "consume . . .
Saxons: / On their enormous Altars built in the terrible North" (*Jerusalem* 83:19–20, E241).[33] Consonant with Damon's shrewd perception, Mars-Molech's arrow is aimed directly and properly at Justice with her scales and, beyond her, at the scepter of the God of This World.

The latter's right hand, it should be noted, rather curiously looses no Jovian thunderbolts and exerts no power but instead rests peacefully to his right beyond the orb of this world. Indeed, it seems to "engender" the human forms that ultimately become part of the Cynthia-Beulah configuration. The gesture, however, is ambiguous, as is appropriate to this crucial transitional stage in the supernal realm of the painting. With its palm, un-Christ-like, away from us, the hand gives rise to the churches to its immediate right (as well as blessing or anointing Britomart below); but should we not, in our "Contemplative Thought," image that palm outward, ushering its human generations toward Beulah and Jerusalem? Corroborating this "transition" from the war-sponsoring sun of this world to Son-Jerusalem (that is, Blake's Jerusalem as the Bride of the Lamb), Cynthia's moon emits an impressive physical light while the archer-sun, despite his fiery nature, has difficulty in illuminating or enlightening *his* world at all. The middle ground below him is noticeably darker than its counterpart below the moon, just as the sun's terrain is more jaggedly rocky than the rolling hills and "vistas" to the left. The New Jerusalem floats firmly (if I may employ that oxymoron) on light-colored clouds while Babylon, almost indistinguishable from its craggy background, sits above a dark cloud and has its tower (Babel) faintly leaning despite its solid foundation of apparent rock. One should recall, perhaps, Spenser's "statelie Towre" in *The Ruines of Time* (ll. 505–18). In any case, by the "time" Blake undoes the Genesis God's division of "day & night in different orderd portions," Jerusalem becomes its light, even as it incorporates Cynthia-Beulah, who, as I have argued, escapes from the physical reality of the moon and hence from the allegory of *The Faerie Queene*.

Such a "transition" is not new to the Blake of the Spenser painting. We find it as early as *America*, in a passage pertinent to the painting and to the misguided wars of Spenser's knights. "Enrag'd" at the American war (in which "Albion is sick" and "America faints"), "the Zenith" vents its rage "As human blood shooting its veins all round the orbed heaven" (4:4–5, E53). Then

> Red rose the clouds from the Atlantic in vast wheels of blood
> And in the red clouds a Wonder o'er the Atlantic sea;
> Intense! naked! a Human fire fierce glowing, as the wedge

Of iron heated in the furnace; his terrible limbs were fire
With myriads of cloudy terrors banners dark & towers
Surrounded.

(4:6–11, E53)

But no "light went thro' the murky atmosphere," only heat, the heat
of corporeal war. This seemingly blood-red "sun" thus turns out to
be not a sun at all, and Blake, who obviously could draw a circle when
he wanted to, presents this terrifying "vision" in his painting as fiery
spiky clouds. Perhaps it is "like a comet," as Albion's Angel first
guesses in *America*; but then again it is "like the planet red" that
"once inclos'd [all] the terrible wandering comets in its sphere," that
is, "Mars [that] wast [once] our center" (5:2–4, E53). The effective
result of this displacement is the blackening of the sun. Only when
"Empire is no more! and . . . the lion & wolf [of corporeal war] shall
cease" can "The Sun . . . [leave] his blackness" to find "a fresher
morning."[34]

This, the only mention of Mars in all of Blake's poetry, is a brilliant
adaptation of the proem to Book V of *The Faerie Queene*, which in turn
underlies or at least informs the sun of this world in the Spenser painting. Spenser begins "The Legend of Artegall or of Justice" (toward
the latter of which Molech-Mars's arrows are aimed in the painting)
with one of his many laments for the lost golden age, but this one,
unlike all others that I know, is cast in language that must have stuck
firmly in Blake's mind. The humanness of that "antique world" has
become (in a stunning locution) "degendered" "into hardest stone"
(proem, 1–2). And

that which all men then did vertue call,
Is now cald vice; and that which vice was hight,
Is now hight vertue, and so vs'd of all:
Right now is wrong, and wrong that was is right,
And all things else in time are chaunged quight.

(St. 4)

Spenser attributes this radical dislocation to the fact that

the heauens reuolution
Is wandred farre from where it first was pight,
And so doe make contrarie constitution
Of all this lower world, toward his dissolution.

(St. 4)

The next several stanzas detail the particulars of this "contrarie
constitution" as a radical shattering of the zodiac, presaged by, in

Ptolemy's time, the sun's rising twice "where he now doth West" and westing twice "where he ought rise aright."

> But most is *Mars* amisse of all the rest,
> And next to him old *Saturne*, that was wont be best.
>
> (St. 8)

Instead of universal peace, goodness, and justice without force, there is now universal war, Mars regnant.

Blake first dramatized this cosmic chaos in his illustrations to *Il Penseroso*, where, as he says in his inscription to "Milton and the Moon," Milton "sees the Moon terrified as one led astray in the midst of her path thro heaven" (E684). Even more germane is the illustration, "Milton and the Spirit of Plato," in which the "Heavens" have become "Venus Jupiter & Mars" with Hermes flying "before as attending on the Heaven of Jupiter" (E685). Helmeted, holding a spear, and accompanied by a "bat bug" (as Grant calls it),[35] Mars sits directly in the center between the "heavens" of Venus (who is vegetating like Daphne and accompanied by Adam and Eve serpentbound, back to back, against the tree of mystery) and Jupiter. Jupiter has a scepter in his left hand and compasses in his right. Over the entire grouping are, as Blake identifies them, "The Three destinies [sitting] on the Circles of Platos Heavens weaving the Thread of Mortal Life," and Lachesis is spread-eagled directly above Mars's head, measuring the span of human life. In the final illustration to *Il Penseroso* (see figure 6), the Zodiac seems to be righting itself since the same four constellations Spenser singles out to illustrate the chaos— Aries, Taurus, Gemini, and Cancer—here appear in proper order. At the same time, it is not too fanciful, I think, to see (with one's eye on Spenser's language in V, proem, 5–6) the Ram (tended improbably by a toe-dancing shepherd) virtually diving beneath Taurus's (undrawn) belly—though clearly not "shouldering" him; Taurus "with his bow-bent horne" having just "butted those two twinnes of *Ioue*" off to the left; and Gemini, as a consequence, landing (now as a single figure) astride, and thence to "crush," the Crab that crawls backward "Into the great *Nemoean* lions groue." But lest we wish to ignore all this and be satisfied with apparent order, Blake inserts Mars (now in the guise of Orion) who rises fiercely with sword brandished to effectively disrupt the "normal" movement of the zodiac.[36]

Blake's little archer in the Spenser painting is no Orion, of course (though his bow may argue a sex change to Diana). Indeed, he seems more Cupidan—perhaps the result of Blake's recall of Phaedria's speech in Book II of *The Faerie Queene*, which we have already seen that he knew well. In making peace between Guyon and Cymochles, she

FIGURE 6.   Blake, *Milton in His Old Age*, plate 12 of his illustrations to
Milton's *L'Allegro* and *Il Penseroso*

(courtesy of the Pierpont Morgan Library)

chastises both for their "Debatefull strife, and cruell enmitie" that "The famous name of knighthood fowly shend" (vi,35). A better strife is that of love, for "*Mars* is *Cupidoes* frend" (ibid.); the canto ends with Pyrochles burning "with implacable fire" in the throes of his lust and rage (stanza 44), a rather neat conflation, for Blake's purposes, of Mars's and Cupid's depredations.

I conclude this perhaps too-long excursus into astronomy and astrology with the reminder that the worst of all the heavenly dislocations in Spenser's conception is the darkening of the sun in its steady declination. Moreover, Spenser invokes Astraea, "Resembling God in his imperiall might," and Elizabeth, "Dread Souerayne Goddesse, that doest highest sit / In seate of iudgement, in th' Almighties stead," to set things right in his universe (V,proem,10–11); and it is that invocation that constitutes the grievous error Blake depicts in his Astraea figure and her scales (zodiacally Virgo and Libra). Filling out this elaborate pictorialization of Spenserian error, Blake positions iron Talus with his flail and spear directly below Virgo-Libra, has Artegall bask self-righteously beneath the blessing of Astraea's left hand, and places directly below Mars his Calidore, the most severely body-armored of all the knights. As we shall see, he is Love-and-War in the fiction of Spenser's Book VI, as Blake read it.

IV

Assuming that my scenario for the supernal realms is at least generally correct in its main points (however arguable some of my particulars may be), a question must arise immediately: What does such an interpretation (or interpretations) of this upper panorama have to do with the characters who function or pose beneath in the mundane, yet at the same time "faerie," world of Blake's painting and Spenser's poem? According to my proposal of a sequence-cum-symmetry in the spatial arrangements of the supernal characters and icons, does this mean that Blake pronounces those characters to Jove's right somehow "better" than those to his left? Una is clearly preferable to Archimago and Duessa in both poets' minds, but is Redcrosse preferable to Calidore, or Guyon to Arthur (or Artegall), or Britomart to Artegall (or Arthur)? Spenser's answer is, of course, in the negative. But if the Palmer is in some sense "obviously better" than Talus, is such a preference one that is in accord with Blakean principles, Spenserian principles, Blake's perception of Spenserian principles, our own principles, or our own perception of Spenserian or Blakean principles? The easy answer is all of these—and though that may seem a kind of comic "cop-out," it does come close to the truth of the matter. The bottom-line question is essentially the same as the one I raised with respect to interpreting *The Marriage of Heaven and Hell.* There we have Devils speaking, Angels speaking, other characters speaking, all "controlled," as it were, by the "speaker," who speaks the entire work; and somewhere in the accents of this mélange is Blake's voice, which is the one that tells us or at least guides us toward seeing what everything "means." In the Spenser painting, Spenser is "speaking," but he speaks through Blake's mouth and hand; and, in addition, Blake himself somehow tells us what it all "means"—including what he understands to be Spenser's meaning and the ways in which that coincides with, or differs from, his own "reading," not merely of *The Faerie Queene* but of the cosmos and its "history." Once again, we are faced with the problem of critical principles, not "merely" interpretive issues or explicative quarrels.

In my discussion of *The Marriage*, I tried to make clear that the "rough basement" of my argument is that the nature, context, and use of Blake's allusions often, if not always, determine (at least fundamentally, if not totally) Blake's position or stance; or, to put that another way, the Blakean meaning inheres in the impact of the allusion and its context on his "own" ostensible presentation. If this sounds excessively arcane or even insanely idiosyncratic as an artistic *modus operandi*, let me place it into two critical-interpretive contexts with which we are all familiar: (1) the necessity of identifying and explicating contexts within Blake's own works in order to perceive Blake's point of view; and (2) the necessity of applying the results of (1), as well as the lines and contexts of another poet's work, to learning what Blake "says," graphically, about that work and about man and the cosmos generally in his "illustrations" to that other poet. (A similar critical procedure is also used in commenting upon the "meaning" of Blake's graphic "quotations" from other artists.) What I have tried to do, then, in my commentary on the supernal realm of the Spenser painting is not to assume a critical stance that I think (for whatever reasons) is adequate or "good" but rather to allow my critical and interpretive principles to emerge out of my engagement with Spenser and Blake separately and with Spenser-Blake in this one work, the painting. But, if out of that engagement a critical procedure has emerged, it has also bred, in turn, other critical subproblems, including the several I listed at the beginning of this chapter as being inherent in Grant and Brown's and Damon's interpretations of the painting. The third one I listed has now become, at this point, crucial (I have briefly subscribed to it in my remarks on the positioning of Talus-Artegall-Calidore and Una): the assumption that the supernal realm is parallel to, reflective of, or even a "guide" to the signification of the sublunary world of Spenser's characters themselves.

My own sense of the validity of this principle may be apparent already in my focus on the complex skein of ambiguities that informs the supernal panorama-sequence-symmetry. If one draws connecting lines (from heads, spears, finger, eyes, whole figures) between lower and upper worlds, the results are far from neat (pace Grant, Brown, and Damon). Artegall, for example, points to one basin of Astraea's scales, not to Justice herself (to Libra, not Virgo), and Jove's scepter points at Arthur, but his hand hangs gently above Britomart. Calidore points with his spear to nothing distinguishable, Redcrosse with his to a far wing of the New Jerusalem, Guyon misses St. Paul's dome with his, Arthur gestures vaguely (perhaps at the city or the sunarcher or both), and Britomart magnanimously calls all her compatriots, "good" and "bad" alike, out for a final bow. Even the "world" cradled in front of Jove hovers oddly—over whom? Marinell, say Grant and Brown (GB67). Marinell?

The problems here are almost infinitely multipliable and to cite other "peculiarities" would be of a little help. A more fruitful approach seems to me to concentrate on how such problems arise in the first place, that is, the fundamental slipperiness of Blake's supernal "allegory," depending upon one's angle of perception. The key issue is one of identity rather than of "meaning" or abstract equivalencies. If Astraea is Astraea, certain meanings follow; but if, because of her scales, we identify her as Justice, Astraea must follow as well as Libra. Similarly, the God of This World is clearly that, since he has the whole world in his hand—or rather, his beard; yet he does not really "have" it because the world is buoyed up by angels, and he neither looks at it nor seems much interested in controlling it. If we focus on his scepter, he must be a king, but he wears a dazzlingly elaborate halo, not a crown; and if he is Jove (Spenser's or anybody else's), one has to wonder where his thunderbolts are and why his right hand seems so gently unarmed. And so on. What Blake has done, then, is not merely to create ambiguous figures but to tempt us to identifications and then not fulfill (at least entirely) our expectations for those identifications. If Justice has scales, where is her "usual" sword? If the moon is Cynthia, why is she haloed and soaring out of it? And if the sun is merely the sun, why is it lopsided and red, emitting little light? I have already suggested some answers to these questions, their very shiftiness arguing implicitly that, if the supernal realms "control" the significance of the mundane characters, such "control" as they exert shifts wildly with second, third, and fourth double takes at the precise nature of the supernal agencies of control. Let us turn from these realms, then, to the characters themselves.

CHAPTER SIX

The Characters in Spenser's Faerie Queene, II

ALTHOUGH GRANT and Brown do not advance the principle overtly, they do imply in a number of their descriptions of the characters that there is some meaningful relationship between a character in the main procession and the supernal realm if a spear or gesture or general positioning of the character by extension intersects in some way with a figure or a detail above. For the most part, however, they do not pursue the interpretive implications of these intersections as Kiralis does in his analysis of the Chaucer painting. Without impugning either the legitimacy or the value of such spear pointing and hand gestures, I should like to begin my study of the processional characters without reference to them, concentrating instead on the few seemingly firm associations of the mundane with the supernal, based on simple vertical symmetries.

I have already commented on the God of This World's spatial "embrace" of Britomart and Artegall (perhaps even of the two "halves" of the entire procession) as well as on his globe that apparently, and curiously, leads to nothing below despite its centrality above. And I have noted the seeming appropriateness (both positive-Spenserian and negative-Blakean) of Astraea's position over Talus, though her scales are divided (as it were) between Talus and Artegall, and the left basin hangs oddly over the figures that Grant and Brown identify as Amoret and Scudamore. Cynthia hovers over both Una and the Palmer, but the moon itself (like Jove's globe and part of Astraea's scales) hangs over the less distinct background characters that have been identified as Belphoebe and Timias (GB64–65).[1] It is hard to make much of that odd tetrad. Even more peculiarly, the red sun and its resident archer—perhaps Mars-Orc—hang directly above Book VI of *The Faerie Queene*. While it might be argued that the restored pastoralism of Book VI justifies a steady sun rather than an inconstant (or slivered) moon, Blake's consistent association of the moon with Beulah, pastoralism, and innocence tends to confute that hypothesis. Moreover, Pastorella, Spenser's "innocent," is likened to "Great *Gloriana*, greatest Maiesty" (VI,x,28), whose alter ego in the supernal realms of Spenser's poem is Cynthia, not Hyperion. And then there is the question (raised in chapter 5) of whether the sun is really the sun at all. More like Mars, it shines therefore (insofar as its rays penetrate the middle distance at all), not on Pastorella or the Graces but on Calidore, whom, despite costume changes in Book VI from armor to shepherd's weeds to armor over shepherd's weeds, Blake presents as the most all-encompassing and formidably armored of all the knights in the painting. As such, he is a kind of quotation from the antibardic, not to say antipastoral and certainly anti-imaginative, warriors of Blake's illustrations to Gray's *The Bard*, *The Fatal Sisters*, and especially *The Descent of Odin* and *The Triumphs of Owen*.[2] His scimitarlike sword (not present in the Gray illustrations) should give one pause, especially since the only wearer of a scimitar in *The Faerie Queene* is Radigund (V,v,3). More of her in the next chapter, but here it is worth observing that there is no other scimitar in Blake's works, graphic or poetic.

To add to the apparent confusions inherent in tracing even vertical intersections, let me add one more. The poet-figure (whose identity, I have argued, poses special problems) sits directly over Artegall's head as well as above Jove's sceptre. He is under a rainbow, to be sure, and that is obviously good. But the rainbow seems to emanate from Jove's aurora borealis and terminates, to our right, in the right wing of the spread-winged Presence; and that is apparently bad. I have already guessed at some resolution of these assorted "confusions" and confusing contraries in my earlier discussion of the poet-figure, but further clarification will emerge shortly. Additional obvious equivalences, and frustrations, emerge from this downward vertical approach. The Tower of Babel "governs" nothing below except Calidore's right arm; it is not over Archimago or Duessa, although it more or less hovers appropriately over the Blatant Beast's mouth. Then again it may be construed as hovering over the rump of Calidore's horse. Perhaps Blake intended it to control, in some sense, the entire final panel of the design. That is clearly what Damon thought, since he identifies Blake's Duessa and Archimago merely as the "young woman and . . . old man" who are "Babylonian captives." The Gothic structure to Jove's right that I have identified as a vaginal chapel is actually above Glauce, not Britomart, and St. Paul's dome vaguely hangs over the space between "Satyrane" (GB66) and the head of Britomart's horse. The dazzling spires of the upper left, however, are solidly above (though not quite centered on) Redcrosse's head. If we lower our sights to the middle realms, assuming Grant and Brown's identifications are reasonably correct (GB78–80), the structures and places more or less sequentially, left to right, mirror the progress from Book I to Book VI but end distressingly and frustratingly in the countryside on the far right, peopled only "with various indistinct figures" and no buildings or caves.[3] Thus, our eye movement from left to right, both for the characters and the middle stratum, runs counter to clock time (the zodiacal "movement") as well as to the symbolic significance of the supernal realm. Left to right is hardly the road to the New Jerusalem in the upper left. Instead, it leads to Book VI, where Blake has transformed Meliboe's pastoral paradise into a rugged, rocky wilderness in the middle ground, which is as inappropriate for Pastorella as it would be for *The Shepheardes Calender* or *Songs of Innocence*.

Blake's conflicting movements in the painting thus suggest that our reading of *The Faerie Queene* in proper order will lead us but to Duessa, Archimago, and the Blatant Beast. The logical conclusion to this perception is that we must read the poem backward to find evidence of Spenser's poetic genius (and hence the New Jerusalem), a rather predictably diabolical and infernal procedure in the sense of those terms established by *The Marriage of Heaven and Hell*. Although certain scenes, castles, caves, and other structures seem to have some relationship to the appropriate (or near appropriate) main characters in the foreground, such vertical, or foreground-background, symmetry as Blake teases us into seeing collapses into the severity and contrariness of his left-to-right design. In light of this "confusion," one can sympathize with Grant and Brown's constant need to explain away Blake's "misplacement" of these icons and of the characters themselves.

If, however, we adopt the principle of identification and interpretation I have argued for with respect to the supernal realms, the whole idea of misplacement is vitiated. For Blake not only is presenting us a kind of contrary to his Chaucer painting (with its reverse direction and palpable movement) but, by his design and ambiguous configurations, is exemplifying or emblemizing his sense of the "organization" of *The Faerie Queene*. That is to say, by deliberately deforming or deorganizing Spenser's poem, Blake re-forms it in both significations of that word. Or, to put the matter another way, the body or corpus of the poem is merely that portion of its imaginative "soul" (its truth) perceived by the five senses. By depersonifying the Spenserian personification allegories, Blake will reverse the procedure of the priests in *The Marriage*: where they "realize" and "abstract" the deities from their respective objects, he will un-realize Spenser's moral abstraction and re-reify them as annihilable error—annihilable, of course, only if we as "spectators" approach them "on the Fiery Chariot of [our] Contemplative Thought" and literally see them out of existence. "Error is Created"—by priests (whether in the guise of poets or not)—while "Truth is Eternal Error or Creation will be Burned Up & then & not till then Truth or Eternity will appear It is Burnt up the Moment Men cease to behold it" (*Vision of the Last Judgment*, E560, 565). Finally, if we combine my earlier idea of the coinstantaneous perception of the whole in one "gripe" (as Spenser defines that in his Letter to Raleigh) with the nonprogress of the procession and the idea of ambiguousness of identity, we shall come much closer to understanding what is really going on in the tableau. Or, rather, what it is, really and unchangeably.

But even as I shall argue that Blake's Spenser painting is a kind of contrary to his depiction of the Canterbury pilgrims, it will become apparent that I share certain basic critical or perceptual principles established by Betsy Bowden in her fine essay on the Chaucer.[4] The interpretive problems in the two are interestingly related, if in somewhat skewed fashion. In the Chaucer, the "reader"-viewer must cope not only with the relationship between Chaucer's text and Blake's pictorialization of it but with the relationship between Blake's own commentary on the painting (and on Chaucer's text) and the painting itself. In the Spenser, these relationships are painting to text and, to a lesser extent, painting and text to Spenser's "commentary" (the Letter to Raleigh), now complicated further by the relationship between the Spenser painting and the Chaucer painting. Bowden points out that, paradoxically, Blake's language in *The Descriptive Catalogue* essay on Chaucer is heavily punctuated with "vague, abstract terms . . . non-descriptive, non-individualized words applied to general classes of mankind by the man who said, 'To Generalize is to be an Idiot'" (B165). She might well have gone on to cite the statement by Sir Joshua Reynolds that prompted this vitriolic marginal jotting: a "disposition to abstractions, to generalizing and classification, is the great glory of the human mind" (E641). We ought to worry, then, when we find that it is precisely this Reynoldsesque mental "glory" for which Blake particularly praises Chaucer: "As Newton numbered the stars, and as Linneus numbered the plants, so Chaucer numbered the classes of men" (*Descriptive Catalogue*, E533)—even as Blake must be remembering his anger at Reynolds for not knowing that "Every Class is Individual."[5]

Bowden concludes from these paradoxes that "Blake . . . is purposely teasing the reader with the inaccuracy and ambiguity inherent in such abstract language, and thus forcing his audience to look instead at the picture" (B165). Furthermore, while she acknowledges and employs one of Kiralis's basic principles ("binary relationships")—followed as well, though less rigorously, by Grant and Brown—Bowden perceives that "within the frozen time and space of this picture, a constant cell-like bisection and re-bisection of types goes on, such that a given figure may be the spectre of one character, the complementary completing half of another, and the contrary of a third" (B165). As a result, there is an "ambiguity inherent in all but a few of these 'eternal principles or characters of human life'" (B180). For example, "the Pardoner/Summoner combines with Monk/Friar, such that Pardoner/Summoner seems the discarded spectrous shadow of the whole bundle Pardoner/Summoner/Monk/Friar. . . . Simultaneously, in the rear half of the procession, the Parson/Plowman joins forces with Doctor/Lawyer, to balance with the four churchmen ahead" (B189) (see figure 3). Without entering into debate with Bowden about the minute particulars of her analysis, her exposure of the shifting identities, fractionated portions of identity, binary oppositions, and complementarities (not to mention interrelated foursomes and even eightsomes) calls into serious doubt Blake's assertions in *The Descriptive Catalogue* that the pilgrims "are the characters which compose all ages and nations," unalterable except in name or title (E532). But if they really *are* "the physiognomies or lineaments of universal human life" (E532–33), the shiftiness of their physiognomies and lineaments (as well as their various permutative combinations) in Blake's painting constitutes an unremittingly biting criticism of Chaucer's "numbering" of the classes of men. What the painting accomplishes is precisely their unnumbering, a bold and necessarily complex effort to retrieve "eternal principles," "eternal attributes, or divine names" (E536) from the vicissitudes of human character and their all-too-allegorical personifications. As well, Blake clearly intends to undeify Chaucer's types (uncomfortably godlike in their lack of proper names) and make them "sacrifice to Man," that is to say, to restore them to the wholeness of which they are but fragmented shadows or ratios. That wholeness "is Jesus the Saviour, the vine of eternity" (E536).

If we read Chaucer through Blake's eyes (not through his commentative essay), he is "sublime" (E535). Otherwise, he is a mere numberer, a cataloguer or taxonomist of "the vegetable world," over which his "Fairies," like Shakespeare's, "rule": "let them [the fairies] be so considered, and then the poet will be understood, and not else" (*Descriptive Catalogue*, E535). While this odd identification of Chaucer's characters as fairies may seem on the surface to be a kind of compliment (it follows Blake's chastising of painters who dress "Shakespeare's Witches in Macbeth . . . for the stage" rather than "as Shakespeare intended"), it is in fact a stern condemnation of what both poets create in their respective ages. As "Goddesses of Destiny" the witches are uncomfortably like Blake's own Vala or Nature, "allegoric and mental signification[s]" that have been turned "into corporeal command" (*Descriptive Catalogue*, E543). Thus, instead of consisting of "facsimile presentations of merely mortal and perishing substances," Blake's painting will "elevate" those substances to the "visionary." Otherwise, "if Mr. B.'s Canterbury Pilgrims had been done by any other power than that of the poetic visionary, it would have been as dull as his adversary's," that is, rival engraver Thomas Stothard's *Pilgrimage to Canterbury*.[6] In other words, painting Chaucer's characters exactly as Chaucer presents them, no matter who the painter, would eventuate in a dull copy of the mundane, an imitation of Chaucer's "angelic" side, as opposed to his essential membership in the devil's party (these terms are, of course, borrowed from Blake's critique of *Paradise Lost* in *The Marriage of Heaven and Hell*—E35).

Fairies, for Blake, are consistently associated with the four elements and this world of Generation ("they know not of Regeneration"); "in the aggregate they are named Satan / And Rahab":

The Fairies, Nymphs, Gnomes & Genii of the Four Elements
Unforgiving & unalterable: these cannot be Regenerated
But must be Created, for they know only of Generation
These are the Gods of the Kingdoms of the Earth: in contrarious
And cruel opposition: Element against Element, opposed in War
Not Mental, as the Wars of Eternity, but a Corporeal Strife.
(*Milton* 31[34]:18–25,E130)

The problem in *The Canterbury Tales*, as Blake perceived it, is Chaucer's fundamental error in making the "Host . . . a leader of the age," "the Knight . . . a true Hero," and the Squire "the germ of perhaps greater perfection still, as he blends literature and the arts with his warlike studies" (*Descriptive Catalogue*, E533). The "cause" of this error is Chaucer's "Reasoning Spectre," who "Stands between the Vegetative Man & his Immortal Imagination" (*Jerusalem* 32[36]: 23–24,E178) and turns vision into history, essence into allegorical identity, and imaginative truth into fairy-tale error, instead of the other way around. This sort of transformation seems to me the burden of the troublesome "pre-Preludium" plate iii of *Europe* (E60), which appears in only two of the twelve known copies of the poem. In it a fairy appears to the first-person speaker and ultimately is credited with having "dictated EUROPE" to the speaker-become-writer. But, that this fairy is hardly an appropriate muse of prophecy is suggested by several important details in the text, not to mention that the entire passage is an oblique parody of the *Introduction* to *Songs of Innocence*, with its child on a cloud inspiring the piper to play, sing, and ultimately write (E7). The "muse" of *Europe*, clearly no child floating in gravity-defying fashion above the piper's head, sits corporeally on Samuel Johnson's "streak'd Tulip," an unpropitious perch at best. The speaker, who oddly and suspiciously "started from the trees," catches the fairy in his "hat as boys knock down a butterfly."[7] Taking "possession" of the fairy, who thus becomes "*My* Fairy" (my italics) obedient to command, the speaker asks as unimaginative a question as Blake could muster for him: "Then tell me, what is the material world, and is it dead?" The fairy responds promisingly by saying he will "shew you all alive / The world, when every particle of dust breathes forth its joy"; but this apparently "right" perception is unmistakably sabotaged by the preceding lines in which the fairy must first be commanded and then wined and dined "on love-thoughts" and "sparkling poetic fancies." Once "tipsie" on that inane poetical liquor, he can "sing . . . to this soft lute." The involuted perverseness of this "inspiration" for the writer of *Europe* is clear not only from the speaker's first inspiring the fairy with "poetic fancies" so that the fairy can reinspire the speaker-writer but also from the fairy's laughing aloud to hear the "Wild flowers" "whimper" when the speaker plucks these "love-thoughts" to feed to the fairy.

Despite its title, then (*Europe a Prophecy*), the "prophecy" proper becomes a kind of antiprophecy, Blake's manipulation of Milton's *Nativity Ode* leading but to the generation of a "secret child," who turns out to be "terrible Orc," the fiery spirit of revolution, the light of whose fury descends on "the vineyards of red France" but is powerless to prevent Britain's vote for counterrevolutionary war against France, what Erdman calls "the English crusade of 1793–1794."[8] If, as Erdman further argues, Blake is not only hopeful but also enthusiastic about the prospects for a new Orc-induced dispensation, in *America*, as Deen points out, Orc's "apocalypse" eventuates not only through revolutionary war but a veritable Armageddon; and in *Europe* Orc's centrality means clearly that Los "has not yet become the champion of humanity in what deserves to be called Mental Fight rather than warfare."[9] In *America* Orc may be seen as "capable of soaring free," but *Europe* itself describes (and enacts) a "suspension or stasis" that will be broken only by Los, who calls his sons (artworks) "to the strife of blood" at the end of the poem.[10] We are not told, significantly, what they *do*. Thus, to reveal the error of the dictating fairy in summoning from the prophetic poet's brain a terrible, secret child whose agency is rage and war, and to reveal as well the necessity of imaginative apocalypse rather than Armageddon, Blake employs an extraordinary obscurity and "complicated web of myth." "Nowhere," Erdman says, "is Blake's symbolism more cryptic; nowhere do so many new characters appear in such fleeting contexts; nowhere is there such sly shifting from one level of discourse to another, such difficulties with ambiguities of punctuation and sudden changes of pace."[11] What Erdman calls the poem's "mythological envelope," then, includes not merely perversions, or at least wrenchings, of Milton's ode proper (these have been well documented) but a perversion of Milton's "Heav'nly Muse" into Blake's fairy, both "afford[ing] a present to the infant God," a "verse" or "hymn" or "solemn strain, / To welcome him to his new abode" (*Nativity Ode*, ll. 15–18). Both presents are to the wrong gods, inspired by the wrong muses, and written by the "wrong" writers; hence Blake's complicated, obscure maneuverings to allow the *real*, "diabolical" prophecy to shine through the "histories" of both "angelic" poets' words.[12]

If we return now to the Spenser painting with all this in mind, as well as with our eye on Blake's Gray illustration of "Spenser Creating His Fairies" (see figure 2), we should be able to see that at least a part of Spenser's "problem" is the same as that of Chaucer and Shakespeare: fairies are rulers of the vegetable universe. To examine Blake's version of Spenser's major fairies, it is difficult to know exactly where to begin since, as we shall see, the visionary movements throughout the frozenness of the physical tableau are dazzling. For want of a method that presents itself as obviously better, and following Blake's encouragement as well as Spenser's order, let us begin at the beginning, with the first (or left-hand) grouping: Dwarf, Dragon, Redcrosse, Una, Lion, and Ass (see figure 7). Perfect Spenser—almost. Una's Dwarf "lasie seemd in being euer last," perhaps "wearied," Spenser suggests, "with bearing of her bag / Of needments." She also leads a "milke white lambe" (I,i,6,4). Blake's Dwarf leads the procession, not merely positionally but physically, for he holds the ass's rein firmly in his clenched left hand. And he is haloed. Blake's reversal of his position in Spenser, taken along with his omission of Una's lamb, thus has the effect of merging Dwarf and lamb into a haloed child who leads. Spenser obviously should have read Isaiah more carefully, particularly chapter 11: "and a little child shall lead them."[13] Indeed, the rest of Isaiah 11:6 is pertinent here, for among those that the little child shall lead are the wolf and lamb, leopard and kid, calf and young lion—and "dust shall be the serpent's meat" (Isa. 65:25), precisely what Spenser's dragon seems to be eating. Moreover, Isaiah's child has "righteousness" as "the gir-

FIGURE 7. Detail of left quarter of *The Characters in Spenser's Faerie Queene*

(*courtesy of* Blake: An Illustrated Quarterly)

dle of his loins, and faithfulness the girdle of his reins" (Isa. 11:5), that is, the loincloth of Blake's otherwise naked child. The contrary pictorialization would be "loins girt about with truth, and having on the breastplate of righteousness" and "the whole armour of God," as Paul prescribes (Eph. 6:13–14), as Spenser (following Paul) costumes his knights, and as Calidore (the pastoralist and hence the "proper" evoker of Blake's children of Innocence) paradoxically demonstrates most severely. J. B. Fletcher long ago translated Una's leading of the "Lamb in leash" as "Innocence led by Truth. But, on the literal side, for Una to drag that poor Lamb along with her on her long quest would be an outrage."[14] Blake thought so too, but not out of allegiance to any society for the prevention of cruelty to animals. He simply corrects Spenser's error and, in good Blakean fashion, has Truth led by Innocence.

More specifically, however, it is the ass itself that is led by the Dwarf-child. Humility becomes the "vehicle" of Truth, not to mention the reenactment of Christ's triumphant entry into Jerusalem, "lowly, and riding upon an ass" (Zech. 9:9; Matt. 21:5 has Christ "meek"). Blake thus charges Spenser with conforming strictly to the Bible's yoking of truth, humility, and Christ and with being unwilling (with his patriotic eye on Gloriana) to elevate Una to the status of the Virgin Mary as Blake does. But, if elevation it be, it is a wry one for, as Randel Helms reminds us, "the Virgin Birth is alien to his Christology. . . . Blake is deeply concerned with the nature of a Christ born fully of and by the flesh."[15] Hence the extraordinary section "f " of *The Everlasting Gospel* with its momentary conflation of the Virgin Mary, Mary Magdalene, and the woman taken in adultery (E521) in order to attack the Old Testamental legalistic notions of chastity, punishment, and sacrifice for sin. What is truly sinful to Blake is a "dark pretence to Chastity" that blasphemes both love and God. What is *called* "a shame & Sin" is "Loves Temple that God dwelleth in"; what *is* a shame and sin is the female "secret hidden Shrine" (*Everlasting Gospel*, E522). In *Jerusalem* it is the "Secret Place" into which "a pompous High Priest" enters, "a False Holiness hid within the Center" (69:38–44, E223), and by extension, the "secret tabernacle / And [the] ark & holy place" of the Whore of Babylon (68:49–50, E222).

Lest this analysis of Blake's Una appear wildly idiosyncratic—especially given her striking demureness—we need to recall first that, late in Book I, Una is described as "that faire virgin" and is associated with Diana (xii,7). More tellingly, when the troop of "comely virgins" enters Una's triumphal homecoming scene, they throw

> Themselues to ground with gratious humblesse bent,
> And her ador'd by honorable name,
> Lifting to heauen her euerlasting fame:
> Then on her head they set a girland greene,
> And crowned her twixt earnest and twixt game;
> Who in her self-resemblance well beseene,
> Did seeme such, as she was, a goodly maiden Queene.

(xii,8)

This echo of Spenser's May festival in *The Shepheardes Calender* ("Maye," ll. 20–33), would have sat ill in Blake's imagination, had he recognized it, but even more damning to Spenser is the hint of virginal majesty before which other virgins humble themselves. Blake's retort, in his running conversation with (and thus conversion of) Spenser, is his presentation of Una as a graphic quotation of his Wife of Bath (see figure 3), who sits her horse precisely as Una does the ass, whose extraordinary, gaudy headgear includes the origins of Una's halo, and whose right hand holds the Whore of Babylon's infamous cup of fornications while Una points with her right forefinger to something in her Urizenic book of moral law (the "truth").[16] In this light Blake "reads" Spenser's Una as a kind of Vala, "a pretence of love to destroy love," a "pretence of Moral Virtue, fill'd with Revenge and Law," a "pretence of Religion to destroy Religion" (*Jerusalem* 17:26, E161; 36[40]:35, E182; 38[43]:36, E185), "a dark pretence to Chastity" (*Everlasting Gospel*, E522). But, as we shall, it is not the only light in which we are to see Blake's Una.

Before studying her "other side," however, we need to pursue a bit further the Spenserian truth-humility-Christ configuration that Blake places at the head of his pictorialized procession. As might be expected, given the extraordinary echoing in Una of Blake's Wife of Bath, Spenser is wrong again in his biblically sanctioned notion of humility, emblemized in the ass, as Blake explains in detail in *The Everlasting Gospel*. There Jesus does say, as we would expect him to do, given our own benightedness, "Follow me I am meek & lowly of heart," but he says it "with most consummate Art" to confound "the Scribes & Pharisees" and "the Heathen Schools" (E519, 518). Had he been able to read these lines, Spenser would have missed this tonality, and hence for Blake the error he commits is the cardinal error of all Pharisees:

> If he had been Antichrist Creeping Jesus
> Hed have done any thing to please us
> Gone sneaking into Synagogues
> And not usd the Elders & Priests like dogs

> But Humble as a Lamb or Ass
> Obeyd himself to Caiaphas.

(E519–20)

But "God wants not Man to Humble himself" for "Humble to God Haughty to Man." "If thou humblest thyself thou humblest me," God says to Jesus;

> Thou also dwellst in Eternity
> Thou art a Man God is no more
> Thine own humanity learn to adore.

(E520)

Finally and summarily—devastating as a criticism of the conventional Lamb, Spenser's Una, and Redcrosse's submission to the enforcement by Humiltá of "stouping low" to enter the House of Holiness—Blake writes: "Humility is only Doubt," which in turn "is Self Contradiction" or the soul's "Reasoning upon its own Dark Fiction" (E520). As unveiled as Una is in Blake's painting, the veil with which Spenser equips her (I,i,4) is still very much there as she "reads" her Urizenic book without looking at it (had there been Braille in Blake's day, it would have been perfect for him).[17]

Although I have "accounted for" the dragon in Blake's Isaiahan tableau, its sharing of the lead, by a head, is of some additional interest. For Blake, Error and Truth are coterminous in this world. "All Life consists of these Two Throwing off Error . . . from our company continually & recieving Truth . . . into our Company Continually. . . . whenever any Individual Rejects Error & Embraces Truth a Last Judgment passes upon that Individual" (*Vision of the Last Judgment*, E562). No slaying of the Dragon is necessary, for error is but a creation of the mind of man; "Error or Creation will be Burned Up & then & not till then Truth or Eternity will appear It is Burnt up the Moment Men cease to behold it" (ibid., E565). Appropriately, then, Blake pictures Redcrosse and his threatening horse's hooves above the dragon's head as an inadequate, even erroneous, "response" to Error. Perhaps that is why the hooves remain merely poised and ironically describe an outer halo over and around the more precise one with which Blake endows his Dwarf-child. With complementary appropriateness, the child simply does not behold either the dragon or the descending hooves, nor does (seemingly) the Lion or the Ass or Una notice the dragon—all of them no doubt being "led" to that imaginative unseeing. In *The Faerie Queene*, however, after Una identifies the "darksome hole" that Redcrosse, she, and the Dwarf are about to enter as the "wandring wood" of "Errours den," Spenser

207

has the Dwarf fearfully cry, "Fly fly"; "this is no place for liuing men" (I,i,13). And, though Spenser does not tell us in so many words, apparently the Dwarf does fly, only reappearing a full forty-eight stanzas later in the next canto—after Redcrosse has slain the dragon, after Archimago's more devilish error, false Una, tries to vamp Redcrosse in his bed, and after that arch-imager creates for Redcrosse a "real" Una whose bed is defiled by another. It is *that* Redcrosse, and *that* Una, it seems to me, that Blake portrays in the painting, for both obviously need leading.

But there is yet another possible association that Blake's Dwarf-child gathers unto itself—one which, if true, suggests as strongly as anything in the painting the nature of Blake's reading of *The Faerie Queene*. Arthur, we recall, is Spenser's "Magnificence," the embodiment in perfection of all the other virtues exemplified in the extant six books, plus presumably the six more that would have completed the Fairy Queen's living year and all time—the image of eternity. Arthur (not to mention the idea of Magnificence) has been variously interpreted and endlessly argued over by Spenserian critics. I shall have more to say about him in chapter 7, but the scholarly dispute is as irrelevant to my purposes as it was to Blake's. In any case, it is the general "truth" enunciated by Spenser in the Letter to Raleigh that underlies the "possible association" of Arthur with Blake's portrayal of the Dwarf-child in the painting. The connection hinges rather precariously on a pun, albeit a precariousness mitigated considerably by Blake's demonstrable fascination with and insistent exploitation of the fundamental polysemousness of language, precisely in the sense that Maureen Quilligan claims for Spenser's language (and for that of several other allegorists from the Middle Ages to the present).[18] I take it as a given, then, that Blake was not averse to hanging a matter of considerable gravity and importance upon a pun. As *The Faerie Queene* progresses, Spenser (not without precedent, of course) refers to Arthur increasingly as "the royall child" (IV,viii,44—this actually is the first such reference). In V, viii, 32 he is "the bold child"; in V, x, 8 and 13 simply "the childe"; and in VI, viii, 15 "the noble childe." The only other knight to whom the term is applied is, perhaps significantly, Timias, Arthur's squire, whose full knighthood ("childe-hood") is yet some years away.

Arthur's first appearance in the poem, while auspicious for Spenser, could hardly have been so to Blake, given the details of Spenser's elaborate Homeric description of his armor (I,vii,29–36). To Blake, that is precisely the armor of holiness of Ephesians, as I have previously noted with respect to Redcrosse, but here matters are worse since Arthur's shield is centered by a "pretious stone" "Shapt like a

Ladies head,'' for Blake as fine a graven image of the Virgin-Faerie Queene as one could ask for. In *Milton*, then, it is no accident that Blake equips a "Shadowy *Female*" (my italics) with such armor—to battle not dragons but Milton:

> For I will put on the Human Form & take the Image of God
> Even Pity & Humanity but my Clothing shall be Cruelty
> And I will put on Holiness as a breastplate & as a helmet
> And all my ornaments shall be of the gold of broken hearts
> And the precious stones of anxiety & care & desperation & death
> And repentance for sin & sorrow & punishment & fear.
>
> (18[20]:19–24, E111)

Terrified at this, Orc argues against her resolve:

> Wherefore dost thou Create & Weave this Satan for a Covering
> . . . .
> When wilt thou put on the Female Form as in times of old
> With a Garment of Pity & Compassion like the Garment of God.
>
> (18[20]:30–35, E112)

Yet, just as Arthur's "glitterand armour" includes "a bauldrick braue . . . / That shynd, like twinkling stars, with stons most pretious rare," so in *The Four Zoas* VIII, the serpent-formed Orc himself rises

> among the Constellations of Urizen
> A crest of fire rose on his forehead red as the carbuncle
> Beneath down to his eyelids scales of pearl then gold & silver
> Immingled with the ruby overspread his Visage down
> His furious neck writhing contortive in dire budding pains
> The scaly armour shot out. Stubborn down his back & bosom
> The Emerald Onyx Sapphire jasper beryl amethyst
> Strove in terrific emulation
>
> (E373)

—all calculated "To undermine the World of Los." "The Soldiers named it Satan" (E374).

Thus, Blake's habitual portrayal in his graphic work of Satan in form-fitting body armor, equipped with sword and shield, severely undercuts Spenser's Arthur as a perfect champion. More accurately, Arthur and Redcrosse, in their spectrous aspect, are Satan. Redeemed, all the knights, regathered in Arthur, *is* (the singular verb here an appropriate Blakism) the child-childe, the "collection" of "the scatterd portions of his immortal body" (as *The Four Zoas* VIII puts it—E385) that, by the "time" of the apocalypse in *Jerusalem*, is no mere "collection" but an incarnation or identification of the Divine Humanity (or Human Divinity). In this light, Blake may well have read into the figure of Archimago-as-Redcrosse some evidence of Spenser's poetic genius alive, however faint and struggling beneath the crushing panoply of love and war, for it is he, not the true Redcrosse, that Una saves from certain death at the hands of Sansloy (I,iii,37).

Thus, Blake provides us no fewer than three Redcrosses: as a personification of vengeful war (richly armored and armed knight, a prototypical Arthur); as Archimago (inherent perhaps in the look Blake's Redcrosse gives Una, one that cannot be described as "holy"—just as his "defending himself" with his shield against the power of her truth or virginity is hardly Spenserian); and, finally, as a "child" (childe). The first of these we shall come to once again in due course, as we move down (up?) the line toward Arthur *in propria persona*; the second is but a fleeting suggestion by Blake and will not be repeated elsewhere in the procession; and the third "reappears" in our second look at Una to discover her nonspectrous, non-Babylonian self.

We have already seen that, in one sense, she is a conventional and therefore un-Blakean Virgin Mary, her haloed head, demeanor, posture on the ass, and gesture all tending to corroborate that identification. If, in Blake's eyes, she is a pregnant Mary (a traditional exegetical interpretation based on Luke 2:4–5), her proleptic relationship in the painting to the Dwarf-child leading her is biblically (as well as imaginatively) correct—a quite extraordinary reconstitution of Spenser's misconception. As others have noted, Blake gives Una no veil despite Spenser's careful noting of it, the standard Spenserian gloss being that Truth cannot be fully perceived until one is "purified" or initiated into its mysteries, as Redcrosse is in the House of Holiness. To Blake, however, "He who does not Know Truth at Sight is unworthy of Her Notice," a marginal comment in Reynolds's *Discourses* countering the latter's assertion that "beside real, there is also apparent truth" (E659). In his painting of the Last Judgment, Blake employs "a Cloud of Women & Children . . . fleeing from the rolling Cloud which separates the Wicked from the Seats of Bliss" to represent "those who tho willing were too weak to Reject Error without the Assistance & *Countenance* of those Already in the Truth" (E563; my italics). Redcrosse may be part of that cloud.

Blake not only rejects the common Renaissance notion that Truth is veiled in some way but also interprets it as a measure of Spenser's own error in *The Faerie Queene* as a whole; for its "dark conceite" that continually veils the truth "beneath" the allegory is but Spenser's veiled Una writ large. In its most devastating sense, Spenser's allegorical-virginal veil over the face of truth is Blake's Vala (pronounced Veila)—Nature draped over the face of Eternity. *The Four Zoas*, therefore, presents Vala as a parody of Mary: "Vala was pregnant & brought forth Urizen Prince of Light."[19] It is not necessary to read Una-as-Mary into this passage to recognize the appropriateness of such a gestation to Blake's corrective critique of Spenser in the painting. Vala's city is Babylon, and she herself is "the Goddess Virgin-Mother" (*Jerusalem* 18:29, E163). With her continual weaving (and wearing) of veils, her association with the curtains hiding the ark and covenant, her being the "shadow" of Jerusalem, and so on, Vala is a kind of Spenserian import into Blake's eclectic mythologizing. Her world is, alas, Spenser's world of fairy—at once classics-dominated (the figure of Jove regnant) and, as we have seen with respect to Blake's fairies, Nature-dominated (the spread-winged presence); but it is also, to misappropriate Blake's phrasing from the Bard's speech in *Milton*, earthly Glory-Power-Dominion-dominated, as the entire panoply of knights "errant" (Blake would have liked that error-suffused word) in courtly service to a virgin queen makes all too abundantly clear.[20] Freed of her veil, Blake's Una is not, then, the *Virgin* Mary but the Mary of *The Everlasting Gospel* as well as the woman Jerusalem, whose alter-configuration, the city, shines dazzlingly in its truth above her head in the painting.

In this light, Una's book is redeemed by Blake from its Urizenic implications. Spenser, of course, endows her with no book; but there are two relevant books in Book I of *The Faerie Queene*. The one Redcrosse gives to Arthur in exchange for Arthur's gift of virtuous balm in their pledge of mutual friendship is "his Saueours testament / . . . writ with golden letters rich and braue; / A worke of wondrous grace, and able soules to saue" (ix,19). If the book in Una's lap is intended to reflect this gift, as I believe it is, one cannot deny the imaginative significance of (1) Blake's stealing it ("translating" it) from the soiled hands of Spenser's Holiness, who immediately ignores the book and falls prey to Despaire and the temptation to suicide; (2) granting it to Una, via the Arthur who defeats Orgoglio and Duessa by "accepting" Una's "simple selfe, and seruice euermore" (viii,27); and (3) thereby iconicizing her as, in a sense, the book itself. In the painting Una instructs us, not Redcrosse, who is behind her, shield at the ready, and who, if he is indeed listening, shows little sign of it. Nor does he look at the book, despite Una's indicating some text with her right hand. Perhaps he is meant to be seen as blinded, or at least dazzled, by "The blazing brightnesse of her beauties beame," which he recognizes as the sign of "a goodly maiden Queen" (I,xii,8); or perhaps he is about to prance off the left side of Blake's picture to leave

"*Vna* . . . to mourne" (I,xii,41)—both equally damnable attitudes to Blake. As to the book itself, what distinguishes it is its visible red letters, a detail that associates Una firmly, as Spenser does, with Fidelia, the contrary of Duessa-Fidessa who mesmerizes Redcrosse into his disastrous "misreading" of the same book.

Rudely unveiled by Sansloy, and hence delegalized and de-Urizenized, Una's beauty shines forth "as brightest skye" (I,vi,4); so Fidelia

> Like sunny beames threw from her Christall face,
> That could haue dazd the rash beholders sight,
> And round about her head did shine like heauens light.
> (x,12)

Like Una, she is "araied all in lilly white," but without the dark wimple of mourning, and she carries in her left hand "A booke, that was both signd and seald with blood, / Wherein darke things were writ, hard to be vnderstood" (x,13)—Spenser referring to 2 Peter 3:16 and Revelation 5ff. Peter is speaking of Paul's epistles, but Blake would have applauded (as Spenser did) Peter's warning about misreading: "in all his epistles . . . are some things hard to be understood, which they that are unlearned and unstable wrest, as they do also the other scriptures, into their own destruction." In Revelation the book is "in the right hand of him that sat on the throne," and "no man was found worthy to open and read the book, neither [as in the case of Blake's Redcrosse] to look thereon."[21] Redcrosse is put to school to Fidelia's book, which "opened his dull eyes, that light mote in them shine" (x,18). From one point of view, Blake interpreted Redcrosse's being instilled with this "celestiall discipline" (x,18) to become God's warrior as his learning to be not merely Saint George but also Arthur.[22] In this sense, Blake no doubt would have been pleased to find that the immediate reaction of Holiness to this teaching is an intensified sense of his own sinfulness, a loathing of the world, despair, and the temptation to self-destruction—the inevitable end of holy Christian "warfare." Such warfare leads to the raising "up of Mystery the Virgin Harlot Mother of War" and to the institution of "Heaven as a Punisher & Hell as One under Punishment: / With Laws from Plato & his Greeks to renew the Trojan Gods / In Albion; & to deny the value of the Saviours blood" (*Milton* 22[24]:48–54, E117–18)—that blood in which Una-Fidelia's book is writ. As a consequence, "No Faith is in all the Earth: the Book of God is trodden under Foot" (ibid., l. 60). For Blake, however, "The Jewish & Christian Testaments are An original derivation from the Poetic Genius" (E1) and are indeed "the Great Code of Art" (*Laocoön*, E274), "translated as well as written by the Holy Ghost'' (letter to James Blake, E727). By giving Fidelia's book to Una, Blake ingeniously transmits "Fidelia" through Una to his Dwarf-child—for it is "He who respects the Infants faith" that "Triumphs over Hell & Death" (*Auguries of Innocence*, E492). Fidelia's "sacred Booke," we should recall is

> with bloud ywrit,
> That none could read, except she did them teach,
> She vnto him disclosed euery whit,
> And heauenly documents thereout did preach.
>
> (I,x,19)

This is precisely what Blake's Una is doing, and in so doing she becomes in a sense Blake's Jerusalem as well as her eponymous poem *Jerusalem*, which Blake himself labels in a revealing afterthought, "The Song of Jerusalem" (E259). In other words, she is a major redemptive image by which Blake can correct Spenser's angelic, spectrous poeticizing, for

> Man is adjoind to Man by his Emanative portion:
> Who is Jerusalem in every individual Man: and her
> Shadow is Vala, builded by the Reasoning power in Man.
>
> (*Jerusalem* 39 [44]:38–40, E187)

Moreover, for Blake, Jerusalem is the "Bride" of "The Lamb of God"—hence the True Church of the Song of Solomon—as well as "the Emanation of the Giant Albion" (*Jerusalem* 27, E171), Blake's macrocosmic version of Mary and Joseph. The key to this relationship is in the remarkable moving vision the "Divine Voice" vouchsafes to the despairing Jerusalem separated from Albion: "Behold," says the Divine Voice,

> behold Joseph & Mary
> And be comforted O Jerusalem in the Visions of Jehovah Elohim

She looked & saw Joseph the Carpenter in Nazareth & Mary
His espoused Wife. And Mary said, If thou put me away from thee
Dost thou not murder me? Joseph spoke in anger & fury. Should I
Marry a Harlot & an Adultress? Mary answered, Art thou more pure
Than thy Maker who forgiveth Sins & calls against Her that is Lost
Tho She hates. he calls her again in love. I love my dear Joseph
But he driveth me away from his presence. yet I hear the voice of God
In the voice of my Husband. tho he is angry for a moment, he will not
Utterly cast me away. if I were pure, never could I taste the sweets
Of the Forgive[ne]ss of Sins! if I were holy! I never could behold the
     tears

213

Of love! of him who loves me in the midst of his anger in furnace of
   fire.

Ah my Mary: said Joseph: weeping over & embracing her closely in
His arms: Doth he forgive Jerusalem & not exact Purity from her who
   is
Polluted. I heard his voice in my sleep & his Angel in my dream:
Saying, Doth Jehovah Forgive a Debt only on condition that it shall
Be Payed? Doth he Forgive Pollution only on conditions of Purity
That Debt is not Forgiven! That Pollution is not Forgiven
Such is the Forgiveness of the Gods, the Moral Virtues of the
Heathen, whose tender Mercies are Cruelty. But Jehovahs Salvation
Is without Money & without Price, in the Continual Forgiveness of
   Sins
In the Perpetual Mutual Sacrifice in Great Eternity! for behold!
There is none that liveth & Sinneth not! And this is the Covenant
Of Jehovah: If you Forgive one-another, so shall Jehovah Forgive
   You:
That He Himself may Dwell among You. Fear not then to take
To thee Mary thy Wife, for she is with Child by the Holy Ghost.
                                                 (61:1–27, E211–212)

I quote this long passage not only because of its great beauty but because it serves as a kind of epitome of Blake's unhappiness with Spenser's religion—parallel to his disaffection with that of Milton. In her
despair and uncertainty, the voice of Jerusalem-Mary echoes across
the Blakean landscape with these words: "Am I Jerusalem the lost
Adultress? or am I / Babylon come up to Jerusalem?"—precisely the
ambiguity of Blake's Una. Blake reveals the truth of the matter in the
extraordinary coda to the above passage from *Jerusalem*:

   Mary leaned her side against Jerusalem, Jerusalem recieved
   The Infant into her hands in the Visions of Jehovah
                                                 (61:47–48, E212)

—that is, the infant Jesus becomes at once child of Mary-Jerusalem,
Eternal Groom to Jerusalem's Bride, and the redeemed Albion-
Adam to Jerusalem's emanation-Eve.[23]
   With this stunning series of "events" in mind, we can now recognize, in yet another double take of Blake's painting, that Una's posture on the ass, even as it echoes that of the Wife of Bath, also repeats
that of the poet-artist-Blake to the right of God (now perhaps to be
seen as Christ Jehovah; see figure 9). Their legs are crossed identically and, even more important, Una-Mary-Jerusalem's right hand
exactly repeats that of the artist (perhaps now a redeemed Spenser)—

she reading-"seeing" what he writes. In this light, Blake's painting may be taken as her unveiling of Spenser's essential truth, a transformation of one of the Proverbs of Hell ("Truth can never be told so as to be understood, and not be believ'd") into a visual criticism of Spenser's telling. Just so, the reversed Dwarf and Una configuration tells us not merely that a little child shall lead them but that Truth can only be "told so as to be understood" if it is told and "understood" by the imagination—or, as the Bard says in *Milton*,

> According to the inspiration of the Poetic Genius
> Who is the eternal all-protecting Divine Humanity
> To whom be Glory & Power & Dominion Evermore Amen.
> (14:1-3, E108)

Grant and Brown identify the "domed doorless building" directly above Una's head as "perhaps the castle of Celia" (GB78). It seems an excellent guess, given the associations I have just described. Not only does Una's book descend, as it were, from Cælia's "auntient house not farre away" (I,x,3) but its doorlessness and windowlessness are splendidly appropriate to Blake's conception of the lack of illumination inherent in Spenser's kind of holiness. (One is reminded of the chapel built "in the midst" of Blake's *Garden of Love*, the gates of which are shut "And Thou shalt not. writ over the door.")[24] Spenser provides an entry, but, as I have noted, it is biblically "streight and narrow," enforcing the "stouping low" of Una and Redcrosse (x,5). "Holiness is not The Price of Enterance into Heaven," Blake wrote in *A Vision of the Last Judgment* (E564), for "Holiness" is an attribute not of the Human Form Divine but of "the Spectre of Man, the Holy Reasoning Power," in which "is closed the Abomination of Desolation" and whose abiding place is in the "Heavens of Chastity & Uncircumcision" (*Jerusalem* 10:15-16, E153; 49:64, E199). Los's advice consistently is to "Go! put off Holiness / And put on Intellect," that is, Imagination (*Jerusalem* 91:55-56, E252). Thus, if Cælia's house is geographically located in Blake's design between Eden (just above Una's left hand) and the New Jerusalem (the keys to which "are to thy hand behight / By wise *Fidelia*"—I,x,50), the road from innocence to the higher innocence is neither the one that Redcrosse travels in *The Faerie Queene* nor one that Blake could sanction.

In this first character grouping, then, we have a visionary epitome not only of Book I but of the entire *Faerie Queene*. No mere portrait of characters, or even of eternal principles of human nature, as in the Chaucer painting, it presents to us a set of iconographic signals by which we can read Una's-Spenser's book. Redcrosse is Redcrosse or Arthur or Archimago or, redemptively, the Christ implicit in the "tender swadling band" in which he is clothed in history to be "rescued" by "a Faerie" (x,65)—the same Christ Blake emblemizes in his Dwarf-child clad in swaddling clout. It all depends upon our perception. Una is Una, the Virgin Mary, Blake's Mary, Fidelia, and Jerusalem, the agent of Spenser's redemption. Of the two, Redcrosse clearly comes off a distant second best. Except for the faint suggestion of redemption inherent in Blake's child-childe in swaddling bands, he is diminished virtually beyond repair from his paragon status in *The Faerie Queene*. If, as A. C. Hamilton and other Spenser scholars claim, "Book I provides the basis and structure for the whole poem,"[25] Blake's "Book I" does the same, for none of his knights fares any better than does Redcrosse. In one sense, at least, all of them are versions of Blake's basic conception of Chaucer's knight (see figure 3), though not necessarily a wholesale recapitulation of his minute particulars. Partly taken in by the careful ironies of Blake's prose description of Chaucer's knight, Kiralis contrasts his guarding "against temporal oppression" with Chaucer's self-portrait of the Poet who warns "about eternal oppression."[26] Bowden, however, compares him "to Blake's armored figures elsewhere—the Ghost of a Flea, the soldiers around the Whore of Babylon in the Bible series, the Satanic 'Fire' in *Gates of Paradise*, the Warrior in *The Grave* [illustrations], and so on"—concluding that, "with his segmented armor plating," Blake's Chaucerian Knight "seems not merely unparticularized, but also sinister."[27]

While "sinister" seems not quite applicable to Blake's Redcrosse (although his eyes and facial expression hardly inspire confidence or trust), it might well fit Blake's Guyon and Calidore—and, as we shall see, it is not entirely inappropriate to Britomart, Arthur, and Artegall. What must be kept in mind in viewing all of Blake's knights, however, is what I believe is his norm for all Christian warriors, the horseman of Revelation 19:

> And I saw heaven opened, and behold a white
> horse; and he that sat upon him was called
> Faithful and True, and in righteousness he doth
> judge and make war. (v.11)

This "knight" wears no armor, and his "sword" is the (s)word that "out of his mouth goeth . . . that with it he would smite the nations." Moreover, in a revealing echo of the "man child" of the "woman clothed with the sun" (Rev. 12:1–5)—the latter surely a relative of Blake's Una—"he shall rule . . . with a rod of iron" (Rev. 19:15,

12:5). Both passages in turn typologically echo Isaiah 11: "And there shall come forth a rod out of the stem of Jesse, and a Branch shall grow out of his roots. . . . and he shall smite the earth with the rod of his mouth and with the breath of his lips shall he slay the wicked" (vv. 1, 4). All three passages, of course, represent a tranformation of the rod of Old Testamental punishment as well as the magical rod of Aaron. Faithful and True's "name is called The Word of God" (Rev. 19:13); he is precisely what Blake means in *Jerusalem* by "a Visionary form dramatic" (98:28, E257), from whose tongue "redounds" the defeat of both "the beast" and "the false prophet," who are "both . . . cast alive into a lake of fire burning with brimstone" (v. 20). This verse may be the source of Blake's curious quatrain, in reversed writing, on plate 37[41] of *Jerusalem* (E184), originally drafted in his *Notebook*:

> Each Man is in his Spectre's power
> Untill the arrival of that hour
> When his Humanity awake
> And cast his Spectre into the Lake.
>
> (E810)

But with no lake mentioned in the text of the *Jerusalem* plate or on neighboring plates, one wonders whether Blake's inspiration for the passage came from Book II of *The Faerie Queene* where Maleger, accompanied by Impotence and Impatience, is described in distinctly spectrous terms: he is "pale and wan as ashes . . ., / His bodie lean and meagre," "skin all withered," and "as cold and drery as a Snake" (II,xi,22). Even more tantalizing, however, is the fact that he is "of such subtile substance and vnsound, / That like a ghost he seem'd, whose graue-clothes were vnbound" (st. 20). Consequently, when Arthur finally runs him through, "Ne drop of bloud appeared shed to bee," and Maleger, though pierced again and again by Arthur's sword, "freshly as at first, prepared himselfe to fight" (st. 38), a "lifelesse shadow" with seeming eternal life (st. 44).

Thus for Blake, appropriately, neither Arthur's omnipotent sword, Morddure, nor his reason is effective against this spectre:

> His [Arthur's] wonder farre exceeded reasons reach,
>   That he began to doubt his dazeled sight,
>   And oft of error did himself appeach:
>   Flesh without bloud, a person without spright,
>   Wounds without hurt, a bodie without might,
>   That could doe harme, yet could not harmed bee,
>   That could not die, yet seem'd a mortall wight,

That was most strong in most infirmitee;
Like did he neuer heare, like did he neuer see.

(St. 40)

One could not find a better definition of Blake's conception of the Spectre of Man, which is itself the reasoning power in Arthur and is, therefore, impervious to physical assault or reasonable outwitting (not to say ''understanding''). Maleger is thus a ''wonder'' that elicits Arthur's baffled wondering. As well, Spenser's stanza might serve here as a definition of the kind of allegorical figment Blake most fundamentally objects to in Spenser, a congeries of vices, the lusts of the flesh, given life via a name. At the same time, Maleger (like the Adam of Genesis) draws his strength from Earth, which ''his mother was, and first him bore'' (st. 44)—Blake's Vala or the fallen Urthona. Therefore, physically ''killing'' him and consigning him ''to graue terrestriall'' paradoxically restores him to ''life''; the ''reasonable'' thing to do to destroy him becomes allegorically the rebirth of Blake's reasoning Spectre. Thus, just as Blake turns upside down Maleger's assault on Alma as the battering of the senses against the citadel of the soul, making it thereby the assault of Reason against man's divine humanity,[28] so he transforms Spenser's Arthur momentarily into ''Humanity awake'' (that is, the Imagination),[29] and Maleger ends up in the lake: ''So end of that Carles dayes, and his owne paines did make'' (st. 46). If he is to Spenser, as F. J. Child long ago suggested, ''disease,''[30] for Blake he is the ultimate Urizenic disease that wars against the human form divine, his own ratiocinative faculty with its mind-forged manacles which constructs allegories unannihilable except by the sort of antiallegories or counterlanguage Los (and Blake) create to cast all spectres in the lake. In Blake's mature symbology, the lake is the lake of Udan-Adan, ''the condition of formlessness, of the indefinite'';[31] thus, the odd maneuver of throwing one's Spectre in the lake is not merely to de-form it but to un-form it, to reverse Genesis as it were. Corporately, Los's counterlanguage emanates into the sword out of the mouth of Revelation, which, as The Word, casts all fallen words (the language of Babel) ''alive into a lake of fire burning with brimstone''—and which, in Blake's leading configuration in the Spenser painting, is embodied as the true ''Faithful and True'' (as opposed to Spenser's Redcrosse and Una, even as he images their redeemed essences) in the Dwarf-child-childe-Lamb-Christ-Imagination-''image of truth new-born.''

Some attention must also be paid to the animal component of this first figure grouping in Blake's painting. Although the specifics do not quite match, I am inclined to see this rather tight clustering of ass, lion, horse, and dragon as a version of that aspect of the apocalypse of *Jerusalem* in which "the Words of the Mutual Covenant Divine" appear

On Chariots of gold & jewels with Living Creatures starry & flaming
With every Colour, Lion, Tyger, Horse, Elephant . . .
And the all wondrous Serpent clothed in gems & rich array . . .

—all "humanizing" in "the Forgiveness of Sins according to the Covenant of Jehovah" (98:41–45, E258). Without attempting a Blakean bestiary here (something, incidentally, that still needs to be done in Blake studies), I assert nothing new by associating this somewhat odd foursome with Revelation's four "beasts": lion, calf, one unspecified but with "a face as a man," and eagle (4:7); but I do point particularly to "a Lamb" that stands "in the midst of the throne and of the four beasts" (5:6). He "shall lead them unto living fountains of waters" (7:17). Although it seems an interpretive evasion, the very lack of similarity among these three foursomes, as well as the confusing ambiguities and even contradictions inherent in their separate significations in Blake's works (not to mention in the Bible),[32] argue for their all being "equal," as it were. They are the quaternaries humanized as simply "*The* Four Living Creatures" (98:24; my italics), which, in Blake's ambiguous syntax and lack of punctuation, are also "*The* Four Living . . . Chariots" whose "Horses" (l. 13; Blake's plural here is revealing) are "Fourfold." "Urizen & Luvah & Tharmas & Urthona" are now "risen" into "Albions Bosom: Then Albion stood before Jesus in the Clouds / Of Heaven Fourfold among the Visions of God in Eternity" (96:41–43, E256).

The contrary view is that Redcrosse's horse is *Redcrosse's* horse (surely one of Blake's famous "horses of instruction," especially given the Spenserian rigors of the House of Holinesse); Una's ass is the conventionally humble, meek, and mild Christ; the lion is destructive wrath as well as the legendary protector of Elizabethan virginity; and the dragon is Revelation's "that old serpent, called the Devil, and Satan" and Spenser's "that old Dragon" of canto xi, Book I. They are the very stuff of allegories, as in Lucifera's palace (dragon, peacock, ass, swine, goat, camel, wolf, lion) and all other Spenserian zoos. Corporately they are "the beast that . . . was" but, if we see it aright, "is not," the beast that "from the foundation of the world . . . was, and is not, and yet is." Those who "behold" it are those "whose names were not [and shall not be] written in the book of life" (Rev. 17:8). No domesticated peaceful cohabitation will do, no lions lying down with lambs (or asses), nor horses with tigers, nor man with serpents. That is the pap of fairy tales, what Blake calls in the *Jerusalem* apocalypse "the Covenant of Priam, the Moral Virtues of the Heathen" (98:46, E258), "an allegorical abode where existence hath never come" (*Europe* 5:7, E62). The Revelation beast, we should recall, is shut up in the bottomless pit for only a thousand years, "and after that he must be loosed a little season" (20:3). For Blake, alas, it is eternally loose in *The Faerie Queene*, the Blatant Beast writ large; and unlike the ringing assurance of the close of *Jerusalem*, Spenser was but able to muster the somewhat forlorn, even (after Book VI) tattered, hope of being granted "that Sabaoths sight" that will lay all dragons to eternal rest (VII,viii,2).

One final note—this with respect to Blake's visionary geography—to link the Spenser painting with the Chaucer, as well as Redcrosse (and indeed all Spenser's knights) with Blake's Arthur. In *Jerusalem* Blake writes with disarming conventionality, "Rahab Babylon the Great hath destroyed Jerusalem"; but then, as if to deliberately unconventionalize the obvious, he adds: "Bath stood upon the Severn with Merlin & Bladud & Arthur / The Cup of Rabab in his hand" (75:1–3, E230). Elsewhere in *Jerusalem* (37[41]:1, E183), "Bath . . . is Legions," a rather nice double entendre on the Gospel of Mark's "unclean spirit" whose "name is Legion" (5:2, 9) as well as on the name of the city that, according to legend, King Bladud founded and in which King Arthur was crowned and established his court, Legions. In eternity the "healing City" and one of "wisdom in midst of Poetic / Fervor" (*Jerusalem* 40[45]:1, E187), Bath is transformed in this world from "benevolent / . . . physician" to "poisoner: the best and worst in Heaven and Hell" (37[41]:1–2, E183). There is little doubt that such a "history" is implicit in Blake's Wife of Bath, his Chaucerian Rahab, and therefore, "she" is the very antithesis of Chaucer's Canterbury. But, characerically, not of Blake's Canterbury—for, as Damon shrewdly noticed, in Blake's establishment of the "four pillars" of Los's "throne" in *Milton*, where we expect to find Canterbury, we find Legions ("London & Bath & Legions & Edinburgh"), just as where we expect to find York (in Blake's principal Cathedral-cities quaternary), we find Bath.[33] Chaucer's pilgrimage, then (pilgrimage itself being a "fallen" conception, like "progress"), is ultimately self-defeating, for it proceeds to Canterbury, which is Bath, and then presumably returns to the equally corrupted cathedral cities of the rest of the pilgrims.[34] All are embodiments of state religion, and hence—to return to Merlin, Bladud, and Arthur—all are, in a sense, Arthurian as well as Rahabian.[35] At one point, Los (Blake) directs the villain "Skofield" to identify himself as to whether "he is Bath or if he is Canterbury / Tell him to be no more dubious: demand explicit words" (*Jerusalem* 17:59, E162). This, Blake's only known use of "dubious" in verse or prose, is a wonderful bit of word-play, for, as I have anticipated, Skofield is both "cities." We should not be surprised to find that "his Emanation is Gwinevera" (*Jerusalem* 71:39, E225) and that, even more Arthur-like, he is "let loose upon [the] Saxons."[36] Spectrous Bath (Canterbury) thus "equals" Rahab, Arthur, Chaucer's Wife, Babylon, physician-turned-poisoner, and a host of others, a rather splendid example in itself of a kind of superallegorizing to deliver all individuals (readers) from all allegories.

Merlin's and Bladud's roles in this composite may be less clear but they are no less crucial. From Milton's *History of Britain*, Blake would have discovered that Bladud not only built Bath but, Merlin-like (and Archimago-like), "taught Necromancie: till having made him Wings to fly, he fell down upon the Temple of *Apollo* in *Trinovant* [London], and so dy'd."[37] Moreover, in *The Faerie Queene* it is Merlin who forges Arthur's armor just as Bladud fashions the weapons and armor of Britomart.[38] If Blake perceived Spenser's Arthur to be in any sense at all a "version" (even a misconceived one) of his own Albion, Blake's efforts to redeem Albion are appropriately Herculean. More accurately, Blake's Arthur is a considerably lesser figure than Spenser's, the conceptual diminution itself perhaps as acerbic a comment as Blake could make on his lost cause. For Arthur is, fundamentally, one of the kings created by Rahab and Tirzah, armed by the necromancers (or false prophets) Merlin-Bladud-Archimago, marshalling his power in Bath-Legions as Satan-Legion, and functioning in *Jerusalem* as a male counterpart to Vala-Babylon. No wonder Blake presents him as he does in his painting in the guise of Redcrosse, for he is the very Dragon-antiChrist he purports to slay.

Blake's pictorialization of Arthur *in propria persona*, however, is central not to this first group but to the center of the entire rest of the "procession." To that we may now turn with what I trust is greater confidence in our ability to read Blake's "vision of Spenser" aright.

CHAPTER SEVEN

The Characters in Spenser's Faerie Queene, III

T HE DETAILED examination I have just accorded the Redcrosse-Una-Dwarf group is justified, I believe, by its paradigmatic configuration and by its implications both for *The Faerie Queene* and for Blake's painting. It reflects as well my sense of Blake's restructuring of Spenser's work, for although the latter's six-book arrangement is reflected in the six major groupings or panels of the painting, it does not require much study to notice that Book IV is missing. One could argue, I suppose, that it is not possible to graphically epitomize Book IV, by its very nature, especially since it has no titular knight; perhaps that difficulty contributed to Blake's artistic decision. But if we remember that the fourth book "defines" friendship, we might well wonder if Blake, at least in one sense, conceived of the entire painting as his Book IV, wherein is "ensampled" his dictum that "Opposition is true Friendship."[1] For Spenser, friendship is cemented by "vertue . . . that bindeth harts most sure" (IV,ii,29), but more crucially for Blake it is epitomized in *The Faerie Queene* in the Temple of Venus, the outer gate of which is guarded by Doubt and Delay, the inner gate by Daunger, and the "porch" of which is manned by Loue and Hate, whose endless strife is prevented only by the constant vigilance of Concord, "Mother of blessed *Peace*, and *Friendship* trew" (x,12–34).

> By her the heauen is in his course contained
> And all the world in state vnmoued stands,
> As their Almightie maker first ordained,
> And bound them with inuiolable bands;
> Else would the waters ouerflow the lands.
> And fire deuoure the ayre, and hell then quight,
> But that she holds them with her blessed hands.
> She is the nourse of pleasure and delight,
> And vnto *Venus* grace the gate doth open right.

(St. 35)

Venus herself, an archetypal Blakean male female and female male who "Begets and eke conceiues" like Blake's Vala and whose altar is the center of "Great sorts of louers piteously complayning" in good Petrarchan fashion, is attended by Womanhood (in whose lap the Petrarchan Amoret sits), Shamefastnesse, Cherefulnesse, Modestie, Curtesie, Silence, and Obedience—all in all a pantheon that could not have been constructed more exactly to be an anathema to Blake. And the fact that Scudamour "rescues" Amoret from the temple is no salvation for Spenser, for their hermaphroditic union in the cancelled ending of Book III was sufficient unto itself to damn them irretrievably in Blake's eyes—not to mention Spenser's telling admission in Book IV that Scudamour "conquers" the "vertuous Amoret" (x,Argument).

The Characters in Spenser's Faerie Queene, then, may be considered quite properly as Blake's "severe contentions of friendship" with Spenser, "the burning fire of [the former's] thought" reconstituting the poem in the image of a kind of apocalypse, a revelation of the fundamental imaginative truth of Spenser's vision that is so obdurately obscured by the spectrous "selfhood" of his moral-allegorical vehicle. If Blake's fallen Los "is the Vehicular Form" of the unfallen Urthona (as all the other zoas and their myriad entourages are vehicular forms of their eternal identities),[2] Blake well may have regarded *The Faerie Queene* as the vehicular form of Spenser himself—or at least the fallen, fragmented form (Arthur) of his own fallen, fragmented Albion, virtually irretrievable because of the absence of an Imagination (Jesus-Los-Poetic Genius) adequate to vehicularize it. Milton was able to redeem himself in *Milton*; but in the Spenser painting it might be argued that Blake regarded Spenser as needing his "friend" Jesus-Blake to lead him to the light. Although one need not subscribe to this suggestion of a monumental arrogance on Blake's part to "read" the Spenser painting aright, it is well to remember the tone of Blake's satiric notebook epigrams, the motto of which may be taken to be, "I found them blind I taught them how to see" (E508). The most outrageous epitome of these epigrams is the scatological "redemption" of Friedrich Klopstock, who, in effect, put himself (and his poem *The Messiah*) forward as *the* successor to Milton:

> If Blake could do this when he rose up from shite
> What might he not do if he sat down to write[3]

—or paint?

To return to the structuring of the Spenser painting (see figure 4) the Redcrosse-Una-Dwarf grouping is made carefully discrete from the other five major groups, insulated as it is by the powerful vertical line of the Palmer. His robe is darker than any other form of dress in the painting and his both-feet-on-the-ground stationariness and backward glance make him a virtual parenthesis mark. Moreover, with ideological as well as geometric precision, he is complemented by Talus's closing parenthesis mark. In this light the painting divides itself into three groups: that of Redcrosse, the triple configuration between the Palmer and Talus, and the "concluding" Arthur-Calidore apparent coupling. At the same time, as I suggested at the close of chapter 6, the first of these is so isolated that one might well see the entire remainder of the procession as a single group, in the exact center of which is an ambiguous Artegall, who, as we shall see, is also Arthur and who cavorts on his horse directly below the "imaginative center" of the supernal realms, the figure of the poet-artist. Then again, Britomart claims centrality in her mimicking of the gestural embrace of Blake's portrait of Chaucer's Host (even to the exact duplication, in reverse, of the leg positioning of the Host's horse); and so do "Artegall" with his hand waving and Arthur with his expansive gesture, not to mention "God" signaling Britomart and Artegall to be his center.

Blake's point seems to be, then, that *The Faerie Queene* has so many self-proclaimed centers that it has no center; in the language of his annotations to Reynolds, the "One Central Form Composed of all other Forms" (E648) is missing. That central form, as early as the Lavater annotations, is for Blake the God who is "the vortex, the centre, the comparative point from which [man] sets out, on which he fixes, to which he irresistibly returns."[4] It is the "Center" that, in *The Four Zoas*, Urizen's "Web of Religion" "misplaces," "altering the Vortexes" (VIII, E375) so that what is eternally "Within" becomes "Without, . . . the Selfish Center" (*Jerusalem* 71:6–7, E225). As Lavater said in his third aphorism, "As in looking upward each beholder thinks himself the centre of the sky; so Nature formed her individuals, that each must see himself the centre of being."[5] That, alas, is what Spenser's spectrous "natural" self did—an error corroborated and exacerbated by his abandoning to unexplained limbo the only possibility of redemption as Blake saw it, the Dwarf. With studied contrariousness, then, Blake's pictorial attribution of physical insignificance to the Dwarf in a land of giant forms is his paradoxical magnification of the Child's ultimate power (an idea Blake surely found at least confirmed in Milton's *Nativity Ode*).

One other aspect of Blake's postural stationing of Spenser's characters is also to the point. Beginning with the somewhat subtle suggestion of Redcrosse's head, there is a kind of backward directional motif countering the horses' apparent movement forward. The Palmer glances backward (curiously at Guyon's horse), Guyon is in sharp right profile, Britomart and Artegall peek to their left, and Calidore virtually twists himself backward off his mount. I shall comment on Arthur's obvious exception to this "rule" in a moment, but I reserve full discussion of his role in the painting until later in this chapter. Despite Arthur's forward look, given the persistent pattern of back-wardness, one must imagine some significance in the fact that the only left profiles (of the "major" characters) are those of the Dwarf-child and Talus, the latter of whose seeming "right vision" is com-promised severely by his sideways both-feet-on-the-ground stance that echoes in reverse that of the Palmer. Similarly, Duessa's and Ar-chimago's left profiles are directed downward to the Blatant Beast and, at the same time, accentuate their even greater immobility. Of all the pedestrians, only the child strides, as well as looks (sees), for-ward, his modest advance a giant step.

Blake's Arthur, as in Spenser, not only has no "book" but may be said to have no "place" in the poem or in the painting. Thus, he interrupts, as it were, the various symmetries to which I have re-ferred. Where he stands in the painting is Book V, but we already have Book V, Artegall and Talus, in the Palmer-Talus bracketed "middle" panel. Moreover, the overlap of Arthur's horse's hind-quarters with Calidore's horse seems to slide him into Book VI, even as Astraea's left arm and palm-down hand include him in Book V. Finally, he seems to include himself in Book V by "quoting" Arte-gall's hand-waving, and Talus keeps him from fading out of Book V by holding the reins of Arthur's horse in mimicry of the Palmer's holding those of Guyon's horse. Part of this "confusion" is due to Blake's omission of Book IV, but at this point it is the better part of valor to postpone a major engagement with that confusion (not to say contradictions, contraries, and mirrorings) in order to fill out my sense of what seems to be Blake's basic tripartite scheme. In the ex-treme right panel, then, Calidore properly dominates, his face as sharply turned to the right as Guyon's, his spear echoing Guyon's (and to a lesser extent Redcrosse's), and his right arm extended downward (as Redcrosse's and Guyon's are upward) and to the right toward Duessa, Archimago, and the Blatant Beast. Even his curved sword, lower left leg, and stirrup move our eyes down and back, away not only from the middle group (with or without Arthur) but from the entire procession (see figure 8).

As the final panel, bracketing (with the Dwarf-Una-Redcrosse panel) the entire middle of *The Faerie Queene* (Books II–V), the Cali-dore panel ought to have some meaningful relationship with its oppo-site number.[6] The most obvious indication of such a relationship is

FIGURE 8.   Detail of right quarter of *The Characters in Spenser's Faerie Queene*

(*courtesy of* Blake: An Illustrated Quarterly)

the wildly out-of-sequence presence here of Duessa and Archimago, neither of whom figures in Book VI, neither of whom ever comes into contact with (or even within sight of) Calidore or the Blatant Beast. But, along with Spenser's critics at least since Upton, Blake surely regarded the Blatant Beast as a reincarnation of "that old Dragon," Erroure, and as such an appropriate bestiary emblem for the two archdeceivers. Despite the apparently "reigning" sun above this panel, as I noted earlier, Blake has drawn a scene of darkness, unilluminated by sun or moon; it is the darkness to which all this world (and hence the world of *The Faerie Queene*) will return in the same diurnal round, echoed in reverse by the supernal configuration of sun and moon. With that round, the beast reappears and Babylon resumes her ascendant power in Duessas of various names as well as in Blake's Tower of Babel above her head—Blake's Child-Word but a Dwarf once more, lost somewhere in the thickets, perhaps even in the forests of the night, of Spenser's fairyland. No apocalyptic words, as those of the book in Una's lap, "conclude" Spenser's vision in the poem, but rather language in its most (and doubly) debased form, Duessan-Archimagoan allegory and the virtually physical destructiveness of the Blatant Beast (who, though physically muzzled, cannot be muzzled, as Spenser himself knew all too well).

Blake surely identified with Spenser in that last stanza of Book VI, for the "blatant beasts" in his own life and career were legion. But he also knew that the contumely of others was but surety of the rightness of his vision and of his words.

> My title as Genius thus is provd
> Not Praisd by Hayley nor by Flaxman lovd,

he wrote in his *Notebook* (E505); and, again:

> I mock thee not tho I by thee am Mocked
> Thou callst me Madman but I call thee blockhead.

(E507)

If Blake's Duessa is at least partially stripped to her ugliness and Archimago is firmly bound, they too know the power of the Blatant Beast's tongues.[7] The fixity of their staring down upon him may well be Blake's revelation to us that, although dragons are slayable, endlessly slayable, the false words of a diseased imagination have an awful power over our souls. The Lilliputian humans that bind the Brobdingnagian beast[8] suggest, in their futility, the silly ineffectiveness of the Brobdingnagian Calidore binding the Lilliputian Blatant Beast (an act rendered even more futile by Blake's transformation of Calidore's "capture" of the beast into a ridiculous hand gesture).

In one sense, then, what Blake angrily leaves us with is Archimago as Spenser, physically more Michelangeloesque and powerful than any other character in the painting, but old and still consorting with a very much alive Duessa who is, in this sense, the two-ness of Spenser's poem, its fundamental allegorical deceptiveness. As unattractive as Blake makes her, she is not, in this *Faerie Queene*, stripped naked to her monstrously repulsive essential self. The venom of the beast that Spenser prays his verse will "escape" has already infected it mightily, and, if unchecked by Blake, will ramp on either through the poem in reverse or back through the right border of the painting (where we see the rest of its scales and batlike spines) to enter the world of the first panel once again as "that old Dragon."

Aside from the Blatant Beast-Dragon connection and the waving of Calidore's hand as a Blakean *reductio* not only of his binding the Beast but of worldly warriors squelching language, we need to know now what all this has to do with Spenser's Book VI. His proem is marginally helpful in this regard. Spenser calls upon the muses to

> Reuele to me the sacred noursery
>   Of vertue, which with you [the muses] doth there remaine,
>   Where it in siluer bowre does hidden ly
>   From view of men, and wicked worlds disdaine.
>   Since it at first was by the Gods with paine
>   Planted in earth, being deriu'd at furst
>   From heauenly seedes of bounty soueraine,
>   And by them long with carefull labour nurst,
> Till it to ripenesse grew, and forth to honour burst.
>
> (St. 3)

Blake, I think, read this "noursery" as Spenser's deluded metaphor of the state of innocence, couched paradoxically in the very "fallen" language Calidore is dedicated to eradicate or control. Perhaps he read the passage as an unfortunate echoing of the Cave of Mammon episode in Book II. To hide his "pretious hils from straungers enuious sight," Mammon pours his gold "Into the hollow earth, them there to hide" (vii,6). Guyon's response to this action reiterates the trope of riches hidden "From the worldes eye," which Mammon in turn translates into the "graces" that he pours "out vnto all" (st. 7–8): "the worldes blis" (32), "the fountaine of the worldes good" (38), and the Garden of Proserpine (51ff). And those graces, Blake would have remembered, include the very "Honour . . . and all this worldes good" that "in the hollow earth haue their eternall brood" (8).

But, whether or not he made this particular connection, his critical eye would not have missed Spenser's hidden silver bower as a sacred nursery of virtue, the very language employed here a measure of Spenser's benightedness. There is a sinister appropriateness, then, to Book VI's thematic introduction: as Mammon secretes his "virtue" in Proserpine's bowers, virtue (like Astraea) now has fled this "wicked world" and hides itself "From view of men" in a "siluer bowre" on Mount Parnassus. Even worse, the origin of virtue is "the Gods," who "with paine / Planted in earth" the "heauenly seedes of bounty soueraine" and then nursed them "with carefull labour" until they burst forth "to honour"—and the "fruit of honour and all chast desire" (III,v,52).[9] In Book IV the

> antique age yet in the infancie
> Of time, did liue then like an innocent,
> In simple truth and blamelesse chastitie,
> Ne then of guile had made experiment,
> But voide of vile and treacherous intent,
> Held vertue for it selfe in soueraine awe:
> Then loyall loue had royall regiment,
> And each vnto his lust did make a lawe,
> From all forbidden things his liking to withdraw.
>
> (viii,30)

The right spirit is there, Blake saw, but its articulation and verbalization reveal the depths of error from which he undertook to extricate Spenser.

Moreover, the pattern of *The Faerie Queene* as a whole, culminating in a "retreat" to the realms of innocence, surely would have recalled to Blake his own *Book of Thel* and *Tiriel*: after five books of moral virtues based squarely on the validity of the senses and their warfare (Thel's grave plot), Spenser flees back to his version of the Vales of Har, complete with Adam and Eve (Blake's Har and Heva in *Tiriel*, Spenser's Meliboe and "his aged Beldame")[10] and a Thel alter ego, Pastorella. The Brigants' capture of Pastorella and her imprisonment in their gravelike home may well have contributed to Blake's conception of Thel's grave plot. Pastorella "thought her self in hell," a place "not so well seene [Spenser adds] as felt" (VI,x,42–43).

> But for to tell the dolefull dreriment,
> And pittifull complaints, which there she made,
> Where day and night she nought did but lament
> Her wretched life, shut vp in deadly shade,
> And waste her goodly beauty, which did fade
> Like to a flowre.
>
> (St.44)

If Blake indeed recalled this passage, he rather shrewdly transfers Pastorella's lament *in* the grave to Thel's persistent whining, prior to entering her grave plot, about not being of use, about fading, and so on—impressive "proof" that Thel has already fallen well before she enters the grave. Her experience in the grave with her "Brigants" is thus a terrifying enactment of her essential (that is, mental) fallenness into the world of the senses. In Spenser, true to the male aspect of Blake's conception of the grave in *Thel*, the Brigant captain views his prisoner "With lustfull eyes" and pursues his courtship with "barbarous heart" inly burning "with flames most raging whot" (an obvious echo by Spenser of Amoret's mental-physical ordeal in Busirane's castle), as well as "With looks, with words, with gifts" (xi,3–4). And Pastorella's resultant "sickenesse" (which she feigns to ward off the Brigant's advances) "was not of the body but the mynde" (st. 8), echoing not only Amoret but Britomart after her vision of Artegall in Merlin's magic glass.

The parallel of Thel and Pastorella, though inexact, is a powerful confirmation of the illusoriness of innocence or its mental precariousness, as well as of the delusion inherent in any attempt to perpetuate it or to try to "recover" it by an act of will. When innocence becomes a retreat, it becomes a parody of innocence, which is to say, when innocence is perceived to be a retreat, the perceiver is no longer innocent. *Nurses Song* in *Songs of Experience* (E23) is a particularly fine example of such misperception, as is the more "Spenserian" *The Garden of Love* (E26). In the latter, the speaker "went" to the garden of love (that obviously *was* there), but what he "saw" is "what [he] never had seen": a chapel where he "used to play on the green" (the reference is to Blake's *The Echoing Green* of *Songs of Innocence*), graves (where "many sweet flowers" were before), and "Priests in black gowns, . . . walking their rounds" (the unusual internal rhyme underscoring the interiority of the speaker's entire "new" perception of the garden). Thus, the priestly "briars" that bind the speaker's "joys & desires" are but externalizations of his own mind-forged manacles transforming his world from innocent freedom and impulse to one of forbidding terror and restraint. That "world" (a mental world or "state of the soul," as the subtitle of the *Songs* tells us) is also one in which *The Divine Image* (Mercy-Pity-Peace-Love) of *Songs of Innocence* (E12) has "become" a shadow of itself, *The Human Abstract* of *Songs of Experience* (E27). In that state, the virtues that corporately and indissolubly "is" (to borrow Blake's crucial singular verb from *The Divine Image*) become not merely plural but discrete and, as it were, manufactured:

> Pity would be no more,
> If we did not make somebody Poor:
> And Mercy no more could be,
> If all were as happy as we;
>
> And mutual fear brings peace;
> Till the selfish loves increase.

Spenser was correct, then, to say that "vertues seat is deepe within the mynd, / And not in outward shows, but inward thoughts defynd" (VI,proem,5), but the world of Meliboe that he presents is to Blake ersatz, a physical retreat *from* the world, and thus a kind of abstract *of* the world. Meliboe confesses that, in his "pride of youth," he "disdain'd amongst [his] equall peares / To follow sheepe, and shepheards base attire" in favor of the "roiall court" where he "did sell [him] selfe for yearely hire, / And in the Princes gardin daily wrought" (ix,24). There, like Blake's speaker in *The Garden of Love*, he "beheld such vainenesse, as I neuer thought" and after "ten yeares" of so "excluding" himself "From natiue home" and its "sweet peace," he returns to his "sheepe againe" (st. 24–25). What Blake depicts in his Spenser painting is the cruel delusion, as I called it, the utter and terrible folly of Meliboe's "reachieved" innocence, presided over by a Calidore who is not merely armored but whose very skin is plated (as in a number of Blake's graphic renditions of Satan). Such an innocence is populated by neither Meliboes nor sheep but by the bowed, though hardly defeated, Har-Archimago and Heva-Duessa and their "flock," the many-tongued Blatant Beast (I leave aside for the moment the mysterious head beneath Calidore's horse).

Calidore's vision on Mount Acidale is the same illusion, called up by the pastoral poet (Colin-Spenser) and promptly destroyed by the nonpoet Calidore's attempt to "realize" its grand fiction (or truth)— just as we saw the young man of *The Crystal Cabinet* do with equal unsuccess in chapter 2. In one sense, then, for Blake, Pastorella (as her name suggests) is such a "realization" (or "abstraction," to borrow *The Marriage*'s verbal equation—E38), an allegorical epitome of Meliboe's world; and Blake would have been delighted to find that the first threat to her illusory status is a tiger, which

> forth out of the wood did rise,
> That with fell clawes full of fierce gourmandize,
> And greedy mouth, wide gaping like hell gate.
>
> (x,34)

Miraculously, with "no weapon, but his shepheards hooke," Calidore not only subdues the tiger but hews "off his head" which, like a
hunter's trophy, he lays "Before the feete of the faire *Pastorell*" (st.
36). The patent absurdity of this entire scene (aside from Calidore's
having nothing in hand to "hew" with) would have been to Blake
vivid proof of Spenser's fundamental error in Book VI, for to slay the
tiger is to sacrifice energy in favor of a world of lambs—theologically,
to evoke the meekness and humility of Christ rather than his energetic
power (imagination). To Spenser, this tiger is no doubt the same one
that Maleger rides in the senses' siege of the Castle of Alma
(II,xi,26).

Commensurate with his reconceiving of Spenser's conception (the
cogs of his wheel turning against the cogs of Spenser's adverse wheel),
Blake, in his painting of Book VI, gives us neither Pastorella nor
Meliboe, Colin Clout nor Coridon, Claribell nor Bellamoure, child
nor mother, lamb nor shepherd. No "immortal day" is here (*Night*,
Songs of Innocence, E14), only the sun of this world, no humanized universe but rather the night of Blake's Innocence deepened to the forests of the night of *The Tyger* and of Spenser's Blatant Beast and Brigants. To be sure, those forests are absent from Blake's final panel but,
as I have noted, the landscape of "innocence" in the middle distance
of the Book VI panel is just as forbiddingly ominous in its spectral
rocky barrenness. In light of all these absences, one wonders all the
more to whom the bodiless head under, or just to the right of, Calidore's horse's rear hooves, belongs. As Grant and Brown note, he
certainly "resists certain identification" (GB71). Their three
guesses—the Brigant chief, Braggadocchio, and Malbecco—seem to
me improbable enough to encourage my own guess, the only one I
can imagine as consonant with Blake's purposes in this Book VI
grouping, as I have defined it. Grant and Brown's conjectural identification of the object the figure is holding as "an open book" is, I
believe, far shrewder than they know, for the figure must be that of
one of Spenser's "gentle Poets" who are rent continually by the beast
"without regard of person or of time" (xii,40). With rather savage
irony, however, it is Calidore's horse that seems to hammer the figure, still clutching his book, into the ground, the courtly-Aristotelian-
moral-chivalric trappings of Spenser's poem quite literally running
its poetry, its evidence of Spenser's poetic genius beneath all that allegorical armor plate, into the ground. Although hardly in the remotest
sense a "portrait" of Spenser, the head, hands, and open book may
be, corporately, Blake's iconographic redaction of Spenser's concluding reference to the entire *Faerie Queene* as "this homely verse, of many
meanest" (VI,xii,41). At the same time, the portrait, if portrait it just

may be, is not entirely unlike that of Blake's Chaucer in the *Heads of the Poets* series, which includes a similar headdress, line of the nose, slanted mustache, and jowl whiskers—and Chaucer, as we have seen, unhappily fell prey to *his* knight, and allegorizing, in very much the same way that Spenser does. I see less resemblance to the *Heads of the Poets* Spenser except for the lower lips of both the head-with-book and the smartly courtierlike Spenser. If there are analogies elsewhere in Blake's graphic works, I am not aware of them,[11] so let us proceed to some conclusions about Calidore.

For Blake, it now should be clear that Book VI *is* Calidore, Spenser's conception of this knight of "'courtesie" doubly damnable as the embodiment of courtiership and as false shepherd, his homely "weed" invisible beneath his form-fitting armor plate in the painting. A pastoral hero is itself a contradiction in terms, and thus Blake forces upon Spenser a confession of the error to which he is attracted so mightily that it usurps the place in his poem that ought to be occupied by the New Jerusalem, or by an "identified" Arthur-Albion the Grand Man, or by the Dwarf-Child as Christ, by *some* Human Form Divine. Calidore's human form divine sheathed in iron emerges as the obverse of Talus, the latter—made of iron yet the only naked human form in the pageant—an astringent comment in himself on Spenser's Justice. "The Human Dress" of Blake's spectrous version of *The Divine Image*, we should recall, is "forged Iron" (E32); and the ineffectuality of Talus's justice is exemplified parodically to Blake by Calidore's absence, "hunting in the woods (as was his trade)" (VI,x,39), when Meliboe and his world are destroyed pitilessly by the Brigants. Finally, we may see Calidore therefore as yet another Arthur (whose pose and arm gestures he mirrors in reverse), for in Spenser it is Arthur, not Calidore, who is so completely armored that "from top to toe no place appeared bare" (I,vii,29).

The structural problem with *The Faerie Queene*, in Blake's eyes, is that it is built backward—from the eradication of error and a vision of the New Jerusalem, through the state of experience, to innocence; or from apocalyptic prophecy to pastoral. The circularity of Blake's panorama that I noted earlier is not exact in this respect, for "innocence" (hands *un*bloodied, be it noted) sits cradled as Ruddymane in the Palmer's arm squarely under the mooniness of Beulah; then "grows" through Books II–VI (experience) to emerge beyond Duessa, Archimago, and the Blatant Beast's out-of-the-picture-frame bodily life into the unitary conception of the Dwarf-Child-Una of the first panel, full under the blaze of the New Jerusalem. Supernally, Blake's sequence is the same, though we may also wish to see it as Eden (New Jerusalem) to Beulah (Cynthia) to Generation (the God of this World and Astraea) to Ulro (Babel-London-false sun). As in Emily Dickinson's well-known poem, the horses' heads are pointed toward eternity, but none of Spenser's characters except the Dwarf-Child (who walks) seems to care.

II

Now we may turn to what I have defined as the middle group or panel in the tripartite version of Blake's artistic structure. Since its multiple ambiguities and elusive shifts of identity are quite literally mind-boggling, it is well to begin with some stabilities: the stolid verticality of the Palmer and Talus (see figures 9 and 10). Although not precisely symmetrical in the horizontal proportions of the overall design, they are nevertheless obvious as well as intractable contraries, in both Spenser and Blake. The Palmer's reason, guidance, prudence, and restraint in Book II are precisely what Talus lacks—for the latter is a blood-lusty slaughterer without pity. His Blakean nakedness makes him as ultimate a perversion of the human form divine as is Calidore, ''dressed'' in forged iron. That, without Spenserian sanction, he leads the horse of the character Grant and Brown identify as Arthur (GB69–70) is as devastating a comment on Arthur as is Arthur's passive acquiescence (he holds no reins) to being led by the iron man. Arthur's vaguely upturned eyes thus brand him an arch-hypocrite, a Redcrosse-like figure of ''Religion hid in War,'' the explicitly scaly armor about his left thigh a certain badge of Blake's Satan.[12] In this light, he becomes along with Talus a contrary to the Palmer, who is, if not War hid in Religion, so to speak, at least the religious sanction accorded war in Blake's mythography. The Palmer's prominent cowl (see figure 7) accordingly is that of Blake's Prester Serpent, his dark robe hiding the human lineaments divine. As Warren Stevenson notes, Blake's allusion is to ''Prester John, the legendary Christian priest-king of the medieval orient,''[13] whom Blake transforms in *The Four Zoas* into the self-proclaimed ''Priest of God.'' His ''Cowl'' was ''placd'' there by God ''in times of Everlasting,'' Blake says, and he ''runs / Along the ranks crying Listen . . . ye warriors'' to the word of God:

Go forth & guide my battles. like the jointed spine
Of Man I made thee when I blotted Man from life & light
Take thou the Seven Diseases of Man store them for times to come
In store houses in secret places that I will tell thee of
To be my great & awful curses at the time appointed.[14]

FIGURE 9.   Detail of center-right quarter of *The Characters in Spenser's Faerie Queene*

(courtesy of Blake: An Illustrated Quarterly)

FIGURE 10.   Detail of center-left quarter of *The Characters in Spenser's
Faerie Queene*

(courtesy of Blake: An Illustrated Quarterly)

Blake's self-quotation in the "jointed spine" phrase is from the self-evolution of Urizen in *The Book of Urizen* (10:35–43; 11:1, E75) and the seven diseases a perverse appropriation of "the seven last plagues" of Revelation 15, but the cowled priest-serpent reference is fully sufficient to fix the Palmer's eternal identity: his hidden lineaments are Talus's iron nakedness "full of the wrath of God" (Rev. 15:7).

Spenser's Palmer thus becomes, in Blake's painterly eye, a diabolical parody of Chaucer's poor Parson, at least as Blake describes the latter in *A Descriptive Catalogue*: "an Apostle, a real Messenger of Heaven, sent in every age for its light and its warmth. This man is beloved and venerated by all, and neglected by all: He serves all, and is served by none; he is, according to Christ's definition, the greatest of his age" (E535). The problem with such men, Blake goes on, is that "you will not easily distinguish him from the Friar or the Pardoner . . . and their counsel, you will continue to follow"[15]—as Guyon does and, worse, as Spenser approves. Here one major aspect of Blake's mental fight with Spenser is joined, as one might expect, over religion. Blake's Palmer is one of "the religious" who maintain that "Good is the passive that obeys Reason" (*Marriage of Heaven and Hell*, E34). While Guyon, to Blake, is hardly a figure of Energy (as is evident from his formless robe, strangulating iron collar, armored cowl, and backward posture)—and thus not approbatively "Evil" in the upside-down parlance of *The Marriage*[16]—together he and the Palmer play out essentially the same error that Milton commits in his "history" of the restraint of desire, *Paradise Lost*. In Spenserian language, that great epic is an essay on temperance, on those who do and do not restrain desire. The following passage from *The Marriage*, then, may be taken as Blake's capsule summary of both Milton's and Spenser's epics: "Those who restrain desire, do so because theirs is weak enough to be restrained; and the restrainer or reason usurps its place & governs the unwilling. And being restraind it by degrees becomes passive till it is only the shadow of desire" (E34). In Milton the "Governor or Reason is call'd Messiah." In Spenser he is "called" the Palmer.

The parallel is imprecise, but the manifold relationships between Spenser's Book II and Milton's *Comus*, as they have been analyzed in expansive detail by A. Kent Hieatt,[17] would not have escaped Blake's notice. He was fond of alluding to *Comus* for obvious reasons, most notably the archetypal clash between the active "Evil" of Comus himself and the rational self-restraint, virginity, and passivity of the "Good" Lady, whose "Spenserian principle" is, as Hieatt says, embodied in "the Britomart of *Faerie Queene* III, IV, and V." "What

Spenser's work seems to provide,'' he goes on, ''unlike any of the other influences, is a model of what is really going on in *Comus*, in terms of structural mythic formulations for moral ideas.'' In addition, Book II provided the ''mental furniture'' that ''exerted great leverage on the choice of incident and the patterns of embodiment for the themes of temptation, ensnarement, and final abstention in Milton's two epics.'' At the core of this pattern is ''God-given reason,'' which ''falls in us from its due regality'' and is reclaimed from both ''passionate, invidious selfhood'' and ''besotted pleasure-seeking.''[18]

While such language (which might well be Spenser's and Milton's) is hardly Blakean, it does not take much to transform it, as Blake did, into the language of energy and the imagination, as opposed to rational self-enslavement. Guyon's temptations are three, as are Christ's in *Paradise Regained*; Spenser's Mammon, in Milton's imagination, is Satan; the temptation in Eden is (among other Spenserian antecedents) a refurbished Guyon–Bower of Bliss scene as well as typologically Christ's ordeal in the wilderness; and so on. The parallels are obvious and well documented. That Blake was a less acute reader of Spenser and Milton is hard to imagine, and it should be no surprise that his works are filled with blissful bowers, Edens (fallen and unfallen), Duessas, Mammons, Archimagos, Petrarchan lovers, and so on—not to mention the full panoply of Milton's canvasses.

If we return now to Blake's Palmer (see figure 7), we can appreciate the fittingness of his immobility and backward looking, as well as his firm control of Guyon's cropped-tailed horse with severely clipped and groomed mane (all perhaps images of restraint).[19] Guyon ignores him in favor of sternly (or is it longingly?) glancing at Britomart, whom he does not meet in Book II but almost attacks (except for the Palmer's intervention) in Book III. If, as Spenser critics repeatedly have pointed out, Book II mirrors the movement of Book I on a more mundane level, Blake (who must have appreciated the parallels) completely divorces them by having both the Palmer and Guyon look back from Redcrosse and Una, and hence forward in Spenser's poem—another example of Blake's confuting Spenser's brand of external orderliness. Whether or not the three figures behind the Palmer and Guyon are, left to right, Belphoebe, Timias, and Sylvanus, as Grant and Brown suggest (I shall not argue their identities here), it is patently clear that they are in bad company. The woman stands directly beneath Diana's moon, head ''next to'' Spenser's virginal Eden; the central figure is infected with Blake's mailed-cowl disease; and even the melancholy right-hand figure has an upturned collar whose line clearly repeats that of the Palmer. No wonder the child the Palmer holds has lost his halo; it has become the Palmer's cowl.

Guyon is to Blake far less interesting than the Palmer, for Guyon is a follower, not a leader of his age (see figure 10). Oppressively helmed, his youthfully propitious curly hair not having a chance, Guyon deceptively disguises his armor with a cloak, and thus "becomes" Calidore:

> So forth they [Calidore and Coridon] goe together (God before)
>   Both clad in shepheards weeds agreeably,
>   And both with shepheards hooks: But *Calidore*
>   Had vnderneath, him armed priuily.
>
> (VI,xi,36)

This possible relationship between Guyon and Calidore is the more tantalizing for Spenser's parenthetical phrase. Guyon's "God before" is the Palmer, leading the knight's horse with rigid arm, while Guyon himself presents his back to the conventionally embracing arms of the God-Child cradled in the Palmer's other arm. Moreover, in connection with the Palmer's gaze, we might now interpret that gaze as appropriate to a "horse of instruction" (cropped, clipped, and gaited). Guyon's maniacal excess in his destruction of the Bower of Bliss thus becomes mirrored both in his ignoring of the Palmer and the child as well as in the latent violence of his armor, what may well be his lascivious leer, and his poised spear that mirrors in reverse Calidore's.

Both Guyon and Calidore are as much pretenders to pastoral innocence, then, as the Palmer is to a solicitous and loving father; and the facial expressions of all three betray the pretense. In *The Faerie Queene* only Guyon decisively enacts his "true nature"—in the viciousness, unrestraint, and quintessential intemperance-grown-to-rage that is but implicit in the Palmer's self-righteousness. In a sense, Guyon is Blake's Bromion to the Palmer's Theotormon, the latter, in *Visions of the Daughters of Albion*, that "knowing, artful, secret, fearful, cautious, trembling hypocrite" who brands "all the virgin joys / Of life as harlots" (E49–50), the former the legitimizer of his rape of Oothoon by offering to marry her to Theotormon. I hasten to add what is perhaps obvious: Blake is no champion of Acrasia or of the Verdants who submit to her wiles. In Oothoon's own words, she will become an Acrasia if she submits to Theotormon's religion of chastity, a "crafty slave of selfish holiness," "a whore indeed" as well as a pimp, for, Acrasia-like,

> silken nets and traps of adamant will Oothoon spread,
> And catch for thee [Theotormon] girls of mild silver, or of furious
>   gold;
> I'll lie beside thee on a bank & view their wanton play
> In lovely copulation bliss on bliss with Theotormon
>
> (E50)

—C. S. Lewis's Cissie and Flossie no doubt.[20] The "rewards of continence" are Guyon's "self enjoyings of self denial" (E50) that burst out in his "rigour pittilesse" and "tempest of . . . wrathfulness" in turning "bliss to balefulnesse" (II,xii,83). Perhaps Blake sensed Spenser's tone of regret—or, at least, of seeming regret—at the holocaust:

> Their groues he feld, their gardins did deface,
> Their arbers spoyle, their Cabinets suppresse,
> Their banket houses burne, their buildings race,
> And of the fairest late, now made the fowlest place.
>
> (St. 83)

Be that as it may, Blake did take great satisfaction in Spenser's leaving us with Grille, that emblem of "the mind of beastly man." Despite Guyon's Bromion-like self-satisfaction at the effectiveness of his corrective (Bromion says his children "are obedient, they resist not, they obey the scourge" and "the violent"—E46), Grille *chooses* "to be a beast, and lack intelligence" and thus to delight "in filth and foule incontinence" (II,xii,87).

Appropriately, then, Grille looms inordinately large in Blake's imaginative rendering of *The Faerie Queene*,[21] the closing bracket to Book II even as he introduces Book III by holding on to Britomart's horse (see figure 10). He stands leering libidinously and triumphantly at Guyon, mouth open as if verbalizing the "miscall" (that is, the reviling) Spenser has him direct at the Palmer for retransforming him "from hoggish forme . . . to natural" (II,xii,86); at the same time he points—as if promising or forecasting—to the House of Busirane, where he will "reappear" as Busirane himself (or, more accurately, as the excesses of the Mask of Cupid). Damon interprets this figure as Guyon's own essential animality.[22] On the surface, there seems some virtue in such an identification, given Guyon's performance in the bower. But as I have argued, it is Guyon's temperance itself that erupts in that rage, not his lust or animality. Accordingly, Blake presents him with the shaft of his spear lying across the ruined bower (now become, perhaps, the eternal Cave of Mammon that Guyon does not, cannot, destroy),[23] its point directed at the religious sanction of St. Paul's Cathedral, his determined glare level with the bower-cave as if to stare its existence out of his "pure" mind (even as he fixedly ogles Britomart).

The positioning of Grille at this point is functional for Blake in another way: as the spectator's eyes are about to enter the Book of Chastity, Blake alludes *in* Grille to the opening stanza of canto iii (just as Spenser, in that stanza, alludes *to* Grille):

> Most sacred fire, that burnest mightily
> In liuing brests, ykindled first aboue,
> Emongst th'eternall spheres and lamping sky,
> And thence pourd into men, which men call Loue;
> Not that same, which doth base affections moue
> In brutish minds, and filthy lust inflame.

What Blake is about to demonstrate in his "reading" of the Britomart-Amoret story is that the difference between these two kinds of love is illusory. Although the one is basest lust and the other is Petrarchan, neither is "Blakean." Both are an excess, the one of unrestraint of animal appetite (the predatoriness that chases Florimell endlessly throughout *The Faerie Queene*), the other of unrestrained restraint (virginity) or, to use the Renaissance phrase Blake must have interpreted as a hilarious and nefarious tautology, "chaste desire." I would like to think, then, that the road Blake paints as leading from Acrasia-Mammon's bower-cave above Grille's head to Busirane's "pallace' (Spenser's word, though he applies it to Acrasia's residence, not Busirane's) is the "road of excess" that I discussed at length in chapter 3. Britomart's excess is the more absurd to Blake for its being caused by a mere "shade and semblant" of her courtier (III,ii,38). Moreover, he would not have failed to remember that her excesses extend well into Book V where, now in a prodigality of jealous rage at Talus's news of Artegall's surrender to Radigund ("in harlots bondage tide," as Talus puts it—vi,11), she throws a fit "Like as a wayward childe" (vi,14):

> And then she in her wrathfull will did cast,
> How to reuenge that blot of honour blent;
> To fight with him, and goodly die her last:
> And then againe she did her selfe torment,
> Inflicting on her selfe his punishment.
> A while she walkt, and chauft; a while she threw
> Her selfe vppon her bed, and did lament.
>
> (V,vi,13)

At the inception of this enduring "fit" in Book III, Glauce tells Britomart that it is a "Monster of your mind" but then, paradoxically to Blake, defines it as an "affection nothing straunge" as opposed to that "more vncouth thing," "filthy lust, contrarie vnto kind."[24] It is precisely this false, Spenserian contrary that Blake makes one in the Grille-Britomart linkage, a linkage that he confirms brilliantly by aligning his Britomart with Chaucer's Wife of Bath. Without exploring fully that identification here, we can say that Britomart "becomes" not merely Spenser's Britomart and Chaucer's Wife of Bath but also Amoret in her Busiranic nightmare, all wrapped up neatly in Blake's equation of Virginity-Chastity-Whoredom. Similarly, Blake's Grille "becomes" the embodiment of Britomart-Wife's lechery, the Busiranic "monster" in Britomart's mind, in addition to Busirane "himself"; then, successively, he "becomes" the Foster in Book III who chases Florimell (another alter ego of Britomart-Amoret); the witch's son of Book III, vii (who "loves" Britomart "in his brutish mind"); the hyena that the witch looses after Florimell—another "Monster" (vii,28), as Spenser calls him; Ollyphant, the monstrous, lecherous twin of the equally lustful Argante, who ("men say") copulated with each other even in the womb (vii,47–48); even the fisherman who saves Florimell from the hyena's clutches only to attack her in his "greedy lust" (viii,25–27); and so on. The list seems endless and as fruitless to pursue as Florimell. What the list "proves" is the uncanny rightness of Blake's insertion of his half-man, half-animal (the hairy remnants of the latter clearly visible in the painting) as a transition from Book II to Book III. Despite his destruction of the Bower of Bliss, Blake's Guyon not only succeeds in eliminating no lust from Spenser's world but by his intemperate temperance reinstalls Acrasia-Grille as the guiding force of the rest of Blake's procession. In this sense Blake's Britomart *is* Acrasia.

In my roster of Grille's reincarnations in *The Faerie Queene* (none of whom I can find in Blake's painting), I omitted the one that Blake decided was crucial—Talus, the iron man of blood lust (see figure 9). He is both a mirror image in reverse of the Palmer and, with Grille, the closing "bracket" for Blake's two central figures, Britomart and Artegall. While this identification of the focal pair (GB66–69) is unexceptionable in one sense, it ignores the enormous impact of the Grille-Talus bracketing upon the stage-center figures. Without attention to the brackets, we have the obvious: Britomart and Artegall reigning rather grandly over the mundane pageant—as Blake has Chaucer's Host reign over the pilgrims with an expansive gesture identical to Britomart's, and as the God of This World supernally reigns over, indeed gesturally embraces, the Spenserian pair. But, as is the case so often in Blake's work—graphic and poetic—the obvious is a kind of perceptual trap, one into which Damon, Grant, and Brown all fall to a greater or lesser degree in their interpretations of this section of the painting: namely, the assumption that Blake paints Spenser's characters rather than the characters *in* Spenser's *Faerie Queene*. The difference is more than a semantic quibble, as is suggested by Blake's careful statement in *A Descriptive Catalogue* that what he paints are "The characters *of* Chaucer's Pilgrims" (E532), not *Chaucer's* pilgrims. Therefore, Blake tells us, he alters and "varies" the "heads and forms of his personages" (E533). In addition, although he pays momentary lip service to Chaucer's sequential presentation of his characters in the General Prologue ("as Chaucer has . . . placed them . . . in his prologue"—E533), in fact he departs from the Prologue's order immediately after listing the Friar and Monk by putting the Tapiser next, along with the Pardoner, Summoner, and Manciple, the latter three not mentioned until near the end of the Prologue. He also conflates the Webbe, Tapiser, and Dyer into a single character, a weaver-dyer, perhaps in order to include Chaucer as a "pilgrim" and still remain within the announced·parameter of "nyne and twenty . . . sondry folk." Both kinds of manipulation eventuate in the groupings Kiralis, quite properly, concentrates upon in his analysis, groupings "justified" on a variety of grounds: the order of the Prologue, relative social "rank and fashion," the logic of "attendants on those" of above-common rank accompanying those they serve, and contrast and/or similarity of characterization and symbolic signification. But far more interesting than these—in many ways predictable—organizing principles, is Blake's disarmingly overt imposition of what seems to be his own "philosophy" upon Chaucer's sequence or groupings. Thus, for example, he places the Sergeant at Law next to the "Good Parson" because, as he says, "I wish men of Law would always ride with [the Parson and Plowman], and take their counsel, especially in all difficult points" (E535). Similarly, with respect to his stationing of the Clerk and Chaucer side by side, Blake says he suggests thereby that "the youthful clerk had put himself under the tuition of the mature poet. Let the Philosopher always be the servant and scholar of inspiration and all will be happy" (E537). The end product is a pictorializing neither of Chaucer's characters nor Blake's "version" of Chaucer's characters, but of the characteral essences of the characters. Perhaps those essences are, indeed, "what Chaucer has left hidden" and what Blake disingenuously says he will "say no more" about "nor expose" (E537).

With this distinction in mind, let us take a longer look at Blake's rendering of what he sees "hidden" in Spenser's Britomart (see figures 9 and 10). "Attached" to Grille, Blake linking the two via the horse's bridle, Britomart poses rather regally and confidently no-hands, yielding her mind to Grille (he is her "mental monster") while feasting her eyes on the dashing Artegall. As we have seen, her dress and posture are a visual quotation of Blake's Wife of Bath. The explicit equation is devastatingly un-Spenserian, but more important, it is Blake's revelation to us that Spenser angelically reverses Chaucer in the same fashion as Blake's speaker in *The Marriage of Heaven and Hell* reverses the roles of Satan and Messiah in *Paradise Lost*—except, of course, that Spenser reverses them the wrong way. For him, Britomart is ideal, questing for an ideal mate and resisting all temptation along the way. For Blake, she is the Whore of Babylon, the eternal virgin of holiness, the epitome of moral virtue, a fallen "Daughter of Albion" to whom cruelty is delight in the true Petrarchan fashion that I examined at length in chapter 2. And he knew, if Spenser did not, that she will get no closer to marriage with Artegall than their almost-touching hands in the painting. Indeed, he appears to be leading her on with his right hand even as he turns his head away from her. Karl Kiralis's extended analysis of the Wife as Blake's Rahab is thus thoroughly pertinent to Blake's Britomart, a "female-male" version of Blake's "Male-Females, the Dragon Forms / Religion hid in War" (*Milton* 37[41]: 42–43, E138). The religion that does the hiding for Blake's Britomart is a version of the Palmer's, the religion of chastity, even as her diaphanous outer garment associates her with Acrasia's "religion":

> [she] was arayd, or rather disarayd,
> All in a vele of silke and siluer thin,
> That hid no whit her alabaster skin,
> But rather shewd more white, if more might bee:
> More subtile web *Arachne* cannot spin,
> Nor the fine nets, which oft we wouen see
> Of scorched deaw, do not in th'aire more lightly flee.

> (II,xii,77)

Even without that graphic allusion with its wonderful Petrarchan net image, the silken veil that hides neither armored undergarment (it appears to be, in part, a chastity belt) nor her fundamental nakedness is perfectly adequate to make the same satiric point.

But there is more to this extraordinary figure. If, as I suggested earlier, Kiralis rather overdoes his coupling of the Prioress as Tirzah with the Wife's Rahab,[25] there is little doubt that Blake intended both his villainesses to play a role in his conception of Britomart. That is to say, more bluntly than Blake's painterly rendition suggests, she is both whore and virginally cruel Petrarchan mistress. Both, for example, Acrasia-Arachne-like, weave "mantles," webs of torture

Mantles of despair girdles of bitter compunction shoes of indolence
Veils of ignorance covering from head to feet with a cold web.

(*Four Zoas* VIII, E376–77)

But it is Tirzah who laments in the excessive accents of Britomart's
lovesick "dying":

> If thou dost go away from me I shall consume upon the rocks
>
> . . . .
>
> My soul is seven furnaces incessant roars the bellows
> Upon my terribly flaming heart the molten metal runs
> In channels thro my fiery limbs O love O pity O pain
> O the pangs the bitter pangs of love forsaken

(VIII, E379)

—a passage from *The Four Zoas* that Blake liked so well he incorporated it into *Jerusalem* (67:46–55, E211); and by that time, Rahab has
become the mother of Tirzah, both of them now major components of
Vala (Nature, or the spectrous, fallen form of Blake's Jerusalem).
The permutations of these two figures in Blake's prophecies are dizzying, and in some sense they are all incorporated into the stunning
"simplicity" of his Britomart. As if to emulate that verbal tactic in
visual Spenserian terms, in an unusually bold move even for Blake,
he clearly merges with his Britomart-Rahab-Tirzah figure, at once
whore and virgin coquette, Amoret (perhaps even Hellenore) and
Belphoebe, knight errantry and Petrarchism[26]—all becoming the
right-hand agent, so to speak, of the God of This World over her
head, whose right hand symbolically anoints "them."

I choose my verb advisedly here, for Blake's Britomart, as a universally recognized "guize" of Queen Elizabeth in Spenser's poem,
and as Rahab-Tirzah in Blake's mythology, appears quite startlingly
in Blake's heretofore unrecognized portrait of Elizabeth on plate 53 of
Jerusalem (see figure 11). His model is the famous engraving by Francis Delaram (after Nicholas Hilliard's painting) that serves as the
frontispiece to Darcie's translation of Camden's *Annales* (1625) (see figure 12). In it Elizabeth's throne of state describes precisely the rising and expanding arcs on either side of Vala in her Rahab aspect.[27]
The Camden portrait has no triple crown as Blake's does, but Elizabeth's coiffure rises in a triple tier of tight curls topped by a roughly
pyramidal headpiece that Blake geometricizes to a triangle; and
Britomart's feathered headdress is trifoliate. The Camden headdress
is also topped with a feather (though only one), ringed with eleven
stars; Blake's Rahab has twelve, plus Cynthia's crescent moon and
the earth, in the flaring wings of Rahab's throne. In the Camden, a

245

FIGURE 11. Blake, plate 53 of *Jerusalem*

(courtesy of the Associated University Presses)

miniature spiky sun rests in a crescent moon-ark surrounded by stars above Elizabeth's left shoulder. Blake's Rahab is enthroned in the center of a giant sunflower just as the head of Camden's Elizabeth is enthroned on her characteristic ruff, Britomart's bodice-collar echoing the sunflower's petals—not to mention the "petals" of the Wife of Bath's collar in Blake's Chaucer painting. Finally, the Camden Elizabeth radiates light as the sun of the universe—an image on which Spenser plays endless variations—while Rahab eclipses the sun, and Britomart (it is hard to resist) just beams.

And so that is Blake's Britomart. We may now turn to her heart's desire, the Knight of Justice, whose Spenserian character is as severely qualified in Blake's painting by Talus's fearsome presence and fixed scowl as Britomart's was by Grille's control of her horse (see figure 9). Artegall, as I have noted, stoutly ignores Britomart's coy glance and thus "fits" the scenario I have been developing. But we should wonder, I think, where his Achilles shield is, his "crest . . . covered with a couchant Hound" and the cyphers on his armor (III,ii,25). Instead of these, Blake endows him with a bright crimson cape and a crown, the latter of which Grant and Brown (GB67) rationalize away as the one he is promised in Merlin's prophecy (III,iii,29). No character in *The Faerie Queene* wears such a cape, but in Blake's *The French Revolution*, the nobles wear "the red robe of terror, the crown of oppression, the shoes of contempt, and . . . / The girdle of war."[28] Blake later modulates this early, simplistic conception into

FIGURE 12. Francis Delaram, after Nicholas Hilliard, frontispiece to
William Camden's *Annales: The True and Royall History of the
Famous Empresse Elizabeth*, trans. A. Darcie (1625)
(courtesy of the Wilson Library, University of North Carolina)

Vala's "Scarlet robes & Gems" (*Four Zoas* VIII, E378), the source of which is Revelation's "MYSTERY, BABYLON THE GREAT, THE MOTHER OF HARLOTS AND ABOMINATIONS OF THE EARTH," who wears scarlet and purple and is "decked with gold and precious stones and pearls" (Rev. 17:4–5). Only the redeemed wear white robes, "made . . . white in the blood of the Lamb" (7:14). Moreover, and even more pointedly appropriate, in Blake's *Vision of the Last Judgment*, Pilate is clothed in scarlet; he represents those "who Calumniate & Murder under Pretence of Holiness & Justice" (E558). Artegall and Britomart are thus tarred by Blake with precisely the same brush; Britomartegall is a hermaphroditic union of War-hid-in-Religion with Religion-hid-in-War, of Blake's Female Male with his Male Female. At one point in *Milton* (in a passage too long to quote here), the "Twofold form Hermaphroditic: and the Double-sexed; / The Female-male & the Male-female" self-divide to stand before Milton "in their beauty, & in cruelties of holiness," "Two yet but one: each in the other sweet reflected" (19[21]:32–34; 20[22]:1, E113). Blake turns Merlin's prophecy of the rise of Britomart and Artegall's race of "Captaines" who, through war and conquest, will "amend" all kingdoms (III,iii,23) into Revelation's vision of the downfall of all kingdoms who "make war with the Lamb" (17:14).

The passages from Revelation I have cited, the uses to which Blake puts them in his own poetry, and the un-Artegall aspects of Artegall all suggest a crucial further ramification of the Britomart-Artegall relationship. With her elaborate triple-feathered headdress and his crown and distinctive royal cape (neither of which has any precedent in Spenser), these two figures "become" Gloriana and Arthur, Spenser's "mistaken" vision of Jerusalem and Albion. In Spenser's proem to Book III, Britomart is explicitly associated with Gloriana as well as with Elizabeth (for it is in her "Soueraines brest" that Chastity is "shrined"), Raleigh's earthly Cynthia (also Elizabeth, of course), and Belphoebe. This synonymizing is consistent in Spenser's poem once Britomart appears, and by Book VI in the pageant of Graces, Gloriana is described precisely as if she were Britomart:

> Diuine resemblaunce, beauty soueraine rare,
> Firme Chastity, that spight ne blemish dare.

> (x,27)

In the succeeding stanza Gloriana-Britomart is delineated by Spenser himself (benightedly, since the description is of Pastorella) as the "Sunne of the world, great glory of the sky, / That all the earth doest lighten with thy rayes, / Great *Gloriana*, greatest Maiesty." In a sense, then (powerfully anticipated in the Camden Elizabeth and

Vala-Rahab-Tirzah connection), Blake's Britomart is a surrogate God of This World, anointed by his right hand, while Artegall-Arthur is his other surrogate, appropriately knighted and crowned by the God of This World's Merlinesque scepter. No wonder Blake has them both take such a grand (if musical-comedic) curtain call, ushered on stage once more by the magnanimous gesture of the "real" Arthur to their left.

This yielding of the floor by Arthur is, in a sense, his acknowledgment of himself in Artegall, which should remind us that Arthur's quest for Gloriana and Britomart's for Artegall are in themselves mirror images. Both begin with the same sort of vision, the critical difference between the two being the eroticism of Arthur's dream as contrasted to Britomart's chaste revelation. The apparent difference evaporates, however, when we recognize that the "virgin queen" becomes, on the one hand, the cruel fair of Petrarchism tormenting her lover and, on the other, the eternal harlot—both part of the make-up of Blake's Britomart. If, for Spenser, Arthur is intended as the sum of all the virtues of *The Faerie Queene*, for Blake he is the epitome of Moral Virtue (enforced, as it were, by Artegall's and Talus's brand of justice). In Blakean terms, he is a fallen version of the already fallen Albion, just as Spenser's Gloriana-Elizabeth is a similarly doubly fallen Jerusalem. As the separated Luvah and Vala say in *The Four Zoas*, in the natural world "Whether this is Jerusalem or Babylon we know not / All is confusion" (E831). Later in the *Zoas*, it is Rahab (Wife of Bath-Britomart) who takes "Jerusalem / Captive A Willing Captive by delusive arts impelld / To worship Urizens Dragon form" (VIII, E385). Another passage in *Jerusalem* seems almost a direct reference to Arthur's dream. Albion laments:

> Jerusalem! Jerusalem! deluding shadow of Albion!
> Daughter of my phantasy! unlawful pleasure! Albions curse.
> (23:1–2, E168)

While these analogues and citations are all useful (they could easily be multiplied), it is Blake himself in *A Descriptive Catalogue* who makes the relationship between Arthur and Albion explicit: "The stories of Arthur are the acts of Albion, applied to a Prince of the fifth century"; and "all the fables of Arthur and his round table; of the warlike naked Britons; of Merlin; of Arthur's conquest of the whole world; of his death, or sleep, and promise to return again . . . All these things are written in Eden" (E542–43)—and "written" in Blake's painting of *The Characters in Spenser's Faerie Queene* as well as in his prophecies. Among the "acts of Albion" in *Jerusalem* that are most pertinent to the painting, in addition to those more general citations I have already provided, is one on the plate immediately following Blake's version of the Camden Queen Elizabeth. The Vala-Elizabeth figure on the sunflower is a double spectre (Jerusalem to Elizabeth to Vala), even triple if we count Vala's allegorical signification as Nature; just so, Albion is trebly spectrified by Blake into "the hard cold restrictive Spectre . . . named Arthur," who is also, allegorically, man's "Rational Power." Thus, Arthur-as-Spectre says,

> I am God O Sons of Men! . . .
> Am I not Bacon & Newton & Locke who teach Humility to Man!
> Who teach Doubt & Experiment & my two Wings Voltaire:
>   Rousseau.
> Where is that Friend of Sinners! that Rebel against my Laws!
> Who teaches Belief in the Nations, & an unknown Eternal Life
> Come hither into the Desart & turn these stones to bread.
> Vain foolish Man! wilt thou believe without Experiment?
> And build a World of Phantasy upon my Great Abyss?
> A World of Shapes in craving lust & devouring appetite.
>   (54:15–24, E203–4)

The references to Christ (the Imagination) and Satan's temptation in *Paradise Regained* are obvious and powerfully enriching, and they therefore inform Blake's painting of *King* Arthur (Damon's and Grant and Brown's Artegall) as well, for he thus becomes Satan to Britomart's Babylon. Blake's hints at this identification, even without the assistance of the *Jerusalem* passage, may be seen in Arthur's subtly scaled rump, exposed to us under his crimson cloak of royalty, and in the gems studding his horse's cinch. As Grant and Brown say, without noting his "Arthurness," "he is the most ornate and kingly figure in the procession" (GB69).

As if in response to Arthur's proclamation, and reflecting her throned state on the preceding plate, Vala-Rahab-Elizabeth-Britomart bitterly claims her superiority: "thou O Male," she cries to Arthur,

> Thou art
> Thyself Female, a Male: a breeder of Seed: a Son & Husband: & Lo.
> The Human Divine is Womans Shadow, a Vapor in the summers
>   heat
> Go assume Papal dignity thou Spectre, thou Male Harlot! Arthur
> Divide into the Kings of Europe in times remote O Woman-born
> And Woman-nourishd & Woman-educated & Woman-scorn'd!
>   (64:12–17, E215)

If Blake's "marriage" of these two on center stage is his graphic presentation of The Idea of Spenser's *Faerie Queene*, Spenser is indeed in "big trouble." I shall try to attend to that matter, and Blake's "response" to it later; but here I shall take advantage of what may be, in the ringing charge of Vala's final words, a reference to Artegall's "relationship" to Radigund, as a means of easing into Blake's problem figure, the Arthur-Artegall-Arthur of his Book V panel, firmly held in place by the Palmer's alter ego, Talus.

Radigund (for Blake at least) is Britomart-Gloriana redivivus,[29] Spenser's description of her sallying forth from the city's gate perhaps contributory to Blake's posturing of Britomart: "With stately port and proud magnificence" (V,v,4). This female-male, the scourge of all knights, challenges Artegall on the condition that, if she vanquish him, "he shall obay / My law, and euer to my lore be bound" (iv,49). The ensuing personal combat is much like all of Spenser's others, but some of its particulars are peculiarly Blakean. Having downed Radigund after a bloody round or two, Artegall unlaces her helmet to reveal her face—which beams forth in Spenser's lines to the same effect as previous descriptions of Belphoebe, Britomart, and Gloriana—not to say Amoret and Florimell:

> But when as he discouered had her face,
>   He saw his senses straunge astonishment,
>   A miracle of natures goodly grace,
>   In her faire visage voide of ornament.

(v,12)

Spenser even daringly associates her face with the moon, heretofore the sole province of Gloriana-Cynthia. "At sight thereof" Artegall's heart is "Empierced . . . with pittifull regard," more sorely wounded now than by any previous incursions of Radigund's sword; and he has no way of knowing what Los says in *Milton*, "I should have remember'd that pity divides the soul / And man, unmans" (8:19–20, E102). Instead, Artegall tosses his sword aside, "Cursing his hand that had that visage mard" (v,13). Blake cannot have forgotten the scene.

Nor did he forget its aftermath: Radigund's merciless and cruel renewal of the fight, Artegall's repeated unknightly, Braggadocchio-like appeals for mercy, and his final surrender of his shield, the last remnant of his manhood (hence Blake provides him with none in the painting).[30] Spenser's condemnation of him is unequivocal, however un-Blakean his reasons:

> So was he ouercome, not ouercome,
>   But to her yeelded of his owne accord;

Yet was he iustly damned by the doome
Of his own mouth, that spake so warelesse word,
To be her thrall, and seruice her afford.

(v,17)

Completely in thrall now to "that Amazons proud law" (st. 22), Artegall is turned into a Female-Male to "complete" Radigund's Male-
Femaleness. Dressed "In womans weedes" according to "her will,"
Artegall plies a distaff (st. 20, 22), a splendidly realized Blakean icon
of the human mind's (and heart's) enslavement of itself and/or the
surrender of the Blakean human form divine to the Female Will.
Spenser is at this point content to draw the familiar Renaissance
moral of the female's proper subservience to the male: "Vertuous
women"

wisely vnderstand,
That they were borne to base humilitie,
Vnlesse the heauens them left to lawfull soueraintie.

(St. 25)

Here in the very midst of one of his most Blakean scenes, Spenser
backslides into the angel's party, for subservience obviously has no
role in Blake's idea of the marriage of contraries for either male or
female.[31] But, more important, is the jolt of Spenser's last line, which
as early a critic as John Jortin (followed by others) claims Spenser
inserted "on account of Queen Elizabeth."[32] If a queen is involved,
male subservience to her is especially proper in Spenser's world
(hence his word *lawfull*): Gloriana, the Faerie Queene, Rahab-Tir-
zah-Vala-Female Will, "the Abomination of Desolation / Religion
hid in War," "Mystery Babylon the Great," and so on. And her
"distaff" is Arthur.

III

This brings us to the fifth major character in Blake's line-up, Damon, Grant, and Brown's Arthur, here standing-in (so to speak) for
the titular character of Book V, Artegall (see figures 8 and 9). But
while his unique crest, elaborately described by Spenser (I,vii,37)
and duly imitated by Blake, does proclaim this figure as Arthur, he is
bereft of the blinding shield wherein his greatest power lies. To argue
that Blake places him here because his most extensive role in *The
Faerie Queene* is in Book V (GB69) is to misconstrue completely Blake's
intent and to subscribe to the principles of Spenserian order that
Blake is at such pains to demolish. Thus, just as Blake's Britomart is
led by Grille, "Arthur" is led by Talus. That is to say, Arthur "be-

comes'' (mentally, essentially) animalistic vengeance and bloodthirst as Britomart mentally submitted to her own virginal lust. Arthur's vaguely upcast ''holy look'' (GB70) is rather wonderfully hypocritical.[33] To underscore this double pairing, Blake limns both Britomart's and Arthur's horses as immobile as their riders, the ''quests'' of both halted effectively by their respective bestial ''grooms'' or ''squires.'' Indeed, Arthur's horse is the silliest looking one in the entire painting (''smiling'' stupidly somewhat as the Parson's does in the Chaucer painting). It is as well the darkest of all the mounts (whatever that might connote).

Just as Arthur is, in some sense, encapsulated in (as well as fragmented into) each of the knights in Blake's painting, so here he is Arthur playing Artegall—or Artegall playing Arthur, it really makes no difference. As holiness, temperance, chastity, and justice in Books I, II, III, and IV, respectively (Artegall being displaced from Book V to Book IV in Blake's plan),[34] Arthur in book-panel V is all four of these ''virtues,'' which are as much ''the four pillars of tyranny'' and ''of Satans Throne'' as are the ''Temperance, Prudence, Justice, Fortitude'' in Blake's *Milton*.[35] From a complementary vantage point, Spenser's sequence of holiness, temperance, and chastity leading to friendship (this last effectively annihilated by Blake whether his ''Book IV figure'' be read as Artegall or Arthur) is in Blake's ''version'' of Book V subsumed by the Arthur to whom each of the preceding four ''virtues'' contributes. The first three intensify Blake's aversion to their Spenserian claims to be the bases of justice, and the fourth is perverted from the severe mental contentions that signal Blakean friendship to the merciless ravages of Talus-executed ''contention.'' On the introductory plate to the third chapter of *Jerusalem*, Blake writes, ''Friendship cannot exist without Forgiveness of Sins continually'' (52:prose, E201). The Arthur-Artegall (or Artegall-Arthur) of Blake's Book V is accordingly an epitome of Blake's attack on the Deists in the remainder of this same plate:

> Man must & will have Some Religion; if he has not the Religion of Jesus, he will have the Religion of Satan, & will erect the Synagogue of Satan. calling the Prince of this World, God; and destroying all who do not worship Satan under the Name of God. . . . Every Religion that Preaches Vengeance for Sin is the Religion of the Enemy & Avenger; and not the Forgiver of Sin, and their God is Satan, Named by the Divine Name Your Religion O Deists: Deism, is the Worship of the God of this World by the means of what you call Natural Religion and Natural Philosophy, and of Natural Morality or Self-Righteousness,

the Selfish Virtues of the Natural Heart. This was the Religion of the Pharisees who murderd Jesus. (E201)

Blake's God of This World thus anoints Artegall-Arthur (directly under his scepter) as "the Prince of this World," but he points the scepter unerringly at Arthur-Artegall; Arthur-Artegall defers gesturally to Artegall-Arthur (who points to Astraea's scales); Talus conjoins the two, linking his flail to the latter and his spear to the former, while residing unmoved (and unmovable) under the Goddess of Justice; and, finally, Arthur-Artegall directs us with his eyes to Astraea, with his right hand to the bifurcated hermaphroditic terror (Britomartegall), and with his left to Mars in his bloody cloud, to Calidore's spearhead, and to the London-Babylon cityscape in the upper right. This stunning set of configurations is not quite all of the *Jerusalem* third-chapter preface, but it is close.

With such significations and implications in mind, we can now recognize Arthur-Artegall's "skirt of scaly mail" as more than a mere "criticism" (GB70), for the linked scales identify Arthur-Artegall as Satan himself, whose pretence to holiness is so splendidly imaged in Arthur's vaguely upturned eyes, as well as so effectively undercut by his dragon-plumed headdress. Spenser defines "Ivstice" as the

> Most sacred vertue . . . of all the rest,
> Resembling God in his imperiall might.
>
> (V,proem,10)

But Talus-like justice under the auspices of God's earthly imperial surrogate is but vengeance pure and simple to Blake; and "he who takes vengeance alone is the criminal of Providence" (one is reminded again of Guyon's wanton fury at the end of Book II).[36] I doubt that Blake saw a minim of difference between Talus and Artegall, or even if he did, there were still too many passages in *The Faerie Queene* that would have blurred the difference immeasurably. For example, when Talus, cave-man style, drags Munera by the hair out of her castle "and fowly did array, / Withouten pitty of her goodly hew," Artegall momentarily is tempted to pity:

> Yet for no pitty would he change the course
>   Of Iustice, which in *Talus* hand did lye;
>   Who rudely hayld her forth without remorse,
>   Still holding vp her suppliant hands on hye,
>   And kneeling at his feete submissiuely.
>   But he her suppliant hands, those hands of gold,
>   And eke her feete, those feete of siluer trye,
>   Which sought vnrighteousness, and iustice sold,
> Chopt off, and nayld on high, that all might them behold.[37]

There is no question here that Blake had little sympathy for Munera either, for she is a kind of female Mammon; but he would have been appalled nonetheless by Talus's (and Spenser's) horrible perversion of the crucifixion: "Christs Crucifix shall be made an excuse for Executing Criminals" (penciled note in *The Four Zoas* manuscript, E697). For Blake, the question was not whether a man (or woman) was good or evil, for "Good & Evil are Qualities in Every Man," but rather what a man does: "by their Works ye shall know them" (*Vision of the Last Judgment*, E563, 564). And again:

> I care not whether a Man is Good or Evil; all that I care
> Is whether he is a Wise Man or a Fool. Go! put off Holiness
> And put on Intellect.
>
> (*Jerusalem* 91:54–56, E252)

Here, as elsewhere, Artegall is the worst kind of fool, a man without "Intellect" (Imagination). Similarly, in the episode of the so-called (but not by Spenser) Egalitarian Giant, Artegall instructs him in a long dull speech on the principles of "right" justice as well as the rightness of things (Pope's "Whatever is, is right"), only to allow Talus to drown him. After, Palmer-like, restraining Guyon from killing Braggadocchio (V,iii,30–36), Artegall in the next canto magnanimously refuses to attack the women besieging Terpine, but sends Talus "To wrecke on them their follies hardyment" (iv,24), thus reasserting Spenser's "motto" in the first stanza of the canto, "powre is the right hand of Iustice truely hight."[38]

There are countless other complementary incidents in Book V involving Talus's relationship both to Artegall and to Arthur, but perhaps the most telling is Spenser's parabolic episode of the Temple of Isis. Although Blake had already assigned "Osiris: Isis: Orus: in Egypt" to his conglomerate "monstrous Churches of Beulah, the Gods of Ulro dark" (*Milton* 37[41]:16–27, E137–38), he might well have been encouraged by Spenser to glimpse in the Isis episode as well the "eternal" Britomart hidden in the spectrous image he gives her in his painting; for it is she, not Artegall, who enters the temple to learn the New Testament principles of mercy and "equity" (Talus is refused admittance). The epitomizing emblem of the episode depicts Isis (Equity) with her foot on the crocodile-god, Osiris ("forged guile, / And open force"), who is her husband and is at least contributory to the scaly mail on Blake's Artegall-Arthur (V,vii,7). When Artegall-Talus exerts neither guile nor force, the result is degradation and slavery by Blake's Female Will, Spenser's Radigund—a parodic version of Isis's stomping on Osiris's neck; but this picture in turn yields to that of Britomart-Isis, with little equity and no mercy, hacking off Radigund-Isis's head, even as she lessons the feminized Artegall that the pride of "fleshly force" comes to nought (vii,34,40). And Talus slaughters everyone in sight. To these fundamental Spenserian implications of the Isis-Osiris emblem, however, Blake surely would have added the Female Will grinding her heel on the head of the suffering Petrarchan lover, or the Whore of Babylon conspiring with Satanic "justice," or even Milton's and the Bible's woman bruising the head of the serpent (they are all the same).

In the Spenser painting, Blake visually incorporates much of this by a rather oversubtle, but splendidly apt, ironic transference, one "sanctioned" by Britomart's dream "Vnder the wings of *Isis*" (vii,12). The visual clue is Artegall-Arthur's royal red cape. Dreaming of "doing sacrifize / To *Isis*, deckt with Mitre on her hed" (*vide* Blake's *Jerusalem* 53 portrait of the Camden triple-crowned Elizabeth-Rahab), Britomart envisions Isis's priestly "linnen stole" "transfigured / . . . to robe of scarlet red, / And Moone-like Mitre [the headdress of Isis's priests] to a Crowne of gold" (vii,13). But, as a skilled practitioner of the art of grammatical, syntactical ambiguity, Blake would have seen in Spenser's language the same artfulness:

> Her [Britomart] seem'd, as she was doing sacrifize
> To *Isis*, deckt with Mitre on her head,
> And linnen stole after those Priestes guize,
> All sodainely she saw transfigured
> Her [Isis-Britomart's] linnen stole to robe of scarlet red
> And Moone-like Mitre to a Crowne of Gold,
> That euen she her selfe much wondered
> At such a chaunge, and ioyed to behold
> Her selfe, adorn'd with gems and iewels manifold.
>
> (vii,13)

This passage is followed, in Britomart's dream, by the remarkable stanzas 15 and 16, in which Artegall-Crocodile-Osiris is tamed by Britomart-Isis's power ("her rod") into his Radigund-enforced role once again; or into groveling Petrarchan lover, who here succeeds, however, in his *Amoretti*-like suit not to "marry" his mistress but simply to copulate with her:

> turning all his pride to humblesse meeke,
> Him selfe before her feete he lowly threw,
> And gan for grace and loue of her to seeke:
> Which she accepting, he so neare her drew,
> That of his game she soone enwombed grew,
> And forth did bring a Lion of great might;
> That shortly did all other beasts subdew.
>
> (St. 16)

Spenser's own genius for characeral multiplicities is dazzlingly displayed here, for, as Britomart earlier fell "prostrate" before the idol of Isis (st. 7), so here Artegall emulates that obeisance and fealty before Britomart *as* Isis—which is to say that Britomart becomes Gloriana-Elizabeth-Cynthia to Artegall's Arthur.

Thus, following Spenser to the letter, Blake graphically transfers Isis's "Crowne of gold" (st. 6) and Britomart's (st. 13), plus the "robe of scarlet red," to Artegall-Arthur (st. 23), and he sends the bestial offspring of their coupling to the head of his pictorial line to glare menacingly at the Dwarf-Child.[39] The priest's interpretation of her dream is thus just right for Blake: the "Magnificke Virgin," already "in queint disguise," cannot hide her "state from being vnderstood" (st. 21) and thus appears in the guise of Elizabeth. Her/their progeny's exemplification of "powre extreame" (st. 23) promises as fully unpromising (to Blake) a future history as the one Merlin foretells in Book III (where even he is so "dismayd" at the "ghastly spectacle" he stays further telling—iii,50). When Artegall and Arthur arrive in Mercilla's palace and in the trial of Duessa are stationed by Spenser on either side of "that gratious Queene" upon her lion-bedecked throne (V,ix,37,27), Blake was certain to have "read" the tableau as Arthur-Artegall spectrously bifurcated and flanking Mercilla-Britomart-Elizabeth, before whose "Angel-like" presence "kings and kesars at her feet did them prostrate" (ix,29), precisely as Britomart and Artegall had prostrated themselves before Isis.

I have already discussed this trial in connection with Astraea's dominant presence above Artegall-Arthur, Talus, and Arthur-Artegall, but what I did not note in that context is Mercilla's metaphorically "elevated" state in a passage Blake clearly literalizes in his vision of Astraea:

> All ouer her a cloth of state was spred,
>   Not of rich tissew, nor of cloth of gold,
>   Nor of ought else, that may be richest red,
>   But like a cloud, as likest may be told,
>   That her brode spreading wings did wyde vnfold:
>   Whose skirts were bordred with bright sunny beams,
>   Glistring like gold, amongst the plights enrold
>   And here and there shooting forth siluer streames.
>
>   (ix,28)

The Satanic mockery of "justice," mercy, and the forgiveness of sins that, in its historical signification, embarrassed Spenser into the tortured, fudgingly ambiguous rhetoric I noted earlier emanates in the embodiment of Mercilla's Duessan, duplicitous performance in

Blake's resurrection of Duessa at the "end" of his painting. And surely he recollected that, "inspired" by and in complicity with Mercilla, Arthur goes on to wage a pitiless (one might say Mercilla-less) war to restore Belge's city to her. He disembowels Geryoneo for good measure, and Artegall "sics" Talus on the mob besieging Burbon and Flourdelis, beheads Grantorto, and allows Talus to slaughter all and sundry willy-nilly. Finally (to Blake it must have been blessedly), prevented by Spenser from doing anything constructive (such as reforming the "ragged commonweale" depressed by Grantorto), Artegall is "recalled" to the Faerie Court.

Perhaps we can see more clearly now why Blake chose to make Artegall-Arthur regnant in "Book IV" of the Spenser painting. Analogous to Britomart's vision of Artegall in Merlin's world of glass, Friendship for Blake is that state of the soul which "Looks for no other heaven than their Beloved & in him sees all reflected as in a Glass of Eternal Diamond" (*Vision of the Last Judgment*, E560). When that eternity of love and friendship is shattered (which Blake emblemizes as "Every ornament of perfection, and every labour of love, / In all the Garden of Eden" becoming "an envied horror, and a remembrance of jealousy: / And every Act a Crime, and Albion the punisher and judge")—when that happens, "willing sacrifice of Self" (friendship) is turned "to sacrifice of (miscall'd) Enemies / For Atonement." And the atonement is executed on the "Altars" of "Justice, and Truth" (*Jerusalem* 28:1-4, 20-23, E174). Artegall-Arthur is thus, for Blake, as much a perversion of friendship as his "emanation" Britomart is of love. Their prospective union, Britomartegall, is doomed to hermaphroditism, what Blake elsewhere calls in a trenchant phrase, "unnatural consanguinities and friendships / Horrid" (*Jerusalem* 28:7-8, E174).

Blake would have regarded Spenser's centering of Book IV as a whole in the distinctly unfriendly battles for Florimell-Venus's girdle to be imaginatively appropriate, not least because Spenser spectrously has Satyrane display the girdle at the tournament "in an arke / Of gold" (Blake's "natural" or spectrous arks are consistently images of female genitalia hidden behind religious curtains).[40] Were this not fortunate (or depressing) enough for Blake, Britomart wins the tournament and the girdle—with which Blake magnanimously endows her in his painting. As a result, she becomes the recipient of "The fayrest Ladie" as her "Paramore"—much to Artegall's "despight" and anger, especially as he (in disguise) had already been unceremoniously unhorsed by Britomart in the tournament (IV,v,8-9). To emulate Spenser's dispatch with the whole messy business, let me say quickly that the prize is the false Florimell (Duessa), "The sight of whom once seene did all the rest dismay,'' but Britomart refuses her and departs with Amoret, an ''unnatural consanguinity'' indeed (st. 13-20). In the wake of their departure unfriendly strife reerupts, the entire episode not only a Petrarchan metaphor gone berserk but a solid basis for Blake's association of his Britomart with Amoret's ordeal in the House of Busirane.

To claim, as I seem to be doing, that Blake's painting of the Britomart-Artegall-Talus-Arthur grouping ''says'' all that I have adduced from it, in the total design of Blake's *Faerie Queene* procession and in Blake's other works, is absurd. I make no such claim. At the same time, it is well worth recalling Blake's own minutely particularized exegesis of his painting of *A Vision of the Last Judgment*, an essay that firmly establishes his critical principles with respect to how to ''read'' one of his paintings:

> Every Man has Eyes Nose & Mouth this Every Idiot knows but he who enters into & discriminates most minutely the Manners & Intentions the [here Blake wrote, then deleted, the word ''Expression''] Characters in all their branches is the alone Wise or Sensible Man & on this discrimination All Art is founded. I intreat then that the Spectator will attend to the Hands & Feet to the Lineaments of the Countenances they are all descriptive of Character & not a line is drawn without intention & that most discriminate & particular.[41]

But Blake was as precise with texts as he was with the minute particularity of drawing. It is rarely noticed, for example, that the main fault he finds (coming back to it again and again, even though he criticizes the painterly technique) with Stothard's version of Chaucer's pilgrims—which, through the perfidy and venery of Robert Cromek, preempted Blake's own—is that Stothard could not *read*; and ''When men cannot read they should not pretend to paint'' (*Descriptive Catalogue*, E538-40).

The subtext, or pretext, of the Last Judgment painting is, of course, the Bible, which Blake cites faithfully (sometimes by chapter and verse) throughout his exegesis, bringing to bear upon this pretext the errors and successes of such intermediate imitations (or, as he calls them in *All Religions Are One*, ''different reception[s]'' of or ''derivation[s] from the Poetic Genius''—E1) as those of ''the Greek Poets,'' ''Apuleius's Golden Ass & Ovid's Metamorphosis,'' *Pilgrim's Progress*, ''Rafal Mich Angelo,'' ''Paine & Voltaire,'' and so on (E554, 556, 562, 564). So too does *The Characters in Spenser's Faerie Queene* have its equally obvious pretext, a ''testament'' that all too often displays evidence of "the confined nature of bodily sensation" (E1). Though understandable, then (for even "The Jewish & Christian Testaments" suffer from it), such sensory confinement in Spenser's case mightily obscures "the Poetic Genius" from which his testament is derived. If it is presumptuous or even arrogant to claim wisdom for my entering into and discriminating "most minutely the Manners & Intentions of the Characters in all their branches," I would still hope that I have been, even amid my enthusiasm, "Sensible."

IV

Blake's Book VI need not detain us long, given what I have said of it already, but a few additional words are in order, especially in light of Blake's careful "overlapping" of Books VI and V, and of Calidore and Arthur-Artegall, the latter the only visual or spatial intersection among the mounted primary knights (see figure 8). It is possible to construe Calidore's horse as being spooked forward (back) into Book V, but I am inclined to think that what draws Calidore into the central sphere of influence of Britomart-Artegall-Talus-Arthur is his sharing with them an especially handsome, not to say regal, saddle blanket and his bearing of a scimitar, which aligns him (now meaningfully) with Radigund (V,v,3,9). As we have seen, all four of the central quadrumvirate have major dealings with her. Beyond that, Blake may have subscribed to what many Spenserians argue, namely, that "courtesy approaches the perfection of all the virtues." Such perfection eventuates "when all aspects of the several visionary surrogates of the Faerie Queene herself coalesce to bring us to the brink of Arthur's union with her"—for he *is*, not merely emblemizes, the full fruition of courtesy in his "magnificence," as Spenser announces that in his Letter to Raleigh.[42]

Yet Blake's pictorialization of Book VI subscribes to no such apocalyptic aspiration, much less its achievement. I have already suggested that Blake's Calidore, armed "From top to toe" so that "no place appeared bare," is a visual quotation of Arthur's first appearance in Spenser's poem (I,vii,29). In one sense, then, he *is* the "real" Arthur. As a corollary to that perception, Spenser's magnificent armoring of Arthur becomes, to Blake, Arthur's magnificence. And to the extent that that virtue-of-all-virtues reappears in the guise of Calidorean courtesy, its affective (or effective) magnificence paradoxically witnesses (permits?) the merciless annihilation of the fond fiction of Meliboe's pastoral paradise of memory and the even fonder imaginative vision on the Acidalian mount. The abysmally fallen Albion in Blake's *Jerusalem* does very much the same thing to the "real" (that is, imaginative) paradise within him: fleeing regeneration, he is "revengeful," covering

His face and bosom with petrific hardness, and his hands
And feet, lest any should enter his bosom & embrace
His hidden heart; his Emanation wept & trembled within him:
Uttering not his jealousy, but hiding it as with
Iron and steel, dark and opake, with clouds & tempests brooding:
. . . .
Turning from Universal Love petrific as he went,
His cold against the warmth of Eden rag'd with loud
Thunders of deadly war (the fever of the human soul).
$\qquad\qquad\qquad\qquad\qquad\qquad\qquad\qquad$ (33[37]:12; 34[38]:1–9,E179)

Blake's Calidore thus appropriately displays nothing of the "comely guize" with which Spenser endows him (VI,i,2), what Blake would call the Human Form Divine; and in his first adventure, he cleaves Maleffort's "head asunder to his chin," gratuitously slays "the Porter [of Crudor's castle] on the flore" (i,23), and, if we are to believe Briana at all, "all her people murdred with outragious might" (st. 29). His battle with Crudor is among the most vengeful and blood-drenched in all of *The Faerie Queene*:

They hew'd their helmes, and plates asunder brake
As they had potshares bene; for nought mote slake
Their greedy vengeaunces, but goary blood,
That at the last like to a purple lake
Of bloudy gore congeal'd about them stood,
Which from their riuen sides forth gushed like a flood.
$\qquad\qquad\qquad\qquad\qquad\qquad\qquad\qquad\qquad\qquad$ (St. 37)

When Calidore finally grants Crudor mercy, it is to force him to "stoupe to ground with meeke humilitie" (st. 38), a mutual self-damning that would have been no more attractive to Blake than the happy reunion, peace, and restored marriage of Briana's supreme insolence, "high disdaine," "proud despite" (not to say crude sexual blackmail) with Crudor's basest cruelty.

When we turn to Arthur in Book VI, outside the lure of the restored Eden of Meliboe and even outside the only slightly less unreal world of Bellamoure and Claribell, we find him and the Saluage Man repeating the endless savage round of Artegall and Talus, Artegall leaving them to it by disappearing for good before Book VI is well begun (i,10). Although Spenser bravely introduces his book with the oft-quoted motto, "vertues seat is deepe within the mynd, / And not in outward shows, but inward thoughts defynd'' (proem,5), Blake may well have translated that truth visually into what he must have regarded as a reincarnation of his Talus—for the Saluage Man is "naked without needfull vestiments" but "invulnerable made by Magicke leare" (iv,4). If Blake even noticed, or cared about, the Saluage's rescue of Calepine from Turpine, Spenser's simile would have effectively undercut the virtue of that act: as the Saluage grows more and more "enraged," "Like to a Tygre that hath mist his pray," he flies again at Turpine "with mad mood," unhorses him, and, his blood-lust still unslaked, chases the now unweaponed (though remounted) Turpine until "He wearie woxe, and backe return'd againe" (iv,6–9). Then, when Arthur, who by now has taken the Saluage Man as his squire, catches up to Turpine two cantos later, the Saluage once again "enraged grew" and not only slaughters Turpine's "homely groome" but with "his teeth and nailes, in present vew, / Him rudely rent, and all to peeces tore" (vi,22). Arthur professorially lectures Turpine on the virtues and prerequisites of knightliness, as Artegall lectured the Egalitarian Giant—and the Saluage Man simultaneously reenacts Talus's "Sherman march" through the assembled throngs.

By canto viii, Arthur finally seems to be getting Spenser's message. At Mirabella's urging, he spares Disdaine as earlier he had spared Sir Enias, but the momentary respite from vengeful violence (perhaps suspect in itself, given Mirabella's nature as well as Disdaine's) is shattered immediately as the Saluage man in his curtain performance "flew vpon" Scorn "like a greedy kight / Vnto some carrion offered to his sight," and, reprising his earlier depradations on Turpine's groom, plucks him down "with his nayles and teeth"

> to hale, and teare, and scratch, and bite;
> And from him taking his owne whip, therewith
> So sore him scourgeth, that the bloud downe followeth.

(viii,28)

Spenser adds that he would have whipped Scorn to death if it had not been for "the Ladies cry," alerting Arthur (st. 29). It is poor consolation, and Blake takes no note of it, though he surely remembered that, at this point, Arthur disappears from the poem, never to surface again—leaving the rest of the book in the hands of his faithful surrogate, Calidore. Artegall-Arthur and Arthur-Artegall, Calidore-Arthur and Arthur-Calidore, show no signs of "redemption" in Blake's elaborate portraiture—unless we see some augury of that redemption in the fact that the artist-poet (now a Blakeanized Spenser) sits Loslike at his task directly over the head of the crimson-cloaked centerpiece of Spenser's poem. And in Blake's art.

CHAPTER EIGHT

Spenser's Spenser and Blake's Spenser

U PON ''TRYING OUT'' the substance of chapters 5 through 7 on my Spenserian colleague Professor A. Leigh DeNeef, his response was perhaps predictable: ''But that is a Spenserian reading of *The Faerie Queene*.'' Without his sanction, I should like to interpret that response in two basically different but related ways: (1) that what I am saying Blake saw in Spenser was what Spenser saw in Spenser, and (2) that what I am saying Blake saw in Spenser is what modern Spenser criticism says is in Spenser. The first of these aside for a moment since it is by far the more complicated critical issue, let me turn to the second. Although perforce the references and quotations I have made to Spenser criticism are selective, I believe that the majority of Spenser scholars and critics would subscribe to the general contours of my remarks.

C. S. Lewis seems the logical place to begin, for from his analysis all others in many respects proceed. In his enduringly readable and profitable *Allegory of Love*, he concluded that ''Spenser must have intended a final book on Arthur and Gloriana which would have stood to the whole poem as [the] central or focal cantos stand to their several books.''[1] What I have suggested about Blake's perception of *The Faerie Queene* as a whole is, in effect, that it participates in this assumption, but only insofar as Blake is able to transform Lewis's structural principle into the imaginative center of *his Faerie Queene*—Arthur and Gloriana as the seductive centerfold. Perhaps he ''believed'' the Letter to Raleigh, perhaps not, though he certainly read it with interest. His ''belief'' does not matter. What does matter is what he understood to be Spenser's bold and startling claim that the entire work is susceptible to a coinstantaneous ''gripe'' of the hand and eye. Without reference to Spenser, Frye once fantasized that all of the plates of *Jerusalem* hung on the walls of his office ''so that the frontispiece will have the second plate on one side and the last plate on the other,'' a "simultaneous conceptual pattern" with the viewer not merely physically in the center of the pattern but perceptually as well as actually (that is to say, imaginatively) *in* the poem.[2] Analogous to Los-Blake's graphically realized frontispiece-entrance into *Jerusalem* and the triumphant Los of plate 100 turning us back into the poem once more, the "movement" in Blake's Spenser painting is from the leading Dwarf-Child and Dragon to Duessa, Archimago, and the Blatant Beast and back again. The cyclicity, however, inheres only in the temporality of apparent sequence, that is, the "procession" that we are forced to watch as spectators *ab extra*, our vision confined to the deliberately elongated and framed rectangle. Eternity inheres in the simultaneity of perception achievable only by drawing the viewer into the center so that no real circumference obtrudes to limit his imaginative participation in the wholeness of the painting-poem. As Blake said in *A Vision of the Last Judgment*,

> If the Spectator could Enter into these Images in his Imagination approaching them on the Fiery Chariot of his Contemplative Thought if he could Enter into . . . [the "bosom" of these characters] or could make a Friend & Companion of one of these Images of wonder which always intreats him to leave mortal things as he must know then would he arise from his Grave then would he meet the Lord in the Air & then he would be happy. (E560)

The *Faerie Queene* painting is no *Last Judgment*, but there is no doubt that it is "A Vision of . . .," however mired it may seem to be in the slough of allegory—or, to put that another way, no matter how Blake, with monumental perversity, traps the viewer again and again into perceptual allegoresis.

A similar perspective upon *The Faerie Queene* and Blake by a non-Blakean non-Spenserian may be found in Martin Price's *To the Palace of Wisdom*, to which I have already referred, and whose title quotation from Blake's Proverbs of Hell may be taken here as charting the imaginative "direction" of both Spenser's and Blake's creations. In Spenser, Price points out, following countless Spenser critics, "the extravagances of chivalric romance are only the outward surface of a spiritual movement within the heroes. Spenser's scene is a landscape of soul, embodied in sinister palaces or castles, deserts of despair, fountains of renewal; his dragons and witches are the temptations that live within the soul." If, as he concludes, instead of characters Blake creates "states," the movement of the soul or psyche from one to another of which "may be apparent transformations of identity,"[3] Price might very well have extended that idea (a keystone of all modern Blake criticism) to Blake's perception of Spenser's "landscape of soul." Were they also Blake critics, a number of Spenserians would agree with this extension, I think, for they characterize *The Faerie Queene* as, in the words of A. Kent Hieatt, "not the accurate and evocative miming of character and action viewed from without, but the shape of internal experience, the inscape of our feelings." If that last phrase could be construed as meaning our imaginative life, Blake would surely agree, as indeed he might (though he would be suspicious of the terminology) with Hieatt's conclusion: "All . . . is felt in a kind of total lyrical spectrum or universal field-relation of sensibility, and is given by the poet a local habitation and a name."[4]

My own debts to the work of Nelson, Hamilton, Berger, MacCaffrey, Nohrnberg, and a host of other Spenserians—not to mention the foundational scholarship of the *Spenser Variorum*—are enormous; but I must confess to a kind of discipleship (I suppose it might be called) to my excolleague Kathleen Williams's *Spenser's World of Glass*.[5] Every student of Blake should read it—not merely to learn about Spenser but to learn about Blake. To try to summarize her work here would be to no purpose, but some selected points are especially germane to the second of my extrapolations from Professor DeNeef's response to my analysis of Blake's Spenser painting.

Williams begins by identifying the milieu as well as the "world" of *The Faerie Queene* as "very close to what it feels like to be living in a world whose significance is only dimly and occasionally discernible." All the knights ("specialized versions of ourselves" rather than virtues personified) try, not always successfully, "to make sense out of the persons and situations they encounter" (Wxiii). Their quests "are hard because the way is hard to see, and things are so hard to distinguish: as in our own life, meanings are not readily discernible in events and so the right choice is difficult, or one is not aware of making a choice at all until the moment is past and we are committed to something we were scarcely conscious of" (W7). Choice and "the way" may not be Blakean language (though some might argue that it is),[6] but, semantics aside, it is difficult not to see, through Williams's eyes, Blake's characters groping, lost, in the similar labyrinthine ways of their own minds, gropings externalized and displayed in his version of a monster-, dragon-, magician-, warrior-, damsel-, and villain-ridden landscape. When we can apprehend, through what Blake calls our "Contemplative Thought," that Archimago and Fidessa are the evidence of Redcrosse's senses and Una of his imagination, we will be seeing through, not with, Blake's own eyes and will trouble ourselves less over Spenser's terminology (Redcrosse's true perception as "the eye of reason"—I,ii,5). Or, untroubling ourselves, we may make the appropriate translation of Spenser's "reason" into a redeemed and restored Urizen, the "Prince of Light" (*Four Zoas* IX, E389). Similarly, if Redcrosse's battles are "in, and for, his own soul or for the release of Adam who is himself,"[7] we are just as surely privileged participants in the battles of Blake's mythographic creations, all ultimately subsumable in Albion who must struggle not only for his own release but for the release of Jerusalem, who is also himself.

In more spacious terms, as Radzinowicz points out in an essay Williams cites approvingly, "the union of male and female in marriage was endlessly likened" during the Renaissance (and earlier) to the union of imagination and mind, spirit and flesh, and numerous other contraries "in the individual personality."[8] While there is no need to claim that Blake discovered this principle in Spenser, there is every reason to believe that his own conception of marriage was confirmed by Spenser's example (with due "adjustment" for the un-Blakean ScudAmoret "hermaphrodite"). Along the same lines, as "the twin themes of love and war" in the proem to Book I "grow more dominant as the poem proceeds" (W46), so Blake's painting reflects not only that growth but the endless wars of sex and dominion waged by his own characters. "What we call peace or concord—inner peace or peace between persons or states," Williams goes on, "is often but continual jar, the peace of mutual hostility in deadlock, what Blake calls mutual fear" (W46). Just so—and Blake, as I have shown, found such "peace" as abundantly in *The Faerie Queene* as his own imagination incorporated it into his epics. He would have appreciated, therefore, Spenser's perception of the continual "confusing or the debasing of love and war and honour" (W50), Blake's own phrase being "confused perturbation & strife & honour & pride" (*Four Zoas* IX, E390), one that I shall return to presently.

As true unity to Blake was the harmonious yet dynamic marriage of contraries (as distinct from their reconciliation or balance, a "Unity" that "is the cloke of folly"),[9] so for Spenser, a man of his times, this "dialectic unity, a coexistence of contraries," as Ernst Cassirer notes in his *Essay on Man*, underlies "much of the practical morality and the psychological insight of the Renaissance tradition."[10] Blake parts company with Spenser precisely at the junction point of the contraries, the principle of the desired mean between extremes (for Blake, simply and sweepingly, there is no mean) and the applicability of that entire concept to a practical morality. A central (perhaps *the* central) aspect of Blake's quarrel with Spenser is here, and Blake scholars and critics well might profit from regarding Blake's work as not merely the case against Bacon, Newton, and

Locke, or even as an effort to redeem their imaginative selves from spectrous embrace, but also as a radical revision of the ancient doctrine of *discordia concors*. Subscribing to the received notion that this doctrine is at the core of Spenser's *Faerie Queene*, Williams must interpret Britomart, for example, as "completeness as woman and warriour, an armed figure like Minerva or Venus armata, in whom feminine and masculine qualities are balanced" (W91). She is, then, as A. C. Hamilton says (without irony or prejudice), "the female Arthur"[11]—or, he might have added, Arthur is the male Britomart. There, for Blake, is the rub, as we have seen (perhaps all too abundantly). "War is energy Enslavd" (*Four Zoas* IX, E390), and sex divorced from imagination is not merely the pride and lust of the flesh but the wars of dominion, male over female, female over male.

As Blake makes clear in *The Four Zoas* in a long speech by "the Eternal Man," it is not Love that is at fault but the rational religion of Urizen that creates, sanctions, and sustains the depredations of fallen love (Blake's Luvah). "My anger against thee," the Eternal Man thunders to Urizen,

> is greater than against this Luvah
> For war is energy Enslavd but thy religion
> The first author of this war & the distracting of honest minds
> Into confused perturbation & strife & honour & pride
> Is a deceit so detestable that I will cast thee out
> If thou repentest not & leave thee as a rotton branch to be burnd
> With Mystery the Harlot & with Satan for Ever & Ever.
>
> (IX, E390)

This passage might well be understood as Blake's chastisement of Spenser, that sullied "Prince of Poets": the fourth line is as neat an encapsulation of *The Faerie Queene* as one might wish to find. Given Blake's acute verbal memory, he actually (and astonishingly) may be alluding here to a passage in Book II of *The Faerie Queene* where Spenser makes a particular point about the word "perturbation" (its unique appearance in his poetry). To temperance, Spenser says, there is "no greater enimy, / Then stubborne perturbation";

> To which right well the wise do giue that name,
> For it the goodly peace of stayed mindes
> Does ouerthrow, and troublous warre proclame:
> His owne woes authour, who so bound it findes.
>
> (v,1)

Spenser is introducing us to Pyrochles, who seems an unlikely Blakean "honest mind," but the relationship between Spenser's "troublous warre" and Blake's "war," "strife & honour & pride" seems more than fortuitous.[12]

The connection is confirmed in Milton's borrowing of the temperance-Pyrochles passage to characterize Satan's self-deceit and archdeceivership. Abjuring God's sovereignty and embracing evil as his good,

> each passion dimmed his face
> Thrice changed with pale, ire, envy, and despair,
> Which marred his borrowed visage, and betrayed
> Him counterfeit, if any eye beheld.
> For heav'nly minds from such distempers foul
> Are ever clear. Whereof he soon aware,
> Each perturbation smoothed with outward calm,
> Artificer of fraud; and was the first
> That practised falsehood under saintly show,
> Deep malice to conceal, couched with revenge.
>
> (*Paradise Lost* IV,114–23)

Here is Milton's version (intended or not) of Archimago disguised as the Redcrosse Knight—or so Blake would have recognized it. Further, he would have associated Archimago-Satan with the ultimate deception of Adam and Eve in *Paradise Lost*. Foully fallen, they are described by Milton as

> discount'nanced both, and discomposed;
> Love was not in their looks, either to God
> Or to each other, but apparent guilt,
> And shame, and perturbation, and despair,
> Anger, and obstinacy, and hate, and guile.
>
> (X,110–14)

This discountenancing is a brilliant dramatization by Milton of the discomposition (deforming, even unforming) of the "human face divine," Blake's "human form divine," Spenser's "stayd mindes"; the spectrous diminution of Milton's and Blake's phrases in Spenser's is a measure of Spenser's submergence of his poetic genius.

If we return now to the Hamiltonian notion of Britomart as a "female Arthur," her opposite number exemplifies a brand of completeness and balance that is equally pernicious. The "marriage" of such false contraries (*negations* is Blake's term) would be fully as monstrous as the eternal perpetuation of Petrarchan warfare between them. The former would be Blake's version of *discordia concors*, the latter of *concordia discors*. Spenser's erroneous embrace of the former, in Blake's imaginative logic, amounts to his embrace of the latter—a virgin queen and a warrior eunuch.

From the preceding discussion one can see just how "detestable" a "deceit" (in Blake's eyes) Spenser perpetrated upon his readers in the creation of *The Faerie Queene*, pace the Spenserians' proper recognition of Spenser's ideological desiderata.

It is an enormous tribute to his acuity as a reader of Spenser, however, not to say to his general critical capacities, that Blake came to see his Renaissance predecessor (when he was his imaginative, "true" self) as no devotee of Petrarchism.[13] I have dealt in detail with Blake's stealing from the *Amoretti* for his own anti-Petrarchism, but, in light of his views on Britomart-Elizabeth and Arthur, it must be noted here that he had to regard Spenser's "solution" to the "Petrarchan problem"—Christian marriage—as equally pernicious. Perhaps that is one of the reasons he turned the *Epithalamion* on its head in his own *To Morning* and *To the Evening Star* of *Poetical Sketches*.[14] Be that as it may, so far as I can tell, *The Fowre Hymnes* play no role in Blake's poetry, perhaps because he regarded them as, somehow, a "natural" culmination of the sequence from Petrarchism (*Amoretti*) to human marriage (*Epithalamion*) to the Dantean, Platonic, Plotinian (it does not matter) union of the soul with God. He did appreciate, I am convinced, Spenser's steady jibing at lovesickness in *The Faerie Queene*, from Britomart to Arthur to Scudamore and Amoret to Cupid's shenanigans to Belphoebe and Timias—and on and on—but how much of Spenser's "satire," and the fundamental tenets underlying that satire, he apprehended is impossible to say.

From the *Poetical Sketches* at least through *The Four Zoas*, Blake seems to have discovered in larger measure than he first realized that Spenser's poetry was a good deal more than a tissue of Petrarchisms, calendars, and cycles of seasons, months, and days. When that realization dawned and gained strength, even as his conviction of grievous errors lying at the base of Spenser's "system" hardened, one might imagine, in the spirit of Walter Savage Landor's *Imaginary Conversations* (1824–53), these two poets, so like and so unlike at the same time, engaged in the sort of contentious conversation Blake regarded as true friendship. In the middle of *Jerusalem*, Blake has Albion, in his fallen condition, crying out for "righteousness & justice" and chastising his "friend" Los for "worshipping" the Blakean or imaginative contrary of these virtues, "mercy." Los-Blake replies as follows to his friend, Albion-Spenser:

> Righteousness & justice I give thee in return
> For thy righteousness! but I add mercy also, and bind
> Thee from destroying these little ones: am I to be only
> Merciful to thee and cruel to all that thou hatest
> Thou wast the Image of God surrounded by the Four Zoa's

Three thou hast slain! I am the Fourth: thou canst not destroy me.
Thou art in Error; trouble me not with thy righteousness.
I have innocence to defend and ignorance to instruct:
I have no time for seeming; and little arts of compliment,
In morality and virtue: in self-glorying and pride.

(42:9–28, E189)

The sort of righteousness Albion-Spenser demands is but the sanction for his own self-righteousness, the necessary stance (however softened, disguised, or modified) of the allegorist who "affirms rules of conduct and powers of soul he would label 'virtuous.'" These last are Angus Fletcher's words, and he goes on to say that, therefore, "the reader is forced into an attitude either of acceptance or rebellion, and for this reason there is room for more than a merely aesthetic dislike" of allegory.[15] That is Blake's position: aesthetics is, in a sense, irrelevant to the issue. Spenser's self-righteousness is, to Blake, destructive of the very "little ones" it purports to defend. Being merciful to the creator of allegory and cruel to his embodiments of all that he hates is to accept the imaginative validity of the allegorist's presuppositions. Los-Blake thus rejects both, and if Albion-Spenser has been successful in compromising the eternal principles that are the other three zoas, Los-Blake proclaims his invulnerability to the onslaught of similar error cloaked in compliments to Gloriana-Elizabeth as well as in the self-glorying and pride of the knights who serve her equally self-glorying self. Someone must keep the divine vision in a time of trouble.

"Therefore," Los-Blake concludes,

I break thy bonds of righteousness; I crush thy messengers!
That they may not crush me and mine: do thou be righteous,
And I will return it; otherwise I defy thy worst revenge:
Consider me as thine enemy. . . .
But destroy not these little ones, nor mock the Lords anointed:
Destroy not by Moral Virtue, the little ones whom he hath chosen!
The little ones whom he hath chosen in preference to thee.
He hath cast thee off for ever; the little ones he hath anointed!
The Selfhood is for ever accursed from the Divine presence.

(42:37–45, 189–90)

In other words, defiantly righteous in his enmity-friendship, Los-Blake must create a system or be enslaved by that of Albion-Spenser; and he creates it to deliver all individuals from all systems, the antiallegorical allegory I spoke of earlier. "So Los spoke," the passage concludes, "then turn'd his face & wept for Albion." It is an affecting, warmly moving, intensely human moment, as well as a moment of vision; for it reveals Los-Blake as a Christ-like forgiver of sins, seeing in his "enemy" Albion-Spenser the perduring glimmerings of the divine vision now so awfully obscured, even denied. But if Albion's divine vision is restored to its pristine, shining fullness in the resounding apocalypse of *Jerusalem*, by that time Blake seems to have forgotten his visionary interlude with Spenser, for only Bacon, Newton, Locke, Milton, Shakespeare, and Chaucer appear in the "Chariots of the Almighty." Nevertheless, as we shall see shortly, there is a chariot reserved for Spenser after all.

Before I hail it into view, some further comments on critical method and allegory are in order. I doubt that Blake read Book VI precisely as Williams does, or even Books IV and V her way, but that is not my point here. The critical principles she employs to examine *The Faerie Queene* are not only mine (perhaps those of most Blakeans) in reading Blake but also, I am convinced, Blake's principles in reading Spenser. For example, to discern (not merely to interpret) Amoret's imprisonment by Busirane as the state of her mind—a *victim*, in Blake's terminology, of mind-forged manacles—is to be not only a fine reader of Spenser but a fit audience for Blake. At one point Williams—a Blake critic aborning if I ever saw one (alas gone from us now)—writes rather wistfully that "Of all poems *The Faerie Queene* perhaps suffers most from an attempt at definitiveness" (W138n), from a critical Urizenicism that Newman Ivey White wittily called long ago (with respect to interpretations of Shelley's *Prometheus Unbound*) "every man his own allegorist."[16] Amid the welter of references, actions, and descriptions looking "back and forth in a process of encircling and unfolding," for the critic to halt such "a lingering style" and comfortably label its particulars is to misconstrue entirely both Spenser and Blake. If "lingering style" sounds Spenserian, it is—Williams's apt term for Spenser's stanza and its epitomizing of the entire movement of *The Faerie Queene*. If the "back and forth" phrase sounds Blakean, it is—Williams again, describing that "movement" of *The Faerie Queene*,[17] as Blake graphically "describes" *The Characters in Spenser's Faerie Queene*.

II

As may have become apparent by now, my extrapolation from the first of Professor DeNeef's two responses—that what I am saying Blake saw in Spenser is what Spenser saw in Spenser—has already been addressed, to some extent, and qualified. Blake parted company with Spenser over issues at least similar to those that led him to "attack" Milton in *The Marriage of Heaven and Hell* and to "redeem" him (or, more properly, to provide him the opportunity to redeem himself) in *Milton*. The key question about the Blake-Spenser relationship, the question I have been addressing one way or another in the previous chapters, is whether Blake found Spenser similarly, not to say equally, redeemable, and if so, on what grounds. Our answer to those questions can help to decide whether or not Blake read Spenser as Spenser wanted to be read.

In his Letter to Raleigh, Spenser begins by acknowledging the risks inherent in all allegories: they are but "doubtfully . . . construed"— or are subject to doubtful construing. *The Faerie Queene* in particular, he seems to say, is doubtful for it is not stationary or merely emblematic but "a continued Allegory, or darke conceit," one that has a "general intention and meaning" as well as "particular purposes or by-accidents therein occasioned." The general intention presumably is the well-known one of fashioning "a gentleman or noble person in vertuous and gentle discipline" in the person of Arthur, a "pourtraict" that is "the image of a brave knight, perfected in the twelve private morall vertues." It is this general intention, worldly and social in nature, that Blake perceived as susceptible of collapsing or degenerating into Milton's error of not being able to penetrate the woods for concentration on the trees. Spenser himself even seems to confess to that very error, for his "clowdily enwrapping" of his central matter "in Allegoricall devises" is occasioned, he says, by "the vse of these days, seeing all things accounted by their showes, and nothing esteemed of, that is not delightfull and pleasing to commune sence." Such cloudy wrappings constitute Blake's "Fable or Allegory," that "totally distinct & inferior kind of Poetry" that does not present "what Eternally Exists. Really & Unchangeably" but rather only "their showes" ("what is Calld Corporeal") to please the "commune sence." But, according to Blake, "what is Calld Corporeal Nobody Knows of its Dwelling Place it is in Fallacy & its Existence an Imposture." Its existence obtains but "in the Mind of a Fool," that is, the Fall-acious mind—Blake's misspelling surely deliberate. Such a mind inhabits the man of "Corporeal Understanding" (Spenser's "commune sence"), who is himself an "Imposture" as well as the agent of metaphysical imposition, quite in the sense Blake explored that most human of phenomena in plates 17–20 of *The Marriage of Heaven and Hell*. Blake's "Sublime Allegory . . . addressd to the Intellectual powers while it is altogether hidden from the Corporeal Understanding," he may well have related to what Spenser mysteriously calls the "particular purposes or by-accidents . . . occasioned" by, and occurring within, the "generall ende" or "general intention," whose vehicle is the ostensibility, and understandability, of the conceit.[18]

Conceit is not a word in Blake's regular vocabulary, but he does pick it up from Sir Joshua Reynolds, who, in deploring the art student's search for novelty, writes, "The productions of such minds are seldom distinguished by an air of originality; they are anticipated in their happiest efforts; and if they are found to differ in anything from their predecessors, it is only in irregular sallies, and trifling conceits." Blake's marginal response is: "Thus Reynolds Depreciates the Efforts of Inventive Genius Trifling Conceits are better than Colouring without any meaning at all" (E644). If I am right about Blake's perceiving in Spenser's mysterious allusion to a kind of underpurpose or "by-accident" something at least approaching his own conception of sublime allegory,[19] the comment on Reynolds suggests a kind of quadripartite hierarchy of poetic (or, more broadly, artistic) products of inventive genius: conceits (especially "trifling" ones), dark conceits (or "Allegoricall devises"), and sublime allegories, beneath all three of which lies mere "coloring" to hide a vacuous imagination.

"Coloring," Blake knew, is what appeals to the "vse of these dayes" because "all things [are] accounted by their showes, and nothing esteemed of, that is not delightfull and pleasing to commune sence." Anything is better than that, even trifling conceits, the product of earnest inventive effort. Dark conceits, like those one finds in *Pilgrim's Progress* and the "Fables" of "the Greek Poets" (and, we might add, in Spenser) are "Seldom without some Vision," but only Vision itself, of course, is sublime allegory. But whether this particular, (probably) overingenious schematization is valid or not, Blake's implicitly hierarchical order of inventive products is firmly tied to, as well as emanative from, modes of perception. Perhaps he associated them in his mind with the single vision that is "Newton's sleep" (coloring), two-fold vision (trifling conceits), three-fold vision (dark conceits—generation as an "image" of regeneration), and four-fold vision (the imagination, which "marries" generation and regeneration without its copulative process of imaging).

Even more interesting and revealing, however, is Blake's assertion that, to the extent that the artist (or reader) turns his eyes to such "showes" as Spenser speaks of, he turns his "Eyes outward to Self. losing the Divine Vision" (*Four Zoas* II, E313). But, "He who sees the Infinite in all things sees God. He who sees the Ratio only sees himself only" (*There Is No Natural Religion*, E3). The perceptual acrobatics here are fascinating, for to turn one's eyes outward (rather than inward) to see one's self necessitates, or is the result of, externalizing one's visual powers in a kind of allegorical other self. Contrariwise, to see eternity, those same powers become windows into the self through which the imagination contemplates itself in the act of imagining or inventing—spectatorship at, as well as participation in, a mental cinema. In his provocative essay, "The Visionary Cinema of Romantic Poetry," Harold Bloom remarks (about Blake's prophecies), "To visualize a poem, and a visionary poem at that, is to see what cannot be seen." What he finds in the prophecies is "argument—passionate, beautiful argument between mutually tormented consciousnesses"; and Blake "stations the disputants in a context informed by conceptual images, images that either poise themselves just within the visible, or compel a new kind of visibility to appear."[20] Although he makes no reference to Blake's Spenser painting, Bloom's argument might be taken as defining what I have been trying to define—the painting as at once Blake's "passionate, beautiful argument" with Spenser, as *the* argument of the characters in Spenser's *Faerie Queene*, and as *the* argument (in its other sense) of *The Faerie Queene*.

The essential nature of Blake's critique of Spenser in the painting, then, is of necessity twofold in another sense, addressing its outward shows to our corporeal understanding while at the same time probing and sublimely allegorizing its dark conceit. Perhaps this vehicular principle, Spenserian as well as Blakean, helps to explain Blake's reversal in the Spenser of the direction Chaucer's pilgrims travel. However unpalatable, even nefarious and Satanic, most of the pilgrims are, the figure of the Host seems to be urging the entire procession in the "right" direction, east toward Canterbury. But, although Blake does make use of (however inconsistently) left as west and right as east in his graphic work, the eternal "directions" are otherwise: "The East is Inwards: & the West is Outwards every way," he wrote in *Jerusalem* (14:30, E158). Thus, he describes his own role in *Jerusalem* as the "great task" of "open[ing] the Eternal Worlds, to open the immortal Eyes / Of Man inwards into the Worlds of Thought: into Eternity / Ever expanding in the Bosom of God. the Human Imagination" (5:17–20, E147). In the Spenser painting, the outward show moves (insofar as it "moves" at all) westward, faithful to Spenser's unimaginative eye turned outward to self. Yet, as I have noted more than once, the light of the supernal realms suffusing the mundane world of fairy loves and wars emanates in truth from the New Jerusalem in the upper "west" (which has now become the imaginatively geographical east), haloing as it does (or manifesting itself as the haloes of) Cynthia, Eden, Una, and the Dwarf-Child (see figure 7). In this "light" they are, inwardly, Jerusalem the city and the woman, the "bride & wife" of "the Lamb of God" figured in the painting as Dwarf-Child-(absent Spenserian) Lamb. Thus, in *The Four Zoas* the "Eternal Man" says,

Behold Jerusalem in whose bosom the Lamb of God
Is seen tho slain before her Gates he self renewd remains
Eternal. . . .

. . . .
Thus shall the male & female live the life of Eternity
Because the Lamb of God Creates himself a bride & wife
That we his Children evermore may live in Jerusalem
Which now descendeth out of heaven a City yet a Woman
Mother of myriads redeemd & born in her spiritual palaces
By a New Spiritual birth Regenerated from Death.

(IX, E391)

"And every English Child is seen, / Children of Jesus & his Bride" (*Jerusalem* 27:19–20, E172). Blake's Dwarf-Child thus gathers unto himself the roles of Bridegroom, Father, and Son ("Know that after Christs death, he became Jehovah"),[21] who *is* also the eternal Albion-and-his-emanation-Jerusalem, Blake's "Eternal Man," as well as "the Divine Family":

they were One in Him. A Human Vision!
Human Divine, Jesus the Saviour, blessed for ever and ever.

(*Jerusalem* 36[40]:44–46, E182)

Eastward (that is, to the imaginative west), the "light" of The God of This World in Blake's painting (see figures 9 and 10), with his "elaborately compounded headdress" (GB82), is that of the Urizenic red sun (which Blake images in The God of This World's red halo):

The Sun reddning like a fierce lion in his chains
Descended to the sound of instruments that drownd the noise
Of the hoarse wheels & the terrific howlings of wild beasts
That dragd the wheels of the Suns chariot & they [Urizen's sons] put
    the Sun
Into the temple of Urizen to give light to the Abyss
To light the War by day to hide his secret beams by night
For he divided day & night in different orderd portions
The day for war the night for secret religion in his temple.

(*Four Zoas* VII, E361)

The rest of the God of This World's headdress, cogged first around the red halo and then black-spiked over the cloud that encaves him, is that of Blake's poem prefatory to the fourth chapter of *Jerusalem*:

I stood among my valleys of the south
And saw a flame of fire, even as a Wheel
Of fire surrounding all the heavens: it went

From west to east against the current of
Creation, and devourd all things in its loud
Fury & thundering course round heaven & earth
By it the Sun was rolld into an orb:
By it the Moon faded into a globe,
Travelling thro the night: for from its dire
And restless fury, Man himself shrunk up
Into a little root a fathom long.
And I asked a Watcher & a Holy-One
Its Name? he answered. It is the Wheel of Religion
I wept & said. Is this the law of Jesus
This terrible devouring sword turning every way
He answerd; Jesus died because he strove
Against the current of this Wheel: its Name
Is Caiaphas, the dark Preacher of Death
Of sin, of sorrow, & of punishment.

(77:1–19, E232)

Finally, to the far east (eternal west) is Mars (see figure 8), whose "sun" has de-formed itself to a red cloud with blood-red spearlike rays (the wheel of fire of the above poem), deilluminating the rocky wasteland of Babylon. That deillumination is the ultimate "darkening" of London to the left of "God," imaged in St. Paul's dome; and the dome, we should note, is as geographically (benightedly) "correct" in being east of London as Jerusalem is geographically "incorrect" in being placed west of London.[22] All (or most) things in Spenser, therefore, are according to their shows, while in Blake's "version" of Spenser, they are also the contraries of their shows. Perhaps the closest Spenser comes to anticipating Blake's perception as "truer" is his acknowledgment that his poem is backwards: "The beginning therefore of my history, if it were to be told by an Historiographer, should be the twelfth booke, which is the last"—but, sadly, even here he is "wrong" in having the alternatives backward: his poem as a "history," his "true poet" or poetic genius as a historiographer.

Part of Spenser's appeal to "commune sence" is the six-book consecutive structure, which Blake emulates and corrects in the variety of ways I have demonstrated; but, although Spenser regards his "Methode" of "doctrine by ensample" as more "profitable and gratious" than "good discipline deliuered plainly in way of precepts, or sermoned at large" (the latter precisely the method Blake parodies into oblivion in *The Marriage of Heaven and Hell*), Blake estimated the externally wooden allegory of knightly personifications of moral virtues to be fully as pernicious as appeals to common sense. As I suggest in appendix B, the same problem obtains in *Pilgrim's Progress*, there exacerbated nearly beyond repair. If we read Blake's Urizen as Reason, Los as Imagination, and so on, we reduce Blake's prophecies to the same "structure." So too with the Spenser painting. As the repetitive action or "plot" of Blake's prophecies from *The Book of Urizen* through *Jerusalem* emerges only dimly, if at all, through the dazzling array and "confusion" of points of view calculated to baffle the corporeal understanding, *The Characters in Spenser's Faerie Queene* baffles our ocular powers (even as it seduces them) to read with "commune sence." This is, in Bloom's words, "a dangerous freedom," but "explorations that are not apocalyptic are, to Blake, exploitations; they lead to religions of concealment."[23] Quest romance, character in the ordinary sense, and sequential action and plot (however internalized and intervolved) are all concentered in the concealment of the "darke conceit." In the Spenser painting, then, Blake's attack is on precisely that appeal to reader delight and pleasure commensurate with "the use of these dayes" to which Spenser felt compelled to acquiesce, an infection that, comparable to Milton's succumbing to the uses of his days and Bunyan's to his, led Spenser to all but capitulate to those uses. Or at least he sufficiently pandered to them to obscure mightily his affiliation with Blake's devil's party, "the line of vision." To Blake, one cannot have it both ways. The "spectrous Fiend" that plagued Blake for "twenty years" before he was able to subdue it to write *Jerusalem*[24] is in this sense Blake's Blatant Beast. It is far too powerful to be subdued by Spenser's kind of mental warfare—as Spenser, clearly much to Blake's regret, confesses at the end of Book VI.

The immediate "occasion" of Blake's elation over his subduing of the fiend in 1804 is his having completed the writing (though not the etching and illuminating) of *Milton*, a poem enacting not only Milton's self-redemption but also Blake's. For both labored under "the general malady & infection from the silly Greek & Latin slaves of the Sword" that produced the "Stolen and Perverted Writings of Homer & Ovid: of Plato & Cicero. which all Men ought to contemn," and that also "curbd" both "Shakespeare & Milton." "We do not want either Greek or Roman Models if we are but just & true to our own Imaginations, those Worlds of Eternity in which we shall live for ever; in Jesus our Lord" (*Milton* 1: prose preface, E95). With (to Blake) studied obtuseness, Spenser confesses his own "infection" with the same "malady": "I haue followed all the antique Poets historicall, first Homere . . . then Virgil . . . after him Ariosto . . . and lately Tasso . . . By ensample of which excellente Poets, I labour to pourtraict in Arthure . . . the image of a braue knight, perfected in the twelve priuate morall vertues, as Aristotle hath diuised.'' For Blake, this end merely exacerbated the perniciousness of the means:

> Aristotle says Characters are either Good or Bad: now Goodness or Badness has nothing to do with Character. an Apple tree a Pear tree a Horse a Lion, are Characters but a Good Apple tree or a Bad, is an Apple tree still: a Horse is not more a Lion for being a Bad Horse. that is its Character; its Goodness or Badness is another consideration.
>
> It is the same with the Moral of a whole Poem as with the Moral Goodness of its parts Unity & Morality, are secondary considerations & belong to Philosophy & not to Poetry, to Exception & not to Rule, to Accident & not to Substance. the Ancients calld it eating of the tree of good & evil. (*On Homers Poetry*, E269–70)

''Greece & Rome'' were like ''Babylon & Egypt,'' ''destroyers of all Art'' rather than the ''parents of Arts & Sciences as they pretend. . . . Homer Virgil & Ovid confirm this opinion'' (*On Virgil*, E270). In relying on their ''ensample,'' Spenser created not art, not poetry, not ''substance,'' not vision but allegory addressed to corporeal ''commune sence.'' To allegorize rather rudely out of context Jane Aptekar's commentary on Book V of *The Faerie Queene*, ''''men doomed to live in a fallen, iron world, a world of force and fraud, a world from which justice has departed, must execute such imperfect justice as under the circumstances they can.''[25] Such behavior on the part of the artist is more than nonsense to Blake; it is an unforgivable annihilation of the Poetic Genius, the ''true Man,'' in one's self, a capitulation to error and the God of This World.

But Blake was a good enough critic to recognize that, except for the complete and perfect nonartist (the devotee and purveyor of mere coloring under the guise of invention), malice was not criticism. In a letter to the editor of *The Monthly Magazine*, for example, published in the 1 July 1806 issue, he publicly attacked ''those wretches who, under pretence of criticism, use the dagger and the poison'' (E768). True criticism was to him both ''fair'' and ''candid.'' The immense difference between the two may be seen by comparing *The Marriage of Heaven and Hell* with *Milton*. In the former, Swedenborg, a nonartist, is treated to the dagger and the poison: like Stothard's painting of Chaucer's Canterbury Pilgrims, his work is ''not worthy any man's respect or care'' (*Descriptive Catalogue*, E540). Thus, Swedenborg's only reappearance in Blake's poetry after *The Marriage* is as a Samson who allowed himself to be ''shorn by the Churches.''[26] Similarly extreme, perhaps the prime examples in his writings of candor and fairness degenerated to the dagger and the poison, are his satiric *Notebook* epigrams at the expense of a notably unvisionary company: Klopstock, Joanna Southcott, Stothard (who becomes "Stewhard"), Hayley, Robert Cromek (who becomes "Screwmuch" as well as the name of a disease), Flaxman (who becomes, wittily, "Jack Hemp"), the engraver Schiavonetti (who becomes "Assassinetti"), the engraver Bartolozzi (who becomes "Bartolloze"), Reynolds (who becomes "Sir Jehoshuan"), and a number of others (see E500–517).

So, what is candid and fair about *The Characters in Spenser's Faerie Queene,* at least sufficiently fair for us to regard it as I have, earlier in this chapter, the severe contention of friend with friend? Let me try to answer that question in two ways, one Miltonic (and I trust not pure fancy), the other Spenserian.

In a note for chapter 7, I pointed out that Blake's Arthur (the figure in the painting that I discussed as Arthur-Artegall) is the identical twin of the Archangel Michael escorting Adam and Eve from Eden in Blake's painting of "The Expulsion" (*Paradise Lost* XII). Pursuing earlier comments on this design by Kester Svendsen and Merritt Hughes, Joseph Wittreich regards the illustration as

> an epilogue to Milton's poem and [as], therefore, an epitome of its action. The serpent recalls the fall (its cause), the thunderbolt the action that immediately ensues (the judgment); and the fall and judgment together point to the ultimate consequence of transgression (man's expulsion from Eden). . . . The thorns at once symbolize the world of experience—its misery, fever, and fret—that Milton so vividly portrayed in the biblical versions of Book XI and that man now enters; and they anticipate the coming of Christ, who, through his passion and death, will restore man to a paradise happier far than the one from which he was exiled.

The four horsemen in the illustration are the Four Horsemen of the Apocalypse, who, though Milton does not refer to them in his text, nevertheless look "forward to the time when 'God shall wipe away all Tears . . .; and there shall be no more death, neither sorrow, nor crying' (Rev. 21:4)."[27] Thus, although Michael ushers Adam and Eve "from Eden into the world of Satan" and Blake pictures that faithfully (thorns, tares, menacing serpent), he also juxtaposes the fact, as it were, with its imaginative signification—Michael guiding them neither east nor west but, as Wittreich suggests, "inward, . . . where a new and happier paradise will be raised."[28]

If the Arthur of Blake's Spenser painting is, in one of his guises, Michael redivivus, he also performs both acts, ushering his "travellers" (who comprise himself) "outward to Satans seat" even as he ushers those same travelers "inward to Golgonooza" (Los's City of Art) on the way to Eternity (*Milton* 17[19]:29–30, E111). This is precisely the way Blake conceives of his own task in *Jerusalem*, "to open the immortal Eyes / Of Man inwards into the Worlds of Thought: into Eternity / Ever expanding in the Bosom of God. the Human Imagination" (5:18–20, E147)—Spenser's Dwarf, Blake's Child, "going forward forward irresistible from Eternity to Eternity" (98:27, E257). The parallel is neat, even startling—yet not so neat, for left "behind" in the painting, apparently, are Calidore, Duessa, Archimago, and the Blatant Beast. The last three one can understand, for "Error can never be redeemd in all Eternity" (*Four Zoas* IX, E390). But Calidore? The answer here may be implicit in my analysis of Blake's portrait of him, Courtesy as the epitome of all the other knights as well as the essence of Arthur's magnificence—his body literally of iron, totally de-forming the Human Form Divine with its "iron brace" (*Auguries of Innocence*, E492) into the horrible and unredeemable parody Blake entitled with mordant ferocity *A Divine Image*:

> The Human Dress, is forged Iron
> The Human Form, a fiery Forge.
> The Human Face, a Furnace seal'd
> The Human Heart, its hungry Gorge.
>
> (E32)

No wonder, then, that the face of Calidore is the least human of any in the procession—Blake's pictorialization, I would like to believe, of Milton's phrase in *Comus* (l. 698), "vizored falsehood and base forgery," and hence, as Error incarnate, unredeemable.[29]

My "Spenserian answer" to my own question about Blake's fairness and candor goes something like this. Blake did not need the Letter to Raleigh to discover that, in *The Faerie Queene*, Spenser's Arthur was Redcrosse-Guyon-Artegall-Calidore (his four zoas, as it were), that Britomart is Belphoebe-Amoret-Florimell (supernally Cynthia-Diana-Phoebus), that the God of This World is Mammon-Jove-Gloriana-Elizabeth, and so on. If Spenser's phantasmagoria of shifting identities seems to focus our attention on the fallen world of Generation and its multifaced "evils," it is not without significance that Blake's, in his prophecies as well as in his Spenser painting, does too. If, in our misguided efforts to create order out of apparent chaos, we as readers abstract "an over-riding plan" (as Spenser does, after the fact, in his Letter to Raleigh) that can be "schematically displayed" (as Blake seems to do in his painting), that is our problem, not theirs.[30] "All Human Forms identified" as one, yet several, "living going forth & returning," are perceivable (that is, readable, visualizable, apprehendable) only in the "Planetary lives of Years Months Days & Hours." When those "forms" awake "into his Bosom in the Life of Immortality" and are "identified" as the "substantial" yet "essential" Human Form Divine and "named" (as their emanations "are named Jerusalem"), it-they have become "portions of eternity too great for the eye of man."[31] In order for us to "see" them in the here-and-now of Spenser's poem and Blake's painting, we must "Enter into" those "Images in [our] Imagination"—which is to say we must "cease to behold" "Error or Creation": it "will be Burned Up & then & not till then Truth or Eternity will appear" (*Vision of the Last Judgment*, E560, 565). To put it somewhat crudely with respect to Spenser, when Arthur is burned up, Christ will appear as the "knight" of Revelation, who is "identified" as the Dwarf-Child of Blake's painting.

Following a now well-established critical "line of vision" that emphasizes Spenser's considerable debt to Revelation, Wittreich, with Milton in mind on the one hand and Blake on the other, has argued persuasively that *The Faerie Queene* is a prophecy, not an allegory, at least in the ordinary sense of personification allegory. As the Spenser critics who precede him have seen, there is a "principle of synchronism" at work in Spenser's poem so that "the cumulative effect is not of a linear movement; instead one episode flows into another, this character merges with that one. In the end, *The Faerie Queene* is one vision, variously repeated, each time from a different perspective, with each new angle of vision contributing to the poem's final clarity."[32] The model for this vision is Revelation (as Josephine Waters Bennett noted long ago).[33] But, as numerous scholars acknowledge, the apocalyptic promise of Book I fades progressively as the poem proceeds (for all its typological interanimations), first to the fond vision on Mt. Acidale, thence to Meliboe's impossible paradise, thence to the wistful close of the truncated Mutabilitie Cantos. And before this last, the Blatant Beast is loose again, even as Book VI tends to distance vision from reality and in the process deny a connection between them.[34] It is precisely this distancing that Blake found nullified, triumphantly, by Milton; and it is this distancing that determined the "shape" of Blake's painting of Spenser's characters. Pastoral, as we have seen in my discussion of Calidore and Book VI, is simply an insufficient imagination, to Blake the sort of wish fulfillment documented so tellingly by Arthur O. Lovejoy in his *Documentary History of*

Primitivism.[35] The Blatant Beast, in all his metamorphoses, "spareth" it not "But rends without regard of person or of time." But unlike Spenser, Blake refuses to settle, beyond pastoral, for a debate between Mutability and Nature, both of whose contestants are wrong, both of whom (whichever is the greater does not matter) cause "this state of life" to be "so tickle" (VII,viii,1). More than that, encouraged by Milton's example, Blake fully embraces what to Spenser is all but a forlorn hope, "that Sabaoths sight" which permits a vision of "all things firmely stayd / Vpon the pillours of Eternity / That is contrayr to *Mutabilitie*" (viii,2).

If, as E. K. Chambers observes, Spenser in *The Faerie Queene* (and even more in *The Shepheardes Calender*) made "pastoral a thing of significance for English writers," he nevertheless sensed the limitations of its forms and thus prepared the way for Milton's subjection of pastoral to even greater, more radical criticism.[36] By Blake's time the genre had grown effete if not moribund, and his *Songs of Innocence* are, in a sense, a heroic effort to instill it with life once again. But after *Songs of Experience*'s satiric attack on pastoral fragility and the dangers of stubbornly persisting in its world, Blake demoted it, as it were, to a mythological-biblical Beulah-land, the "higher" form of Ulro but nonetheless a fragile if merciful fiction for all that, a holding action against eternal Chaos and old night. Blake, I think, regarded Spenser's "heaven" and "eternity" as a similar Beulah-land, neither prelapsarian Eden nor the New Jerusalem. Although Redcrosse marries Una, from their union springs no "new-born heir" as in Milton's "rewrite" in his *Nativity Ode* of Book I of *The Faerie Queene* and as in Blake's invention of the Christ-Child leading Spenser's characters. Compounding this signal error, Spenser sends Redcrosse to serve "that great Faerie Queene," the Whore of Babylon, in appropriate "warlike wize," and Una is peremptorily "left to mourne" (I,xii,18, 41). No wonder Blake has Una, though unveiled by Spenser at the end of Book I, reassume the "blake stole" of mourning she wears when we meet her. Similarly, Britomart and Artegall never manage more than a Platonic liaison, Spenser cancels the union of Scudamore and Amoret, Arthur never finds his Faerie Queene, and Calidore is left alone and palely loitering, apparently having given up his pursuit of the Blatant Beast even as he deserts Pastorella. But Guyon may be the worst off of all, for he, in a sense, becomes the Palmer (is that the Palmer's robe Blake clothes him with, the cowl now a helmet?); or, uncloaked, he becomes Calidore. And, without even the Ruddymane with which Blake endows his Palmer, Guyon wanders celibate through Books III, IV, and V to disappear and be heard of no more. Blake's summary of all this is inherent in the fact that not one single character in his Spenserian procession even looks at, much less moves toward, the New Jerusalem or the Dwarf-Child-Christ.

Despite these strictures, I do not quarrel with Wittreich's drawing of the "line of vision" from Revelation to Spenser, Milton, and Blake. For if he is disappointingly absent, by name, from Blake's various honor rolls, and most conspicuously absent from the "Milton & Shakespeare & Chaucer" triumvirate of *Jerusalem*, Spenser is still the only poet aside from Chaucer to be granted a nonsequential "illustration," that is to say (if I may employ this horrendous compound coinage), a nonsequential-text-aligned set or series of illustrations. All the others (the Gray, Bunyan, Young, Shakespeare, Dante—even Milton) depend entirely for their effectiveness on specific texts within the book or books, poem or poems illustrated, the specificity of the "imitation" being the heart of Blake's idea of imitation as criticism. This imitation-criticism constitutes Blake's redemption of such poetic genius as he perceives flickering, more or less brightly, in his "model." Blake's *Milton* is a different matter entirely, for, as I have already noted, it is a Blakean vehicle for Milton's own self-redemption. And so is the Chaucer painting.[37] And the Spenser. These three poems (like the Job series) are the highest tribute Blake could possibly pay to his predecessors in the line of vision. They must be allowed, therefore, to take their places in his critical-artistic canon alongside the epitome of such "imitative" homage, *A Vision of the Last Judgment*, Blake's Revelation.

Appendixes

Spenser and Blake's Thel

I N M Y S E C O N D chapter I tried to demonstrate that due recognition of the Spenser allusions in the grave passage of *Thel* reveals the profound influence Spenser's formulations in the *Amoretti* and related passages in *The Faerie Queene* had not only upon the
language of the voice of sorrow's speech but upon Blake's entire conception of Thel's career in the poem. There are other dimensions of
Spenserian influence that enrich Blake's poem considerably, however, but that do not lend themselves to harmonious inclusion in
chapter 2.

In *Blake's Composite Art* (see chap. 1, n. 25), W. J. T. Mitchell argues that *The Book of Thel* "is primarily a story about dying" (p.
81)—and, he might have added, about the Renaissance idea of sexual
dying as well. Metaphorically, "*Thel* is a story of dying as growing up
as being born," "of a young woman who questions her own usefulness and purpose in a world where everything dies or fades away, and
who is given the opportunity to explore death in order to come to her
own conclusions" (pp. 82–83). Implicit in this thesis is the notion that
Thel is also a story about the nature of one's identity: "Thel's problem is that she lacks the faith, spontaneity, and selflessness of her
comforters [Lily, Cloud, Clod of Clay], and insists on clinging to her
present identity" as the Virgin Queen of the Vales of Har (p. 87).
Finally, Mitchell describes "the moral framework" of the poem as a
kind of "inversion of the values of Genesis: man does not die when he
falls from grace; he falls from grace when he fails to learn how to die"
(p. 89).

Without attempting to respond directly to all of these points, I wish
to propose that, in addition to its Petrarchan progenitors, a familiar
section of Book I of *The Faerie Queene* lies behind the grave section of
Thel (plate 6, E6) and that our recognition of this "borrowing" enables us to appreciate, perhaps even more fully than via its anti-

Petrarchism, that *Thel* is a severe attack upon the underpinnings of Spenser's Book I and the language in which it is couched.

In that book, still suffering from his battle with the giant Orgoglio and his subsequent entombment in Ignaro's dungeon, the Redcrosse Knight (having been freed by Arthur) travels on with Una. "So as they traueiled, lo they gan epsy" galloping furiously toward them Trevisan, who has just barely extricated himself from the mental clutches of Despaire (ix,21) and who is still so terrified that he hesitates to tell his tale to Arthur for fear Despaire "comes fast after mee" (25). "Feare nought," says Redcrosse, "no daunger now is nye," thereby providing Blake perhaps with the matron Clay's assuagement of Thel's anxiety: "fear nothing. enter with thy virgin feet" (5:17). The locution is unextraordinary to be sure and by itself signals little more than coincidence, but as I proceed, I trust that gradually it will assume at least the significance of a Blakean verbal gesture or semaphore, alerting us to his allusive intent. Leaving the phrase aside for the moment, let us return to Spenser's scene.

Calmed somewhat by Arthur's importunings, Trevisan does stay to recount the suicide of his friend Sir Terwin:

> But I more fearfull, or more luckie wight,
> Dismayd with that deformed dismall sight,
> Fled fast away, halfe dead with dying feare:
> Ne yet assur'd of life by you, Sir knight,
> Whose like infirmitie like chaunce may beare:
> But God you neuer let his [Despaire's] charmed speeches heare.
>
> (I,ix,30)

Redcrosse rather obtusely pooh-poohs the power of words, whether in charmed speeches or not, in a passage Blake appropriated, in part, for the voice of sorrow's speech:

> How may a man (said he) with idle speach
> Be woune, to spoyle the Castle of his health?
> I wote (quoth [Trevisan] whom triall late did teach),
> That like would not for all this worldes wealth:
> His subtill tongue, like dropping honny, mealt'th
> Into the hart, and searcheth euery vaine
> That ere one be aware, by secret stealth
> His powre is reft, and weaknesse doth remaine.
> O neuer Sir desire to try his guilefull traine.
>
> (St.31)

In his self-righteous self-confidence, Redcrosse listens to the warning without understanding what Trevisan knows all too well, the power

of "a Tongue impress'd with honey from every wind," as Blake re-
phrased Spenser's words in a line of the grave speech (6:16). Like
Thel, Redcrosse's prideful self-image, nurtured and corroborated by
his physical victories over the likes of Erroure, Sansfoy, and Orgoglio, will not permit him to be intimidated by the powers of words,
whether they be the voice of experience (Trevisan) or the voice expe-
rienced (Despaire). Appropriately, then, Spenser has Redcrosse reason that Despaire, despite Trevisan's eloquent testimony, surely cannot be endowed with the "enchanting voice" and "bait of honied
words" the Chorus of *Samson Agonistes* credits to Dalila; his must be "a
rougher tongue" like that of the giant Harapha (ll. 1065–68). So, says
Redcrosse,

> hence I shall neuer rest,
> Till I that treachours art haue heard and tride.
>
> (St. 32)

Had he Guyon's Palmer as his guide and stay, Redcrosse well might
have been restrained from entertaining such a foolhardy quest against
words; but his travel-partner Una is unaccountably silent as they both
push on to Despaire's "dwelling."
  They find his "house"

> low in an hollow caue,
> Fare vnderneath a craggie clift upight,
> Darke, dolefull, drearie, like a greedie graue.
>
> (St. 33)

No "couches of the dead" nor "fibrous roots / Of every heart [that]
on earth infixes deep its restless twists" (*Thel* 6:3–4) are apparent in
Despaire's abode, but Blake's lines are a metaphorical transformation of Spenser's scenery:

> And all about old stockes and stubs of trees,
>   Whereon nor fruit, nor leafe was euer seene,
>   Did hang vpon the ragged rocky knees;
>   On which had many wretches hanged beene,
>   Whose carcases were scattered on the greene
> And throwne about the cliffs.
>
> (St. 34)

What Thel sees upon first entering the grave is, in Blake's generaliz-
ing phrase, "the secrets of the land unknown," a phrase borrowed
perhaps from Duessa's account of the primordial origins of "griesly
Night" who "sawst the secrets of the world vnmade" (I,v,22).
  Unlike Thel, Redcrosse is brashly unterrified and pontificates to
Despaire that he will avenge Sir Terwin's death:

What iustice can be iudge against thee right,
What thine owne bloud to price his bloud, here shed in sight?
(I,ix,37)

But, like Thel, he does not reckon with the power of Despaire, of words, of despair. As Despaire delivers his casuistical speech, Spenser deftly allows us to witness the words insinuating themselves into Redcrosse's consciousness until they become his words, even his thoughts, "As he were charmed with inchaunted rimes" (st. 48). Once Despaire becomes internalized as despair, the knight, his hand provided now with "a dagger sharpe and keene," struggles mightily, at length vainly, with himself:

> his hand did quake,
> And tremble like a leafe of Aspin greene,
> And troubled bloud through his pale face was seene
> To come, and goe with tydings from the hart,
> As it a running messenger had beene.
> At last resolu'd to worke his finall smart,
> He lifted vp his hand, that backe againe did start.
>
> (St. 51)

At this point, at long last, the silent Una takes a hand, snatches the knife from him, and recalls him to his sworn duty to slay the dragon—but not without berating him in remarkably un-Una-like fashion as a "fraile, feeble, fleshly wight" (st. 52). The charge might well have been leveled at Thel; indeed, it is the sum and substance of the voice's "lesson" delivered from her grave plot.

What Una basically reminds Redcrosse of, rather than his vow, is what he should have known as a Christian warrior, namely, that words are "vaine" and that "diuelish thoughts" should ne'er "dismay" his "constant spright" (which till now in Book I has been notably inconstant, even Duessan). "Where iustice growes," Una goes on to proverbialize, "there grows eke greater grace, / The which doth quench the brond of hellish smart," and the "accurst hand-writing" on man's brain "doth deface" (st. 53).

Before commenting further on this sequence with respect to *The Book of Thel*, we need to see what Blake does with this "brond." In a twelve-line passage that he deleted from the undated manuscript of *Tiriel*, that is either the origin or a later redaction of *Thel*'s grave speech and that includes the exact words of lines 3–4 of "Thel's Motto," we find Spenser's "brond":

> Dost thou not see that men cannot be formed all alike
> Some nostrild wide breathing out blood. Some close shut up

In silent deceit. poisons inhaling from the morning rose
With daggers hid beneath their lips & poison in their tongue
Or eyed with little sparks of Hell or with infernal brands
Flinging flames of discontent & plagues of dark despair.

(E815)

Although the pertinence of the passage to Despaire's consummately artful speech to Redcrosse is undeniable, the penultimate two lines obviously cannot apply to Spenser's Despaire, whose "hollow eyne / Lookt deadly dull, and stared as astound" (I,ix,35). But among those pulling Lucifera's coach in the Triumph of Pride, to which Duessa-as-Fidessa brings the deluded, inconstant Redcrosse, is Wrath, "fierce reuenging Wrath," such as Redcrosse displays upon first confronting Despaire. "Loth for to be led" (as is Redcrosse with respect to Una),

> in his hand a burning brond he hath,
> The which he brandisheth about his hed;
> His eyes did hurle forth sparkles fiery red,
>
> . . . .
>
> And on his dagger still his hand he held
> Trembling through hasty rage, when choler in him sweld.

(I,iv,33)

Blake would have appreciated how Spenser himself shrewdly connects this passage to Redcrosse's mental struggle with despair and suicidal thoughts. Still playing the role of knight in shining armor that pride, the arch-sin, has confirmed in him as his true self-image, Redcrosse nearly fatally experiences the stripping of that self-image in favor of the arch-form of the arch-sin, despair, wonderfully personified by Spenser at this moment as wrath against one's self. Thus, the knight lifts up his hand to stab himself, lowers it, then raises it again as if compelled against his will. Wrath, dagger always in hand, "of his hands . . . had no gouernement, / Ne car'd for bond in his auengement." Redcrosse's initial rage and desire for revenge against Despaire (in the interests of equity to the dead Sir Terwin) becomes Redcrosse's uncontrollable desire to slay his own despair—obviously a multiple self-damnation in the eyes of Blake, not to say Spenser himself.

The bottom-line question for us, of course, is: what has all this to do with *The Book of Thel* and how does it help us to read that poem aright? If Thel's "problem" is, as Mitchell claims, her lack of "faith as well as of spontaneity and selflessness" (p. 87), then Spenser's "solution" to Redcrosse's comparable "problem"—Una's intervention to prevent his suicide—would seem to Blake somehow right. As

Una says earlier when her champion is losing the battle with Erroure, "Add faith vnto your force" (i,19). But she also adds the sort of "advice" Trevisan implicitly gives Redcrosse before he even enters Despaire's cave: "Strangle her, else she sure will strangle you" (ibid.), a logical kill-or-be-killed philosophy that would have grated harshly on Blake's ears. Una offers no such counsel in the Despaire episode but rather takes matters into her own hands and saves the hapless Redcrosse from himself, thereby assuming the role of "grace" that is "greater" than the "iustice" of killing Despaire. As Spenser's final stanza in the canto (ix,54) demonstrates, and as Blake himself knew, even Despaire cannot "kill" despair.

Mitchell's otherwise exemplary summary of the alternative readings of Genesis he sees reflected in *Thel* thus skews the lines of Blake's argument in the poem. To Blake, Spenser is wrong in believing what Genesis suggests, that man does die when he falls from grace; but it is also wrong to impute to Blake the belief that, because Thel has not learned "how to die," she "falls from grace." Grace has nothing to do with the matter—as indeed the bulk of Mitchell's own argument paradoxically shows—for it implies a state of sin from which the graceless one may be redeemed, hardly a Blakean idea even this early in his career, as a number of his annotations to Lavater's *Aphorisms on Man* amply show. Thel's *sin*, if we can extricate that term for a moment from its conventionally moral implications, is a function of her identity as Queen of the Vales of Har, a virgin to boot. As such, she is so self-conscious a self that she is almost obsessed with the possibility of vanishing from her "pearly throne" to some limbo where no one "shall find my place" (2:12). Rephrasing this fear after receiving her first "lesson" to the contrary by the Lily, Thel laments, "I pass away. yet I complain, and no one hears my voice" (3:4); and yet again, after the Cloud delivers his homily, "I fade away, / And all shall say, without a use this shining woman liv'd" (3:21-22). In other words, she wants the world to beat a path to her door, as it were, and when she dies she wants to be mourned—by someone, anyone. (I shall return to the matter of "use" in a moment.) Like all of Blake's embodiments of Selfhood, she must have an "other" subservient to herself—a mental construct that iconicizes itself as the fundamental act of the Female Will. Without such others in her world, she is queen over a vacuous realm. No wonder she longs to lie down gentle in that good night

> And gentle sleep the sleep of death. and gentle hear the voice
> Of him that walketh in the garden in the evening time.
>
> (1:13-14)

That is, she will become the second Eve in the second Eden and for a second time exert her power over Adam. "And all is done as I have told," as Blake concludes his later and more complex "history" of this cycle in *The Mental Traveller* (E486).

Thel's mental struggle in Despaire's cave, then, is no more successful than Redcrosse's, and Blake's allusive counterpointing is a striking instance of his early capacity to seduce his reader into interpretive traps. While Thel wishes to die because she is of no "use," Spenser brings Redcrosse to the brink of death at his own hands, despite his chivalric vows of usefulness. Just as Trevisan "Fled fast away" (I,ix,30) from Despaire only to be plagued throughout his final appearance in the poem with fear and despair, so too Thel "Fled back unhindered," Blake leaving it to the reader to fill in the blanks of her mental state after she reaches the Vales of Har once more. Even when he returns to Despaire's cave leading Redcrosse and Una, Trevisan "for dread and dolefull teene, / Would faine haue fled" again—and there Spenser leaves him without telling us whether the "they" who "enter" the "darkesome caue" in the next stanza include Trevisan, whether he does flee when Redcrosse and Una enter, or whether he stands there eterne in fear and dread and despair—however "free" of Despaire.

A second aspect of Blake's extraordinary counterpointing is inherent in Despaire's speech to Redcrosse, the gist of which, in the language of *Thel*, is that the "children of the spring" are "born but to smile & fall" (1:7), the very physical evanescence and facts of life Thel wishes to transcend. Moreover, Despaire's argument hinges in part on the rightness of Redcrosse's dying now, before the time "ordaynd by destinie" (st. 42), because he has sinned enough for a lifetime:

> Why then doest thou, O man of sin, desire
>   To draw thy dayes forth to their last degree?
> Is not the measure of thy sinfull hire
> High heaped vp with huge iniquitie,
> Against the day of wrath, to burden thee?
> Is not enough, that to this Ladie milde
> Thou falsed hast thy faith with periurie,
> And sold thy selfe to serue *Duessa* vilde,
> With whom in all abuse thou hast thy selfe defilde?
>
> (St. 46)

He then quotes the very law of Him "From highest heauen" that Thel believes and that precipitates her ultimate despair: "Die shall all flesh"; "Let euery sinner die" (st. 47). Translated into the metaphysics of *The Book of Thel*, the entire argument of Despaire imputes both sinfulness and irrevocable enchainment on the wheel and rack of time to Thel herself. That is to say, both a sense of sin and of temporality govern her mind. Her sin (or sins), however, are not Redcrosse's but rather the fundamental Blakean sins of unimaginativeness and inaction; for, as we know from his annotations to Lavater, "Vice" is "the omission of act in self" as well as the more obvious "hindering of act in another." "Whatever is Negative is Vice," Blake goes on, "all Act ["from Individual propensity"—deleted] is Virtue" (E601).

Thel's problem, then, is not that "she lacks faith." That is Redcrosse's problem. Nor is it that she lacks "spontaneity" or "selflessness" in the conventional altruistic sense explained to her by the Lily, Cloud, and Clod of Clay. Dying to be the "food" of anything is hardly the road to Blake's paradise or the palace of wisdom. What she lacks is the virtue of action (not the same, of course, as virtuous action). She begins by lamenting her evanescence in the most egregiously sentimental and conventional terms, wishing only to "gentle sleep the sleep of death"—even that tired metaphor suffused with the languor of inaction. Then she likens herself to "a faint cloud" floating through the day's skies until it vanishes from everyone's sight (2:11–12). To be sure, she "walk[s] through the vales of Har," but she does not feed "the little flowers," merely smells them; she hears the birds but feeds them not (3:18–20)—Blake's language in the passage careful enough to leave unanswered the question of why she does not feed either. What she does do is "delight" in them (3:21). And, finally, she longs to be "cherish'd" with "milk and oil" (5:10–11). The emptiness of it all is an echo or anticipation of the life of those imbecilic aged infants, Har and Heva, who cling to their memories (Mnetha, their "governess" and protector) to avoid acting in their world in *Tiriel*.

In Spenser's world, Redcrosse is hardly inactive when we first meet him, though it is difficult to believe Blake cheered the slaying of dragons (even when they are called Erroure) as the way to New Jerusalem. But, more important, as Book I proceeds, Redcrosse's action comes more and more under the spell of Duessa and Archimago, by whom he is repeatedly undone (separated the while from Una, in whom Blake perceived at least the rudiments, however benightedly iconicized, of Imagination). It is "right," then, in Blake's mental transformation of Spenser's sequence, that Redcrosse become a man of inaction through Duessa's "merciful" saving of him from certain death by Orgoglio and his subsequent imprisonment in the dungeon of ignorance (Ignaro)—perhaps to Blake the bottomless pit of unimaginativeness. Thus, it comes as no surprise that, when Arthur, in search of Redcrosse, "entred in" (cf. Blake's "enter'd in," 6:2), he falls down "a deepe descent" from which "with an hollow, dreary, murmuring voyce / . . . piteous plaints and dolours did resound" (viii,38; cf. Blake's "Dolours & lamentations," 6:7). And, uncannily apropos Blake's purposes in *Thel*, it is Redcrosse's voice that we hear from his "grave," its accents those of Blake's "voice of sorrow," here interpreting Arthur's entry as that of someone "which brings me happy choyce / Of death, that here lye dying euery stound, / Yet liue perforce in balefull darkenesse bound" (st. 38). In other words, in the double grip of Despaire and Ignaro, Redcrosse wishes to "gentle sleep the sleep of death" without much caring whether he hears "the voice / Of him that walketh in the garden in the evening time" (*Thel* 1:13–14).

Through Una, Spenser interprets Redcrosse in this plight as "of your selfe . . . berobbed," a "misseeming" of his true "hew" (I,viii,42). For Blake, Thel's selfhood would indeed be berobbed had she not fled the rigors of what Blake will later call "self-annihilation"; and what she flees back to is the "misseeming" that in Blake is equatable with one's self-created image of one's self—"*like* a watry bow and *like* a parting cloud. / *Like* a reflection in a glass. *like* shadows in the water. / *Like* dreams of infants. *like* a smile upon an infants face, / *Like* the doves voice, *like* transient day, *like* music in the air" (1:8–11)—the similes brilliantly emblemizing both a deliberate self-construct and a fiction. Moreover, when she is presented with the palpable reality of her images in the persons of Lily, Cloud, and Clod of Clay, she finds that she is not as like them as she thought or wished or hoped. She is not like the Lily, she says, but "like a faint cloud" (2:11); upon meeting the Cloud she says, "I fear that I am not like thee" (3:17). What she is like, indeed is, is the composite image of the grave speech: ear, eye, tongue, nostril, the "touch" of sexuality—the human form human that, perceived unsimilitudinously, is the Human Form Divine, The Divine Image as Blake's song of innocence of that title emblemizes that percept (E12–13). This Divine Image is, of course, the human-divine form of Blake's idea of "virtue," its Mercy-Pity-Peace-Love that "*Is* God" and "*Is* Man" being a far cry from Redcrosse's warlike holiness accompanied by the truth of the church.

While all this seems ample to damn both Thel and Spenser, Blake is not quite finished with his "heroine" or his Renaissance predecessor. After his ordeals of inaction with Orgoglio and Despaire, Redcrosse is taken by Una to the House of Holinesse. Spenser's opening stanza of this tenth canto of Book I is rather remarkably applicable to

The Book of Thel with but little "translation":

> What man is he, that boasts of fleshly might,
>   And vaine assurance of mortality,
>   Which all too soone, as it doth come to fight,
>   Against spirituall foes, yeelds by and by,
>   Or from the field most cowardly doth fly?

Thel boasts no fleshly might, and she is painfully devoid of assurance of any kind, even as she implicitly subscribes to the validity of both in her mind by fleeing back to her pearly throne, her "shining" lot, and her virgin queenship over the Vales of Har. When it comes to the mental fight that the grave's "reality" reveals to her as the way things really are (as opposed to her Lockean images of the way things are in her mind), she most cowardly doth fly this field of battle against the mental foes Blake will later call spectres. Thus, Spenser's "lesson" in the rest of the first stanza of the canto is rather severely countered:

> Ne let the man ascribe it to his skill,
>   That thorough grace hath gained victory.
>   If any strength we haue, it is to ill,
>   But all the good is Gods, both power and eke will.

Grace, good, power, and will become Blake's imagination—the grace, good, power, and will that Thel lacks but does not know she lacks.

For Blake, then, Spenser sinks deeper into error by having Truth and the Church bring Redcrosse to the House of Holinesse, a sinking that *The Book of Thel* reveals by its echoing of Redcrosse's entry therein. Caelia's place is "an auntient house not farre away" (cf. the Matron Clay's "house" over the "roof" of which Thel's moans fly, 5:15-16), "Renowmd throughout the world for sacred lore, / And pure vnspotted life" (Blake's implicit irony is very nearly vicious). It is "gouernd" through "wisedome of a matrone graue and hore" (I,x,3). Blake's turning the last phrase into a double pun is little short of spectacular: Matron Clay = grave = "matrone graue," not to mention the earth as whore, her wisdom delivered by the voice of sorrow from the archetypal Grave. Lest this seem merely explicative ingenuity rather than a tribute to Blake's extraordinary sensitivity to, and memory of, even individual words in the writers from whom he stole, we need to recall that a "Porter" (as in *Thel*) opens the door to the castle of holiness and that he is the Humiltá that Spenser regards Redcrosse (and would have regarded Thel) as lacking. Redcrosse and Una "passe in stouping low; / For streight and narrow was the way" (st. 5); but instead of meeting the visceralness of Blake's senses, they meet in turn Zele, Reuerence, Faith, Hope, Obedience, Amendment, Penance, Remorse, Repentance, and finally Charissa—a notably unBlakean pantheon. But Charissa does hand Redcrosse to Mercy to guide "his weaker wandring steps" along "the ready path" to "heauen" (st. 33–34), seemingly righting a procedure that began so wrong. But quite unlike Blake, Mercy submits Redcrosse to "an holy Hospitall," whose doctors are seven beadsmen dedicated to teaching the conventional religious opposites of, or cures for, the seven deadly sins to which Spenser earlier subjected Redcrosse in Lucifera's House of Pride.

The most un-Blakean, yet curiously Blakean, ministration of all to Redcrosse's sinfulness is exercised by Patience, who works on the "disease of grieued conscience." When Redcrosse does not respond to "salues and med'cines," and

> yet the cause and root of all his ill,
> Inward corruption, and infected sin,
> Not purg'd nor heald, behind remained still,
> And festring sore did rankle yet within,
> Close creeping twixt the marrow and the skin.
> Which to extirpe, he [Patience] laid him priuily
> Down in a darkesome lowly place farre in,
> Whereas he meant his corrosiues to apply.
>
> (x,25)

This remarkable passage, containing the only corrosives in all of Spenser, recalls the famous corrosives of *The Marriage of Heaven and Hell* that "in Hell are salutary and medicinal, melting apparent surfaces away, and displaying the infinite which was hid" (E39). Whether this argues that *The Marriage* and *Thel* are being composed at virtually the same time or not, the most important thing to notice about Spenser's corrosives is that they lead not to the hidden infiniteness of Redcrosse's Human Form Divine but to utter humiliation and dehumanization:

> In ashes and sackcloth he did array
>   His daintie corse [Thel's "grave" again?], proud humors to
>   abate,
>   And dieted with fasting euery day,
>   The swelling of his wounds to mitigate,
>   And *made him pray* [my italics] both earely and eke late:
>   And euer as superfluous flesh did rot
>   *Amendment* readie still at hand did wayt,
>   To pluck it out with pincers firie whot,
> That soone in him was left no one corrupted iot.
>
> (St. 26)

What is left is a literal Blakean spectre who, now thoroughly "holy," can glimpse "The new *Hierusalem*" (st. 57).

Obviously not wanting to submit her selfhood to such corrosives, much less acknowledge the "apparent surface" of her sense-dominated self that corrosives will melt away, Thel precipitately retreats to her own garden of holiness, assuming perhaps that thereby her unsuperfluous flesh will be left without "one corrupted iot" and, even more pointedly, assuming once again "control" of the Vales-Veils of Har that, in Blake, will shortly become Vala-Veila, the "goddess" Nature, not to mention the Whore of Babylon (the spectrous "version" of the New Jerusalem). But it is not necessary to invoke these later formulations anachronistically to appreciate what Blake accomplishes very nicely in *The Book of Thel* without them. It is necessary to invoke Spenser, however, to avoid resting one's case with respect to the "meaning" of Thel's entry into, and flight from, the grave upon assumptions as misleading (and even erroneous) as hers. Mitchell concludes: "Thel enters the earth's household . . . with the assumption that her fate is in the hands of a just and merciful deity" (p. 93), a conclusion drawn from what she learns from the Clod of Clay's assurance that God not only loves even the worm and protects it from "the evil foot" but cherishes it "With milk and oil" (5:9–11). But, Mitchell says, she discovers in the grave "that this god does not exist," that he is but "a manifestation of Thel's wishful (or fearful) thinking" (p. 93). "What is left?" is obviously the right question to ask at this point, and Mitchell asks it, only to answer subjunctively with what Thel may have really learned, what she must do to be a true Blakean "heroine," and why therefore we should not criticize her for returning to the Vales of Har, a return he regards as "ambiguous."

As I have tried to show, however, there is no ambiguity once we recognize Blake's "Spenserianizing" of the poem, of the grave, of Thel's flight, indeed of her entire philosophizing. It is to my point, then, that true to her misreading (often deliberately, at best obtusely) of her first two interviews—with Lily and Cloud—Thel badly misreads the Clod of Clay's message as well. That interview is prepared for subtly but meticulously by Blake in the Cloud's introduction to it. Taking his cue from Thel's definition of her state as one in which she not only "fades away" but lives a "shining woman" without use except "to be at death the food of worms" (3:21–23), the Cloud calls up the devouring worm; but it miraculously appears to Thel's eyes in most undevouring guise as an image of "weakness" and "helplessness" perched upon the equally "humble," "modest," "weak" "Lilly's leaf" (1:16–22; 3:30). "Astonish'd" because her previous mental image of the eternal worm is thus belied by her new perception, Thel repeatedly questions the "reality" of the Lockean object that so confounds her "idea": "Art thou a Worm? . . . art thou but a Worm?" And again: "Is this a Worm?" And, precisely as she "images" her own life on plate 1 (which, we must now recall, includes neither worm nor clod of clay), she now "translates" the worm not only into an "image of weakness" but into a simile, "like an infant" with no mother to cherish it "with mothers smiles." Blake thus has the Clod of Clay arise as that mother, "pitying" and bowing over "the weeping infant" (the simile now become the fact in Thel's mind) and "exhaling" her "life . . . / In milky fondness" upon it (4:1–9).

But the Clod knows more than Thel wishes to know—or perhaps even to hear spoken—namely, that the Clay is the "mother" of all God's "chillun," including the infant-sorrow Thel, who has "leapt" into "the dangerous world . . . / Helpless, naked, piping loud" (*Infant Sorrow*, E28, the lines echoing *Thel* 4:5) and who indulges in her own version of the song of experience's final lines:

> Bound and weary I thought best
> To sulk upon my mothers breast.

Infant Sorrow was written after Blake first drafted *The Book of Thel* but, as Erdman and others have noted, at least the final plate of *Thel* (the grave passage) and "Thel's Motto" cannot have been etched earlier than 1791, suggesting that final revisions in the nonextant manuscript of the rest of *Thel* may well have been executed contemporaneously with Blake's *Notebook* drafting of poems for *Songs of Experience*, including a considerably longer version of *Infant Sorrow*. It is not without interest that this earlier version of the song of experience includes what may be distant echoes of *Thel*: she "delights" in the birds and flowers while the infant seeks "only for delight"; she "delights . . . no more" because she "fades away" while, for the infant, "No delight was to be found" upon "the nettly ground" (E797). The verbal similarities are uncompelling, however, nor are they necessary for us to recognize that Blake's much revised *Notebook* draft of *Infant Sorrow* was at some stage planned as, in Erdman's words, "a compact cycle-poem (compare 'The Mental Traveller') from infancy to grey hairs" (E798), perhaps then a version, however attenuated and transformed, of what I have claimed as the cycle of *Thel*.

If we return now to Thel's conversation with the Clod of Clay, we find her curiously misapplying what she hears. In her sermon on selflessness ("we live not for ourselves"), the Clod presents herself as "the meanest thing," yet one on whose head "he that loves the lowly, pours his oil . . . / And kisses me, and binds his nuptial bands around my breast''—and, in culmination, gives to her "a crown that none can take away" (4:11, 5:1-4). This "wisdom" is in itself suspect, but Thel rather wilfully transfers God's cherishing and anointing of the Clay to the Worm, and thereby to herself:

> That God would love a Worm I knew, and punish the evil foot
> That wilful, bruis'd its helpless form: but that he cherish'd it
> With milk and oil, I never knew; and therefore did I weep.
>
> (5:9-11)

The Clod has said no such thing. Rather she "exhales" her life "In milky fondness" upon the Worm; she mentions no "evil" feet or divine punishment, and it is she herself whom God cherishes with oil. Blake's "message" is clear. Still wrapped firmly within herself despite all that the Lily and Cloud have told her of "life," Thel turns the Clod's climactic lesson into an assertion of an avenging God who will protect her from "evil," anoint her with milk and oil, and therefore reaffirm her sovereignty (the Clay's "crown") over the Vales of Har.

The lesson delivered by the voice of sorrow from the grave violently shatters her new-found complacency, and for Blake, that lesson is the "true wisdom" behind the sentimental façades of the three previous speeches. Despite her imaging herself as like those interlocutors, capped by her warping of the Clod's speech into an identification of herself with helpless, infant Worm, Thel is unlike any of them—to Blake. What is "tested" in the poem, then, is her fundamental humanity, her humanness, her sensory identity as well as her imaginative (not imagined) identity. Put somewhat crudely but not inaccurately, she wishes to remain a pure soul once she finds out that she is an "impure" body. Her "white veil" (5:7) is "in reality" that "little curtain of flesh on the bed of [her] desire," but, as in all three of her previous interviews, she prefers the image to the thing. Back in Har's vales (veils), she can "safely" (protected by God against "evil") live the life she images to herself, one that Blake has steadily exposed as a sham in his reiterated epithets for her: "the lovely maid" (1:16), "mistress of the vales of Har" (2:1), "Queen of the vales" (2:13), "the virgin" (3:1,7), "this shining woman" (3:22), "virgin of the skies" (3:25), "pensive queen" (3:29—the language of eighteenth-century melancholy poetry here a deft maneuver by Blake), "daughter of beauty" (5:7; again the language is subversive), "Queen of the vales" once more (5:14), followed by simply "Queen" with "virgin feet" (5:16-17).

This litany of implicit pejoratives, delivered unpejoratively and in humility by Thel's subjects as well as dead-panned by Blake himself as narrator, exerts a perverse pressure on what the Lily, Cloud, and Clod seem to deliver so "correctly," not to say engagingly, as wisdom. The Lily, for example, abides in "humble grass" and "lowly vales" and is, like Thel, a "gentle maid of silent valleys. and of modest brooks" (1:15, 17, 22). Though she "melts" finally, she will "flourish in eternal vales"—so conventional an image of immortality that it is remarkable we have all "believed" it despite its wonderful pun in "vales" and the resultant irony in "flourish." After the Lily "bowd her modest head" in self-deprecation and obeisance, the Cloud appears with his curiously "golden head" (crowned?) and pontificates in the same syrupy, predictable terms. Although he touts love, peace, and "raptures holy" as his destiny after death, he curiously belies the natural cycle to which he belongs by claiming that, once "link'd in a golden band" with the "weeping virgin" dew, they will "never part." Of course they will, every day, the diurnal dissolution of their marriage as much a fact of life as the daily new-Cloud-new-dew wedding and subsequent dissolution. Thus, when the Cloud presents the eternal, devouring worm as an image of his wisdom and doctrine of use, Thel neatly sidesteps it, preferring the Worm as infant to its reality as harbinger of her final "interview" in the grave. Like the Lily, the Clod too is "humble" as well as "mean," "cold," "dark," and "lowly"—Blake's climactic portrait of self-humbling appropriate perhaps to natural law but hardly a law governing the idea of "The Divine Image" in man.

In sum, Thel is steadily misinformed, equated by each of the speakers with themselves. That is, they "realize" her images. She is righter than she ever comes to know about her denial of "likeness" to them—or at least to Lily and Cloud—that denial paradoxically intensified by her choice of likeness to the very Worm for which, inevitably, she will be food. In *There Is No Natural Religion* Blake wrote, "If any could desire what he is incapable of possessing, despair must be his eternal lot" (E2). Exactly. And there is where Spenser comes in. But, as Blake also says in the same tractate, "The desire of Man [is] Infinite" and, since that is so, "the possession is Infinite & himself Infinite." It is what Thel could not possibly learn from Nature's denizens nor from the grave, nor will she ever know as one "who sees the Ratio only" and therefore "sees [herself] only." For her, God does not become as she is so that she "may be as he is" (E3). She constructs her own image of God who reigns, loves the helpless, and punishes evil feet that tromp wilfully on the helpless, that is to say, the God of the Old Testament. When the voice of sorrow from the grave rudely questions this theosophy, Thel refuses to recognize the image that the voice presents as hers. Queen, virgin, maid, infant—

"Vales" and veils—are. Thus, she reenters the land of her images that for her has now become the "eternal vales" of the Lily, the "ten-fold life, . . . love, . . . peace, and raptures holy" of the Cloud, and the cradle of a parodic "Infant Joy," that is, an ersatz Eternity or New Jerusalem "wherein," as Spenser put it, "eternall peace and happinesse doth dwell" (I,x,55) and wherein reside God's "chosen people purg'd from sinfull guilt" (st. 56).

> Now are they Saints all in that Citie sam,
> More deare vnto their God, then younglings to their dam.
>
> (St. 57)

Thel, the eternal Virgin Queen, once more eternally "protected" in the womb by her virgin veil, is now a saint.

Blake, Bunyan, Pilgrimages, and Allegory

ALTHOUGH THIS is not the place to enter into a full-scale discussion of Bunyanesque allegory or of Blake's "response" to Bunyan, since I have made some comments about Blake's antipathy to progresses or pilgrimages, some word on the subject is in order. Commentary on Blake's illustrations to *The Pilgrim's Progress* is sparse; extended commentary is nonexistent. Although we know that in 1810 or so Blake thought "Pilgrims Progress . . . full" of "Vision" (*A Vision of the Last Judgment*, E554), the general consensus among Blake scholars about his attitude toward the work is that stated by Morris Eaves in *William Blake's Theory of Art* (see chap. 1, n. 12), namely, that it is a "memory-guided" mockery (p. 38). Accordingly, so the argument goes, Blake's illustrations to the *Progress* are his "most direct illustrations since *Tiriel*," as S. Foster Damon says in *A Blake Dictionary* (see chap. 1, n. 1), p. 62. In his "Los, Pilgrim of Eternity" in *Blake's Sublime Allegory* (see chap. 1, n. 9), however, E. J. Rose argues that it is only "in the mind of the [imaginative] reader" that "Christian ceases to be a cold earth wanderer . . . and becomes a true pilgrim," and that Blake was such a reader, as is evidenced by his "corrective" illustrations to *Pilgrim's Progress* late in his life (p. 99). The most detailed essay on Blake and Bunyan is Geoffrey Keynes's introduction to *The Pilgrim's Progress Illustrated with 29 Watercolour Paintings by William Blake*, ed. G. B. Harrison (New York: The Limited Editions Club, 1941), more conveniently available in Keynes's *Blake Studies* (London: Rupert Hart-Davis, 1949, or, in its second edition, in which the Blake-Bunyan essay is unchanged—see chap. 1, n. 47). As befits Keynes's introduction of the entire series to students of Blake and Bunyan, his essay is almost entirely factual and descriptive, its critical comments severely limited, for example, to the "allegorical and visionary qualities" of

Bunyan's work that "would have attracted [Blake] from an early age" (2d ed., p. 165).

Most recently, these neglected designs have been rescued from critical indifference or easy assumptions by Gerda Norvig, whose *The Designing Vision: Blake's Illustrations of Bunyan's "Pilgrim's Progress"* is in press and who was kind enough to loan me her manuscript. She notes that James T. Wills, as well, "has also recently completed a dissertation on the drawings and is currently compiling notes on them for the Frick Collection catalogue" (p. 13); the Frick is the gallery where the drawings reside. It would be impossible for me to try to do justice in brief space to Professor Norvig's fine, detailed study, but for what I have to say below, I am much indebted to her work (I have not seen Wills's dissertation).

The range of critical "responses" to *The Pilgrim's Progress* by Renaissance and seventeenth-century scholars describes a spectrum similar to that in studies of Blake and Bunyan. On the conventional side (a term that, I hasten to add, I use here nonpejoratively) are comments like those of John R. Knott, Jr., in *Milton's Pastoral Vision* (Chicago: University of Chicago Press, 1971), who sees Bunyan, like other Puritan writers, conceiving of his pilgrimage as "a linear, historical journey and not a journey of the mind to God" (p. 31), an argument he pursues even more vigorously in "Bunyan's Gospel Day: A Reading of *The Pilgrim's Progress*," *English Literary Renaissance* 3 (1973): 443–61, in the context of an attack on Stanley Fish's reading (to which I shall turn in a moment). Near the other end of the critical scale is Isabel MacCaffrey, in *Spenser's Allegory: The Anatomy of Imagination* (see chap. 4, n. 46), who, while acknowledging that, "for most of its length," *Pilgrim's Progress* "is a continued metaphor," finds that its "fictiveness opens into vision at the climax of both Parts"—citing with approval Blake's remark about Bunyan's "vision" (p. 65). Somewhere in the middle is Barbara Kiefer Lewalski's "Typological Symbolism and the 'Progress of the Soul' in Seventeenth-Century Literature," in *The Literary Uses of Typology*, ed. Earl Miner (Princeton: Princeton University Press, 1976); see, for example pp. 106ff. This entire critical spectrum is anticipated by Coleridge's famous comment in *Table Talk*: Bunyan's "piety was baffled by his genius, and the Bunyan of Parnassus had the better of the Bunyan of the Conventicle" (quoted by Roberta Florence Brinkley in her *Coleridge on the Seventeenth Century* [Durham: Duke University Press, 1955], p. 475).

Aside from MacCaffrey's brief comments, the only "Blakean" readings of *Pilgrim's Progress* that I have found (other than Norvig's) are Stanley Fish's in *Self-Consuming Artifacts* (Berkeley and Los

Angeles: University of California Press, 1972) and Brian Nellist's
"*The Pilgrim's Progress* and Allegory," in *"The Pilgrim's Progress":
Critical and Historical Views*, ed. Vincent Newey (Totowa, N.J.:
Barnes & Noble, 1980). Fish's argument, briefly, is that Bunyan's
intention was to "[disqualify] his work as a vehicle of the insight it
pretends to convey"; that is, Bunyan's art militates against the readers' becoming "captives of a literal and incorrect reading" (pp. 225–
26). The reader, "in order to affirm the primacy" of the "dimension
that is not available in the visible configurations" of the work (scene
and/or character), "must (like Christian) interpret the language of
spatial configuration in such a way as to deny its claims to referential
adequacy" (p. 228). Thus, although the work has "the illusion of a
progress," it is "antiprogressive" (p. 229); and if we "believe in the
metaphor of the journey and in the pilgrim's *progress*," contrary to
Bunyan's purpose, we will assert a belief in ourselves and "prefer the
operation of [our] discursive intellect to the revealed word of God"
(pp. 229, 237). In this sense, *The Pilgrim's Progress* is "the ultimate
self-consuming artifact, for the insights it yields are inseparable from
the demonstration of the inadequacy of its own forms, which are also
the forms of the reader's understanding" (p. 264). It is a provocative
reading to be sure, and in essence it is what I think we all would like to
think was Blake's way of reading the work.

But I do not think it was. As Norvig points out, disarmingly and I
think correctly, Blake's phrase describing the work ("full of vision")
is clearly not the same as hailing it as Vision (capital "V"). It takes
no ingenuity at all to argue that "full of vision" strongly implies that
Pilgrim's Progress is something other than *a* vision, but that, perhaps
like *Paradise Lost*, its vision is often obscured by the something else.
Thus, Norvig says: "The fact that Bunyan's characters frequently
maintained both a didacticly reductive attitude towards the symbol
on the one hand, and a naive, concretistic approach on the other, only
increased what Blake regarded as the unfortunate allegoric dimension
of the *Progress*. For each attitude represented a mode of belief that
served sectarian needs and detracted from the reader's direct confrontation with the vision as an eternal state, stripped of doctrinal or
historical accident" (p. 152). Blake, however, as Norvig demonstrates in persuasive detail in her sequential analysis of each illustration, "shifts the focus of Bunyan's story away from Christian's spiritual development [the narrative journey] and on to the individuation
process of the dreamer" (p. 389)—not exactly a Fishian "reading,"
but close. What Norvig does not stress is that Blake's "shift" realle-
gorizes Bunyan's narrative even as it deallegorizes its Puritan emphasis on reprobation and election, on what perhaps the most eminent

Bunyan scholar, Roger Sharrock, calls the familiar Puritan stages of the soul's progress: "conviction of sin, legality, justification, sanctification, and growth in grace" (*John Bunyan: The Pilgrim's Progress* [London: Edward Arnold, 1966], p. 26). Now this is as unlikely a Blakean litany as one might conjure up, but, aside from its particular language, it tends to reinforce a point I have made frequently in this book, namely, that Blake allegorizes in order to deallegorize. That is to say, the very excesses of Bunyan's Puritan historiography as well as theology become, in Blake's graphic version of the *Progress*, the allegorical unidirectional, linear movement, comparable to the linear movement of time against which the pictorialized (hence externalized) allegory of what Norvig describes as an individuation process is pitted—cogs in the wheel to turn the adverse wheel in Blake's metaphor elsewhere. Or, in my less incisive language, Blake, in his illustrations to Bunyan, is necessarily an allegorical antiallegorist. What Fish (and Coleridge) claim for Bunyan's artistry, then, was insufficient in Blake's eyes to fully rescue Bunyan's vision from the confines of the restrictive vehicle (formal, theological, and figurative) that contained it; or, to invoke a familiar conception from *The Marriage of Heaven and Hell*, the body of Bunyan's work is not only "that portion of soul perceived by the five senses" but "the bound and outward circumference" obscuring whatever of soul may be reflective of Bunyan's true (that is, un-Puritan) vision. At worst, the formal aspects of the *Progress* constitute a kind of "Negation," "a false Body: an Incrustation over [the vision's] Immortal / Spirit; a Selfhood, which must be put off & annihilated alway / To cleanse the Face of [the] Spirit" (*Milton* 41[48]:34–37, E142).

To Blake, I believe, "any pilgrimage," as Donald R. Howard puts it succinctly in his *Writers and Pilgrims* (Berkeley and Los Angeles: University of California Press, 1980), "was a symbolical journey to the Heavenly Jerusalem but of necessity a real, physical journey too" (p. 16). The consequent allegorical construct, "like the Puritan world view, . . . implicated man in a psychology of doubt and postponement, of secrecy and restraint," anathematically emblemized, to Blake, in Bunyan's idea of "figuration as a veil placed over another reality," a curtaining of "a discrete and separable substance," a "homiletic allegorizing of Christian's dream journey" (Norvig, pp. 77, 63, 60).

Blake's idea of pilgrims, then, is more nearly that of Milton in his presentation of the "Paradise of Fools" in Book III of *Paradise Lost*: "eremites and friars / White, black, and gray, with all their trumpery," "pilgrims [who] roam" and stray "so far to seek / In Golgotha him dead who lives in heav'n"; and those who see "Saint Peter at heav'n's wicket'' seeming ''To wait them with his keys,'' only find that when they ''lift their feet'' ''at foot / Of heav'n's ascent,'' they are blown ''transverse ten thousand leagues awry / Into the devious air'' and ''upwhirled aloft / . . . o'er the backside of the world'' (ll. 474–77, 484–94). The mightiness of Blake's struggle to redeem, or make possible the self-redemption of, Milton, Spenser, Chaucer, and Bunyan (at least these) can only be appreciated, it seems to me, if we acknowledge the benighted depths into which they allowed their visions to descend.

Allegory and Typology

A NY ATTEMPT to distinguish the essential sameness (to Blake) of *allegory* and *typology*, I am aware, threatens participation in some of the same confusions over the two terms that continue to plague critics as well as biblical exegetes. Tannenbaum's and Wittreich's positions, as I have presented them in chapter 4, are essentially Auerbachian, but Blake's, I believe, is basically Gnostic. Christian biblical exegesis transformed the theosophy of the Old Testament into a metaphysic, that is to say, it allegorized the Old Testament into the New, distinguishing thereby the new "system" from the Judaic old, love and forgiveness from law and punishment, in effect, soul from body. Whereas the Christian dispensation metaphorically links the fate of the individual and his community in history with the progressive working out of God's design, the Gnostics tended to link the inner life of the individual with immutable and transcendent reality, with a "timeless knowing," as Harold Bloom defines *Gnosis* in *Agon: Towards a Theory of Revisionism* (New York: Oxford University Press, 1982). To Blake, the New Testament is not the "fulfillment" of the old, then, and most importantly, it is not his "Everlasting Gospel." That gospel is The Word, in the sense that the four gospels are the fragmented Word, competing for the truth of history (precisely the "problem" of Blake's fallen zoas). Hence Blake's heroic efforts to detemporalize his visions, to present a simultaneous canonical book, as it were, to deliver individuals from *système* (which is a spatial and temporal conceptualizing of the fictions of the "ancient poets" of *The Marriage*). The most balanced and informative presentation of Blake's knowledge and use of Gnostic materials is Stuart Curran's "Blake and the Gnostic Hyle: A Double Negative," *Blake Studies* 4 (1972): 117-33. Although it is not what I am arguing for or against in my use of the term *Gnosis*, Curran's article is well worth reading in the context of allegory's relationship to typology.

As to the sharpness of Wittreich's and Tannenbaum's distinction between *typology* and *allegory*, it is, for the study of Blake a false distinction to try to make at all. *Tropology* might have been, for them, a more accurate contrast to allegory, although even that term has its problems—as does Auerbach's *figural*. Although the literature on all four terms is enormous, Earl Miner's edition of essays by various hands, *Literary Uses of Typology* (Princeton: Princeton University Press, 1977), is at least a convenient starting place for those who would pursue the subject further. In his preface, Miner himself points out that "to early Christians, typological interpretation was involved in prophecy, moral allegory, and eschatology," but "like theological exegesis itself, literary practice commonly adapts the strict sense [of typology: OT types > NT antitypes] to freer ends" (pp. ix–x). Moreover, the various Jerusalems in literature, for example, as well as in ritual, "may be read literally or fictionally, typologically or tropologically" (p. xii). In his important "Afterword" to the collection, however, Miner presents polysemousness ("multiplicity of representation") as working "contrarily" to the exemplary meaning of the OT-type / NT-antitype typological paradigm. Robert Hollander thus argues that Prudentius's *Psychomachia*, to which (or at least to the conception implicit in which) Blake's work has been likened, is both allegorical and typological ("Typology and Secular Literature," pp. 13–15). And Karlfried Froehlich (in "'Always to Keep the Literal Sense in Holy Scripture Means to Kill One's Soul': The State of Biblical Hermeneutics at the Beginning of the Fifteenth Century") cites Rudolf Bultmann's point that both allegory and typology "are based on the same assumptions about time and history and that they can not be sharply distinguished one from the other" (p. 21n). D. W. Robertson, who is not represented by an essay in the volume, nevertheless assumes a position of major importance in the debate by way of Thomas P. Roche, Jr.'s prominent citation in his essay on Tasso of Robertson's *A Preface to Chaucer* (Princeton: Princeton University Press, 1962), especially pp. 189ff, and of his article, "The Question of 'Typology' and the Wakefield *Mactatio Abel*," *American Benedictine Review* 25 (1974): especially pp. 160ff. Particularly pertinent to the "confusion" I mentioned is Robertson's assertion in *A Preface to Chaucer* that "typology employs allegory to imply tropology, which is its ultimate aim."

But the most important essay for the study of Blake (and the only one that refers to Blake, if briefly) is Paul J. Korshin's "The Development of Abstracted Typology in England, 1650–1820" (pp. 147–203), a part of his larger study, *Typologies in England, 1650–1820* (Princeton: Princeton University Press, 1982). Two of his points must detain us briefly. The first is the interesting relationship he draws between his notion of "abstracted typology" and the seventeenth-century "Character" (Theophrastian or Hallian). Both Theophrastus's and Hall's characters are portraits of "a generalized class of individuals that are—and always will be—everywhere the same" (pp. 160–61). Korshin then goes on to argue that such portraits are "types" and hence "prefigurative personages," prefigurative not of Christ (or some other ideal) but of the person-type's "behavior" anywhere anytime. Thus, the erstwhile strictly defined typology becomes a kind of "imagistic technique" by which the reader learns to recognize, in Joseph Hall's words, "the face" of good and evil. This is precisely (though Korshin does not draw the connection even when discussing Blake's Chaucer essay) Blake's idea of physiognomy, which I have already indicated is not a term of praise for Chaucer's "charactery." And the "watering down" that Korshin perceives occurring in the seventeenth century lends additional credence to Arnold Kettle's perception, in *An Introduction to the English Novel* (London: Hutchinson's University Library, 1951), that *Pilgrim's Progress* "is the link between the medieval allegory and the moral fable of the eighteenth century" (p. 142).

Korshin's second point is his remark about the "central position [that] prefigurative structures occupy in [Blake's] poetry," whereby "types" are presented "as prefigurations of the eternal, universal harmony which is the ultimate goal of *Jerusalem*" (pp. 193–94). As with Wittreich and Tannenbaum, I think this quite wrong. If indeed Blake uses types this way, the structure of the poetry itself (or "structures" as Stuart Curran has taught us, importantly, to say: "The Structures of *Jerusalem*," in Curran and Wittreich, *Blake's Sublime Allegory*, pp. 329–46) argues that all types are but types of types, none preceding or eventuating from or repeating another, so that a reader's insistence on the functioning of type and antitype in the prophecies is a reflection of that reader's allegorizing the poem, or (essentially the same thing) accepting Los's allegory as Blake's.

Spenser's Ireland and Blake's Erin

ACCORDING TO historians of Ireland, its name, from the Old Irish Erinn (dative case of Erin or the modern Eire), was well established by the fifth century (Arthur's era, as Blake himself noted) as applicable to Pict and Celt alike, who were known as Fir Erenn, the men of Ireland. In *Milton* Blake makes this same identification: "Erins Land, Ireland ancient nation" (39[44]: 45, E141). In *Jerusalem* "Erins Land" is said to be "toward the north" (39[44]:26, E187), but if we notice that this skewed geographical placing in the lap of the fallen Urizen is engineered by a spectre bent upon creating his own religion, we will recognize that Erin's proper place is the east. Damon associates Erin with Blake's "philosophy of love,"[1] and the eternal abode of the corresponding zoa, Luvah, is the east. If one looks at the map of the British Isles, however, Ireland is its westernmost territory. This is the state of things in our fallen universe, a condition precipitated by Blake's archetypal Fall of the eternal zoas from their "proper" realms "toward the Center," that is, toward what we would imagine as chaos. To prevent this ultimate cataclysm and to provide a "rough basement" upon which to rebuild, Los "alter'd the poles of the world, east, west & north & south" (*Milton* 9:17, E103). Otherwise in the South there would be "a burning fire; in the East a void. / In the West, a world of raging waters; in the North a solid, / Unfathomable" (19[21]:21–24, E112–13). That is, we would have the four elements alone without a spark of human life and hence with no chance for "Kingdoms & Nations & Families of the Earth," much less "England & Scotland & Ireland" (*Jerusalem* 16:33–34, E160). Los's altering of the poles, then, orders the chaos, but because he too is fallen, his constructive effort stabilizes the universe according to geographic rather than eternal "propriety"—an aspect of his tireless efforts to create a system by which to liberate all individuals from all earthly systems.

Rearranged, Urizen is now in the North, Urthona in the South, Luvah in the West, and Tharmas in the East; or, geographically, Scotland North, England South, Ireland West, and Wales East. As is obvious (Wales is clearly north of England, and west), Blake's scheme is not mathematically elegant, and there are numerous other complications and ramifications I shall ignore here as well, but the general outline I have given is both true to Blake and sufficient for my purposes. The important thing to remember is that Los's realignment is a fallen conception and that the zoas so realigned are now their spectrous selves, with their "divorced" emanations now under the dominion of the fallen versions of their opposite zoas. Accordingly, Erin, the emanation of Tharmas and the embodiment of healthy, energetic sexuality, falls prey to Luvah's Spectre, lust and hate; and Luvah's emanation, Vala, becomes fallen Nature and the Whore of Babylon under the aegis of a spectral Tharmas, who is identified with "the Vegetated Tongue even the Devouring Tongue" (*Jerusalem* 14:4, E158), the sense of Touch that is now verboten and hence, in Blake's parlance, a "closed gate."

But there is always a residuum of "unfallenness" clinging to the constitutive make-up of Blake's zoas and their emanations. That residuum is what Los preserves by his heroic act of creating a Generation that is the "image" of regeneration (the mirror metaphor reflecting the topsy-turvy upside-downness of the fallen world and the deities or daemons of its four corners). Blake calls Erin's residuum the "spaces of Erin" (*Jerusalem* 9:34, E152), sharply distinguishable from the numbered, weighed, and measured spaces of Ireland on the map of the British Isles. Those imaginative spaces become the "location" of Los's furnaces and the building of Golgonooza, for they "reach'd from the starry heighth, to the starry depth."[2] Erin's geographically real place in the west, Ireland, becomes, in her absence, a place where "whatever enters: / Becomes Sexual, & is Created, and Vegetated, and Born"—so uncannily like the Ireland of Yeats's Byzantium poems that it is difficult not to believe that he, as a pioneer Blakean, constructed part of his East-West, Byzantium-Ireland contrary out of his acute appreciation of Blake's myth. "A Sexual Machine," Blake acidly calls Ireland, "an Aged Virgin Form" that "In love & jealousy immingled" is called "Religion" (*Jerusalem* 39[44]:21–22, 25–27, E186–87). In the "spaces of Erin" Beulah is also fashioned, mercifully woven by Los's emanation, Enitharmon. There "the loves / Of Beulah" are woven by all the Emanations as "sweet" and promising "visions" "for Jerusalem & Shiloh, in immortal Golgonooza / Concentering in the majestic form of Erin" (*Jerusalem* 86:41–45, E245).

In the apocalypse of *Jerusalem*, the zoas and their emanations disappear as physical presences to reassume their mental-eternal realities and "stations." That is, they are "reabsorbed" into the body of Albion and Jerusalem. The Imaginative Man thus stands fourfold once more, "facing" all the compass points at once, such geographical "directions" and "places" no longer functions of a space that has become infinity and a historical time that has become eternity. Both infinity and eternity are what is "preserved," so to speak, in Erin's spaces. Facing no "spaces" but rather all space, the Divine Humanity can still go "forward irresistible from Eternity to Eternity" (98:27, E257).

That, by way of these "spaces of Erin" and an Ireland fallen into the West, Blake may be said to incorporate the Irish Spenser into his cosmogony and apocalyptic vision seems a bit much to claim, I will admit. But I would like to examine the proposition a little further, emboldened some by the conspicuous presence of Beulah (Cynthia and the crescent moon) in Blake's painting of *The Faerie Queene* characters.

In the Mutabilitie Cantos, to which Blake alludes more than once in his work, Spenser locates the "triall" of Mutabilitie on "Arlohill":

> That is the highest head (in all mens sights)
> Of my old father *Mole*, whom Shepheards quill
> Renowmed hath with hymnes fit for a rurall skill.
>
> (VII,vi,36)

It is a realm of pastoral innocence, a Spenserian, Irish Beulah; and like Blake's innocence, it was ravaged (just as Meliboe's Elysium was in Book VI of *The Faerie Queene*) by wolves and thieves "made the most vnpleasant, and most ill" (VII,vi,55, 37). Originally (Blake's "Eternity," Spenser's Eden), it is the Eden of Una's parents (in which she is the resident "innocent, as that same lambe") before they are "expeld" by "that infernall fiend" (I,i,5); it is the east as opposed to Duessa-Fidessa's west, of which her sire is "Emperour";[3] and it is the "litle hillocke" upon which Calidore first espies Pastorella, and, of course, the Acidalian Mount (VI,ix,8; x,6ff). But it is also more specifically Ireland:

> *Ireland* florished in fame
> Of wealths and goodnesse, far aboue the rest
> Of all that beare the *British* Islands name,
> The Gods them vs'd (for pleasure and for rest)
> Oft to resort there-to, when seem'd them best:

But none of all there-in more pleasure found,
Then *Cynthia*; that is soueraine Queene profest
Of woods and forrests, which therein abound,
Sprinkled with wholsom waters, more than most on ground.
(VII,vi,38)

Arlo Hill is thus the "home" of Elizabeth, the Faerie Queene, the very "moony spaces" that in *The Four Zoas* are originally named Ona (deleted by Blake to become Eno) and that become, in *Milton* and *Jerusalem*, Enitharmon's "space," "Beulahs moony shades & hills"—in Spenser's mythology, the realm of pastoral (Pastorella).[4] Here Jerusalem is "protected" until such time as Albion awakes from his nightmarish sleep and, reclaiming all emanations (*in toto* "they are named Jerusalem") as his bride, "becomes" one with the Lamb of God. In Blake's earliest version of this marriage, in *The Four Zoas*,

the Lamb of God Creates himself a bride & wife
That we his Children evermore may live in Jerusalem
Which now descendeth out of heaven a City yet a Woman
Mother of myriads redeemd & born in her spiritual places.
(IX, E391)

The implicative permutations of all this are a little dizzying. Spenser's Elizabeth is the Fairy Queen is Cynthia is Ireland is Una is the Moon—and is, therefore, relegated by Blake to his fallen, upside-down universe, albeit "protected" from further ravagement and division by the moony shade of Beulah. The irony is severe: Elizabeth, the Virgin Queen, Belphoebe, Cynthia-Diana, Una, et al. are only seemingly "regenerated" through the ministrations of earthly marriage, the biblical land of Beulah. In Blake's vision of *The Faerie Queene* as well as in the originating "realities" of Spenser's poem, none of them is ever united (much less reunited) with her eternal counterpart. At best they remain "asleep" and separate in Beulah-Cynthia's "moony" rest; at worst they slip from Beulah's precarious poise into the "torments of love and jealousy" and the bloody corporeality of war in Blake's Ulro. To put that into the terms of the spatial-geo-graphical paradigm I outlined above, the Spectre of Luvah (fallen love and war) and Erin remain firmly in the west, "away from resurrection, energy, and Imagination . . . toward death, Nature's speciality."[5] Other formulations are possible, of course, since Blake's west, like all his "places," is connotatively rich beyond our fallen language's capacities to articulate. According to Morris Eaves, "the estate of the West is essentially a large graveyard, and its chateau and its great charnel house is the church," its book of laws the Bible as

"Sacred Code."[6] Though he does not say so, it is the "garden of love" of Blake's poem of that title, replete with chapel, priests, graves, and an entry gate over which Dante's motto, reinterpreted, is inscribed—"Thou shalt not"—Blake's emblematic antecedent for the "closed gate" of the west in his later mythopoeic formulations.

If we return now to Spenser's Mutabilitie Cantos, we find that Mutabilitie herself, in the opening stanza, "creates," as it were, the very land of faerie that Spenser seems to erect against her usurpation:

> she . . . her selfe began to reare,
> Gainst all the Gods, and th'empire sought from them to beare.

For she, like Blake's Urizen (and ultimately each and all of his four zoas), aspired to

> Rule and dominion to her selfe to gaine;
> That as a Goddesse, men might her admire,
> And heauenly honours yield. . . .
> At first, on earth she sought it to obtaine;
> Where she such proofe and sad examples shewed
> Of her great power, to many ones great paine,
> That not men onely (whom she soone subdewed)
> But eke all other creatures, her bad dooings rewed.
>
> For, she the face of earthly things so changed,
> That all which Nature had establisht first
> In good estate, and in meet order ranged,
> She did pervert, and all their statutes burst:
> And all the worlds faire frame (which none yet durst
> Of Gods or men to alter or misguide)
> She alter'd quite, and made them all accurst
> That God had blest; and did at first prouide
> In that still happy state for euer to abide.
>
> Ne shee the lawes of Nature onely brake,
> But eke of Iustice, and of Policie;
> And wrong of right, and bad of good did make,
> And death for life exchanged foolishlie.

> (VII,vi,4–6)

The parallels to Blake's conception of the Fall and Los's heroic efforts to undo it are so extraordinary that one wonders why the passage has not been cited before—especially as it is immediately followed by Mutabilitie's attempt to unseat Cynthia as the first step in her realignment of the heavens and their resident gods. And that act is followed in turn by the antecedent to Milton's council of fallen angels in Pandemonium, Jove's summoning of his cohorts "to aduise"

> What way is best to driue her [Mutabilitie] to retire;
> Whether by open force, or counsell wise.

> (VII,vi,21)

But however much Blake would have appreciated Milton's remarkable "correction" of Spenser's error (Jove to Satan, Mutabilitie to God), his seventeenth-century predecessor in the line of vision merely surrendered *his* poetic genius to the "new angelicism" of institutionalized Christianity, in which all things (in Spenser's conception) are changed but yet remain the same the more they are changed. Thus, the whole history of western thought, from the classics through Chaucer, Spenser, and Milton, constitutes the error Blake (and in his "fiction," Los) must undo[7]—by (it bears repeating) creating a system by which individuals, including those in the line of vision, may be delivered from all systems.

The debate on Arlo Hill, then, is hardly apocalyptic to Blake, who, in his imaginative conflation of Spenser's and Milton's "systems," perceives it to be Mutabilitie-God arguing her/his case before the throne of Jove-Satan. At the same time, as the curious and much worried-over episode of Diana and Faunus would have revealed to him, Arlo Hill was the "right" place for this absurd debate, after all.

Having bribed Molanna, the maid of Cynthia (now become Diana), to secretly get a look at Diana bathing ("to compasse his desire"), Faunus is discovered and made the quarry of Diana and her huntress maidens; and, "full of indignation," Diana takes her wrath and revenge out on the pastoral innocence of Arlo Hill itself:

> Thence-forth she left; and parting from the place,
> There-on an heauy haplesse curse did lay,
> To weet, that Wolues, where she was wont to space,
> Should harbor'd be, and all those Woods deface,
> And Thieues should rob and spoile that Coast around.
> Since which, those Woods, and all that goodly Chase,
> Doth to this day with Wolues and Thieues abound:
> Which too-too true that lands in-dwellers since haue found.

> (vi,55)

Spenser's earlier version of this is in Merlin's prophetic history lesson delivered to Britomart. There one of Artegall's mighty descendents, Careticus, King of all "great Britainee," is conquered by "Great *Gormond*," who, once "Ireland [is] subdewd,"

> in his furie all shall ouerrunne,
> And holy Church with faithlesse hands deface,
> That thy sad people vtterly fordonne,
> Shall to the vtmost mountaines fly apace:
> Was neuer so great wast in any place,
> Nor so fowle outrage doen by liuing men:
> For all thy Cities they shall sacke and race,
> And the greene grasse, that groweth, they shall bren,
> That euen the wild beast shall dy in starued den.
>
> (III,iii,32–34)

Wasteland or no, in the former passage, Blake's forest of the night and its ravening beasts (and men) have clearly taken over. In either scenario of the rape of Ireland, Cynthia-Diana-Erin's eternal "space" is in very bad shape indeed; or, to put that in terms of Blake's fallen cosmology, Beulah has become Ulro. It is this geographical space in the west (in both its Beulah and its Ulro aspect) that Spenser conjures up once again to present his "vision" of the triumph of Nature-Mutabilitie over all, and it may be as well his vision of *The Faerie Queene*.

The reigning queen of this space, then, is not "merely" Elizabeth-Cynthia-Diana-Britomart et al. but Nature, Blake's Vala, who, upon Arlo Hill "forth issewed," veiled as a parodic Jerusalem-bride, her questionable sex surely "griding" (to use a good Blakean word that he stole from Spenser) Blake even more:

> Whether she man or woman inly were,
> That could not any creature well descry:
> For, with a veile that wimpled euery where
> Her head and face were hid, that mote to none appeare.
>
> (VII,vii,5)

Why her face was hidden Spenser says he does not know; perhaps because it was too terrible to look upon, perhaps too dazzlingly beautiful. That Spenser prefers the latter interpretation is clear from the seventh stanza where, to Blake blasphemously, he associates this "vision" with that of the three men who saw God on Mount Tabor (1 Sam. 10:3ff), the experience that leads to Saul's conversion. To Blake, then, it is meet and right that Nature-Vala-Satan-Jove triumph over Mutabilitie-God. That is, "right" for Spenser; and Blake duly enshrines Spenser's hermaphroditic God as the God of This World in *The Faerie Queene* painting, "confirm'd in his imperiall see" (VII,vii,59).

If, as Isabel MacCaffrey concludes, in Book VII Spenser "confesses his helplessness," acknowledging "the limits of his art," no such confession or acknowledgement could possibly have been a part of the furniture of Blake's mind. For him there is no such thing as "the human limits of imagining." "The ultimately satisfying poem," MacCaffrey finally asserts to extricate herself from her own dilemma, is the one God writes. Exactly; and, as she says, "it will not be an allegorical fiction."[8] It will be what I have called an "antiallegorical allegory," one in which Erin (and all her related eternals) will be reinstated to her eternal "place" in the bosom of the Lamb of God, the east where she belongs, where we all belong, "Inwards." For "without," she is "the Covering Cherub & within him Satan / And Rahab, in an outside which is fallacious" (*Milton* 37[41]:8–9, E137).

Notes

I. SPENSER AND BLAKE

1. S. Foster Damon, *A Blake Dictionary* (Providence: Brown University Press, 1965), p. 383. So far as I can see, there has been little advance beyond this position in the criticism and scholarship of the last twenty years. The closest we can come to an "advance" is the unpursued suggestion of Morton D. Paley in *Energy and the Imagination: A Study of the Development of Blake's Thought* (Oxford: Clarendon Press, 1970): "In writing *Vala* [*The Four Zoas*], Blake freely adapted the method of Spenser [in *The Faerie Queene*]. The attempts of the Zoas to reunite with their separated female counterparts recall Spenser's knights in quest of their lost or abducted ladies. Blake's subject, like Spenser's, is the making of a whole man. Both use the conventions of the *psychomachia* to define the mind's division against itself." But Blake goes beyond Spenser "in making the poem more of a projection of the mind's processes and less of a moralized allegory" (pp. 95–96). Although I take issue with the phrase "the making of a whole man" as accurate when applied to Blake's efforts (*restoration* of the whole man who *is*, eternally, is more like it), Paley's perception is sound. My other differences with his formulation of that perception (as well as an extension of it considerably beyond the confines of *The Four Zoas*) will become apparent as I proceed.

2. This painting is described more extensively than in Damon and is analyzed, however tentatively, by John E. Grant and Robert E. Brown in "Blake's Vision of Spenser's *Faerie Queene*: A Report and an Anatomy," *Blake Newsletter* 8 (1974–75): 56–85—which contains, indispensably, a fold-out facsimile of the painting as well as black and white blow-ups of its several sections and several useful diagrammatic schema.

3. "Blake's Miltonizing of Chatterton," *Blake Newsletter* 11 (1977): 27–29; "Blake, Gray, and the Illustrations," *Criticism* 19 (1977): 118–40; "Blake's 'I Saw a Chapel All of Gold,'" *Colby Library Quarterly* 15 (1979): 37–47; "Antithetical Structure in Blake's *Poetical Sketches*," *Studies in Romanticism* 20 (1981): 143–62; "Edmund Spenser and Blake's Printing House in Hell," *South Atlantic Quarterly* 81 (1982): 311–22; and *Blake's Prelude: "Poetical Sketches"* (Baltimore: Johns Hopkins University Press, 1982).

4. John Hollander, *The Figure of Echo* (Berkeley and Los Angeles: University of California Press, 1981), pp. 68, 88–89.

5. John Beer, "Influence and Independence in Blake," in *Interpreting Blake*, ed. Michael Phillips (Cambridge: Cambridge University Press, 1978), pp. 200–201. "Intensive effects" are those that include "some unusual feature of the proposed source . . . or something markedly distinctive in the author's usage"; "extensive effects" occur "where two or more noteworthy parallels between the proposed source and the later work may be found. . . . In all cases, obviously, uniqueness is at a premium" (p. 201).

6. See Hollander, *The Figure of Echo*, p. 141, where he describes this figure as "a wrenching of sense hovering between the brilliant and the disreputable." The only emendation I would make with respect to Blake is that his catachreses are more often than not both brilliant and disreputable, the latter in its root Latin sense of, roughly, a reversed rethinking. As Hollander points out earlier in his book, "the revisionary power of allusive echo generates new figuration" (p. ix).

7. Plate 11, line 5, in David V. Erdman, *The Poetry and Prose of William Blake*, newly rev. ed. (Berkeley and Los Angeles: University of California Press, 1982), p. 154. All future citations to Blake's works, in text and notes, will be to this edition by plate and line numbers (where appropriate), with E prefixed to the page number.

8. Damon, *A Blake Dictionary*, p. 383. For a more sophisticated and elaborate study of various "general influences" on Blake, see Northrop Frye's remarkable chapter, "The Word within the Word," *Fearful Symmetry* (Princeton: Princeton University Press, 1947), chap. 5, especially pp. 125–43. In *Shelley's Mythmaking* (1959; Ithaca, N.Y.: Cornell University Press, 1969), Harold Bloom has some provocative comments on Spenser's general influence on Blake, although he does concentrate rather narrowly on *Muiopotmos* and the Garden of Adonis episode of *The Faerie Queene*. In 1969, John F. A. Heath-Stubbs stated the obvious: Blake's "debt to Spenser still requires investigation"—*The Pastoral* (London: Oxford University Press), p. 63.

9. See Joseph A. Wittreich, Jr.'s *Angel of Apocalypse* (Madison: University of Wisconsin Press, 1975) as well as several of his articles preliminary to, and revised in, that book: "William Blake: Illustrator-Interpreter of *Paradise Regained*," in *Calm of Mind*, ed. Wittreich (Cleveland: Case Western Reserve University Press, 1971), pp. 93–132; "'Sublime Allegory': Blake's Epic Manifesto and the Milton Tradition," *Blake Studies* 4 (1972): 15–44; "Opening the Seals: Blake's Epics and the Milton Tradition," in *Blake's Sublime Allegory*, ed. Stuart Curran and Wittreich (Madison: University of Wisconsin Press, 1973), pp. 23–58. Also see his preface to and essay in *Milton and the Line of Vision*, ed. Wittreich (Madison: University of Wisconsin Press, 1975), pp. xiii–xix, 97–142; and, most recently, *Visionary Poetics* (San Marino, Calif.: Henry E. Huntington Library, 1979). A significant extension of a number of Wittreich's points, not to say Frye's in *Fearful Symmetry*, is Leslie Tannenbaum's *Biblical Tradition in Blake's Early Prophecies: The Great Code of Art* (Princeton University Press, 1982), and, of course, Frye's own ultimate

extension of the fundamental principles of *Fearful Symmetry* in *The Great Code* (New York: Harcourt Brace Jovanovich, 1982).

10. Damon, *Blake Dictionary*, p. 383. Damon's commentary on Blake's Spenser painting is on pp. 383–85. See also my quotation from Paley's *Energy and Imagination* in note 1 above. The disrepute into which allegory fell progressively from Spenser's day to the Romantic Period needs no rehearsal here, nor does the extraordinary campaign by twentieth-century critics to redeem it in one way or another. I shall have occasion to refer to a number of these "redeemers" as I proceed, and my debts to them (as well as to others uncited herein) are considerable, but it is at least worth speculating here about whether Blake is a seminal force, as we say, in that campaign, acknowledged or not by the redeemers. Ten years after his monumental study of Blake, *Fearful Symmetry*, Frye could say, unabashedly, that all literary interpretation is allegorical (*allegoresis*), and, further, that *allegoresis* in its conventional sense is not even necessary because the commentary is already indicated in the text—*Anatomy of Criticism* (1957; New York: Atheneum, 1967), pp. 89–90.

11. See note 2 above.

12. *Public Address*, E581. Jean Hagstrum was the first to offer the emendation, "Poco-Piud," for the up-till-then accepted reading, "Poco-Pend." Along with "Niggling" it means, as Morris Eaves says, "adornments of the subject by techniques of high finishing" (*William Blake's Theory of Art* [Princeton: Princeton University Press, 1982], p. 69). See also Blake's *Notebook* poem, "To Venetian Artists" (E515), and Erdman's notes (E882).

13. See, e.g., Blake's *A Descriptive Catalogue of Pictures* (E529–30 and passim), *Public Address* (E574–82 passim), annotations to Reynolds's *Discourses* (E635ff), and a number of the epigrams and satirical poems in his *Notebook* (E510–15).

14. Donald D. Ault, *Visionary Physics* (Chicago: University of Chicago Press, 1974); F. B. Curtis, "Blake and the 'Moment of Time': An Eighteenth-Century Controversy in Mathematics," *Philological Quarterly* 51 (1972): 460–70; Stuart Peterfreund, "Blake and Newton: Argument as Art, Argument as Science," in *Studies in Eighteenth-Century Culture*, vol. 10, ed. Harry C. Payne (Madison: University of Wisconsin Press, 1981), pp. 205–26. On Blake and Locke, all study must begin with Frye's chapter, "The Case against Locke," in *Fearful Symmetry*; see also Harald A. Kittel, "*The Book of Urizen* and *An Essay Concerning Human Understanding*," in *Interpreting Blake*, ed. Phillips, pp. 111–44, and David Simpson's comments on this essay in his review of the book in *Blake: An Illustrated Quarterly* 14 (1980–81): 124–25. On Blake and Bacon there has been little or no advance over the preliminary essay by Sir Geoffrey Keynes, "William Blake and Sir Francis Bacon," in *Blake Studies* (Oxford: Clarendon Press, 1971), pp. 90–97; my "Blake, Bacon, Dante, and Sir Geoffrey Keynes," *Criticism* 1 (1959): 265–70—both of these dealing with Blake's annotations to Bacon's *Essays* (E609–22)—and Mark Schorer's "William Blake and the Cosmic Nadir," *Sewanee Review* 43 (1935): 210–21. See also Mark L. Greenberg, "Blake's 'Science,'" *Studies in Eighteenth-Century Culture*, vol. 12 (1983), pp. 115–30.

15. The worst thing about these painters, according to Blake at the outset of his annotations to Reynolds's *Discourses* ("This Man was Hired to Depress Art"), was that "Rubens & the Venetians," for example, not only were "Opposite in every thing to True Art" but "they Meant to be so they were hired for this Purpose" (E635, 655). Blake calls the hirers "Satans" (E642), but in his *Descriptive Catalogue*, the offending painters themselves become the demons that needed to be exorcised from his own imagination (E547–48). That they were unredeemable in Blake's eyes is suggested by his attempt in his 1809 exhibition to "remove" them from his mind by exposing "their vile tricks," which were the work of "no Mind" (E547, 578). The only "cure" for this is "Aqua fortis" poured "on the Name of the Wicked" to turn them "into an Ornament & an Example to be Avoided by Some and Imitated by Others if they Please" (*Public Address*, E579).

16. It should be noted, however, that a host of writers and artists from whom Blake borrowed are also absent from his visionary-company lists as well as from his groupings of artistic lost souls: e.g., Gray, Collins, the Wartons, Thomson, Donne, Drayton, Addison, Cowper, Macpherson, not to mention the disparate figures referred to one way or another in *An Island in the Moon*: Chatterton, Epicurus, Pythagoras, James Harris, Pindar, Giotto, Plutarch, John Hunter, Hervey, St. Jerome, Hume, Goethe, Johnson, Handel, and Fielding.

17. Gleckner, *Blake's Prelude*, chap. 2; Damon, *Blake Dictionary*, p. 383.

18. For Spenser's reception by eighteenth-century poets, see Earl R. Wasserman, *Elizabethan Poetry in the Eighteenth Century*, in *Illinois Studies in Language and Literature*, vol. 32, nos. 2–3 (Urbana: University of Illinois Press, 1947), especially pp. 92ff. It is unlikely that Blake's "some Vision" refers to the proportion of imagination to fancy in Spenser, but it is not without significance that, for the eighteenth century (even its "establishment"), Spenser "became the symbol of fancy, just as Shakespeare did of imagination and nature." Moreover, "like Homer and Virgil," Spenser, to the eighteenth century, "had combined the *utile* with the *dulce* by the use of a moral allegory, and hence had fulfilled the twofold purpose of poetry" (pp. 94–95). But not to Blake, of course. In an unpublished essay, "The Problem of Originality and Blake's *Poetical Sketches*," delivered as a paper at the 1983 Modern Language Association meeting, Stuart Peterfreund disputed my earlier characterization of the *Imitation of Spencer* as a redaction of eighteenth-century neo-Spenserianism, interpreting the poem instead as an early example of Blake's criticism of Spenser: "Spenser . . . is in several senses a classic case of what happens when one begins at the wrong step in the sequence and takes allegory or fable as vision, confusing the actions of naming with the true first act of recognizing the infinite in otherness" (p. 25). His demonstration of this is via the "golden rod" of line 29 of the poem and the "Spenserian" speaker's confusing of Aaron and Moses' rod as Mercury's caduceus. That is to say, the "classicizing tendency" of Blake's speaker is self-damning.

19. Nowhere does Blake say, or even hint, that he admires Spenser. On the idea of "admiration," however, he has this to say (among more positive usages related to Michelangelo, Raphael, et al.):

Thank God I never was sent to school
To learn to admire the works of a Fool [first version deleted]
To be Flogd into following the Style of a Fool.

(E510, 870)

On the other hand, although they never make it into Blake's pantheon, he says unequivocally, "I own myself an admirer of Ossian equally with any other Poet whatever Rowley & Chatterton also" (E666). For the basis for this admiration see my *Blake's Prelude*, pp. 117–18, 136–39.

20. Harold Bloom, in his "Commentary" included in Erdman's edition of Blake, does suggest, however, that in plate 4 of *Jerusalem* "there may be a memory . . . of Spenser's marriage of the Thames and the Medway" (E929). If so—and Blake's "locating" the two rivers in Beulah (his "state" of marriage) seems to suggest as much—the fact that the "jealous fears" of Albion lead him to "hide" his ostensible spouse and "dissemble" his jealousy (E147) hardly suggests a sympathetic reading by Blake of canto xi, Book IV of *The Faerie Queene*. But see Morton D. Paley's comment on the passage in *The Continuing City: William Blake's "Jerusalem"* (Oxford: Clarendon Press, 1983), p. 198.

21. Rosemond Tuve, *Seasons and Months: Studies in a Tradition of Middle English Poetry* (Paris: J. Gamber, 1933), p. 58. See my "Blake's Seasons," *Studies in English Literature* 5 (1965): 533–51 and its expanded version in chapter 4 of *Blake's Prelude*; Geoffrey Hartman's "Blake and the 'Progress of Poesy,'" in *William Blake: Essays for S. Foster Damon*, ed. Alvin H. Rosenfeld (Providence: Brown University Press, 1969), pp. 57–68; and Irene Chayes's "Blake and the Seasons of the Poet," *Studies in Romanticism* 11 (1972): 225–40.

22. It is worth noting in this connection that Spenser introduces *The Faerie Queene* with his intent to "blazon broad emongst [the] learned throng" the "Fierce warres and faithfull loues" of "Knights and Ladies" (I,proem,1) and that, in one sense at least, Blake does the same thing, with all-too-obvious differences, in "The torments of Love & Jealousy" and consequent assorted "wars" in *The Four Zoas*. Spenser also announces his decision "For trumpets sterne to chaunge mine Oaten reeds" just as Blake describes his first epic effort in terms of "the march of long resounding strong heroic Verse / Marshalld in order for the day of Intellectual Battle" (E300). Although Blake's reference is more directly to Milton's Preface to *Paradise Lost* ("The measure is English heroic verse"), as is the remainder of his subtitle ("The Death and Judgement of Albion the Ancient Man"), the impact of Spenser on *The Four Zoas* seems to me substantial. A further clue may inhere in Blake's introductory reference to Urthona's emanations propagating "Fairies of Albion," which "afterwards [become] Gods of the Heathen" (E301). The intracanonical reference here is clearly to the remarkable plate 11 of *The Marriage of Heaven and Hell*, in which the tutelary gods created by the "ancient poets" in their animation of "all sensible objects" become, in the hands of priests, no longer "mental deities" but "realized" gods. Although the entire idea was commonplace, Blake may well have found it "explained"

in Hesiod's *Theogony* or Hobbes's *Leviathan*. Here is Hobbes:

There is almost nothing that has a name, that has not been esteemed amongst the Gentiles, in one place or another, a God, or Divell; or by their Poets feigned to be inanimated, inhabited, or possessed by some Spirit or other. . . . the same Legislators of the Gentiles have added their Images, both in Picture, and Sculpture; that the more ignorant sort, (that is to say, the most part, or generality of the people,) thinking the Gods for whose representation they were made, were really included, and as it were housed within them, might so much the more stand in feare of them. . . . And therefore the first Founders, and Legislators of Common-wealths amongst the Gentiles, whose ends were only to keep the people in obedience . . . have in all places taken care; First, to imprint in their minds a beliefe, that those precepts which they gave concerning Religion, might not be thought to proceed from their own device, but from the dictates of some God, or other Spirit. (A. R. Waller, ed., Cambridge University Press, 1904, pp. 73–76)

In addition to Blake's fundamental purpose of exposing the self-serving power play that is the origin of priesthood (or the method by which poetry is debased to religion), the passage is also a thumbnail sketch of how poetic vision is narrowed to allegorical constructs. John Beer has located an interesting "source" for the idea and *The Marriage* passage in John Ogilvie's *The Theology of Plato, compared with the Principles of Oriental and Grecian Philosophers* (London: J. Deighton, 1793), even while admitting that the date of Ogilvie's work makes it impossible for Blake to have seen it before etching *The Marriage*; hence, " it is safest to treat the parallels merely as coincidental, and as indications of a contemporary 'climate of thought' " ("Influence and Independence in Blake," pp. 247–48). Jean Hagstrum agrees, in his *William Blake: Poet and Painter* (Chicago: University of Chicago Press, 1964): "The doyen of neoclassical aestheticians, the Abbe du Bos, has said that 'allegorical personages are such as have no real existence, but have been conceived and brought forth merely by the imagination of painters, from whom they have received a name, a body, and attributes' " (p. 19).

23. David V. Erdman, *The Notebook of William Blake* (Oxford: Clarendon Press, 1973), pp. 7 and N75. '

24. There was, however, at least one painting of the episode in the eighteenth century, Thomas Daniell's *The Babe with the Bloody Hands* (1781), which was exhibited at the Royal Academy. The fullest study to date of the attractiveness of *The Faerie Queene* to painters and book-illustrators is Laurel Bradley, "Eighteenth-Century Paintings and Illustrations of Spenser's *Faerie Queene*: A Study in Taste," *Marsyas: Studies in the History of Art* 20 (1979–80): 31–51, although Norman Farmer is currently preparing a book-length treatment of the subject. My information on the Daniell comes from Bradley.

25. Thomas Minnick, "On Blake and Milton," (Ph.D. diss., Ohio State University, 1973), quoted by W. J. T. Mitchell, *Blake's Composite Art* (Princeton: Princeton University Press, 1978), p. 122 and note.

26. On Spenser's being at "one with current Elizabethan thought" in the Garden of Adonis section, see Brents Stirling, "The Philosophy of Spenser's 'Garden of Adonis,'" *PMLA* 49 (1934): 501–38, summarized in *The Works of Edmund Spenser: A Variorum Edition*, ed. Edwin Greenlaw et al. (Baltimore: Johns Hopkins Press, 1934), 2, pp. 347–52. As the Special Editor of this volume, Frederick M. Padelford, notes, "Mr. Stirling clears the ground of much lumber accumulated in previous discussion," the highlights of that "lumber" appearing as well in appendix 3 to the volume. While much additional lumber has been cut since Stirling's essay, none of it, I think, need detain us further here. From Blake's point of view, the "Scheme of the Garden" is the way Stirling sees it as well: "the story of creation, first hinted at, then told thrice over" (p. 352).

27. *A Vision of the Last Judgment*, E556, 555. For an excellent account of "identity" in Blake, although with minimal attention to "essence," see Leonard W. Deen, *Conversing in Paradise: Poetic Genius and Identity-as-Community in Blake's Los* (Columbia: University of Missouri Press, 1983).

28. E. J. Rose, "'Forms Eternal Exist For-ever': The Covenant of the Harvest in Blake's Prophetic Poems," in *Blake's Visionary Forms Dramatic*, ed. David V. Erdman and John E. Grant (Princeton: Princeton University Press, 1970), p. 456. For Blake, "Time is the *mercy* of Eternity" (*Milton* 24[26]:72, E121; my italics), not the avenue *to* eternity. Thus all pilgrimages in Blake are "mortal pilgrimages" of specified, biblical length (usually sixty or seventy years), and despite their occasional brightness (as in Milton's "bright pilgrimage of sixty years"—*Milton* 15[17]:52, E110), they are but earthly imagings of man's eternal life, bound to and in time, necessitating the self-redemption chronicled in *Milton* and *Jerusalem*. I suppose this conception is in some sense "fundamentally Christian," but I do not believe that is what Rose means by the term. For more on Blake's idea of pilgrimages, see chapter 5 in this volume; I might add here a reference to Barbara Nolan's *The Gothic Visionary Perspective* (Princeton: Princeton University Press, 1977), in which she defines "Gothic visionary art" as "essentially an art of edification" that is presented, of necessity, in terms of "the temporal, narrative route to spiritual transformation" through, *successively*, "examination of conscience, confession and contrition" (pp. xv, 135). Thus, we never "lose the sense of the linear fictional context" even as we are reminded always of the "mental geography . . . operating in its own visionary time scheme" (p. 152). Nolan's examples of what she calls "The Later Medieval Spiritual Quest" (the title of her fourth chapter) are *Pearl* and *Piers Plowman*.

29. Sir Geoffrey Keynes, ed., *The Gates of Paradise* (London: Trianon Press, 1968) 2:41; Erdman, *Notebook*, p. 16.

30. Erdman, *Notebook*, p. 16; Emblem 4 is on p. N19. Erdman's photograph of this *Notebook* page indicates clearly that the fourth word of line 3 is "thou," not "now," as in his transcription of the line. It is no doubt too fanciful to suggest that the emblem is Blake's version of Spenser's Genius attiring the "thousand naked babes" who "attend" him, clothing them "with sinfull mire" and sending them "forth to liue in mortall state"— which to Blake, of course, is death.

31. The influence of the emblem tradition as a whole must take precedence, of course, most particularly John Wynne's *Choice Emblems, Natural, Historical, Fabulous, Moral and Divine* (London: George Riley, 1772), from which Blake borrowed for his *Notebook* emblem series (see Erdman, *Notebook*, p. 9 and note 2). *The Shepheardes Calender* also would not have been far from Blake's mind.

32. Irene Tayler, *Blake's Illustrations to the Poems of Gray* (Princeton: Princeton University Press, 1971), pp. 104–5. All the quotations from Tayler are from these pages, numbered in the text in parentheses.

33. For the particulars of Hayley's arrangements with Blake and the revised lists of poets to be included, see Gerald E. Bentley, Jr., *Blake Records* (Oxford: Clarendon Press, 1969), pp. 69–70. The earliest reproduction of all eighteen is Thomas Wright, ed., *The Heads of the Poets by William Blake* (Olney: The Blake Society, 1925), unfortunately with a number of erroneous identifications of the portraits. Kenneth Povey, in "Blake's 'Heads of Poets,'" *Notes and Queries* 151 (1926): 57–58, corrected these errors. Not until 1969, however, was there a new "edition" of the *Heads* by William Wells in connection with a Manchester Art Gallery exhibit of the *Heads* and forty-seven additional works (six by Blake) that were thought to provide "iconographical sources" for Blake. Wells's booklet is entitled *William Blake's "Heads of the Poets" for Turret House, the Residence of William Hayley, Felpham* (Manchester, 1969).

34. In his introduction, Wright indicates that these notes (from which both my quotations are taken) were supplied by S. L. Coulthurst of the photography firm of Flatters, Milborne, and McKechnie of Manchester, which took the photographs for Wright's *Heads*.

35. Edith J. Morley, ed., *Letters on Chivalry and Romance* (London: Henry Frowde, 1911), p. 115.

36. "On Virgil" (E270). Although this particular formulation of the opposition between Gothic and Greco-Roman art is not made until circa 1820, Blake's preoccupation during his apprenticeship with James Basire with Gothic monuments and architecture argues an early date for his preference—even if it is about the turn of the century before the "classics" become a favorite whipping boy of his. For a splendid explication of Blake's transformation of classical principles into his own aesthetic, see Morris Eaves, *William Blake's Theory of Art.*

37. Tayler, *Blake's Illustrations to the Poems of Gray*, p. 103. It is worth noting that, although Gray's note in the 1768 edition of his *Poems* acknowledges his debt in these lines to the Proem of *The Faerie Queene*, Blake ignores both the note and the Proem to focus on "fairy Fiction" and its relationship to "Truth severe."

38. In the 1768 *Poems of Mr. Gray*, however, Gray added a note: "Progress of Poetry from Greece to Italy, and from Italy to England. Chaucer was not unacquainted with the writing of Dante or of Petrarch. The Earl of Surrey and Sir Tho. Wyatt had travelled to Italy, and formed their taste there; Spenser imitated the Italian writers; Milton improved on them."— *The Poems of Thomas Gray, William Collins, Oliver Goldsmith*, ed. Roger Lonsdale (London:

Longman, 1969), p. 170n. Gray's implicit "ranking" of Milton over Spenser here obviously has a bearing on his omission of Spenser from *The Progress*, and it anticipates Blake's similar ranking, although Blake's reasons are more complex.

39. Lonsdale, *Poems of Gray, Collins, Goldsmith*, pp. xv, xvii.

40. William Mason, in his *The Poems of Mr. Gray* (1775; York: A. Ward, 1778), says, however, that in the last epode of "The Bard" Gray "praises Spenser only *for his allegory*" (1, 124; Mason's italics). In a letter of 12 January 1768, however, Gray described himself in no uncertain terms as "naturally no friend to allegory" (4, 217). Cf. Wasserman's conclusion that "it was . . . the painter and the allegorist, not the narrative poet or the poetic technician, that the eighteenth century admired" (*Elizabethan Poetry in the Eighteenth Century*, p. 100), but he says little of Gray.

41. By way of contrast, see the first two stanzas of Collins's "Ode on the Poetical Character" and their praise of Spenser and *The Faerie Queene*.

42. Lonsdale cites a number of possible sources for these lines in addition to Spenser: *Paradise Lost*, IV,293; Dryden's *Religio Laici*, l. 233; Young's *Night Thoughts*, V,70; *II Henry VI*, IV,iv,5; Dryden's *Lucretius*, III,198; Pope's *January and May*, l. 231; and others—all, or most, in themselves deriving from Spenser. See Lonsdale, *Poems of Gray, Collins, Goldsmith*, pp. 198–99, notes.

43. Blake, *All Religions Are One*, E2. If I am right about the physiognomy of Spenser here, Blake is clearly indicating that neither Gray's Spenser in his poem nor Spenser's Spenser (as it were) in *his* poem is *the* Poetic Genius.

44. Although Gray's phrase "a form divine," as applied to Elizabeth, is indeterminate and poetically conventional at least since Dryden, Blake would not have missed the phrase's travesty of his idea of the human form divine, the Imagination, Jesus Christ. See Lonsdale, *Poems of Gray, Collins, Goldsmith*, p. 197n; and Blake's *The Divine Image* in *Songs of Innocence* (E12–13) and *A Divine Image* in *Songs of Experience* (E32).

45. Tayler connects the two pictured episodes with "Truth severe" and "fairy Fiction" but acknowledges her puzzlement at Blake's choices: "Neither of them [is] obviously pertinent to the other or to Gray's poem" (105–6), and thus "more likely" Blake "wished merely to indicate that these are the stuff of Spenser's poetic art, indications of the variety of his visionary knowledge" (107). Her identification of both scenes as exempla of Spenser's "'fairies' themselves" (105) adds confusion to puzzlement. The Cave of Despair episode was one of the favorite subjects for painters, although not quite so popular (as one might expect) as Una. According to Bradley, Fuseli's 1769 *Cave of Despair* is the earliest of these paintings, and there is little doubt that Blake knew it. Benjamin West has one in 1773; Mortimer, one in 1778 and *A Head of Despaire* in 1779; and in 1819 the Royal Academy held a competition on the subject. See Bradley, "Eighteenth-Century Paintings and Illustrations," pp. 37ff.

46. Despite the fact that, in the 1768 edition of his poems, Gray's note to these lines makes clear that he is referring to Shakespeare, Blake's "reading" of the lines need not have had Shakespeare in mind at all, of course.

47. See Sir Geoffrey Keynes's essay on "Blake's Library" in his *Blake Studies*, 2d ed. (Oxford: Clarendon Press, 1971), p. 161, and Gerald E. Bentley, Jr., *Blake Books* (Oxford: Clarendon Press, 1977), pp. 681, 689. The issue of the *Literary Gazette* Bentley refers to is that of 18 August 1827, the article a Blake obituary (pp. 540–41). It should be noted here that neither the Chapman nor the Vellutello was very expensive in Blake's time (Bentley, *Blake Records* [Oxford: Clarendon Press, 1969], p. 349n).

48. Frederick Tatham, "Life of Blake," in *The Letters of William Blake*, ed. Archibald G. B. Russell (New York: Scribner, 1906). The full text of the life appears in Bentley's *Blake Records*, pp. 508–35; Tatham's comments on Blake's library are on pp. 526–27. More extensive (and, as Keynes notes, more "hyperbolic") comments appear in a letter late in Tatham's life (1864), the text of it in Keynes's *Blake Studies*, p. 157.

49. Ernest de Selincourt, ed., *The Poetical Works of Edmund Spenser* (Oxford: Clarendon Press, 1910), p. 507. This edition has four frontispieces and three illustrations, all by Louis DuGuernier, some commentary on which may be found in Bradley, "Eighteenth-Century Paintings and Illustrations," p. 32. Her conclusion that the artist "apparently did not read the six books thoroughly" is sound.

50. Ibid., p. 508.

51. John Upton, ed., *Spenser's Faerie Queene*, 2 vols. (London: J. and R. Tonson, 1758), 1, p. xxvi.

52. The engravings were for John Flaxman's *Compositions from the Works, Days, and Theogony of Hesiod* (London: Longman, Hurst, Rees, Orme & Brown, 1817). Thomas Cooke's translation was steadily available in various editions up through Johnson's *The Works of the English Poets*. Indeed, some lines from Blake's *Poetical Sketches* poem, *An Imitation of Spencer*, may very well owe something to Cooke's translation. After Perseus slays Medusa,

> Then started out, when you began to bleed,
> The great Chrysaor, and the gallant steed
> Call'd Pegasus, a name not given in vain,
> Born near the fountains of the spacious main.
> His birth will great Chrysaor's name unfold,
> When in his hand glitter'd the sword of gold;
> Mounted on Pegasus he soar'd above,
> And sought the palace of almighty Jove;
> Loaded with light'ning through the skies he rode,
> And bore it with the thunder to the god.

This quote is from Cooke's *Hesiod's Theogony or The Generation of the Gods*, in *The Works of the English Poets*, ed. Samuel Johnson (London: J. Johnson, 1810), vol. 20 (the passage above is ll. 444–53). Blake's lines are a prayer to Mercury to help his "lab'ring sense" to fly

> As the wing'd eagle scorns the tow'ry fence
> Of Alpine hills round his high aery,
> And searches thro' the corners of the sky,
> Sports in the clouds to hear the thunder's sound,

And sees the winged lightnings as they fly,
  Then, bosom'd in an amber cloud, around
Plumes his wide wings, and seeks Sol's palace high.

(E421)

Although the metaphors are unequal (Pegasus, eagle), the language and conception, even in their very conventionality, are oddly similar to Cooke's. Moreover, one wonders whether Blake made any connection between Hesiod's Chrysaor and his "sword of gold" and Artegall's sword in *The Faerie Queene*, "Chrysaor." E. H. Blakeney, in his edition of Book V of *The Faerie Queene* (London: Blackie, 1914), cites the *Theogony* passage as a source for Spenser's conception, according to the *Spenser Variorum*, 5, p. 165.

53. Frye, *Fearful Symmetry*, p. 284.

54. The passages from Bacon that I have quoted all appear in Cooke's essay, p. 774 of Johnson's *Works of the English Poets*, cited in note 52 above. Prior to the section Cooke selects, Bacon writes further: "The earlier antiquity lies buried in silence and oblivion, excepting the remains we have of it in sacred writ. This silence was succeeded by poetical fables. . . . great numbers, to procure the sanction of antiquity to their own notions and inventions, have miserably wrested and abused the fables of the ancients"— *The Moral and Historical Works of Lord Bacon*, ed. Joseph Devey (London: George Bell, 1909), p. 200.

55. In 1808 or so Blake wrote, in the margins of his copy of Reynolds's *Discourses*, "I read Burkes Treatise when very Young at the same time I read Locke on Human Understanding & Bacons Advancement of Learning." (E660); and in 1799, in a letter to Rev. John Trusler, he quoted (accurately) from the first edition of the *Advancement* (E703). It seems at least possible, then, that Blake had read *The Wisdom of the Ancients* before writing *The Marriage*. Interestingly, given his low opinion of Bacon as part of the infernal triumvirate—Bacon-Newton-Locke—he continued to purchase and read Bacon up through the turn of the century; the edition of the *Essays Moral, Economical and Political* that he annotated was dated 1798.

56. Upton's discussion appears in *Spenser's Faerie Queene*, 2, p. 461. Milton does not use the phrase in connection with Mammon in either of his appearances (in Books I and II) in *Paradise Lost*. In his annotations to Bishop Watson's *An Apology for the Bible* (London: T. Evans, 1797) Blake wrote, "They seem to Forget that there is a God. of This World. A God Worshipd in this World as God & Set above all that is calld God" (E618). I might note here in passing that Upton calls especial attention to Spenser's use of the word "corrosives" in *The Faerie Queene*, I,x,25, where they will be applied to Redcrosse to "extirpe" his "Inward corruption, and infected sin." In *The Marriage*, in connection with Blake's vow to print "in the infernal method," corrosives are said to be "in Hell . . . salutary and medicinal" (E39). The echo, if echo it be, is faint, but it is possible at least that Redcrosse's hard-won vision of the "new *Hierusalem*" was somewhere in the back of Blake's mind when presenting his own idea of how man can perceive "the infinite which was hid."

57. The full title of Birch's edition is *The Faerie Queene, By Edmund Spenser. With an exact Collation of the Two Original Editions, Published by Himself at London*

in Quarto; the Former containing the first Three Books printed in 1590, and the Latter the Six Books in 1596. To which are now added, A new Life of the Author, and also A Glossary. Adorn'd with thirty-two Copper-Plates, from the Original Drawings of the late W. Kent, Esq; Architect and principal Painter to his Majesty (London: J. Brindley and S. Wright, 1751). The "new Life" is largely Hughes's warmed over. Kent's illustrations, so far as I know, have never been reprinted. There are fifteen in Book I, five in Book II, four in Book III, three in Book IV, one in Book V, and four in Book VI. Aside from the fact that Kent was nearing his death, the distribution is perhaps of some interest—even significance—as an index to eighteenth-century taste and preference (or national pride in England's patron saint). Wasserman's exhaustive research for his *Elizabethan Poetry in the Eighteenth Century* turned up more imitations, "translations," and continuations of Book I than of any other book (see pp. 100ff. and his bibliography of "Poems Influenced by Spenser's *Faerie Queene*" from 1706 to 1802, pp. 260–68). Nothing in Kent's illustrations could be conceived as "sources" for Blake's painting, but it is at least interesting in light of Blake's only known quotation from *The Faerie Queene*, accompanying the *Notebook* emblem discussed earlier in this chapter, that two of the five illustrations in Book II deal with the Amavia-Mordant-Ruddymane episode.

58. Margaret Jourdain, *The Work of William Kent* (London: Country Life; New York: Scribner's, 1948), p. 43.

59. Jeffrey P. Eichholz, "William Kent's Career as Literary Illustrator," *Bulletin of the New York Public Library* 70 (1966): 621, 644. Eichholz tries mightily, but unsuccessfully, to reconcile Kent's reflection in his illustrations of "the aesthetic tastes of the period" and the "artistic spirit of . . . the Augustan age" with what he calls Kent's "grotesque mode"—"disproportion in the drawing of the human figure; the presence of fantastic scenes and creatures; elaborate and fanciful decoration of artifacts; the use of deceptive perspectives in the composition of landscapes" (pp. 620–21, 645). Spenser was often claimed as a powerful influence on eighteenth-century gardening, specifically on what Bishop Hurd in his *Letters on Chivalry and Romance* called "the Gothic method of design in Gardening." See, e.g., Jim Corder, "Spencer [*sic*] and the Eighteenth-Century Informal Garden," *Notes & Queries* 204 (January 1959): 19–21; A. R. Humphries, *William Shenstone: An Eighteenth-Century Portrait* (Cambridge: Cambridge University Press, 1949), pp. 127f; Kenneth Woodbridge, "William Kent as Landscape-Gardener: A Reappraisal," *Apollo* 149 (n.s.) (July 1974): 126–37; and *The Works of William Mason*, 4 vols. (London: T. Cadell & W. Daires, 1811), 1, p. 385.

60. The "distressing conventionality" I perceive in the illustrations is something like Hazlitt's judgment of an art exhibit at the British Institution in 1814. He ridicules the paintings as "done by the book . . . with the characters and story correctly expressed by uplifted eyes or hands, according to old receipt-books for the passions, and with all the hardness and inflexibility of figures carved in wood" ("The Morning *Chronicle*, 5 February 1814," in *The Complete Works of William Hazlitt*, ed. P. P. Howe [London and Toronto: J. M. Dent, 1934], 18, p. 10). Elsewhere Hazlitt reflects his own view of Spenser's achievement: "Spenser, a poet to whom justice will never be done till a

painter of equal genius arises to embody the dazzling and enchanting creations of his pen'' (*Works*, 20, p. 240). Kent was obviously not this man, but one
must wonder whether Blake would have been, had Hazlitt had the opportunity to see Blake's Spenser painting.

61. Jourdain, *Work of William Kent*, p. 73. The Walpole quotations are
from his *Anecdotes of Painting in England* (Strawberry Hill: T. Farmer, 1762).
Even though Walpole's judgment is narrowly derived, one cannot ignore
Jourdain's own implicitly negative response to Kent's drawings or Wasser-
man's judgment of them as ''miserable'' partly because Kent attributed ''to
Spenser's picturesque description his own taste in gardening'' (Wasserman,
Elizabethan Poetry in the Eighteenth Century, p. 95), not ''his architectural bent''
(Jourdain, p. 73). I tend to agree, although in the context of Spenser criti-
cism as well as Blake's criticism of Spenser, I still find them at least interest-
ing and worthy of greater notice.

62. See note 60 above.

63. Henry J. Todd, ed., *The Works of Edmund Spenser* (London: F. C. and
J. Rivington, 1805). In his essay, ''Spenser's Eighteenth-Century Readers
and the Question of Unity in *The Faerie Queene*,'' *University of Toronto Quarterly*
46 (1976–77), Herbert F. Tucker, Jr. calls Upton ''the hero of the Johns
Hopkins *Variorum* edition'' and (''in a sense'') ''the father of all forms of
latter-day Spenser criticism'' (pp. 328, 333). It is not without significance,
then (pace de Selincourt's statement quoted earlier), that in the 1778 eight-
volume *The Poetical Works of Edmund Spenser* in Bell's *The Poets of Great Britain*,
the text is listed in the subtitle as ''From the text of Mr. Upton.'' Aikin's
1802 edition, despite its being not entirely faithful to Upton, is entitled *The
Poetical Works of Edmund Spenser, from the text of J. Upton* (London: J. Heath), as
are its subsequent editions in 1806 (published by Kearsley, with the Stothard
illustrations), 1810 (published by J. Sharpe), 1819, and 1842.

64. Frye, *Fearful Symmetry*, pp. 318–19. Elsewhere in his book Frye equates
Orc with Adonis, Beulah with the Garden of Adonis, Duessa with Rahab, and
Archimago ''more or less'' with Urizen (pp. 143, 228). But he also says, provocatively, that ''the Arthurian legend contains many reminiscences of the more
ancient one of Albion, of whom Arthur himself is a distorted reminiscence'' (p.
142). The point, of course, is the same as Blake's own: ''The stories of Arthur
are the acts of Albion, applied to a Prince of the Fifth century'' (*A Descriptive
Catalogue*, E543). In one sense, it is Spenser's particular ''application'' that
Blake attacks. An interesting analysis of Blake's own ''application'' (without
reference to Spenser's Arthur) is David Worrall's ''Blakes *Jerusalem* and the Visionary History of Britain,'' *Studies in Romanticism* 16 (1977): 189–216.

65. Frye, *Fearful Symmetry*, p. 158.

II. THE TORMENTS OF LOVE AND
JEALOUSY

1. Gleckner, *Blake's Prelude* (see chap. 1, n. 3).
2. William Wordsworth, Preface to *The Excursion* (1814 ed.), *The Poetical*

Works of Wordsworth, ed. Thomas Hutchinson, rev. Ernest de Selincourt (London: Oxford University Press, 1904), p. 754.

3. The sort of "using" I have in mind is that defined by Hollander in *The Figure of Echo* (see chap. 1, n. 4) as catachresis or *abusio*, "a wrenching of sense hovering between the brilliant and the disreputable" (p. 141).

4. Jean Hagstrum, "Babylon Revisited, or the Story of Luvah and Vala," in *Blake's Sublime Allegory*, ed. Stuart Curran and Joseph A. Wittreich (see chap. 1, n. 9), p. 101. His argument that Babylon is "a hideous perversion of Beulah" (p. 106) has some pertinence to what I shall say of *The Book of Thel*, below.

5. Frye, *Fearful Symmetry* (see chap. 1, n. 8), p. 75.

6. Blake did not need Spenser to establish this analogy, of course, for he was perfectly familiar with the Venus-Mars paradigm. But the fact that Britomart, an obvious *Venus armata*, occupies as central a place in his painting of *The Faerie Queene* characters as she does in Spenser's epic argues strongly that his exploitation of the paradigm (and his ignoring of Venus and Mars) is based in large part on Spenser's "versions" of it. See the following chapters on the painting.

7. Ll. 274, 277, 283–84. Elsewhere in the "Hymne" lust "dare not to heauen fly, / But like a moldwarpe in the earth doth ly" (ll. 181–82), perhaps a source for, and certainly an analogy to, the mole passage in "Thel's Motto," as it stands in opposition to the eagle's flight (in Spenser's terms) heavenward. Complementarily, restraint of desire in the "Hymne" becomes the same as insatiable, infinite desire for an "image" or "phantasy" (ll. 197–203).

8. David Wagenknecht's provocative study, *Blake's Night: William Blake and the Idea of Pastoral* (Cambridge: Harvard University Press, 1973), with its many references to the *Calender*, seems to argue against my position here; but Wagenknecht's central point is not that Blake was "influenced" by Spenser's pastoral but rather that a study of the *Calender* can help to lead us to an understanding of Blake's *idea* of pastoral (pp. 4–5).

9. Isabel MacCaffrey, "Allegory and Pastoral in *The Shepheardes Calender*," in *Critical Essays on Spenser from "ELH"* (Baltimore: Johns Hopkins Press, 1970), pp. 117, 120. In connection with my earlier discussion of Blake's general ignoring of the specifics of the *Calender*, see MacCaffrey's comments on Blake on pp. 122–23; Nancy Jo Hoffman's contrary view of Spenser in *Spenser's Pastorals* (Baltimore: Johns Hopkins University Press, 1977), especially p. 24; and Ruth Samson Luborsky's "The Illustrations to *The Shepheardes Calender*," in *Spenser Studies*, vol. 2 (Pittsburgh: University of Pittsburgh Press, 1981), pp. 3–53, in which she demonstrates what Blake surely perceived in this rather crude example of "composite Art," namely, that "the calendrical in all its forms, including books of hours and almanacs, is the most pervasive visual element in the cuts." "By repeating these conventions . . . [they] establish in the reader's mind a continuity with . . . early Virgil and calendrical blocks" (pp. 19, 43).

10. Kathleen Williams, *Spenser's World of Glass* (Berkeley and Los Angeles: University of California Press, 1966), p. 203.

11. The main interpretations are those of Nancy Bogen, *William Blake: The Book of Thel* (Providence: Brown University Press, 1971); Irene Chayes, "The Presence of Cupid and Psyche," in *Blake's Visionary Forms Dramatic*, ed. David V. Erdman and John E. Grant (see chap. 1, n. 28), pp. 214–43; Mitchell, *Blake's Composite Art* (see chap. 1, n. 25), pp. 83ff (I shall deal with this important reading in some detail below); and two recent more-or-less Ricoeurian readings, Marjorie Levinson's "'The Book of Thel' by William Blake: A Critical Reading," *ELH* 47 (1980): 287–303; and James E. Swearingen's unpublished book, "William Blake: The Summons and Consent to Be," pp. 17–36. See also my *Piper and the Bard: A Study of William Blake* (Detroit: Wayne State University Press, 1959), pp. 161–74. In *Blake and Tradition* (Princeton: Princeton University Press, 1968), Kathleen Raine asserts that "*Thel*, in mood, theme, and imagery, is close to Spenser," but then she tarnishes her perception by identifying that theme as merely mutability and by aligning Thel's lament with that of "Spenser's Venus, as immortal mother of the mortal creatures" (1, pp. 100, 103).

12. Eighteenth-century editions of these poets are far from rare. For example, Daniel's *Poetical Works* appeared in two volumes in 1717–18, Sidney's *Works* in 1724–25 and 1739, Surrey's and Wyatt's in 1717 and 1728, Drayton's *Works* in 1748 and 1753, and Davies' in 1773, not to mention the inclusion of all of these in Robert Anderson's *Works of the British Poets* (London: John & Arthur Arch, 1793–95). Should we need reminding, there are a number of compilations of Petrarchisms: Lisle Cecil John, *The Elizabethan Sonnet Sequences* (New York: Columbia University Press, 1938); Lu Emily Pearson, *Elizabethan Love Conventions* (Berkeley and Los Angeles: University of California Press, 1933); J. W. Lever, *The Elizabethan Love Sonnet* (London: Methuen, 1956). Several Blake critics have noted the Petrarchism of the voice from the grave, but only Mitchell has interesting things to say about that fact in his *Blake's Composite Art*.

13. In a not entirely unrelated connection, C. S. Lewis, in *The Allegory of Love* (London: Oxford University Press, 1936), characterizes Spenser's Mask of Cupid as "a picture of the deep human suffering which underlies" courtly love (p. 341). My comments on the Mask follow in due course.

14. "The Art of Dancing a Poem," in Robert Dodsley, *A Collection of Poems* (London: J. Hughes, 1758), 3, 147; see also "Song" (1, 378).

15. A measure of Blake's increasing attenuation of the Petrarchan origins of this and the remainder of the voice of sorrow's speech may be seen in *Milton* 5: 19–37 (E99). It is possible that Blake also had in mind, in connection with the ear as well as with his subsequent line on the tongue, Milton's Belial, whose "tongue / Dropped manna, and could make the worse appear / The better reason"; he was "To vice industrious," yet "he pleased the ear" (*Paradise Lost*, II,112–17). Cf. Patrick Cullen, *Infernal Triad* (Princeton: Princeton University Press, 1974), pp. 102–3; also John M. Steadman's essay on the Sirens, *Modern Language Review* 58 (1962): 560–65.

16. It is worth noting that the *Spenser Variorum* lists neither analogues nor precedents for the language of this sonnet.

17. Similar to, indeed corroborative of, my interpretation is E. B. Mur-

ray's informative essay, "Thel, *Thelyphthora*, and the Daughters of Albion," *Studies in Romanticism* 20 (1981): 275–97. While Murray takes little notice of the Petrarchism in the voice of sorrow's speech, he does establish that speech as "a dialogue made up of identical or congruent word patterns which, at least at that expressive level, are understood by each [sex] in the monologue for two as saying different things to them about their relationship" (p. 291). That is, "the grave-site voice . . . represents a parallel identification of apparent opposites," a kind of "psychic identity" of woman (which Murray regards, persuasively, as the etymological signification of Thel's name) and man (p. 291n). See especially Murray's line-by-line reading of the voice of sorrow's speech (pp. 292–93).

18. See my analysis of Blake's *Samson* in *Blake's Prelude*, pp. 136–47. Mary Lynn Johnson makes the same point in an unpublished paper delivered to the Missouri Philological Association in 1982, "Woman as Symbol in Blake's Illustrations of the Book of Judges."

19. Ll. 678–80. Cf. *Paradise Lost*, II,183–84, and Shakespeare's Sonnet 102.

20. This phrase is a unique one in Blake's works. In *Mythology and the Romantic Tradition in English Poetry* (1937; New York: Norton, 1963), Douglas Bush records no nineteenth-century use of the Zeus-Danaë myth prior to the Victorians, and Kathleen Raine's wide-ranging research in *Blake and Tradition* makes no mention of it.

21. *Paradise Lost*, IX,579–85. The phrase "honied words" is from *Samson Agonistes* (l. 1066), not *Paradise Lost*, but my seemingly rude conflation of Satan and Dalila, a commonplace of Renaissance typologizing of the Samson story, is not inapropos in the context of *The Book of Thel*. Blake makes use of Milton's apple again in *The Human Abstract* of *Songs of Experience*, where, following the tantalizingly Petrarchan "Cruelty" ("selfish loves") knitting a "snare" and spreading his/her "baits with care," Humility sprouts from Cruelty's hypocritical tears to bear "the fruit of Deceit / Ruddy and sweet to eat" (E27). Altogether, the poem is a brilliant epitome of Blake's attitude toward Milton's Fall as well as his effortless blending of Petrarchan elements into that attitude.

22. *Paradise Lost*, IX,1034–45.

23. O. B. Hardison, "*Amoretti* and the *Dolce Stil Nuovo*," *English Literary Renaissance* 2 (1972): 210.

24. It might well be argued here that Blake's reading of the *Amoretti* is obtuse; whether that obtuseness is deliberate or not is, I think, a moot aspect of the question. The old-fashioned view of the sequence is epitomized by Lu Emily Pearson, in *Elizabethan Love Conventions*: Spenser is "the most genuine Petrarchan of all the Elizabethans" (p. 162). At least as early as the 1950s (and no doubt before), the sonnets came to be seen as "largely concerned with a denigration of the romance cult of courtly love and the substitution of a new theme: the triumph of virtuous courtship in betrothal and holy matrimony" (Lever, *Elizabethan Love Sonnet*, p. 23). This view, which is essentially the same as Hardison's, is then extended to argue that Spenser deliberately affects the Petrarchisms in his "search for the ideal method of winning the lady's hand" (William C. Johnson, "Amor and Spenser's *Amoretti*," *English*

Studies 54 [1973]: 218) or, more wittily, that the poet seems to say: " 'These
are the conventions of love . . . ; these are the usual rituals of courtships'; he
will gladly pay these tribute, and even overpay them, since that is what his
delightful damsel seems to expect, and she thoroughly deserves this state; at
the same time a girl of her deep wit will know exactly how to take them, in the
spirit offered" (Louis Martz, "*The Amoretti*: 'Most Goodly Temperature,'"
in *The Prince of Poets*, ed. John R. Elliott, Jr. [New York: New York University Press, 1968], p. 128). For Blake, neither winning the lady's hand nor
conventional (and conventionally religious) betrothal and holy matrimony is
any better than the repression of desire demanded and sanctioned by any
other fundamentally religious code. His choice, then (and I believe it was a
choice), to take a readerly position anticipative of Pearson's, is evidence of
his attempt to expose the core of both kinds of error, *amor courtois* and Cardinal Bembo's *amor razionale*.

25. On the Prolific and the Devourer, see *The Marriage of Heaven and Hell*,
E40; on being lost and found, see my *Piper and the Bard*, chap. 5; and on
dying, see Mitchell, *Blake's Composite Art*, pp. 83ff.

26. William C. Johnson, "Amor and Spenser's *Amoretti*," p. 221.

27. Richard A. Lanham, "*Astrophel and Stella*: Pure and Impure Persua-
sion," *English Literary Renaissance* 2 (1972): 102, 104.

28. William C. Johnson, "Amor and Spenser's *Amoretti*," p. 221.

29. See, e.g., Robert Kellogg's argument, in "Thought's Astonishment
and the Dark Conceit of Spenser's *Amoretti*," in Elliott, *The Prince of Poets*,
that the *Amoretti* is a kind of allegory; for "allegory and the conceit do not
hide or veil or conceal meaning: they are rationalizing and analyzing devices
without which Western man could not have illuminated the dark conceits of
his own nature" (p. 147). If Blake regarded the *Amoretti* this way, it is little
wonder that he pillories it so severely.

30. Cf. Graham Hough's distinction, in *A Preface to the Faerie Queene* (London: Duckworth, 1963), between Ariosto's Bradamante, who is chaste, and
Britomart, who is Chastity, chastity considered by Spenser "not as abstinence" or even as temperance but as an "active, honest, and devoted love"
(p. 170).

31. A. Leigh DeNeef, *Spenser and the Motives of Metaphor* (Durham, N.C.:
Duke University Press, 1982), pp. 114–15 (Colie's point appears on p. 115).
DeNeef also acknowledges Harry Berger's witty conception, which is found
in *The Allegorical Temper* (1957; n.p.: Archon books, 1967), pp. 133–49. See
also Paul Alpers, *The Poetry of "The Faerie Queene"* (Princeton: Princeton University Press, 1967), pp. 186–95, 387–95, and Williams, *Spenser's World of
Glass*, pp. 48–49. Williams further identifies Belphoebe as a blend of love and
war fully in the hunt/chase tradition of Petrarchism and argues that Spenser
makes "the confusing or the debasing of love and war" "one of his major
organizing themes" (p. 50)—one that is, I believe, at the heart of Blake's
exploration of the "torments of love and jealousy."

32. One is reminded in this connection of Berger's point that (like Thel's
Vales of Har) "Belphoebe and her world are withdrawn from and untouched
by the stain of sin; to this extent she represents an impossible ideal around

whose radiance Spenser calls up the darker echoes of what her condition leaves out" (*The Allegorical Temper*, p. 149).

33. Frye was the first, so far as I know, to make this connection (*Fearful Symmetry*, pp. 228, 234); Elaine M. Kauver develops it in "Landscape of the Mind: Blake's Garden Symbolism," *Blake Studies* 9 (1980): 57–73. Echoing Raine in *Blake and Tradition* (1, p. 100), Kauver notes (p. 63) the connection between Blake's "terrific porter" and Spenser's porter of the Garden of Adonis. To further associate the grave with the Bower of Bliss, as Frye and Kauver do, seems to me to be seriously misleading.

34. For a more extensive discussion of the Spenserian nature of *The Book of Thel* and of the remarkable sophistication of Blake's absorption of the very fabric of Spenser's matter into his poetry even as early as 1789–90, see appendix A.

35. Kathleen Williams describes Amoret's imprisonment by Busirane as a "state of mind," an imprisonment by Amoret herself "in her own mind" (*Spenser's World of Glass*, pp. 107–8). James Nohrnberg, in *The Analogy of "The Faerie Queene"* (Princeton: Princeton University Press, 1976), relates the "quite explicitly emblematic" House of Busirane to an Alciati emblem entitled "Virtuous Love Conquering Vicious Love" (pp. 479–80). Long ago, C. S. Lewis argued that the Busirane episode records the final literary defeat of the ideal of courtly love by the ideal of marriage (*The Allegory of Love*, pp. 338ff); as such, it might well have been seen by Blake as another, more elaborate "version" of the *Amoretti*. It is worth noting here, then, that Blake's designs to Milton's *Comus* present the Lady's "entire encounter with Comus as the lady's fantasy, based on her fears of sexual man as a dangerous enchanter whose powers, if she should succumb to them, could destroy her human identity" (Irene Tayler, "Blake's *Comus* Designs," *Blake Studies* 4 [1972]: 76). If that is the case, as I think it is, Blake's imaginative conflating of Spenser, Milton, and his own Thel is quite extraordinary. Cf. Marjorie Levinson's analysis of *Thel* as a "narrative of psychosexual development" ("'The Book of Thel' by William Blake").

36. Damon, *Blake Dictionary* (see chap. 1, n. 1), pp. 181–82; *Milton* 19[21]:32–33 (E113). Other references in Blake to the hermaphrodite may be found on the pages cited in Damon. The opposite of hermaphroditism in Blake is androgyny, as Damon notes, citing Ovid, Plato, Spenser, and Genesis as his sources for this conception, although he gives no indication as to where in *The Faerie Queene* this is to be found.

37. Janet Gezari, "Borne to Live and Die," in *Eterne in Mutabilitie: The Unity of "The Faerie Queene,"* ed. Kenneth J. Atchity (n.p.: Archon Books, 1972), pp. 51–52. Thomas P. Roche, Jr., makes the point and develops it far more extensively in "The Challenge to Chastity: Britomart at the House of Busyrane," *PMLA* 76 (1961): 340–44, and, in revised form, in *The Kindly Flame: A Study of "The Faerie Queene" III and IV* (Princeton: Princeton University Press, 1964).

38. *Europe* 5:5–7, E62. Mary Lynn Johnson's perception in "Recent Reconstructions of Blake's Milton and *Milton: A Poem*," *Milton and the Romantics*

2 (1976): 1–10, is apropos: *Europe*'s "main target is female domination (especially in Mariolotry and worship of the Petrarchan mistress)" (p. 8).

39. E. B. Murray has recently reminded us that Blake did not begin learning Greek until more than ten years after he had written *The Book of Thel*, thus calling into serious doubt earlier attempts to characterize Thel via Greek etymology. Far more persuasive is Murray's contention that "the only apposite meaning Blake could have supposed his prospective contemporary audience to associate with the word 'Thel' was the word 'female.'" The widespread flap in the periodical press over the Rev. Martin Madan's book, *Thelyphthora; or A Treatise on Female Ruin* . . . (London: J. Dodsley, 1780–81), made this virtually common knowledge. On the whole of *Thel*, indeed, see Murray's "Thel, *Thelyphthora*, and the Daughters of Albion" (the quotation above appears on p. 276).

40. DeNeef, *Spenser and the Motives of Metaphor*, p. 160. See also Lewis, *The Allegory of Love*, pp. 330–33.

41. In "Thel, *Thelyphthora*, and the Daughters of Albion," Murray comes to quite different conclusions about Oothoon's magnanimity (see especially pp. 290, 296), as do David V. Erdman, *Blake: Prophet against Empire* (Garden City, N.Y.: Doubleday, 1969), pp. 226–42 and Deen, *Conversing in Paradise* (see chap. 1, n. 27), pp. 50–57. Although the impossible situation she finds herself in cannot be adjudged her fault, the fact remains that her generous offer to Theotormon of "girls of mild silver, or of furious gold" (7:24, E50) does not change anything; her final status in the poem is constituted by "wails," "woes," and "sighs."

42. The fullest reading is that of Hazard Adams, *William Blake: A Reading of the Shorter Poems* (Seattle: University of Washington Press, 1963), pp. 129–31, but see also Harold Bloom, *Blake's Apocalypse* (1963; Garden City, N.Y.: Doubleday, 1965), pp. 315–16, and Frye, *Fearful Symmetry*, p. 266.

43. Sidney Lee, *An English Garner: Elizabethan Sonnets* (New York: E. P. Dutton, 1904), pp. xciv–xcv.

44. *The Works of Edmund Spenser: A Variorum Edition*, ed. Edwin Greenlaw et al. (Baltimore: Johns Hopkins Press, 1947), 7 (part 2), p. 473—hereafter cited as *Spenser Variorum*. Cf. Ted-Larry Petworth, "The Net for the Soul: A Renaissance Conceit and the Songs of Songs," *Romance Notes* 13 (1971): 159–64, who says that Spenser's treatment of the conceit is "probably its fullest . . . in English" (p. 161).

45. For this and other variants, see E859.

46. *Jerusalem* 88:31 (E247). The entire passage is worth quoting as an example of Blake's most mature "Petrarchism": Enitharmon proclaims the world "Womans World" in which she will "weave / A triple Female Tabernacle for Moral Law"

That he who loves Jesus may loathe terrified Female love
Till God himself become a Male subservient to the Female

. . . .

> So speaking she sat down on Sussex shore singing lulling
> Cadences, & playing in sweet intoxication among the glistening
> Fibres of Los. . . .
>
> (88:16–25)

> In triumph the reasoning Spectre smiles
>
> in mockery & scorn
> Knowing himself the author of their divisions & shrinkings, gratified
> At their contentions, . . .
> The Man who respects Woman shall be despised by Woman
> And deadly cunning & mean abjectness only, shall enjoy them
> For I will make their places of joy & love, excrementitious
> Continually building, continually destroying in Family feuds
> While you are under the dominion of a jealous Female
> Unpermanent for ever because of love & jealousy.
>
> (88:34–42)

"Unpermanent for ever": what a wonderful oxymoronic epitome of Petrarchism!

47. Blake may have taken the word *intreat* from Spenser's *Amoretti*, 17 and 30, although *entreat* occurs once in Milton, in his Psalm 88. Blake used Milton's spelling twice (both in letters), but his frequent poetic use of the word, in various forms, is in Spenser's spelling. The most likely "source," however, is the Bible, where *intreat* in its several forms and spelled with an *i* is employed extensively. The (by now in the poem) predictable difference in Blake's usage is the speaker's intreating of abstractions made concrete through his clothing metaphor, while in the Bible it is God who is most often intreated or supplicated: "I intreated thy favour with my whole heart: be merciful unto me according to thy word" (Psalms 119:58); "if a man sin against the LORD, who shall intreat for him?" (1 Samuel 2:25). Blake's speaker's supplications to the abstracted gods of his Petrarchan world are thus thrown into even greater relief.

48. This is clearly, it seems to me, a rewrite of the *Four Zoas* line I quoted earlier, "I have taught pale artifice to spread his nets upon the morning" (E325).

49. The mooniness of Beulah is most clearly explicated in *The Four Zoas* I (E303) and *Milton* 30[33]–31[34] (E129–30). Its delusoriness is dramatized by Blake's constant use of "shadow," "shadowy," or "shadowiness" to characterize it.

50. The similarity here with a passage in *Visions of the Daughters of Albion* (Oothoon's reflecting of Theotormon's "image pure"), commented upon earlier, is, to say the least, striking.

51. Such deluded attempts at seizing the unseizable are frequent in the prophetic books, particularly *The Four Zoas* (see, e.g., E324, 344, and 381–82).

52. The effect is similar to that in the fourth "Memorable Fancy" of *The Marriage of Heaven and Hell* (E41–42), where all that the speaker and the Angel

see is "owing to" their respective "metaphysics." In this light, it is a serious mistake to relate *The Crystal Cabinet* to *Jerusalem* 37[41]:15–22, as John Sutherland does in "Blake: A Crisis of Love and Jealousy," *PMLA* 87 (1972): 429. My reading of the poem, however, is generally corroborated, albeit from a quite different point of view, in Deen's *Conversing in Paradise*, p. 116. Indeed, he sees the "Weeping Woman pale reclind" as passing "from threefold Beulah into twofold Generation—into the world of 'The Mental Traveller.'"

53. One wonders whether somewhere in the back of his mind Blake did not recall Pandora. In *Paradise Lost*, Milton associates Eve with Pandora, who "ensnared / Mankind with her fair looks" and to avenge herself on Prometheus loosed all ills from her box upon the world (Hesiod, *Works and Days*, ll. 70ff). Blake's only reference to Pandora by name is in his very early manuscript fragment "then She bore Pale desire": "in Cities . . . [Man's] Pride made a Goddess. fair or Image rather till knowledge animated it. 'twas Calld Selflove. The Gods admiring loaded her with Gifts as once Pandora She 'mongst men was Sent. and worser ills attended by her far. She was a Goddess Powerful & bore Conceit and Shame bore honour & made league with Pride & Policy doth dwell with her by whom she [had] Mistrust & Suspition" (E448).

54. Night the Second (E313). Cf. Nights the Sixth (E350–51) and Seventh (E368).

55. Brian Wilkie and Mary Lynn Johnson, *Blake's "Four Zoas": The Design of a Dream* (Cambridge: Harvard University Press, 1978). They mention courtly love only once (p. 59), but it is in connection with what they describe as Enitharmon's "radiantly beautiful but sinister anthem of female domination" in Night the Second (E323–24), "one of the most metrically elaborate passages in the *Zoas*." I look briefly at this passage below, but the very fact that Blake lavishes so much attention on it is, in itself, an index of the convention's persistent power in his imagination. Wilkie and Johnson's concluding remark is to my entire point in this chapter: "experientially Enitharmon's hymn expresses perfectly the heady exhilaration of winning in the adversary form of the game of love. Such victories, Blake reminds us, are sham ones, deceptions not only of one's lover-opponent but of oneself"; it is thus "both an exposition and an exposé of the tradition of courtly love" (p. 59). Wagenknecht, in *Blake's Night*, even more pointedly, if tentatively, says that Enitharmon's hymn has "more than one suggestion of Spenser in it" (p. 199), and Paley, in *Energy and the Imagination*, goes so far as to say that in the *Zoas* "Blake freely adapted the method of Spenser. The attempts of the Zoas to reunite with their separated female counterparts recall Spenser's knights in quest of their lost or abducted ladies. Blake's subject, like Spenser's, is the making of a whole man. Both use the conventions of the *psychomachia* to define the mind's division against itself" (pp. 95–96). I have some serious objections to making the analogy thus simply (as will be seen in my chapters on Blake's painting of *The Faerie Queene* characters), but Paley's general perception is clearly sound.

56. The King James Version is: "For we wrestle not against flesh and

blood, but against principalities, against powers, against the rulers of the darkness of this world, against spiritual wickedness in high places" (Eph. 6:12).

57. Lewis, *The Allegory of Love*, p. 20.

58. Andrew M. Cooper makes the same point in "Blake's Escape from Mythology," *Studies in Romanticism* 20 (1981): 107–8.

59. With respect to pastoralism, see Thomas Weiskel's shrewd comment, in his review of Wagenknecht's *Blake's Night, Studies in Romanticism* 13 (1974), that "were the later Blake a pastoralist, he would have found his need and desire to revise Generation into the image of Re-generation impossible to realize, i.e., impossibly compromised by fictionality" (p. 175). That indeed may be the way Blake perceived Spenser's dilemma (or error) in Book VI of *The Faerie Queene*, where the deliberate, Virgilian fictionality of *The Shepheardes Calender* resurfaces, despite Colin's broken pipe, in a pastoral ostensibly freed from time and calendricity to be located with "vertues seal . . . deepe within the mind" (VI,proem,v). But Blake would have recognized that, even in the bravura of the proem, Spenser's plan for the book was doomed, for the "image" of regenerative virtue (its "faire . . . pattern") is his "soueraine Lady Queene" and her "Faire Lords and Ladies, which about you dwell, / And doe adorne your Court." The fictionality of Meliboe's never-never land replete with Pastorellas and Coridons borrowed from *The Shepheardes Calender* never had a chance. Compromised in the proem, it is utterly destroyed in the book, and Spenser-Orpheus is unable to keep the Blatant-Beast-Cerburus in tow, much less annihilate his militant, indeed ferocious, fictional antifictionality. If Colin's pipe is glued together once more for one last try, the glue is an insufficient imagination to preclude the sweeping back of nature, history, even art into the recycling of cycles from which they, momently, seem to be rescued. And Spenser, surely much to Blake's disappointment, must settle for the hope that his "rimes" may "please," since such pleasing *"now"* is all that is "counted wisemens threasure." No wonder, then, that Mutabilitie comes next, "the betrayal," as Michael O'Connell puts it in a slightly different context, "that lies in experience somewhere beyond the fiction" (*Mirror and Veil: The Historical Dimension of Spenser's "Faerie Queene"* [Chapel Hill: University of North Carolina Press, 1977], p. 192). O'Connell, however, does not read Book VII as I believe Blake did, for he entitles his chapter on it "Escape from Mutability."

60. E95. Nancy M. Goslee, in " 'In Englands green & pleasant Land': The Building of Vision in Blake's Stanzas from *Milton*," *Studies in Romanticism* 13 (1974): 114–19, notes this "reworking of images" from the "Petrarchan or Ovidian convention of love as warfare," amalgamated now with Elijah's "chariot of fire" in 2 Kings 2:2 and Christ's war-chariot in *Paradise Lost*, VI, 750ff., which is based largely on the Book of Ezekiel, as well as with Blake's own more radical notion of "the Fiery Chariot of . . . Contemplative Thought" (*Vision of the Last Judgment*, E560). On pages 119–25, she demonstrates a similar development of the bow image, though without reference to its Petrarchist origins or analogues.

61. Wilkie and Johnson, *Blake's "Four Zoas,"* p. 59.

62. For an important analysis of friendship, brotherhood, and love, see Michael Ferber, "Blake's Idea of Brotherhood," *PMLA* 93 (1978): 438–47. See also Deen, *Conversing in Paradise*, especially pp. 163–64, 201–4. Unaccountably, he takes no notice of Ferber.

63. Helen McNeil, "The Formal Art of *The Four Zoas*," in *Visionary Forms Dramatic*, p. 374.

64. For a meticulous analysis of many of these, see John E. Grant, "Visions in *Vala*: A Consideration of Some Pictures in the Manuscript," in *Blake's Sublime Allegory*, pp. 141–202.

65. McNeil, "The Formal Art of *The Four Zoas*," p. 388.

66. Jean Hagstrum, "Babylon Revisited, or the Story of Luvah and Vala," in *Blake's Sublime Allegory*, p. 113.

67. Harold Bloom, "Commentary," E967.

68. McNeil, "The Formal Art of *The Four Zoas*," p. 373.

69. More or less on this idea, but without reference to Blake, see Mark D. Seem's interesting article, "Liberation of Difference: Toward a Theory of Antiliterature," *New Literary History* 5 (1973): 119–33, and Michel Foucault's "L'Ordre du discours," trans. Rupert Swyer, appended to Foucault's *The Archeology of Knowledge* (New York: Pantheon Books, 1972), p. 229.

III. ROADS OF EXCESS

1. Northrop Frye, "The Road of Excess," in *Myth and Symbol: Critical Approaches and Applications*, ed. Bernice Slote (Lincoln: University of Nebraska Press, 1963), pp. 3–20, repr. in Frye, *The Stubborn Structure* (Ithaca, N.Y.: Cornell University Press, 1970), pp. 160–74; Martin Price, *To the Palace of Wisdom* (Garden City, N.Y.: Doubleday, 1964). The quotations that follow appear on pp. 161 and vii, respectively.

2. I distinguish here between those critics who constantly refer to or summarize *The Marriage* as the clearest and most convenient encapsulation of Blakean ideas and those who attempt to deal with it as a work of art.

3. Harold Bloom, "Dialectic in *The Marriage of Heaven and Hell*," *PMLA* 73 (1958): 501–4, repr. in *English Romantic Poets: Modern Essays in Criticism*, ed. M. H. Abrams (London: Oxford University Press, 1960), p. 76; Bloom, *Blake's Apocalypse* (see chap. 2, n. 42), p. 76.

4. Frye, *Fearful Symmetry* (see chap. 2, n. 6), p. 198.

5. Bloom, *Blake's Apocalypse*, pp. 77–78; "Dialectic in *The Marriage of Heaven and Hell*," p. 80; *Blake's Apocalypse*, pp. 78, 82–84. It is also worth noting here that, in dealing with plate 16 (on the Prolific and Devourer), Bloom writes, "If ever Blake speaks straight, forgoing all irony . . . it is here" (*Blake's Apocalypse*, p. 91).

6. See Leslie Tannenbaum, "Blake's News from Hell: *The Marriage of Heaven and Hell* and the Lucianic Tradition," *ELH* 43 (1976): 74–99.

7. Bloom, *Blake's Apocalypse*, pp. 85–86, 88. The "problem" of how to read *The Marriage* is at least analogous to that in reading what Robert M.

Adams calls "open" works, that is, those that engage in a "double-dealing which creates a formality chiefly to outrage it." See his *Strains of Discord: Studies in Literary Openness* (Ithaca, N.Y.: Cornell University Press, 1958). See also Stephen C. Behrendt, "Art as Deceptive Intruder: Audience Entrapment in Eighteenth-Century Verbal and Visual Art," *Papers on Language and Literature* 19 (1983): 37–52, in which he associates Adams's idea with the notion of "multistable images," by which an artist or poet violates "our presumptions and expectations" in his invoking of "clear, particular schemata when he is in fact conjuring up entirely different ones." On such imagery, see Fred Attneave, "Multistability in Perception," *Scientific American* 225 (December 1971): 70.

8. Bloom, *Blake's Apocalypse*, p. 83. My following discussion of the Devil's sentence is a shorter version of my "Blake's Miltonizing of Chatterton" (see chap. 1, n. 3).

9. It could be argued that Blake transforms this conventional concept of grace into his own idea of the "Poetic Genius," for "the forms of all things are derived from their Genius. which by the Ancients was call'd an Angel & Spirit & Demon." Furthermore, "The Religions of all Nations are derived from each Nations different reception of the Poetic Genius which is every where call'd the Spirit of Prophecy," that different reception being due "to the weaknesses of every individual" and every nation (*All Religions Are One*, E1). In this sense, the Devil's question has to do with the uncertainty or adaptative nature of our reception of this bird-angel, certainly an idea that is not unconsonant with Blake's point in the Proverbs and in *The Marriage* as a whole.

10. It is worth noting here that, just as the very "existence" in *The Marriage* of Angels and Devils is indebted to a fundamentally erroneous conceptual split, so the Prolific and Devourer (which Blake defines as, in effect, functions of each other in the third paragraph of plate 16) are reified into entities by abstracting an "aspect" of that functioning as if it were already "realized."

11. Cf. the significantly similar distinction between two modes of perception after Adam and Eve fall: "each the other viewing," they "Soon found their eyes how opened, and their minds how darkened" (IX,1052–54), clearly a part of Blake's imaginative construct in his ostensible "borrowing" from Chatterton.

12. III,691, 676, 694–98. Uriel's speech may well contain a clue to a proper reading of *The Marriage*. He congratulates Satan for his "desire . . . to know / The works of God," the excessiveness of that desire leading him from his "empyreal mansion thus alone, / To witness with [his] eyes what some perhaps / Contented with report hear only in heav'n" (III,694–95, 699–701). Such "report" is, of course, what we, as readers, receive from the speaker of *The Marriage*: the traveler in Hell brings back its proverbs and presents them to us for our delectation and education; plate 14 constitutes a report by the speaker of what he has "heard from Hell''; the "Printing-house in Hell" Memorable Fancy is an account of the speaker's visit there; and so on. The reader, then, needs to travel from the "empyreal mansion" of a

mind lulled into easy acceptance of a first-hand report of "real" experience "to witness with [his own] eyes," whose perceptions will be cleansed by the corrosive fires of intellect. Cf. *Jerusalem* 3 (E145), where Blake, addressing "the Public," hears directly "Within the unfathomd caverns of [his] Ear" the voice of God speaking "in thunder and in fire! / Thunder of Thought, & flames of fierce desire: / Even from the Depths of Hell his voice I hear." God's voice emanates thus from both heaven and hell, but the former speaks to the mind "Thunder of Thought," the latter (that portion of heaven perceived by the five senses) to the ear. "Therefore," says Blake, "I print"—to the eye of the mind, for it is there that "Heaven, Earth & Hell, henceforth shall live in harmony" (*Jerusalem* 3, E145). Cf. *The Marriage* 14 (E39). For a splendid explication of this sort of "marriage," see Eaves, *William Blake's Theory of Art* (see chap. 1, n. 12), and Deen, *Conversing in Paradise* (see chap. 1, n. 27).

13. David Wagenknecht makes a similar point, although not specifically with respect to *The Marriage*, in his review of *William Blake: Essays in Honour of Sir Geoffrey Keynes*, ed. M. D. Paley and M. Phillips (Oxford: Clarendon Press, 1973), in *Studies in Romanticism* 13 (1974): 166.

14. Bloom, *Blake's Apocalypse*, p. 79.

15. In *A Vision of the Last Judgment*, Blake wrote: "the Knave who is Converted to Deism & the Knave who is Converted to Christianity is still a Knave but he himself will not know it. . . . Christ comes as he came at first to deliver those who were bound under the Knave not to deliver the Knave" (E564). In *Milton* Blake comes in one sense to deliver Milton, the true poet that he does not know he is, from his bondage to Milton, the "knave"; or, more accurately (but essentially the same thing), *Milton* is the enabling means for Milton, the true poet (that is, Christ or the Imagination), to redeem himself from Milton, the false poet (the knavery of Satan or the Puritan moral arbiter and accuser). For "No man can Embrace True Art till he has Explord & Cast out False Art" (E562). *Milton* is Milton's "last judgment" (see the end of the first paragraph on E562).

16. *The Four Zoas* IX, E390. Cf. Blake's moving account of his own struggle with error's power, "that spectrous Fiend," in his letter to Hayley of 23 October 1804 (E756).

17. Frye, *Fearful Symmetry*, p. 83; Eaves, *William Blake's Theory of Art*, p. 73; Bloom, *Blake's Apocalypse*, p. 71. A position similar to Bloom's is taken by Robert N. Essick, in "Preludium: Meditations on a Fiery Pegasus," in *Blake in His Time*, ed. Essick and Donald Pearce (Bloomington: Indiana University Press, 1978), pp. 9–10. Such a "balance" as Essick defines is more Coleridgean than Blakean; at worst it is a metaphor for decorum, as Eaves demonstrates (pp. 145–55). Eaves further argues that the "decorum" of *Jerusalem*, indeed of all Blake's works, is in reality synthesis, not balance—synthesis of conception with execution and of artist with work and of audience with all of those (p. 157). On the increasing emphasis in the latter half of the seventeenth century on "concord" almost to the exclusion of "discord," see Edward W. Tayler, *Literary Criticism of 17th-Century England* (New York: Knopf, 1967), pp. 18–20. Blake's lone reference to the principle of *concordia*

discors and its perniciousness is in *Jerusalem*, where "Harmonies of Concords & Discords / Opposed to Melody" are equated with "Lights & Shades, opposed to Outline" and "Abstraction opposed to the Visions of Imagination" (74:23–26, E229).

18. *Public Address*, E581. See also "Blakes Apology for his Catalogue" (E505).

19. Frye says categorically that "Blake wrote such aphorisms as 'The road of excess leads to the palace of wisdom' with one eye on the Greek 'Nothing in excess' " (*Fearful Symmetry*, p. 64). The *locus classicus* for the idea is Aristotle's *Nichomachean Ethics*. See also W. D. Ross, *Aristotle* (London: Methuen, 1923), pp. 195ff. Although it seems a small point, perhaps, it is useful to notice that Blake's proverb does not read, "Excess leads to the palace of wisdom" (or just to wisdom)—a point, then, that contributes to solidifying Spenser's road-monitor figure of Excesse as a bona fide allusion.

20. Bloom, *Blake's Apocalypse*, p. 70.

21. More simply perhaps, the *concept* of "inlets" or "outlets" presupposes the duality that *The Marriage* is presumably dedicated to annihilate. Inlets, then, may suggest an objectivism that is as pernicious as the subjectivism implicit in outlets.

22. See my essay, "Blake and the Senses," *Studies in Romanticism* 5 (1965): 1–15.

23. Blake's line near the end of *The Marriage* has been misread consistently as his personal promise to us to write a "Bible of Hell" and to deliver it to us ("the world"), whether we want it or not. Such a bible would emanate from precisely the same "confident insolence sprouting from systematic reasoning" characteristic of angels, who "have the vanity to speak of themselves as the only wise" (E44, 42). The speaker of *The Marriage* (not Blake) says that, now that he has given us the book of Proverbs, he will give us the whole bible, which (he says) "I have also." "One Law for the Lion & Ox" is no worse than some other law, no matter how contrarious. Oppression is oppression; *all* bibles and sacred codes are the causes of error.

24. *Marriage* 3 (E34). These same chapters of Isaiah are also the major source for the "Argument" to *The Marriage*. One wonders whether Isaiah 63 was not also in Blake's mind:

> Who is this that cometh from Edom, with dyed garments
> from Bozrah? this that is glorious in his apparel, travelling
> in the greatness of his strength? . . .
> . . . .
> I have trodden the winepress alone; and of the people
> there was none with me. . . .
> . . . .
> And I looked, and there was none to help; and I
> wondered that there was none to uphold: therefore
> mine own arm brought salvation unto me. . . .
> . . . .
> For, behold, I create new heavens and a new

earth; and the former shall not be remembered, nor
come into mind.

(Isa. 63:1, 3, 5; 65:17)

25. Byron, *Don Juan*, XIV,xvii.

26. There has been, predictably, much ado about Guyon's wanton destruction of the Bower, the preponderance of commentary ignoring the uncontrollable violence of stanza 83 or rationalizing it one way or another to preserve Guyon's achievement of his allegorical signification. But there are a few darker notes. Berger, for example, in *The Allegorical Temper* (see chap. 2, n. 31), characterizes Guyon's final action as "a Puritan frenzy," but even he rationalizes it in terms of Guyon's reaction to the power of his own lustful interest in the striptease of the two nymphs C. S. Lewis once called "Cissie" and "Flossie" (p. 218). Lewis's more sober perception, that the Bower is not merely "a picture of lawless, that is, unwedded love" but "of the whole sexual nature in disease" (*The Allegory of Love*, p. 332), is clearly pertinent to Blake's reading of the passage. For Guyon, as temperance (or even continence), to destroy the "improvement of sensual enjoyment" is one thing (in that case the road of excess may well lead to the palace of wisdom), but for Guyon to annihilate excess in order to purge love of its unlawfulness is perhaps even the greater crime. Blake's excess, then, *may* be aimed more at the Palmer than at Guyon, since the Greeks associated wisdom with prudence. See Kathleen Williams, *Spenser's World of Glass* (see chap. 2, n. 10), pp. 35–40.

27. A number of Spenser's critics (and Blake's, as I noted earlier) tend to identify Milton's Eden as at least a potential Bower of Bliss, with Eve as its incipient Acrasia. If that is so, it gives the final lie to the Proverb of Hell about excess as Blakean wisdom. See, e.g., A. Bartlett Giamatti, *The Earthly Paradise and the Renaissance Epic* (Princeton: Princeton University Press, 1966), pp. 302–30.

28. For an earlier and somewhat different version of my analysis of the poem, see "Blake's 'I Saw a Chapel All of Gold' " (see chap. 1, n. 3). The only intelligent reading prior to my attempt at one is Hazard Adams's in *William Blake: A Reading of the Shorter Poems* (see chap. 1, n. 42), pp. 240–42.

29. Blake employs "Verulam" in his own poetry elsewhere, once in *Europe* (where, as in Spenser and contrary to fact, it is situated on the Thames) and five times in *Jerusalem*, where it is one of the cathedral cities associated with the Four Zoas. That its Zoa is Urizen *may* have some pertinence to "I Saw a Chapel," but I am inclined to agree with Damon, in *A Blake Dictionary* (see chap. 1, n. 1), that Blake chose the name "because Francis Bacon, who 'put an end to Faith,' . . . was created Baron Verulam and is buried in St. Michael's, which was partly constructed out of Verulam's ruins" (p. 434).

30. W. L. Renwick, in *Spenser Variorum*, 7 (part 2), p. 305; see also *The Faerie Queene*, V,x,27ff; xi,21–32.

31. Blake no doubt had in mind as well Solomon's "house of the Lord," built for the ark and the covenant (hence for Blake, a symbol of religious secrecy, priesthood, and the oppressive law of the ten commandments'

"thou shalt nots"). It is furnished with "altars of gold, and the table of gold, whereupon the shewbread was. . . . and the hinges of gold, both for the doors of the inner house, the most holy place, and for the doors of the house, to wit, of the temple" (1 Kings 7:48–50). For an elaboration of the idea of secret religion and its relationship to repressed sexuality, see Urizen's "temple of love" in *The Four Zoas* VII (E361).

32. Hazard Adams, *William Blake: A Reading of the Shorter Poems*, p. 240.

33. The graves are, of course, the same as the one Thel enters and flees from, the Petrarchan unfulfillment of desire enforced by reason, here personified by the equal militancy and power of priestly religion. In *The Lilly* of *Songs of Experience*, it is a "*modest* Rose" that "puts forth a thorn" (E25, my italics), the same modesty that, in *Visions of the Daughters of Albion*, leads to dissembling, the weaving of Petrarchan nets, and to becoming a "knowing, artful, secret, fearful, cautious, trembling hypocrite" (E49)—as good a description of the speaker of *The Garden of Love* as one might find.

34. Thus, as Damon summarizes, Orc assumes serpent form in *The Four Zoas* to encircle man with the twenty-seven folds of the false heavens or churches "in forms of priesthood," thus becoming his own opposite (Damon, *Blake Dictionary*, p. 365). Relevant passages in the *Zoas* include Nights the Seventh (E356) and the Eighth (E382, 383–84). See Damon's entire entry under "Serpent," pp. 365–66.

35. Although Andrew Marvell, in his poem dedicatory to the second edition of *Paradise Lost* (1674), interprets the biblical Samson's act as one of "spite" and "revenge," and although biblical commentators before and after 1674 (especially in the eighteenth and nineteenth centuries) agree, only a small handful of critics regard Milton's Samson as performing a negative, destructive act, one of carnal warfare. But, as I have argued elsewhere, Blake consistently regarded it this way. See my analysis of *Samson* in *Blake's Prelude*, pp. 139–47, and, for the divergent views of Milton critics, see the notes on pp. 187–90 of that book.

36. It is reproduced in Kathleen Raine, *Blake and Tradition* (see chap. 2, n. 11), 1, 196. She relates the drawing to "I Saw a Chapel" but then goes on to suggest that "Blake is following the tradition which calls the Blessed Virgin the 'Domus aurea' (House of Gold) in the litany addressed to her." More to Blake's point is John E. Grant's commentary on the drawing (which is on page 44 of *The Four Zoas* manuscript and is reproduced in Grant's essay) in "Visions in *Vala*" (see chap. 2, n. 64), pp. 163–64, and plate 16. Chapels in Blake, of course, graduate into tabernacles, the hiding place of the ark and convenant as well as the female genitalia. See, e.g., *Jerusalem* 69:38–44:

> Hence the Infernal Veil grows in the disobedient Female:
> Which Jesus rends & the whole Druid Law removes away
> From the Inner Sanctuary: a False Holiness hid within the Center,
> For the Sanctuary of Eden. is in the Camp: in the Outline,
> In the Circumference: & every Minute Particular is Holy:
> Embraces are Cominglings: from the Head even to the Feet;
> And not a pompous High Priest entering by a Secret Place.

That the serpent in "I Saw a Chapel" is no Jesus goes without saying.

37. See note 35 above.

38. I,i,20. Cf. the monster from within Geryoneo's chapel altar, whom Arthur slays and from whose pierced entrails gush "Most vgly filth, and poyson" into "a puddle of contagion." Like Guyon, Arthur then "did all to peeces breake" the "Idoll" and "foyle / In filthy durt, and left so in the loathely soyle" (V,xi,31–33).

39. Damon, *Blake Dictionary*, p. 366. Earlier Damon was far less certain about the meaning of the poem; see *William Blake: His Philosophy and Symbols* (New York: Houghton Mifflin, 1924), p. 287, where he pronounces it an "enigma."

40. The *OED* defines *sty* as "An abode of bestial lust, or of moral pollution generally; a place inhabited or frequented by the morally degraded." Whereas Blake may have meant merely that the sty is "cleaner" than the defiled chapel and the serpent (something like Oothoon's insisting in *Visions of the Daughters of Albion* on her soul's purity, despite her physical defilement), it is more likely that he is turning the traditional idea of "bestial lust" and "moral pollution" inside out—a polemical ploy, as it were, similar to his familiar championing of harlotry. Cf. Milton's argument in the *Tetrachordon* against maintaining at all costs a marriage in which "coupling" is the sole bond: "What is this, besides tyranny, but to turn nature upside down, to make both religion, and the minde of man wait upon the slavish errands of the body, and not the body to follow either the sanctity, or the sovranty of the mind unspeakably wrong'd, and with all equity complaining? what is this but to abuse the sacred and misterious bed of mariage to be the compulsive stie of an ungratefull and malignant lust, stirr'd up only from a carnall acrimony, without either love or peace, or regard to any thing holy or human"—*Complete Prose Works of John Milton* (New Haven: Yale University Press; London: Oxford University Press, 1959), 2 (ed. Ernest Sirluck), 599–60. That Blake would have rejected not only Milton's puritanical streak here but also the logic of either/or should by now be obvious from my discussion of *The Marriage*.

41. Michael E. Holstein, "Crooked Roads without Improvement: Blake's 'Proverbs of Hell,'" *Genre* 8 (1975): 36.

42. David V. Erdman (with Tom Dargan and Marlene Deverell-Van Meter), "Reading the Illuminations of Blake's *Marriage of Heaven and Hell*," in *William Blake: Essays in Honour of Sir Geoffrey Keynes*, ed. Paley and Phillips, pp. 190–91. See also Erdman's "Postscript: The Cave in the Chambers," in *William Blake: Essays for S. Foster Damon*, ed. Alvin H. Rosenfeld (see chap. 1, n. 21), pp. 410–13.

43. David V. Erdman, *The Illuminated Blake* (Garden City, N.Y.: Anchor Books / Doubleday, 1974), p. 11.

44. For a thorough examination of Blake's relationship to Swedenborg, see Morton D. Paley, " 'A New Heaven Is Begun': William Blake and Swedenborgianism," *Blake: An Illustrated Quarterly* 13 (1979): 64–90; see also J. G. Davies, *The Theology of William Blake* (Oxford: Clarendon Press, 1948), pp. 31–53. Paley dates Blake's repudiation of Swedenborg, after his earlier

general interest in Swedenborg's works, as 1790, the year in which he at least began *The Marriage.*

45. Samuel Taylor Coleridge, *Biographia Literaria*, chap. 14. It is tempting to try to discover other "parallels" in Coleridge's thinking to Blakean conceptions. For example, although Blake would not be sympathetic to Coleridge's distinction between the primary and secondary imagination, the notion, expressed most clearly by Richard Harter Fogle in *The Idea of Coleridge's Criticism* (Berkeley and Los Angeles: University of California Press, 1962), that the imagination is a copulative agent is at least interestingly similar to the power that effects, and indeed constitutes, Blake's "marriage."

46. Eaves, *William Blake's Theory of Art*, p. 73.

47. Bloom, "Dialectic in *The Marriage of Heaven and Hell*," *English Romantic Poets: Modern Essays in Criticism*, p. 79.

48. Robert Essick, "The Altering Eye: Blake's Vision in the *Tiriel* Designs," in *William Blake: Essays in Honour of Sir Geoffrey Keynes*, ed. Paley and Phillips, pp. 50–65. Essick's description of Tiriel as "one of Blake's travellers" who, in their impercipience, "learn nothing of spiritual wisdom from the lands they physically visit" (p. 51) has, then, a rather striking pertinence to the traveler in Hell who narrates *The Marriage.* Essick's citation of *All Religions Are One* is appropriate to both: "As none traveling over known lands can find out the unknown. So from already acquired knowledge Man could not acquire more" (E1). Finally, it is worth noting that *Tiriel* was written just prior to Blake's initial effort to compose *The Marriage.* On the pejorative implicit in the phrase "Memorable Fancy," see also Cooper, "Blake's Escape from Mythology" (see chap. 2, n. 58), 86n.

49. For a discussion of the important Blakean and Spenserian idea of naming and calling, see chapter 4 in this volume.

50. The speaker's garbled, even slanted versions of Isaiah and Ezekiel in the final two paragraphs of the "Memorable Fancy" (E39) are to my point. Isaiah walks "naked and barefoot three years" not because he's emulating Diogenes but "for a sign and wonder upon Egypt and Ethiopia. So shall the king of Assyria lead away the Egyptians prisoners, and the Ethiopians captives, young and old, naked and barefoot, even with their buttocks uncovered, to the shame of Egypt" (Isa. 20:2–3). Ezekiel eats dung not to raise "other men into a perception of the infinite" (E39) but because God orders him to do so in the day of hard famine in order to take on the iniquity of the Israelites eating "defiled bread." Similarly, he lies on his left side to "bear [the] iniquity" of Israel and on his right to "bear the iniquity of the house of Judah (Ezek. 4:4–6, 9–15).

51. E42. Blake even more severely undercuts such knowledge in *An Island* by having the Lawgiver confuse his reading of Hervey's *Meditations* with *Theron and Aspasia.* With wry appropriateness, Blake then has Obtuse Angle take up the same book and read "till the other was quite tir'd out," after which Scopprell takes up "a book" (which Blake might very well have intended to be the same book) that turns out to be "An Easy of Huming Understanding by John Lookye Gent" (E456). The fragment ends with (presumably) Quid, who is usually regarded (probably incorrectly) as Blake,

announcing his grand project of having all the writing in his book "Engraved instead of Printed & at every other leaf a high finishd print all in three Volumes folio, & sell them a hundred pounds a piece." His unnamed female companion, obviously impressed, says, "whoever will not have them will be ignorant fools & will not deserve to live" (E465). The fact that Quid will have them engraved, that he will include high-finished prints (niggled or poco piud, as Blake contemptuously will later call that technique of ornamentation), and that the female's language anticipates that of the speaker of *The Marriage* at the end of plate 24 all urge the relevance of *An Island* to the library of plate 15.

52. Mark L. Greenberg makes a similar point about *The Marriage* itself in his 1982 paper delivered at the American Society for Eighteenth-Century Studies (Houston, Texas), "Blake's *Marriage of Heaven and Hell* as Menippean Satire: Technology and Literary Form." It is worth recalling here Blake's remarkable image of the printing press in *Milton*. There Los lays the "cogs" of his prophetic words in the "human brain" against the "cogs of the adverse wheel" to reverse that adverse wheel's error-producing turning (27[29]:8–10, E124). Translated simplistically but not inaccurately, this means that, without the imagination's unceasing efforts, the adverse wheel turns irresistibly forward to produce either illusion (the product of a senses-memory-fancy ratio) or "the same dull round over again" (*There Is No Natural Religion*, E1), that is, books for libraries. The fact that Los here employs the "tools" of his nemesis and thus produces a book, however much that book is an "anti-book," I shall address later in this chapter.

53. That Blake was especially taken with the Mammon episode is attested to by his vignette of Guyon, Mammon, and Mammon's "fiend" in the twelfth design of his illustrations to Gray's *The Bard*—see figure 2 in chapter 1 of this volume—and by his *Notebook* poem, "I Rose Up at the Dawn of Day" (E481). The Gray is reproduced in and analyzed by Irene Tayler in *Blake's Illustrations to the Poems of Gray* (see chap. 1, n. 32).

54. It is at least possible, then, that the Mammon episode figures as well in the grave-speech of Blake's *Book of Thel*, which I examined in chapter 2. The relevant line is "an Eye of gifts & graces, show'ring fruits and coined gold!" (E6). Mammon describes his gold as both "graces" and "giftes," in sum, "eye-glutting gaine" (II,vii,8–9). Blake's "fruits," then, may well derive from those of the Garden of Proserpine (vii,51ff.), which contains, among other things, "fruit of gold" (vii,54), including the golden apple Ate used to precipitate the Trojan War.

55. This aspect of the allusion calls into serious doubt the prevailing assumption, most fully articulated by Erdman, that Blake's six chambers are modeled on the six days of creation. If that is so, as it may be in one sense, what is created is, of course, the physical universe—Nature—as well as a "firmament" that God, like the "religious" of plate 3 of *The Marriage*, "calls" "Heaven." Paradoxically Blakean, then, is Spenser's conception of the physical body of man divided into six chambers—yet hardly Blake's "human form divine," as we shall see.

56. One wonders in this context whether the eighteenth-century-inherited

terminology of one of Blake's Proverbs of Hell is not a redaction of Alma's proportional castle: "The head Sublime, the heart Pathos, the Genitals Beauty, the hands & feet Proportion" (E37). The entire idea of "proportion" is proposed by Spenser, in geometric terminology, in stanza 22, thereby occasioning a torrent of learned commentary, from Sir Kenelm Digby's *Observations on the 22d. Stanza in the 9th Canto of the 2d. Book of Spencers Faery Queen* in 1644 right down to the present. Digby's notion, briefly, is that the circle is the soul, the triangle the body, and, as Spenser adds, at the base is "a quadrate," what Upton in his edition of Spenser (the one I believe Blake used) calls the "sacred quaternion" of the classical virtues: temperance, justice, fortitude, and prudence (*Spenser's Faerie Queene*, 2, pp. 480–81). Thus, we could say that what was already allegorized, by Pythagoras say, is reallegorized by the Renaissance and Spenser and reallegorized again by Blake in *The Marriage* to make nonsense of the entire mental process of allegorizing that is inherent in the geometry of Spenser's conception. For a sampling of the interpretations of stanza 22 up to the third decade of the twentieth century, see the *Spenser Variorum*, 2, pp. 472–85. Greenberg (see chap. 3, n. 52) perceptively reminds us that cast metal for printing was described in human terms, including shoulders, feet, back, and face.

57. In *The Allegorical Temper*, Berger defines Phantastes' productions as "images-phantasms of what the senses receive" (p. 86); hence, they are associated directly with memory. Michael Murrin, in *The Allegorical Epic* (Chicago: University of Chicago Press, 1980), goes further to say that "Spenser associates Phantastes with folly and madness" (p. 134).

58. As Berger describes the chamber walls, they "picture individual events which reason has permeated, a world constructed according to the plans of human intellect, practical affairs measured and ordered by the ingression of reason" (*The Allegorical Temper*, p. 83).

59. Although not allegories in the conventional sense, the two books read by Arthur and Guyon are to the point here: Arthur's is the history of "Albion" (precisely what Blake will essay in *Jerusalem*) and Guyon's is the "fanciful" "*Antiquitie* of *Faerie* lond," which includes Guyon's direct descent from "Elfe" as well as Gloriana's—the Faerie Queene, Elizabeth herself. This, says Spenser in his proem to the Book, is, along with his own legend of Temperance, a "matter of iust memory," not a "painted forgery" (a phrase that Blake had to take personally as well as one he conceptually absorbed into the Printing house in Hell "Memorable Fancy").

60. Erdman, *The Illuminated Blake*, pp. 112–13.

61. Erdman, "Postscript: The Cave in the Chambers," pp. 412–13.

62. Ibid.

63. *Spenser Variorum*, 2, pp. 336–37.

64. For a summary of Blake's reference to the eagle as genius, see Damon, *Blake Dictionary*, p. 112.

65. *Visions of the Daughters of Albion* 2:13–17, E46. The ambiguity of the eagle that is exploited so complexly by Blake in the printing-house Fancy is initiated in the *Visions* for, in addition to Theotormon's punitive Jovian eagles, there is also (with what it would be pleasant to believe is a subtle Spen-

serian reference to Mammon's cave) the eagle that "scorn[s] the earth & despise[s] the treasures beneath" (5:39, E49).

66. Perhaps at this point it is worth recalling that the viper is a *poisonous* snake. While that fact supports the hellishly oriented metaphysics of *The Marriage* in the same way that the speaker assures us that the corrosive fires of hell are not "torment and insanity" but "salutary and medicinal" (E35, 39), the *Notebook* poem "I Saw a Chapel All of Gold," with its poisonous serpent, argues precisely the opposite—namely, that one excess breeds but another.

67. How extraordinary if it is true, as Erdman claims, that "body" to the left of the title of the prison-house plate and soul to the right "are threaded together by the line that writes 'Fancy,' " and, even more marvelously, that "after the words about transmitting knowledge there is a continuous worm-serpent-tendril of curves and loops, ending ironically in a Shandean delete sign" ("Reading the Illuminations," p. 191).

68. Max Plowman, *An Introduction to the Study of Blake* (London and Toronto: J. M. Dent, 1927), pp. 136–37, 161–62; also, his facsimile edition of *The Marriage of Heaven and Hell* (London and Toronto: J. M. Dent, 1927), p. 13.

IV. CALLING AND NAMING

1. Wittreich, *Visionary Poetics* (see chap. 1, n. 9), p. 6. See also Wittreich, *Milton and the Line of Vision* (chap. 1, n. 9), where in his preface he defines the line as extending from the Bible to Chaucer, Sidney, Spenser, Milton, "the major Romantics, and many moderns" (p. xiv).

2. This pattern of biblical interrelationships, says Wittreich, "is archetypal for those that exist between *The Canterbury Tales* and *The Faerie Queene*, between *The Faerie Queene* and *Paradise Lost*, between Milton's epics and those of Blake, and between Blake's epics and the lyric-epic vision of Yeats or the epical novels of Joyce" (*Milton and the Line of Vision*, p. xv).

3. See the entirety of chapter 1 of Wittreich, *Visionary Poetics*, which is entitled "Revelation's 'New' Form." My quotations are from, respectively, pp. 18, 39, 42, and 28. See also Tannenbaum, *Biblical Tradition in Blake's Early Prophecies* (chap. 1, n. 9), especially chaps. 1–3.

4. Annotations to Bacon's *Essays*, E623.

5. See, e.g., Josephine Waters Bennett, *The Evolution of The Faerie Queene* (Chicago: University of Chicago Press, 1942), chap. 5; Kathleen Williams, "Milton, Greatest Spenserian," in *Milton and the Line of Vision*, pp. 25–55; and John E. Hankins, "Spenser and the Revelation of St. John," in *Essential Articles for the Study of Edmund Spenser*, ed. A. C. Hamilton (Hamden, Conn.: Archon Books, 1972), pp. 40–57 (orig. pub. *PMLA* 60 [145]: 364–81). Angus Fletcher, in *The Prophetic Moment* (Chicago: University of Chicago Press, 1971), has argued that "Spenser is . . . resolutely opposed to apocalypse, in spite of his periodically apocalyptic symbolism" and that this is "perhaps" why Blake regarded Spenser as having "failed to free himself in his prophetic calling, despite a continuous drive toward this freedom" (pp. 67, 10).

6. Northrop Frye, *Five Essays on Milton's Epics* (London: Routledge and Kegan Paul, 1965), pp. 95–98.

7. See my essays, "Romanticism and the Self-Annihilation of Language," *Criticism* 18 (1976): 173–89; and "Most Holy Forms of Thought: Some Observations on Blake's Language," *ELH* 41 (1974): 555–77, repr. in *ELH Essays for Earl R. Wasserman*, ed. Ronald Paulson and Arnold Stein (Baltimore: Johns Hopkins University Press, 1974), pp. 262–84. See also W. J. T. Mitchell, "Blake's Radical Comedy: Dramatic Structure as Meaning in *Milton*," in *Blake's Sublime Allegory* (see chap. 1, n. 9), pp. 306–7; and Cooper, "Blake's Escape from Mythology" (see chap. 2, n. 58), pp. 91, 108.

8. Hazard Adams, "Blake and the Philosophy of Literary Symbolism," *New Literary History* 5 (1973): 142.

9. Maureen Quilligan, *The Language of Allegory* (Ithaca, N.Y.: Cornell University Press, 1979), p. 85 and n. Not entirely unrelated to my mention of "conversation" in the preceding paragraph, as well as to the issues of language and Spenser's efforts to redeem it, is DeNeef's *Spenser and the Motives of Metaphor* (see chap. 2, n. 31), especially chap. 6. See also, on conversation as conversion, Marjorie O. Boyle, *Erasmus on Language and Method in Theology* (Toronto: University of Toronto Press, 1977). On polysemous language in Blake, see Nelson Hilton, *Literal Imagination: Blake's Vision of Words* (Berkeley and Los Angeles: University of California Press, 1983) as well as his review of Quilligan in *Blake: An Illustrated Quarterly* 14 (1980–81): 135–37.

10. Murray Krieger, "'A Waking Dream': The Symbolic Alternative to Allegory," in *Allegory, Myth, and Symbol*, Harvard English Studies 9, ed. Morton W. Bloomfield (Cambridge, Mass.: Harvard University Press, 1981), p. 4.

11. Samuel Levin, "Allegorical Language," in *Allegory, Myth, and Symbol*, pp. 25–27. See also his *Semantics of Metaphor* (Baltimore: Johns Hopkins University Press, 1977).

12. Quilligan, *Language of Allegory*, p. 80. Cf. A. C. Hamilton, "Our New Poet: Spenser, 'Well of English Undefyld,'" in *A Theatre for Spenserians*, ed. Judith M. Kennedy and James A. Reither (Toronto: University of Toronto Press, 1973), p. 121. See also A. Bartlett Giamatti's discussion of Proteus as both *vates* and *magus* and of Archimago as Spenser's version of the Proteus myth in "Proteus Unbound," in *The Disciplines of Criticism*, ed. Peter Demetz, Thomas Greene, and Lowry Nelson, Jr. (New Haven, Conn.: Yale University Press, 1968), as well as his *Play of Double Senses* (Englewood Cliffs, N.J.: Prentice-Hall, 1975), in which, among a number of things pertinent to the study of Blake's language, he remarks that one of the epic's lessons is "that words, fictions, appearances are misleading or dangerous. . . . They are creations in language that warn against the power of words" (p. 25). On this "power," see Quilligan, *Language of Allegory*, p. 163, and Walter J. Ong, *The Presence of the Word* (New York: Simon & Shuster, 1970).

13. Wittreich, *Visionary Poetics*, p. 68. Earlier Angus Fletcher, in *Allegory: The Theory of a Symbolic Mode* (Ithaca, N.Y.: Cornell University Press, 1964), reminds us that the allegorist "requires some kind of hierarchical matrix, some abiding cosmic structure, on which to base his fictions" and then goes

on to characterize *The Faerie Queene* as "a largely idealized defense of the Establishment" (pp. 239, 272). Nevertheless, somewhat like Quilligan, he also argues that Spenser's epic is "built upon clusters of 'antithetical primal words,'" single terms that contain "diametrically opposed meanings, allowing for paradoxes and ironies at the heart of" the antiestablishmentarian allegory (p. 302).

14. A. Kent Hieatt, *Chaucer, Spenser, Milton* (Montreal: McGill-Queen's University Press, 1975), p. 223. Blake's perverse image of "a gentleman or noble person" of "vertuous and gentle discipline" is Robert Watson, Bishop of Landaff, whose response to Paine's *The Age of Reason*, entitled *An Apology for the Bible* (see chap. 1, n. 56), Blake heavily and angrily annotated. See especially his first annotation to Letter 1 on E612. Also pertinent to the subject of self-discipline is Blake's letter to John Linnell of 1 February 1826 about "a cold in [his] stomach" and his charge that Bacon would have attributed it to "want of Discipline": "Sr Francis Bacon is a Liar. No discipline will turn one Man into another even in the least particle. & such Discipline I call Presumption & Folly I have tried it too much not to know this & am very sorry for all such who may be led to such ostentatious Exertion against their Eternal Existence itself because it is Mental Rebellion against the Holy Spirit & fit only for a Soldier of Satan to perform" (E775).

15. Rosalie Colie, *Paradoxica Epidemica* (Princeton: Princeton University Press, 1966), p. 350. Giamatti's example, in *Play of Double Senses*, will serve well here: "The substance of Courtesy is achieved only after Calidore reassumes his armor beneath his shepherd's clothing"; before that, he is but "the image of Courtesy" (p. 68).

16. Williams, *Spenser's World of Glass* (see chap. 2, n. 10), pp. xiii–xiv, xvi. At the other end of the spectrum is Charles Moorman, in *A Knyght There Was* (Lexington: University of Kentucky Press, 1967), who reductively describes Spenser's knights as "merely pegs on which to hang allegories"; "a literary device," not a human character (pp. 135, 141). As Berger says, quoting Allen Tate from *Reactionary Essays* (New York: Scribner, 1936), "if Spenser did write [that] kind of poetry . . . then readers are justified in feeling that it is . . . 'aesthetic creation at a low level of intensity'"— *The Allegorical Temper* (see chap. 3, n. 26), p. 187.

17. This is a commonplace in Spenser criticism. For example, Thomas Greene, in *The Descent from Heaven* (New Haven, Conn.: Yale University Press, 1963), says that "the status and meaning and concreteness of all the manifold figures of the poem shift and fade and recombine" (p. 331). See also Wittreich, *Visionary Poetics*, pp. 237–38; Giamatti, *Play of Double Senses*, p. 107ff.; and Patricia A. Parker, *Inescapable Romance* (Princeton: Princeton University Press, 1979), in which she remarks on "the dangerous proliferation of lookalikes through 'Faerie lond'" (p. 70).

18. Spenser's terminology is basically Aristotelian. In the *De Anima*, he writes: "There is one class of existent things which we call substance, including under that term, firstly, matter which in itself is not this or that; secondly, shape or form, in virtue of which the term this or that is at once applied; thirdly, the whole make up of matter and form. Matter is identical with po-

tentiality, form with actuality" (*Spenser Variorum*, 3, p. 258). See also James I. Wimsatt, *Allegory and Mirror* (New York: Pegasus, 1970), pp. 26–27. It is at least interesting to note that John E. Hankins, in *Source and Meaning in Spenser's Allegory* (Oxford: Clarendon Press, 1971), appropriately entitles a section of his treatment of the Garden of Adonis "The Wheel of Generation" (pp. 272–77). Such cycles are anathema to Blake. For other comments by Blake on "accident" and "substance," as both distinct from "essence," see his annotations to Lavater, E596 (where "essence" is equated with "genius") and E600 (where Lavater is chastised for making "every thing originate in its accident"), and *Milton* 29[31]:35–36, E128 (where "Accident [is] formed / Into Substance & Principle, by the Cruelties of Demonstration").

19. My quotations are from, successively, *Book of Urizen* 3:26 (E71), *Four Zoas* IV (E335), *Four Zoas* IV (E335), *Book of Urizen* 7:8–9 (E74), and *Four Zoas* IV (E335). In *A Vision of the Last Judgment*, Blake attacks the notion "that before [Adam, deleted] the Creation All was Solitude & Chaos This is the most pernicious Idea that can enter the Mind as it . . . Limits All Existence to Creation & to Chaos To the Time & Space fixed by the Corporeal Vegetative Eye & leaves the Man who entertains such an Idea the habitation of Unbelieving Demons Eternity Exists and All things in Eternity Independent of Creation" (E563). Blake presumably regarded Spenser to be such a man.

20. Cf. Tannenbaum's observation that "taken literally, Genesis is a justification of [Blake's] Angels' party. It is an account of God's attempt to create a species of beings who will obey him and of his eventual success in finding a chosen few among the largely disobedient creation" (*Biblical Tradition*, p. 223). In an earlier essay, "Blake's Art of Crypsis: *The Book of Urizen* and Genesis," *Blake Studies* 5 (1972): 141–64, Tannenbaum characterizes Genesis as an "inverted Apocalypse" (p. 162). His entire essay is pertinent to what I later have to say of Blake's idea of Genesis. See also Philip J. Gallagher, "The Word Made Flesh: Blake's 'A Poison Tree' and the Book of Genesis," *Studies in Romanticism* 16 (1977): 237–49.

21. See, e.g., *Book of Urizen* 3:36–39 (E71), *Jerusalem* 98:35–37 (E258), *Four Zoas* II (E322) and IX (E406), and especially *Jerusalem* 5:17–20 (E147).

22. E596. The term *tincture* is alchemical and Hermetic, a confusing body of terminology that Blake may have read in Paracelsus or perhaps in Thomas Vaughan's *Coelum Terrae* (1650), *Lumen de Lumine* (1651), *Anthroposophia Theomagica* (1650), and *Magia Adamica* (1650)—at least according to Kathleen Raine, who finds virtually all of Blake's imagery and language here when she is not locating them in Boehme, Thomas Taylor's translations of Plotinus, Hermes Trismegistus, and assorted other esoterica. See her *Blake and Tradition* (chap. 2, n. 11), 2 vols., passim.

23. E533. In a most interesting essay, "Character in an Eighteenth-Century Context," *The Eighteenth Century* 24 (1983), Patrick Coleman remarks upon the age's compulsion to classify and hence its "idea of characterization as . . . the discursive 'placing' of an entity in the spectrum of being" (pp. 52, 57). The relationship to naming, as I discuss that, is remarkably close.

24. Michael Murrin, *Veil of Allegory* (Chicago: University of Chicago Press, 1969), p. 198. Earlier Murrin distinguishes between the traditional,

hierarchical levels of audience perception (literal, moral, allegorical) that he finds in evidence in *The Faerie Queene* and Blake's "reversal" of those levels. Thus, Spenser designs his epic for an upper-class audience of initiates, a kind of "inner circle," giving "profit to the few and [mere] pleasure to the many" (p. 15). Murrin also suggests what Wittreich and Tannenbaum have recently "proved," namely, that Blake's "comments on vision poetry might have pleased an Alexandrian exegete of the Bible" (p. 199); see Wittreich's *Visionary Poetics* and Tannenbaum's *Biblical Tradition*.

25. Wittreich, *Visionary Poetics*, p. 29. As Hieatt and others have shown, places in Spenser may also be disguised, the most prominent perhaps being the Bower of Bliss in which, Hieatt says, in *Chaucer, Spenser, Milton*, "the sensuality is disguised with all the courtly sentimental trappings of love poetry, but ultimately signifies the surrender of rationality, the substituted love of a creature in place of the Creator, and the abandonment of the Christian call to honourable action in this world" (p. 223).

26. Thus, as *The Marriage* passage continues, "this history has been adopted by both parties," biblical and Miltonic, the moral allegory of both equally disreputable, demanding both Blake's *Milton* and his illustrations to the Book of Job, in addition to his own "everlasting gospel."

27. Parker, *Inescapable Romance*, p. 68; Millar MacLure, "Spenser and the Ruins of Time," in *A Theatre for Spenserians*, ed. Kennedy and Reither, p. 10. See also Quilligan, *Language of Allegory*, p. 163.

28. Genesis 5:1–2. This "flashback" structure—in which Genesis is identified as "the book of the generations of Adam" for the first time in chapter 5 and the "day" of creation is "introduced" again—may account for Blake's seemingly peculiar structure of the first two "chapters" of *The Book of Urizen*, in which chapter 2 begins by parodically mimicking Genesis 1:1–2: "In the beginning God created the heaven and the earth. And the earth was without form" becomes Blake's "Earth was not." Then Blake transfers the next word of Genesis 1:2, *void*, to his Preludium as the place where "the primeval Priest" assumes his power (E70). In his extraordinary study of *The Art of Biblical Narrative* (New York: Basic Books, 1981), Robert Alter characterizes these initial verses of Genesis as "numerically ordered," creation proceeding "through a rhythmic process of incremental repetition." Moreover, "creation . . . advances through a series of balanced pairings, which in most instances are binary oppositions," God splitting

> off the realm of earth from the realm of heaven, sets luminaries in the heavens to shine on the earth, creates the birds of the heavens above together with the swarming things of the seas below. Darkness and light, night and day, evening and morning, water and sky, water and dry land, sun and moon, grass and trees, bird and sea-creatures, beast of the field and creeping thing of the earth, human male and female—each moment of creation is conceived as a balancing of opposites or a bifurcation producing difference. . . . Before the appearance of animate creatures, the governing verb, after the reiterated verbs of God's speaking, is 'to divide,' sug-

gesting that the writer was quite aware of defining creation as a
series of bifurcations or splittings-off. . . . Everything is ordered,
set in its appointed place, and contained within a symmetrical
frame. . . . Law, manifested in the symmetrical dividings . . .
and in the divine speech that initiates each stage of creation is the
underlying characteristic of the world as God makes it. (pp. 142–
44)

See also Tannenbaum's point, in "Blake's Art of Crypsis," that *The Book of Urizen* reflects both main originary versions of Genesis, thus presenting us with the "God of Creation as self-divided" into the Elohim and Jahweh (pp. 145–46). Alter's analysis of the two versions of Genesis comes to somewhat different, though not unrelated, conclusions.

29. Tannenbaum, *Biblical Tradition*, p. 223.

30. Ibid., pp. 219–20. Tannenbaum's point that it is a prelapsarian Adam who names would not have been lost on Blake either. His Adam is, by definition, postlapsarian.

31. V. A. DeLuca, "Proper Names in the Structural Design of Blake's Myth-Making," *Blake Studies* 8 (1978): 9. Cf., for example, Gustaf Wingren, *Man and the Incarnation*, trans. Ross MacKenzie (Philadelphia: Muhlenberg Press, 1959): "A man moves among his fellow-beings, speaks to them and has dealings with them. In the case of the divine Word—the *Verbum*—there is no progression to a certain point at which it assumes human substance and then communicates the divine to mankind. Rather, the concept of the *Word* shatters the concept of substance" (p. 89). Wingren's use of the terms *progression* and *substance* makes the passage unusually pertinent to Blake's use of the same words as well as to his implicit ideas of the Word.

32. This, I believe, is what the contrarious poem of *Songs of Experience*, *Infant Sorrow*, is about. The joy that is the essence of the identity, infant, becomes an infantile "sorrow," "born" of the sorrows of mother and father ("My mother groand! my father wept"), an abstraction of abstractions. When Infant Sorrow thus "leaps" into the world, he is only a simile ("similitude" is Blake's more graphic and precise word), "Like a fiend in a cloud," which is then "realized" into form by his "fathers hands" and "swadling bands" (E28). The relationship of this "birth" to the genesis and shaping of Adam, as well as to the incarnation of the Word in the corporeal Jesus Christ, should be obvious.

33. DeLuca, "Proper Names in the Structural Design of Blake's Myth-Making," pp. 20–22. See also DeLuca's earlier article on the nonexplanatoriness of this kind of Blakean name, "Ariston's Immortal Palace: Icon and Allegory in Blake's Prophecies," *Criticism* 12 (1970): 1–19 (especially 10–11, 13).

34. I exclude Bunyan, whom Blake may well have read early in his life, because of the simplistically allegorical namings of his characters and places, which surely led Blake to regard *Pilgrim's Progress* as, in Eaves's words, a "memory-guided" mockery (*William Blake's Theory of Art* [see chap. 1, n. 12], p. 38). For a brief discussion of the way (or ways) in which Blake may have read Bunyan, see my appendix B.

35. Karl Kroeber, "Delivering *Jerusalem*," in *Blake's Sublime Allegory*, ed. Curran and Wittreich, pp. 347–67. What I have termed his *misguidedness* stems from his extraordinary perception of *Jerusalem* as "a relatively straightforward exposition of a religious vision" which contains "little verbal or rhetorical ingenuity" (pp. 365, 349). Kroeber has since retracted much of this essay, although I do not know whether his denigration of puns has been exorcised by the work of such scholars as Quilligan (*Language of Allegory*) and Hilton (*Literal Imagination*). Newman Ivey White's classic essay, relevant in many ways to the problem of how to read Blake, is "Shelley's *Prometheus Unbound*, or Every Man His Own Allegorist," *PMLA* 40 (1925): 172–84.

36. Kroeber, "Delivering *Jerusalem*," pp. 349–50. Kroeber cites G. N. Leech, "Linguistics and the Figures of Rhetoric," in *Essays on Style and Language*, ed. Roger Fowler (London: Routledge and Kegan Paul, 1966), pp. 135–56, as his source for applying the linguistician's terms *paradigmatic* and *syntagmatic* to literary analysis. The core of Kroeber's argument against Frye's (to him erroneous) assumption that archetypal criticism is appropriate to Blake's composite art need not detain us here, but I might add that recent applications of anti-Fryean, new-new criticism to Blake seem to me to dearchetypalize and deallegorize him only to reallegorize him in different terms; see, e.g., Levinson's " 'The Book of Thel' by William Blake" (see chap. 2, n. 11).

37. W. J. T. Mitchell, E. J. Rose, and David E. James all make similar points about Urizen; see, respectively, "Poetic and Pictorial Imagery in Blake's *The Book of Urizen*," *Eighteenth Century Studies* 3 (1969): 83–107, and "Blake's Radical Comedy," pp. 281–307; "Blake's *Milton*: The Poet as Poem," *Blake Studies* 1 (1968): 16–38; *Written Within and Without: A Study of Blake's "Milton"* (Frankfurt am Main: Peter Lang, 1978), p. 43.

38. Kroeber, "Delivering *Jerusalem*," pp. 353–54. The italics are Kroeber's.

39. Rose, "Los, Pilgrim of Eternity," in *Blake's Sublime Allegory*, pp. 86, 93.

40. Mitchell, "Blake's Radical Comedy," p. 281.

41. Parker, in *Inescapable Romance*, identifies Spenser's giving form to Errour in *The Faerie Queene* (I,i,14–16) as "a kind of freezing, a process which Blake called clarifying the Body of Error, reducing it by making it appear" (p. 67). Although there is no phrase, "Body of Error," in Blake so far as I know, and although her final phrase is inexact, I argue in the next three chapters that that is precisely what Blake's painting of *The Faerie Queene* characters does.

42. Morton W. Bloomfield, "A Grammatical Approach to Personification Allegory," in Bloomfield, *Essays and Explorations* (Cambridge, Mass.: Harvard University Press, 1970), p. 259. In the second half of his sentence, Bloomfield is quoting Owen Barfield, *Saving the Appearances: A Study in Idolatry* (London: Faber & Faber, 1957), p. 86. Bloomfield's essay originally appeared in *Modern Philology* 60 (1963): 161–71.

43. Angus Fletcher, *Allegory: The Theory of a Symbolic Mode*, pp. 333, 306.

44. Bloomfield, "A Grammatical Approach to Personification Allegory," p. 250.

45. Ibid.; Levin, "Allegorical Language," p. 25.

46. Barfield, *Saving the Appearances*, p. 86. See also p. 30, where he describes this process as one of endowing the unmanifest with manifestness, using a phenomenon as a name for what is not phenomenal. Isabel MacCaffrey also notes the cerebration involved in this procedure in *Spenser's Allegory: The Anatomy of Imagination* (Princeton: Princeton University Press, 1976): "Allegory belongs to the fallen world . . .; it is an invention of mind on its own, trying to make sense of experience in a benighted universe" (p. 34). In John's gospel, as Augustine rephrases it, however, "the Word of God was made flesh, but more assuredly not changed into flesh," the infant Jesus being "the paradoxical unspeaking Word; God" (I borrow here from Quilligan, *Language of Allegory*, p. 161; "in fans" is Latin for nonspeaker).

47. See Erdman, *The Notebook of William Blake* (chap. 1, n. 23), pp. 7 and N75 and my discussion of this emblem in chapter 1 above.

48. Betsy Bowden, "The Artistic and Interpretive Context of Blake's *Canterbury Pilgrims*," *Blake: An Illustrated Quarterly* 13 (1980): 180–81. Karl Kiralis's essay is "William Blake as an Intellectual and Spiritual Guide to Chaucer's *Canterbury Pilgrims*," *Blake Studies* 1 (1969): 139–90. See also Warren Stevenson, "Interpreting Blake's *Canterbury Pilgrims*," *Colby Library Quarterly* 13 (1977): 115–26; Orphia Jane Allen, "Blake's Archetypal Criticism: *The Canterbury Pilgrims*," *Genre* 2 (1978): 173–89; and Mary Ellen Reisner, "William Blake and Westminster Abbey," in *Man and Nature*, ed. Roger L. Emerson, Gilles Girard, and Roseann Runte (London, Ontario: University of Western Ontario, 1982), pp. 185–98. In light of Bowden's judgment of Redcrosse, it is interesting that Edwin Honig, in *Dark Conceit* (New York: Oxford University Press, 1966), argues that *The Faerie Queene* is "a poem that justifies not the ways of God to man but the ways of man to man" (pp. 97–98). Blake would have liked that perception.

49. Williams, *Spenser's World of Glass*, pp. xix, 32. In light of her point, one must wonder about Rose's claim that Blake's "symbolic figures are . . . not allegorical abstractions or mythological people and gods, but energizing *images in action*" ("Los, Pilgrim of Eternity," p. 86; my italics). Certainly closer to the "truth" is Mitchell's perception that Urizen, e.g., "is not a man 'representing reason'" but rather "*is* reason, a particular mode of consciousness" ("Blake's Radical Comedy," p. 281).

50. Williams, *Spenser's World of Glass*, p. 107.

51. *Milton* 32[35]:32–33 (E132); *Jerusalem* 84:31–85:1 (E243). Much effort has been expended trying to resolve Blake's apparent contradiction between a state as something that changes and as something permanent. The problem is that this is the wrong "contrary," as it were; for the contrary to all states is no state, the Imagination—just as the contrary of the sexual contraries is Humanness. Los creates states as a hedge against "Eternal Death" (*Jerusalem* 73:40, E229), and, as in the Genesis creation, all such states are names. As perceived by the unimaginative eye, they "remain permanent for ever" like countries (Blake's analogy in *Jerusalem* 73:44 is a crucial one)

through which the pilgrim, consulting his map of reality, passes. To the imaginative eye, however, as distinct from that of the earthly traveler, the states are but historical manifestations of the Divine Humanity: "Adam Noah Abraham Moses Samuel David Ezekiel" (73:41). "So *Men* pass on" (my italics) in history, their names being a "permanent" record in this world of their traveling. But imaginative "Human Existence itself" neither travels nor passes on. It simply *is*, its apparent states (that is, those that appear in history) but illusions, allegorical figments created by Los to dissipate "the rocky forms of Death" or endless nonentity (73:43). Thus in *Jerusalem* 31[35], "the Divine hand" not only founds "the Two Limits, Satan and Adam"—limits which "in every Human bosom . . . stand"—but "creates" them in the first place "to deliver Individuals evermore" from states (ll. 1-3, 15-16, 18, E177-78). When "distant," all states "appear as One Man" (that is, the "unstate" that is the Human Imagination), "but as you approach they appear Multitudes of Nations" (*Vision of the Last Judgment*, E556-57). This One Man is "The Spiritual States of the Soul," which "are all Eternal," as distinct from "Man [in] his Present State" (*Jerusalem* 52, E200). In sum, states are allegories. On travelers, pilgrims, and pilgrimages in Blake, see appendix B in this volume.

52. On Busirane's "penning" (imprisoning, writing) Amoret "in a web of pernicious metaphor" and hence in a world "created" out of the abuse of language, see Quilligan, *Language of Allegory*, pp. 84-85, and DeNeef, *Spenser and the Motives of Metaphor*, pp. 191-92, n. 16.

53. Angus Fletcher, *Allegory: The Theory of a Symbolic Mode*, p. 272. Fletcher is speaking of Spenser's conception (his "largely idealized defense of the Establishment"), not Blake's conception of Spenser. Other Sper.ser scholars hold similar views of Gloriana.

54. Giamatti, "Proteus Unbound"; see also his larger study, *Play of Double Senses*, as well as DeNeef's point that Archimago, by virture of his "double-metaphored" name, is "both text and conceit" and "the creator of the text" (*Spenser and the Motives of Metaphor*, p. 95). The latter point is made as well by Nohrnberg, *The Analogy of "The Faerie Queene"* (see chap. 2, n. 35), who characterizes "all allegory [as] a Duessan [or Archimagoan] enterprise" (pp. 109-10). One wonders whether Blake had Proteus (either Spenser's or his predecessors') in mind even as early as *Tiriel*, for there Ijim regards Tiriel as a Protean "fiend" rather than the "real thing," taking the forms, at various times, of lion, tiger, river, cloud, serpent, toad or newt, rock, or poisonous shrub (E281). Similarly, in *America* the "shadowy daughter of Urthona" perceives Orc to be a fallen "image of God . . . in darkness of Africa," a serpent, an eagle, a lion, a whale, a fire (1:11-16, 2:8-15, E51-52). Neither of these characters, of course, is a *vates*.

55. One should be reminded here of the grave risk Los-Blake runs in thus "realizing" error. If we, the reader-viewers, do not perceive (realize) that it is error and thus the not-real, we simply and disastrously embrace the "wrong" truth precisely as Redcrosse does—and in our embrace, we form laws based upon it "and [call] them / The eternal laws of God" (*Book of Urizen* 28:6-7, E83). That is, we become self-enslaving allegorists—or, as Blake

says again and again, we become what we behold. In other terms, Los may convince us, to our everlasting regret, to believe in the "system" he creates, lest he be enslaved by ours.

56. Berger, *Allegorical Temper*, p. 224. It is useful to note here that in Book II it is the Palmer (reason, prudence) who deallegorizes Acrasia's victims, thus "proving" to Blake not only Spenser's fundamental misconception of the imagination but Milton's as well in the latter's borrowings in *Comus* from both opening books of *The Faerie Queene*; for it is "the visage" that Comus's "pleasing poison / . . . quite transforms," "unmolding reason's mintage / Charactered in the face" (ll. 524–30). The connections here between Spenser and Milton are critical commonplaces, but the most extensive and detailed analysis of the "iconographical parallels" that embody Milton's "themes of temptation, ensnarement, and final abstention" may be found in Hieatt, *Chaucer, Spenser, Milton*.

57. DeNeef, *Spenser and the Motives of Metaphor*, pp. 130–31. See also Harry Berger, "The Prospect of Imagination," *Studies in English Literature* 1 (1961): especially p. 100.

58. DeNeef, *Spenser and the Motives of Metaphor*, p. 130.

59. *The Four Zoas* VIII (E379), *Jerusalem* 68:5–6 (E221). The *Four Zoas* passage culminates in: "Thus was the Lamb of God condemnd to Death / They naild him upon the tree of Mystery" (E379); and the *Jerusalem* passage is preceded by: "The Twelve Daughters in Rahab & Tirzah have circumscribed the Brain / Beneath [the skull] & pierced it thro the midst with a golden pin" (67:41–42, E220). Elizabeth-Mercilla is portrayed in Blake's Spenser painting as Rahab-Tirzah, among others.

60. DeNeef, *Spenser and the Motives of Metaphor*, p. 132.

61. Annotations to Reynolds's *Discourses* (E636); Annotations to Bishop Watson's *An Apology for the Bible* (E611). Cf. William Cowper's apparitional appearance to Blake, saying "Can you not make me truly insane. . . . O that in the bosom of God I was hid. You [i.e. Blake] retain health & yet are as mad as any of us all—over us all—mad as a refuge from unbelief—from Bacon Newton & Locke" (Annotations to Spurzheim's *Observations on Insanity*, E663). In a letter to Richard Phillips, "the Newtonian" is one "who reads Not & cannot Read" because he "is opressed by his own Reasonings & Experiments" (E769).

62. Letter to George Cumberland (E704) complaining about Trusler's "advice," probably written on the same day Blake received and responded to Trusler's letter itself. The "Superstition" phrase is taken from what Mona Wilson, in *The Life of William Blake* (1927; New York: Oxford University Press, 1949), claims is Trusler's "endorsement" of Blake's letter to him: "Blake, dim'd with Superstition" (p. 82). Erdman does not record the endorsement.

63. Upton, *Spenser's Faerie Queene* (see chap. 1, n. 51), 2, 528. Such mirrors as Merlin supplies to Britomart are, of course, commonplace in medieval literature. A useful study of them and their relationship to allegories is Wimsatt's *Allegory and Mirror*. Of especial pertinence to Blake and his continuing analysis of the implications of Petrarchism is the fact that, in *The Ro-*

mance of the Rose, when the lover looks into the pool to discover two beautiful crystals reflecting the whole garden of love, what he dis-covers in the depths of his own eyes is "the broad range of attractive experiences available to him in this garden" (Wimsatt, p. 69). It is possible that Blake was aware of the *Romance*'s trope and used it for his own purposes in his "Crystal Cabinet" poem (see chapter 2), but even had he not been, Merlin's "world of glas" that showed "in perfect sight / What ever thing was in the world contayned" would have served him just as well, especially in the entire context of Brito-mart's Petrarchan languishment.

64. Williams, *Spenser's World of Glass*, p. 91. Williams also sees her as, un-Blakeanly, "strength and love" blended, and hence "a point of reference for all those knights and ladies who, singly and jointly, fail to achieve concord," an image thus of perfect *discordia concors* as well as of "chaste affection" (pp. 93, 97).

65. *Faerie Queene* III,ii,4. This passage also contains the famous "blun-der," as Upton calls it—Spenser's forgetting that it is Redcrosse, not Guyon, who is traveling with Britomart. If Blake noticed it at all, he would have been delighted by the confusion of names, especially in the very heart of a discus-sion about dissembling and disguise.

66. On names as breeders of names in Spenser, see especially Jonathan Goldberg, *Endlesse Work: Spenser and the Structures of Discourse* (Baltimore: Johns Hopkins University Press, 1981); in Blake, see DeLuca, "Proper Names in the Structural Design of Blake's Myth-making," especially p. 11: "the generating principle of Blake's name-formations . . . resides in an au-tonomous linguistic activity and not in appropriate associations derived from the function of the characters." Nohrnberg's argument about the potential "marriage" of names in *The Faerie Queene* (e.g., Britomart + Artegall = Britomartegall) comes to precisely the opposite conclusion from that of De-Luca (see *Analogy of "The Faerie Queene*," p. 607). On Blake's names, see also Aaron Fogel's interesting essay, "Pictures of Speech: On Blake's Poetic," *Studies in Romanticism* 21 (1982): 217–42, especially pp. 217–23.

67. Hamilton, " 'Well of English Undefyld,' " p. 113 (my italics). Archi-mago only divides her *from* herself, or, more properly, Redcrosse perceives her to be "divided."

68. Honig, *Dark Conceit*, p. 63.

69. Angus Fletcher, *Allegory: The Theory of a Symbolic Mode*, pp. 195f.

70. DeLuca, "Proper Names in the Structural Design of Blake's Myth-making," pp. 10, 18–19.

71. Nohrnberg, *Analogy of " The Faerie Queene*," p. 607.

72. Diana Hume George, *Blake and Freud* (Ithaca, N.Y.: Cornell Univer-sity Press, 1980), p. 177.

73. Russell Fraser, *The Language of Adam* (New York: Columbia Univer-sity Press, 1977), p. 171. On the other hand, Murrin, in *The Veil of Allegory*, argues that "one could never really diagram the allegory of *The Faerie Queene*" (p. 56).

74. Honig, *Dark Conceit*, p. 53. On this point, see also MacCaffrey, *Spen-ser's Allegory*, pp. 37–38, and Alpers, *The Poetry of " The Faerie Queene*" (see

chap. 2, n. 31), pp. 330–33. This is surely why Spenser's epic moves toward resolution (concord)—not apocalypse, as in Blake—and why his names are merely similitudes or images in Blake's terminology. On this score, we might recall that the title-page epigraph to *Pilgrim's Progress* is "I have used Similitudes" (Hosea 12:10). See also Paul's "allegory," as he calls it, of Abraham's two sons in Galatians 4:22–31, which I might appropriate here as the difference between Spenser's "children" (born of the bondwoman "after the flesh") and those of Blake (born of the freewoman, "the children of promise").

75. William Nelson, *The Poetry of Edmund Spenser* (New York: Columbia University Press, 1963), p. 174.

76. Angus Fletcher, *Allegory: The Theory of a Symbolic Mode*, pp. 195–96. With but uncertain success Blake, in *A Descriptive Catalogue*, attempts to distinguish between "facsimile representations of merely mortal and perishing substances" (whether true or false in Spenser's sense is an erroneous alternative) and "visionary conception" or "representations of spiritual existence of God's immortal, to the mortal perishing organ of sight. . . . A Spirit and a Vision are not . . . a cloudy vapour or a nothing: they are organized and minutely articulated beyond all that the mortal and perishing nature can produce" (E541).

77. Isabel MacCaffrey (as well as other Spenserians) regards Book VI as the least allegorical (if allegorical at all) of the entire work: "the innocents in this book are all *human* characters, neither personifications nor 'ensamples' like Una or Florimell or Amoret" (*Spenser's Allegory*, p. 408). Humphrey Tonkin makes a similar but not quite so sweeping claim in *Spenser's Courteous Pastoral* (Oxford: Clarendon Press, 1972).

78. Wittreich, " 'Sublime Allegory' " (see chap. 1, n. 9), p. 32. Tannenbaum extends Wittreich's argument substantially in *Biblical Tradition in Blake's Early Prophecies*; he also offers a distinction between allegory and typology. Blake employs the latter, not the former, he says, thus "identifying" typology with vision (pp. 107–8).

79. Pertinent here is Deen's observation, in the context of his fine explication of Blake's *Mental Traveller*, that even "Mental Travelling is an evasion of Mental Fight" (*Conversing in Paradise*, [see chap. 1, n. 27], p. 87). On the relationship of allegory to typology and the pertinence of both to the study of Blake, see appendix C in this volume.

80. Wittreich, " 'Sublime Allegory,' " p. 35. Angus Fletcher makes the same point in *Allegory: The Theory of a Symbolic Mode*; see especially pp. 306, 333.

81. Since Blake added an Italian translation of a phrase in Boyd's English version (see E885), it is possible to argue that these annotations are contemporary with the Dante illustrations. Without denying that possibility (which does not entirely invalidate my point), it is worth noting that Blake annotated only Boyd's "Historical Notes," not his translation, and may well have returned to the translation itself while preparing his Dante illustrations.

82. Thomas Warton's *Observations on the Fairy Queen* (1754) and Richard

Hurd's *Lectures on Chivalry and Romance* (1762), both of which gave Spenser new life and legitimacy, as it were, did not effect a sudden glorious revolution in the taste of the reading public; that remained largely for the Romantic poets, notably Keats, to achieve. The disabusing of the public of error was precisely Blake's motivation for his one art exhibition: "Mr. B. appeals to the Public, from the judgment of those narrow blinking eyes, that have too long governed art in a dark corner" (Preface to *A Descriptive Catalogue*, E529). The villains here are the enemies of "real Art, as it was left us by *Raphael* and *Albert Durer, Michael Angelo*, and *Julio Romano*; stripped from the Ignorances of *Rubens* and *Rembrandt, Titian* and *Correggio*" (E528). Incidentally, it is not without interest that, for all his learning, wide reading, and linguistic skills, Warton shows no evidence in the *Observations* of having read Dante—a quick review of the book yielding Dante's name only once, in a footnote reference to his terza rima. Hurd does not mention Dante at all.

83. Hamilton, "'Well of English Undefyld,'" p. 121. I have some doubts about the purity of Adamic language, as I have already indicated, but I fully share the spirit of Hamilton's remarks. Quilligan's *Language of Allegory* extends Hamilton's point considerably, and Hilton's *Literal Imagination* applies the idea excitingly to Blake.

84. Gleckner, "Blake's Verbal Technique," in *William Blake: Essays for S. Foster Damon* (see chap. 3, n. 42), pp. 330–32.

85. Successively, my quotations in this sentence are from *The Book of Urizen*, 4:26 (E72), *A Descriptive Catalogue* (E543), *Milton* 31[34]:25 (E130), and *The Four Zoas* I (E313).

86. I have borrowed this term from Fredric V. Bogel's fine discussion of the language of eighteenth-century literature, "The Rhetoric of Substantiality," *Eighteenth-Century Studies* 12 (1979): 457–80. See also Greenberg's alliance of such "rhetoric" to the seventeenth-century *res-et-verba* campaign to delimit language's referential function, and, as well, to "the ideal of Adamic naming," in "Blake's 'Science,'" *Studies in Eighteenth-Century Culture* (see chap. 1, n. 14), pp. 118–19.

87. Wittreich, *Angel of Apocalypse* (see chap. 1, n. 9), pp. 112–13. Wittreich's quoted phrase is E. J. Rose's in "Blake's Illustrations for *Paradise Lost, L'Allegro*, and *Il Penseroso*: A Thematic Reading," *Hartford Studies in Literature* 2 (1970): 56. Rather fortuitously (for my purposes), Wittreich here moves beyond his earlier assertions about Blake's typology to say, with reference to Blake's *Paradise Regained* illustrations: "at the same time that Blake revised the tradition of synoptic illustration he eschewed the tradition of typology, except where, wishing to subvert the tradition, he used it against itself" (p. 111). See also Wittreich's more extensive argument in "William Blake: Illustrator-Interpreter of *Paradise Regained*," in *Calm of Mind* (see chap. 1, n. 9), pp. 93–132.

88. Wittreich, *Angel of Apocalypse*, p. 145.

89. E. J. Rose, "Blake's Metaphoric States," *Blake Studies* 4 (1971): 14.

90. Cf. Mark L. Greenberg's point, in the essay cited above in note 86, that like all deities, for Blake "all language . . . resides in the human breast

. . . language as a constitutive imaginative force, ontologically prior to its ostensible referent'' (p. 120). See also Deen's study of "conversation" in Blake, and of Identity as Community, in *Conversing in Paradise*.

V. *THE CHARACTERS IN SPENSER'S FAIRIE QUEENE*, I

1. Grant and Brown, "Blake's Vision of Spenser's *Faerie Queene*" (see chap. 1, n. 2); Damon, *Blake Dictionary* (see chap. 1, n. 1), pp. 383–85. Subsequent references to the former will be made parenthetically in my text as GB plus the page number; the latter's essay is brief enough as to require no further page references except where the source of my quotation is unclear. Spenserians also have generally ignored the painting; Helena Shire is one of the very few, if not the only attempt at even a minicommentary—and, alas, it is well nigh disastrous. Blake "makes us . . . aware of moral and spiritual values implicit in Spenser's poetry''; ''Virtue . . . pass[es] from God down to earth through love and . . . return[s] through magnanimity in action''; and Calidore's hand ''is outstretched in benediction to a couple bowing humbly and bound (Serena and Calepine)'' are but three samples. See her *Preface to Spenser* (London: Longman, 1978), pp. 116–17.

2. Kiralis, ''William Blake as an Intellectual and Spiritual Guide to Chaucer's *Canterbury Pilgrims*'' (see chap. 4, n. 48), hereafter referred to parenthetically in the text as KK plus the page number.

3. In her fascinating essay, ''Effigies of Power: Pitt and Fox as Canterbury Pilgrims,'' *Eighteenth-Century Studies* 12 (1979): 481–503, in which Blake's Pardoner is established as a portrait of William Pitt and the Summoner as Charles James Fox, Mary Ellen Reisner adds an important historical dimension to Kiralis's pairings and groupings of Blake's pilgrims. As well, she sees in the two pilgrims a set of Blakean contraries, both of which are instructively ''bad'' or error-ridden—somewhat the same way I have argued that both angels and devils in *The Marriage of Heaven and Hell* are ''wrong.'' Quoting from Walter C. Curry's *Chaucer and the Mediaeval Sciences*, rev. ed. (London: Allen and Unwin, 1960), she notes that, although the Pardoner boasts about ''a joly wenche in every toun,'' he ''carries upon his body and has stamped upon his mind and character the marks of what is known to medieval physiognomists as a *eunuchus ex nativitate*,'' matching Pitt's well-known and maliciously publicized celibacy and life-long continence (''the immaculate minister''). The Summoner, however, is in Chaucer ''hoot . . . and lecherous as a sparwe,'' matching Fox's publicized escapades with the likes of the Duchess of Devonshire, Perdita Robinson, and Elizabeth Armistead. The Pardoner's severely backward-looking posture on his-her horse should remind us of Guyon's in the Spenser painting and, moreover, the red cross emblazoned on the Pardoner's back aligns him-her to Blake's Redcrosse. Even more devastating, perhaps, is Chaucer's suggestion of the Pardoner's homosexuality (which Blake may well have interpreted as his ''mar-

riage" to the Palmer). On this suggestion, see Monica E. McAlpine, "The Pardoner's Homosexuality and How It Matters," *PMLA* 95 (1980): 8–22—a point, incidentally, that Reisner stops short of. Blake did not.

4. One wonders, at least, whether Blake is alluding here not merely to the six-book *Faerie Queene* but to the "planned" double twelve-book structure Spenser projects in the Letter to Raleigh, which would represent a full "visionary" day. He would hardly have missed this insistent numerological sentence in the letter: "The beginning therefore of my history, if it were to be told by an Historiographer, should be the twelfth book, which is the last, where I devise that the Faery Queene kept her Annuall feste xii. dayes, vppon which xii. seuerall dayes, the occasions of the xii. seueral aduentures hapned, which being vndertaken by xii. seuerall knights, are in these xii books seuerally handled and discoursed." Blake's own numbers are similarly fascinating, but I have not allowed myself the indulgence of constructing innumerable numerological equivalencies and analogues in Spenser's and Blake's works. I wish someone would, though.

5. But see Nohrnberg's argument, in *Analogy of "The Faerie Queene"* (see chap. 2, n. 35), that "Spenser orders his poem in parallel strata, and presents it 'horizontally,' in agreement with the picture plane" (p. 22). Murrin argues, however, in *The Veil of Allegory* (see chap. 4, n. 24), that "one could never really diagram the allegory of *The Faerie Queene*" (p. 56), because, as Rosemond Tuve points out in *Allegorical Imagery* (Princeton: Princeton University Press, 1966), "Spenser's favorite and usual function for allegorical images is precisely [Jean de Meun's] enacted dialectic which 'opens' some large philosophical questions to the view" (p. 327). This is why, Tuve claims, "the *Faerie Queene* has never been satisfactorily illustrated" (ibid.)—William Kent's illustrations, which I commented upon in chapter 1, being a signal example of such unsatisfactoriness.

6. Cf. Millar MacLure's observation, in "Spenser and the Ruins of Time" (see chap. 4, n. 27), that from the ruins of time only new seeds of future ruins sprout: "the vegetable creation is renewed, for Nature's clock is circular" (p. 15), is precisely Blake's "same dull round . . . of a universe" that "soon become[s] a mill with complicated wheels" (*There Is No Natural Religion*, E2). We might well recall Blake's alternate versions of Los's (and his own) task, as a cogged machine (printing press) to reverse the erroneous turning of "adverse" machines and as a mill so constructed as to liberate man from all mills (see p. 154 above).

7. I have discussed this point in greater detail in my *Blake's Prelude* (see chap. 1, n. 3), q.v., especially "cycle," "sequence," and "time" in the index. For other cycles in Blake—historical, political, and erotic—see Frye on the "Orc Cycle" in *Fearful Symmetry* (chap. 1, n. 8), chap. 7; Erdman, "A Note on the 'Orc Cycle,'" in *Blake's Visionary Forms Dramatic* (see chap. 1, n. 28), pp. 112–14; and Deen (on what he calls the "Eros Cycle") in *Conversing in Paradise* (see chap. 1, n. 27), especially pp. 91–97, 113–14. In connection with my earlier exploration of Blake's use of Petrarchism, Deen's analysis of *The Mental Traveller* includes this perceptive comment: "Blake seems to see male suffering in erotic poetry, 'the akeing heart' and 'lovesick eye,' as a

trivialized recall of the human sacrifice once aimed at renewing the immortal life of a cyclical fertility goddess'' (p. 114).

8. E555. It is interesting at least, perhaps crucial, to note that, immediately following this passage, Blake writes to himself: ''Query the Above ought to follow the description'' (E555). The orderly description of the painting, in other words, is a falsification of the coinstantaneousness of its events' occurrence, but it is necessary, as Blake says in his explanation of the design to Ozias Humphry, ''for the accomodation of those who at least give it the honor of attention'' (E552). Accordingly, the assertion of its ''aggregate Imaginations'' properly being reassumed instantaneously in the spectator's ''Imaginative Eye,'' Blake wisely thought should appear after he fractionated the painting's imaginative wholeness, its ''image'' of the One Man.

9. Henry Summerfield, ''Blake and the Names Divine,'' *Blake: An Illustrated Quarterly* 15 (1981): 14–22.

10. On this latter figure, see the cited references in Summerfield's note 34 (''Blake and the Names Divine,'' p. 21).

11. 29[31]:49 (E128). These are the four principal classical virtues, which Blake translates (in his previous line) into ''the four iron pillars of Satan's Throne.'' His source, should he have needed one in particular, is most likely book 4 of Plato's *Republic.*

12. Erdman, *The Illuminated Blake* (see chap. 3, n. 43), p. 24. The plate is reproduced on the same page.

13. Reproduced in Irene Tayler, *Blake's Illustrations to the Poems of Gray* (see chap. 1, n. 32).

14. Erdman, *The Illuminated Blake*, p. 316. The plate is also reproduced on E184. I am indebted to Erdman for calling my attention to the small figure seated on the hair and between the wings of the zoa Urthona on page 136 of *The Four Zoas* (Night IX). Urthona's three tiers of wings lead Erdman to associate him with the six-winged seraphim seen by Isaiah, and he further conjectures that, below Urthona's chin, one pair of wings cradle the live coal that was laid on the mouth of Isaiah (6:4–7). The small figure on Urthona's head is writing in a book open on his left, The Poet writing ''out of'' or on the wings of Imagination.

15. GB83. Although the flying posture of this figure is hardly unique in Blake's graphic canon, it seems to me strikingly close to that of ''A Muse'' (Blake's title) in the final design for Gray's *Progress of Poesy*, which also contains the table of contents of Blake's designs to *The Bard*. As Irene Tayler suggests, ''the muse seems to be handing her lyre up to someone else—perhaps to the poetic vision of the next poem, 'The Bard' '' (*Blake's Illustrations to the Poems of Gray*, p. 94). That Gray's version of the progress theme in *The Progress of Poesy* has the ''line of vision'' proceeding westerly to Shakespeare, Milton, and Dryden (omitting, prominently, Spenser as well as Chaucer) was clear evidence to Blake of Gray's benightedness in that poem. But Blake may have regarded that error as redeemed (at least in part) by Gray's inclusion of Spenser in *The Bard* (the operative cause of Blake's substantial graphic magnification of his presence there?). The ''someone else'' to whom Blake's muse in the Gray design hands the harp turns out to be, then, for Gray as

well as for Blake, regressively Spenser and "the ancient poets" of Blake's *Marriage of Heaven and Hell* (Los's cogs in the wheel to turn the adverse wheel?).

16. Erdman, *The Illuminated Blake*, p. 107.

17. Jenijoy LaBelle, "Blake's Visions and Re-visions of Michelangelo," in *Blake in His Time* (see chap. 3, n. 17), p. 20. Both the Ghisi and Blake's drawing are reproduced in this book. Although LaBelle does not say so, it is certainly possible that Blake saw some version of Michelangelo's original that included the hovering "shadowy spirit."

18. Ibid., p. 21. A provocative analogue to the Michelangelo, and to Blake's "version" of it in the Spenser painting, is the tripartite design of reading-writing-copying (and perhaps "influencing") on plate 10 of *The Marriage of Heaven and Hell*.

19. DeNeef, *Spenser and the Motives of Metaphor* (see chap. 2, n. 31), chap. 6. Unless otherwise indicated, all my quotations in the following discussion are from this book, acknowledged by parenthetical page numbers. There are a number of other excellent discussions of the epic poet in his poem, in the Renaissance and earlier, but DeNeef's analysis of *The Faerie Queene*, as I trust will become apparent, is the most pertinent to my purposes here.

20. Nohrnberg, *Analogy of "The Faerie Queene,"* p. 105; DeNeef, *Spenser and the Motives of Metaphor*, p. 95.

21. Summerfield, "Blake and the Names Divine," p. 20.

22. S. Foster Damon, *William Blake: His Philosophy and Symbols* (1924; New York: Peter Smith, 1947) pp. 426–27. The best introduction to what I have called this geography and genealogy (not to mention numerology) is still Northrop Frye's "Notes for a Commentary on *Milton*," in *The Divine Vision*, ed. Vivian de Sola Pinto (London: Victor Gollancz, 1957), pp. 99–137. See also the passages in Frye's *Fearful Symmetry*, referred to under "zodiac" in the index (p. 462).

23. Harold Bloom, Commentary to Erdman's *Complete Poetry and Prose of William Blake*, E926.

24. These abstractions constitute, therefore, Blake's "Female Space" (*Milton* 10[11]:6, E104), which Frye wittily defines as, "like a 'harlot coy' increasing her price by pretending to be a virgin," continually retreating "from the perceiver" ("Notes for a Commentary on *Milton*," pp. 115–16). Quite coincidentally, while not entirely inapropos my mention of Astraea as the Female Will, Frye in his next sentence lays to rest the question of Blake's antifeminism that continues to disturb recent commentators: "The perceiver," he says, "is a human being, who may be a man or woman—in other words Blake's 'female will' has nothing to do with human women except when women dramatize it in their sexual rituals, as they do, for instance, in the Courtly Love convention" (p. 116) (see chapter 2 in this volume). Among the recent worriers over Blake's "male chauvinism," which is generally regarded as inherited from Milton and Genesis (not to say the eighteenth century), are Susan Fox, in "The Female as Metaphor in William Blake's Poetry" *Critical Inquiry* 3 (1977): 507–19, and Anne K. Mellor, "Blake's Portrayal of Women," *Blake: An Illustrated Quarterly* 16 (1982–83): 148–55.

25. *The Faerie Queene*, V,i,11. "Sixt in her degree" means the sixth month, August, in the old calendar.

26. *Spenser Variorum*, 5, p. 166. Upton, *Spenser's Faerie Queene* (see chap. 1, n. 51), makes the distinction between the traditional Talus as judge (hence, somehow "brazen") and Spenser's Talus as executioner (hence, iron man). Warton in his *Observations* (see chap. 4, n. 82) makes the same point. Blake's conflation of the two metals and roles in his Urizenic God of This World thus acquires an additional imaginative dimension. At one point Blake identifies "Satans' holy Trinity" as "The Accuser The Judge & The Executioner" (E672), and elsewhere Satan sets himself up as "God the judge of all," holding "the Balances of Right & Just" (*Milton* 38[43]:50–51, 54, E139–40). I find it amusing that one modern commentator, B. E. C. Davis (*Edmund Spenser: A Critical Study* [New York: Cambridge University Press, 1933]), rather bitterly laments Spenser's introduction of Talus: "neither authority nor the demands of allegory can palliate the offence of admitting this grotesque automaton, Thor with his hammer but without his humour, upon the shores of old romance. Talus is a very affront to the hero's [Artegall's] dignity, a lapse on the part of Spenser that can only be attributed to waning power" (*Spenser Variorum*, 5, p. 298).

27. H. S. V. Jones, *A Spenser Handbook* (New York: F. S. Crofts, 1930), quoted in *Spenser Variorum*, 5, pp. 295–96.

28. Kate M. Warren, *The Faerie Queene by Edmund Spenser*, 6 vols. (Westminster: Archibald Constable, 1897–1900), quoted in *Spenser Variorum*, 5, p. 272.

29. This illustration and Young's text are in Blake's design #151 (*Night Thoughts* 4). Morton D. Paley, in "Blake's *Night Thoughts*: An Exploration of the Fallen World," in *William Blake: Essays for S. Foster Damon* (see chap. 4, n. 84), identifies this scale-holder as "Virtue" (p. 144), despite the text's specifying "reason," as Thomas H. Helmstadter notices in "Blake and the Age of Reason: Spectres in the *Night Thoughts*," *Blake Studies* 5 (1972): 138.

30. Nicholas Warner, "Blake's Moon-Ark Symbolism," *Blake: An Illustrated Quarterly* 14 (1980): 44. In one of the most recent analyses of *Jerusalem*, *The Continuing City: William Blake's "Jerusalem"* (see chap. 1, n. 20), Paley accepts the entirety of Warner's comforting analysis, but in the other recent book on the poem, *William Blake's "Jerusalem"* (Rutherford, N.J. and London: Fairleigh Dickinson University and Associated University Presses, 1982), Minna Doskow cites the crescent moons of *Jerusalem* 8, 14, 18, 20, 24, and 33, among other plates, as "symbolizing the fallen female" and Vala's "fallen version of religion" (p. 86).

31. Warner, "Blake's Moon-Ark Symbolism," p. 53. The plate is reproduced on the following page. Unlike Warner, Erdman notes the "lower moon's turning, impossibly, its wrong side to the lower sun" but does not pursue the impossibility (*The Illuminated Blake*, p. 312). He also correctly counts the stars in the middle distance of this plate as twenty-one but does not connect them with the Ptolemeic twenty-one constellations of the northern hemisphere—and hence, by a series of Blakean "equations," with Satan's "monstrous dishumanizd terrors." These last are incorporated into Blake's

characteristically Satanic bat-wingedness of the hovering, pterodactyl-like perversion of the Holy Ghost. See Doskow, *William Blake's "Jerusalem,"* p. 86 and my comments on page 182 above.

32. I am inclined to dispute Grant and Brown's identification of the structure to the right of St. Paul's dome as "Gothic" (Damon's suggestion of the Bower of Bliss is completely off the mark; see figure 10). Its portal, unlike all Blake's other Gothic portals, is narrowed to an uncharacteristic sliverlike aperture, and its spire (really only half a spire) is oddly off-center. None of the human figures enter or seem disposed to even try. The incommensurability of the entire configuration with Los's entry into the portal of *Jerusalem* in plate 1 of that poem argues that the structure is more likely one of Blake's twenty-seven churches or heavens of historical, dogmatic Christianity, which culminate in Abraham, Moses, Solomon, Paul, Constantine, Charlemaine, and Luther—"And where Luther ends Adam begins again in Eternal Circle" (*Jerusalem* 75:24, E231). These final "Seven are the Male Females: the Dragon Forms / The Female hid within a Male: thus Rahab is reveald / Mystery Babylon the Great"; "Thus are the Heavens formed by Los within the Mundane Shell" (*Jerusalem* 75:17–20, 23, E231). I see the sliverlike aperture, then, as vaginal, a replica of the genital shrine or chapel entrance in Blake's extraordinary drawing in the *Vala* (*Four Zoas*) manuscript reproduced in Kathleen Raine, *Blake and Tradition* (see chap. 2, n. 11), 1, p. 196. See also Grant's comments on this drawing, in "Visions in *Vala*" (see chap. 2, n. 64), pp. 163–64, in which the *Vala* drawing is reproduced as plate 16; also see my earlier analysis in this volume of Blake's manuscript poem, "I Saw a Chapel All of Gold." It is hardly accidental, then, that Blake positions this vaginal chapel directly above (actually slightly to the left because of "God's" right hand) Britomart, who, as we shall see, is intimately related to both.

33. I have borrowed freely here from Damon's *Blake Dictionary*, respectively, pp. 384, 283–84, 146.

34. "A Song of Liberty," *The Marriage of Heaven and Hell* (E45); *America* 6:13 (E53). For an earnest, if finally vain (and even misguided) attempt to unravel the complexities of Mars in *America*, see Michael Ferber, "Mars and the Planets Three in *America*," *Blake: An Illustrated Quarterly* 15 (1981–82): 136–37. He does properly demolish, however, Rodney M. and Mary R. Baine's silly Swedenborgian reading of the passage in *English Language Notes* 13 (1975): 14–18. See also David V. Erdman's analysis of "*America*: New Expanses," in Erdman and Grant, *Visionary Forms Dramatic*, especially pp. 106–10.

35. John E. Grant, "Blake's Designs for *L'Allegro* and *Il Penseroso*," *Blake Newsletter* 4 (1971): 128. For a somewhat different interpretation of the companion poems, see Rose, "Blake's Illustrations for *Paradise Lost*, *L'Allegro* and *Il Penseroso* (see chap. 4, n. 87), pp. 40–67.

36. Whether or not the scene is "wintry" and hence ominous in that sense, as Rose argues (in the essay cited in note 35 above), I cannot agree with Grant's sanguine conclusion that here "the starry heavens [are] humanized" and all is well once again. Milton in his mossy cell or cave, a gigantic open book beside him lit only by a candle, seems hardly a compelling image

of enlightenment in Blake's sense, despite the light irradiating from his head (see figure 6). But that aside, if we concentrate on the heavens alone, Grant's admitting to the Gemini's apparent fighting with each and to the shepherd's wearing a hat like that of the benighted figures in the fifth and sixth designs, and then pleading specially for Blake's "respectfulness" toward Orion elsewhere, hardly constitute a persuasive argument for a *Pippa Passes* view of these supernal realms. Grant's "conclusion" is from part 2 of the *L'Allegro-Il Penseroso* article, in *Blake Newsletter* 5 (1971–72): 202; the other points I have cited are from part 1, p. 134.

VI. *THE CHARACTERS IN SPENSER'S FAERIE QUEENE,* II

1. See figure 7. His particular armor seems to support this identification. More crucially, Timias's proximity to Guyon may reflect his allusion to the Bower of Bliss when he awakes from his swoon to find Belphoebe hovering over him:

> Mercy deare Lord (said he) what grace is this,
> That thou hast shewed to me sinfull wight,
> To send thine Angell from her bowre of blis,
> To comfort me in my distressed plight?

> (III,v,35)

If it is Timias, though, and the female he faces is Belphoebe, I have no other idea as to why they are where they are in the painting. To argue, on one of Kiralis's principles, that Belphoebe and Amoretta (the figure under Arthur's left elbow) are "female counterparts . . . almost equidistant . . . from the integral figure of Britomart" (GB65) and hence that they "complete the 'female character'" (GB69) is, I think, to confuse Chaucer with Spenser—not to say, in Blake's Spenser painting, the background with the foreground.

2. See particularly *The Bard* illustration 11, the armor on Guyon in illustration 12, the head armor of *The Fatal Sisters* 7–8 and 10, the armored figures of *The Descent of Odin* 1–3 and 8–9, and *The Triumphs of Owen* 4–5—all reproduced in Irene Tayler, *Blake's Illustrations to the Poems of Gray* (see chap. 1, n. 32).

3. To be sure, the painting is much deteriorated in this area (see figure 8), and "if there were originally no other important features" there, "it would be remarkable" (GB80). Nevertheless, the rocky barrenness is still striking as a counterecho of Meliboe's realm.

4. Bowden, "The Artistic and Interpretive Context of Blake's 'Canterbury Pilgrims,'" (see chap. 4, n. 48), pp. 164–90. Subsequent references to the essay will be parenthetical in my text as B plus the page number.

5. E648. On this taxonomic numbering, see Patrick Coleman's interesting essay on "Character in an Eighteenth-Century Context," (see chap. 4, n. 23), pp. 51–63, especially his analysis of the eighteenth-century's compulsion to classify, to create (as it were) artificial constructs of separateness (spe-

cies), which are then named. See also Jonathan Bennett, *Locke, Berkeley, Hume* (Oxford: Oxford University Press, 1971), pp. 120–23, whom Coleman cites on Locke's conceding the impossibility of discovering the nature of the "essences" of things and man's necessarily settling for words that are but arbitrary signs for objects.

6. The behind-the-scenes villain in the public appearance of Stothard's *Canterbury Pilgrims* before Blake's "version" was Robert Hartley Cromek, whom Erdman describes as a "duplicitous" and "unscrupulous promoter and mediocre engraver," who more than once sold Blake down the river for a buck. The best account of Cromek's several dealings with Blake is Erdman's in *Blake: Prophet against Empire* (see chap. 2, n. 41), pp. 434–40, from which I have taken the above-quoted characterization. Specifically on the Chaucer-painting affair, Stothard's preempting of the field, and Cromek's role in that, see Mona Wilson, *The Life of William Blake*, 3d ed., ed. Geoffrey Keynes (Oxford: Oxford University Press, 1971), pp. 232–41, and Bowden's "The Artistic and Interpretive Context of Blake's 'Canterbury Pilgrims,'" p. 170. Stothard's version is reprinted (reduced) in Kiralis, "William Blake as an Intellectual and Spiritual Guide to Chaucer's *Canterbury Pilgrims*," (see chap. 4, n. 48), p. 181 (fig. 2). In his *Notebook*, Blake savagely pillories Stothard as "Stewhard" and Cromek as "Screwmuch" (E503–4) as well as characterizing Cromek as a disease (E505). Other venemous jottings at their expense may be found on E508, 509, 510.

7. The unpropitiousness of this act may be measured by the contrary physical inaction of the piper with respect to the child in *Introduction* to *Innocence*, but it is more starkly underscored by Blake's manuscript poems "Eternity" (E470), repeated with slight variation under "Several Questions Answerd" (E474) and in "The Fairy" (E475). A seemingly "good" fairy appears in a poem scribbled on a single sheet bearing a drawing on the reverse side of "The Infant Hercules" (E481–82, and Erdman's textual note E858). In a letter to me, Erdman argues that the fairy of plate iii of *Europe* is merely amoral and thus neither condemnable nor suspect as the inspiration for or dictator of a prophetic poem such as *Europe*. I am afraid that I can square this interpretation with neither the details of plate iii nor the passage from *Milton* I quote in the text, a poem that Blake was working on at least by the time the *Europe* prefatory plate was etched.

8. Erdman, *Blake: Prophet against Empire*, p. 211. Blake's perverse uses of the *Nativity Ode* are well documented by Michael J. Tolley in "Europe: 'to those ychain'd in sleep,'" in *Blake's Visionary Forms Dramatic* (see chap. 1, n. 28), pp. 115–45. As I am, Tolley is far less sanguine than Erdman about the role of Orc in the poem, calling "Blake in *Europe* . . . a prophet of doom" and arguing his unhappiness with Erdman's "identification [of] Orc with Christ" (p. 144). He is firm, however, about asserting that "Blake, when writing *Europe*, had not yet projected Orc's perversion" to his role in *The Four Zoas* as a "Serpent round the tree of Mystery"; "his Prophecy was written in the hope that Orc would continue to expand" (p. 145n). I think both Erdman and Tolley are wrong—or at least that their emphases are wrong. Somewhere in the recesses of his mind, Blake may have clung to the possibility that

Orc could expand or soar, but I tend to agree with Deen that, after the "clearing away" effected by the Lambeth prophecies through the confrontations of Orc and Urizen, Blake did not quite "know what to put in place of what was cleared away"—or if he knew the general contours of what to put in the void, he was less than certain how Los and his sons would effect it. See Deen's *Conversing in Paradise* (see chap. 1, n. 27), p. 78. Other negative views of *Europe* and of Orc include W. J. T. Mitchell's in "Blake's Composite Art," in *Blake's Visionary Forms Dramatic* ("Orc *is* Urizen" and Urizen *is* Orc, because "the tyrant inevitably begets the revolutionary reaction against his rule" and because "the spirit of violent rebellion always degenerates into oppression when it has gained power"—p. 80 and n.); Robert E. Simmons's in "*Urizen*: The Symmetry of Fear," ibid., pp. 160–61, especially 161n; Minna Doskow's in "William Blake's *America*: The Story of a Revolution Betrayed," *Blake Studies* 8 (1979): 167–86; and the most extensive and balanced treatment, E. J. Rose's "Good-Bye to Orc and All That," *Blake Studies* 4 (1972): 135–51. All of these analyses are in one way or another based on Frye's pioneering discussion of the "Orc cycle" in *Fearful Symmetry* (see chap. 1, n. 8), pp. 206–35, the uses of which in the context of the Lambeth prophecies Erdman argues as misapplications and a "wander[ing] far astray"—"A Note on the 'Orc Cycle'" (see chap. 5, n. 7), p. 112.

9. Erdman, *Blake: Prophet against Empire*, p. 224; Deen, *Conversing in Paradise*, pp. 51, 59.

10. Erdman, footnote comment on Simmons's "*Urizen*: The Symmetry of Fear," p. 161n.

11. Erdman, *Blake: Prophet against Empire*, p. 211.

12. Carol P. Kowle's attempt to dovetail plate iii neatly into the rest of the poem by regarding it "as an important guide to the meaning of the entire prophecy" is, I believe, a misleading analysis; see her "Plate iii and the Meaning of *Europe*," *Blake Studies* 8 (1978): 89–99.

13. Isaiah 11:6. As Grant and Brown point out (GB64), the Dwarf does lead Una and Arthur to Orgoglio's castle, where Redcrosse is imprisoned, in I, viii, 1–2, but that passage is not the one to which Blake is alluding. One wonders whether Blake recalled that Isaiah 11 recounts the Lord's efforts "to recover the remnant of his people," assembling "the outcasts of Israel" and gathering "together the dispersed of Judah from the four corners of the earth" (11:11–12); "And there shall be an highway for the remnant of his people" (v. 16). Are the new Jerusalem and the "one church" of Isaiah 65–66 the "true" destination of Spenser's "pilgrims"?

14. J. B. Fletcher, "The Painter of the Poets," *Studies in Philology* 14 (1917): 164, noted in *Spenser Variorum*, 1, p. 178.

15. Randel Helms, "The Genesis of *The Everlasting Gospel*," *Blake Studies* 9 (1980): 130. The other principal reading of *The Everlasting Gospel* is by David V. Erdman, "Terrible Blake in His Pride: An Essay on *The Everlasting Gospel*," in *From Sensibility to Romanticism: Essays Presented to Frederick A. Pottle*, ed. Frederick W. Hilles and Harold Bloom (London: Oxford University Press, 1965), pp. 331–56.

16. In "William Blake and Westminster Abbey" (see chap. 4, n. 48),

Mary Ellen Reisner suggests that the Wife's costume is based at least in part on Queen Elizabeth's effigies (see especially pp. 194–95); but see also John F. Plummer, "The Wife of Bath's Hat as Sexual Metaphor," *English Language Notes* 1 (1980): 89–90.

17. Cf. the title-page design of *The Book of Urizen* and Morris Eaves's fine analysis of it, "The Title-page of *The Book of Urizen*," in *William Blake: Essays in Honour of Sir Geoffrey Keynes* (see chap. 3, n. 13), pp. 225–30. See also plate 11 on which George III is pictured as a Satanic batwinged Pope who, with "his brazen Book, / That Kings & Priests had copied on Earth" open before him, stares stonily directly at us.

18. See Quilligan, *Language of Allegory* (see chap. 4, n. 9) and, more to my point, Hilton's *Literal Imagination* (also chap. 4, n. 9).

19. Night the Seventh (E358). It is noteworthy that Blake here is echoing the originating "allegory" of Genesis that I have already dealt with, for "Urizen Prince of Light" is also identified in *The Four Zoas* passage as "First born of Generation," that is, of Nature. Further parodying the Genesis God's creation of man, Blake pursues his identification of the God of This World and Adam as follows:

> Then behold a wonder to the Eyes
> Of the now fallen Man a double form Vala appeard. A Male
> And female shuddring pale.
>
> (E358)

Blake shrewdly appropriated the phrase "Prince of Light" from Milton's *Nativity Ode* (l. 62), where also "The winds with wonder" are hushed at the birth (l. 64). He may have taken a cue for his Dwarf-child from the ode: "Our babe, to show his Godhead true, / Can in his swaddling bands control the damned crew" of "all the gods beside," including "Typhon huge ending in snaky twine" (ll. 225–28).

20. *Milton* 14[15]:3 (E108). Blake's terms are here applied to "the Poetic Genius / Who is the eternal all-protecting Divine Humanity" and whose words are "Truth" (13[14]:51, E107).

21. Revelation 5:1, 4. Should Blake have needed prompting to locate these biblical sources of Spenser's conception, he would have found them in Upton's notes to the edition of *The Faerie Queene* that I have argued (see chapter 1) Blake most relied on. With or without Upton's help, he would also have recognized in Spenser's stanza 20 of canto x the attribution of prophetic "powre, and puissance great" to Fidelia via the allusions to Joshua 10:12, Exodus 14:21–31, and Matthew 21:21.

22. Redcrosse as St. George suggests a possible relationship with Urizen, Blake's archetypal plowman. As Frye reminds us (*Fearful Symmetry*, p. 335), "the plowman is traditional in the English epic as a symbol of the visionary," and he mentions Langland's Piers, Chaucer's "idealized plowman," and Spenser's St. George. But just as Urizen surrenders his eternal plow in favor of his sceptre and iron laws, so Spenser's *Georgos* is "prickt with courage, and [his] forces pryde" and goes "To Faery court . . . to seeke for fame, / And proue [his] puissaunt armes, as seemes [him] best became" (I,x,66). He is

thus elevated to "Saint *George* of mery England, the signe of victoree" (st. 61), not to mention his becoming a war cry. His fighting "that old Dragon," then, would be to Blake a measure of Spenser's benightedness, a fallen Urizen combatting the very error he embodies. One might add as well that beating one's plowshare into a sword hardly becomes the artist-visionary whose graver-plow should be dedicated to the annihilation of all apparent surfaces in order to reveal the infinite that was hid.

23. It is at least fortuitous for my purposes that three plates later in *Jerusalem* Vala, under the domination of the "Mundane Shell," cries:

> The Human is but a Worm, & thou O Male: Thou art
> Thyself Female, a Male: a breeder of Seed: a Son & Husband: & Lo.
> The Human Divine is Womans Shadow, a Vapor in the summers heat
> Go assume Papal dignity thou Spectre, thou Male Harlot! Arthur
> Divide into the Kings of Europe in times remote O Woman-born
> And Woman-nourishd & Woman-educated & Woman-scorn'd!
>
> (64:12–17, E215)

The Faerie Queene is "times remote"? Perhaps. In any case, I shall have occasion to discuss this passage once again, in connection with Blake's portrayal of Arthur in the painting. I might also note here that Blake's Una may be a quotation of Mary in his 1799 painting, *The Flight into Egypt*. Mary is seated on her ass precisely as Una is, facing to her half-right with nearly identical features. Her hood is very similar to Una's but her halo is flatter and without spikey rays. Finally, Mary holds the Christ child rather than Una's book in her lap.

24. E26. See also "I Saw a Chapel All of Gold" and my analysis of it (pp. 87–97 above) in the context of Blake's numerous allusions to Spenser. Perhaps there is some intended significance, then, in Blake's locating Redcrosse directly between the House of Holinesse and what Grant and Brown identify, correctly I believe, as Despaire's cave (GB78). Either way, Redcrosse is a goner. Damon's identification of the bearded figure in the cave as Spenser is absurd, for his reading his book intently and raising a forefinger, not to mention his ancient-of-days beardedness, his distant echoing of plate 9, and the reversed repeat in his attendant figure of plate 10 of *The Book of Urizen* all mark him as the Urizen of "One King, one God, one Law" (E72). The two graphic designs may be seen in *The Illuminated Blake*, ed. Erdman (see chap. 3, n. 43), pp. 191, 192.

25. A. C. Hamilton, *The Structure of Allegory in "The Faerie Queene"* (Oxford: Clarendon Press, 1961), p. 192. Williams, in *Spenser's World of Glass* (see chap. 2, n. 10), argues that Redcrosse "stands behind" all the other knights "and often in their quests we are reminded of him" (p. 33).

26. Kiralis, "William Blake as an Intellectual and Spiritual Guide to Chaucer's *Canterbury Pilgrims*," p. 142. In his note 6 (p. 189), however, Kiralis adds: "But in view of Blake's well-known antipathy to physical war and his inscription beside the title in the third state [of the illustration]—'The use of Money & its Wars. / An Allegory of Idolatry or Politics.'—it seems unlikely that he would consider the warrior Knight altogether favorably." If, as

Erdman has suggested to me, Blake had more approval for the good warriors in Chaucer who fought oppressors, there is little evidence of that in the Chaucer painting (see n. 27 below). For an analysis of the four (or five) states of the painting, see Kiralis, pp. 174–77, and Sir Geoffrey Keynes, *Engravings by William Blake, The Separate Plates: A Catalogue Raisonné* (Dublin: E. Walker, 1956), pp. 45–49. Erdman dates the inscription to which Kiralis refers circa 1820 (E687). Its apparent sweeping damnation of Chaucer to angelhood is equally applicable to *The Faerie Queene*.

27. Bowden, "The Artistic and Interpretive Context of Blake's 'Canterbury Pilgrims,'" p. 180. She also argues, correctly I believe, that Blake's "Knight, as an eternal type, takes it upon himself to define man's oppressor," but "with the rules and trappings of chivalry, he guards against forces that man—if left to his own inspiration—might embrace rather than fear" (p. 181).

28. See my analysis of the siege of Alma's castle in chapter 2 of this volume.

29. In stanza 31, the downed Arthur, aided by Timias, revives "As one awakt out of long slombering shade" to unite "all his powres to purge himselfe from blame." The "blame," of course, derives from his reason being momently "defeated" by the senses, and his "purge" consists of breaking "his caitiue bands" (st. 33). Mind-forged manacles? On Blake's idea of a sleeping Humanity, see the passages indexed under "Humanity" in *A Concordance to the Writings of William Blake*, ed. David V. Erdman (Ithaca, N.Y.: Cornell University Press, 1967), 2, pp. 948–49.

30. F. J. Child, *The Poetical Works of Edmund Spenser*, 5 vols. (Boston, 1855), cited in *Spenser Variorum*, 2, p. 343. Upton, in his edition of *The Faerie Queene* (London, 1758), rather charmingly notes Maleger's "gloominess," which, he says, "is to be destroyed by a chearful raising your thoughts above muck and durt and earthly things, and by a spiritualizing exaltation" (*Spenser Variorum*, 2, p. 347)—the right idea, the wrong terminology.

31. Damon, *Blake Dictionary*, p. 416. In *Jerusalem* (7:24, E149), Blake associates Udan-Adan with the Flood, God's version of Los's creative undoing (or uncreating).

32. For a generous sampling of these confused and often contradictory significations, consult Damon's animal entries in *A Blake Dictionary*.

33. *Milton* 39[44]:35, E140; Damon, *Blake Dictionary*, p. 69.

34. On pilgrimages as Blake perceived them, see appendix B in this volume. It must be intentional that, although Blake describes his painting (in *A Descriptive Catalogue*, E532) as consisting of Chaucer plus "nine and twenty Pilgrims," there are really only twenty-eight—plus "Our Host" (whose "cathedral" is the Tabarde Inn). For a list and discussion of Blake's twenty-eight cathedral cities, see Damon, *Blake Dictionary*, pp. 71–74. Kiralis's feeling that Blake's "miscounting" Chaucer's pilgrims is not "forgivable," then, is surely misplaced (see p. 173 of his essay on the Chaucer painting).

35. Although he sees redemptive aspects (that I do not share) in Blake's perception of Arthur, Frye deserves much credit for connecting Blake's Arthur with Satan and the Covering Cherub (*Fearful Symmetry*, p. 142). Blake's

more sanguine view of Milton's redeemability, then, may rest in part on his rejection of the Arthurian myth as false and his adoption (however flawed) of the biblical myth in its place.

36. *Jerusalem* 38[43]:51, E185. For a full account of the origin of Blake's mythological Skofield and his manifold significations and characeral relationships, see Damon's *Blake Dictionary*, pp. 360–61.

37. *The Works of John Milton* (New York: Columbia University Press, 1932), vol. 10, ed. George P. Krapp, pp. 17–18. Geoffrey of Monmouth has almost identical phrasing; see *The British History of Geoffrey of Monmouth*, trans. A. Thompson, ed. J. A. Giles (London: James Bohn, 1842), pp. 31–32. More complete than Milton, Geoffrey's history contains references to the "eight and twenty cities" of Britain (p. 3), the origin and significance of the city of Legions (pp. 53, 191–95), and Merlin's supervision of the bringing of the Druid stones from Ireland to Stonehenge (pp. 158–60).

38. *Faerie Queene* III,iii,60. In Book II, in a kind of Blakean redeemed form, Bladud is presented as a master of the arts of peace whom Huddibras emulates to mollify the "stubborne harts" of those bent on "wearie warres" (x,25). But even there Spenser acknowledges that he, "at last contending to excell / The reach of men, through flight into fond mischief fell" (st. 26). Incidentally, for what it is worth, Spenser spells the names of Lear's daughters as Gonorill, Regan, and Cordeill; Geoffrey of Monmouth as Gonorilla, Regan, and Cordeilla; and Blake as Gonorill, Ragan, and Cordella.

VII. *THE CHARACTERS IN SPENSER'S FAERIE QUEENE*, III

1. *The Marriage of Heaven and Hell*, E42. Elsewhere Blake lauds friendship, associating it with love, benevolence, and the forgiveness of sins, but his conception of it is as far removed from Venusian love as it is from the principle of *discordia concors*. The former is a product of "Worshipping the Maternal / Humanity" (*Jerusalem* 90:65–66, E25), the latter the "peace" that only "mutual fear brings" (*The Human Abstract*, E27). As Los says in *Jerusalem*, "I never made friends but by spiritual gifts; / By severe contentions of friendship & the burning fire of thought" (91:16–17, E251). Thus, Albion's severe contentions with "his Friend" Jesus (who is "the likeness & similitude of Los") lead to Jesus' dying so that Albion might live—which is to say, Albion's dying so that Jesus might live in him: "every kindness to another is a little Death / In the Divine Image nor can Man exist but by Brotherhood" (*Jerusalem* 96:3–32, E255–56). For excellent analyses of brotherhood in Blake, see Michael Ferber, "Blake's Idea of Brotherhood" (see chap. 2, n. 62), and Leonard W. Deen, *Conversing in Paradise* (see chap. 1, n. 27). For a convenient presentation of the way I believe Blake read Book IV of *The Faerie Queene*, see John E. Hankins's chapter, "The Moral Allegory of Friendship, Chastity, and Love" in *Source and Meaning in Spenser's Allegory* (see chap. 4, n. 18), pp. 141–70. But it is also possible that Blake perceived the power of Ate and Sclaunder dominating the book in somewhat the same way that I have

argued he read Excesse in Book II. As A. Leigh DeNeef suggests, in *Spenser and the Motives of Metaphor* (see chap. 2, n. 31), the apparent triumph of concord, friendship, and love in the marriage of Thames and Medway essentially "excludes man from its celebration. . . . The world of man, it seems, is exactly where Spenser left it, controlled by destructive and deforming forces" (p. 124).

2. *Jerusalem* 53:1 (E202). Similarly, "Lazarus . . . is the Vehicular Body of Albion the Redeemd" (*Milton* 24[26]:27, E120).

3. The poem (E500–501) begins "When Klopstock England defied," and Blake is summoned from his privy seat to perform marvelous ministrations for poor Klopstock. On the "relationship" between the two, see F. E. Pierce, "Blake and Klopstock," *Studies in Philology* 25 (1928): 11–26; Frye, *Fearful Symmetry*, p. 329; and Mona Wilson, *The Life of William Blake* (see chap. 6, n. 6), p. 141. One might cite Blake's annotations as well, the general tenor of which is epitomized by his opening fusillade against Sir Joshua Reynolds: "This Man was Hired to Depress Art This is the opinion of Will Blake my Proofs of this Opinion are given in the following notes" (E635); or again: "How I did secretly Rage. I also spoke my Mind" (E639).

4. The language here is from Lavater's aphorism 14, which Blake bracketed and labeled "Pure gold" (E584).

5. E584. Blake makes no direct comment on this aphorism but refers us to what is, in effect, his "translation" of it in his marginal comments on aphorisms 533 ("man is the ark of God . . . man is either the ark of God or a phantom of the earth & of the water") and 630 ("our Lord is the word of God & every thing on earth is the word of God & in its essence is God")—E596, 599. See also aphorisms 549 (E596), which Blake designates as "true worship," and 554 (E597), on which he comments, "human nature is the image of God." Both are cross-referenced in his note to aphorism 630.

6. Although it is more than possible that I have missed something in the vast sea of Spenser scholarship and criticism, I am inclined to agree with Isabel MacCaffrey in *Spenser's Allegory* (see chap. 4, n. 46), that "the many filiations between Book I and Book VI still need to be worked out in detail" (p. 401n). She details several of these filiations in part 4 of her book, subtitled "Book VI: The Paradise Within," and also cites suggestive comments on the matter by Thomas Roche, *The Kindly Flame* (see chap. 2, n. 37), p. 200; Alastair Fowler, *Triumphal Forms* (Cambridge: Cambridge University Press, 1970), p. 111; and Maurice Evans, *Spenser's Anatomy of Heroism* (Cambridge: Cambridge University Press, 1970), pp. 18–19. See also A. C. Hamilton, *The Structure of Allegory in "The Faerie Queene,"* (chap. 6, n. 25), pp. 205–6; and, for a different view of Book VI, Stanley N. Stewart's "Sir Calidore and 'Closure,'" *Studies in English Literature* 24 (1984): 69–86. My analysis of the "filiation" between the two books is what I perceive to be Blake's view of the matter, which, although it may well coincide with that of the best of Spenser's critics, is uniquely his own powerful reading of the relationship, at once less and more subtle (but certainly bolder) than theirs.

7. As early as the 1770s, in the manuscript fragment, "Then She Bore Pale Desire," Blake transforms "Babel with thousand tongues" ("Confu-

sion it was calld'') into ''Envy,'' which ''hath a Serpents head of fearful bulk hissing with hundred tongues, her poisnous breath breeds Satire foul Contagion from which none are free'' (E446). In *Jerusalem*, the Covering Cherub as ''a Human Dragon terrible'' stretches itself ''over Europe & Asia''; its ''Head dark, deadly, in its Brain incloses a reflexion / Of Eden all perverted . . . many tongued / And many mouthd'' (89:9–16, E248). In defending the Bible against the Bishop of Landaff's ''apology'' for it in response to Paine's *Age of Reason*, Blake charges the Bishop with defending the Antichrist. Thus, he affectingly confesses that ''To defend the Bible in this year 1798 would cost a man his life The Beast & the Whore rule without controls'' (E611–12).

8. Of these, one leads the beast by a chain-leash, one pulls tight the cords of the net over its mouth, and one seems to be tightening (or fastening) its collar. For an excellent enlargement of this scene, see GB72.

9. My aligning of the proem of Book VI with Spenser's minihymn on the ''faire flowre'' of ''chastity and vertue virginall'' in Book III is sanctioned by Spenser's own near self-quotation (which Blake may well have noticed): ''God'' plants this flower ''In Paradize,'' and the muses ''dight'' their garlands with it to make a crown such as ''Angels weare before Gods tribunall'' (III,v,52–53). Moreover, ''Ne poysnous Envy iustly can empaire / The prayse of . . . fresh flowring Maidenhead'' (Belphoebe), who is not only chaste but courteous, kind, ''Tempred with grace, and goodly modesty'' (st. 55).

10. In this connection, one wonders whether the aged Archimago and Duessa, though in one sense peculiarly out of place in Blake's Book VI, do not ''belong'' there after all as echoes of the aged Har and Heva of *Tiriel*. As imbecilic aged infants in that poem, they refuse to acknowledge their self-entrapment in the world of Experience and are content to dwell in memory (personified by their ''nurse'' Mnetha) of days gone by. Blake's sepia illustrations to the poem lend some further credence to this possibly outrageous suggestion.

11. Perhaps the best candidate, however, is plate 54 of *Jerusalem*, which occurs in an Arthurian context. As ''the hard cold constrictive Spectre,'' Arthur pronounces himself to be ''God O Sons of Men! I am your Rational Power! / Am I not Bacon & Newton & Locke who teach Humility to Man! / Who teach Doubt & Experiment.'' A few lines later, he calls upon ''that Rebel against my Laws'' to ''Come hither into the Desart & turn these stones to bread'' (E203–4). If indeed this is a kind of gloss on the painting's bodiless figure, that figure is a bizarre conflation of Arthur-as-Spectre, the rational power (all head and no body-energy), Bacon-Newton-Locke actively ''teaching'' out of their books of knowledge, and the ''Druid Rocks round Canaan'' into which *Jerusalem*'s Arthur ''constricts.'' The appropriateness of such a conflation to Blake's interpretation of Book VI is inherent both in ''Courtesy'' stomping ''Reason'' and (as I shall interpret him shortly) Calidore-as-Arthur clobbering Arthur. For a relevant reading of *Jerusalem* 54 without reference to Spenser, see David Worrall, ''Blake's *Jerusalem* and the Visionary History of Britain'' (see chap. 1, n. 64), pp. 199ff. Damon's conjecture (which Grant and Brown reject) that there is ''a heap of stones'' under Cali-

dore's horse's hooves may well be a shrewd guess, especially since the "book" looks suspiciously like Urizen's stone tablets.

12. Blake uses the quoted phrase several times, the earliest in *Milton*, where it sums up "the Male-Females, the Dragon Forms" component of his "Twenty-seven Heavens & their Churches": Abraham, Moses, Solomon, Paul, Constantine, Charlemaine, and Luther (37[41]:35–43, E138). In *Jerusalem*, the same seven are again identified as "Religion hid in War," but here Bath, Merlin, Bladud, and Arthur share the appellation by virtue of Arthur's holding "The Cup of Rahab in his hand," the cup of "her Poisons Twenty-seven-fold / And all her Twenty-seven Heavens now hid & now reveal'd" (75:1–20, E230–31). In plate 89 of *Jerusalem*, Blake uses the phrase, "Religion hid in War," to describe the "Double Female . . . within the Tabernacle" who, on the outside, is "a Warlike Mighty-one / Of dreadful power, sitting upon Horeb pondering dire / And mighty preparations mustering multitudes innumerable / Of warlike Sons"; "They become One with the Antichrist & are absorbd in him" (ll. 52–62, E249).

13. Warren Stevenson, *The Poems of William Blake* (London: Longman, 1971), p. 394n.

14. *The Four Zoas*, Night the Seventh, E363. The Prester Serpent is illustrated on this page as a hooded cobra. Interestingly, in *America*, it is "the Bard of Albion" (here not the Albion of *Jerusalem* but the British suppressors of the American Revolution) who has "a cowl of flesh [grow] o'er his head" and, like the Calidore of Blake's Spenser painting, "scales" form "on his back & ribs" (15:16–17, E57). Erdman identifies the figure as England's then poet-laureate William Whitehead—*Blake: Prophet against Empire* (see chap. 2, n. 41), p. 61—but in Blake's ahistorical myth any poetic royal sympathizer, including Spenser, will do. Perhaps not coincidentally, the Palmer's baldness recalls Tiriel, Blake's first effort to present his archetypal father-priest-king triune tyrant. In the sepia designs he executed for the poem, Tiriel is not only bald and bearded but always garbed in a black gown (without cowl, however). The Palmer's otherwise curious parodying of innumerable Renaissance Madonna-and-child configurations may be related to the closing passage of *Tiriel*, where "The child springs from the womb. the father ready stands to form / The infant head." "Such was Tiriel," says the eponymous character, "Compelld to pray repugnant & to humble the immortal spirit / Till I am subtil as a serpent in a paradise" (E285). Blake portrays Chaucer's Monk and Friar with cowls virtually identical to the Palmer's, but both of these figures are neatly tonsured. Both are also characters "of a mixed kind," the Friar "with constitutional gaiety enough to make him a master of all the pleasures of the world," the Monk "a man of luxury, pride and pleasure." That Blake groups them with the Pardoner, Summoner, and Manciple is obviously inauspicious in ways that transcend his own given reason for that grouping, that they are "all . . . above the common rank in life or attendants on those who were so" (E533–34).

15. Both Kiralis and Bowden regard Blake's Parson as entirely benevolent, a "perfect and selfless practitioner of Christianity" (Kiralis, "William Blake as an Intellectual and Spiritual Guide," [see chap. 4, n. 48], p. 144).

Maybe so. Blake surely says so unequivocally in the *Descriptive Catalogue* quotations. But there is something odd about Blake's becoming "less misleading" in his prose commentary "concerning the characters in the second half of the [Chaucer] procession" (Bowden, "The Artistic and Interpretive Context of Blake's *Canterbury Pilgrims*" [see chap. 4, n. 48], p. 186). I find it difficult to accept his black gown, black hat, stolid staring eyes, "comfortable-looking shoes" (Kiralis, p. 149), and bob-tailed horse as any more auspicious than the dress and regalia of other less "perfect" characters. It can hardly be true, as Kiralis argues (p. 149), that Blake, "given the religious framework of the *Canterbury Tales*, accepts Chaucer's and the Parson's religion" indicated by the "solid church tower . . . over the head of the Parson." How this entire portrait and churchly sanction translate into what Kiralis calls "enthusiastic superstition," which is for the Parson "a true religion, a spiritual reality and not a dead orthodoxy," is beyond me. I think he is a Palmer, stared at, with appropriate lasciviousness, by the Wife of Bath.

16. As I noted in chapter 3, the energy Guyon does express is the perverted Orcian destructiveness bred of excessive self-repression, the demonic, mad wrath of the courtier "Incapacity," whose mistress is Prudence (*The Marriage of Heaven and Hell*, proverb 4, E35). Cf. Frye's perception, in "The Structure of Imagery in *The Faerie Queene*," in *Fables of Identity* (New York: Harcourt, Brace & World, 1963), that "in his whole moral complex" Guyon is "something of a male Diana" (p. 164).

17. A. Kent Hieatt, *Chaucer, Spenser, Milton* (see chap. 4, n. 14). It is worth noting here that Hieatt links Guyon's archcontrary, Pyrochles, to Milton's Satan (p. 217).

18. Ibid., pp. 164, 154–55, 166, 215, respectively.

19. In light of my gloomier view of Blake's Chaucerian Parson in note 15 above, it is worth noting here that Guyon's horse—mane, tail, and legs—is virtually identical to the Parson's. If, as Damon says (*Blake Dictionary*, p. 79), in the Chaucer painting Blake demonstrates that he "knew his horse-flesh," perhaps in the interim between the two paintings he learned enough about equestrianism to make Guyon's horse, unlike the Parson's, the only gaited trotter in the "race." Alas, the pilgrim Chaucer's is too in *Chaucers Canterbury Pilgrims*.

20. As I noted earlier, Deen's interpretation of Oothoon is considerably more positive (and hopeful) than mine. See his *Conversing in Paradise*, chap. 3, as well as the similarly positive view of E. B. Murray in "Thel, *Thelophthora*, and the Daughters of Albion" (see chap. 2, n. 17).

21. Grant and Brown's identification of this figure as Satyrane seems to me unsupportable (GB66), for despite his woodsman training, he is "all armd in rugged steele vnfilde," wears a helmet, and bears "in his Scutchin . . . a Satyres head" (III,vii,30).

22. Damon, *Blake Dictionary*, p. 384.

23. So Grant and Brown identify it (GB79).

24. *Faerie Queene* III,ii,40. It would be pleasant to think that this conjunction in *The Faerie Queene* of the words "Monster" and "affection" gave rise to

Blake's "Thought alone can make monsters, but the affections cannot" (Annotations to Swedenborg's *Divine Love and Divine Wisdom*, E603).

25. Although Erdman, among others, disputes Kiralis's firm Blakean identifications of the Wife of Bath as Rahab and the Prioress as Tirzah in his Chaucer painting, Blake's verbal and visual links between the Prioress and the Summoner and Pardoner leave little doubt about what Blake thought of the Lady Abbess. She is, he says, "of the first rank; rich and honoured" (E533), but it cannot be accidental that he uses identical language to describe the Summoner: "rich and honoured in the rank of which he holds the destiny" (E535). The Prioress has long blond hair like the Pardoner and displays two crosses to "equal" his more ostentatious one. We must also wonder at least at her peaked headdress, her wispily covered decolletage, and the prominent beads and brooch hanging from her right wrist—all more demure versions of the Wife of Bath's more blatant sporting of similar costume details. Britomart, then, is a kind of secular (or Petrarchan) Prioress coupled with her Wife-of-Bathhood; and if we are to see at all the Prioress as Chaucer's "version" of Blake's Jerusalem, Chaucer's allegiance to Jerusalem's fallen version, Vala, could not be made more obvious. In Blake's Spenser painting, the Prioress is "corrected" by the figure of Una in her "redeemed" aspect, as I analyzed that in chapter 6.

26. Perhaps Blake recalled that Chaucer's Wife of Bath wore a hat "As brood as is a bokeler or a targe" as well as "on hir feet a paire of spores sharpe" (the latter he includes explicitly in his Chaucer painting); her implicit knight-errantry ("she konde muchel of wandrynge by the weye") is thus coupled neatly with "Of remedies of love she knew per chaunce, / For she konde of that art the olde daunce." The Wife herself confirms her Britomartian character in her long prologue to her tale: "For certes, I am al Venerien / In feelynge, and myn herte is Marcien."

27. In *Portraits of Queene Elizabeth I* (Oxford: Clarendon Press, 1963), Roy C. Strong describes the imagery as "that of the Virgin Mary as the Woman of the Apocalypse" (p. 154). The engraving exists in four states and there is a copy of it, by Gerrit Mountin, in a 1629 edition of Camden's *Annales*. Erdman's description of the design in *The Illuminated Blake* (see chap. 3, n. 43), p. 332, is also most apt, even without reference to Elizabeth.

28. *The French Revolution*, lines 222–23 (E296). The warmonger Duke of Burgundy is "Cloth'd in flames of crimson" (l. 86, E290). See also lines 188–89 (E294).

29. She is also, appropriately, Belphoebe, as Spenser himself suggests by way of her "Camis light," buskins, and other details employed upon Belphoebe's first appearance (II,iii,26–30)—not the least of which is Spenser's curious mention of the "ham" of both. In turn, it is clear from the following details that Blake had Belphoebe's description in mind when creating his Britomart: "Knit with a golden bauldricke, which forelay / Athwart her snowy brest, and did diuide / Her daintie paps; which like young fruit in May / Now little gan swell, and being tide, / Through her thin weed their places only signifide" (st. 29); "Her yellow lockes crisped, like golden wyre,

/ About her shoulders weren loosely shed'' and "low behind her backe were scattered'' (st. 30). Although more often than not Radigund is associated by Spenser scholars with Mary, Queen of Scots, since Kate M. Warren's 1897–1900 edition of *The Faerie Queene* (see chap. 5, n. 28), she has also been identified, as Warren puts it, with "Queen Elizabeth herself, in some of her many moods'' (*Spenser Variorum*, 5, p. 202).

30. Radigund also breaks his sword (v,21) despite its being Merlin-forged. Are we to imagine Artegall-Arthur's sword, seemingly on the far side of his horse, to be actually on the near side (as the "real" Arthur's is to the right of Talus) with no blade or point visible?

31. There has been continual dispute on this point in Blake studies, usually (but not exclusively) revolving around Blake's employment of Mary Wollstonecraft's *Vindication of the Rights of Women* in *Visions of the Daughters of Albion*. The latest salvo in the critical war includes virtually the entire issue of *Blake: An Illustrated Quarterly* 16 (1982–83), most notably the essays by Anne K. Mellor, Alicia Ostriker, and Michael Ackland. See also Susan Fox, "The Female as Metaphor in William Blake's Poetry" (see chap. 5, n. 24).

32. John Jortin, *Remarks on Spenser's Poems* (London, 1734), quoted in *Spenser Variorum*, 5, p. 204.

33. This hypocrisy is underscored by a brilliant graphic self-allusion to Blake's illustration of Milton's Archangel Michael conducting Adam and Eve out of Eden (plate 9 of the Boston Museum of Fine Arts version), where Michael's physiognomy, even to the eyes, is identical to Arthur's. Milton's description of Michael appropriately refers to Artegall-Arthur as well:

> th' Archangel soon drew nigh,
> Not in his shape celestial, but as a man
> Clad to meet man; over his lucid arms
> A military vest of purple flowed,
> Livelier than Meliboean. . . .
> . . . .
> His starry helm unbuckled showed him prime
> In manhood where youth ended; by his side
> As in a glistering zodiac hung the sword,
> Satan's dire dread.
>
> (*Paradise Lost*, XI,238–48)

Michael's sword is Artegall's Chrysaor:

> For of most perfect metall it was made,
> Tempred with Adamant amongst the same,
> . . . .
> . . . there no substance was so firme and hard,
> But it would pierce or cleaue, where so it came;
> Ne any armour could his dint out ward,
> But wheresoeuer it did light, it throughly shard.
>
> (V,i,10)

Milton's condensed version of this is: "the sword / Of Michael from the armory of God / Was giv'n him tempered so, that neither keen / Nor solid might resist that edge: it met / The sword of Satan with steep force to smite / Descending, and in half cut sheer" (VI,320–25). The fact that Artegall-Arthur's sword is Jove's, transmitted to the knight by Astraea, is no more propitious in Blake's eyes than Michael's physical arming from the armory of God. The similar arming of Redcrosse and Spenser's sanctioning of that armor by reference to the famous Ephesians passage, both of which I discussed earlier, may well argue for Blake's extension of Redcrosse's alter-avatars to Michael as well.

34. Although I earlier suggested other reasons for Blake's omission of Book IV in his pageant, Artegall's presence in that spot may be Blake's acerbic comment on the nature of Spenser's friendship, perhaps best exemplified by the necessity of Cambina's using her magic rod and cup of Nepenthe to terminate the ferocious battles of Cambell with Priamond, Diamond, and Triamond (IV,iii,48). That Blake would have interpreted Nepenthe as an opiate seems to me beyond question—or, more precisely, as the cup of poisonous religion with which he steadily equips Vala, the Whore of Babylon. He may have associated Cambina as well with Milton's Comus and his cup and wand; and he certainly saw her as an alter ego of canto x's Concord, about whom I have already written as one of Spenser's principal errors in *The Faerie Queene*—the elevation of *discordia concors* to the level of cardinal virtue. See note 1, chapter 7, above and its reference to DeNeef's provocative argument, that Ate and Sclaunder dominate—even triumph in—Book IV, not concord or friendship. Whether or not he read Book IV that way, however, Blake would have been appalled that the wedding climaxing the book is achieved under the auspices of Proteus-Archimago. On Proteus, see A. Bartlett Giamatti, *Play of Double Senses* (see chap. 4, n. 12).

35. *Milton* 29[31]:48–49, E128. Blake found an interesting translation of these in Bacon's "Of Sedition and Troubles," where "the four pillars of government" are "religion, justice, counsel, and treasure." Blake's wry marginal comment is: "Four Pillars of different heights and Sizes"—suggesting clearly that Baconian government is propped with almost comic precariousness; but then, as he says in an earlier notation, "It was a Common opinion in the Court of Queen Elizabeth that Knavery Is Wisdom" (E624, 620).

36. *Jerusalem* 45[31]:32, E194. In light of Arthur's frequent identification with grace, another passage in *Jerusalem* is at least provocatively fortuitous: "Vengeance is the destroyer of Grace & Repentance in the bosom / Of the injurer: in which the Divine Lamb is cruelly slain" (25:10–11, E170). One of Blake's inscriptions on the unfinished Dante illustrations reads: "Whatever Book is for Vengeance for Sin & whatever Book is Against the Forgiveness of Sins is not of the Father but of Satan the Accuser & Father of Hell" (E690).

37. V,ii,26. Is this the suppliant damsel ignored by the knight under the shadows of a castle wall in the pencil sketch Blake drew in his *Notebook*, and of which I have already spoken in chapter 1? See Erdman, *The Notebook of William Blake* (see chap. 1, n. 23), pp. N18, 77.

38. In light of Talus's career in *The Faerie Queene*, and of Blake's carefully

particularized portrait of him, one wonders, at least, whether a passage in *The Four Zoas*, Night the Sixth, was inspired by Talus or, more likely, whether Blake's epitomizing of his career in the Spenser painting was in part inspired by *The Four Zoas* passage:

> A spectre Vast appeard whose feet & legs with iron scaled
> . . . .
> In his hand a knotted Club whose knots like mountains frownd
> Desart among the Stars them withering with its ridges cold
> Black scales of iron arm the dread visage iron spikes instead
> Of hair shoot from his orbed scull. his glowing eyes
> Burn like two furnaces.

(E352)

I have already commented upon Blake's association of Talus with Urizen and his books of iron and brass (see p. 179), but it is still worth noting here that, in *The Four Zoas*, Blake equips Urizen with a flail (IX,E402)—although there, to be sure, it is the flail used in the final apocalyptic harvest. Notwithstanding his ignoring of Urizen's flail (which should at least seem odd to us since he is the eternal plowman-zoa), see E. J. Rose's discussion of harvests in Blake, "'Forms Eternal Exist For-ever'" (see chap. 1, n. 28), pp. 443–62. See also Brian Wilkie and Mary Lynn Johnson's commentary on Night the Ninth of *The Four Zoas* in *Blake's "Four Zoas"* (see chap. 2, n. 55), pp. 207–37.

39. Since Blake, in *A Vision of the Last Judgment*, indicates his familiarity with Apuleius as well as Ovid (E556), it is at least possible that he remembered what Charles Osgood (*Spenser Variorum*, 5, p. 216) claims as Spenser's source—the story of Lucius the Ass, who is restored to human form and becomes a priest of Isis and Osiris. Is that Lucius-as-ass that Una is riding neck-in-neck with the lion? For what it is worth, Upton, in his edition of *The Faerie Queene*, states that Spenser erred in not making the Isis priests bald (*Spenser Variorum*, 5, p. 217). The Palmer? Cf. Ezekiel 44:17, 20, to which Upton refers.

40. See, for example, *The Four Zoas* VIII (E377 and E378); *Milton* 37[41]: 40, 41[48]: 25–27 (E138, 142–43); *Jerusalem* 68:14–15, 49–50 (E221, 222), 74:14–15 (E231). For Blake's redemptive ark images, which in a sense redeem Cynthia from her "infection from the silly Greek & Latin slaves of the Sword" (*Milton* 1: prose preface, E95), see Nicholas Warner, "Blake's Moon-Ark Symbolism" (see chap. 5, n. 30), pp. 44–59. Warner, however, finds Blake's "negative adaptation" of Jacob Bryant's Ark of Osiris in a *Jerusalem* passage "curious," since Bryant associates it with resurrection. Because Blake read Bryant's *Analysis of Antient Mythology*, even contributing a tailpiece (moon-ark, dove, and rainbow) to the third volume of the 1807 edition, one wonders whether Blake "read into" the Isis Church episode of *The Faerie Queene* this fortuitous connection.

41. E560. See also Blake's second draft of the prospectus for his Chaucer fresco, in which he specifies that "every Character & every Expression, every Lineament of Head Hand & Foot. every particular of Dress or Costume.

where every horse is appropriate to his Rider''—all ''is minutely labour'd . . . even to the Stuffs & Embroidery of the Garments. the hair upon the Horses'' (E568).

42. I quote Hamilton, who is typical on this point, in *The Structure of Allegory in ''The Faerie Queene, ''* pp. 192, 191. He also claims that Arthur's ''defining virtue above all [the others in Books I–V] is his Courtesy'' (p. 191).

VIII. SPENSER'S SPENSER AND BLAKE'S SPENSER

1. C. S. Lewis, *The Allegory of Love* (see chap. 2, n. 13), pp. 336–37.

2. Northrop Frye, ''The Road of Excess,'' in Frye, *The Stubborn Structure* (see chap. 3, n. 1), p. 163; orig. pub. in Bernice Slote, ed., *Myth and Symbol* (see chap. 3, n. 1).

3. Martin Price, *To the Palace of Wisdom* (see chap. 3, n. 1), pp. 433–34.

4. A. Kent Hieatt, *Chaucer, Spenser, Milton* (see chap. 4, n. 14), p. 149. Ever since Coleridge's famous characterization of the ''locale'' of *The Faerie Queene* as ''mental space,'' the point, however it is phrased or translated, has become a commonplace in Spenser criticism. Donald R. Howard interestingly applies it to Chaucer as well, in ''Flying through Space: Chaucer and Milton,'' in *Milton and the Line of Vision*, ed. Joseph A. Wittreich, Jr. (see chap. 1, n. 9), pp. 3–23 (see especially p. 15). The general acceptance of the idea has become the springboard for denying the possibility of illustrating or even diagraming *The Faerie Queene* satisfactorily; see, for example, Graham Hough, *A Preface to The Faerie Queene* (see chap. 2, n. 30), pp. 93–94; Rosemond Tuve, *Allegorical Imagery* (see chap. 5, n. 5), p. 327; and Michael Murrin, *The Veil of Allegory* (see chap. 4, n. 24), p. 56. In light of Kiralis's and Grant and Brown's reliance on various symmetries in their analyses of, respectively, Blake's Chaucer and Spenser paintings, one needs Robert E. Simmons's reminder, in ''*Urizen*: The Symmetry of Fear'' (see chap. 6, n. 8), that symmetry is ''the generalizing and abstracting habit of reducing the world to similars and opposites, ups and downs, lefts and rights, rights and wrongs'' (p. 165).

5. Kathleen Williams, *Spenser's World of Glass* (see chap. 2, n. 10). Subsequent references will be parenthetical by page number preceded by W.

6. See, for example, Leslie Brisman's *Milton's Poetry of Choice and Its Romantic Heirs* (Ithaca, N.Y.: Cornell University Press, 1973).

7. Williams, *Spenser's World of Glass*, p. 32.

8. M. A. N. Radzinowicz, ''Eve and Dalila: Renovation and Hardening of the Heart,'' in *Reason and the Imagination*, ed. J. A. Mazzeo (New York: Columbia University Press, 1962), p. 163, cited in Williams, *Spenser's World of Glass*, p. 41n.

9. *On Homer's Poetry*, E269. And ''Folly,'' we should remember from the Proverbs of Hell, ''is the cloke of knavery'' (E36).

10. Ernst Cassirer, *Essay on Man* (New Haven, Conn.: Yale University Press, 1944), p. 222; Williams, *Spenser's World of Glass*, p. 77.

11. A. C. Hamilton, *The Structure of Allegory in "The Faerie Queene"* (see chap. 6, n. 25), p. 129. The hermaphroditism of Britomartegall (or Britomarthur) and Blake's pictorializing of it-her-him as another Wife of Bath should remind us that in the Wife of Bath's prologue she describes herself as "al Venerien / In feelynge, and myn herte is Marcien" (ll. 609–10). Furthermore, her tale, though not of loves and wars, is a parodic Arthurian chivalric legend in which the errant (in both senses of the word) knight ends up by putting himself in the "wise governance" of the old hag who thereby, as in the Radigund-Artegall story, gets of him "maistrie" and "may chese and governe as [she] lest" (ll. 1231–37). When she lifts her Una-like veil-"curtyn," she reveals herself to be Una to the knight's Redcrosse (ll. 1249–54). We should also remember that the knight discovers the old hag on his quest only after, Calidore-like, causing the dancing "ladyes foure and twenty" to vanish upon his appearance, leaving not Pastorella, but the hag (ll. 989–99). Blake would have loved every minute of the Wife's performance.

12. John Upton may have jogged Blake's verbal memory (should it have needed jogging), for he makes an extended comment on the word *perturbation*, citing Cicero as Spenser's source (*Spenser Variorum*, 2, pp. 233–34).

13. On Spenser's criticism of Petrarchism see, for example, Thomas P. Roche, Jr., *The Kindly Flame* (see chap. 2, n. 37), pp. 72–99; Paul Alpers, *The Poetry of The Faerie Queene* (see chap. 2, n. 31), pp. 16–18, 400ff; Mark Rose, *Heroic Love* (Cambridge, Mass.: Harvard University Press, 1968), pp. 121–28; and Isabel MacCaffrey, *Spenser's Allegory* (see chap. 4, n. 46), pp. 111–16.

14. See my analyses of those poems in *Blake's Prelude* (see chap. 1, n. 3), chap. 5.

15. Angus Fletcher, *Allegory: The Theory of a Symbolic Mode* (see chap. 4, p. 13), p. 306.

16. Newman Ivey White, "Shelley's *Prometheus Unbound*" (see chap. 4, n. 35).

17. Williams, *Spenser's World of Glass*, p. 152. Such a view of *The Faerie Queene*'s structure and movement is not unique in Spenser studies. What is unusual is James Nohrnberg's assertion (almost as if with Blake's painting in mind) that "Spenser orders his poem in parallel strata, and presents it 'horizontally' in agreement with the picture plane"—*The Analogy of "The Faerie Queene"* (see chap. 2, n. 35), p. 76. More "Blakean" is Hieatt's view, in *Chaucer, Spenser, Milton*, that in Spenser's "visionary landscape" the "denizens are positionally or typographically, rather than individually, defined, and that their significance as characters is necessarily liable to sudden slippage." But even he regards "processional, successive, hierarchical" arrangements as crucial to our "reading" of such landscapes (p. 218). Cf. Angus Fletcher's comments on "allegorical painting and the emblematic poetry that takes after it" in *Allegory: The Theory of a Symbolic Mode*, p. 87. One paradigmatic procedure for "reading" that I like, though it appears in a quite unrelated context, is Ira Clark's characterization of the poetry of Edward Taylor, in *Christ Revealed: The History of the Neotypological Lyric in the English Renaissance* (Gainesville: University Presses of Florida, 1982): Taylor "faith-

fully left it to Christ to weave out of fallen, tattered repetitions of image, word, pun, broken syntax, and sounds the whole brilliant white raiment which covers poets and poems incapable of expressing transcendence'' (p. 184). If we changed his "Christ" to "Imagination," there are much worse ways to describe reading-viewing Blake as poet or graphic artist.

18. The quotations from Blake in this paragraph are from *A Vision of the Last Judgment* (E554, 565) and his letter to Thomas Butts of 6 July 1803 (E730).

19. In this regard it is interesting that Harry Berger, in *The Allegorical Temper* (see chap. 2, n. 31), suggests as the "burden" of his study that "such purposes and by-accidents comprise the bulk of " *The Faerie Queene* (p. 161); accordingly, he distinguishes between "allegory as a general 'habit of thought' " and "Spenser's allegorical practice as embodied in this poem" (p. 177).

20. Harold Bloom, "The Visionary Cinema of Romantic Poetry," in *William Blake: Essays for S. Foster Damon*, ed. Alvin H. Rosenfeld (see chap. 4, n. 84), pp. 27, 22.

21. *Marriage of Heaven and Hell*, E35.

22. Although I did not mention it in my discussion of the supernal realms of Blake's painting, it should be noted that the St. Paul's dome is precisely that of Blake's drawing, *Theotormon Woven* (Theotormon, we recall, is the self-repressed, self-righteous, self-pitying theocratic and paralyzed "lover" of Oothoon in *Visions of the Daughters of Albion*). The drawing is plate 2 of *Blake's Sublime Allegory*, ed. Stuart Curran and Joseph A. Wittreich, Jr. (see chap. 1, n. 9). On the whole idea of weaving in Blake, see Morton D. Paley's essay in this volume, "The Figure of the Garment in *The Four Zoas*, *Milton*, and *Jerusalem*," pp. 119–39, and Nelson Hilton, *Literal Imagination: Blake's Vision of Words* (see chap. 4, n. 9), chap. 6.

23. Bloom, "The Visionary Cinema of Romantic Poetry," pp. 18, 24.

24. Letter to William Hayley, 23 October 1804, E756. See also Erdman's discussion of the compositional dates of both *Milton* and *Jerusalem*, E806–7, 808–9. Blake, incidentally, identifies the fiend as "the Jupiter of the Greeks, an iron-hearted tyrant" (E756), obviously Spenser's fiend as well, according to Blake's painting.

25. Jane Aptekar, *Icons of Justice* (New York: Columbia University Press, 1969), p. 124. I suspect her reading of Artegall, Talus, et al. is not an adequate response to Spenser's achievement in the book, but, as I have indicated in my analysis of Blake's painting, Blake clearly read Book V as she does.

26. *Milton* 22[24]:50, E117. His error, says Blake, was his "Shewing the Transgressors in Hell, the proud Warriors in Heaven: / Heaven as a Punisher & Hell as One under Punishment: / With Laws from Plato & his Greeks to renew the Trojan Gods, / In Albion" (22[24]:51–54, E118). It was Spenser's "problem" as well.

27. Wittreich, *Angel of Apocalypse* (see chap. 1, n. 9), pp. 95–96; Kester Svendsen's interpretation is in "John Martin and the Expulsion Scene of *Paradise Lost*," *Studies in English Literature* 1 (1961): 70; Merritt Hughes's in "Some Illustrators of Milton: The Expulsion from Paradise," in *Milton Stud-*

ies in Honor of Harris Francis Fletcher, ed. G. Blakemore Evans et al. (Urbana: University of Illinois Press, 1961), pp. 65–66. The most recent interpretation of the design, essentially an expansion on and development of Wittreich's analysis, is that of Stephen C. Behrendt, *The Moment of Explosion: Blake and the Illustration of Milton* (Lincoln: University of Nebraska Press, 1983), pp. 174–77. With respect to Michael's traditional typological signification as Christlike warrior, and thus Blake's aligning him imaginatively with Redcrosse, it is especially noteworthy that, in this culminating design of the *Paradise Lost* series, Michael is swordless and (perhaps more important), in the later Boston Museum version, seems to plant his heel firmly on the serpent rather than, as in the Huntington Library version, stepping over it. Corroboratively, while Adam and Eve look upward and backward—gesturing a forlorn farewell to the lost paradise—in the Huntington copy, the later version presents them looking down at the serpent under Michael's heel with a mixture of astonishment and awe. The Michael who leads them thus becomes the internalized Christian-warrior-become-the-Imagination that is, to Blake, the agency of their self-redemption.

28. Wittreich, *Angel of Apocalypse*, pp. 87, 97. Wittreich actually writes that the movement in the illustration is "downward and inward." He should have said "imaginatively upward and inward" even as the "literal" design moves outward (to the spectator) and down (Adam and Eve's bent heads). To Blake, "travellers from Eternity. pass outward to Satans seat, / But travellers to Eternity. pass inward to Golgonooza" (*Milton* 17[19]:29–30, E111; Golgonooza is Los's City of Art). And "what is Above is Within" (*Jerusalem* 71:6, E225).

29. In line with my interpretation of Michael-as-Arthur-as-Michael, I might mention here my idea that Blake's Spenser painting as a whole recapitulates in a way Michael's entire vision, for Adam's benefit, of "what shall come in future days / To thee and to thy offspring" (*Paradise Lost*, XI,357–58); from Intemperance and brutish vice (ll. 472ff), to Mammon's Cave (ll. 564ff), to the wanton women and their amorous nets (ll. 580ff), to the "cruel tournaments" of war (ll. 638ff) and human glory (ll. 694ff), to "Justice and temperance, truth and faith forgot" before the Flood (ll. 711ff), to Babel (XII,24ff), to royal tyranny (ll. 63ff), and so on through Book XII, leading to the "return / Of him so lately promised to thy aid, / The Woman's Seed," the "dissolving" of "Satan with his perverted world" (ll. 541–47), and the *Paradise Regained* inherent in Blake's "reading" of the Expulsion. I leave it to others to do what they will with what I offer only as a nice idea.

30. The quoted phrases are Hough's, in *A Preface to The Faerie Queene*, p. 94.

31. The quotations, except for the last (which is from *The Marriage of Heaven and Hell*, E36), are from *Jerusalem* 99, E258.

32. Wittreich, *Visionary Poetics* (see chap. 1, n. 9), pp. 39, 65. As Wittreich makes clear in his book's dedication and preface, his greatest debt on these points is to Williams's *Spenser's World of Glass*, although she is not the only one to hold this view.

33. Josephine Waters Bennett, *The Evolution of "The Faerie Queene"* (see

chap. 4, n. 5). See also John E. Hankins, *Source and Meaning in Spenser's Allegory* (see chap. 4, n. 18).

34. A number of Spenser scholars make this point, but see especially Patricia A. Parker, *Inescapable Romance* (see chap. 4, n. 17).

35. Arthur O. Lovejoy, *Documentary History of Primitivism* (Baltimore: Johns Hopkins Press, 1935).

36. E. K. Chambers, *English Pastorals* (London: Blackie and Sons, 1895), p. xix; and Kathleen Williams, "Milton, Greatest Spenserian" in Wittreich, *Milton and the Line of Vision* (see chap. 4, n. 5). She includes Milton's radicalizing of traditional epic in her argument.

37. This is obviously not the place to develop this idea, unsuggested by any of the four major commentators on the Chaucer painting. Of the four, Betsy Bowden's, as I have suggested before, is the most provocative and "correct," though even she is unwilling to go so far as I. Nevertheless, Blake's patterning (or at least paralleling) of his prose commentary on his painting in *A Descriptive Catalogue* on Dryden's in *Fables Ancient and Modern*, and his attribution to Chaucer's *Canterbury Tales* of the commission of the errors of Dryden's perception suggest strongly that Chaucer's fundamental errors were similar to Spenser's. Therefore, as horrendous as they were, they were subject to redemption via Blake's provision of a context within which Chaucer could discover that he was of that devil's party after all, even if he did not know it when executing his pilgrimage. Bowden will only go so far as to say that Blake's language in parts of his commentary suggests that he "seems not to care about Chaucer's exact sense so much as about making the words tell his own Blakean meaning" ("The Artistic and Interpretive Context of Blake's *Canterbury Pilgrims*"—see chap. 4, n. 48). It would have been better had she said "making the picture tell his own Blakean meaning," but neither is quite enough. I hope someone will do more.

APPENDIX D. SPENSER'S IRELAND AND BLAKE'S ERIN

1. S. Foster Damon, *A Blake Dictionary* (see chap. 1, n. 1), p. 128.

2. *Jerusalem* 11:12, E154; 12:23, E155. Perhaps Blake thus intends them to encompass the fallen Urizen (for "the North is Breadth") and the fallen Urthona, his opposite number (for "the South is Heighth & Depth"), as well as the fallen Tharmas's west (which "is Outwards every way") and Erin's native east, where the fallen Luvah resides (which "is Inwards")—*Jerusalem* 14:29–30, E158.

3. *Faerie Queene* I,xii,26. Tiriel, we should recall, in Blake's poem of that title, is "king of the west"; with his "Queene of all the western plains," Myratana, he is deposed and expelled by his serpent sons (E278, 276–77). Blake's poem is a travesty of the biblical and Miltonic Eden story, in which Tiriel plays the role of Satan-God, Har and Heva become Adam and Eve, the latter foursome vegetating, in their "Fall," into imbecilic infants desperately clinging to the memory (Mnetha) of their pastoral innocence. But *Tiriel*

may also be at least a distant reminiscence of Book I of *The Faerie Queene*, the "right" ending of which would be Una's father "outstretchd . . . in awful death" (her mother, Myratana, already dead) in the fallen paradise of Har and Heva, led there by his daughter Hela-Una (E285). One hesitates to push such an interpretation too hard, but it is worth remembering that the titular character of Blake's *A Little Girl Lost* (written, to be sure, after *Tiriel*) is named Ona, who "In the Age of Gold" lived "in garden bright" and whose father condemns her love for a youth as "a crime" (E29). In the related manuscript draft of *Infant Sorrow* (E799), he, with "holy book" in hand, "Pronouncd curses on [her] head / And bound [her] in a mirtle shade" (lawful marriage). Several Blake scholars have suggested that Blake's Ona is his "version" of Una (both, we note, are "one"), the most compelling evidence for this, aside from what I have suggested, being the career of Lyca in the almost identically titled *The Little Girl Lost* and *The Little Girl Found* (E20–22), poems that include a lion who acts tantalizingly like Una's. Blake even gives the lion an Elizabethan crown, and he may be quoting Spenser (II,i,41) in the last line of *A Little Girl Lost* ("That shakes the blossoms of my hoary hair"), with its odd word, *blossoms* (E30).

4. *The Four Zoas* I, E304 and 824; *Milton* 30[33]:5, E129; *Jerusalem* 48:24, E197. On Blake's Ona, see note 3. I cannot imagine that Ona's momentary presence here (changed by Blake to an even clearer anagrammatic "one") is unrelated to the little-girl-lost poems and to Spenser's Una.

5. Morris Eaves, "A Reading of Blake's *Marriage of Heaven and Hell*, Plates 17–20: On and Under the Estate of the West," *Blake Studies* 4 (1972): 111.

6. Ibid., p. 113. It is at least interesting that, in his sonnet prefatory to Lewes Lewkenor's *The Commonwealth and Government of Venice* (1599), Spenser describes the "antique *Babel*" as "Empresse of the West" but the "second Babell" as "tyrant of the West." It is a fugitive poem that Blake could easily have seen since it was first published in Thomas Warton's *Observations on the Fairy Queen*, 2d ed. (London, 1762), 2, 246–47.

7. Leopold Damrosch makes a similar point in *Symbol and Truth in Blake's Myth* (Princeton: Princeton University Press, 1980), pp. 114 and passim.

8. Isabel MacCaffrey, *Spenser's Allegory* (see chap. 4, n. 46), pp. 431–32.

Index

Adam: in Bible, 127–29, 148, 151, 153,
155, 157, 218, 293; in Blake's *Paradise
Lost* illustrations, 279; elsewhere in
Blake, 85, 122, 135, 152, 154, 191, 214;
Milton's, 36–37, 48, 76, 80–81, 125,
128, 268; in Spenser, 135, 266

Adams, Hazard, 88, 90, 93, 96–97, 118

Aikin, John, 23; edition of *Faerie Queene*
by, 24

Albion (character in Blake), 28, 48, 52,
56, 57, 58, 66, 70, 118, 130, 131, 152,
171, 180, 186–87, 219, 221, 249, 258,
260–61, 269–71, 323n.20; and Arthur,
223, 233, 249–50; and Jerusalem, 61,
147, 213–14, 248, 266, 275, 313–14

Allegory: Bacon on, 22; Blake on (including *Faerie Queene*'s), 3, 20, 39–40, 44,
51–52, 54, 56, 67, 69–70, 97–98, 101–4,
109–13, 118, 120, 124, 130–33, 135,
140–44, 148–49, 152–54, 156–57, 168,
175, 178, 198, 200–201, 210–11, 218–19,
221, 227–28, 264, 270–74, 276–78,
303–7, 350n.56; John Hughes on Spenser's, 20–21; nature of, 118–19,
124–25, 133, 150, 270, 281, 321n.10,
324n.22, 358n.46, 359nn. 51, 54; and
typology, 308–10

Alter, Robert, 355n.28

Amoret: in Blake's *Faerie Queene* painting,
163–65, 196, 245; and Blake's *Thel*,
41–43, 136; in *Faerie Queene*, 16, 33, 39,
135–37, 145, 147, 154, 223, 230,
241–42, 251, 259, 266, 269, 271, 280,
282

Amoretti, 3, 5, 6, 27, 36, 37, 39, 41, 62, 64,
65, 68, 168, 256, 287; as allegory,

335n.29; marriage in, 5, 43, 269;
Petrarchism in, 5–6, 28, 31, 33–35,
49–50, 53–54, 68, 78, 269, 334n.24

Aptekar, Jane, 278, 387n.25

Archimago: as allegorist, 140, 174–75,
227; in Blake's *Faerie Queene* painting,
143, 149, 166–67, 193, 197–98, 225–28,
231, 233, 264, 280, 378n.10; and
disguise, 125, 144; in *Faerie Queene*, 6,
23, 79, 137–40, 208, 210, 221, 238,
265, 268, 294; and Proteus, 138–39,
175, 359n.54

Ariosto, 175, 277

Aristotle, 80, 121–22, 150, 168, 232,
278, 353n.18; Blake on, 278

Artegall: in Blake's *Faerie Queene* painting,
165, 193–95, 196–97, 216, 224–25, 242,
244, 246–49, 250–60, 262, 279; as
Blake's Satan, 254; in *Faerie Queene*, 23,
64, 141–42, 145–48, 181, 190, 230,
241, 248, 251, 255–58, 261–62, 280,
282, 316; as Petrarchan lover, 256.
See also Justice; Talus

Arthur: and Blake's Albion, 223, 233,
250; in Blake's *Descriptive Catalogue*,
249; in Blake's *Faerie Queene* painting,
165–67, 187, 193, 195, 210, 216,
220–21, 224–25, 233, 249–60, 262, 263,
279–80; as Blake's Satan, 209, 234,
254; as childe, 208–10; in *Faerie Queene*,
16, 23, 26, 59, 107, 113, 133, 140, 142,
145, 147–48, 168, 181, 186, 211–12,
217–18, 221, 248, 252, 255, 257–58,
260–62, 263, 267–69, 272, 277–78,
280–82, 288, 295, 350n.59; in Gray's
The Bard, 16; in *Jerusalem*, 220–21, 250

Auerbach, Erich, 308-9
Ault, Donald D., 4

Babylon: in Bible, 248; in Blake's *Faerie Queene* painting, 164, 166, 177, 185-86, 188-89, 197, 227, 234, 254, 276; in Blake's poetry, 93, 211, 214, 221, 249, 252, 256, 278; Whore of: in Blake, 178, 205, 220, 298, 312; Blake's Wife of Bath as, 206; Britomart as, in Blake's *Faerie Queene* painting, 145, 244, 250; Faerie Queene as, 282
Bacon, Sir Francis, 158, 266; in Blake's works, 4, 250, 271, 353n.14; "Of Sedition and Troubles," 383n.35; *Wisdom of the Ancients*, 22, 329nn. 54, 55,
Barfield, Owen, 134
Beer, John, 2, 320n.5, 324n.22
Bennett, Josephine Waters, 281
Berger, Harry, 41, 141, 265, 335n.32, 345n.26, 350n.57, 387n.19
Berkeley, Bishop George, *Siris*, 19; Blake's annotations to, 140, 158
Bible, 1, 3, 6, 10, 20, 60, 66, 77, 85, 104, 111, 117, 120, 143, 150, 156, 158, 212, 256, 259, 314; Blake's illustrations to, 216, 283; sublimity in, 9, 156
—books of: 1 Chronicles, 116; 1 Corinthians, 22; Daniel, 59, 61, 88, 153; Ecclesiastes, 119, 151; Ephesians, 58-59, 187, 205, 208, 339n.56, Exodus, 4, 124, 373n.21; Ezekiel, 340n.60, 348n.50; Galatians, 362n.74; Genesis, 4, 70, 83, 121, 127-29, 131-32, 153, 157, 188-89, 218, 287, 292, 354n.20, 355n.28, 373n.19; Isaiah, 59, 61, 85, 101, 203-5, 217, 344n.24, 348n.50, 366n.14, 372n.13; Job, 126; John, 22, 129, 131, 133-34, 157, 358n.46; Joshua, 373n.21; 1 Kings, 346n.31; 2 Kings, 340n.60; Luke, 210; Mark, 220; Matthew, 103, 205, 373n.21; 2 Peter, 212; Proverbs, 119, 151; Psalms, 61, 338n.47; Revelation, 3, 59, 60, 61, 111, 117, 125, 129, 149, 156, 176, 183-84, 212, 216-17, 218-20, 237, 248, 279, 281, 283; 1 Samuel, 317, 338n.47; Song of Solomon, 69, 89, 93, 213; Zechariah, 205
Birch, Thomas, 24, 329-30n.57; *Faerie Queene* edition of, 23, 330n.57
Blake, William: allusion, technique of,

1-2, 28, 73, 77, 173, 194; Beulah, idea of, in, 43-44, 67, 70, 181-83, 185-86, 188-89, 197, 233, 255, 282, 313-14, 317, 323n.20; energy, idea of, in, 78-79, 82-83, 237-38; Female Will, idea of, in, 28-29, 35, 44, 47-48, 145, 178, 252, 255-56, 292; Genius, idea of, in, 13, 78-79, 116, 215, 223; identity, idea of, in, 7-8, 123, 153, 223; on pilgrimages, 9, 131, 137, 168, 185, 220, 303-7, 325n.28, 358-59n.51; sexual warfare in works of, 28, 33, 35-36, 39, 47, 55, 64-65, 68-69, 90, 118, 266-67; Ulro, idea of, in, 47-48, 67, 121, 182, 234, 255, 282, 314, 317; vision, idea of, in, 3-5, 51, 99, 120, 124, 131, 139-40, 150, 152, 156, 169-70, 201, 264, 273, 305. *See also under* Allegory; Chastity; Contraries; Disguise; Excess; Friendship; Generation; Hermaphroditism; Imagination; Innocence; Justice; Marriage; Nature; Pastoralism; Petrarchism; Prudence; Reason; Temperance; Time; Typology; War, Intellectual; Zodiac
—annotations by: *see under* Berkeley; Dante; Lavater; Reynolds; Swedenborg; Watson
—characters in (other than Adam; Albion; Arthur; Babylon, Whore of; Christ; Elizabeth I; Eve; Har; Heva; Jerusalem; Los; Oothoon; Orc; Rahab; Satan; Theotormon; Tirzah; Urizen; Vala, qq. v.): Ahania, 63, 65; Bladud, 220-21; Bromion, 45-46, 114, 121, 239-40; Enion, 21, 55, 138-40; Enitharmon, 44, 55, 62-63, 65, 92, 139, 147, 152, 339n.55; Erin, 48, 50, 311-18; Isis, 255; Leutha, 21; Luvah, 67-69, 219, 249, 267, 311-12, 314; Merlin, 220-21, 249; Molech, 180-90; Ololon, 182-83; Osiris, 255; Tharmas, 21, 55, 138-40, 219, 312; Urthona, 59, 60, 154, 218, 219, 223, 312, 323n.22
—graphic works of: *Heads of the Poets*, 10-13, 17, 123; illustrations to *Il Penseroso*, 171, 191-92, 369n.36; *Theotormon Woven*, 387n.22. *See also under* Bible; Bunyan, John; *Canterbury Tales, The*; *Comus*; Dante; *Faerie Queene, The Characters in Spenser's*; Ghisi, Adam; Gray, Thomas; Hervey, James; Hesiod,

Theogony; Paradise Lost; Paradise Re-gained; Young, Edward
—places in: Bath, 220–21; Canterbury, 220–21. *See also* Babylon; Jerusalem
—writings (other than *Descriptive Cata-logue; Europe; Four Zoas, The; Jerusalem; Marriage of Heaven and Hell, The; Milton; Notebook; Poetical Sketches; Songs of Inno-cence and of Experience; Thel, The Book of; Tiriel; Urizen, The Book of; Vision of the Last Judgment; Visions of the Daughters of Albion*, qq. v.): *All Religions Are One*, 9–10, 78–79, 104, 171, 259–60, 342n.9; *America*, 91–92, 114–15, 188–90, 202; *Auguries of Innocence*, 169, 177, 213, 280; *For Children: The Gates of Paradise*, 6, 10, 216; *The Crystal Cabinet*, 53–58, 63, 64, 231, 338n.52; *The Everlasting Gospel*, 169, 205, 206, 211; *The French Revolu-tion*, 131, 178, 246; *The Golden Net*, 47–53, 58, 64; *On Homer's Poetry*, 21, 278; *An Island in the Moon*, 57, 104, 150–51, 322n.16, 348n.51; *Laocoön*, 36, 178, 212; *The Mental Traveller*, 53, 63, 185, 293, 299; *Public Address*, 176, 322n.15; *Song of Los*, 51; *There is No Natural Religion*, 9, 83, 154, 185, 273, 301; *On Virgil*, 21, 278, 326n.36
Bloom, Harold, 71–72, 77–78, 82, 100, 274, 277, 308, 320n.8, 323n.20
Bloomfield, Morton, 133
Bogel, Fredric V., 363n.86
Bowden, Betsy, 134, 199–200, 216, 389n.37
Bradley, Laurel, 324n.24
Britomart: and Acrasia, 242, 244; in Blake's *Faerie Queene* painting, 12, 16, 137, 145, 165, 185, 189, 193, 195, 196–97, 216, 224–25, 238, 240–55, 258–60, 381nn. 25, 29; and Blake's Rahab, 244–45, 250; and Blake's Tirzah, 245; and Blake's Whore of Babylon, 250; and Blake's Wife of Bath, 242, 244; in *Faerie Queene*, 16, 23, 39, 42, 47, 64–65, 133, 136–37, 144–48, 154, 230, 237, 241, 244, 248, 251, 255–59, 267–69, 280, 282, 316–17; as Petrarchan mistress, 144, 244–45, 249. *See also* Chastity
Brown, Robert E. *See* Grant, John E.
Bunyan, John, 4, 120, 150, 158, 303–7; Blake's illustrations to, 283, 303–6;

Pilgrim's Progress, 3, 259, 273, 277, 303–6
Busirane, 33, 36, 39, 135–36, 154, 230, 242, 259, 271; as allegorist, 137; and Blake's *Book of Thel*, 41–42; House of, in Blake's *Faerie Queene* painting, 240–41. *See also* Cupid, Mask of
Byron, Lord, 86, 150, 158

Camden, William, *Annales*, frontispiece to, 245–47, 248, 250, 256, 381n.27
Camoëns, Luis de, 11
Canterbury Tales, The, 2, 123, 151, 201; Blake's painting of, 120, 151, 156, 158–68, 198–99, 215, 220, 224, 246, 274, 283, 384n.41; Stothard's painting of, 23–24, 159, 201, 259, 278, 371n.6
—characters in: Bailey, Harry, 161–65, 201, 224, 242, 274, 372n.16; Citizens, 161–62; Clerk, 159, 161, 243; Franklin, 161–62; Friar, 23, 160, 200, 237, 243, 379n.14; Knight, 134, 159–61, 163, 166, 201, 216, 233, 374n.26, 375n.27; Lawyer, 200, 243; Maniple, 160, 243, 379n.14; Merchant, 159–60; 162; Miller, 159–61; Monk, 23, 160, 200, 243, 379n.14; Nun's Priest, 160; Par-doner, 60–61, 163, 200, 237, 243, 364n.3, 379n.14, 381n.25; Parson, 161–62, 200, 237, 243, 253, 379–80n.15; Physician, 161, 200; Plowman, 161–62, 200, 243; Poet, 159–61, 216, 243; Prioress, 160–63, 165, 244, 381n.25; Squire, 159, 161–62, 201; Squire's Yoeman, 159, 162; Summoner, 200, 243, 364n.3, 379n.14, 381n.25; Tapiser, 243; Wife of Bath, 159–62, 165, 206, 214, 220–21, 242, 244, 246, 249, 381n.26, 386n.11
Cassirer, Ernst, 266
Chambers, E. K., 282
Chastity: Blake on, 50, 69, 95, 119, 180–81, 186, 205–6, 215, 239, 242, 253; in Milton, 80; in Spenser, 36, 80, 97, 137, 145, 184–85, 229, 244, 248, 253, 335n.30. *See also* Britomart
Chatterton, Thomas, 73–74, 323n.19
Chaucer, Geoffrey, 4, 20, 137, 155–56, 203, 244, 271, 307, 316; Blake's *Descrip-tive Catalogue* essay on, 26, 120–21, 123, 126, 130, 134, 140, 199–201, 237, 243,

Chaucer (*cont'd.*)
310, 389n.37; Blake's portrait of, 11,
233. *See also Canterbury Tales, The*
Child, F. J., 218
Christ: and Arthur, 26, 281; in Bible,
129, 133, 205; in Blake, 8–9, 37, 66,
69–70, 85, 122, 130, 139, 156, 170,
177, 187, 189, 200, 205–7, 213, 214,
218–19, 223, 255, 274–76, 277, 314,
376n.1; in Milton, 30, 48–49, 77,
125–26, 156, 237–38, 244, 250; in
Spenser, 29, 187, 205, 206, 211, 219,
232. *See also* Dwarf, in Blake's *Faerie
Queene* painting; Imagination, in Blake
Church, Ralph, 24; *Faerie Queene* edition
of, 23
Cicero, 11, 145, 277
Clark, Ira, 356n.17
Coleman, Patrick, 354n.23
Coleridge, Samuel Taylor, 99, 126, 135,
150, 156, 159, 304, 306, 348n.45
Colie, Rosalie, 41, 119–20, 149
Comus, 42, 80, 83, 280, 360n.56; Blake's
illustrations to, 336n.35; and Blake's
''I Saw a Chapel All of Gold,'' 94–97;
and *Faerie Queene*, 237–38
Contraries: Blake's idea of, 71–72, 77, 82,
84, 87, 103–4, 110, 123–24, 153, 186,
234, 252, 268; in Milton, 84; in Spen-
ser, 84, 118, 136, 234, 242, 266. *See also*
Marriage
Cooke, Thomas, translation of Hesiod's
Theogony, 21–22, 328n.52
Courtly Love. *See* Petrarchism
Cowper, William, 11, 360n.61
Cromek, Robert H., 259, 279, 371n.6
Cupid, 49, 73, 138, 174, 193, 269; Mask
of, 33, 42–43, 135–36, 240. *See also*
Amoret; Busirane
Curran, Stuart, 308, 310
Curtis, F. B., 4
Cynthia, 11, 245; in Blake's *Faerie Queene*
painting, 169, 177, 181–86, 188–89,
195, 196, 233, 274, 313; in *Faerie Queene*,
23, 251, 257, 280, 314–17; Raleigh's,
248

Damon, S. Foster, 1, 2, 3, 4–5, 94, 97,
158, 162–66, 177–78, 182–83, 188–89,
194–95, 197, 220, 240, 242, 250, 252,
303, 311, 346n.34

Daniel, Samuel, 31; *Delia*, 34, 49, 53;
eighteenth-century editions of, 333n.12
Dante, 19, 150, 158, 269, 315; Blake's
annotations to 150, 362n.81; in Blake's
Heads of the Poets, 11; Blake's illustra-
tions to, 19, 283, 362n.81, 383n.36
Davis, B. E. C., 368n.26
Deen, Leonard, 202, 365n.7, 372n.8
DeLuca, Vincent, 129–30, 147, 361n.66
Demosthenes, 11
DeNeef, A. Leigh, 142–43, 173–75, 263,
265, 271
Descriptive Catalogue, 362n.76; Arthur in,
249; attack on Stothard in, 24, 259,
278; Chaucer essay in, *see under* Chau-
cer; fairies in, 200–201; Preface to,
363n.82; comments on Swedenborg in,
108
DeSelincourt, Ernest, 19
Despaire, Cave of: and Blake's *Book of
Thel*, 288–95; in Blake's *Faerie Queene*
painting, 374n.24; in Blake's Gray
illustrations, 16–17; in *Faerie Queene*,
211, 288–95; paintings of, 327n.45
Diana, 178, 238; in Blake, 191; in *Faerie
Queene*, 23, 145, 205, 280, 314, 316–17
Disguise: in allegory-prophecy, 124–25;
in Blake, 44, 125, 144, 149, 220–21; in
Milton, 125, 268; in *Faerie Queene*, 136,
138–41, 144–47, 149, 174–75, 355n.25
Doskow, Minna, 368n.30
Dragon: in Bible, 183–84, 219–20; in
Blake's *Faerie Queene* painting, 166–67,
184, 203, 207, 221, 228, 264; in Blake's
poetry, 56, 207, 244, 249; in *Faerie
Queene*, 6, 134, 184, 208, 219–20, 227
Drayton, Michael, 31, 34, 49, 53, 55;
eighteenth-century editions of, 333n.12
Dryden, John, 19; Blake on, 4, 78, 134;
in Blake's *Heads of the Poets*, 11; *Fables
Ancient and Modern*, 389n.37
Duessa: as allegorist, 140–41, 227–28; in
Blake's *Faerie Queene* painting, 143, 149,
166–67, 193, 197–98, 225–28, 231, 233,
258, 264, 280, 378n.10; and disguise,
144; in *Faerie Queene*, 6, 79, 134, 137,
145, 149, 156, 179, 211–12, 238,
257–58, 289–91, 293–94, 313
Dwarf: in Blake's *Faerie Queene* painting,
166–67, 184–85, 203–5, 207–8, 210,
213, 215–16, 218, 222–27, 233–34,
257, 264, 274–75, 280–83; in *Faerie*

Queene, 184, 203, 207-8, 233, 280; Stothard's painting of, 25

Eaves, Morris, 77, 100, 303, 314-15, 321n.12
Eichholz, Jeffrey, 24, 330n.59
Elizabeth I: in Blake's *Faerie Queene* painting, 181; in Blake's Gray illustrations, 15-16; in Blake's *Jerusalem*, 245-46; in Blake's Spenser portrait in *Heads of the Poets*, 11; frontispiece portrait of, in Camden's *Annales*, 245-47, 248, 250, 256; in Spenser, 65, 142, 147, 174, 180, 185-86, 193, 219, 245, 248-49, 252, 257, 270, 280, 314, 317. *See also Faerie Queene, The*, characters in, Gloriana
Ercilla y Zúñiga, Alonso de, 11
Erdman, David V., 6, 10, 98, 110-13, 171-72, 202-3, 299, 351n.67, 366n.14, 368n.31, 371n.7
Essick, Robert N., 100, 348n.48
Europe, 39, 82-83, 147, 188, 220, 337n.38, 371nn. 7, 8; fairy in, 201-3
Eve: in Bible, 128, 153, 293; in Blake's *Paradise Lost* illustrations, 279; in Blake's poetry, 191, 214; in *Paradise Lost*, 36, 76, 83, 268
Excess, idea of: in Blake, 71, 76-79, 81-83, 86, 94, 97, 113, 241, 344n.19, 345n.26; in Milton, 76, 80-81; in Spenser, 78-80, 86, 97, 106-8, 115, 118
Experience, Blake's state of. *See* Generation; Nature

Faerie Queene, The: and Blake's *Book of Thel*, 36-39, 41, 43, 287-98, 349n.54; and Blake's *Marriage of Heaven and Hell*, 85-87, 97-98, 105-10; Blake's *Notebook* quotation from, 6, 10, 19-20, 134, 150; and *Comus*, 237-38; DuGuernier's illustrations to, 19, 328n.49; eighteenth-century editions of, 18-26; Epistle to Harvey in, 155-56; Kent illustrations to, 23-25, 330-31nn. 57, 59, 60; and language, 119, 151, 154-55, 227-28; Letter to Raleigh in, 59, 119, 130, 133, 168, 199, 208, 260, 263, 272, 280-81; Mutabilitie Cantos in, 5, 7, 27, 133, 149, 168-69, 281-82, 313-18; and Revelation, 117, 281; Stothard's illustrations to, 23-25; Warton and Hurd

on, 12-13, 21; Zodiac in, 190-91. *See also under* Allegory; Disguise; Hermaphroditism; Innocence; Nature; Pastoralism; Petrarchism; Reason; Zodiac
—characters in (other than Amoret; Archimago; Artegall; Arthur; Britomart; Busirane; Cynthia; Dragon; Duessa; Dwarf; Guyon; Palmer; Radigund; Redcrosse; Ruddymane; Talus; Una; Venus, qq. v.): Acrasia, 10, 79-80, 86, 96, 107, 134, 239, 241-42, 244; Agdistes, 79; Alma, 80, 105, 107-10, 113, 115, 218, 232; Amavia, 6, 10; Argante, 147, 242; Astraea, 178-79, 193, 229; Bacchante, 147; Basciante, 147; Belge, 89, 258; Bellamoure, 148, 232, 261; Bladud, 221, 376n.38; Belphoebe, 16, 23, 41-42, 137, 145, 248, 251, 269, 280, 314, 381n.29; Blatant Beast, 93-94, 97, 137, 142, 148, 220, 227, 281-82; Bon Font, 142-43; Braggadocchio, 232, 251, 255; Briana, 261; Brigants, 44, 229-30, 232-33; Burbon, 258; Calepine, 262; Calidore, 93, 145, 148, 149, 232, 261-62, 313; Cambina, 383n.34; Celia, 61, 215, 296; Charissa, 297; Claribell, 148, 232, 261; Clarinda, 64; Colin Clout, 231-32; Coridon, 232, 239; Crudor, 261; Cymochles, 73, 80, 191; Egalitarian Giant, 255, 262; Elissa, 79, 80; Erroure, 207, 227, 289, 292, 294; Eumnestes, 104, 109, 112, 115; Excesse, 78-80, 86, 95-97; Faunus, 316-17; Fidelia, 212-13, 215-16; Fidessa, 140, 212, 265, 291, 313; Florimell, 16, 137, 145-47, 241-42, 251, 258-59, 280; Flourdelis, 258; Fradubio, 140; Fraelissa, 140; Furor, 79; Gardante, 147; Genius, 7, 41, 78-79, 86, 95; Geryoneo, 89, 258, 347n.38; Glauce, 144-45, 241; Gloriana, 16, 65, 113, 137, 142, 145, 168, 186, 197, 205, 209, 248-49, 251-52, 257, 263, 270, 280, 282, 314; Grantorto, 258; Grille, 80, 87, 96-97, 240; Hellenore, 148, 245; Ignaro, 288, 294-95; Iocante, 147; Isis, 145, 148, 255-57; Lucifera, 219, 291, 297; Malbecco, 232; Maleffort, 261; Maleger, 79, 107, 217-18, 232; Mammon, 17, 22, 73, 80, 98, 105-8, 112-15, 228-29, 238, 240, 241, 255,

Faerie Queene (cont'd.)
280; Medina, 80; Meliboe, 44, 198, 231-33, 260-61, 281, 313; Mercilla, 137, 141-42, 179-80, 257-58; Merlin, 145, 221, 230, 246, 248, 257-58, 316; Mirabella, 262; Mordant, 10, 79; Munera, 254-55; Noctante, 147; Occasion, 79; Orgoglio, 211, 288-89, 294-95; Osiris, 145, 148, 255-56; Paridell, 148; Parlante, 147; Pastorella, 148, 197-98, 231-32, 248, 282, 313-14; Perissa, 79, 80; Phaedria, 79, 191-93; Phantastes, 107, 109, 137, 350n.57; Philotime, 107; Pyrochles, 73, 79, 193, 267-68; Saluage Man, 261-62; Sansfoy, 289; Sansloy, 80, 138, 210, 212; Satyrane, 146-47, 258; Scudamore, 41-42, 136, 147, 223, 266, 269, 282; Sylvanus, 238; Telamond, 148; Terpine, 255; Terwin, 288-89, 291; Timias, 208, 269; Trevisan, 288-89, 292-93; Turpine, 262
—places in (other than Despaire, Cave of; Jerusalem; Mammon's Cave; Venus, qq. v.): Acidale, Mount, 231, 260, 281, 313; Adonis, Garden of, 7, 9, 62-63, 79, 84, 120-23, 320n.8, 325n.26; Arlo Hill, 313-14, 316-17; Bower of Bliss, 10, 39, 78, 86, 94-97, 107, 114, 238, 239, 242, 336n.33, 345n.26; Castle Ioyeous, 46, 146; Cleopolis, 61, 186; House of Holinesse, 61, 186-87, 207, 210, 215, 219, 295-97; House of Temperance, 33, 38, 105, 107-10, 115; Isis Church, 145-46, 255; Temple of Venus, 222
Faerie Queene, The Characters in Spenser's, 1, 3, 6, 12, 16, 22, 26, 27, 120, 123, 137, 143, 145, 149-51, 271, 274, 277, 279, 281, 283, 314; analyzed, 158-262; date of, 25
—characters in (other than Amoret; Archimago; Artegall; Arthur; Britomart; Cynthia; Dragon; Duessa; Dwarf; God of This World; Guyon; Mars; Palmer; Redcrosse; Ruddymane; Talus; Una, qq. v.): Astraea, 170-72, 176-82, 185-86, 188-89, 193, 195, 196, 225, 234, 254, 257; Belphoebe, 167, 181, 196, 238, 245, 370n.1; Blatant Beast, 143, 149, 165-67, 175, 197-98, 225-28, 231-33, 264, 280; Calidore, 12, 149, 165, 167, 193-95, 197, 205, 216, 224-28, 231, 233-34, 239, 254, 260-62, 280, 282; Grille, 240-44, 246, 252; poet-artist figure, 170-77, 180, 185, 197, 214, 224, 262; Scudamore, 167, 196; spread-winged presence, 170-72, 176, 180, 197, 211; Timias, 167, 196, 238, 370n.1; torsoless head, 167, 231, 232-33, 378n.11
—places in (other than Babylon; Despaire, Cave of; Jerusalem, qq. v.): Bower of Bliss, 240; House of Busirane, 240-41; House of Holinesse, 215

Ferber, Michael, 341n.62

Fish, Stanley, 304-5

Flaxman, John, 21, 227, 279

Fletcher, Angus, 133, 137, 147, 148, 270, 351n.5, 352n.13

Fletcher, Giles, 125

Fletcher, J. B., 205

Four Zoas, The, 6, 28, 47, 64, 121, 132, 138, 179, 188, 209, 211, 224, 234, 245, 248-49, 255, 266, 267, 269, 273, 275, 280, 314, 319n.1, 323n.22, 384n.38; apocalypse in, 60, 274-75; and *The Crystal Cabinet*, 55, 57; Enitharmon's "canticle" in, 62-63, 65, fairies in, 59; illustrations for, 67-68; and "I Saw a Chapel All of Gold," 92-93; and *Milton*, 68; Petrarchism in, 51, 58, 62-63, 67

Fraser, Russell, 148

Friendship: in Blake, 66, 70, 175, 222-23, 253, 258, 270, 279, 376n.1; in Spenser, 222, 253, 383n.34. *See also* War, Intellectual

Frye, Northrop, 21, 25-26, 28, 71-72, 77, 118, 263, 320n.8, 321n.10, 331n.64, 367nn. 22, 24

Fuseli, Henry, 143, 327n.45

Gainsborough, Thomas, 143

Gay, John, Kent's illustrations to poems of, 24

Generation: and allegory, 149, 152; Blake's idea of, 7-8, 44, 67, 69, 90, 100, 130, 188, 201, 233, 273, 280, 312. *See also Faerie Queene, The*, places in, Adonis, Garden of

George, Diana Hume, 148

Gezari, Janet, 43

Ghisi, Adam, Blake's drawing of Daniel after, 172-73

Giamatti, A. Bartlett, 138, 140, 352n.12, 353n.15

God of This World: in Blake's *Faerie Queene* painting, 170-71, 176-77, 185-86, 189, 193, 195, 196-97, 211, 214, 224, 233-34, 242, 245, 249, 254, 275-76, 317; in Blake's writings, 253, 278, 368n.26; in Milton, 23; Spenser's Mammon as, 22, 114. *See also* Jove; Urizen

Goslee, Nancy, 340n.60

Grant, John E., 191; with Robert E. Brown, essay on Blake's *Faerie Queene* painting, 3, 158, 164-67, 170-72, 174, 176, 181-82, 185, 188, 194-96, 198, 200, 215, 232, 234, 238, 242, 246, 250, 252, 369n.32, 370n.1

Gray, Thomas, 150, 326n.37, 327nn. 40, 43, 44; *The Bard*, 12-13, 15, 18, 113, 171, 366n.15; Blake's illustrations to *Poems* of, 10, 12-18, 22, 113, 171, 197, 203, 283, 366n.15, 370n.2; *The Descent of Odin*, 197; *The Fatal Sisters*, 197; *Ode on the Spring*, 13, 15, 18; *The Progress of Poesy*, 13, 326n.38, 366n.15

Greenberg, Mark, 112, 363nn. 86, 90

Guyon: and Blake's Bromion, 239-40; in Blake's *Faerie Queene* painting, 163, 165, 193, 195, 216, 225, 237-42; in Blake's Gray illustrations, 16; in *Faerie Queene*, 6, 39, 73, 78, 80, 85-87, 90, 93-97, 98, 105, 107-8, 112-15, 133, 145-46, 148, 187, 191, 228, 237-38, 240, 254-55, 280, 282, 350n.59. *See also* Temperance

Hagstrum, Jean, 28, 68, 321n.12, 324n.22

Hamilton, A. C., 147, 151, 154-55, 216, 265, 267-68

Har, 38, 43, 294; as Blake's Archimago, 231; as parodic Adam, 100, 229

Hardison, O. B., 37

Hayley, William, 10-11, 123; in Blake's *Notebook*, 227, 279

Hazlitt, William, 25, 330-31n.60

Helms, Randel, 205

Hermaphroditism: Blake on, 42-43, 129, 136, 148, 153, 223, 248, 258, 336n.36; in *Faerie Queene*, 42-43, 136, 148, 223, 266, 317. *See also* Marriage

Hervey, James, *Meditations Among the Tombs*, 104, 151; Blake's painting of, 151, 168, 169

Hesiod, *Theogony*, 324n.22; Blake's illustrations to, 21

Heva, 38; as Blake's Duessa, 231; as parodic Eve, 100, 229; and Thel, 39, 43, 294

Hieatt, A. Kent, 237-38, 265, 355n.25, 386n.17

Hobbes, Thomas, *Leviathan*, 324n.22

Hollander, John, 1-2, 320n.6

Hollander, Robert, 309

Homer, 25, 60, 73, 150, 158, 208, 277-78; Blake's copy of, 19; in Blake's *Heads of the Poets*, 11

Honig, Edwin, 147

Howard, Donald R., 306

Hughes, John, *Works of Mr. Edmund Spenser*, 19-23, 25

Hughes, Merritt, 279

Hurd, Bishop Richard, 12-13, 18, 21, 362-63n.82

Imagination: in Blake, 85, 99, 101, 108-10, 120, 122-24, 133-34, 135, 139, 148, 170, 176, 184-85, 187, 215, 218, 223, 227, 238, 255, 264, 273-74, 277, 296, 318; in Spenser, 107, 109, 118, 136-37, 174, 360n.56

Innocence: Blake's idea of, 43, 90, 205, 215, 228, 230-33; in *Faerie Queene*, 228-29, 231

Jerusalem: in Bible, 61, 184, 306; in Blake's *Faerie Queene* painting, 164, 166, 177, 183, 185-86, 188-89, 195, 198, 215-16, 233, 274, 276, 283; in Blake's writings, 61, 70, 130, 147, 161-62, 180, 185, 211, 220, 245, 248-50, 266, 275, 281, 294, 313-14, 317; as Mary, in Blake, 213-14; in *Faerie Queene*, 61, 184, 186, 233, 282, 298, 302; Una as, in Blake's painting, 211, 213

Jerusalem, 2, 4, 6, 28, 47, 58, 67, 129, 131, 155-56, 213, 263, 277, 310, 314; apocalypse in, 7, 85, 118, 218-19, 271, 313; and *Crystal Cabinet*, 56-57; and mythology, 59

—individual plates quoted or commented on (individual plate numbers are in italic): *1*, 264, 369n.32; *3*, 343n.12; *4*, 323n.10; *5*, 274, 280; *9*, 312; *10*, 44, 110, 123, 152-53, 215; *11*, 41, 111, 153; *12*, 111, 153; *13*, 115; *14*, 274, 312,

Jerusalem (cont'd.)
389n.3; *16*, 311; *17*, 206, 220; *18*, 211; *23*, 249; *25*, 383n.36; *27*, 213, 275; *28*, 66, 258; *29[33]*, 70; *31[35]*, 359n.51; *32[36]*, 40, 186, 201; *33[37]*, 182, 261; *34[38]*, 69, 261; *36[40]*, 118, 152, 171, 206, 275; *37[41]*, 186, 217, 220; *38[43]*, 51, 206; *39[44]*, 47–48, 213, 311–12; *40[45]*, 220; *41[46]*, 123; *42*, 122, 269–70; *44[30]*; 186; *49*, 50, 215; *52*, 69, 253, 359n.51; *53*, 245–46, 256; *54*, 70, 250, 378n.11; *58*, 69; *61*, 213–14; *64*, 250, 374n.23; *67*, 245, 360n.59; *68*, 205; *69*, 180–81, 205, 346n.36; *70*, 56–57; *71*, 221, 224; *73*, 358n.51; *74*, 101, 344n.17; *75*, 220, 369n.32, 379n.12; *77*, 275–76; *79*, 70; *83*, 189; *88*, 108, 337n.46; *89*, 56, 378n.7, 379n.12; *90*, 69, 128; *91*, 66, 78, 93, 120, 215, 255; *96*, 66, 219, 376n.1; *97*, 70, 180; *98*, 9, 31, 108–9, 118–19, 130, 132, 217, 219–20, 280, 313; *99*, 7–9, 157; *100*, 264
Johnson, Mary Lynn, 57, 62, 65, 339n.55
Johnson, Samuel, 202
Johnson, William C., 39
Jonson, Ben, 151, 155
Jortin, John, 252
Jourdain, Margaret, 24
Jove, 138, 280, 316–17; in Blake's *Faerie Queene* painting, 177, 185, 193, 195–97, 211; and Danaë, 35–36; in Spenser, 316. *See also* God of This World
Justice: Blake on, 78, 119, 141, 170, 179, 233, 248, 253–54, 256, 258, 269; in Spenser, 141, 170, 181, 233, 249, 253–55, 257–58, 278, 290. *See also* Artegall; *Faerie Queene, The*, characters in, Astraea; *Faerie Queene, The Characters in Spenser's*, characters in, Astraea; Talus

Keats, John, 54, 150
Kellogg, Robert, 335n.29
Keynes, Sir Geoffrey, 10, 25, 303–4
Kiralis, Karl, 134, 158–64, 196, 200, 216, 243–44, 374n.26, 380n.14
Klopstock, Friedrich, 11, 223, 279, 377n.3
Knott, John R., 304
Korshin, Paul, 309–10

Krieger, Murray, 118
Kroeber, Karl, 131–32, 136, 357n.35

LaBelle, Jenijoy, 172
Lavater, John Casper, 9, 123; *Aphorisms on Man*, 7, 121, 224, 292; Blake's annotations to, 46, 121, 123, 224, 292, 294, 354n.18, 377n.5
Lee, Sidney, 49
Lever, J. W., 334–35n.24
Levin, Samuel, 118–19
Lewalski, Barbara Kiefer, 304
Lewis, C. S., 42, 58, 59, 63–64, 240, 263, 345n.26
Linnaeus, Carolus, 123, 199
Locke, John, 67, 82, 99, 104–5, 124, 158, 267, 296, 299; in Blake's works, 4, 57, 250, 271
Lonsdale, Roger, 13
Los, 51, 55, 60, 93, 112, 115, 130, 180, 188, 209, 215, 220, 223, 251, 264, 269–71, 277, 280; and Ahania, 63; as allegorist, 52, 69, 111, 140, 154, 218, 270, 310; in Blake's *Faerie Queene* painting, 172, 176, 262; and Enitharmon, 62–63, 65, 139; as Petrarchan lover, 63, 69; as poet, 69, 154–55; printing press of, 154, 176, 349n.52; as prophet, 78, 153; task of, 2, 26, 40, 68–69, 110–11, 118–19, 121–22, 132, 139, 152, 171, 175, 202, 311–12, 315–16, 359n.55

MacCaffrey, Isabel, 30–31, 265, 304, 317–18, 358n.46, 362n.77, 377n.6
McNeil, Helen, 67
Mammon's Cave: and Blake's *Book of Thel*, 349n.54; in Blake's Gray illustrations, 16, 22; and Blake's *Marriage of Heaven and Hell*, 105–6; in *Faerie Queene*, 17, 73, 105–7, 112–15, 228–29, 240
Marriage: Blake's idea of, 5, 28, 46, 53, 85, 103–4, 113, 115, 124, 136, 147, 153, 252, 266, 268–69, 273, 314; in Milton, 347n.40; in Spenser, 5, 37, 45, 65, 147, 266, 268–69, 377n.1. *See also* Contraries; Hermaphroditism
Marriage of Heaven and Hell, The, 4, 5, 26, 28, 71–78, 81–87, 94, 128, 130–31, 134, 138, 149, 153, 163, 169, 170, 172, 175–76, 194, 198, 237, 276, 278, 297, 342n.12; as allegory, 133; allusion to

Index

Chatterton in, 73–74; allusions to Milton in, 74–76; allusions to Spenser in, 85–87, 97–98, 105–10; "The Argument" in, 101, 344n.24; Bible of Hell in, 104, 344n.23; body and soul in, 8, 29, 79, 82–83, 102, 306; criticism of Milton in, 4, 76–77, 85, 91, 101, 103, 126, 143, 156, 244, 271; desire and restraint in, 29, 32, 101, 237; idea of imposition in, 85, 103, 143, 272; improvement of sensual enjoyment in, 96; Isaiah and Ezekiel in, 84–85, 102, 348n.50; Lucianic pattern of, 72; origin of priesthood in, 21, 22, 29–30, 35, 44, 51–52, 54, 101–2, 110–11, 123–24, 126, 198, 308, 323n.22; printing house in Hell in, 98–110, 143; prolific and devourer in, 65–66, 75, 342n.10; Proverbs of Hell in, 71–73, 76, 81, 90, 96, 102, 108, 119, 215, 264

Mars: in Blake's *America*, 190; in Blake's *Faerie Queene* painting, 188–91, 193, 196–97, 254, 276; in Blake's *Il Penseroso* illustrations, 191; in *Faerie Queene*, 145, 174, 193

Martz, Louis, 335n.24

Mary, Virgin: Blake on, 205, 211, 213–14; in Blake's *Faerie Queene* painting, 205, 210, 216; in Spenser, 147

Mental Fight, Blake's idea of. *See* Friendship; War, Intellectual

Michelangelo, 4, 175, 228, 259; painting of Daniel, 172–73

Milton, 6, 26, 47, 48, 58, 65, 67, 129, 130, 154–55, 183, 185, 187, 209, 215, 220, 223, 244, 272, 278, 280, 283, 306, 314, 318; Bard in, 153–54, 211; and *The Four Zoas*, 68; and mythology, 59; Petrarchan metaphors in, 60

—individual plates quoted or commented on (individual plate numbers are in italic): *1*, 60, 277; *2*, 28, 153; *4*, 53; *8*, 251; *9*, 311; *11[12]*, 77, 129; *14[15]*, 122; *19[21]*, 248, 311; *22[24]*, 212; *27[29]*, 68, 154; *28[30]*, 53, 132; *29[31]*, 78, 122; *30[33]*, 183; *31[34]*, 186, 201; *32[35]*, 135; *37[41]*, 178, 255; *39[44]*, 311; *41[46]*, 37, 66, 132

Milton, John, 1, 60, 61, 66, 79–80, 82, 84, 86, 119, 158, 214, 256, 271–72, 277, 307, 343n.15; Blake's illustrations to poems of: *see under* poem titles;

Blake's portrait of, 11; debts to Spenser, 38, 42, 65, 237–38, 268; in Gray's *The Bard*, 18; in Gray's *Progress of Poesy*, 13; and language, 156; and Revelation, 117, 149–50, 281–83; sublime allegory in, 3; and wives, 48. *See also under* Christ; Disguise; Excess; Marriage; Pastoralism; Prudence; Reason; Satan; Temperance

—works of (other than *Comus; On the Morning of Christ's Nativity; Paradise Lost; Paradise Regained; Samson Agonistes*, qq. v.): *L'Allegro*, 6; *History of Britain*, 220–21; *Il Penseroso*, 6, 171, 191–92, 369n.36; *Tetrachordon*, 347n.40

Miner, Earl, 309

Mitchell, W. J. T., 44–45, 132, 287, 291–92, 298, 358n.49

Murray, E. B., 333–34n.17, 337n.39

Murrin, Michael, 124, 350n.57, 354n.24, 365n.5

Nature: in Blake, 31, 41–43, 47, 62, 83, 121–22, 170, 176, 186, 201, 211, 245, 250, 298, 312, 314; in his Gray illustrations, 15; in Spenser, 7–9, 41–42, 62–63, 79, 121, 133, 148, 282, 315, 317

Nellist, Brian, 305

Nelson, William, 148, 265

Newton, Isaac, 57, 123, 158, 183, 199, 266; in Blake's works, 4, 78, 250, 271, 273

Nohrnberg, James, 147–48, 174, 265, 365n.5, 386n.17

Nolan, Barbara, 325n.28

Norvig, Gerda, 304–6

Notebook, Blake's, 299, 325n.30; emblems in, 6, 10, 134, 326n.31; *Faerie Queene* quotation in, 6, 10, 19–20, 97–98; individual poems in: "Abstinence sows sand all over," 90; "Each Man is in his Spectre's power," 217; "To God," 31; "I fear'd the fury of my wind," 90; "I found them blind," 223; "Imitation of Pope," 32; *Infant Sorrow*, draft of, 299; "I Saw a Chapel All of Gold," 87–97, 346n.36; "The look of love alarms," 52; "When Klopstock England defied," 223, 377n.3; satiric epigrams in, 227, 279

O'Connell, Michael, 340n.59
On the Morning of Christ's Nativity, 139, 179, 188, 224, 282, 373n.19; and Blake's *Europe*, 202-3, 371n.8
Oothoon, 35, 47, 63, 114-15, 121, 337n.41; and anti-Petrarchism, 45-46; and Spenser's Acrasia, 239-40
Orc, 92-93, 147, 188, 202-3, 209; and Blake's "I Saw a Chapel All of Gold," 90; critical debate over, 371n.8; as Mars, in Blake's *Faerie Queene* painting, 196; "Orc Cycle," 96, 185, 346n.34, 372n.8; and Spenser's Guyon, 114; as viper, 114-16
Otway, Thomas, 11
Ovid, 28, 34, 59, 73, 150, 259, 277-78

Paley, Morton, D., 319n.1
Palmer, in Blake's *Faerie Queene* painting, 165, 167, 181, 193, 196, 224-25, 233-34, 238-39, 242, 251, 282; and Chaucer's Parson, 237; in *Faerie Queene*, 39, 78, 80, 86-87, 96-97, 187, 237, 240, 244, 255, 282, 289, 360n.56; as Prester Serpent in Blake's painting, 234-37, 379n.14
Paradise Lost, 6, 60-61, 80, 82, 84, 117, 126-28, 143, 178, 268, 306-7, 316, 323n.22; allusions to, in Blake's *Marriage of Heaven and Hell*, 74-77, 81; Blake on, 4, 30, 75-77, 81-84, 101, 126, 237, 244, 305; and Blake's *Golden Net*, 48; Blake's illustrations to, 279-80, 382n.33, 388nn.26-28; and Blake's "I Saw a Chapel All of Gold," 91; and Blake's *Thel*, 48; disguise in, 125; and Dryden, 4, 78
—characters in (other than Adam; Eve; Christ; Satan, qq. v.): Beelzebub, 74-75; Belial, 48-49; 333n.15; Michael, 48, 80-81, 126, 388n.29; Moloch, 188; Raphael, 91, 125; Sin and Death, 75, 126, 156; Uriel, 76, 342n.12
Paradise Regained, 23, 37, 74, 117, 156, 250; and Blake's *Golden Net*, 48-49; Blake's illustrations to, 156; disguise in, 125; and Spenser's Guyon, 238
Parker, Patricia, 127, 357n.41
Pastoralism: Blake on, 40, 233, 281-82, 340n.59; in Blake's works, 31, 197; in *Faerie Queene*, 196, 229-31, 233, 239,
281-82, 313-14; 340n.59; in *Milton*, 282; in *Shepheardes Calender*, 282
Pearson, Lu Emily, 334n.24
Peterfreund, Stuart, 4, 322n.18
Petrarch, Francesco, 28, 31, 34, 49, 57, 62
Petrarchism, 238, 241, 367n.24; and allegory, 67; in *Amoretti*, 5-6, 28, 31-35, 49-50, 53-54, 68, 78, 269, 334n.24; Blake's use of, 28-70; passim, 245, 256, 269, 334n.21, 337n.46; in *Faerie Queene*, 41, 43, 58, 64, 74, 144-45, 223, 249, 256, 259, 268-69
Plato, 29, 45, 179, 191, 212, 269, 277
Plowman, Max, 116
Poetical Sketches, 1, 4-6, 7, 9, 25, 30, 99; influence of Spenser in, 27-28; poems in: *To the Evening Star*, 5, 28, 269; *Fair Elenor*, 99; *An Imitation of Spencer*, 4-5, 6, 322n.18, 328n.52; *King Edward the Third*, 28, 134; *Mad Song*, 40; *Memory Hither Come*, 99-100; *To Morning*, 5, 28, 269; *To the Muses*, 5; poems on the seasons, 5
Pope, Alexander, 4, 40, 134, 255; in Blake's *Heads of the Poets*, 11; *Pastorals*, 5; *The Rape of the Lock*, 31-32
Price, Martin, 71, 264
Prudence: Blake on, 78, 84, 119, 170, 253; in *Milton*, 80; in Spenser, 80, 87. *See also* Palmer

Quilligan, Maureen, 118-19, 155, 208

Radigund, 197, 255-56, 260; and Artegall, 64, 145, 241, 251-52; as Elizabeth, 382n.29; fight with Britomart, 65
Radzinowicz, M. A. N., 266
Rahab, 56-57, 181, 201, 220-21, 245-46, 249, 252, 256, 318; Britomart as, in Blake's *Faerie Queene* painting, 244-45, 250; Wife of Bath as, in Blake's Chaucer painting, 160, 162, 244. *See also* Babylon, Whore of; Tirzah; Vala
Raine, Kathleen, 346n.36
Reason: Blake on, 8, 39, 44, 65, 77-79, 81-82, 85, 101, 104, 110, 124, 126, 153, 207, 213, 215, 218, 237, 250; in *Milton*, 80-81, 96, 126, 237-38; in Spenser, 8, 39, 65, 80-81, 96-97, 107, 109, 136, 266-267
Redcrosse: Archimago as, 138-39, 210, 268; in Blake's *Faerie Queene* painting,

163, 165–67, 187, 193, 195, 197–98,
203, 207–8, 210–12, 216, 219, 221,
222–25, 234, 238, 374n.24; and Blake's
Satan, 209; in *Faerie Queene*, 6, 59, 61,
133, 135, 138–40, 145, 148, 184, 187,
207–12, 215, 218, 220, 265–66, 268,
280, 282, 288–97, 373n.22; Stothard's
painting of, 25
Reisner, Mary Ellen, 364n.3
Rembrandt, Blake on, 4, 134
Renwick, W. L., 88
Reynolds, Sir Joshua, 143, 158; Blake's
annotations to *Discourses* of, 120, 199,
210, 224, 273, 322n.15, 329n.55,
377n.3; in Blake's *Notebook*, 279
Robertson, D. W., 309
Roche, Thomas P., 309
Romance of the Rose, 89, 360–61n.63
Rose, E. J., 9, 132, 156, 303, 325n.28,
358n.49
Rousseau, Jean Jacques, in Blake's
works, 250
Rubens, Peter Paul, Blake on, 4, 322n.15
Ruddymane: in Blake's *Faerie Queene*
painting, 167, 233, 239, 282; in Blake's
Notebook, 6, 10; in *Faerie Queene*, 6, 10;
Thomas Daniell painting of, 324n.24

Samson Agonistes, 35–36, 94, 117, 289;
and Blake's "I Saw a Chapel All of
Gold," 91–92; critical debate over,
346n.35
Satan: in Bible, 219; in Blake, 69–70, 77,
93, 122, 126, 128–29, 132, 135, 152,
178, 186, 201, 209, 221, 231, 234,
253–54, 267, 280, 318, 368n.26; as
Lucifer, 125–26; in Milton, 36, 48–49,
74–76, 79, 125–26, 238, 244, 250,
268, 316
Shakespeare, William, 28, 31, 45, 53,
158, 162, 200–201, 203, 277, 322n.18;
in Blake's *Heads of the Poets*, 11; in
Gray's *Progress of Poesy*, 13; in *Jerusalem*,
4, 271, 283
Sharrock, Roger, 306
Shelley, Percy Bysshe, 78, 131, 150, 154,
271
Shepheardes Calender, The, 3, 6, 27, 31, 198,
332n.9; Blake on, 5, 30; "Maye" in,
206, pastoralism of, 282; prefatory
epistle to Harvey in, 155; time in, 30,
168

Sidney, Sir Philip, 31; *Astrophel and Stella*,
32, 34, 39, 49; eighteenth-century editions of, 333n.12
Simmons, Robert E., 385n.4
Songs of Innocence and of Experience, 5, 28,
30, 31, 55, 58, 100, 104, 198, 282; individual poems in: *A Divine Image*, 80,
233, 280; *The Divine Image*, 52, 82, 102,
179, 230, 295; *The Echoing Green*, 100,
230; *The Garden of Love*, 88–89, 215,
230–31, 315, 346n.33; *The Human
Abstract*, 66, 80, 230–31, 334n.21; *Holy
Thursday (Innocence)*, 186; *Infant Joy*,
130, 302; *Infant Sorrow*, 17, 56, 299,
356n.32; *Introduction (Innocence)*, 172,
202; *The Lamb*, 129; *The Lilly*, 346n.33;
The Little Boy Lost, 100; *Night*, 232;
Nurses Song (Experience), 125, 230; *The
Tyger*, 232; *To Tirzah*, 130
Spenser, Edmund: in Blake's illustrations
to Gray's *Poems*, 13–18, 113, 171, 203;
Blake's portrait of, in *Heads of the Poets*,
10–12, 13, 17, 123, 233; Chatterton's
allusions to, 73–74; Gray's allusions to,
13; influence of, in Blake's *Poetical
Sketches*, 27–28; Milton's debts to, 38, 42,
65, 237–38, 268. *See also under* Chastity;
Christ; Contraries; Elizabeth I; Excess;
Friendship; Imagination; Justice; Mar-
riage; Nature; Petrarchism; Prudence;
Reason; Temperance; Time; Typology
—works (other than *Amoretti; Faerie Queene;
Shepheardes Calender*, qq. v.): *Colin Clouts
Come Home Again*, 27; *Epithalamion*, 3, 5,
6, 27, 47, 65, 168, 269; *Fowre Hymns*, 3,
27, 269; "Hymne of Heauenly Love,"
29–30, 74, 332n.7; *Muiopotmos*, 27,
320n.8; *Prothalamion*, 3, 5, 27, 65; *Ruines
of Rome*, 88; *Ruines of Time*, 169, 189;
Teares of the Muses, 5, 6, 27; *Theatre for
Worldlings*, 5; *Virgils Gnat*, 27
Stevenson, Warren, 234
Stirling, Brents, 325n.26
Stothard, Thomas: in Blake's *Notebook*,
279; illustrations to *Faerie Queene*, 23–25;
painting of Canterbury pilgrims, 23,
24, 159, 201, 259, 278, 371n.6
Summerfield, Henry, 170, 177
Svendsen, Kester, 279
Swedenborg, Emmanuel, 9, 72, 77, 85,
111, 123, 137; in Blake's *Descriptive
Catalogue*, 108; in Blake's *Marriage of*

Swedenborg (*cont'd.*)
   Heaven and Hell, 71, 98–100, 103–5; as a
      "shorn Samson," in Blake, 278; works
      of: *A Treatise concerning Heaven and Hell*,
      7, 84, 99 (Blake's annotations to, 84);
      *The Wisdom of Angels, concerning Divine
      Love and Divine Wisdom*, 7, 84 (Blake's
      annotations to, 7, 84, 123, 137)

Talus: in Blake's *Faerie Queene* painting,
      167, 170, 179–80, 184, 193–94, 196,
      224–25, 233–34, 237, 242, 246, 251–52,
      254–55, 257, 259–60, 262, 383n.38; and
      Blake's Urizen, 179–80; in *Faerie Queene*,
      148, 181, 241, 249, 253, 255–56, 258,
      261–62; Upton on, 368n.26. *See also*
      Justice
Tannenbaum, Leslie, 127–28, 149,
      308–10, 354n.20
Tasso, Torquato, 28, 277; in Blake's
      Heads of the Poets, 11
Tayler, Irene, 11–13, 15–18, 327n.45,
      366n.15
Temperance: Blake on, 39, 78, 119, 170,
      242, 253; in Milton, 80, 82, 237; in
      Spenser, 39, 80, 82, 86, 97, 107, 113,
      118, 133, 253, 267. *See also* Guyon;
      Faerie Queene, places in, House of Tem-
      perance
Thel, The Book of, 6, 28, 46–47, 58, 136,
      143, 230, 287–302, 334n.17, 337n.39;
      allusions to *Faerie Queene* in, 36–39, 41,
      43, 287–98, 349n.54; and *Paradise Lost*,
      48; pastoralism in, 39–40, 43–44, 59,
      229–30; Petrarchism in, 31–45; Thel
      in, passim
Theotormon, 35, 114, 121, 240; Blake's
      drawing of, 387n.22; as Petrarchan
      lover, 45–47; and Spenser's Palmer,
      239
Thomson, James, *The Seasons*, 5; Kent's
      illustrations to, 24
Time: Blake on, 5, 9, 30, 42, 169, 281,
      308; in Spenser, 5, 8, 30, 42, 63, 124,
      168–69
Tiriel, 40, 43, 100, 229, 290–91, 294, 303,
      359n.54, 379n.14, 389n.3; mock pasto-
      ralism of, 38–39; and Spenser's Meli-
      boe, 229. *See also* Har; Heva
Tirzah, 221, 245, 249, 252; Prioress as,
      in Blake's Chaucer painting, 160, 162,
      244

Titian: Blake on, 4, 134; painting of Zeus
      and Danaë, 36
Todd, H. J., 19; *Works of Edmund Spen-
      ser*, 25
Tolley, Michael J., 371n.8
Trusler, Rev. John, 99, 143, 360n.62
Tuve, Rosemond, 5, 365n.5
Typology: and allegory, 308–10; in Blake,
      149, 153, 156, 363n.87; in Spenser,
      149, 281

Una: in Blake's *Faerie Queene* painting,
      163, 165–66, 184, 188, 193–94, 196,
      203–8, 210–16, 219, 222–23, 225–27,
      233, 238, 274, 282, 374n.23; as Blake's
      Jerusalem, 211, 213–14; and Blake's
      Ona, 390nn. 3, 4; and Blake's Vala,
      206; false, 138–39, 208; Stothard's
      painting of, 25; as Virgin Mary,
      210–11, 214; as Wife of Bath, in Blake's
      Chaucer painting, 206
Upton, John, 20, 145, 179–80, 227,
      329n.56, 331n.63, 368n.26, 373n.21,
      375n.30, 386n.12; edition of *Faerie
      Queene*, 21, 22–23, 25, 179
Urizen, 31, 47, 57, 62, 67, 81, 82, 83–84,
      114, 151–54, 178, 185, 206–7, 209, 218,
      224, 237, 267, 277, 311–12, 315; and
      Ahania, 65; in Blake's *Faerie Queene*
      painting, 170, 177, 275; as the Creator,
      121–22, 127, 132, 140–41, 188–89; as
      Dragon, 249; and reason, 131; re-
      deemed, 85, 266; and Spenser's Talus,
      179–80; and Vala, 211
Urizen, The Book of, 41–42, 51, 81, 84, 88,
      127–29, 131, 132, 140–41, 151, 180,
      237, 277, 355n.28; and Genesis, 121–22,
      153; origin of allegory in, 152–53

Vala, 31, 39, 47, 55, 70, 83, 162, 201,
      213, 218, 221, 223, 298; as Covering
      Cherub, 56; as Elizabeth, 250; and
      Luvah, 67, 249, 312; as parodic Jeru-
      salem, 317; as parodic Virgin Mary,
      211; and Rahab, 57, 245, 249–52; and
      Una, in Blake's *Faerie Queene* painting,
      206, 211; as Whore of Babylon, 248.
      See also Nature
Venus, 188–89, 191, 267; in *Faerie Queene*,
      41, 42, 63, 145, 147, 174, 223, 258
Virgil, 25, 73, 150, 158, 174–75, 278;
      and epic, 21, 277

Vision of the Last Judgment, A, 3, 9, 115, 120, 141, 169-70, 187, 207, 210, 248, 255, 259, 264, 283, 303, 343n.15, 354n.19, 366n.8; on allegory, 40, 52, 97, 272; "Church Universal" in, 182-84; idea of error in, 199, 281; idea of friendship in, 258; idea of holiness in, 215; on imagination (vision), 99, 120

Visions of the Daughters of Albion, 6, 21, 28, 35, 63, 121, 239; and Mary Wollstonecraft, 382n.31; Petrarchism and anti-Petrarchism in, 45-47. *See also* Oothoon; Theotormon

Vogler, Thomas, 57

Voltaire, 259; in Blake's *Heads of the Poets*, 11; in Blake's *Jerusalem*, 250

War, Intellectual, Blake's idea of, 60, 104, 110-11, 117-18, 152, 201-2, 237, 253, 277. *See also* Friendship

Warner, Nicholas, 182

Warren, Kate, 382n.29

Warton, Thomas, 12-13, 18, 21; *Observations on the Fairy Queen*, 362n.82

Wasserman, Earl R., 322n.18, 327n.40

Watson, Bishop Robert, *Apology for the Bible*, 4, 353n.14; Blake's annotations to, 4, 329n.56, 353n.14, 378n.7

Weiskel, Thomas, 340n.59

Wells, William, 11, 326n.33

Wilkie, Brian, 57, 62, 65, 339n.55

Williams, Kathleen, 30-31, 120, 134-35, 145, 265-67, 271, 335n.31, 361n.64

Wimsatt, James, 360-61n.63

Wingren, Gustaf, 356n.31

Wittreich, Joseph A., 2-3, 117, 119, 125, 149-50, 156, 279, 281, 283, 308-10, 363n.87

Wollstonecraft, Mary, *Vindication of the Rights of Women*, 382n.31

Wordsworth, William, 27, 158

Wright, Thomas, 326nn. 33, 34

Yeats, William Butler, 312

Young, Edward, *Night Thoughts*, 104, 150-51; Blake's illustrations to, 151, 181, 283, 368n.29

Zodiac: in Blake, 178, 180, 191, 193, 195, 198; in *Faerie Queene*, 190-91; signs of: Aries, 191; Cancer, 191; Gemini, 191; Leo, 191; Libra, 178, 180, 193, 195; Sagittarius, 180; Scorpio, 180; Taurus, 191; Virgo, 178, 180, 193, 195

THE JOHNS HOPKINS UNIVERSITY PRESS

BLAKE AND SPENSER

This book was composed in Baskerville text
and Weiss display type by Action Composition Company,
Baltimore, Maryland.
It was designed by Cynthia W. Hotvedt
and printed on 50-lb. Glatfelter Offset paper.
It was bound in Holliston Kingston Natural
book cloth by Thomson-Shore, Inc.,
Dexter, Michigan.